Contents

2008 update

2008

2008 update

2008

Antenatal care

routine care for the healthy pregnant woman

National C
and Childr

Commissic
for Health

March 2008

This is a partial up
New or amended
grey bar in the ma

RCOG Press

Published by the **RCOG Press** at the Royal College of Obstetricians and Gynaecologists, 27 Sussex Place, Regent's Park, London NW1 4RG

www.rcog.org.uk

Registered charity no. 213280

First published 2008

2nd edition © 2008 National Collaborating Centre for Women's and Children's Health
1st edition published in 2003

ISBN 978-1-904752-46-2

NCC-WCH Editor: Andrew Welsh
Original design: FiSH Books, London
Typesetting: Andrew Welsh
Proofreading: Katharine Timberlake (Reedmace Editing)
Index: Jan Ross (Merrall-Ross (Wales) Ltd)
Printed by Henry Ling Ltd, The Dorset Press, Dorchester DT1 1HD

2008 update

2008 update

Guideline Development Group membership and acknowledgements

Original (2003) version

Guideline Development Group

Peter Brocklehurst	Group Leader
Belinda Ackerman	Midwife
Brian Cook	General Practitioner
Joanie Dimavicius	Consumer
Helen Edwards	Radiographer
Gill Gyte	Consumer
Shahid Husain	Neonatologist
Gwyneth Lewis	Confidential Enquiry into Maternal Deaths
Tim Overton	Obstetrician
Gill Roberts	RCOG Patient Information Specialist
Stephen Robson	Obstetrician
Julia Sanders	Midwife
Anne White	General Practitioner
Jane Thomas	Director NCC-WCH
Sue Lee	Research Fellow NCC-WCH
Jennifer Gray	Informatics Specialist NCC-WCH
Natalie Terry	Administrative support NCC-WCH
Hannah Rose Douglas	Health Economist, London School of Hygiene and Tropical Medicine
Dimitra Lambrelli	Health Economist London School of Hygiene and Tropical Medicine

Acknowledgments

Additional support was also received from:
- David Asomani, Anna Burt, Heather Brown, Susan Davidson, Gregory Eliovson, Susan Murray and Alex McNeil at the National Collaborating Centre for Women's and Children's Health.
- Stravros Petrou at the National Perinatal Epidemiology Unit and Kirsten Duckitt at the John Radcliffe Hospital, Oxford.
- Members of the previous Antenatal Care Guideline Development Group: John Spencer (Chairman), J Bradley, Jean Chapple, R Cranna, Marion Hall, Marcia Kelson, Catherine McCormack, Ralph Settatree, Lindsay Smith, L Turner, Martin Whittle, Julie Wray.
- The Patient Involvement Unit, whose glossary we have amended for use in this guideline.
- The Three Centres Consensus Guidelines on Antenatal Care, Mercy Hospital for Women, Monash Medical Centre (Southern Health) and The Royal Women's Hospital (Women's & Children's Health), Melbourne 2001, whose work we benefited from in the development of this guideline.

Stakeholder organisations

Action on Pre-Eclampsia (APEC)
Antenatal Results and Choices
Association for Continence Advice (ACA)
Association for Improvements in Maternity Services (AIMS)

Association of Radical Midwives
Association of the British Pharmaceuticals Industry(ABPI)
Aventis Pasteur MSD
Brighton Healthcare NHS Trust
British Association of Paediatric Surgeons
British Association of Perinatal Medicine
British Dietetic Association
British Maternal and Fetal Medicine Society
British Medical Association
British National Formulary
British Psychological Society
BUPA
Chartered Society of Physiotherapy
CIS'ters
Department of Health
Evidence based Midwifery Network
Faculty of Public Health Medicine
Gateshead Primary Care Trust
General Medical Council
Group B Strep Support
Health Development Agency
Hospital Infection Society
Isabel Medical Charity
Maternity Alliance
Mental Health Foundation
Monmouthshire Local Health Group
National Childbirth Trust
NHS Quality Improvement Scotland
Nottingham City Hospital
Obstetric Anaesthetists Association
Royal College of General Practitioners
Royal College of General Practitioners Wales
Royal College of Midwives
Royal College of Nursing
Royal College of Obstetricians and Gynaecologists
Royal College of Paediatrics and Child Health
Royal College of Pathologists
Royal College of Psychiatrists
Royal College of Radiologists
Royal Pharmaceutical Society of Great Britain
Royal Society of Medicine
Scottish Intercollegiate Guidelines Network (SIGN)
Sickle Cell Society
Society and College of Radiographers
STEPS
Survivors Trust
Twins and Multiple Births Association (TAMBA)
UK Coalition of People Living with HIV and AIDS
UK National Screening Committee
UK Pain Society
United Kingdom Association of Sonographers
Victim Support
Welsh Assembly Government (formerly National Assembly for Wales)
West Gloucestershire Primary Care Trust
Young Minds

Peer reviewers

Susan Bewley, Leanne Bricker, Howard Cuckle, Andrew Dawson, Viv Dickinson, Grace Edwards, Jason Gardosi, Duncan Irons, Deirdre Murphy, Tim Reynolds, Jilly Rosser, Lindsay Smith, John Spencer, Pat Tookey, Derek Tuffnell, Gavin Young.

2008 update

Guideline Development Group

GDG members

Rhona Hughes	Group Leader
Jane Anderson	Ultrasound Radiographer
Chris Barry	General Practitioner
Marie Benton	Service User Representative
Jennifer Elliott	Service User Representative
Nina Khazaezadeh	Consultant Midwife and Supervisor of Midwives
Rachel Knowles	Medical Research Council Clinical Public Health Research Fellow
Tim Overton	Consultant Obstetrician
Katie Yiannouzis	Head of Midwifery

National Collaborating Centre for Women's and Children's Health (NCC-WCH) staff

Rupert Franklin	Work-Programme Coordinator
Eva Gautam-Aitken	Work-Programme Coordinator
Paul Jacklin	Senior Health Economist
Rajesh Khanna	Senior Research Fellow
Rintaro Mori	Research Fellow
Francesco Moscone	Health Economist
Debbie Pledge	Senior Information Scientist
Jeff Round	Health Economist
Anuradha Sekhri	Research Fellow
Roz Ullman	Senior Research Fellow
Martin Whittle	Co-Director in Women's Health

External advisers

Guy Rooney	Genitourinary Medicine Specialist
Anne Longton	Health Visitor
Fiona Ford	Dietician
Jane Hawdon	Consultant Neonataologist

Acknowledgments

Additional support was also received from:
- Anna Bancsi, Angela Kraut, Moira Mugglestone and Martin Dougherty at the NCC-WCH
- Allison Streetly, Programme Director for the NHS Sickle Cell and Thalassaemia Screening Programme.
- Andrew Welsh, freelance guideline editor, whose editorial support was invaluable in the production of this guideline.
- Group Dynamics, who provided the voting equipment for the Assessment Tool consensus meeting.

Stakeholder organisations

Academic Division of Midwifery, University of Nottingham
Action on Pre-Eclampsia
Addenbrooke's NHS Trust
All Wales Birth Centre Group
Antenatal Screening Wales
Association for Psychoanalytic Psychotherapy in the NHS
Association for Spina Bifida & Hydrocephalus (ASBAH)
Association of Breastfeeding Mothers
Association of British Clinical Diabetologists
Association of Chartered Physiotherapists in Women's Health

Association of Medical Microbiologists
Association of the British Pharmaceuticals Industry (ABPI)
Baby Lifeline
Barnsley Acute Trust
Barnsley PCT
BDF Newlife (Birth Defects Foundation)
Bedfont Scientific Ltd
Bedfordshire PCT
Berkshire Healthcare NHS Trust
Birmingham Women's Healthcare Trust
Birth Trauma Association
Bradford & Airedale PCT
Bradford Teaching Hospitals NHS Foundation Trust
Brighton & Sussex University Hospitals Trust
Bristol Health Services Plan
British Association for Counselling and Psychotherapy
British Dietetic Association
British HIV Association (BHIVA)
British Hypertension Society
British Maternal and Fetal Medicine Society
British National Formulary (BNF)
British Psychological Society
Calderdale PCT
CASPE
CEMACH
Chartered Society of Physiotherapy
Chelsea & Westminster NHS Foundation Trust
Chronic Conditions Collaborating Centre
CIS'ters
CO-Awareness
Commission for Social Care Inspection
Community Practitioners and Health Visitors Association
Connecting for Health
Cotswold and Vale PCT
Croydon PCT
Cytyc UK Ltd
Department of Health, Social Security and Public Safety of Northern Ireland
Derbyshire Mental Health Services NHS Trust
Det Norske Veritas – NHSLA Schemes
Doula UK
Down's Syndrome Association
Dudley Group of Hospitals NHS Trust
English National Forum of LSA Midwifery Officers
Epsom & St Helier University Hospitals NHS Trust
Evidence-based Midwifery Network
Faculty of Family Planning and Reproductive Health Care
Faculty of Public Health
Foundation for the Study of Infant Deaths
Gateshead PCT
Gloucestershire Acute Trust
Gloucestershire Hospitals NHS Foundation Trust
Group B Strep Support
Guy's and St Thomas' NHS Foundation Trust
Health Protection Agency
Healthcare Commission
Homerton University Hospital NHS Foundation Trust
Huntleigh Healthcare
King's College Hospital NHS Trust

2008 update

ix

2008 update

Liverpool PCT
Liverpool Women's Hospital NHS Trust
Luton and Dunstable Hospital NHS Trust
Mast Diagnostics
Medicines and Healthcare products Regulatory Agency (MHRA)
Mid and West Regional MSLC
Milton Keynes PCT
Monica Healthcare Ltd
MRC Centre of Epidemiology for Child Health
National Childbirth Trust
National Chlamydia Screening Programme
National Patient Safety Agency
National Public Health Service – Wales
NHS Direct
NHS Health and Social Care Information Centre
NHS Quality Improvement Scotland
NHS Sickle Cell and Thalassemia Screening Programme
North Tees and Hartlepool NHS Trust
Northwest London Hospitals NHS Trust
Nutrition Society
Obstetric Anaesthetists Association
Partnerships for Children, Families, Women and Maternity
Pelvic Partnership
PERIGON (formerly the NHS Modernisation Agency)
Phoenix Partnership
PNI ORG UK
Positively Women
Post Natal Illness Organisation (PNI)
Primary Care Pharmacists' Association
PRIMIS+
Princess Alexandra Hospital NHS Trust
Queen Mary's Hospital NHS Trust (Sidcup)
Regional Maternity Survey Office
Regional Public Health Group – London
Royal College of General Practitioners
Royal College of Midwives
Royal College of Nursing
Royal College of Obstetricians and Gynaecologists
Royal College of Paediatrics and Child Health
Royal College of Pathologists
Royal College of Psychiatrists
Royal College of Radiologists
Royal Liverpool Children's Trust
Royal Society of Medicine
Salford Royal Hospitals NHS Foundation Trust
Salisbury NHS Foundation Trust
Sandwell and West Birmingham NHS Trust
Sanofi Pasteur MSD
Scottish Executive Health Department
Scottish Intercollegiate Guidelines Network (SIGN)
Sefton PCT
Sheffield South West PCT
Sheffield Teaching Hospitals NHS Trust
Sickle Cell & Thalassaemia Association of Counsellors
Sickle Cell Society
Society and College of Radiographers
Survivors Trust
TIPS Limited

UK Coalition of People Living with HIV & AIDS
UK Forum on Haemoglobin Disorders
UK National Screening Committee
UK Newborn Screening Programme Centre
UK Thalassaemia Society
UNICEF Baby Friendly Initiative
United Lincolnshire Hospitals NHS Trust
University College London Hospitals NHS Foundation Trust
University College London Hospitals NHS Trust
University Hospitals of Leicester
Victim Support
Welsh Assembly Government
Welsh Scientific Advisory Committee (WSAC)
West Middlesex University Hospital NHS Trust
Western Cheshire PCT
Wiltshire PCT
Wirral University Hospital Teaching NHS Trust
Women's Health Research Group
Worcestershire Acute NHS Trust
Worthing and Southlands Hospital NHS Trust
Worthing Hospital
Wyre Forest PCT
York NHS Trust
Yorkshire and Humber Local Supervisory Authority

2008 update

Abbreviations

2008 update

AC	abdominal circumference
ACHOIS	Australian Carbohydrate Intolerance Study in Pregnant Women
ACOG	American College of Obstetricians and Gynecologists
ACTH	adrenocorticotrophic hormone
ADA	American Diabetes Association
AFG	adequate fetal growth
AFI	amniotic fluid index
AFP	alpha-fetoprotein
AIDS	acquired immune deficiency syndrome
ALPHA	Antenatal Psychosocial Health Assessment
ANC	antenatal care
APEC	Action on Pre-eclampsia
APH	antepartum haemorrhage
ASB	asymptomatic bacteriuria
BD	twice a day
BERR	Department for Business, Enterprise and Regulatory Reform
BMC	bone mineral content
BMI	body mass index
BP	blood pressure
BPD	biparietal diameter or bronchopulmonary dysplasia
BV	bacterial vaginosis
BW	birthweight
CAMP	Christie, Atkinson, Munch, Peterson test
$cBG_{120\,min}$	capillary blood glucose 120 minutes after glucose load
CDSC	Communicable Disease Surveillance Centre
CEGEN	Confidential Enquiry into Counselling for Genetic Disorders
cFBG	capillary fasting blood glucose
CFGC	customised fetal growth chart
cfu/ml	colony-forming units per millilitre
CHO	carbohydrate
CI	confidence interval
CINAHL	Cumulative Index to Nursing and Allied Health Literature
CMV	cytomegalovirus
CNS	central nervous system
COMA	Committee on Medical Aspects of Food Policy
CPC	choroid plexus cyst
CRL	crown–rump length
CRP	C-reactive protein
CS	caesarean section
CTG	cardiotocography
DA	direct agglutination test
DARE	Database of Abstracts and Reviews of Effectiveness
df	degrees of freedom
DFA	direct fluorescent antibody test
DNA	deoxyribonucleic acid
DR	detection rate
DS	Down's syndrome
Dx	Diagnosis
eAg	hepatitis e antigen
EB	elementary body

ECV	external cephalic version
EEA	European Economic Area
EFW	estimated fetal weight
EIA	enzyme immunoassay
EL	evidence level
ELISA	enzyme-linked immunosorbent assay
EOGBS	early-onset group B streptococcus
EPDS	Edinburgh Postnatal Depression Scale
EPIC	external intermittent pneumatic compression
EU	European Union
FBC	full blood count
FFN	fetal fibronectin
FGM	female genital mutilation
FGR	fetal growth restriction
fl	femtolitre (10^{-15} litres)
FL	femur length
FPG	fasting plasma glucose
FPR	false positive rate
FTA-abs	fluorescent treponemal antibody – absorbed test
GA	gestational age
GBS	group B streptococcus
GCT	glucose challenge test
GD	gestational diabetes
GDG	Guideline Development Group
GDM	gestational diabetes mellitus
GPP	good practice point
GTT	glucose tolerance test
H/O	history of
HADS	Hospital Anxiety and Depression Scale
Hb	haemoglobin
HBIG	hepatitis B immune globulin
HBsAg	hepatitis B surface antigen
HBV	hepatitis B virus
HC	head circumference
hCG	human chorionic gonadotrophin (can be total or free beta)
β-hCG	beta-human chorionic gonadotrophin
HCV	hepatitis C virus
HDN	haemolytic disease of the newborn
HEED	Health Economic Evaluations Database
HELLP	haemolysis, elevated liver enzymes and low platelet count
HIV	human immunodeficiency virus
HPA	Health Protection Agency
HPLC	high-performance liquid chromatography
HSI	health sector initiative
HT	hypertension
HTA	Health Technology Assessment
ICD-9	International Classification of Diseases, 9th edition
ICER	incremental cost-effectiveness ratio
IFG	inadequate fetal growth
IGT	impaired glucose tolerance
IL	interleukin
IM	intramuscular(ly)
IMDA	interactive multimedia decision aid
IPC	intrapartum care
IPV	intimate partner violence
IU	international unit
IUGR	intrauterine growth restriction
LA	latex agglutination test

LBW	low birthweight
LCR	ligase chain reaction
LE	leucocyte esterase
LGA	large for gestational age
LMP	last menstrual period
LR	likelihood ratio
LR−	negative likelihood ratio
LR+	positive likelihood ratio
LSHTM	London School of Hygiene & Tropical Medicine
MCH	mean corpuscular haemoglobin
MCV	mean corpuscular volume
MeSH	medical subject headings
MIDIRS	Midwives Information and Resource Service
MMIC	Multidimensional Measure of Informed Choice
MoM	multiples of the median
MOMP	major outer membrane protein
MSAFP	maternal serum alpha-fetoprotein
MSHCG	maternal serum beta-human chorionic gonadotrophin
MSS	maternal serum screening
MSU	midstream urine sample
MTCT	mother-to-child transmission
NCC-WCH	National Collaborating Centre for Women's and Children's Health
NCRSP	National Congenital Rubella Surveillance Programme
NEC	necrotising enterocolitis
NFG	normal fetal growth
NHS EED	NHS Economic Evaluations Database
NHS	National Health Service
NICE	National Institute for Health and Clinical Excellence
NICU	neonatal intensive care unit
NNT	number needed to treat
NPI	Neonatal Perception Inventory
NPV	negative predictive value
NS	not significant
NSC	(UK) National Screening Committee
NSF	National Service Framework
NT	nuchal translucency
NTD	neural tube defect
OGTT	oral glucose tolerance test
OH	oligohydramnios
25-OHD	25-hydroxyvitamin D
ONS	Office for National Statistics
OR	odds ratio
OTC	over-the-counter
oz	fluid ounce (28.41 ml)
PAI	Prenatal Attachment Inventory
PAPP-A	pregnancy-associated plasma protein-A
PCR	polymerase chain reaction
PCT	primary care trust
PE	pre-eclampsia
pg	picogram (10^{-12} grams)
PHLS	Public Health Laboratory Service
PI	pulsatility index
PIH	pregnancy-induced hypertension
PPV	positive predictive value
PROM	preterm rupture of the membranes
PTD	preterm delivery
QID	four times a day
RBC	red blood cell

RBG	random blood glucose
RCOG	Royal College of Obstetricians and Gynaecologists
RCT	randomised controlled trial
RhD	rhesus D
RIBA	recombinant immunoblot assay
RNA	ribonucleic acid
ROC	receiver operating characteristic
ROP	retinopathy of prematurity
RPG	random plasma glucose
RPR	rapid plasmin reagin test
RR	relative risk
RST	reagent strip testing
S/D	systolic/diastolic
SACN	Scientific Advisory Committee on Nutrition
SD	standard deviation
SE	socio-economic(ally)
SFH	symphysis–fundal height
SGA	small for gestational age
SIGN	Scottish Intercollegiate Guidelines Network
SP	specificity
SPD	symphysis pubis dysfunction
SPTB	spontaneous preterm birth
ST	sensitivity
STAI	Spielberger State-Trait Anxiety Inventory
T 21/18/13	trisomy 21, 18 or 13
TDS	three times a day
TGA	tranposition of the great arteries
TPHA	*Treponema pallidum* haemagglutination assay
TVS	transvaginal sonography
uE3	unconjugated estriol
UHT	ultra-high-temperature processing
UK	United Kingdom
US CDC	United States Centers for Disease Control and Prevention
US	ultrasound
USPSTF	US Preventive Services Task Force
USS	ultrasound scan
UTI	urinary tract infection
VDRL	Venereal Disease Research Laboratory (test for syphilis)
VE	vaginal examination
WHO	World Health Organization
WMD	weighted mean difference

2008 update

Glossary of terms

Bias Influences on a study that can lead to invalid conclusions about a treatment or intervention. Bias in research can make a treatment look better or worse than it really is. Bias can even make it look as if the treatment works when it actually doesn't. Bias can occur by chance or as a result of systematic errors in the design and execution of a study. Bias can occur at different stages in the research process, e.g. in the collection, analysis, interpretation, publication or review of research data.

Blinding or masking The practice of keeping the investigators or subjects of a study ignorant of the group to which a subject has been assigned. For example, a clinical trial in which the participating patients or their doctors are unaware of whether they (the patients) are taking the experimental drug or a **placebo** (dummy treatment). The purpose of 'blinding' or 'masking' is to protect against **bias**. See also **double-blind study**.

Body mass index (BMI) A person's weight (in kilograms) divided by the square of their height (in metres). It is used as a measure of underweight, overweight or obesity.

Booking The appointment where the woman enters the maternity care pathway, characterised by information giving and detailed history-taking to help the woman choose the most appropriate antenatal care pathway. Also includes measurement of height, weight, blood pressure and blood tests for determining blood group, rubella status and haemoglobin level. Blood and urine samples for screening may also be taken at booking after the woman has been well informed and has given her consent. The booking appointment follows the first contact with a health professional.

Case–control study A study that starts with the identification of a group of individuals sharing the same characteristics (e.g. people with a particular disease) and a suitable comparison (**control**) group (e.g. people without the disease). All subjects are then assessed with respect to things that happened to them in the past, e.g. things that might be related to getting the disease under investigation. Such studies are also called **retrospective** as they look back in time from the outcome to the possible causes.

Case report (or case study) Detailed report on one patient (or case), usually covering the course of that person's disease and their response to treatment.

Case series Description of several cases of a given disease, usually covering the course of the disease and the response to treatment. There is no comparison (**control**) group of patients.

Clinical effectiveness The extent to which a specific treatment or intervention, when used under usual conditions, has a beneficial effect on the course or outcome of a disease compared with no treatment or routine care.

Clinical question The term is sometimes used in guideline development to refer to the questions about treatment and care that are formulated in order to guide the search for research evidence.

Clinical trial A research study conducted with patients which tests out a drug or other intervention to assess its effectiveness and safety. Each trial is designed to answer scientific questions and to find better ways to treat individuals with a specific disease. This general term encompasses **controlled clinical trials** and **randomised controlled trials**.

Cluster A group of patients, rather than an individual, used as a basic unit for investigation. See also **cluster randomisation**.

Cluster randomisation A study in which groups of individuals (eg. attending one GP surgery) are randomly allocated to intervention groups. See also **cluster**.

Cohort A group of people sharing some common characteristic (e.g. patients with the same disease), followed up in a research study for a specified period of time.

Cohort study	An observational study that takes a group (**cohort**) of patients and follows their progress over time in order to measure outcomes such as disease or mortality rates and make comparisons according to the treatments or interventions that patients received. Thus within the study group, subgroups of patients are identified (from information collected about patients) and these groups are compared with respect to outcome, e.g. comparing mortality between one group that received a specific treatment and one group which did not (or between two groups that received different levels of treatment). Cohorts can be assembled in the present and followed into the future (a concurrent or **prospective** cohort study) or identified from past records and followed forward from that time up to the present (a historical or **retrospective** cohort study). Because patients are not randomly allocated to subgroups, these subgroups may be quite different in their characteristics and some adjustment must be made when analysing the results to ensure that the comparison between groups is as fair as possible.
Combined test	A battery of screening tests used together to determine the risk of the unborn baby having Down's Syndrome. The tests are: a nuchal translucency ultrasound scan plus blood tests to measure levels of a beta human chorionic gonadotrophin and pregnancy-associated plasma protein-A. The test should be performed between 11 weeks 0 days and 13 weeks 6 days.
Confidence interval	A way of expressing certainty about the findings from a study or group of studies, using statistical techniques. A confidence interval describes a range of possible effects (of a treatment or intervention) that is consistent with the results of a study or group of studies. A wide confidence interval indicates a lack of certainty or precision about the true size of the clinical effect and is seen in studies with too few patients. Where confidence intervals are narrow they indicate more precise estimates of effects and a larger sample of patients studied. It is usual to interpret a '95%' confidence interval as the range of effects within which we are 95% confident that the true effect lies.
Confounder or confounding variable/factor	Something that influences a study and can contribute to misleading findings if it is not understood and appropriately dealt with.
Consensus methods	A variety of techniques that aim to reach an agreement on a particular issue. Formal consensus methods include **Delphi** or **nominal group techniques**, and consensus development conferences. In the development of a clinical guideline, consensus methods may be used where there is a lack of good research evidence.
Consistency	The extent to which the conclusions of a collection of studies used to support a guideline recommendation are in agreement with each other. See also **homogeneity**.
Control group	A group of patients recruited into a study that receives no treatment, a treatment of known effect, or a **placebo** (dummy treatment), in order to provide a comparison for a group receiving an experimental treatment, such as a new drug.
Controlled clinical trial (CCT)	A study testing a specific drug or other treatment involving two (or more) groups of patients with the same disease. One (the experimental group) receives the treatment that is being tested, and the other (the comparison or **control group**) receives an alternative treatment, a **placebo** (dummy treatment) or no treatment. The two groups are followed up to compare differences in outcomes to see how effective the experimental treatment was. A CCT where patients are randomly allocated to treatment and comparison groups is called a **randomised controlled trial**.
Cost–benefit analysis	A type of economic evaluation where both costs and benefits of healthcare treatment are measured in the same monetary units. If benefits exceed costs, the evaluation would recommend providing the treatment.
Cost-effectiveness	A type of economic evaluation that assesses the additional costs and benefits of doing something different. In cost-effectiveness analysis, the costs and benefits of different treatments are compared. When a new treatment is compared with current care, its additional costs divided by its additional benefits is called the cost-effectiveness ratio. Benefits are measured in natural units, for example, cost per additional heart attack prevented.
Cost–utility analysis	A special form of **cost-effectiveness** analysis where benefit is measured in **quality-adjusted life years (QALYs)**. A treatment is assessed in terms of its ability to extend or improve the quality of life.
Counselling	For the purpose of the guideline, 'counselling' is defined broadly as supportive listening, advice giving and information. The British Association for Counselling and Psychotherapy offers a more specific definition of counselling as a discrete psychological intervention (regular planned meetings of usually 50 minutes in length) which is facilitative, non-directive and/or relationship focused, with the content of sessions largely determined by the service user'.

2008 update

2008 update

Crossover study design	A study comparing two or more interventions in which the participants, upon completion of the course of one treatment, are switched to another. For example, for a comparison of treatments A and B, half the participants are randomly allocated to receive them in the order A, B and half to receive them in the order B, A. A problem with this study design is that the effects of the first treatment may carry over into the period when the second is given. Therefore a crossover study should include an adequate 'wash-out' period, which means allowing sufficient time between stopping one treatment and starting another so that the first treatment has time to wash out of the patient's system.
Cross-sectional study	The observation of a defined set of people at a single point in time or time period – a snapshot. (This type of study contrasts with a **longitudinal study**, which follows a set of people over a period of time.)
Customised fetal growth chart	The customised fetal growth chart (CFGC) is the term used for an individually adjusted standard for fundal height, estimated fetal weight and birthweight which takes into consideration maternal characteristics such as height, country of family origin, cigarette smoking and presence of diabetes.
Delphi technique	A technique used for the purpose of reaching an agreement on a particular issue, without the participants meeting or interacting directly. It involves sending participants a series of postal questionnaires asking them to record their views. After the first questionnaire, participants are asked to give further views in the light of the group feedback. The judgements of the participants are statistically aggregated. See also **consensus methods**.
Detection rate	100% minus **sensitivity**.
Diagnosis	Confirmation of the presence of a disease/disorder.
Diagnostic study	A study to assess the effectiveness of a test or measurement in terms of its ability to accurately detect or exclude a specific disease.
Double-blind study	A study in which neither the subject (patient) nor the observer (investigator or clinician) is aware of which treatment or intervention the subject is receiving. The purpose of **blinding** is to protect against **bias**.
Evidence based	The process of systematically finding, appraising and using research findings as the basis for clinical decisions.
Evidence-based clinical practice	Evidence-based clinical practice involves making decisions about the care of individual patients based on the best research evidence available rather than basing decisions on personal opinions or common practice (which may not always be evidence based). Evidence-based clinical practice therefore involves integrating individual clinical expertise and patient preferences with the best available evidence from research.
Evidence level (EL)	A code (eg. 1++, 1+) linked to an individual study or **systematic review** indicating where it fits in the **hierarchy of evidence** and how well it has adhered to recognised research principles.
Evidence table	A table summarising the results of a collection of studies which, taken together, represent the evidence supporting a particular recommendation or series of recommendations in a guideline.
Exclusion criteria	See **Selection criteria**.
Experimental study	A research study designed to test whether a treatment or intervention has an effect on the course or outcome of a condition or disease, where the conditions of testing are to some extent under the control of the investigator. **Controlled clinical trials** and **randomised controlled trials** are examples of experimental studies.
False positive rate	100% minus **specificity**.
First contact	The initial appointment where the woman first meets a healthcare professional with a confirmed pregnancy. This appointment includes referral into the maternity care pathway and is an opportunity for information giving to ensure the woman is able to make informed decisions about her pregnancy care, including all antenatal screening and to raise awareness about health-related issues that are particularly relevant in early pregnancy.
Gold standard	A method, procedure or measurement that is widely accepted as being the best available.
Gravid	Pregnant.
Guideline	A systematically developed tool that describes aspects of a person's condition and the care to be given. A good guideline makes recommendations based on best research evidence available, rather than opinion. It is used to assist clinician and patient decision making about appropriate health care for specific conditions.

Health economics	A field of conventional economics which examines the benefits of healthcare interventions (e.g. medicines) compared with their financial costs.
Health technology	Health technologies include medicines, medical devices, diagnostic techniques, surgical procedures, health promotion activities and other therapeutic interventions.
Heterogeneity	Or lack of **homogeneity**. The term is used in **meta-analyses** and **systematic reviews** when the results or estimates of effects of treatment from separate studies seem to be very different, in terms of the size of treatment effects, or even to the extent that some indicate beneficial and others suggest adverse treatment effects. Such results may occur as a result of differences between studies in terms of the patient populations, outcome measures, definition of variables or duration of follow up.
Hierarchy of evidence	An established hierarchy of study types, based on the degree of certainty that can be attributed to the conclusions that can be drawn from a well-conducted study. Well-conducted **randomised controlled trials (RCTs)** are at the top of this hierarchy.
Homogeneity	This means that the results of studies included in a **systematic review** or **meta-analysis** are similar and there is no evidence of **heterogeneity**. Results are usually regarded as homogeneous when differences between studies could reasonably be expected to occur by chance. See also **consistency**.
Inclusion criteria	See **selection criteria**.
Integrated test	A battery of screening tests used together to determine the risk of the unborn baby having Down's syndrome. The tests are: a nuchal translucency ultrasound scan plus blood tests to measure levels of a beta human chorionic gonadotrophin (β-hCG)and pregnancy-associated plasma protein-A. These tests should be performed between 11 weeks 0 days and 13 weeks 6 days. This is then followed by a second battery of blood tests: alpha-fetoprotein, uE3 and inhibin A between 15 weeks 0 days and 20 weeks 0 days. The woman waits for results from the second set of tests before she is told her risk level.
Intention-to-treat analysis	An analysis of a clinical trial where particpants are analysed according to the group to which they are initially randomly allocated, regardless of whether or not they had dropped out of the study, fully received the intervention as intended or crossed over to an alternative intervention.
Intervention	Healthcare action intended to benefit the patient, e.g. drug treatment, surgical procedure, psychological therapy.
Likelihood ratio	See **negative likelihood ratio** and **positive likelihood ratio**.
Longitudinal study	A study of the same group of people at more than one point in time. (This type of study contrasts with a **cross-sectional study**, which observes a defined set of people at a single point in time.)
Masking	See **blinding**.
Meta-analysis	Results from a collection of independent studies (investigating the same treatment) are pooled, using statistical techniques to synthesise their findings into a single estimate of a treatment effect. Where studies are not compatible, e.g. because of differences in the study populations or in the outcomes measured, it may be inappropriate or even misleading to statistically pool results in this way. See also **systematic review** and **heterogeneity**.
Multiparous	Having carried more than one pregnancy to a viable stage.
Negative likelihood ratio (LR–)	The negative likelihood ratio describes the probability of having a negative test result in the diseased population compared with that of a non-diseased population and corresponds to the ratio of the false negative rate divided by the true negative rate ((1 – sensitivity)/specificity).
Negative predictive value (NPV)	The proportion of people with a negative test result who do not have the disease (where not having the disease is indicated by the gold test being negative).
Nominal group technique	A technique used for the purpose of reaching an agreement on a particular issue. It uses a variety of postal and direct contact techniques, with individual judgements being aggregated statistically to derive the group judgement. See also **consensus methods**.
Non-experimental study	A study based on subjects selected on the basis of their availability, with no attempt having been made to avoid problems of **bias**.
Nulliparous	Having never given birth to a viable infant.

2008 update

Number needed to treat (NNT)	This measures the impact of a treatment or intervention. It states how many patients need to be treated with the treatment in question in order to prevent an event that would otherwise occur; e.g. if the NNT = 4, then four patients would have to be treated to prevent one bad outcome. The closer the NNT is to one, the better the treatment is. Analogous to the NNT is the number needed to harm (NNH), which is the number of patients that would need to receive a treatment to cause one additional adverse event. e.g. if the NNH = 4, then four patients would have to be treated for one bad outcome to occur.
Observational study	In research about diseases or treatments, this refers to a study in which nature is allowed to take its course. Changes or differences in one characteristic (e.g. whether or not people received a specific treatment or intervention) are studied in relation to changes or differences in other(s) (e.g. whether or not they died), without the intervention of the investigator. There is a greater risk of selection bias than in **experimental studies**.
Odds ratio (OR)	Odds are a way of representing probability, especially familiar from betting. In recent years odds ratios have become widely used in reports of clinical studies. They provide an estimate (usually with a **confidence interval**) for the effect of a treatment. Odds are used to convey the idea of 'risk' and an odds ratio of one between two treatment groups would imply that the risks of an adverse outcome were the same in each group. For rare events the odds ratio and the **relative risk** (which uses actual risks and not odds) will be very similar. See also **relative risk**, **risk ratio**.
Parous	Having borne at least one viable offspring (usually more than 24 weeks of gestation).
Peer review	Review of a study, service or recommendations by those with similar interests and expertise to the people who produced the study findings or recommendations. Peer reviewers can include professional, patient and carer representatives.
Pilot study	A small-scale 'test' of the research instrument. For example, testing out (piloting) a new questionnaire with people who are similar to the population of the study, in order to highlight any problems or areas of concern, which can then be addressed before the full-scale study begins.
Placebo	Placebos are fake or inactive treatments received by participants allocated to the **control group** in a **clinical trial**, which are indistinguishable from the active treatments being given in the experimental group. They are used so that participants are ignorant of their treatment allocation in order to be able to quantify the effect of the experimental treatment over and above any **placebo effect** due to receiving care or attention.
Placebo effect	A beneficial (or adverse) effect produced by a **placebo** and not due to any property of the placebo itself.
Positive likelihood ratio (LR+)	The positive likelihood ratio describes the probability of having a positive test result in the diseased population compared with that of a non-diseased population and corresponds to the ratio of the true positive rate divided by the false positive rate (sensitivity/(1−specificity)).
Positive predictive value (PPV)	The proportion of people with a positive test result who have the condition (where having the condition is indicated by the **gold standard** test being positive).
Power	See **statistical power**.
Prospective study	A study in which people are entered into the research and then followed up over a period of time with future events recorded as they happen. This contrasts with studies that are **retrospective**.
P value	If a study is done to compare two treatments then the P value is the probability of obtaining the results of that study, or something more extreme, if there really was no difference between treatments. (The assumption that there really is no difference between treatments is called the 'null hypothesis'.) Suppose the P value was 0.03. What this means is that, if there really was no difference between treatments, there would only be a 3% chance of getting the kind of results obtained. Since this chance seems quite low we should question the validity of the assumption that there really is no difference between treatments. We would conclude that there probably is a difference between treatments. By convention, where the value of P is below 0.05 (i.e. less than 5%) the result is seen as statistically significant. Where the value of P is 0.001 or less, the result is seen as highly significant. P values just tell us whether an effect can be regarded as statistically significant or not. In no way do they relate to how big the effect might be, for which we need the **confidence interval**.

Qualitative research	Qualitative research is used to explore and understand people's beliefs, experiences, attitudes, behaviour and interactions. It generates non-numerical data, e.g. a patient's description of their pain rather than a measure of pain. In health care, qualitative techniques have been commonly used in research documenting the experience of chronic illness and in studies about the functioning of organisations. Qualitative research techniques such as focus groups and in-depth interviews have been used in one-off projects commissioned by guideline development groups to find out more about the views and experiences of patients and carers.
Quality-adjusted life years (QALYs)	A measure of health outcome that looks at both length of life and quality of life. QALYs are calculated by estimating the years of life remaining for a person following a particular care pathway and weighting each year with a quality of life score (on a zero to one scale). One QALY is equal to 1 year of life in perfect health, or 2 years at 50% health, and so on.
Quantitative research	Research that generates numerical data or data that can be converted into numbers, for example clinical trials or the National Census, which counts people and households.
Random allocation or randomisation	A method that uses the play of chance to assign participants to comparison groups in a research study; for example, by using a random numbers table or a computer-generated random sequence. Random allocation implies that each individual (or each unit in the case of **cluster randomisation**) being entered into a study has the same chance of receiving each of the possible interventions.
Randomised controlled trial	A study to test a specific drug or other treatment in which people are randomly assigned to two (or more) groups: one (the experimental group) receiving the treatment that is being tested, and the other (the comparison or **control group**) receiving an alternative treatment, a **placebo** (dummy treatment) or no treatment. The two groups are followed up to compare differences in outcomes to see how effective the experimental treatment was. (Through randomisation, the groups should be similar in all aspects apart from the treatment they receive during the study.)
Relative risk (RR)	A summary measure which represents the ratio of the risk of a given event or outcome (e.g. an adverse reaction to the drug being tested) in one group of subjects compared with another group. When the 'risk' of the event is the same in the two groups the relative risk is 1. In a study comparing two treatments, a relative risk of 2 would indicate that patients receiving one of the treatments had twice the risk of an undesirable outcome than those receiving the other treatment. Relative risk is sometimes used as a synonym for **risk ratio**.
Reliability	Reliability refers to a method of measurement that consistently gives the same results. For example, someone who has a high score on one occasion tends to have a high score if measured on another occasion very soon afterwards. With physical assessments it is possible for different clinicians to make independent assessments in quick succession and if their assessments tend to agree then the method of assessment is said to be reliable.
Retrospective study	A retrospective study deals with the present and past and does not involve studying future events. This contrasts with studies that are **prospective**.
Risk ratio	Ratio of the risk of an undesirable event or outcome occurring in a group of patients receiving experimental treatment compared with a comparison (**control**) group. The term **relative risk** is sometimes used as a synonym of risk ratio.
Sample	A part of the study's target population from which the subjects of the study will be recruited. If subjects are drawn in an unbiased way from a particular population, the results can be generalised from the sample to the population as a whole.
Screening	Screening is a public health service in which members of a defined population, who do not necessarily perceive they are at risk of, or are already affected by a disease or its complications, are asked a question or offered a test, to identify those individuals who are more likely to be helped than harmed by further tests or treatment to reduce the risk of a disease or its complications.
Selection criteria	Explicit standards used by guideline development groups to decide which studies should be included and excluded from consideration as potential sources of evidence.
Sensitivity	In diagnostic testing, sensitivity refers to the proportion of cases with the target condition correctly identified by the diagnostic test out of all the cases that have the target condition.
Specificity	In diagnostic testing, specificity refers to the proportion of cases without the target condition correctly identified by the diagnostic test out of all the cases that do not have the target condition.

Statistical power	The ability of a study to demonstrate an association or causal relationship between two **variables**, given that an association exists. For example, 80% power in a clinical trial means that the study has a 80% chance of ending up with a *P* value of less than 5% in a statistical test (i.e. a statistically significant treatment effect) if there really was an important difference (e.g. 10% versus 5% mortality) between treatments. If the statistical power of a study is low, the study results will be questionable (the study might have been too small to detect any differences). By convention, 80% is an acceptable level of power. See also *P* **value**.
Study type	The kind of design used for a study. **Randomised controlled trials, case–control studies** and **cohort studies** are all examples of study types.
Systematic review	A review in which evidence from scientific studies has been identified, appraised and synthesised in a methodical way according to predetermined criteria. May or may not include a **meta-analysis**.
Technology appraisal	A technology appraisal, as undertaken by NICE, is the process of determining the clinical and cost-effectiveness of a **health technology**. NICE technology appraisals are designed to provide patients, health professionals and managers with an authoritative source of advice on new and exisiting health technologies.
Test	A procedure conducted to look for a pre-defined target of interest – either in terms of its presence/absence, or the amount/level contained in the body or a body fluid.
Validity	Assessment of how well a tool or instrument measures what it is intended to measure.
Variable	A measurement that can vary within a study, e.g. the age of participants. Variability is present when differences can be seen between different people or within the same person over time, with respect to any characteristic or feature that can be assessed or measured.

2008 update

1 Introduction

1.0 Introduction

The original antenatal care guideline was published by NICE in 2003. Since then a number of important pieces of evidence have become available, particularly concerning gestational diabetes, haemoglobinopathy and ultrasound, so that the update was initiated. This update has also provided an opportunity to look at a number of aspects of antenatal care:

- the development of a method to assess women for whom additional care is necessary (the 'antenatal assessment tool')
- information giving to women
- lifestyle:
  - vitamin D supplementation
  - alcohol consumption
- screening for the baby:
  - use of ultrasound for gestational age assessment and screening for fetal abnormalities
  - methods for determining normal fetal growth
  - placenta praevia
- screening for the mother:
  - haemoglobinopathy screening
  - gestational diabetes
  - pre-eclampsia and preterm labour
  - chlamydia.

1.1 Aim of the guideline

The ethos of this guideline is that pregnancy is a normal physiological process and that, as such, any interventions offered should have known benefits and be acceptable to pregnant women. The guideline has been developed with the following aims: to offer information on best practice for baseline clinical care of all pregnancies and comprehensive information on the antenatal care of the healthy woman with an uncomplicated singleton pregnancy. It provides evidence-based information for clinicians and pregnant women to make decisions about appropriate treatment in specific circumstances. The guideline will complement the Children's National Service Frameworks (England and Wales) (2004) which provides standards for service configuration, with emphasis on how care is delivered and by whom, including issues of ensuring equity of access to care for disadvantaged women and women's views about service provision (For more information, see www.dh.gov.uk/en/Healthcare/NationalServiceFrameworks/ChildrenServices/index.htm for England and www.wales.nhs.uk/ sites3/page.cfm?orgid=334&pid=934 for Wales). The guideline has also drawn on the evidence-based recommendations of the UK National Screening Committee (NSC).

The *Changing Childbirth* report[1] (1993) and *Maternity Matters*[635] (2007) explicitly confirmed that women should be the focus of maternity care with an emphasis on providing choice, easy access and continuity of care. Care during pregnancy should enable a woman to make informed decisions, based on her needs, having discussed matters fully with the professionals involved.

Reviews of women's views on antenatal care, including a comprehensive national survey conducted by the National Perinatal Epidemiology Unit,[994] suggest that key aspects of care valued by women are respect, competence, communication, support and convenience.[2] Access to information and provision of care by the same small group of people are also key aspects of care that lend themselves to a pregnant woman feeling valued as an individual and more in control.[3]

Current models of antenatal care originated in the early decades of the 20th century. The pattern of visits recommended at that time (monthly until 30 weeks, then fortnightly to 36 weeks and then weekly until delivery) is still recognisable today. It has been said that antenatal care has escaped critical assessment.[4] Both the individual components and composite package of antenatal care should conform to the criteria for a successful screening programme, namely that:

- the condition being screened for is an important health problem
- the screening test (further diagnostic test and treatment) is safe and acceptable
- the natural history of the condition is understood
- early detection and treatment has benefit over later detection and treatment
- the screening test is valid and reliable
- treatments or interventions should be effective
- there are adequate facilities for confirming the test results and resources for treatment
- the objectives of screening justify the costs.

A complete list of the NSC criteria for screening can be found in the NSC online library (www. nsc.nhs.uk/library/lib_ind.htm) under the title, *The UK National Screening Committee's criteria for appraising the viability, effectiveness and appropriateness of a screening programme.*

1.2 Areas outside the remit of the guideline

The guideline will not produce standards for service configuration, which have been addressed by the Children's National Service Frameworks (England and Wales), nor will it address quality standard issues (such as laboratory standards), which are addressed by the National Screening Committee.[5]

Although the guideline addresses screening for many of the complications of pregnancy, it does not include information on the investigation and appropriate ongoing management of these complications if they arise in pregnancy (for example, the management of pre-eclampsia, fetal anomalies and multiple pregnancies).

Any aspect of intrapartum and postpartum care has not been included in this guideline. This includes preparation for birth and parenthood, risk factor assessment for intrapartum care, breastfeeding and postnatal depression. These topics will be addressed in future National Institute for Clinical Excellence (NICE) guidelines on intrapartum and postpartum care. In addition, preconception care is not covered in this guideline.

The guideline offers recommendations on baseline clinical care for all pregnant women but it does not offer information on the additional care that some women will require. Pregnant women with the following conditions usually require care additional to that detailed in this guideline:

- cardiac disease, including hypertension
- renal disease
- hepatic disease
- endocrine disorders or diabetes
- psychiatric disorders (on medication)
- haematological disorders, including sickle cell or thalassaemia, thromboembolic disease, autoimmune diseases such as antiphospholipid syndrome
- epilepsy requiring anticonvulsant drugs
- malignant disease
- severe asthma
- drug use such as heroin, cocaine (including crack cocaine) and ecstasy
- HIV or hepatitis B virus (HBV) infected
- cystic fibrosis
- autoimmune disorders
- obesity (body mass index, BMI, 35 kg/m² or more at first contact) or underweight (BMI less than 18 kg/m² at first contact)
- women who may be at higher risk of developing complications e.g. women 40 years and older and women who smoke
- women who are particularly vulnerable (e.g. women 18 years or younger) or who lack social support
- family history of genetic disorder
- multiple pregnancy

- women who have experienced any of the following in previous pregnancies:
  - recurrent miscarriage (three or more consecutive pregnancy losses) or a mid-trimester loss
  - severe pre-eclampsia, HELLP syndrome or eclampsia
  - rhesus isoimmunisation or other significant blood group antibodies
  - uterine surgery including caesarean section, myomectomy or cone biopsy
  - antenatal or postpartum haemorrhage on two occasions
  - retained placenta on two occasions
  - puerperal psychosis
  - grand multiparity (more than six pregnancies)
  - a stillbirth or neonatal death
  - a small-for-gestational-age (SGA) infant (less than fifth centile)
  - a large-for-gestational-age (LGA) infant (greater than 95th centile)
  - a baby weighing less than 2500 g or more than 4500 g
  - a baby with a congenital anomaly (structural or chromosomal).

1.3 For whom is the guideline intended?

This guideline is of relevance to those who work in or use the National Health Service (NHS) in England and Wales:

- professional groups who share in caring for pregnant women, such as obstetricians, midwives, radiographers, physiotherapists, anaesthetists, general practitioners, paediatricians, pharmacists and others
- those with responsibilities for commissioning and planning maternity services, such as primary care trusts in England, Health Commission Wales, public health and trust managers
- pregnant women.

A version of this guideline for pregnant women, their partners and the public is available from the NICE website (www.nice.org.uk/CG062publicinfo) or from NICE publications on 0845 003 7783 (quote reference number N1483).

1.4 Who has developed the guideline?

The Guideline was developed by a multi-professional and lay working group, the Guideline Development Group (GDG), convened by the National Collaborating Centre for Women's and Children's Health (NCC-WCH). Membership included:

- two service user representatives
- two general practitioners
- two midwives
- two obstetricians
- a radiographer
- a neonatologist
- a representative from the Confidential Enquiry into Maternal Deaths (CEMD).

Staff from NCC-WCH provided methodological support for the guideline development process, undertook the systematic searches, retrieval and appraisal of the evidence and wrote successive drafts of the document.

In accordance with the NICE guideline development process,[6] all GDG members have made and updated any declarations of interest.

1.5 Who has developed the guideline update?

The guideline update was developed by a multi-professional and lay working group, the Guideline Development Group (GDG), convened by the National Collaborating Centre for Women's and Children's Health (NCC-WCH). Membership included:

- two service user representatives
- two midwives

2008 update

2008

2008 update

2008 update

- two obstetricians
- a general practitioner
- an ultrasonographer
- an MRC-funded public health research fellow.

Staff from NCC-WCH provided methodological support for the guideline development process, undertook the systematic searches, retrieval and appraisal of the evidence and wrote successive drafts of the document.

In accordance with the NICE guideline development process,[6] all GDG members have made and updated any declarations of interest (Appendix A).

1.6   Guideline methodology

The development of the guideline was commissioned by the National Institute for Health and Clinical Excellence (NICE) and developed in accordance with the guideline development process outlined in *The Guideline Development Process – Information for National Collaborating Centres and Guideline Development Groups*, available from the NICE website (www.nice.org.uk).[6]

Update methodology

The guideline update was developed in accordance with the NICE guideline development process outlined in the 2006 and 2007 editions of the guidelines manual.[632,633] Table 1.1 summarises the key stages of the guideline development process and which version of the process was followed at each stage.

Table 1.1   Stages in the NICE guideline development process and the versions followed at each stage

Stage	2006 version	2007 version
Scoping the guideline (determining what the guideline would and would not cover)	✓	
Preparing the work plan (agreeing timelines, milestones, Guideline Development Group constitution, etc.)	✓	
Forming and running the Guideline Development Group	✓	
Developing clinical questions	✓	
Identifying the evidence	✓	
Reviewing and grading the evidence	✓	✓
Incorporating health economics	✓	✓
Making group decisions and reaching consensus		✓
Linking guidance to other NICE guidance		✓
Creating guideline recommendations		✓
Developing clinical audit criteria		✓
Writing the guideline		✓
Validation (stakeholder consultation on the draft guideline)		✓
Declaration of interests[a]	✓	✓

[a]   The process for declaring interests was extended in November 2006 to cover NCC-WCH staff and to include personal family interests.

Literature search strategy

The aim of the literature review was to identify and synthesise relevant evidence within the published literature, in order to answer the specific clinical questions. Searches were performed using generic and specially developed filters, relevant MeSH (medical subject headings) terms and free-text terms. Details of all literature searches are available upon application to the NCC-WCH.

Guidelines by other development groups were searched for on the National Guidelines Clearinghouse database, the TRIP database and OMNI service on the Internet. The reference lists in these guidelines were checked against the searches to identify any missing evidence.

Searches were carried out for each topic of interest. The Cochrane Database of Systematic Reviews, up to Issue 3, 2003, was searched to identify systematic reviews of randomised controlled trials, with or without meta-analyses and randomised controlled trials. The electronic database, MEDLINE (Ovid version for the period January 1966 to April 2003), EMBASE (Ovid version from January 1980 to April 2003), MIDIRS (Midwives Information and Resource Service), CINAHL (Cumulative Index to Nursing and Allied Health Literature), the British Nursing Index (BNI) and PsychInfo were also searched.

The Database of Abstracts and Reviews of Effectiveness (DARE) was searched. Reference lists of non-systematic review articles and studies obtained from the initial search were reviewed and journals in the RCOG library were hand-searched to identify articles not yet indexed. There was no systematic attempt to search the 'grey literature' (conferences, abstracts, theses and unpublished trials).

A preliminary scrutiny of titles and abstracts was undertaken and full papers were obtained if they appeared to address the GDG's question relevant to the topic. Following a critical review of the full version of the study, articles not relevant to the subject in question were excluded. Studies that did not report on relevant outcomes were also excluded. Submitted evidence from stakeholders was included where the evidence was relevant to the GDG clinical question and when it was either better or equivalent in quality to the research identified in the literature searches.

The economic evaluation included a search of:

- NHS Economic Evaluations Database (NHS EED)
- Health Economic Evaluation Database (HEED)
- Cochrane Database of Systematic Reviews, Issue 3, 2003
- MEDLINE January 1966 to April 2003
- EMBASE 1980 to April 2003.

Relevant experts in the field were contacted for further information.

The search strategies were designed to find any economic study related to specific antenatal screening programmes. Abstracts and database reviews of papers found were reviewed by the health economist and were discarded if they appeared not to contain any economic data or if the focus of the paper did not relate to the precise topic or question being considered (i.e. to screening strategy alternatives that were not relevant to this guideline). Relevant references in the bibliographies of reviewed papers were also identified and reviewed. These were assessed by the health economists against standard criteria.

Literature search strategy for the 2008 update

Relevant published evidence to inform the guideline development process and answer the clinical questions was identified by systematic search strategies. Additionally, stakeholder organisations were invited to submit evidence for consideration by the GDG provided it was relevant to the clinical questions and of equivalent or better quality than evidence identified by the search strategies.

Systematic searches to answer the clinical questions formulated and agreed by the GDG were executed using the following databases via the 'Ovid' platform: Medline (1966 onwards), Embase (1980 onwards), Cumulative Index to Nursing and Allied Health Literature (1982 onwards) and PsycINFO (1967 onwards). The most recent search conducted for the three Cochrane databases (Cochrane Central Register of Controlled Trials, Cochrane Database of Systematic Reviews, and the Database of Abstracts of Reviews of Effects) was during Quarter 1, 2007. Searches to identify economic studies were undertaken using the above databases, and the NHS Economic Evaluations Database (NHS EED).

Search strategies combined relevant controlled vocabulary and natural language in an effort to balance sensitivity and specificity. Unless advised by the GDG, searches were not date specific. Language restrictions were not applied to searches. Both generic and specially developed methodological search filters were used appropriately.

2008 update

There was no systematic attempt to search grey literature (conferences, abstracts, theses and unpublished trials). Hand searching of journals not indexed on the databases was not undertaken.

Towards the end of the guideline development process searches were re-executed, thereby including evidence published and included in the databases up to 8 June 2007. Any evidence published after this date was not included. This date should be considered the starting point for searching for new evidence for future updates to this guideline.

Further details of the search strategies, including the methodological filters employed, are available on an accompanying disc.

Clinical effectiveness

For all the subject areas, evidence from the study designs least subject to sources of bias was included. Where possible, the highest levels of evidence were used, but all papers were reviewed using established guides (see below). Published systematic reviews or meta-analyses were used if available. For subject areas where neither was available, other appropriate experimental or observational studies were sought.

Identified articles were assessed methodologically and the best available evidence was used to form and support the recommendations. The highest level of evidence was selected for each clinical question. Using the evidence-level structure shown in Table 1.2, the retrieved evidence was graded accordingly.

Table 1.2   Structure of evidence levels

Level	Definition
1a	Systematic review and meta-analysis of randomised controlled trials
1b	At least one randomised controlled trial
2a	At least one well-designed controlled study without randomisation
2b	At least one other type of well-designed quasi-experimental study
3	Well-designed non-experimental descriptive studies, such as comparative studies, correlation studies or case studies
4	Expert committee reports or opinions and/or clinical experience of respected authorities

Hierarchy of evidence

The clinical question dictates the highest level of evidence that should be sought. For issues of therapy or treatment, the highest level of evidence is meta-analyses of randomised controlled trials or randomised controlled trials themselves. This would equate to a grade A recommendation.

For issues of prognosis, a cohort study is the best level of evidence available. The best possible level of evidence would equate to a grade B recommendation. It should not be interpreted as an inferior grade of recommendation, as it represents the highest level of evidence attainable for that type of clinical question.

For diagnostic tests, test evaluation studies examining the performance of the test were used if the efficacy of the test was required. Where an evaluation of the effectiveness of the test on management and outcome was required, evidence from randomised controlled trials or cohort studies was sought.

All retrieved articles have been appraised methodologically using established guides. Where appropriate, if a systematic review, meta-analysis or randomised controlled trial existed in relation to a topic, studies of a weaker design were not sought.

The evidence was synthesised using qualitative methods. These involved summarising the content of identified papers in the form of evidence tables and agreeing brief statements that accurately reflect the relevant evidence. Quantitative techniques (meta-analyses) were performed if appropriate and necessary.

For the purposes of this guideline, data are presented as relative risk (RR) where relevant (i.e. in RCTs and cohort studies) or as odds ratios (OR) where relevant (i.e. in systematic reviews of RCTs). Where these data are statistically significant they are also presented as numbers needed to treat (NNT), if relevant.

Appraisal and synthesis of clinical effectiveness evidence for the 2008 update

Evidence relating to clinical effectiveness was reviewed and classified using the established hierarchical system presented in Table 1.3.[632,633] This system reflects the susceptibility to bias that is inherent in particular study designs.

The type of clinical question dictates the highest level of evidence that may be sought. In assessing the quality of the evidence, each study was assigned a quality rating coded as '++', '+' or '−'. For issues of therapy or treatment, the highest possible evidence level (EL) is a well-conducted systematic review or meta-analysis of randomised controlled trials (RCTs; EL = 1++) or an individual RCT (EL = 1+). Studies of poor quality were rated as '−'. Usually, studies rated as '−' should not be used as a basis for making a recommendation, but they can be used to inform recommendations. For issues of prognosis, the highest possible level of evidence is a cohort study (EL = 2). A level of evidence was assigned to each study appraised during the development of the guideline.

For each clinical question, the highest available level of evidence was selected. Where appropriate, for example, if a systematic review, meta-analysis or RCT existed in relation to a question, studies of a weaker design were not considered. Where systematic reviews, meta-analyses and RCTs did not exist, other appropriate experimental or observational studies were sought. For diagnostic tests, test evaluation studies examining the performance of the test were used if the effectiveness (accuracy) of the test was required, but where an evaluation of the effectiveness of the test in the clinical management of patients and the outcome of disease was required, evidence from RCTs or cohort studies was optimal. For studies evaluating the accuracy of a diagnostic test, sensitivity, specificity, positive predictive values (PPVs) and negative predictive values (NPVs) were calculated or quoted where possible (see Table 1.4).

Table 1.3 Levels of evidence for intervention studies

Level	Source of evidence
1++	High-quality meta-analyses, systematic reviews of randomised controlled trials (RCTs), or RCTs with a very low risk of bias
1+	Well-conducted meta-analyses, systematic reviews of RCTs, or RCTs with a low risk of bias
1−	Meta-analyses, systematic reviews of RCTs, or RCTs with a high risk of bias
2++	High-quality systematic reviews of case–control or cohort studies; high-quality case–control or cohort studies with a very low risk of confounding, bias or chance and a high probability that the relationship is causal
2+	Well-conducted case–control or cohort studies with a low risk of confounding, bias or chance and a moderate probability that the relationship is causal
2−	Case–control or cohort studies with a high risk of confounding, bias or chance and a significant risk that the relationship is not causal
3	Non-analytical studies (for example, case reports, case series)
4	Expert opinion, formal consensus

Table 1.4 '2 × 2' table for calculation of diagnostic accuracy parameters

	Reference standard positive	Reference standard negative	Total
Test positive	a (true positive)	b (false positive)	a+b
Test negative	c (false negative)	d (true negative)	c+d
Total	a+c	b+d	a+b+c+d = N (total number of tests in study)

Sensitivity = a/(a+c), specificity = d/(b+d), PPV = a/(a+b), NPV = d/(c+d)

2008 update

The system described above covers studies of treatment effectiveness. However, it is less appropriate for studies reporting accuracy of diagnostic tests. In the absence of a validated ranking system for this type of test, NICE has developed a hierarchy of evidence that takes into account the various factors likely to affect the validity of these studies (see Table 1.5).[633]

Table 1.5   Levels of evidence for studies of the accuracy of diagnostic tests

Level	Type of evidence
Ia	Systematic review (with homogeneity)[a] of level-1 studies[b]
Ib	Level-1 studies[b]
II	Level-2 studies[c]; systematic reviews of level-2 studies
III	Level-3 studies[d]; systematic reviews of level-3 studies
IV	Consensus, expert committee reports or opinions and/or clinical experience without explicit critical appraisal; or based on physiology, bench research or 'first principles'

[a] Homogeneity means there are no or minor variations in the directions and degrees of results between individual studies that are included in the systematic review.

[b] Level-1 studies are studies that use a blind comparison of the test with a validated reference standard (gold standard) in a sample of patients that reflects the population to whom the test would apply.

[c] Level-2 studies are studies that have only one of the following:
  • narrow population (the sample does not reflect the population to whom the test would apply)
  • use a poor reference standard (defined as that where the 'test' is included in the 'reference', or where the 'testing' affects the 'reference')
  • the comparison between the test and reference standard is not blind
  • case–control studies.

[d] Level-3 studies are studies that have at least two or three of the features listed above.

Health economics

In antenatal care, there is a relatively large body of economic literature that has considered the economic costs and consequences of different screening programmes and considered the organisation of antenatal care. The purpose of including economic evidence in a clinical guideline is to allow recommendations to be made not just on the clinical effectiveness of different forms of care, but on the cost-effectiveness as well. The aim is to produce guidance that uses scarce health service resources efficiently; that is, providing the best possible care within resource constraints.

The economic evidence is focused around the different methods of screening, although some work has been undertaken to examine the cost-effectiveness of different patterns of antenatal care (the number of antenatal appointments) and to explore women's preferences for different aspects of their antenatal care. The economic evidence presented in this guideline is not a systematic review of all the economic evidence around antenatal care. It was decided that the health economic input into the guideline should focus on specific topics where the GDG thought that economic evidence would help them to inform their decisions. This approach was made on pragmatic grounds (not all the economic evidence could be reviewed with the resources available) and on the basis that economic evidence should not be based only on the economic literature, but should be consistent with the clinical effectiveness evidence presented in the guideline. Some of the economic evaluation studies did not address the specific alternatives (say, for screening) that were addressed in the guideline. Therefore, for each of the specific topic areas where the economic evidence was reviewed, a simple economic model was developed in order to present the GDG with a coherent picture of the costs and consequences of the decisions based on the clinical and economic evidence. The role of the health economist in this guideline was to review the literature in these specific areas and obtain cost data considered to be the closest to current UK opportunity cost (the value of the resources used, rather than the price or charge).

The approach adopted for this guideline was for the health economic analysis to focus on specific areas. Topics for economic analysis were selected on the following basis by the GDG.

• Does the proposed topic have major resource implications?
• Is there a change of policy involved?

- Are there sufficient data of adequate quality to allow useful review or modelling?
- Is there a lack of consensus among clinicians?
- Is there a particular area with a large amount of uncertainty?

Where the above answers were 'yes', this indicated that further economic analysis including modelling is more likely to be useful.

The GDG identified six areas where the potential impact of alternative strategies could be substantial and where the health economics evidence should focus. These were: screening for asymptomatic bacteriuria, screening for group B streptococcus, screening for syphilis, screening for sickle cell and thalassaemia, ultrasound screening for structural abnormalities and Down's syndrome screening.

For all these topics, a review of the economic evidence was undertaken, followed by simple economic modelling of the cost-effectiveness in England and Wales of different strategies.

The review of the economic evaluation studies included cost-effectiveness studies (only those where an ICER had been determined or could be determined from the data presented). The topic had to focus on the appropriate alternatives (the appropriate clinical question), preferably able to be generalised to the England and Wales setting, and therefore be useful in constructing a simple decision model. The review of the evidence included cost-effectiveness studies, cost-consequence studies (cost of present and future costs only) and high-quality systematic reviews of the evidence. A narrative review of all the evidence is not presented in the main guideline. Appendices B to F shows the way the models have been constructed, the economic and clinical parameters incorporated into each model, the sources of data that have been used (cost data and clinical data), the results of the baseline model and the sensitivity analysis.

Evidence on the cost consequences associated with alternative screening strategies was obtained from various published sources that addressed these issues. The purpose was to obtain good-quality cost data judged by the health economist to be as close as possible to the true opportunity cost of the intervention (screening programme).

The key cost variables considered were:

- the cost of a screening programme (the cost of different screening interventions and the cost of expanding and contracting a screening programme)
- the cost of treatment of women found to be carriers of a disease
- the cost of any adverse or non-therapeutic effects of screening or treatment to the woman
- the cost of the consequences of screening and not screening to the fetus and infant, including fetal loss, ending pregnancy, and the lifetime costs of caring for infants born with disabilities.

Cost data not available from published sources were obtained from the most up-to-date NHS reference cost price list. Some cost data could not be obtained from published sources or from NHS reference costs and, in such cases, an indicative estimate of the likely costs was obtained from the GDG. The range of sources of cost data are set out in the appendix that explains the methodology adopted to construct each of the economic models created for this guideline.

In some cases (e.g. screening for group B streptococcus and syphilis), the economic modelling work could not be completed owing to lack of clinical evidence relating to the different screening options. Appendices C and D provide some discussion of these models that could not be completed in the guideline and areas for future research.

Limitations of the economic evidence in this guideline

Economic analyses have been undertaken alongside a wide range of antenatal screening procedures. A systematic review of antenatal screening was undertaken in 2001.[7] This review found that many of the studies identified were of poor quality, since they did not consider the effects of screening on future health (of mother and baby) but only costs averted by a screening programme.

In this guideline, the costs of screening and the costs of the benefits or harm of screening have been considered simultaneously where possible (i.e. where the data exist). It has not been possible to include many of the consequences of a screening programme because the data do not exist on these less straightforward or measurable outcomes (such as the benefit foregone from ending pregnancy).

The economic analysis of screening methods in the guideline has not been able to consider the following:

- the value to the woman of being given information about the health of her future child
- the value of being able to plan appropriate services for children who are born with disabilities
- the value of a life of a child born with disability, to the child, to the family and to society in general
- the value to a woman of being able to choose whether to end a pregnancy
- the value of a life foregone as a consequence of screening.

The cost-effectiveness studies reviewed for this guideline had narrowly defined endpoints; for example, a case of birth defect detected and subsequently averted as a result of a screening test. Some of the studies have considered the cost consequences of avoiding the birth of an infant with severe disabilities and their long-term care costs. The value of future life foregone (of a healthy or a disabled infant's life) due to screening has not been explicitly considered in any of the economic evidence of antenatal screening. Since economic evaluation should always consider the costs and benefits of an intervention in the widest possible sense, this could be seen as a limitation of the analysis presented in this guideline. The consequences of this are discussed in Appendices B to G as appropriate.

Health economics for the 2008 update

The aim of the economic input into the guideline was to inform the GDG of potential economic issues relating to antenatal care. The health economist helped the GDG by identifying topics within the guideline that might benefit from economic analysis, reviewing the available economic evidence and, where necessary, conducting (or commissioning) economic analysis. Reviews of published health economic evidence are presented alongside the reviews of clinical evidence and are incorporated within the relevant evidence statement and recommendations. For some questions, no published evidence was identified, and decision analytic modelling was undertaken. Results of this modelling are presented in the guideline text where appropriate, with full details in Appendices B to G inclusive.

Economic evaluations in this guideline have been conducted in the form of a cost-effectiveness analysis, with the health effects measured in an appropriate non-monetary outcome indicator. The NICE technology appraisal programme measures outcomes in terms of quality-adjusted life years (QALYs). Where possible, this approach has been used in the development of this guideline. However, where it has not been possible to estimate QALYs gained as a result of an intervention, an alternative measure of effectiveness has been used.

Cost-effectiveness analysis, with the units of effectiveness expressed in QALYs (known as cost–utility analysis) is widely recognised as a useful approach for measuring and comparing the efficiency of different health interventions. The QALY is a measure of health outcome which assigns to each period of time (generally 1 year) a weight, ranging from 0 to 1, corresponding to health-related quality of life during that period. It is one of the most commonly used outcome measures in health economics. A score of 1 corresponds to full health and a score of 0 corresponds to a health state equivalent to death. Negative valuations, implying a health state worse than death, are possible. Health outcomes using this method are measured by the number of years of life in a given health state multiplied by the value of being in that health state.

Forming and grading the recommendations

The GDG was presented with the summaries (text and evidence tables) of the best available research evidence to answer their questions. Recommendations were based on, and explicitly linked to, the evidence that supported them. A recommendation's grade may not necessarily reflect the importance attached to the recommendation. For example, the GDG felt that the principles of woman-centred care that underpin this guideline (Chapter 3) are particularly important but some of these recommendations receive only a D grade or good practice point (GPP).

The GDG worked where possible on an informal consensus basis. Formal consensus methods (modified Delphi techniques or nominal group technique) were employed if required (e.g. grading recommendations or agreeing audit criteria).

The recommendations were then graded according to the level of evidence upon which they were based. The strength of the evidence on which each recommendation is based is shown in Table 1.6. The grading of recommendations will follow that outlined in the Health Technology Assessment (HTA) review *How to develop cost conscious guidelines*.

Table 1.6 Strength of the evidence upon which each recommendation is based

Grade	Definition
A	Directly based on level I evidence
B	Directly based on level II evidence or extrapolated recommendation from level I evidence
C	Directly based on level III evidence or extrapolated recommendation from either level I or II evidence
D	Directly based on level IV evidence or extrapolated recommendation from either level I, II or III evidence
Good practice point (GPP)	The view of the Guideline Development Group
NICE Technology Appraisal	Recommendation taken from a NICE Technology Appraisal

Limited results or data are presented in the text. More comprehensive results and data are available in the relevant evidence tables.

Forming and grading the recommendations for the 2008 update

The updated NICE guideline methodology manual (2007)[633] requires that recommendations are no longer graded. The 2008 recommendations in this update therefore do not have a grade; however, the grade assigned to 2003 recommendations has been left in place.

The Antenatal Assessment Tool was developed using formal consensus methodology (see Chapter 14 for further details).

External review

The guideline has been developed in accordance with the NICE guideline development process.[6] This has included the opportunity for registered stakeholders to comment on the scope of the guideline, the first draft of the full and summary guidelines and the second draft of all versions of the guideline. In addition, the first draft was reviewed by nominated individuals with an interest in antenatal care. All drafts, comments and responses were also reviewed by the independent Guideline Review Panel established by NICE.

The comments made by the stakeholders, peer reviewers and the NICE Guideline Review Panel were collated and presented anonymously for consideration by the GDG. All comments were considered systematically by the GDG and the resulting actions and responses were recorded.

2008 update

2 Summary of recommendations and care pathway

2.1 Key priorities for implementation (key recommendations)

Antenatal information

Pregnant women should be offered information based on the current available evidence together with support to enable them to make informed decisions about their care. This information should include where they will be seen and who will undertake their care.

Lifestyle considerations

All women should be informed at the booking appointment about the importance for their own and their baby's health of maintaining adequate vitamin D stores during pregnancy and whilst breastfeeding. In order to achieve this, women may choose to take 10 micrograms of vitamin D per day, as found in the Healthy Start multivitamin supplement. Particular care should be taken to enquire as to whether women at greatest risk are following advice to take this daily supplement. These include:

- women of South Asian, African, Caribbean or Middle Eastern family origin
- women who have limited exposure to sunlight, such as women who are predominantly housebound, or usually remain covered when outdoors
- women who eat a diet particularly low in vitamin D, such as women who consume no oily fish, eggs, meat, vitamin D-fortified margarine or breakfast cereal
- women with a pre-pregnancy body mass index above 30 kg/m^2.

Screening for haematological conditions

Screening for sickle cell diseases and thalassaemias should be offered to all women as early as possible in pregnancy (ideally by 10 weeks). The type of screening depends upon the prevalence and can be carried out in either primary or secondary care.

Screening for fetal anomalies

Participation in regional congenital anomaly registers and/or UK National Screening Committee-approved audit systems is strongly recommended to facilitate the audit of detection rates.

The 'combined test' (nuchal translucency, beta-human chorionic gonadotrophin, pregnancy-associated plasma protein-A) should be offered to screen for Down's syndrome between 11 weeks 0 days and 13 weeks 6 days. For women who book later in pregnancy the most clinically and cost-effective serum screening test (triple or quadruple test) should be offered between 15 weeks 0 days and 20 weeks 0 days.

Screening for clinical conditions

Screening for gestational diabetes using risk factors is recommended in a healthy population. At the booking appointment, the following risk factors for gestational diabetes should be determined:

- body mass index above 30 kg/m^2
- previous macrosomic baby weighing 4.5 kg or above

- previous gestational diabetes (refer to 'Diabetes in pregnancy' [NICE clinical guideline 63], available from www.nice.org.uk/CG063)
- family history of diabetes (first-degree relative with diabetes)
- family origin with a high prevalence of diabetes:
  - South Asian (specifically women whose country of family origin is India, Pakistan or Bangladesh)
  - black Caribbean
  - Middle Eastern (specifically women whose country of family origin is Saudi Arabia, United Arab Emirates, Iraq, Jordan, Syria, Oman, Qatar, Kuwait, Lebanon or Egypt).

Women with any one of these risk factors should be offered testing for gestational diabetes (refer to 'Diabetes in pregnancy' [NICE clinical guideline 63], available from www.nice.org.uk/CG063).

2.2 Summary of recommendations

Chapter 3 Woman-centred care and informed decision making

Antenatal information
Antenatal information should be given to pregnant women according to the following schedule.

- At the first contact with a healthcare professional:
  - folic acid supplementation
  - food hygiene, including how to reduce the risk of a food-acquired infection
  - lifestyle advice, including smoking cessation, and the implications of recreational drug use and alcohol consumption in pregnancy
  - all antenatal screening, including screening for haemoglobinopathies, the anomaly scan and screening for Down's syndrome, as well as risks and benefits of the screening tests.
- At booking (ideally by 10 weeks):
  - how the baby develops during pregnancy
  - nutrition and diet, including vitamin D supplementation for women at risk of vitamin D deficiency, and details of the 'Healthy Start' programme (www.healthystart.nhs.uk)
  - exercise, including pelvic floor exercises
  - place of birth (refer to 'Intrapartum care' [NICE clinical guideline 55], available from www.nice.org.uk/CG055)
  - pregnancy care pathway
  - breastfeeding, including workshops
  - participant-led antenatal classes
  - further discussion of all antenatal screening
  - discussion of mental health issues (refer to 'Antenatal and postnatal mental health' [NICE clinical guideline 45], available from www.nice.org.uk/CG045).
- Before or at 36 weeks:
  - breastfeeding information, including technique and good management practices that would help a woman succeed, such as detailed in the UNICEF 'Baby Friendly Initiative' (www.babyfriendly.org.uk)
  - preparation for labour and birth, including information about coping with pain in labour and the birth plan
  - recognition of active labour
  - care of the new baby
  - vitamin K prophylaxis
  - newborn screening tests
  - postnatal self-care
  - awareness of 'baby blues' and postnatal depression.
- At 38 weeks:
  - options for management of prolonged pregnancy*.

This can be supported by information such as 'The pregnancy book' (Department of Health 2007) and the use of other relevant resources such as UK National Screening Committee publications and the Midwives Information and Resource Service (MIDIRS) information leaflets (www.infochoice.org).

---

* The clinical guideline 'Induction of labour' is being updated and is expected to be published in June 2008.

2008 update

Information should be given in a form that is easy to understand and accessible to pregnant women with additional needs, such as physical, sensory or learning disabilities, and to pregnant women who do not speak or read English.

Information can also be given in other forms such as audiovisual or touch screen technology; this should be supported by written information.

Pregnant women should be offered information based on the current available evidence together with support to enable them to make informed decisions about their care. This information should include where they will be seen and who will undertake their care.

At each antenatal appointment, healthcare professionals should offer consistent information and clear explanations, and should provide pregnant women with an opportunity to discuss issues and ask questions.

Pregnant women should be offered opportunities to attend participant-led antenatal classes, including breastfeeding workshops.

Women's decisions should be respected, even when this is contrary to the views of the healthcare professional.

Pregnant women should be informed about the purpose of any test before it is performed. The healthcare professional should ensure the woman has understood this information and has sufficient time to make an informed decision. The right of a woman to accept or decline a test should be made clear.

Information about antenatal screening should be provided in a setting where discussion can take place; this may be in a group setting or on a one-to-one basis. This should be done before the booking appointment.

Information about antenatal screening should include balanced and accurate information about the condition being screened for.

Chapter 4 Provision and organisation of care

4.1 Who provides care?
Midwife- and GP-led models of care should be offered for women with an uncomplicated pregnancy. Routine involvement of obstetricians in the care of women with an uncomplicated pregnancy at scheduled times does not appear to improve perinatal outcomes compared with involving obstetricians when complications arise. [A]

4.2 Continuity of care
Antenatal care should be provided by a small group of carers with whom the woman feels comfortable. There should be continuity of care throughout the antenatal period. [A]

A system of clear referral paths should be established so that pregnant women who require additional care are managed and treated by the appropriate specialist teams when problems are identified. [D]

4.3 Where should antenatal appointments take place?
Antenatal care should be readily and easily accessible to all women and should be sensitive to the needs of individual women and the local community. [C]

The environment in which antenatal appointments take place should enable women to discuss sensitive issues such as domestic violence, sexual abuse, psychiatric illness and illicit drug use. [Good practice point]

4.4 Documentation of care
Structured maternity records should be used for antenatal care. [A]

Maternity services should have a system in place whereby women carry their own case notes. [A]

A standardised, national maternity record with an agreed minimum data set should be developed and used. This will help carers to provide the recommended evidence-based care to pregnant women. [Good practice point]

4.5 Frequency of antenatal appointments

A schedule of antenatal appointments should be determined by the function of the appointments. For a woman who is nulliparous with an uncomplicated pregnancy, a schedule of ten appointments should be adequate. For a woman who is parous with an uncomplicated pregnancy, a schedule of seven appointments should be adequate. [B]

Early in pregnancy, all women should receive appropriate written information about the likely number, timing and content of antenatal appointments associated with different options of care and be given an opportunity to discuss this schedule with their midwife or doctor. [D]

Each antenatal appointment should be structured and have focused content. Longer appointments are needed early in pregnancy to allow comprehensive assessment and discussion. Wherever possible, appointments should incorporate routine tests and investigations to minimise inconvenience to women. [D]

4.6 Gestational age assessment: LMP and ultrasound

Pregnant women should be offered an early ultrasound scan between 10 weeks 0 days and 13 weeks 6 days to determine gestational age and to detect multiple pregnancies. This will ensure consistency of gestational age assessment and reduce the incidence of induction of labour for prolonged pregnancy.

Crown–rump length measurement should be used to determine gestational age. If the crown–rump length is above 84 mm, the gestational age should be estimated using head circumference.

Chapter 5 Lifestyle considerations

5.3 Working during pregnancy

Pregnant women should be informed of their maternity rights and benefits. [C]

The majority of women can be reassured that it is safe to continue working during pregnancy. Further information about possible occupational hazards during pregnancy is available from the Health and Safety Executive (www.hse.gov.uk). [D]

A woman's occupation during pregnancy should be ascertained to identify those at increased risk through occupational exposure. [Good practice point]

5.5 Nutritional supplements

Pregnant women (and those intending to become pregnant) should be informed that dietary supplementation with folic acid, before conception and up to 12 weeks of gestation, reduces the risk of having a baby with neural tube defects (anencephaly, spina bifida). The recommended dose is 400 micrograms per day. [A]

Iron supplementation should not be offered routinely to all pregnant women. It does not benefit the mother's or the fetus's health and may have unpleasant maternal side effects. [A]

Pregnant women should be informed that vitamin A supplementation (intake greater than 700 micrograms) might be teratogenic and therefore it should be avoided. Pregnant women should be informed that as liver and liver products may also contain high levels of vitamin A, consumption of these products should also be avoided. [C]

All women should be informed at the booking appointment about the importance for their own and their baby's health of maintaining adequate vitamin D stores during pregnancy and whilst breastfeeding. In order to achieve this, women may choose to take 10 micrograms of vitamin D per day, as found in the Healthy Start multivitamin supplement. Particular care should be taken to enquire as to whether women at greatest risk are following advice to take this daily supplement. These include:

- women of South Asian, African, Caribbean or Middle Eastern family origin
- women who have limited exposure to sunlight, such as women who are predominantly housebound, or usually remain covered when outdoors
- women who eat a diet particularly low in vitamin D, such as women who consume no oily fish, eggs, meat, vitamin D-fortified margarine or breakfast cereal
- women with a pre-pregnancy body mass index above 30 kg/m².

2008 update

5.6 Food-acquired infections
Pregnant women should be offered information on how to reduce the risk of listeriosis by:

- drinking only pasteurised or UHT milk
- not eating ripened soft cheese such as Camembert, Brie and blue-veined cheese (there is no risk with hard cheeses, such as Cheddar, or cottage cheese and processed cheese)
- not eating pâté (of any sort, including vegetable)
- not eating uncooked or undercooked ready-prepared meals. [D]

Pregnant women should be offered information on how to reduce the risk of salmonella infection by:

- avoiding raw or partially cooked eggs or food that may contain them (such as mayonnaise)
- avoiding raw or partially cooked meat, especially poultry. [D]

5.7 Prescribed medicines
Few medicines have been established as safe to use in pregnancy. Prescription medicines should be used as little as possible during pregnancy and should be limited to circumstances where the benefit outweighs the risk. [D]

5.8 Over-the-counter medicines
Pregnant women should be informed that few over-the-counter (OTC) medicines have been established as being safe to take in pregnancy. OTC medicines should be used as little as possible during pregnancy. [D]

5.9 Complementary therapies
Pregnant women should be informed that few complementary therapies have been established as being safe and effective during pregnancy. Women should not assume that such therapies are safe and they should be used as little as possible during pregnancy. [D]

5.10 Exercise in pregnancy
Pregnant women should be informed that beginning or continuing a moderate course of exercise during pregnancy is not associated with adverse outcomes. [A]

Pregnant women should be informed of the potential dangers of certain activities during pregnancy, for example, contact sports, high-impact sports and vigorous racquet sports that may involve the risk of abdominal trauma, falls or excessive joint stress, and scuba diving, which may result in fetal birth defects and fetal decompression disease. [D]

5.11 Sexual intercourse in pregnancy
Pregnant woman should be informed that sexual intercourse in pregnancy is not known to be associated with any adverse outcomes. [B]

5.12 Alcohol and smoking in pregnancy

Alcohol consumption in pregnancy:
Pregnant women and women planning a pregnancy should be advised to avoid drinking alcohol in the first 3 months of pregnancy if possible because it may be associated with an increased risk of miscarriage.

If women choose to drink alcohol during pregnancy they should be advised to drink no more than 1 to 2 UK units once or twice a week (1 unit equals half a pint of ordinary strength lager or beer, or one shot [25 ml] of spirits. One small [125 ml] glass of wine is equal to 1.5 UK units). Although there is uncertainty regarding a safe level of alcohol consumption in pregnancy, at this low level there is no evidence of harm to the unborn baby.

Women should be informed that getting drunk or binge drinking during pregnancy (defined as more than 5 standard drinks or 7.5 UK units on a single occasion) may be harmful to the unborn baby.

Smoking in pregnancy:
At the first contact with the woman, discuss her smoking status, provide information about the risks of smoking to the unborn child and the hazards of exposure to secondhand smoke. Address any concerns she and her partner or family may have about stopping smoking.*

---

* This recommendation is from the NICE public health guidance on smoking cessation (www.nice.org.uk/PH010). Following NICE protocol, the recommendation has been incorporated verbatim into this guideline.

Pregnant women should be informed about the specific risks of smoking during pregnancy (such as the risk of having a baby with low birthweight and preterm birth). The benefits of quitting at any stage should be emphasised. [A]

Offer personalised information, advice and support on how to stop smoking. Encourage pregnant women to use local NHS Stop Smoking Services and the NHS pregnancy smoking helpline, by providing details on when, where and how to access them. Consider visiting pregnant women at home if it is difficult for them to attend specialist services.*

Monitor smoking status and offer smoking cessation advice, encouragement and support throughout the pregnancy and beyond.*

Discuss the risks and benefits of nicotine replacement therapy (NRT) with pregnant women who smoke, particularly those who do not wish to accept the offer of help from the NHS Stop Smoking Service. If a woman expresses a clear wish to receive NRT, use professional judgement when deciding whether to offer a prescription.*

Advise women using nicotine patches to remove them before going to bed.*

This supersedes NICE technology appraisal guidance 39 on NRT and bupropion.*

Women who are unable to quit smoking during pregnancy should be encouraged to reduce smoking. [B]

5.13 Cannabis use in pregnancy
The direct effects of cannabis on the fetus are uncertain but may be harmful. Cannabis use is associated with smoking, which is known to be harmful; therefore women should be discouraged from using cannabis during pregnancy. [C]

5.14 Air travel during pregnancy
Pregnant women should be informed that long-haul air travel is associated with an increased risk of venous thrombosis, although whether or not there is additional risk during pregnancy is unclear. In the general population, wearing correctly fitted compression stockings is effective at reducing the risk. [B]

5.15 Car travel during pregnancy
Pregnant women should be informed about the correct use of seatbelts (that is, three-point seatbelts 'above and below the bump, not over it'). [B]

5.16 Travelling abroad during pregnancy
Pregnant women should be informed that, if they are planning to travel abroad, they should discuss considerations such as flying, vaccinations and travel insurance with their midwife or doctor. [Good practice point]

Chapter 6 Management of common symptoms of pregnancy

6.1 Nausea and vomiting in early pregnancy
Women should be informed that most cases of nausea and vomiting in pregnancy will resolve spontaneously within 16 to 20 weeks of gestation and that nausea and vomiting are not usually associated with a poor pregnancy outcome. If a woman requests or would like to consider treatment, the following interventions appear to be effective in reducing symptoms [A]:

- nonpharmacological:
  - ginger
  - P6 (wrist) acupressure
- pharmacological:
  - antihistamines.

Information about all forms of self-help and nonpharmacological treatments should be made available for pregnant women who have nausea and vomiting. [Good practice point]

---

* This recommendation is from the NICE public health guidance on smoking cessation (www.nice.org.uk/PH010). Following NICE protocol, the recommendation has been incorporated verbatim into this guideline.

6.2 Heartburn
Women who present with symptoms of heartburn in pregnancy should be offered information regarding lifestyle and diet modification. [Good practice point]

Antacids may be offered to women whose heartburn remains troublesome despite lifestyle and diet modification. [A]

6.3 Constipation
Women who present with constipation in pregnancy should be offered information regarding diet modification, such as bran or wheat fibre supplementation. [A]

6.4 Haemorrhoids
In the absence of evidence of the effectiveness of treatments for haemorrhoids in pregnancy, women should be offered information concerning diet modification. If clinical symptoms remain troublesome, standard haemorrhoid creams should be considered. [Good practice point]

6.5 Varicose veins
Women should be informed that varicose veins are a common symptom of pregnancy that will not cause harm and that compression stockings can improve the symptoms but will not prevent varicose veins from emerging. [A]

6.6 Vaginal discharge
Women should be informed that an increase in vaginal discharge is a common physiological change that occurs during pregnancy. If this is associated with itch, soreness, offensive smell or pain on passing urine there maybe an infective cause and investigation should be considered. [Good practice point]

A 1 week course of a topical imidazole is an effective treatment and should be considered for vaginal candidiasis infections in pregnant women. [A]

The effectiveness and safety of oral treatments for vaginal candidiasis in pregnancy is uncertain and these should not be offered. [Good practice point]

6.7 Backache
Women should be informed that exercising in water, massage therapy and group or individual back care classes might help to ease backache during pregnancy. [A]

Chapter 7 Clinical examination of pregnant women

7.1 Measurement of weight and body mass index
Maternal weight and height should be measured at the first antenatal appointment, and the woman's body mass index (BMI) calculated (weight [kg]/height[m]^2). [B]

Repeated weighing during pregnancy should be confined to circumstances where clinical management is likely to be influenced. [C]

7.2 Breast examination
Routine breast examination during antenatal care is not recommended for the promotion of postnatal breastfeeding. [A]

7.3 Pelvic examination
Routine antenatal pelvic examination does not accurately assess gestational age, nor does it accurately predict preterm birth or cephalopelvic disproportion. It is not recommended. [B]

7.4 Female genital mutilation
Pregnant women who have had female genital mutilation should be identified early in antenatal care through sensitive enquiry. Antenatal examination will then allow planning of intrapartum care. [C]

7.5 Domestic violence
Healthcare professionals need to be alert to the symptoms or signs of domestic violence and women should be given the opportunity to disclose domestic violence in an environment in which they feel secure. [D]

7.6 Prediction, detection and initial management of mental disorders
In all communications (including initial referral) with maternity services, healthcare professionals should include information on any relevant history of mental disorder.*

At a woman's first contact with services in both the antenatal and the postnatal periods, healthcare professionals (including midwives, obstetricians, health visitors and GPs) should ask about:

- past or present severe mental illness including schizophrenia, bipolar disorder, psychosis in the postnatal period and severe depression
- previous treatment by a psychiatrist/specialist mental health team, including inpatient care
- a family history of perinatal mental illness.

Other specific predictors, such as poor relationships with her partner, should not be used for the routine prediction of the development of a mental disorder.*

At a woman's first contact with primary care, at her booking visit and postnatally (usually at 4 to 6 weeks and 3 to 4 months), healthcare professionals (including midwives, obstetricians, health visitors and GPs) should ask two questions to identify possible depression.

- During the past month, have you often been bothered by feeling down, depressed or hopeless?
- During the past month, have you often been bothered by having little interest or pleasure in doing things?

A third question should be considered if the woman answers 'yes' to either of the initial questions.

- Is this something you feel you need or want help with?*

After identifying a possible mental disorder in a woman during pregnancy or the postnatal period, further assessment should be considered, in consultation with colleagues if necessary.

- If the healthcare professional or the woman has significant concerns, the woman should normally be referred for further assessment to her GP.
- If the woman has, or is suspected to have, a severe mental illness (for example, bipolar disorder or schizophrenia), she should be referred to a specialist mental health service, including, if appropriate, a specialist perinatal mental health service. This should be discussed with the woman and preferably with her GP.
- The woman's GP should be informed in all cases in which a possible current mental disorder or a history of significant mental disorder is detected, even if no further assessment or referral is made.*

Chapter 8 Screening for haematological conditions

8.1 Anaemia
Pregnant women should be offered screening for anaemia. Screening should take place early in pregnancy (at the booking appointment) and at 28 weeks when other blood screening tests are being performed. This allows enough time for treatment if anaemia is detected. [B]

Haemoglobin levels outside the normal UK range for pregnancy (that is, 11 g/100 ml at first contact and 10.5 g/100 ml at 28 weeks) should be investigated and iron supplementation considered if indicated. [A]

8.2 Blood grouping and red cell alloantibodies
Women should be offered testing for blood group and rhesus D status in early pregnancy. [B]

It is recommended that routine antenatal anti-D prophylaxis is offered to all non-sensitised pregnant women who are rhesus D-negative.† [NICE 2002]

Women should be screened for atypical red cell alloantibodies in early pregnancy and again at 28 weeks, regardless of their rhesus D status. [B]

---

* This recommendation is from the NICE clinical guideline on antenatal and postnatal mental health (see www.nice.org.uk/CG045). Following NICE protocol, the recommendation has been incorporated verbatim into this guideline.

† The technology appraisal guidance 'Guidance on the use of routine antenatal anti-D prophylaxis for RhD-negative women' (NICE technology appraisal 41) is being updated and is expected to be published in June 2008.

Pregnant women with clinically significant atypical red cell alloantibodies should be offered referral to a specialist centre for further investigation and advice on subsequent antenatal management. [D]

If a pregnant woman is rhesus D-negative, consideration should be given to offering partner testing to determine whether the administration of anti-D prophylaxis is necessary. [Good practice point]

8.3 Haemoglobinopathies

Preconception counselling (supportive listening, advice giving and information) and carrier testing should be available to all women who are identified as being at higher risk of haemoglobinopathies, using the Family Origin Questionnaire from the NHS Antenatal and Newborn Screening Programme (www.sickleandthal.org.uk/Documents/F_Origin_Questionnaire.pdf) (see Appendix J).

Information about screening for sickle cell diseases and thalassaemias, including carrier status and the implications of these, should be given to pregnant women at the first contact with a healthcare professional. Refer to Section 3.3 for more information about giving antenatal information.

Screening for sickle cell diseases and thalassaemias should be offered to all women as early as possible in pregnancy (ideally by 10 weeks). The type of screening depends upon the prevalence and can be carried out in either primary or secondary care.

Where prevalence of sickle cell disease is high (fetal prevalence above 1.5 cases per 10 000 pregnancies), laboratory screening (preferably high-performance liquid chromatography) should be offered to all pregnant women to identify carriers of sickle cell disease and/or thalassaemia.

Where prevalence of sickle cell disease is low (fetal prevalence 1.5 cases per 10 000 pregnancies or below), all pregnant women should be offered screening for haemoglobinopathies using the Family Origin Questionnaire (www.sickleandthal.org.uk/Documents/F_Origin_Questionnaire.pdf).

- If the Family Origin Questionnaire indicates a high risk of sickle cell disorders, laboratory screening (preferably high-performance liquid chromatography) should be offered.
- If the mean corpuscular haemoglobin is below 27 picograms, laboratory screening (preferably high-performance liquid chromatography) should be offered.

If the woman is identified as a carrier of a clinically significant haemoglobinopathy then the father of the baby should be offered counselling and appropriate screening without delay. For more details about haemoglobinopathy variants refer to the NHS Antenatal and Newborn Screening Programme (www.sickleandthal.org.uk/Documents/ProgrammeSTAN.pdf).

Chapter 9 Screening for fetal anomalies

9.1 Screening for structural anomalies

Ultrasound screening for fetal anomalies should be routinely offered, normally between 18 weeks 0 days and 20 weeks 6 days.

At the first contact with a healthcare professional, women should be given information about the purpose and implications of the anomaly scan to enable them to make an informed choice as to whether or not to have the scan. The purpose of the scan is to identify fetal anomalies and allow:

- reproductive choice (termination of pregnancy)
- parents to prepare (for any treatment/disability/palliative care/termination of pregnancy)
- managed birth in a specialist centre
- intrauterine therapy.

Women should be informed of the limitations of routine ultrasound screening and that detection rates vary by the type of fetal anomaly, the woman's body mass index and the position of the unborn baby at the time of the scan.

If an anomaly is detected during the anomaly scan pregnant women should be informed of the findings to enable them to make an informed choice as to whether they wish to continue with the pregnancy or have a termination of pregnancy.

Fetal echocardiography involving the four chamber view of the fetal heart and outflow tracts is recommended as part of the routine anomaly scan.

Routine screening for cardiac anomalies using nuchal translucency is not recommended.

When routine ultrasound screening is performed to detect neural tube defects, alpha-fetoprotein testing is not required.

Participation in regional congenital anomaly registers and/or UK National Screening Committee-approved audit systems is strongly recommended to facilitate the audit of detection rates.

9.2 Screening for Down's syndrome

All pregnant women should be offered screening for Down's syndrome. Women should understand that it is their choice to embark on screening for Down's syndrome.

Screening for Down's syndrome should be performed by the end of the first trimester (13 weeks 6 days), but provision should be made to allow later screening (which could be as late as 20 weeks 0 days) for women booking later in pregnancy.

The 'combined test' (nuchal translucency, beta-human chorionic gonadotrophin, pregnancy-associated plasma protein-A) should be offered to screen for Down's syndrome between 11 weeks 0 days and 13 weeks 6 days. For women who book later in pregnancy the most clinically and cost-effective serum screening test (triple or quadruple test) should be offered between 15 weeks 0 days and 20 weeks 0 days.

When it is not possible to measure nuchal translucency, owing to fetal position or raised body mass index, women should be offered serum screening (triple or quadruple test) between 15 weeks 0 days and 20 weeks 0 days.

Information about screening for Down's syndrome should be given to pregnant women at the first contact with a healthcare professional. This will provide the opportunity for further discussion before embarking on screening. (Refer to Section 3.3 for more information about giving antenatal information). Specific information should include:

- the screening pathway for both screen-positive and screen-negative results
- the decisions that need to be made at each point along the pathway and their consequences
- the fact that screening does not provide a definitive diagnosis and a full explanation of the risk score obtained following testing
- information about chorionic villus sampling and amniocentesis
- balanced and accurate information about Down's syndrome.

If a woman receives a screen-positive result for Down's syndrome, she should have rapid access to appropriate counselling by trained staff.

The routine anomaly scan (at 18 weeks 0 days to 20 weeks 6 days) should not be routinely used for Down's syndrome screening using soft markers

The presence of an isolated soft marker, with an exception of increased nuchal fold, on the routine anomaly scan, should not be used to adjust the a priori risk for Down's syndrome.

The presence of an increased nuchal fold (6 mm or above) or two or more soft markers on the routine anomaly scan should prompt the offer of a referral to a fetal medicine specialist or an appropriate healthcare professional with a special interest in fetal medicine.

Chapter 10 Screening for infections

10.1 Asymptomatic bacteriuria

Women should be offered routine screening for asymptomatic bacteriuria by midstream urine culture early in pregnancy. Identification and treatment of asymptomatic bacteriuria reduces the risk of pyelonephritis.

10.2 Asymptomatic bacterial vaginosis

Pregnant women should not be offered routine screening for bacterial vaginosis because the evidence suggests that the identification and treatment of asymptomatic bacterial vaginosis does not lower the risk for preterm birth and other adverse reproductive outcomes. [A]

2008 update

10.3 Chlamydia trachomatis
At the booking appointment, healthcare professionals should inform pregnant women younger than 25 years about the high prevalence of chlamydia infection in their age group, and give details of their local National Chlamydia Screening Programme (www.chlamydiascreening.nhs.uk).

Chlamydia screening should not be offered as part of routine antenatal care.

10.4 Cytomegalovirus
The available evidence does not support routine cytomegalovirus screening in pregnant women and it should not be offered. [B]

10.5 Hepatitis B virus
Serological screening for hepatitis B virus should be offered to pregnant women so that effective postnatal intervention can be offered to infected women to decrease the risk of mother-to-child transmission. [A]

10.6 Hepatitis C virus
Pregnant women should not be offered routine screening for hepatitis C virus because there is insufficient evidence to support its effectiveness and cost-effectiveness.[C]

10.7 HIV
Pregnant women should be offered screening for HIV infection early in antenatal care because appropriate antenatal interventions can reduce mother-to-child transmission of HIV infection. [A]

A system of clear referral paths should be established in each unit or department so that pregnant women who are diagnosed with an HIV infection are managed and treated by the appropriate specialist teams. [D]

10.8 Rubella
Rubella susceptibility screening should be offered early in antenatal care to identify women at risk of contracting rubella infection and to enable vaccination in the postnatal period for the protection of future pregnancies. [B]

10.9 Streptococcus Group B
Pregnant women should not be offered routine antenatal screening for group B streptococcus because evidence of its clinical and cost-effectiveness remains uncertain. [C]

10.10 Syphilis
Screening for syphilis should be offered to all pregnant women at an early stage in antenatal care because treatment of syphilis is beneficial to the mother and baby. [B]

Because syphilis is a rare condition in the UK and a positive result does not necessarily mean that a woman has syphilis, clear paths of referral for the management of pregnant women testing positive for syphilis should be established. [Good practice point]

10.11 Toxoplasmosis
Routine antenatal serological screening for toxoplasmosis should not be offered because the risks of screening may outweigh the potential benefits. [B]

Pregnant women should be informed of primary prevention measures to avoid toxoplasmosis infection, such as:

* washing hands before handling food
* thoroughly washing all fruit and vegetables, including ready-prepared salads, before eating
* thoroughly cooking raw meats and ready-prepared chilled meals
* wearing gloves and thoroughly washing hands after handling soil and gardening
* avoiding cat faeces in cat litter or in soil. [C]

Chapter 11 Screening for clinical conditions

11.1 Gestational diabetes

Screening for gestational diabetes using risk factors is recommended in a healthy population. At the booking appointment, the following risk factors for gestational diabetes should be determined:

- body mass index above 30 kg/m²
- previous macrosomic baby weighing 4.5 kg or above
- previous gestational diabetes (refer to 'Diabetes in pregnancy' [NICE clinical guideline 63], available from www.nice.org.uk/CG063)
- family history of diabetes (first-degree relative with diabetes)
- family origin with a high prevalence of diabetes:
  - South Asian (specifically women whose country of family origin is India, Pakistan or Bangladesh)
  - black Caribbean
  - Middle Eastern (specifically women whose country of family origin is Saudi Arabia, United Arab Emirates, Iraq, Jordan, Syria, Oman, Qatar, Kuwait, Lebanon or Egypt).

Women with any one of these risk factors should be offered testing for gestational diabetes (refer to 'Diabetes in pregnancy' [NICE clinical guideline 63], available from www.nice.org.uk/CG063).

In order to make an informed decision about screening and testing for gestational diabetes, women should be informed that:

- in most women, gestational diabetes will respond to changes in diet and exercise
- some women (between 10% and 20%) will need oral hypoglycaemic agents or insulin therapy if diet and exercise are not effective in controlling gestational diabetes
- if gestational diabetes is not detected and controlled there is a small risk of birth complications such as shoulder dystocia
- a diagnosis of gestational diabetes may lead to increased monitoring and interventions during both pregnancy and labour.

Screening for gestational diabetes using fasting plasma glucose, random blood glucose, glucose challenge test and urinalysis for glucose should not be undertaken.

11.2 Pre-eclampsia

Blood pressure measurement and urinalysis for protein should be carried out at each antenatal visit to screen for pre-eclampsia.

At the booking appointment, the following risk factors for pre-eclampsia should be determined:

- age 40 years or older
- nulliparity
- pregnancy interval of more than 10 years
- family history of pre-eclampsia
- previous history of pre-eclampsia
- body mass index 30 kg/m² or above
- pre-existing vascular disease such as hypertension
- pre-existing renal disease
- multiple pregnancy.

More frequent blood pressure measurements should be considered for pregnant women who have any of the above risk factors.

The presence of significant hypertension and/or proteinuria should alert the healthcare professional to the need for increased surveillance.

Blood pressure should be measured as outlined below:

- remove tight clothing, ensure arm is relaxed and supported at heart level
- use cuff of appropriate size
- inflate cuff to 20–30 mmHg above palpated systolic blood pressure
- lower column slowly, by 2 mmHg per second or per beat
- read blood pressure to the nearest 2 mmHg
- measure diastolic blood pressure as disappearance of sounds (phase V).

2008 update

Hypertension in which there is a single diastolic blood pressure of 110 mmHg or two consecutive readings of 90 mmHg at least 4 hours apart and/or significant proteinuria (1+) should prompt increased surveillance.

If the systolic blood pressure is above 160 mmHg on two consecutive readings at least 4 hours apart, treatment should be considered.

All pregnant women should be made aware of the need to seek immediate advice from a healthcare professional if they experience symptoms of pre-eclampsia. Symptoms include:

- severe headache
- problems with vision, such as blurring or flashing before the eyes
- severe pain just below the ribs
- vomiting
- sudden swelling of the face, hands or feet.

Although there is a great deal of material published on alternative screening methods for pre-eclampsia, none of these has satisfactory sensitivity and specificity, and therefore they are not recommended.

11.3 Preterm birth
Routine screening for preterm labour should not be offered.

11.4 Placenta praevia
Because most low-lying placentas detected at the routine anomaly scan will have resolved by the time the baby is born, only a woman whose placenta extends over the internal cervical os should be offered another transabdominal scan at 32 weeks. If the transabdominal scan is unclear, a transvaginal scan should be offered.

Chapter 12 Fetal growth and wellbeing

Determining fetal growth
Symphysis–fundal height should be measured and recorded at each antenatal appointment from 24 weeks.

Ultrasound estimation of fetal size for suspected large-for-gestational-age unborn babies should not be undertaken in a low-risk population.

Routine Doppler ultrasound should not be used in low-risk pregnancies.

Abdominal palpation for fetal presentation
Fetal presentation should be assessed by abdominal palpation at 36 weeks or later, when presentation is likely to influence the plans for the birth. Routine assessment of presentation by abdominal palpation should not be offered before 36 weeks because it is not always accurate and may be uncomfortable. [C]

Suspected fetal malpresentation should be confirmed by an ultrasound assessment. [Good practice point]

Routine monitoring of fetal movements
Routine formal fetal-movement counting should not be offered. [A]

Auscultation of fetal heart
Auscultation of the fetal heart may confirm that the fetus is alive but is unlikely to have any predictive value and routine listening is therefore not recommended. However, when requested by the mother, auscultation of the fetal heart may provide reassurance. [D]

Cardiotocography
The evidence does not support the routine use of antenatal electronic fetal heart rate monitoring (cardiotocography) for fetal assessment in women with an uncomplicated pregnancy and therefore it should not be offered. [A]

Ultrasound assessment in the third trimester
The evidence does not support the routine use of ultrasound scanning after 24 weeks of gestation and therefore it should not be offered. [A]

Chapter 13 Management of specific clinical conditions

13.1 Pregnancy after 41 weeks (see also Section 4.6 Gestational age assessment)
Prior to formal induction of labour,* women should be offered a vaginal examination for membrane sweeping. [A]

Women with uncomplicated pregnancies should be offered induction of labour* beyond 41 weeks. [A]

From 42 weeks, women who decline induction of labour should be offered increased antenatal monitoring consisting of at least twice-weekly cardiotocography and ultrasound estimation of maximum amniotic pool depth. [Good practice point]

13.2 Breech presentation at term
All women who have an uncomplicated singleton breech pregnancy at 36 weeks should be offered external cephalic version. Exceptions include women in labour and women with a uterine scar or abnormality, fetal compromise, ruptured membranes, vaginal bleeding and medical conditions. [A]

Where it is not possible to schedule an appointment for external cephalic version at 37 weeks, it should be scheduled at 36 weeks. [Good practice point]

2.3   Key priorities for research

Information for pregnant women

Alternative ways of helping healthcare professionals to support pregnant women in making informed decisions should be investigated.

Why this is important
Giving pregnant women relevant information to allow them to make an informed decision remains a challenge to all healthcare professionals. The use of media other than leaflets needs to be systematically studied, and the current available evidence is limited.

Vitamin D

There is a need for research into the effectiveness of routine vitamin D supplementation for pregnant and breastfeeding women.

Why this is important
Although there is some evidence of benefit from vitamin D supplementation for pregnant women at risk of vitamin D deficiency, there is less evidence in the case of pregnant women currently regarded as being at low risk of deficiency. It is possible that there will be health gains resulting from vitamin D supplementation, but further evidence is required.

Chlamydia screening

Further research needs to be undertaken to assess the effectiveness, practicality and acceptability of chlamydia screening in an antenatal setting.

Why this is important
Chlamydia is a significant healthcare issue, especially amongst the young, but the current level of evidence provides an insufficient basis for a recommendation. Of particular importance is the possibility that treatment might reduce the incidence of preterm birth and neonatal complications, and studies should be directed to these areas.

2008 update

---

* The clinical guideline 'Induction of labour' is being updated and is expected to be published in June 2008.

Fetal growth and wellbeing

Further prospective research is required to evaluate the diagnostic value and effectiveness (both clinical and cost-effectiveness) of predicting small-for-gestational-age babies using:

- customised fetal growth charts to plot symphysis–fundal height measurements
- routine ultrasound in the third trimester.

Why this is important
Poor fetal growth is undoubtedly a cause of serious perinatal mortality and morbidity. Unfortunately, the methods by which the condition can be identified antenatally are poorly developed or not tested by rigorous methodology. However, existing evidence suggests that there may be ways in which babies at risk can be identified and appropriately managed to improve outcome, and this should form the basis of the study.

The 'Antenatal assessment tool'

Multicentred validation studies are required in the UK to validate and evaluate the use of the 'Antenatal assessment tool'. Using structured questions, the tool aims to support the routine antenatal care of all women by identifying women who may require additional care. The tool identifies women who:

- can remain within or return to the routine antenatal pathway of care
- may need additional obstetric care for medical reasons
- may need social support and/or medical care for a variety of socially complex reasons.

Why this is important
The idea of some form of assessment tool to help group pregnant women into low-risk (midwifery-only care) and increased-risk (midwifery and obstetric care) categories is not new. The 'Antenatal assessment tool' has been developed using a consensus approach. Once developed, it will be essential to subject the tool to a multicentred validation study. The validated tool should have the potential to identify a third group of women who are particularly vulnerable and at increased risk of maternal and perinatal death.

2.4   Additional research recommendations

2.4.1   2008 recommendations

5.12 Alcohol and smoking in pregnancy
Prospective research is required into the effects of alcohol consumption during pregnancy.

9.1 Screening for structural anomalies
Research should be undertaken to elucidate the relationship between increased nuchal translucency and cardiac defects.

9.2 Screening for Down's syndrome
There should be multicentred studies to evaluate the practicality, cost-effectiveness and acceptability of a two-stage test for Down's syndrome and other screening contingencies including the integrated test.

Further research should be undertaken into the views and understanding of women going through the screening process.

11.1 Gestational diabetes
Is screening for gestational diabetes based on expected local prevalence, with or without modification by risk factors, clinically effective and cost-effective?

11.2 Pre-eclampsia
Further research using large prospective studies should be conducted into the effectiveness and cost-effectiveness of using alpha-fetoprotein, beta-human chorionic gonadotrophin, fetal DNA in maternal blood and uterine artery Dopplers or potentially a combination of these, to detect women at risk of developing pre-eclampsia. Testing should focus particularly on the prediction of early-onset pre-eclampsia, with priority given to blood tests.

11.3 Preterm birth

There is need for future research investigating the value of tests that are cheap and easy to perform such as maternal serum human chorionic gonadotrophin (MSHCG), serum C-reactive protein (CRP) and cervico-vaginal fetal fibrinonectin levels. The diagnostic accuracy and cost-effectiveness of transvaginal ultrasound to measure cervical length and funnelling to identify women at risk of preterm labour should also be investigated.

2.4.2   2003 recommendations for future research

Antenatal care is fortunate to have some areas where research evidence can clearly underpin clinical practice. However, it is noticeable that there are key areas within care where the research evidence is limited. For some of these areas, such as screening for gestational diabetes and first-trimester screening for anomalies, research is under way and results are awaited but for others there is an urgent need to address the gaps in the evidence.

- Effective ways of helping health professionals to support pregnant women in making informed decisions should be investigated. (Chapter 3)
- There is a lack of qualitative research on women's views regarding who provides care during pregnancy. (4.1)
- Alternative methods of providing antenatal information and support, such as drop in services, should be explored. (4.5)
- Research that explores how to ensure women's satisfaction and low morbidity and mortality with a reduced schedule of appointments should be conducted. (4.5)
- Further research to quantify the risk of air travel and to assess the effectiveness of interventions to prevent venous thromboembolism in pregnancy is needed. (5.14)
- More information on maternal and fetal safety for all interventions for nausea and vomiting in pregnancy (except antihistamines) is needed. (6.1)
- Further research into other nonpharmacological treatments for nausea and vomiting in pregnancy is recommended. (6.1)
- Although many treatments exist for backache in pregnancy, there is a lack of research evaluating their safety and effectiveness. (6.7)
- More research on effective treatments for symphysis pubis dysfunction is needed. (6.8)
- There is a lack of research evaluating effective interventions for carpal tunnel syndrome. (6.9)
- Although there are effective screening tools and screening for domestic violence has been shown to be acceptable to women, there is insufficient evidence on the effectiveness of interventions in improving health outcomes for women who have been identified. Therefore evaluation of interventions for domestic violence is urgently needed. (7.5)
- Randomised controlled trials are needed to confirm the beneficial effect of screening for asymptomatic bacteriuria. (10.1)
- Further research into the effectiveness and cost-effectiveness of antenatal screening for streptococcus group B is needed. (10.9)
- Further research is necessary to determine whether tocolysis improves the success rate of external cephalic version. (13.2)

2.5   Care pathway

The care pathway on pages 28–36 is reproduced from the Quick Reference Guide version of this guideline, which is available at www.nice.org.uk/CG062.

Women needing additional care

The guideline makes recommendations on baseline clinical care for all pregnant women. Pregnant women with the following conditions usually require additional care:

- cardiac disease, including hypertension
- renal disease
- endocrine disorders or diabetes requiring insulin
- psychiatric disorders (being treated with medication)
- haematological disorders
- autoimmune disorders
- epilepsy requiring anticonvulsant drugs
- malignant disease
- severe asthma

- use of recreational drugs such as heroin, cocaine (including crack cocaine) and ecstasy
- HIV or HBV infection
- obesity (body mass index 30 kg/m^2 or above) or underweight (body mass index below 18 kg/m^2)
- higher risk of developing complications, for example, women aged 40 and older, women who smoke
- women who are particularly vulnerable (such as teenagers) or who lack social support.

In addition, women who have experienced any of the following in previous pregnancies usually require additional care:

- recurrent miscarriage (three or more)
- preterm birth
- severe pre-eclampsia, HELLP syndrome or eclampsia
- rhesus isoimmunisation or other significant blood group antibodies
- uterine surgery including caesarean section, myomectomy or cone biopsy
- antenatal or postpartum haemorrhage on two occasions
- puerperal psychosis

- grand multiparity (more than six pregnancies)
- a stillbirth or neonatal death
- a small-for-gestational-age infant (below 5th centile)
- a large-for-gestational-age infant (above 95th centile)
- a baby weighing below 2.5 kg or above 4.5 kg
- a baby with a congenital abnormality (structural or chromosomal).

Women needing additional care

2008 update

Antenatal information

Give information that:

- is easily understood by all women, including women with additional needs such as physical, sensory or learning disabilities, and women who do not speak or read English

- enables women to make informed decisions

- is clear, consistent, balanced and accurate, and based on the current evidence

- is supported by written information and may also be provided in different formats.

Remember to:

- respect a woman's decisions, even when her views are contrary to your own

- provide an opportunity for her to discuss concerns and ask questions

- make sure she understands the information

- give her enough time to make decisions

- explain details of antenatal tests and screening in a setting conducive to discussions (group setting or one-to-one). This should happen before the booking appointment.

Information should cover:

- where the woman will be seen and who by

- the likely number, timing and content of antenatal appointments

- participant-led antenatal classes and breastfeeding workshops

- the woman's right to accept or decline a test.

The following pages contain details about information to give to pregnant women at specific times during their pregnancy. This information can be supported by 'The pregnancy book', other relevant resources such as UK National Screening Committee publications and the Midwives Information and Resource Service information leaflets (www.infochoice.org).

2008 update

Basic principles of antenatal care

Midwives and GPs should care for women with an uncomplicated pregnancy, providing continuous care throughout the pregnancy. Obstetricians and specialist teams should be involved where additional care is needed.

Antenatal appointments should take place in a location that women can easily access. The location should be appropriate to the needs of women and their community.

Maternity records should be structured, standardised, national maternity records, held by the woman.

In an uncomplicated pregnancy, there should be 10 appointments for nulliparous women and 7 appointments for parous women.

Each antenatal appointment should have a structure and a focus. Appointments early in pregnancy should be longer to provide information and time for discussion about screening so that women can make informed decisions.

If possible, incorporate routine tests into the appointments to minimise inconvenience to women.

Women should feel able to discuss sensitive issues and disclose problems. Be alert to the symptoms and signs of domestic violence.

Schedule of appointments

First contact with a healthcare professional

Give specific information on:

- folic acid supplements
- food hygiene, including how to reduce the risk of a food-acquired infection
- lifestyle, including smoking cessation, recreational drug use and alcohol consumption
- all antenatal screening, including risks, benefits and limitations of the screening tests.

Give information (supported by written information and antenatal classes), with an opportunity to discuss issues and ask questions.

Be alert to any factors, clinical and/or social, that may affect the health of the woman and baby.

For further information about lifestyle see pages 23–25.

Give information (supported by written information and antenatal classes), with an opportunity to discuss issues and ask questions.

Be alert to any factors, clinical and/or social, that may affect the health of the woman and baby.

Schedule of appointments

Booking appointment (ideally by 10 weeks)

Checks and tests

- Identify women who may need additional care (see pages 8 and 9) and plan pattern of care for the pregnancy.

- Measure height and weight and calculate body mass index.

- Measure blood pressure and test urine for proteinuria.

- Determine risk factors for pre-eclampsia and gestational diabetes (refer to 'Diabetes in pregnancy' [NICE clinical guideline 63], available from www.nice.org.uk/CG063).

- Offer blood tests to check blood group and rhesus D status, and screening for anaemia, haemoglobinopathies, red-cell alloantibodies, hepatitis B virus, HIV, rubella susceptibility and syphilis.

- Offer screening for asymptomatic bacteriuria.

- Inform women younger than 25 years about the high prevalence of chlamydia infection in their age group, and give details of their local National Chlamydia Screening Programme.

- Offer screening for Down's syndrome.

- Offer early ultrasound scan for gestational age assessment and ultrasound screening for structural anomalies.

- Identify women who have had genital mutilation (FGM).

- Ask about any past or present severe mental illness or psychiatric treatment.

- Ask about mood to identify possible depression.

- Ask about the woman's occupation to identify potential risks.

Give specific information on:

- how the baby develops during pregnancy

- nutrition and diet, including vitamin D supplements

- exercise, including pelvic floor exercises

- antenatal screening, including risks and benefits of the screening tests

- the pregnancy care pathway

- planning place of birth (refer to 'Intrapartum care' [NICE clinical guideline 55])

- breastfeeding, including workshops

- participant-led antenatal classes

- maternity benefits.

Give information (supported by written information and antenatal classes), with an opportunity to discuss issues and ask questions.

Be alert to any factors, clinical and/or social, that may affect the health of the woman and baby.

Schedule of appointments

2008 update

Give information (supported by written information and antenatal classes), with an opportunity to discuss issues and ask questions.

Be alert to any factors, clinical and/or social, that may affect the health of the woman and baby.

For women who choose to have screening, arrange as appropriate:

- blood tests (blood group, rhesus D status, screening for anaemia, haemoglobinopathies, red-cell alloantibodies, hepatitis B virus, HIV, rubella susceptibility and syphilis), ideally before 10 weeks

- urine tests (proteinuria and asymptomatic bacteriuria)

- ultrasound scan to determine gestational age using:
  - crown–rump measurement between 10 weeks 0 days and 13 weeks 6 days
  - head circumference if crown–rump length is above 84 mm

- Down's syndrome screening using either:
  - 'combined test' between 11 weeks 0 days and 13 weeks 6 days
  - serum screening test (triple or quadruple test) between 15 weeks 0 days and 20 weeks 0 days

- ultrasound screening for structural anomalies, normally between 18 weeks 0 days and 20 weeks 6 days.

16 weeks
Checks and tests
- Review, discuss and record the results of screening tests.
- Measure blood pressure and test urine for proteinuria.
- Investigate a haemoglobin level below 11 g/100 ml and consider iron supplements.

Give specific information on:
- the routine anomaly scan.

Anomaly scan: 18 to 20 weeks
Checks and tests
- If the woman chooses, an ultrasound scan should be performed between 18 weeks 0 days and 20 weeks 6 days to detect structural anomalies.
- For a woman whose placenta extends across the internal cervical os, offer another scan at 32 weeks.

Give information (supported by written information and antenatal classes), with an opportunity to discuss issues and ask questions.

Be alert to any factors, clinical and/or social, that may affect the health of the woman and baby.

Give information (supported by written information and antenatal classes), with an opportunity to discuss issues and ask questions.

Be alert to any factors, clinical and/or social, that may affect the health of the woman and baby.

25 weeks – *for nulliparous women*
Checks and tests
- Measure blood pressure and test urine for proteinuria.
- Measure and plot symphysis–fundal height.

28 weeks
Checks and tests
- Measure blood pressure and test urine for proteinuria.
- Offer a second screening for anaemia and atypical red-cell alloantibodies.
- Investigate a haemoglobin level below 10.5 g/100 ml and consider iron supplements.
- Offer anti-D prophylaxis to women who are rhesus D-negative[1].
- Measure and plot symphysis–fundal height.

---

[1] The technology appraisal guidance 'Guidance on the use of routine antenatal anti-D prophylaxis for RhD-negative women' (NICE technology appraisal 41) is being updated and is expected to be published in June 2008.

31 weeks – *for nulliparous women*
Checks and tests
- Review, discuss and record the results of screening tests undertaken at 28 weeks.
- Measure blood pressure and test urine for proteinuria.
- Measure and plot symphysis–fundal height.

34 weeks
Checks and tests
- Review, discuss and record the results of screening tests undertaken at 28 weeks.
- Measure blood pressure and test urine for proteinuria.
- Offer a second dose of anti-D prophylaxis to women who are rhesus D-negative[1].
- Measure and plot symphysis–fundal height.

Give specific information on:
- preparation for labour and birth, including the birth plan, recognising active labour and coping with pain.

Give information (supported by written information and antenatal classes), with an opportunity to discuss issues and ask questions.

Be alert to any factors, clinical and/or social, that may affect the health of the woman and baby.

---

[1] The technology appraisal guidance 'Guidance on the use of routine antenatal anti-D prophylaxis for RhD-negative women' (NICE technology appraisal 41) is being updated and is expected to be published in June 2008.

Schedule of appointments

2008 update

Schedule of appointments

Give information (supported by written information and antenatal classes), with an opportunity to discuss issues and ask questions.

Be alert to any factors, clinical and/or social, that may affect the health of the woman and baby.

36 weeks

Checks and tests

- Measure blood pressure and test urine for proteinuria.

- Measure and plot symphysis–fundal height.

- Check the position of the baby. If breech, offer external cephalic version.

Give specific information (at or before 36 weeks) on:

- breastfeeding: technique and good management practices, such as detailed in the UNICEF Baby Friendly Initiative (www.babyfriendly.org.uk)

- care of the new baby, vitamin K prophylaxis and newborn screening tests

- postnatal self-care, awareness of 'baby blues' and postnatal depression.

38 weeks

Checks and tests

- Measure blood pressure and test urine for proteinuria.

- Measure and plot symphysis–fundal height.

Give specific information on:

- options for management of prolonged pregnancy[2].

[2] The clinical guideline 'Induction of labour' is being updated and is expected to be published in June 2008.

40 weeks – *for nulliparous women*

Checks and tests

- Measure blood pressure and test urine for proteinuria.

- Measure and plot symphysis–fundal height.

- Further discussion of management of prolonged pregnancy[2].

41 weeks

Checks and tests

For women who have not given birth by 41 weeks:

- offer a membrane sweep[2]

- offer induction of labour[2]

- measure blood pressure and test urine for proteinuria

- measure and plot symphysis–fundal height.

From 42 weeks, offer women who decline induction of labour increased monitoring (at least twice-weekly cardiotocography and ultrasound examination of maximum amniotic pool depth).

Schedule of appointments

Give information (supported by written information and antenatal classes), with an opportunity to discuss issues and ask questions.

Be alert to any factors, clinical and/or social, that may affect the health of the woman and baby.

[2] The clinical guideline 'Induction of labour' is being updated and is expected to be published in June 2008.

Antenatal interventions NOT routinely recommended

- Repeated maternal weighing.
- Breast or pelvic examination.
- Iron or vitamin A supplements.
- Routine screening for chlamydia, cytomegalovirus, hepatitis C virus, group B streptococcus, toxoplasmosis, bacterial vaginosis.
- Routine Doppler ultrasound in low-risk pregnancies.
- Ultrasound estimation of fetal size for suspected large-for-gestational-age unborn babies.
- Routine screening for preterm labour.
- Routine screening for cardiac anomalies using nuchal translucency.
- Gestational diabetes screening using fasting plasma glucose, random blood glucose, glucose challenge test or urinalysis for glucose.
- Routine fetal-movement counting.
- Routine auscultation of the fetal heart.
- Routine antenatal electronic cardiotocography.
- Routine ultrasound scanning after 24 weeks.

Lifestyle advice

Work	Reassure women that it is usually safe to continue working.
	Ascertain a woman's occupation to identify risk.
	Refer to the Health and Safety Executive (www.hse.gov.uk) for more information.
	Tell women about their maternity rights and benefits.
Nutritional supplements	Recommend supplementation with folic acid before conception and throughout the first 12 weeks (400 micrograms per day).
	Advise women of the importance of vitamin D intake during pregnancy and breastfeeding (10 micrograms per day). Ensure women at risk of deficiency are following this advice.
	Do not recommend routine iron supplementation.
	Advise women of the risk of birth defects associated with vitamin A, and to avoid vitamin A supplementation (above 700 micrograms) and liver products.
Avoiding infection	Advise women how to reduce the risk of listeriosis and salmonella, and how to avoid toxoplasmosis infection.
Medicines	Prescribe as few medicines as possible, and only in circumstances where the benefit outweighs the risk.
	Advise women to use over-the-counter medicines as little as possible.

continued

2008 update

Lifestyle advice

35

Lifestyle advice

Complementary therapies	Advise women that few complementary therapies have been proven as being safe and effective during pregnancy.
Exercise	There is no risk associated with starting or continuing moderate exercise. However, sports that may cause abdominal trauma, falls or excessive joint stress; and scuba diving, should be avoided.
Sexual intercourse	Reassure women that intercourse is thought to be safe during pregnancy.
Alcohol	Advise women planning a pregnancy to avoid alcohol in the first 3 months if possible. If women choose to drink alcohol, advise them to drink no more than 1 to 2 UK units once or twice a week (1 unit equals half a pint of ordinary strength lager or beer, or one shot [25 ml] of spirits. One small [125 ml] glass of wine is equal to 1.5 UK units). At this low level there is no evidence of harm. Advise women to avoid getting drunk and to avoid binge drinking.
Smoking	Discuss smoking status and give information about the risks of smoking during pregnancy. Give information, advice and support on how to stop smoking throughout the pregnancy. Give details of, and encourage women to use, NHS Stop Smoking Services and the NHS pregnancy smoking helpline (0800 169 9 169). Discuss nicotine replacement therapy (NRT). If women are unable to quit, encourage them to reduce smoking.

Cannabis	Discourage women from using cannabis.
Air travel	Long-haul air travel is associated with an increased risk of venous thrombosis, although the possibility of any additional risk in pregnancy is unclear. In the general population, compression stockings are effective in reducing the risk.
Car travel	Advise women that the seat belt should go 'above and below the bump, not over it'.
Travel abroad	Advise women to discuss flying, vaccinations and travel insurance with their midwife or doctor.

Lifestyle advice

3 Woman-centred care and informed decision making

3.1 Introduction

Women, their partners and their families should always be treated with kindness, respect and dignity. The views, beliefs and values of the woman, her partner and her family in relation to her care and that of her baby should be sought and respected at all times.

Women should have the opportunity to make informed decisions about their care and treatment, in partnership with their healthcare professionals. If women do not have the capacity to make decisions, healthcare professionals should follow the Department of Health guidelines – 'Reference guide to consent for examination or treatment' (2001) (available from www.dh.gov.uk). Since April 2007 healthcare professionals need to follow a code of practice accompanying the Mental Capacity Act (summary available from www.dca.gov.uk/menincap/bill-summary.htm).

Good communication between healthcare professionals and women is essential. It should be supported by evidence-based, written information tailored to the woman's needs. Treatment and care, and the information women are given about it, should be culturally appropriate. It should also be accessible to women with additional needs such as physical, sensory or learning disabilities, and to women who do not speak or read English.

Every opportunity should be taken to provide the woman and her partner or other relevant family members with the information and support they need.

3.2 Provision of information

Clinical question
What, how and when information should be offered during the antenatal period to inform women's decisions about care during pregnancy, labour, birth and the postnatal period?

Previous NICE guidance (for the updated recommendations see below)
Pregnant women should offered opportunities to attend antenatal classes and have written information about antenatal care. [A]

Pregnant women should be offered evidence-based information and support to enable them to make informed decisions regarding their care. Information should include details of where they will be seen and who will undertake their care. Addressing women's choices should be recognised as being integral to the decision-making process. [C]

At the first contact, pregnant women should be offered information about pregnancy care services and options available, lifestyle considerations, including dietary information, and screening tests. [C]

Pregnant women should be informed about the purpose of any screening test before it is performed. The right of a woman to accept or decline a test should be made clear. [D]

At each antenatal appointment, midwives and doctors should offer consistent information and clear explanations and should provide pregnant women with an opportunity to discuss issues and ask questions. [D]

Communication and information should be provided in a form that is accessible to pregnant women who have additional needs, such as those with physical, cognitive or sensory disabilities and those who do not speak or read English. [GPP]

2008 update

Future research:
Effective ways of helping health professionals to support pregnant women in making informed decisions should be investigated.

3.2.1   Introduction and background

Informed decision making involves making reasoned choice based on relevant information about the advantages and disadvantages of all the possible courses of action (including taking no action).[8] It requires that the individual has understood both the information provided and the full implications of all the alternative courses of action available. In providing information for women antenatally it is important that healthcare professionals are aware of what informed choice entails and that they provide information in order to facilitate this. The provision of clear information, and time for women to consider decisions and seek additional information, as well as the need for care to be provided in an individualised, woman-focused way are key components of Standard 11 Section 3 of the National Service Framework for Maternity Care (September 2004, www.dh.gov.uk/).

3.2.2   Effectiveness of information giving

Description of included studies
Common areas were chosen to search for evidence regarding the effectiveness of information giving. These were chosen either because of their relevance to this guideline update or because they are areas where a body of evidence was known to exist that could be drawn on to illustrate general principles that could inform the clinical question. The areas chosen were breastfeeding information, dietary information, smoking cessation and travel safety. The section on breastfeeding information includes a Cochrane systematic review and a Health Technology Assessment, an RCT, two cluster RCTs, two controlled trials, a prospective cohort study and two descriptive studies. The section on dietary information comprises five studies: a Cochrane systematic review, an RCT, a prospective cohort study, a qualitative study and a retrospective study.

3.2.3   Breastfeeding information/preparation

Findings
A Cochrane systematic review (2005)[637] examined the interventions that aim to encourage women to breastfeed, to evaluate their effectiveness in terms of changes in the number of women who initiate breastfeeding and to report any other effects of such interventions. [EL = 1+] The review included seven randomised controlled trials (RCTs) with or without blinding of any breastfeeding promotion intervention among healthy low-risk pregnant women with healthy infants. There was no limitation of study by country of origin or language. The outcome measure studied was initiation rate of breastfeeding. The seven studies suffered from a high overall risk of bias due to unclear or inadequate allocation concealment. Regarding attrition bias, three of seven studies reported breastfeeding initiation for all participants. The remaining four studies had up to 25% losses to follow up between recruitment and breastfeeding initiation. A total of 1388 women were included. These seven studies were classified and analysed under three types of intervention: health education, breastfeeding promotion packs, and early mother–infant contact. Five trials involving 582 women showed that breastfeeding education had a significant effect on increasing initiation rates compared with routine care (RR 1.53, 95% CI 1.25 to 1.88). These trials evaluated programmes delivered in the USA to low-income women. It was concluded that the forms of intervention evaluated were effective at increasing breastfeeding initiation rates among women on low incomes in the USA.

A Health Technology Assessment (2000)[638] evaluated the existing evidence to identify which promotion programmes are effective at increasing the number of women who start to breastfeed. [EL = 1+] The review also assessed the impact of such programmes on the duration and exclusivity of breastfeeding. RCTs, non-randomised controlled trials (non-RCTs) with concurrent controls, and before–after studies (cohort and cross-sectional) were included in the review. The study participants included pregnant women, mothers in the immediate postpartum period before the first breastfeed, any participant linked to pregnant women or new mothers, or any participant who may breastfeed in the future, or be linked to a breastfeeding woman in the future. The review included any type of intervention designed to promote the uptake of breastfeeding and the control groups could receive an alternative breastfeeding promotion programme or standard care. A total of 59 studies met the selection criteria, out of which 14 were RCTs, 16 non-RCTs and 29 before–after studies. Interventions were grouped into categories: health education; health sector initiatives (HSI) – general; HSI – Baby Friendly Hospital Initiative (BFHI); HSI – training of health professionals; HSI – US Department of Agriculture's Special Supplemental Nutrition Program for Women, Infants, and Children (WIC); HSI – social support from health professionals; peer support; media campaigns; and multifaceted interventions. The health education intervention was covered in nine RCTs, seven non-RCTs and three before–after studies. The result of this intervention showed that there is limited impact on initiation rates of breastfeeding by giving breastfeeding literature alone, or combined with a more formal, non-interactive method of health education. Small, informal, group health education classes, delivered in the antenatal period, can be an effective intervention to increase initiation rates, and in some cases the duration of breastfeeding, among women from different income or ethnic groups. Two RCTs, three non-RCTs and five before–after studies were included in relation to HSI – WIC. It was found that effective WIC interventions included one-to-one health education in the antenatal period, peer counselling in the ante- and postnatal periods, or a combination of one-to-one health education and peer counselling in the ante- and postnatal periods. WIC programmes were effective at increasing both the initiation and duration of breastfeeding among women of low-income groups in the USA. Regarding HSI – training of health professionals, five before–after studies were included. There is limited evidence but it suggests that these programmes may be useful in improving the knowledge of midwives and nurses. There were no favourable results shown in terms of changes in attitudes of health professionals, or changes in breastfeeding rates. There was one RCT on social support intervention and it did not significantly increase rates of initiation compared with standard care. Two non-RCTs were included related to peer support and showed that peer support programmes, when delivered as a stand-alone intervention to women in low-income groups, to be an effective intervention at increasing initiation rates (and duration) among women who had expressed a wish to breastfeed. Two before–after studies were found related to media campaigns which suggested that a media campaign as a stand-alone intervention, and particularly television commercials, may improve attitudes towards and increase initiation rates of breastfeeding. There was one RCT and ten before–after studies related to multifaceted interventions that found that multifaceted interventions comprising a media campaign and/or a peer support programme combined with structural changes to the health sector (HSI) or, in fewer cases, combined with health education activities are effective in increasing initiation rates (and duration and exclusivity of breastfeeding). It was concluded that there is sufficient evidence of effectiveness to increase the availability of good practice health education programmes.

A cluster RCT in a teaching hospital in North West of England (2005)[639] [EL = 1–] assessed the effectiveness of an antenatal educational breastfeeding intervention which attempted to enable woman to achieve their own target for breastfeeding duration. It was delivered by a lactation consultant to both pregnant women and their attendant midwife. The primary outcome was the proportion that fulfilled their antenatal breastfeeding expectation and the secondary outcomes were the number of women breastfeeding on discharge and at 4 months. Women who expressed a desire to breastfeed at the start of their pregnancy were allocated to either routine antenatal education or an additional single educational group session supervised by a lactation specialist and attended by midwives from their locality. Data were collected using a series of questionnaires and diaries. 1312 women were randomised but 1249 (95%) women were available for analysis. The study results found no difference between the groups in the proportion of women who attained their expected duration of breastfeeding (OR 1.2, 95% CI 0.89 to 1.6). There were no differences between the groups in the uptake of breastfeeding on discharge (OR 1.2, 95% CI 0.8 to 1.7) or exclusively at 4 months (OR 1.1, 95% CI 0.6 to 1.8). The intervention was only available antenatally, and it failed to address the emotional and physical needs of women in the postnatal period. The study included women who expressed a desire to breastfeed so the results cannot be generalised to all women. It was not possible to conceal the study group allocation from the recruiting midwife or to blind the women or the attending midwives from the treatment allocation.

An RCT conducted in Singapore (2007)[640] aimed to address the impact of simple antenatal educational interventions on breastfeeding practice. [EL = 1–] Low-risk antenatal women were randomly assigned to one of the three groups. Group A received breastfeeding educational material and individual coaching from a lactation counsellor. Group B received breastfeeding educational material with no counselling. Group C received routine antenatal care only. A total of 401 women were recruited. The results showed that women who received simple antenatal instruction with a short, single, individual counselling session combined with educational material practised exclusive and predominant breastfeeding more often than women receiving routine care alone at 3 months (OR 2.6, 95% CI 1.2 to 5.4) and 6 months (OR 2.4, 95% CI 1.0 to 5.7) postpartum. More women practised exclusive and predominant breastfeeding at 6 months among women receiving individual counselling compared with women exposed to educational material alone (OR 2.5, 95% CI 1.0 to 6.3). A number of limitations were noted for this trial. There was contamination between the groups and women in the control group came to know about the interventions offered to the other groups simply by speaking to women in those groups. There was insufficient sample size to fulfil power calculations. The most useful breastfeeding intervention includes demonstration of breastfeeding techniques (educational video), one-to-one teaching by a trained lactation counsellor, and a breastfeeding education booklet.

A Canadian RCT (2006)[641] sought to determine the effects of an antenatal breastfeeding workshop on maternal breastfeeding self-efficacy and breastfeeding duration. [EL = 1–] One hundred and one nulliparous women expecting a single child and an uncomplicated birth, and planning to breastfeed were randomised into either the intervention group or the control group. Both groups received standard care and in addition the intervention group attended a 2.5 hour prenatal breastfeeding workshop (based on Bandura's theory of self-efficacy and adult learning principles). The main outcome measures were maternal breastfeeding self-efficacy (measured with a revised breastfeeding self-efficacy scale) and breastfeeding duration (measured at 4 weeks and 8 weeks postpartum). The study suffered from participation bias because the participants were self-selecting. Overall both the groups had higher breastfeeding rates at 8 weeks postpartum when compared with the national statistics. This suggests that owing to the participation bias the participants may have started out more committed to or more confident about breastfeeding than the general population. Higher self-efficacy scores and a higher proportion of exclusively breastfeeding women were seen in the group who attended the workshop as compared with women who did not attend the workshop, although by 8 weeks postpartum this difference was no longer statistically significant (intervention 61.7% versus control 58.9%; $t = -1.60$, 95% CI -6.28 to -0.70; $P = 0.115$).

A US-based non-RCT (1997)[642] examined the effect of specific antenatal breastfeeding information on postpartum rates of breastfeeding among WIC participants. [EL = 1–] This information was provided in group classes by nurse practitioners. A total of 14 women in the experimental group and 17 in the control group received prenatal nutrition education through the WIC programme. The experimental group received at least one breastfeeding education class and a follow-up class was offered but not required. The control group received the standard prenatal education class which included content on the appropriate diet for pregnancy and they were taught that breastfeeding is the preferred method of infant feeding rather than the 'how-to's' of breastfeeding. All participants were interviewed at 1 month postpartum WIC visit. The study suffered from a small sample size and wide variance in the duration of breastfeeding, which led to a low statistical power. The results showed no significant difference in breastfeeding incidence between the two groups. However, there was a significantly higher percentage of women still breastfeeding at 3 and 4 months postpartum in the experimental versus the control group. The control group breastfed for 29.5 ± 43.6 days, while the experimental group breastfed for 76 days ± 104.3 ($P = 0.05$). It was found that multiparous women who had bottle-fed previous children breastfed for a shorter duration (18 ± 22 days) than primiparous women (60 ± 87 days) but this was not statistically significant.

A US-based quasi-randomised controlled trial (1984)[643] was used to determine the effect of prenatal breastfeeding education on maternal reports of success in breastfeeding and maternal perception of the infant. [EL = 1–] All participants were enrolled to attend childbirth education classes and vaginally delivered full-term healthy infants without complication. Forty nulliparous women who desired to breastfeed were randomly assigned to control and experimental groups according to the childbirth class in which they were enrolled. Twenty women attended a prenatal breastfeeding education class and 20 were in the control group. The independent variable used in this study was prenatal breastfeeding education class. The two dependent variables were maternal report of success in breastfeeding and maternal perception of the infant. The maternal perception of the infant variable was measured using the Neonatal Perception Inventory (NPI). The NPI I was administered 1–2 days postpartum and the NPI II was administered at 1 month postpartum. The results showed that there was a significantly higher frequency of success in breastfeeding among primiparous women who received prenatal breastfeeding education as compared with those who did not. There was a significant difference in the NPI I scores in both experimental and control subjects at 1–2 days postpartum. The NPI II scores of the experimental mothers were significantly more positive at 1 month postpartum. Primiparous women in the experimental group reported significantly more positive NPI II scores than the control group.

A quasi-experimental design with pre- and post-intervention groups was carried out in Chile (1996)[644] to assess the impact of five interventions on breastfeeding patterns and duration. [EL = 2] The five interventions were: training the health team in breastfeeding; implementing activities at the prenatal clinic; implementing activities at the hospital; creating an outpatient lactation clinic; and offering the Lactational Amenorrhea Method (LAM) as an initial form of family planning. During the intervention phase, a sixth intervention (prenatal breastfeeding skills group education (PBSGE)) was added for a subset of the women in the intervention group. A subset of 59 women (for the sixth intervention) was drawn from 123 mother/child pairs of the intervention group. The women in the sixth intervention group attended the prenatal breastfeeding skills group education sessions (conducted by a trained nurse-midwife at the outpatient prenatal clinic) during the third trimester of pregnancy. Each session lasted about 20 minutes and the topics covered were breast care, breastfeeding advantages for the infant and for the mother, breastfeeding technique, anatomy and physiology of the mammary gland, prevention of breastfeeding problems, rooming-in, and immediate contact. The five interventions demonstrated a significant increase in full breastfeeding at 6 months (32% to 67%). A significantly higher percentage of the sixth intervention women were fully breastfeeding at 6 months compared with those who received only the five basic interventions (80% versus 65%). The effect was greater among nulliparous women.

An Australian qualitative study (2003)[645] explored the physical, social and emotional experiences influencing women's baby-feeding decisions by investigating women's own decision-making processes. [EL = 3] The study was undertaken with 29 women using face-to-face in-depth interviews that were audiotape-recorded and transcribed verbatim. Data were analysed using thematic analysis. A number of themes were identified in this study that appeared to influence the baby-feeding decision. One of the most dominant themes was the embodied expression of breastfeeding. Another dominant theme was that breastfeeding could be difficult and problematic. It was found that the women sought information from a variety of sources as well as exploring their own understandings of themselves and their breasts. Based on this knowledge the women made their antenatal baby-feeding decisions. These baby-feeding decisions grouped into four thematic groups: 'assuming I'll breastfeed'; 'definitely going to breastfeed'; 'playing it by ear'; and 'definitely going to bottle-feed'. Each of these standpoints was associated with and precipitated a number of behaviours and strategies. It was concluded that there is need for antenatal educators and midwives who provide care in pregnancy to acknowledge a range of experiences and expectations of women and to provide diverse educational opportunities to meet a range of needs.

A US-based descriptive study (1982)[646] sought to determine the relationship between nulliparous women's information on breastfeeding and success in breastfeeding. [EL = 3] The study hypothesis was that pregnant women having relatively more information on breastfeeding would breastfeed their infants beyond 4 weeks, as compared with pregnant women with relatively little information on breastfeeding who would breastfeed their infants for less than 4 weeks. A multiple-choice questionnaire of 26 items was developed to measure the pregnant women's knowledge about breastfeeding. The questionnaire was tested for its validity and was pilot tested on 30 nulliparous women who were not a part of the main study, which yielded a 2 week test–retest reliability of 0.87. A post-delivery mail questionnaire on breastfeeding outcome was completed 5–6 weeks following delivery and the results of the two questionnaires were correlated. The anonymity of the participants was ensured by assigning code numbers to all questionnaires. The results showed that women who breastfed beyond 4 weeks after delivery had higher overall breastfeeding information scores than mothers who breastfed less than 4 weeks. The decision to breastfeed made early in pregnancy was associated with successful breastfeeding whereas the decision to breastfeed made late in pregnancy was associated with unsuccessful breastfeeding. There was a positive correlation between breastfeeding information scores and the number of breastfeeding information sources used by nulliparous women.

2008 update

Evidence summary

There is evidence from RCTs that breastfeeding initiation rates and, in some instances, breastfeeding duration can be improved by antenatal breastfeeding education, particularly if this is interactive and takes place in small informal groups. One-to-one counselling and peer support antenatally are also effective.

3.2.4 Nutrition-related pregnancy interventions

A Cochrane systematic review (1999)[65] assessed the effects of advising pregnant women to increase their energy and protein intakes on those intakes, on gestational weight gain, and on outcome of pregnancy. [EL = 1+] The studies included made controlled comparisons of nutritional advice, whether administered on a one-to-one basis or to groups of women. The interventions included specific advice to increase dietary energy and protein intake. Dietary intake and pregnancy outcome were the main outcome measures. A total of four trials including 1108 women were included. The results showed that advice to increase energy and protein intakes seems to be successful in achieving those goals, but the increases are lower than those reported in trials of actual protein/energy supplementation. The evidence regarding the effects on pregnancy outcome are not reliable, however, as the evidence is drawn from one trial with very wide confidence intervals. None of the trials reported any potential adverse effects that might accompany increased fetal size, such as an increased risk of prolonged labour or caesarean section. It was concluded that nutritional advice appears to be effective in increasing pregnant women's energy and protein intakes, but the effects on fetal, infant or maternal outcomes remain uncertain, and seem likely to be minimal.

A US-based RCT (2004)[647] developed and evaluated a tailored nutrition education CD-ROM program for participants in the Special Supplemental Nutrition Program for Women, Infants and Children (WIC). [EL = 1+] Eligible participants were computer-randomised into either the intervention or the control group. The intervention group completed a baseline survey (lasting approximately 15 minutes), received the intervention programme (soap opera and interactive feedback lasting 20–25 minutes), and answered immediate postpartum questions. The control group completed the surveys but did not receive the intervention until after follow-up. Both groups were asked to return in 1 month for follow-up. At follow-up, intervention participants answered the survey questions whereas control participants completed the survey and received the tailored intervention. The study sample comprised a total of 307 respondents to the follow-up survey (response rate 74.8%). Ninety-six percent of participants were female, 20% were pregnant and 50% were minorities (African-American and other). The main outcome measures included total fat and fruit and vegetable intake, knowledge of low-fat and infant feeding choices, self-efficacy, and stages of change. The results showed that the intervention group members significantly increased self-efficacy and scored significantly higher on both low-fat and infant feeding knowledge compared with controls.

A US-based prospective cohort study (2004)[648] aimed to evaluate the efficacy of an intervention directed at preventing excessive gestational weight gain. [EL = 2+] The study used a historical control group. The intervention group constituted women with normal and overweight pregnancy BMI. The control group consisted of women with normal and overweight BMI from an earlier observational study of postpartum weight retention. One hundred and seventy-nine women in the intervention group had their gestational weight gain monitored by healthcare providers and also received postal patient education. The intervention was designed to encourage pregnant women to gain an amount of weight during pregnancy that is within the range recommended by the Institute of Medicine. It had two major components: a clinical component (that included guidance about and monitoring of gestational weight gain by healthcare providers using new tools in the obstetric charts) and a by-mail patient education programme. Three hundred and eighty-one women formed an historical control group. At 1 year postpartum, 158 women in the intervention group and 359 women in the control group were available for analysis. The study population was monitored from early pregnancy until 1 year postpartum. The results showed that low-income women who received the intervention had a significantly reduced risk of excessive gestational weight gain (OR 0.41, 95% CI 0.20 to 0.81). There was a significantly reduced risk of retaining more than 2.27 kg in low-income overweight women (OR 0.24, 95% CI 0.07 to 0.89).

A Netherlands-based retrospective qualitative study (2005)[649] [EL = 2–] aimed to explore the use of nutrition-related information sources (mass media, social environment and health professionals) and nutrition-related information-seeking behaviours and motives before and throughout pregnancy. In-depth face-to-face interviews of 1 hour with five groups of 12 women (a total of 60 women) from various parts of the Netherlands were conducted at conference rooms or at the respondent's home and women were mainly selected via midwifery practices. The five groups included women who wanted a child, women in their first, second and third trimester of the first pregnancy and women in their first trimester of the second pregnancy. All pregnant women sought or were confronted with at least some pregnancy-specific nutrition information. Three groups of women could be distinguished in relation to the manifestation of nutrition-related information-seeking behaviours during first-time pregnancies: women who feel like a mother from the moment they know that they are pregnant; women who feel like a mother later in pregnancy; and women who do not feel like a mother yet. Each group had its own specific information-seeking behaviour. Women in the first trimester mainly sought nutrition information in the media, such as the internet, books, magazines, 9 month calendars and brochures. In the second trimester, nutrition information was sought from the 9 month calendar (fun and tips) and friends (experienced). Women in the third trimester sought information from friends (information on breastfeeding). The information sources of the second group of women were mainly brochures provided by the midwife and the midwife herself. The third group of women mainly relied on their own common sense. Second-time pregnant women relied on their experience, the midwife and books for specific questions.

A US-based retrospective study (1985)[650] evaluated the effect of intensive nutrition counselling on weight gain of pregnant women and birthweight of their infants. [EL = 2–] Data were collected through retrospective review of medical records. The test group consisted of 114 women who were admitted to the clinic before the 35th week of pregnancy, attended a 30 minute prenatal nutrition class given by the clinic dietician, and were counselled by the clinic dietician at each visit. This group was sampled between the years 1979 and 1981. The control group consisted of 86 women who were admitted to the prenatal clinic before 35th week of pregnancy and attended a 20 minute prenatal nutrition class, and was sampled for the years 1975 to 1977. Two different dieticians worked with the two groups. The results showed that the women in the test group gained 2.5 kg more weight than in the control group. The test group women versus control group women had fewer low birthweight infants (4% versus 13%), although this difference is not statistically significant. They also had infants weighing 100 g more at birth than infants born to women in the control group. It should be noted that women in the intervention group attended antenatal clinic significantly earlier in pregnancy than women in the control group, and had significantly more antenatal consultations.

Evidence summary
There is some evidence of a fair quality from the field of nutritional support that intensive antenatal dietary counselling and support is effective in increasing women's knowledge about healthy eating and can impact upon eating behaviours. There is no evidence linking this with improved pregnancy outcomes, however.

3.2.5 Smoking cessation

Findings
A Cochrane systematic review (2004)[651] [EL = 1+] assessed the effects of smoking cessation programmes during pregnancy on the health of the unborn baby, infant, mother and family. A total of 64 trials were included (51 RCT s with 20 931 women and six cluster-randomised trials with 7500 women). A significant reduction in smoking in the intervention groups of 48 trials was noted (RR 0.94, 95% CI 0.93 to 0.95). Smoking cessation interventions reduced low birthweight (RR 0.81, 95% CI 0.70 to 0.94) and preterm birth (RR 0.84, 95% CI 0.72 to 0.98), and there was a 33 g (95% CI 11 g to 55 g) increase in mean birthweight. The results for very low birthweight, stillbirths, and perinatal or neonatal mortality showed no statistically significant differences between groups. One intervention strategy, rewards plus social support (two trials), resulted in a significantly greater smoking reduction than other strategies (RR 0.77, 95% CI 0.72 to 0.82). Five trials of smoking relapse prevention (over 800 women) showed no statistically significant reduction in relapse.

2008 update

A UK-based prospective study (2002)[652] [EL = 2+] evaluated the impact of the current anti-smoking advice in the UK on smoking habits of women with planned pregnancies. Two hospitals in North London were included whose policy is to provide all women at the first-trimester booking visit with leaflets and direct counselling for women who report that they smoke. Information was collected over a 6 month period at random from women booking for routine antenatal care. The study population included 117 (65%) women who did not currently smoke (non-smokers) and 63 (35%) who were active smokers at the beginning of their pregnancy. Thirty-nine non-smokers were found to be passive smokers. Three women took up smoking during pregnancy. 84.1% of smokers made no change in their smoking behaviour during pregnancy, 11.1% reduced their cigarette consumption and only 4.8% gave up smoking during the first half of pregnancy. None of the partners changed their smoking habits. All women were aware that smoking in pregnancy could be deleterious to their health and that of their unborn baby.

A US-based RCT (2006)[653] [EL = 1+] tested the efficacy of a pregnancy tailored telephone counselling intervention for pregnant smokers. The intervention used a motivational interviewing style. The study hypothesised that telephone counselling would increase smoking cessation rates at the end of pregnancy and 3 months postpartum compared with a control group that was given brief counselling. Pregnant women included in the study were identified as current cigarette smokers if they had smoked at least one cigarette in the past 7 days. The study population of 442 pregnant smokers referred by prenatal providers and a managed care plan were at least 18 years of age and at up to 26 weeks of gestation. Trained counsellors using cognitive–behavioural and motivational interviewing methods called women in the intervention group throughout pregnancy and for 2 months postpartum (a mean of five calls and a mean total contact of 68 minutes). Women in the control group received just one 5 minute counselling call. The results showed that 7 day tobacco abstinence rates in the intervention versus control groups were 10.0% versus 7.5% at the end of pregnancy (OR 1.37, 95% CI 0.69 to 2.70) and 6.7% versus 7.1% at 3 months postpartum (OR 0.93, 95% CI 0.44 to 1.99). The end-of-pregnancy cessation rates increased among 201 light smokers (fewer than 10 cigarettes/day at study enrolment) in the intervention group (intervention 19.1% versus control 8.4%; OR 2.58, 95% CI 1.1 to 6.1) and among 193 smokers who attempted to quit in pregnancy before enrolment (intervention 18.1% versus control 6.8%; OR 3.02, 95% CI 1.15 to 7.94).

A US-based RCT (1993)[654] [EL = 1+] evaluated a brief-contact smoking cessation programme among 57 pregnant women at two urban clinics. All the women were given a specially created videotape or a booklet related to smoking. After this they were randomly assigned to receive either a nurse counselling message or usual care at the clinic. There was no statistically significant difference in smoking status between the two groups. Twelve percent reported smoking cessation at 1 month after entry in the study, 18% reported in the ninth month of pregnancy, and 9% at 1 month postpartum. Over half of the patients attempted to quit smoking in the first month and 68% made at least one quit attempt during the entire study period.

A cluster RCT in New Zealand (2004)[655] [EL = 1+] tested the hypothesis that in a usual primary maternity care setting appropriate interventions delivered by midwives can help women to stop or reduce smoking and facilitate longer duration of breastfeeding. The midwives were stratified by locality and randomly allocated into a control group which provided usual care and three intervention groups. In the first intervention group, a programme of education and support for smoking cessation or reduction was given. In the second one, a programme of education and support for breastfeeding was given. In the third one both programmes were given. A total of 297 women were recruited by 61 midwives. The women who received only the smoking cessation or reduction programme were significantly more likely to have reduced, stopped smoking or maintained smoking changes than women in the control group, at 28 weeks and at 36 weeks of gestation. Women who received both the smoking cessation and breastfeeding education and support programmes were significantly more likely to have changed their smoking behaviour at 36 weeks of gestation than the control group. The postnatal period showed no difference in rates of cessation or reduction between the groups. Also there was no difference in rates of full breastfeeding between the control and intervention groups for women who planned to breastfeed.

2008 update

3.2.6 Travel safety information

Findings

A US-based prospective trial (1985)[656] [EL = 1–] administered a special 30 minute curriculum consisting of a lecture, a motion picture demonstrating the consequences of not using child car safety seats, and a question-and-answer session to couples attending prenatal classes. All parents were telephone interviewed at 4–6 months postpartum. The results showed that 96% of parents who received the special curriculum reported they used a crash-tested child car safety seat, as compared with 78% of those who had not received the curriculum. The compliance significantly rose from 60% before curriculum to 94% after curriculum at a hospital where parents were associated with low compliance (e.g. lower income, low use of seat belts, lower educational level).

A prospective study (1982)[657] [EL = 2–] in the USA investigated the influence of an in-hospital prenatal and postpartum educational programme on the prenatal use of infant car restraints. The participants were given demonstrations and talks on automobile crash statistics in the prenatal course, and in the postpartum period a car safety film on the hospital television, a pamphlet given to each mother and instructions to nurses to encourage parents' purchase and use of car restraints. The results showed that the actual use of infant restraints on the trip home was highest in the pre- plus postnatal education group although it was not statistically significant. There was higher restraint shown in the group given counselling in any period than no counselling.

3.2.7 Alcohol

Findings

Two trials were conducted in the UK (1990)[658] [EL = 1+] that compared three methods of imparting basic information and advice regarding the risks of alcohol in pregnancy at the first visit to the antenatal clinic. The effects on drinking patterns were assessed by written information alone, written information coupled with personalised advice, and written information with personalised advice reinforced by a specially produced video. The written information was in the form of a special edition of the leaflet 'Pregnancy. What you need to know' published by the Health Education Council and available commonly in antenatal clinics during the 1990s. The personalised advice was given by the interviewing doctor. The 4 minute video was designed to encourage pregnant women to reduce their drinking and gave suggestions on how to do so. Trial I had Group 1 (written information) and Group 2 (written information plus verbal reinforcement) and Trial II had Group 3 (written information) and Group 4 (written information plus verbal reinforcement plus video). Three questionnaires were given to the women: the first at their first visit to the clinic, the second at about 28 weeks of gestation and the third in the week immediately prior to delivery. The results showed no significant differences within or between trials in terms of behavioural change. Significantly more women in both arms of Trial II recommended 1 unit or less a day as the safe level of drinking during pregnancy compared with women in Trial I.

3.2.8 Gestational diabetes

Findings

A descriptive study with a retrospective analysis (1995)[659] [EL = 2–] in the USA compared two treatment approaches designed to help women with gestational diabetes manage their pregnancies: a hospital outpatient-based nursing intervention and traditional office-based care provided by obstetricians. A research model was constructed after a literature review that used three variables: input variables (risk factors prior to gestation), moderating variables (conditions that occur during pregnancy), and outcome variables (normal versus abnormal outcomes for mother and infant). The two treatment approaches were compared using this research model. In treatment 1 (nursing intervention) all patients completed the hospital gestational diabetes outpatient education programme regardless of referral source or subsequent treatments by other professionals. In treatment 2 (obstetricians only) all patients were treated by an obstetrician only (i.e. they did not participate in the nursing intervention and were not seen by an endocrinologist, a specialist in internal medicine, or a registered dietician). The study results showed that there was no statistically significant reduction in the risk of abnormal outcomes for mother or infant in either of the treatment approaches.

2008 update

Evidence summary for Sections 3.2.5 to 3.2.8
There is good-quality evidence to show that smoking cessation interventions help women reduce smoking and decrease adverse neonatal outcomes.

Evidence about car travel safety is of poor quality but findings suggest focused antenatal information provision may increase appropriate use of car restraints for babies.

There is a small amount of good-quality evidence on providing information about alcohol consumption in pregnancy that suggests that using a variety of methods does not alter reported behaviour, although it can improve knowledge about recommended safe levels.

3.2.9 How information is given to women antenatally

A total of nine studies (seven RCTs, one cluster controlled trial and one prospective cohort study) have been included in this section. All these studies compared different methods of providing information during the antenatal period in terms of uptake of screening tests, anxiety levels, knowledge, and other outcomes. The methodological quality of the included trials is generally good but no two studies compared similar methods of providing information. The review is further subdivided by the type of information provided, that is, general information about pregnancy/ screening tests or specific information about a disease/complication.

General information about pregnancy/screening tests (three studies)

Description of included studies
A randomised trial comparing three methods of giving information for prenatal testing was conducted in the UK (1995):[12] routine information given in antenatal clinics at the booking visit by the doctor or midwife (control group); extra information given individually before 16 weeks or at an extra hospital visit by a research midwife (individual group); and extra information given to a group of 4–12 women separate from the routine antenatal clinics (class group). [EL = 1+] The study population comprised pregnant women at less than 15 weeks of gestation and they were allocated to the three groups by simple randomisation using sealed opaque envelopes. The main outcome measures evaluated were attendance at the extra information sessions, uptake rates of prenatal screening tests (ultrasound, Down's syndrome, cystic fibrosis, haemoglobinopathy), levels of anxiety, understanding, and satisfaction with decisions. Questions on level of anxiety were administered at 16–18 weeks, 20 weeks, 30 weeks and 6 weeks post-delivery to assess anxiety at different times. Questions on information were administered at 16–18 weeks, and satisfaction questions at 30 and 46 weeks. All analysis was by intention-to-treat analysis but blinding was not specified and sample size calculations were not performed.

A second RCT (2000)[660] was conducted in five antenatal clinics in a university teaching hospital in the UK to compare the effectiveness of a touch screen method with information leaflets for providing women with information about prenatal tests. [EL = 1+] The study population comprised both low- and high-risk pregnant women at booking appointment for antenatal care. After recruitment, baseline information was collected and women were randomly allocated to the intervention (touch screen and information leaflet) or control group (leaflet only) using consecutive sealed opaque envelopes. Use of touch screen was limited to the intervention group by means of a password. The primary outcome measured was women's informed decision making on prenatal testing as measured by their uptake and understanding of the purpose of five screening tests (ultrasound scan at booking, serum screening, detailed anomaly scan, amniocentesis and chorionic villus sampling). Secondary outcomes included women's satisfaction with the information and their anxiety levels. Primary outcomes were assessed by a self-completed postal questionnaire (developed from a validated instrument) at around 16 and then 20 weeks, and anxiety by the Spielberg state-anxiety inventory. Quality control checks were conducted on a random sample of 10% of questionnaires, statistical analysis was done on an intention-to-treat basis, and power and sample size calculations were performed.

A cluster RCT (2002)[13] was conducted in Wales to investigate the effect of leaflets on promoting informed choice in women using maternity services. [EL = 1−] Twelve maternity units each having more than 1000 deliveries annually were grouped into ten clusters (some units shared management or consultants) and randomly assigned to the intervention units (five units receiving set of leaflets) or control units (five units continuing with normal care) by tossing a coin. A set of ten leaflets summarising the evidence on ten decisions that women face during pregnancy and childbirth, and encouraging them to make informed decisions was used as the intervention. In the intervention units some relevant leaflets were given at 10–12 weeks and the rest at 34–36 weeks. Participants included an antenatal sample (women reaching 28 weeks during the 6 week study period) and a postnatal sample (delivering during the study period) of women both prior to introduction of the leaflets and 9 months after they were introduced; thus four groups of participants were identified. The primary outcome measured was the change in proportion of women who reported exercising informed choice, while secondary outcomes were women's levels of knowledge, satisfaction with information, and possible consequences of informed choice. Outcomes were assessed using a postal questionnaire (piloted before use) sent at 28 weeks of gestation for the antenatal sample and 8 weeks post-delivery for the postnatal sample. Power and sample size calculations were performed, analyses were done on intention-to-treat basis and confounding variables were adjusted, but blinding of outcome investigators was not achieved. Moreover, there was selection bias (poor response rate) and the study had low power.

Findings

A total of 1691 women consented to participate in the UK RCT:[12] 567 in the control group, 563 in the individual group and 561 in the class group. The baseline demographic features of the three groups were comparable. Attendance at the extra sessions was low (overall 52%) and was lower at classes than at individual appointments (adjusted OR 0.45, 95% CI 0.35 to 0.58). Uptake of ultrasound at 18 weeks was almost universal (99%) and not affected by either intervention. Low uptake of Down's syndrome screening in the control group improved slightly after the intervention in the individual group (OR 1.45, 95% CI 1.04 to 2.02) but was not affected by extra information given in classes. High uptake of cystic fibrosis screening at the baseline was lowered both in the individual group (OR 0.44, 95% CI 0.20 to 0.97) and the class group (OR 0.39, 95% CI 0.18 to 0.86). Women in the individual group were found to have significantly reduced levels of anxiety at 20 weeks ($P = 0.02$) compared with the control group, and thereafter anxiety was reduced but not significantly. Pregnant women given extra information either at individual level or in classes felt that they had received more relevant information and understood it better. They were also more satisfied with the information received.

In the second RCT[660] of the 1050 women randomised to the intervention group ($n = 524$) and control group ($n = 526$), only 64% returned all three questionnaires and the sample sizes for measuring uptake and understanding were 358 and 376, respectively. There were no significant differences between the intervention and the control groups for the baseline characteristics and reasons or rate of loss to follow-up. More women in the intervention group underwent detailed anomaly scans compared with the control group (94% versus 87%; $P = 0.01$), but for the rest of the screening tests uptake rates were similar. All women in the trial had good baseline knowledge of the screening tests and this increased significantly in both the groups after the intervention, but no apparent greater gain in knowledge was seen among women in the intervention arm compared with the control arm. Levels of anxiety declined significantly among the nulliparous women in the intervention group ($P < 0.001$). Both groups reported high level of satisfaction with the information leaflets (> 95%), and a similar proportion of women in the intervention group reported that they would recommend the touch screen to other women. The authors concluded that touch screen method conferred no additional benefit to that provided by the more traditional method of information leaflet but seemed to reduce anxiety and may be most effective for information provision to selected women, that is, those with relevant adverse history or abnormal results.

In the Welsh cluster RCT[13] the overall response rate was 64% with a rate of 65% (3164/4835) for the antenatal sample and 63% (3288/5235) for the postnatal one. Socio-demographic characteristics of women in the intervention and control units were similar in the antenatal sample, while in the postnatal sample respondents after the intervention were an average 7 months younger. The proportion of women who reported exercising informed choice increased slightly after the intervention in both the units, but there was no significant difference in the change between the two groups for either the antenatal or the postnatal sample. A small increase in satisfaction with information was observed in the antenatal sample of the population in the intervention units compared with the control units (OR 1.40, 95% CI 1.05 to 1.88). However, owing to operational

2008 update

difficulties, just 75% of the women in the intervention units reported receiving at least one of the information leaflets. It was concluded that evidence-based information leaflets were not effective in promoting informed choice in women using maternity services.

Specific information about Down's syndrome screening (four studies)

Description of included studies

An RCT was conducted in Canada (1997)[661] to investigate to what extent a newly revised educational pamphlet on triple screening (developed using consumer consultation and providers' perception and suggestions) improved patient knowledge and to identify subgroups not benefiting from these materials. [EL = 1+] The study population of women with singleton pregnancies at less than 18 weeks of gestation was recruited from six different sites in both urban and rural areas. Participants were randomly allocated (computer-generated random list in a block-randomisation sequence for each site) to receive the pamphlet on triple-marker screening in the intervention group, or a similar-appearing pamphlet on daily activities during pregnancy in the control group. The method of allocation was concealed till the time of enrolment. The primary outcome measure was the Maternal Serum Screening Knowledge Questionnaire (a validated 14-item scale). Blinding of outcome investigators was not specified. Power and sample size calculations were performed.

A second RCT (2004)[662] was conducted in a prenatal diagnosis clinic in the UK to evaluate decision analysis as a technique to facilitate women's decision making about prenatal diagnosis for Down's syndrome using measures of effective decision making. [EL = 1+] Pregnant women receiving a screen-positive maternal serum screening (MSS) test for Down's syndrome (risk ≥ 1 in 250) were randomly allocated to the intervention or the control group using sealed opaque envelopes. Routine consultation based on the MSS result sheet was provided to the women in the control group, while in the intervention group a decision-analysis consultation using three prompts was employed – a decision tree representing test options and consequences, a utility elicitation question prompting women to choose between the burden of having a child with Down's syndrome and that of pregnancy termination, and a threshold graph identifying the alternatives. All the consultations were audiotape-recorded, transcribed and coded. Participants also completed a questionnaire after the consultation and 1 month later after the receipt of their test results. The main outcomes measured were risk perception, test decision, subjective expected utilities, knowledge, informed decision making, conflict in decision making, anxiety, and perceived usefulness of consultation. All the consultations in the two groups were provided by a single professional and calculations for power and sample size performed. Blinding of outcome investigator and intention-to-treat analysis was carried out.

Another RCT conducted in Hong Kong (2004)[663] compared an interactive multimedia decision aid (IMDA) with a leaflet and a video to give information about prenatal screening for Down's syndrome, and to determine women's acceptance of IMDA. [EL = 1+] All Chinese women attending a prenatal clinic in a tertiary hospital before 20 weeks of gestation were invited to participate and offered either an integrated screening test (presenting before 15 weeks) or a serum screening test (presenting after 15 weeks). After informed consent, eligible women were randomised into the intervention group (information leaflet, 30 minute video and then browsing IMDA) or the control group (information leaflet and watching 30 minute video only) by consecutive sealed opaque envelopes. Apart from giving information contained in the leaflet and/or video, the IMDA prompted women to choose their option with information about its implication, and followed it with a frequently asked question and answer session. IMDA could only be accessed in a closed room by women in the intervention group. The primary outcome evaluated was uptake of the screening test, and secondary outcomes measured were women's initial decision, understanding, and satisfaction with the information that they received. The instrument used for measuring outcome was a questionnaire given to both the groups after watching the video, and another one given to the intervention group after the IMDA session. Analysis was done on an intention-to-treat basis, and confounding variables were controlled in evaluating women's acceptance of the decision aid. Sample size was calculated prior to study.

Another UK RCT (2001)[664] was carried out to assess the effect of a Down's syndrome screening video (specifically produced fulfilling all RCOG recommendations) on the test uptake, knowledge, anxiety and worry. [EL = 1−] The study population comprising consecutive pregnant women referred for antenatal care was allocated either to the intervention group (sent the video at home before the hospital booking visit) or the control group who received usual care by a quasi-randomisation technique. All women also received screening information in the form of a leaflet before booking and from a midwife at the time of booking. Outcomes evaluated were test uptake (using record linkage), knowledge (multiple-choice questionnaire with 12 items), worries (multiple-choice questionnaire with 16 items), and anxiety (Hospital Anxiety and Depression scale). Baseline characteristics of the intervention and the control group were not compared. Blinding of outcome investigator was not specified and calculations for sample size and analysis on intention-to-treat basis were not performed.

Findings

Findings from the Canadian RCT[661] showed the success rate of the recruitment process among eligible women to be 94.7% (198/209). Baseline demographic, obstetric and medical factors were similar between the intervention/triple marker screening group ($n = 133$) and the control/daily activity group ($n = 65$). The mean overall knowledge score was significantly higher in the intervention group (0.89 versus 0.52 on a scale from −2 to +2; $P < 0.001$) compared with the control group. Also women receiving pamphlet on triple screening had higher scores for the domains of test characteristics, ancillary tests and target conditions ($P < 0.001$) but not for the domains of indication and timing of tests. These results remained the same even after controlling for potential confounding variables. Subgroups not benefiting from the triple marker screening pamphlet were women aged 25 years and younger and those not speaking English at home. Those who had completed university or postgraduate education had high levels of knowledge with and without the pamphlet.

Findings from the second RCT[662] showed no differences in the socio-demographic characteristics (apart from gestation), risk assessed by MSS test, and return rates of the questionnaires between the two groups. A similar proportion of women chose to have a diagnostic test: 47/58 (81%) in the control group versus 48/59 (81%) in the intervention group. Choice of test did not differ by group allocation, but decision-analysis women evaluated more information during their consultation, both positively and negatively than those in the control group (positive evaluation: mean score 3.18 versus 2.55, $F = 6.30$, $P = 0.01$; negative evaluation: mean score 3.00 versus 2.37, $F = 5.98$, $P = 0.02$). These women also perceived the risk more realistically ($P = 0.05$) and had a lower decisional conflict over time. Decision-analysis consultations lasted about 6 minutes longer but women did not perceive consultations to be any more or less directive, useful or anxiety provoking than the routine ones. No significant differences were observed for the other outcomes.

In the third RCT[663] a total of 201 women were randomised to the intervention ($n = 100$) and the control group ($n = 101$), and the questionnaire was completed by 90% of women in the intervention group and 99% in the control group. The baseline characteristics of the two groups were similar. There were no significant differences in the initial decision for and the final uptake of the screening test between the intervention and the control group (P value for all the tests > 0.05). After watching the video 54.1% of women in the control group and 55.1% in the intervention group reported that they had no more questions. After browsing the IMDA the proportion of women having no more questions increased to 77.0% ($P < 0.001$), and 86.6% of women agreed that IMDA was user-friendly and 78.9% that it was acceptable. A higher proportion of younger women (aged under 35 years) accepted IMDA compared with those over 35 years of age ($P = 0.03$), but the difference was not significant after adjusting for confounding variables.

For the UK quasi-RCT[664] a total of 993 women were allocated to the video group and 1007 to the control group. No statistically significant difference was observed in the screening uptake rate between the two groups (64.2% versus 64.7%). Questionnaires were sent at 17–19 weeks only to the first 1200 women randomised in the two groups and after exclusions the sample sizes were 499 (video group) and 552 (control group). The rate of questionnaire completion was similar between the two groups. Knowledge about screening was increased in the video group with a mean score of 7.3 compared with 6.7 in the control group ($P = 0.0005$), but there was no difference between the two groups in specific worries about abnormalities in the baby, or general anxiety. The outcomes were also evaluated in relation to baseline demographic characteristics of housing tenure and age. Knowledge was found to be significantly higher in owner-occupiers and older age groups, anxiety scores lower in owner-occupiers, and worry scores higher in older age groups. The authors concluded that knowledge of prenatal testing can be increased by using a video, and moreover this can be done without making women more anxious or worried about fetal abnormalities.

Specific information on preterm birth (one study)

Description of included study
Patient education was included as an integral part of a multi-faceted programme aimed at reducing preterm birth deliveries in a province in New York (USA), and this cohort study (1989)[665] examined specifically the effectiveness of patient education in preterm birth prevention. [EL = 2–] All women beginning antenatal care by 36 weeks and not at high risk for preterm birth were enrolled for the study and offered a class about recognising the signs and symptoms of preterm labour. The class consisted of a 15 minute videotape presentation followed by a 15 minute discussion led by a registered nurse staff member where several printed educational materials were also given. Outcomes evaluated were the rates of preterm birth and low birthweight. Blinding of outcome investigators was not specified and confounding variables were not controlled.

Findings
The study population was 2326 women and of these 487 attended the class, with most participating between 24 and 32 weeks of gestational age. There were no significant differences between the class attendees and non-attendees for the baseline demographic and obstetric variables. Women attending classes had babies with a higher mean birthweight ($P = 0.03$) and gestational age ($P = 0.12$), but improvement in gestational age did not reach statistical significance. The preterm birth rate was reduced by 17% and low birthweight rate by 27% among women attending the classes compared with the non-attendees, but these differences were statistically not significant.

Specific information on HIV (one study)

Description of included study
This UK (Scottish) RCT (1998)[666] aimed to determine whether different methods of offering voluntary HIV testing to all pregnant women would lead to significantly different uptake rates, and to assess the impact of these methods on women's satisfaction, anxiety and knowledge. [EL = 1+] All pregnant women booked in a tertiary hospital in the UK were invited to participate in the trial. Four different combinations of providing information using a leaflet sent with the booking information package ('all blood tests information' or 'HIV-specific test information') and discussion with a midwife ('minimal' or 'comprehensive') were compared. After recruitment the participants were computer-randomised into five groups: Group 1 was the control group with no leaflet or discussion; Group 2 was given 'all blood tests' leaflet and 'minimal discussion' by a midwife; Group 3 was given 'all blood tests' leaflet and 'comprehensive discussion' by a midwife; Group 4 given 'HIV-specific test' leaflet and 'minimal discussion' by a midwife; and Group 5 was given 'HIV-specific test' leaflet and 'comprehensive discussion' by a midwife. Except for Group 1, which was offered HIV testing on request, all the other four groups were directly offered the test by the midwife, that is, the policy of universal testing was followed. The key outcomes were uptake of testing and women's knowledge of HIV, satisfaction with consultation, and anxiety. Hospital records along with a questionnaire given to women after discussion with a midwife were used to assess the outcomes. Analysis was done on an intention-to-treat basis and regression used to determine independent predictors of uptake.

Findings
Of the 3505 women randomised at booking, 3024 participated in the study over a 10 month period. Baseline demographic characteristics of the five groups were similar. Uptake rates were 6% for the control group and each of the methods of directly offering the test resulted in a higher uptake than in the control group (χ^2 test, df = 4, $P < 0.0001$). However, there was no significant difference between the four groups where the test was offered directly (χ^2 test, df = 3, $P = 0.37$). The best independent predictor of uptake was being directly offered the test. General knowledge of HIV was good and did not differ significantly by the method of offering testing, but specific knowledge about HIV and benefits of testing increased with the amount of information given (χ^2 test of linear trend, df = 4, $P < 0.001$). No significant difference was found regarding anxiety and satisfaction.

Evidence summary for Section 3.2.9
Evidence from a single trial [EL = 1+] indicates that extra information about screening tests given individually or in a group leads to higher level of satisfaction and understanding among pregnant women. This may, in turn, decrease uptake of some screening tests.

There is high-quality evidence that information leaflets are effective in increasing the knowledge of pregnant women about screening tests (general and for Down's syndrome), and the use of a touch screen method does not improve the uptake rate of screening tests compared with the leaflets.

Evidence from a good-quality trial shows that decision-aid techniques are helpful to pregnant women in making informed choices about the screening tests for Down's syndrome.

Results from a good-quality trial show that using an interactive multimedia decision aid does not improve the uptake of screening tests for Down's syndrome compared with the information provided by leaflets and video.

There is limited evidence on effectiveness of informational material for reducing preterm deliveries. Results from a single cohort study show that educating women using a video film followed by a discussion are ineffective in preventing preterm births.

Evidence from a single good-quality trial indicates that a formal offer of an HIV test accompanied by both written and verbal information leads to a higher uptake of HIV screening tests in pregnant women without increasing their anxiety compared with making the test available on request.

3.2.10 Perspectives of clinicians and women regarding information giving

Three good-quality descriptive studies have been included in this section. The first study explored and compared the perceptions of clinicians and patients regarding screening tests, the second evaluated information provided for Down's syndrome from the perspective of healthcare practitioners only, and the last one looked at the social context with respect to introduction of a new informational leaflet for prenatal care.

Description of included studies
A qualitative descriptive study was conducted in the USA (2005)[667] to explore the interaction between the contrasting perspectives of clinicians and the patients, and consider how differences in their primary orientations might affect efforts to assure patients are making informed decisions about prenatal genetic testing. [EL = 3] This study combined data from a series of related studies and altogether a convenience sample of 40 patients and a convenience snowball sample of 50 clinicians were interviewed along with observations of 101 genetics counselling sessions. Women interviewed were those offered amniocentesis following an abnormal alpha-fetoprotein (AFP) test while the clinicians interviewed included 25 physicians, 20 clinical staff and five genetics counsellors. Patients and clinicians were interviewed from the same clinics and who had interacted with each other in order to capture their contrasting perspectives. The interviews, averaging about 2 hours, were tape-recorded and transcribed, and followed a standardised set of open-ended questions. Information and knowledge content scores were generated from the interviews based on eight informational elements considered important by the clinicians when offering amniocentesis. All phases of data processing and analysis were cross-checked during conference sessions and any discrepancy was addressed.

A qualitative study in the UK (2002)[668] explored the information given to pregnant women and their partners about Down's syndrome from the perspective of healthcare practitioners, and looked at some ways in which this information could be constructed. [EL = 3] Healthcare practitioners whose work was related directly or indirectly to perinatal care were recruited (*n* = 70) using 'snowballing' technique, and their informed consent was taken. Individual interviews lasting between 1 and 2 hours were conducted in the form of semi-structured 'guided conversations'. Most of the interviewees (56/70) then participated in group discussions with an average group size of nine (six participants, two sociologists, one group leader). Groups were of mixed disciplines and seniority and their discussions were tape-recorded, fully transcribed, analysed by content for emergent themes and then coded. Each session lasted approximately 2 hours. Findings of this study are based on the 11 group discussions that took place and do not include data from the interviews held earlier.

2008 update

Qualitative research was conducted independently but alongside the cluster-randomised trial[13] to understand the social context in which the leaflets (ten pairs of informed choice) were used.[14] [EL = 3] The study involved non-participant observation and in-depth interviews with health professionals and pregnant women in both the intervention (five units receiving the leaflets) and the control units (five units continuing normal care). Consultations were observed to identify how the leaflets were used and how informed choice and decision making occurred in practice. Face-to-face interviews were conducted using a semi-structured format to discuss various aspects of information giving (availability, quality and understanding), the meaning of informed choice, and the role of childbearing women in decision making. Sampling was initially 'opportunistic' depending on the availability and willingness to participate, but later became 'selective' to ensure uniform representation of both the health professionals and pregnant women. Towards the end of the intervention period, women who had questioned or declined the choices offered to them and staff who offered information withheld by their colleagues were selectively interviewed to identify the interplay between hierarchy, power and trust.

Findings
One-third of the women interviewed were 25–30 years of age, more than half were married and three-quarters had decided to go for amniocentesis. Almost half of the clinicians interviewed were working in private genetics specialty clinics, 22% were MD with genetics specialty and 10% were genetics counsellors. Of the 101 genetics counselling sessions, women were observed in two-thirds of cases while in the rest they were both observed and interviewed. Broadly, both the clinicians and patients shared the obvious goal of prenatal care of ensuring a healthy pregnancy, but their understanding and orientations to this undertaking were quite different. For the clinicians, consultations were a routine part of their everyday work of trying to identify, prevent and control problems. In contrast, patients considered consultations as a disruption of their routine of nurturing and protecting their pregnancy. While moving through the process of prenatal genetic diagnosis, each defined the shared goal of promoting a healthy pregnancy in strikingly different ways:

* *Meaning of an abnormal screening test* – In the genetics counselling sessions, clinicians usually began by noting that the abnormal screening test only indicates that there might be a problem (specifying a percentage 'risk') and explaining that further testing was required for the diagnosis. Most of the patients (87%) felt anxious with the news and many began crying, while 63% said that they were told nothing about the reason for referral to a genetics specialist and they thought it was a routine prenatal visit.
* *Ultrasound to confirm dates* – For the clinicians, it was a mundane step to verify whether further testing was required and usually occurred without discussion with the patient. The patient on the other hand was primarily concerned with getting information about the wellbeing of the baby.
* *Offer of amniocentesis* – Clinicians were primarily concerned with finding and responding to a problem and 96% described acceptance of testing by the patients as being based on their desire to know the wellbeing of the baby. All the patients accepting the offer of amniocentesis said they had wanted reassurance about the baby's health after the positive screening tests results, while 90% of women declining the offer did it for not willing to risk a miscarriage.

Clinicians discussed all the essential elements of information giving in only 59% of the consultations. Elements most consistently covered were that the test is optional, the risks of the procedure, and the risks for the anomaly, while the least covered elements were the nature of the anomaly and alternatives to amniocentesis. Patients' overall knowledge score averaged about 53% and the elements for which they showed most complete knowledge included reasons for doing amniocentesis, that the test is optional, the nature of the invasive procedure, and what information this test could give. The elements least completely discussed included risk of anomaly, alternatives to amniocentesis and nature of the anomaly.

However, there was no statistical correlation between the completeness of information included in consultants' consultations and the level of knowledge exhibited by the patients during the interviews (Pearson correlation = 0.204; $P = 0.289$).

In the UK qualitative study[668] of the 56 health practitioners who participated in the group discussions there were 20 midwives, 20 doctors, and 16 from a variety of other disciplines. The principal findings from the study were as follows:

- *What women were thought to know about Down's syndrome* – Practitioners felt that more time was spent explaining the complexities of the actual screening process rather than the condition being screened. Moreover, many women did not have adequate knowledge about some of the basic features of Down's syndrome. This was ascribed to fewer births of infants with Down's syndrome and medical innovations shifting people's perception of normality.
- *How information about Down's syndrome is presented* – Although many practitioners felt that their way of providing information influenced decision making by pregnant women, they seldom made any positive and realistic statement about the condition. Leaflets distributed to the pregnant women at the time of booking visit were frequently used to provide information. These leaflets contained little information about Down's syndrome itself and devoted most of its space to the screening process. Many staff members were also reluctant to provide positive aspects of information as they felt that it might not present a realistic picture to the prospective parents.
- *From where do practitioners obtain their knowledge* – Most practitioners themselves had little time and practical experience of dealing with Down's syndrome cases. They relied on medical textbooks, leaflets and articles for knowledge and these sources usually focused on the potential problems of the syndrome and its management strategies.
- *Ways in which information about Down's syndrome was negatively constructed* – The authors explained that lack of access to adequate health care (denial of treatment for common ailments, decreased probability of affected children attending mass screening) along with the difficulty in distinguishing visual/hearing problems from learning disabilities leads to the development of a negative picture about Down's syndrome.

A total of 886 episodes of consultations with pregnant women were observed – 653 held by midwives, 167 by obstetricians and 66 by the obstetric ultrasonographers, and 383 face-to-face interviews were conducted (173 childbearing women, 177 midwives, 28 obstetricians, 12 obstetric ultrasonographers and three obstetric anaesthetists). Although the health professionals were positive about the leaflet and their potential in helping women to make informed choices, the leaflets were seldom used to maximum effect in clinical practice. The various reasons observed were the time constraints, unavailability of choice in regular practice, disagreement among staff with its content or an option given in it, and their distribution usually in a concealed manner or 'wrapped' up with other advertising material. Health professionals were also observed to influence decision making in pregnant women towards technological intervention by conveying information which either minimised the risk of the intervention or emphasised the potential for harm without the intervention. They reinforced notions of 'right' and 'wrong' choices instead of 'informed choices' and this was promoted by their fear of litigation. A strong hierarchy was observed within the maternity services with the obstetricians at the top, midwives and health professionals other than doctors in the middle, and pregnant women at the bottom. This led to concern in midwives about the consequences of recommending options that contradicted obstetrically defined clinical norms. Because of their trust in health professionals, women seldom questioned them or made alternative requests, and this ensured 'informed compliance' rather than 'informed decision making'.

Evidence summary
There is evidence from a well-conducted qualitative study which shows that the process of informed decision making for prenatal screening tests is hampered by inadequate information provided to pregnant women during consultations, and the divergent approaches taken by the information provider (clinicians) and information taker (patients).

Although the healthcare providers intend to provide complete information about Down's syndrome screening and its subsequent pathway to prospective parents, their ability to do so is limited by time constraints, their limited experience of the condition after birth and a lack of factual information given in the sources they used to acquire knowledge about Down's syndrome.

Time constraints, fear of litigation, power hierarchies, and imperativeness of current technological interventions act as barriers in promoting leaflets for informed decision making in maternity care.

2008 update

Women were found to merely comply with the information provided by health professionals and were unable to make an 'informed choice'.

3.2.11 Women's preference for source of information

Description of included study

A retrospective cohort study (2004)[669] was carried out using data from an earlier study to find out: (i) who women perceive as influencing their decision about prenatal screening and diagnosis for birth defects; (ii) who they would have liked to talk more to; and (iii) what sources of information they preferred. [EL = 2+] The sample population comprised pregnant women from 18 hospitals in Australia at approximately 24 weeks of gestation and over 37 years of age at the estimated date of delivery. Questionnaires seeking women's choices and preferences for the above-mentioned three objectives were developed through a process of piloting, and differences between women who did and who did not undergo prenatal testing were examined for each of the objective.

Findings

The sample population for the final analysis included 724 women, with 539 undergoing prenatal testing (tested group) and 185 not having prenatal testing (untested group). The baseline socio-demographic characteristics of the two groups were similar. More than 90% of women in both groups reported that they themselves had a strong influence on their decision to be tested or not, and 70% reported their partner as strongly influencing their decision. Statistically, no significant difference was observed between the two groups for the above parameters, but a significantly higher proportion of women in the tested group were influenced by their doctor or genetics counsellor ($P < 0.001$ for both) and a friend or a nurse ($P < 0.01$ for both). Of women in the tested group, 35.7% were more likely to talk to other women who have had the tests as compared with 21% of women in the untested group ($P < 0.001$). A higher proportion of tested women would have preferred to talk to a genetics counsellor (9.5% versus 8.6%; $P = 0.002$), while women in the untested group were more likely to talk to a pastoral carer (2.5% versus 10.6%; $P < 0.001$). There were no significant differences between the groups with respect to a specialist, general practitioner, friend, nurse/midwife or other pregnant women. In both the tested and the untested groups, the preferred source of getting information was face-to-face discussion or counselling (69.1% tested group versus 47.4% untested group), and the difference between the two groups was statistically significant ($P < 0.001$). The second preferred choice was pamphlet (48.7% versus 42.8%; $P = 0.18$) followed by video (35.2% versus 24.9%; $P = 0.01$). Untested women were significantly more likely than the tested women to say that they were not interested in any information. The authors concluded that since a high proportion of women were responsible for their own decisions about prenatal testing, it is unlikely that universal acceptance and uptake will occur even in this group of women with advanced age. Moreover, there continues to be a need for face-to-face sessions with a doctor or a counsellor in combination with printed information material.

Evidence summary

Evidence shows that the decision on whether or not to undergo a prenatal screening test is usually made by the woman herself. However, those choosing to undergo testing report that healthcare professionals also have a strong influence on their decision. Women prefer getting information from face-to-face discussion or counselling rather than other methods.

3.2.12 Women's views of general antenatal information provision

Description of included studies

Six descriptive studies are included in this section, three conducted in the UK, two in the USA and one from New Zealand.

An English retrospective cross-sectional questionnaire survey (2005)[670] was identified for review that investigated women's views of information giving during the antenatal period. [EL = 3] All women giving birth in the study area during a 3 month period were invited to participate in the survey ($n = 700$), and 329 women returned a completed questionnaire (response rate 47%).

A local English longitudinal, prospective survey (1997)[672] of antenatal classes conducted in one large teaching hospital and National Childbirth Trust classes in the neighbouring area sought men's and women's views concerning class content. [EL = 3] Three questionnaires were distributed to couples (separate questionnaires for men and women), one prior to the commencement of classes, one at the end of the course of antenatal classes, and one after the birth of the baby. The first questionnaire was posted (details of its return are unclear), the second was handed out and returned to the antenatal educator at the end of the final session. It is unclear how the third questionnaire was distributed and returned. The overall response rate for all three questionnaires was 159/400. One open-ended question on each questionnaire asked for respondents' views of class content. The response rates for this question on each questionnaire were 31.5%, 22% and 71%, respectively.

A retrospective, national survey was conducted with a randomly selected sample of women giving birth during a particular month in 1984.[673] [EL = 3] The sample was drawn from ten regions of England stratified by county on a north to south basis. 1920 women were included in the survey and 1508 returned a completed questionnaire (response rate 79%). Women were asked what had been their main sources of information during pregnancy and how useful these had been. (Information received during labour and postpartum was also asked about but will not be reported here.)

A US concurrent mixed methods study[674] conducted in 2003–04 involved 202 (response rate 90%) low-income African-American women in face-to-face interviews to ask their views and experiences of pregnancy and antenatal care. [EL = 3] The study aimed to investigate differences between women with low literacy skills and those with higher literacy skills. A randomly selected subgroup of participants ($n = 40$) carried out a free-list task where participants were asked to list up to ten words or short phrases for 'things you think about when going to the doctor when you are pregnant'. Responses from the free-list task were then subject to cultural consensus analysis (or cultural domain analysis). This technique is used to define how members of group make sense of or understand a particular aspect of life (cognitive domain). Four focus groups were conducted to confirm and explore the items/themes identified through the free-list task. These involved eight women with low literacy skills (defined as up to sixth grade) and ten women with higher literacy skills (at least ninth grade), matched by age and postpartum month. Findings from the focus groups were analysed using a grounded theory approach in order to confirm factor items identified through cultural consensus analysis and to look for meaning in and relationships between items.

A US cross-sectional interview-based descriptive study was conducted in order to identify differences between the health promotion content women wanted to discuss during antenatal consultations and issues actually discussed, and to compare health promotion content of consultations between African-American women and Mexican-American women.[675] [EL = 3] Interviews were conducted with 159 African-American or Mexican-American women with low income recruited from a 'low-risk' antenatal clinic affiliated to a tertiary care hospital (response rate 91%). Within the research interview women were read a list of 27 health promotion topics and asked 'did you want or need information about [topic]' and then they were asked 'did you talk about [topic]?'.

A cross-sectional questionnaire survey carried out in New Zealand (1999)[676] investigated women's information needs and sources. [EL = 3] Recruitment was carried out using posters placed in public places where pregnant and postnatal women were expected to see them. The sample is thus a volunteer sample and it is not possible to compare the sample of respondents with non-respondents. Respondents included women planning a pregnancy ($n = 7$), pregnant women ($n = 30$) and women who had given birth in the previous 3 months ($n = 13$).

Findings
The UK retrospective survey asked women how they preferred information to be provided.[670] Seventy percent of women stated a preference for one-to-one discussion, and a similar proportion cited leaflets as their preferred method. Only 20% indicated that taught classes or discussion groups were the preferred method of receiving information. While the majority of women reported that they understood the written information provided during pregnancy, subgroup analysis revealed an important difference. While 72% of women from professional/semi-professional groups reported that they understood all written materials, only 45.5% of women from non-professional/non-working groups reported this high level of understanding. Over 90% of women expressed that they had been given enough information and an opportunity to make decisions

2008 update

about screening tests. However, women's responses regarding diet, alcohol intake, exercise and smoking indicated that the information received had little or no effect on their attitude or behaviour. When asked whether information they had received influenced their decision about where to give birth, 70% said it had little or no influence. However, the only choices available in the study area were birth in the local hospital or home birth.

Findings from the UK local survey of men and women's views of the content of antenatal classes suggested that both men and women would have preferred more information about the postnatal period to be provided by antenatal classes. This need was apparent at all phases of the survey but was most prominent in the postnatal questionnaire where 95/111 (86%) participants included this topic in their response to an open-ended question. The major category within this theme was information about caring for the new baby.

Findings from the English national survey carried out in 1984 were reported separately for nulliparous and multiparous women.[673] [EL = 3] Almost three-quarters of nulliparous women had attended antenatal classes, but only 6% cited these as the most helpful source of information. Non-professional sources of information (own mother, husband, friends and relatives) were considered the most useful sources of information by 43% of nulliparous women, compared with 24% who reported professional sources (midwife, GP, obstetrician, health visitor) as the most useful. When asked about the amount of information given during pregnancy, 59% of all women said they felt it had been the right amount of information, 20% reported it had been too much and 20% that it had not been enough. A quarter of women felt that they had not been able to discuss all the things they had wanted to during antenatal consultations. Women who were not married, those whose social class was classified as manual and those who did not own their own homes were more likely to report dissatisfaction in this.

Findings from the UK local survey of men and women's views of the content of antenatal classes suggested that both men and women would have preferred more information about the postnatal period to be provided by antenatal classes. This need was apparent at all phases of the survey but most prominent in the postnatal questionnaire where 95/111 (86%) of the participants included this topic in their response to an open-ended question. The major category within this theme was information about caring for the new baby.

Cultural consensus analysis of findings from the US concurrent mixed methods study (n = 9 women with low literacy level; n = 31 women with higher literacy)[674] revealed the following items as most salient when women were asked what they thought about when considering an antenatal appointment (from most to least salient): finding out if everything is OK; long wait; questions (communication with carer); needles (blood tests); woman's weight and hearing the baby's heartbeat. [EL = 3] Items associated with communication between women and their carers were identified as making up an organising theme when women were discussing obstacles to care. This was common across all four focus groups. Women in all groups described ideal communication as communication where each person makes statements that are accurately understood and completely responded to by the other person. Women in all groups valued carers who provided information in a way they could understand, for example where complex concepts or words were 'broken down' in order to make them more easily understood. It was important to women that they were able to tell their carer when they had not understood something so that the carer could explain further.

The US cross-sectional descriptive study[675] involved interviews with 112 African-American women and 47 Mexican-American women, where 72% of the women were younger than 24 years and 65% were multiparous. Thirty-nine percent of women in the sample had less than 12 years of education and 45% had household incomes of less than $1000 per month. Bivariate analysis revealed statistically significant differences ($P < 0.001$) between topics women wanted to discuss and topics actually discussed. Statistical analysis was performed using the Sign test for paired data. Although P values are given, values for the Sign statistic are not reported. Significantly more women wanted or needed information but did not discuss using seatbelts safely, dealing with stress and conflict, family planning, and caring for the new baby. Women did not want or feel they needed information but discussed taking vitamin/mineral supplements, eating specific food groups, drinking adequate amounts of water, stopping specific substance use. More differences were reported between information wanted or needed and information discussed for African-American women compared with Mexican-American women (adjusted regression analysis $R^2 = 0.39$; $P < 0.001$).

Findings from the New Zealand cross-sectional survey showed that the sources pregnant women most often used for information were their midwife (37%), friends (23%) and the GP (13%).[676] Advice from midwives was thought to be useful because it tended to be practical and reassuring. The theme of reassurance was prominent amongst women's responses. Topics that pregnant women wanted information about included: knowing what is normal; how to prepare for birth; coping with labour and birth; how to look after the baby; and what to expect after birth. Multiparous women identified some different information needs including: coping with morning sickness; self-care during pregnancy; birth after caesarean section; and financial needs and options. The educational background of women did not appear to be related to the kind of information needs they reported.

Evidence summary
Most women preferred information to be provided on a face-to-face basis. The extent to which there was an understanding of what was said was dependent upon their working background.

A wide range of information was required, for example, details about screening in pregnancy, advice about smoking cessation, alcohol use and vitamin supplementation, and place of birth and breastfeeding.

3.2.13 Women's views of specific antenatal information interventions

Description of included studies
A further three descriptive studies were identified for inclusion in this section of the review, one international study and two from the USA.

A web-based cross-sectional survey was conducted to identify perceived barriers to, and benefits of, attending a smoking cessation course.[677] [EL = 3] The questionnaire targeted pregnant smokers and pregnant recent ex-smokers. Owing to the nature of the sample selection, details of non-respondents are not available. The survey comprised a 20-item decisional-balance measure, a method devised to help understand why people do or do not change behaviour. Items were based upon emergent themes from a UK focus group ($n = 10$ pregnant women who smoked).

A focus group study conducted in the USA aimed to evaluate women's responses to educational messages concerning the risks and prevention of listeriosis, and to identify preferred delivery methods for such information.[678] [EL = 3] Eight focus groups were carried out, involving a total of 63 pregnant women: 64% of participants were multiparous and 87% were Caucasian. Two focus groups were conducted in four cities selected to provide geographical diversity. In each city one focus group was conducted with women educated to high-school level and one with women educated to college level. Focus groups were videotaped and audio-recorded. Common themes were identified within and across groups.

An older American study published in 1979 interviewed women to discover their perceptions of dietary information and advice provided during pregnancy.[679] [EL = 3] Women were interviewed during an antenatal appointment between 34 and 38 weeks of pregnancy. All women with an estimated date of delivery falling within a specified 2 month period were invited to take part in the study: 92 agreed and were interviewed, a response rate of 86%.

Findings
The web-based survey of smoking cessation advice was completed by 443 women who were pregnant smokers or recent (within previous month) ex-smokers.[677] [EL = 3] Most respondents were from the UK or the USA. The most frequently endorsed barriers to attending a smoking cessation course were 'I am afraid I would disappoint myself' (54.2%), 'I do not tend to seek help for this sort of thing' (40.6%), 'I do not have access to such a course' (40.5%) and 'I do not have time to attend the appointments' (39.8%). The last two barriers were significantly more frequently identified by respondents from the USA compared with those from the UK. The two statements with the least agreement were 'People that are close to me would not support me attending such a course' (9.8%) and 'Stopping smoking is not particularly important to me' (7.6%). The most frequently endorsed benefits of attending a smoking cessation course were 'Advice about managing my cigarette cravings would be useful' (74.2%), 'Praise and encouragement with stopping smoking would be helpful' (70.7%), 'Advice about safe medications to help me stop

2008 update

57

smoking would be useful' (69.2%) and 'Someone checking my progress would be helpful' (64.5%). Approximately half of all respondents agreed with all the benefits statements. Respondents who agreed with the benefits of attending a smoking cessation course were significantly more likely to express an interest in receiving help of this kind (ANOVA, all at $P < 0.01$).

Findings from the US focus group study[678] revealed that most participants were not aware that pregnant women are highly susceptible to food-borne illness. Few women reported receiving information about food safety from healthcare professionals contacted during pregnancy, and none remembered receiving information specifically about listeriosis. Commonly cited sources of information about food safety included books and magazines on antenatal care. Women suggested that written information on listeriosis be provided as part of the antenatal booking information package. Some women felt this written information should be backed up with specific advice from a healthcare professional, either during consultations or at antenatal classes. Most participants reported using books and magazines as a main source of information. College-educated women also reported using the internet as a source of information. Participants felt that knowledge of listeriosis should be improved among the general population and suggested using the media to deliver public health food safety messages.

Findings from the 1979 US interview-based survey showed that, while 75% of women felt pregnant women in general needed dietary advice, only half said that they personally needed such advice.[679] [EL = 3] The most common reasons for this response was that advice was remembered from a previous pregnancy (39%) or that the woman already had a good knowledge of dietary requirements (35%). Only 11% of women reported that they had acquired dietary information from other sources (such as books and leaflets). One-third of respondents reported that complying with dietary advice worried them 'a lot', with the most common concern being excessive weight gain during pregnancy. A similar proportion of women reported difficulty complying with dietary advice, especially that relating to dietary restrictions. When asked about their satisfaction with dietary information only three women reported any shortfall. Dietary information did not appear to be well recalled by women. When asked what was the most useful dietary advice they had received only 36 women (39%) could recall specific dietary information.

Evidence summary
There is poor-quality evidence to show that most women considered information given during pregnancy as being adequate. Most women reported using books and magazines as the main source of information although the evidence is of poor quality.

Advice about smoking cessation and dietary issues do not seem in general to be effective. Dietary advice seemed to be obtained from sources other than the antenatal clinic.

3.3 Antenatal classes

3.3.1 Effectiveness of antenatal classes

Introduction
Antenatal classes are often used to give information regarding pregnancy, birth, infant feeding and parenting. However, antenatal education can encompass a broader concept of educational and supportive measures that help women and their partners to understand and explore their own social, emotional, psychological and physical needs during this time. It is often the aim of classes that through providing this opportunity in a supportive group environment prospective parents will be able to develop self-awareness and confidence in their abilities, experience birth more positively and adjust more successfully to the changes that parenthood brings.

Description of included studies
This review was conducted to investigate the effectiveness of antenatal classes, that is, their impact on specified outcomes. The review comprises one systematic review reporting findings from five RCTs plus four before–after studies and two retrospective cross-sectional studies. Most of the included studies are from the USA and Australia.

A systematic review of six RCTs involving 1443 women was identified for inclusion in this review.[27] [EL = 1+] One of these trials (*n* = 1275) was an evaluation of an intervention aimed specifically at increasing rates of vaginal birth following caesarean section and so will be excluded from this analysis. This leaves five small trials for inclusion here (total *n* = 168). All trials were conducted in either the USA or Canada and published between 1981 and 1999. The intervention included was any structured educational programme, offered to individuals or groups, relating to preparation for childbirth, caring for a baby and adjustment to parenthood, compared with 'usual care' (not always described). Outcome measures included: knowledge acquisition; anxiety; woman's sense of control/active decision making; pain and pain relief; obstetric interventions; breastfeeding; and psychological adjustment to parenthood.

A UK retrospective survey conducted in 1994 investigated the reported usefulness of coping strategies taught in antenatal classes.[680] [EL = 3] Antenatal classes aimed to provide women with a range of three coping strategies from which to choose to help them cope with labour: change of position; relaxation; and 'sighing out slowly' breathing. All three strategies were practised during the antenatal sessions and women were encouraged to practise further at home. Women who had attended at least four of the five antenatal sessions were interviewed 72 hours after the birth of their baby (*n* = 121).

A US descriptive study (2003)[681] investigated the effects of antenatal classes on women's beliefs and perceptions of childbirth. [EL = 3] The study used a validated 64-item questionnaire, the Utah Test for the Childbearing Year, to assess four areas of women's beliefs and attitudes about childbirth: fear of childbirth; childbearing locus of control; passive compliance versus active participation in childbirth; and personal values about childbearing and childrearing. The scale was administered to women before and after attendance at a series of antenatal classes which focused on building women's capacity to be active participants in their labour. Fifty-seven women from ten sets of antenatal classes completed the pre-test questionnaire, 42 of whom also completed the post-test questionnaire.

A US questionnaire-based survey conducted in 1994 compared couples' (*n* = 119) self-care agency before and after attendance at a series of antenatal classes.[682] [EL = 3] Self-care agency was measured using the Appraisal of Self-care Agency Scale developed by Evers (1986).

An Australian before and after questionnaire-based study conducted in 2000 compared a course of four participant-led classes with four traditional classes.[683] [EL = 3] The participant-led classes were designed to identify and address couples' fears and concerns regarding childbirth and parenting. The four traditional classes focused on breathing and relaxation techniques and preparation for labour. Couples registering for classes at the study hospital were alternately allocated to either the participant-led classes (*n* = 36 couples) or the traditional classes (*n* = 34 couples).

A second Australian questionnaire-based survey (1991)[684] investigated nulliparous women's reasons for non-attendance at antenatal classes, knowledge acquired at classes and satisfaction with the antenatal programme. [EL = 3] In the first phase of the study all nulliparous women giving birth in a large teaching hospital in a 4 month period were invited to complete a questionnaire within 3 days of giving birth. A final sample of 325 women (response rate 91%) completed this phase of the study. In the second phase of the study, aimed at assessing levels of acquired knowledge and satisfaction following attendance at classes, all women and their partners attending classes over a 3 month period were invited to participate. A pre-test questionnaire was distributed for completion prior to attending the first class and a post-test questionnaire was distributed, completed and collected during the fourth and final session. Both questionnaires were completed by 117 women (response rate 82%) and 82 men (response rate (58%).

An Australian retrospective cross-sectional study (2002)[685] compared couples expecting their first baby who had attended an expanded course of antenatal classes aimed at preparing couples for parenting and early lifestyle changes following childbirth (*n* = 19 couples) with those of couples attending standard classes (*n* = 14 couples). [EL = 3] The classes provided in the intervention group utilised adult learning principles, including needs identification and shared knowledge and experiences facilitated through same-sex discussion groups. Participants comprised a convenience sample with final response rates of 64% for the intervention group and 47% for the comparison group.

Findings

Owing to heterogeneity of included studies in the systematic review, meta-analysis of study findings could not be conducted.[27] [EL = 1+] Amongst the five RCTs, no consistent results were seen. No trials reported on labour and birth outcomes, anxiety, or breastfeeding. Knowledge acquisition and baby care competencies were investigated. One small study ($n = 10$) showed greater frequency of maternal attachment behaviours when specific maternal attachment preparation was included in the classes compared with standard classes without this component (WMD 52.60 points, 95% CI 21.82 to 83.38). Two other studies showed greater knowledge acquisition, one in relation to fathers' parenting knowledge preparation ($n = 28$; WMD 9.55, 95% CI 1.25 to 17.85), the other compared expanded childbirth education classes with standard/ usual classes ($n = 48$; WMD 1.62, 95% CI 0.49 to 2.75). There is concern over selection bias in the latter study however, since some exclusion criteria were applied post-randomisation, and reported baseline differences were not controlled for in the analysis.

The 1994 UK retrospective interview-based study found that 88% of women ($n = 106$) used 'sighing out slowly' breathing, 51% ($n = 61$) used change of position and 40% ($n = 48$) used a relaxation technique. Almost all women (98%) were accompanied by a birth partner during labour. The most common effects reported for 'sighing out slowly' breathing was that of relaxation/calming (36%) and distraction (34%). Relaxation techniques were reported by 33% of the women who used it as being effective in providing relaxation. Only 12% of women who used this technique reported that it provided a distraction. Change of position was reported by 14% of women as providing a distraction, while only 6% found it relaxing. Change in position was the most effective in terms of pain relief with 22% of women reporting that it provided some pain relief. Nineteen percent of women who used 'sighing out slowly' breathing and 12% of those who used relaxation techniques reported that they provided some pain relief. A minority of women found the coping strategy (strategies) used of minimal or no benefit ('sighing out slowly' breathing 7%; change of position 9%; relaxation 12%).

The 2003 US before–after study found that women's mean scores for fear of childbirth and passive compliance versus active participation decreased significantly after participation in the antenatal classes (fear ($n = 37$) 9.68 versus 8.32, $P < 0.05$; compliance versus active participation ($n = 38$) 3.84 versus 2.89, $P < 0.02$). This shift suggests a decrease in fear of childbirth and a shift from passive compliance towards active participation. There was no significant change in scores for locus of control ($n = 41$; $x = 1.98$ versus 1.49) and personal values about childbearing ($n = 39$; $x = 4.03$ versus 3.97). It is not known whether or not these changes in questionnaire scores relate to changes in women's experience of childbirth.

The second US before–after study[682] found that self-care agency was very high in women and men both before and after attendance at a series of antenatal classes. For women there was no significant difference between scores obtained before and after antenatal classes (mean score pre-class 97.1; post class 97.5). Men did show a significant increase following class attendance (mean scores 91.3 and 94.7). It is unclear whether or how this increase may have impacted on self-care behaviour.

Findings from the first Australian study[683] showed that women who attended participant-led antenatal classes reported significantly higher levels of increased knowledge relating to childbirth, baby care and becoming a parent than women attending traditional classes ($F (1,59) = 11.89$, $P < 0.01$). This difference was not evident for men attending the classes ($F (1,57) = 2.59$, NS). Women in the intervention group also reported higher level of preparedness for the experience of pregnancy ($t = 3.05$, $P < 0.01$) and for self-care following birth ($t = 3.12$, $P < 0.01$). No differences were found for preparedness for labour, birth, mood and lifestyle changes following birth, or caring for the baby. Again, no differences were found for men's reported preparedness for any of the factors investigated. Both men and women in the intervention group were significantly more satisfied with the way classes were presented and the topics included in the classes compared with couples in the traditional classes.

The second Australian questionnaire-based survey (1991)[684] found that 82% of nulliparous women attended antenatal classes, the majority of whom (83%) attended classes provided by the hospital where they were booked to give birth. Women who chose to attend classes were older, of a higher educational level, more likely to be married or living as married, and more likely to have private health insurance than women who chose not to attend. The most common reasons for not attending antenatal classes were that women felt they knew all that they wanted to know about pregnancy and giving birth (18% of non-attenders) or did not have time to attend classes (15%). Stepwise logistic regression analysis was used to investigate the possible effects of attendance at classes on three health-related behaviours (breastfeeding, cigarette smoking and knowledge of community services), five aspects of satisfaction with childbirth and three intrapartum interventions (use of pethidine, epidural and forceps birth). This analysis revealed that demographic factors had greater association with these outcomes than attendance at antenatal classes. Women's and men's knowledge of issues relating to pregnancy and childbirth increased significantly following attendance at antenatal classes across all topic areas measured. Most of the course components were rated as either 'very' or 'quite' useful by the majority of respondents. Of the 24 items included, 17 were rated as very or quite useful by at least 70% of participants. Items relating to labour were rated as very or quite useful by over 90% of participants. Items with fewer ratings of very or quite useful were family planning, baby health centres, and nutrition and weight gain.

Findings from the Australian retrospective study[685] showed no significant differences between the intervention and control groups in the type of antenatal care chosen nor place of birth (no figures reported). Significantly more women in the intervention group stated that their labour had been 'managed as [they] liked' (84% versus 43%; $\chi^2 = 5.4$, $P < 0.05$). No significant differences were found between the two groups regarding women's experience of pain or views of pain relief used during labour (again figures not given). Women in the intervention group were also more likely to rate their parenting experience more highly than women in the control group (mean score on parenting rating scale $x = 89.4$ versus 83.6; $t(31) = 2.06$, $P < 0.05$). No significant difference was seen between the two groups regarding adjustment to life change following birth (mean score $x = 38.0$ versus 37.0; $t(31) = 0.36$, NS). Open-ended responses to the questionnaire indicated that 70% of the women and 85% of the men in the intervention group felt as prepared as they could have been for parenting compared with 25% of the women and 40% of the men in the comparison group (numbers of participants not given).

3.3.2 Women's experiences and views of antenatal classes

While a number of studies were identified which addressed women's views of antenatal classes, the majority were of very poor methodological quality. As a result, only seven descriptive studies were included in the final review, four from the UK, two from Australia and one conducted in Canada.

Description of included studies

A longitudinal questionnaire survey was conducted in England (2000)[671] to investigate women's views of information giving in maternity care. [EL = 3] Invitations to participate in the survey and the first questionnaire were posted to all women booked for a first appointment in a randomly selected month. Sixty women completed a questionnaire at five time points during their maternity care (before booking, following the 20 week ultrasound scan, after 34 weeks, on the postnatal ward, and at time of community discharge (14–28 days after birth)), representing a final response rate of 60/475.

A UK retrospective cross-sectional questionnaire survey (2005)[670] was also identified for review that investigated women's views of information giving during the antenatal period. [EL = 3] All women giving birth in the study area during a 3 month period were invited to participate in the survey (n = 700). Three hundred and twenty-nine women returned a completed questionnaire (response rate 47%).

A local English longitudinal, prospective survey (1997)[672] of antenatal classes conducted in one large teaching hospital and National Childbirth Trust classes in the neighbouring area sought men and women's views concerning class content. [EL = 3] Three questionnaires were distributed to couples (separate questionnaires for men and for women), one prior to the commencement of classes, one at the end of the course of antenatal classes, and one after the birth of the baby. The first questionnaire was posted (details of its return are unclear), the second was handed out and returned to the antenatal educator at the end of the final session. It is unclear how the third questionnaire was distributed and returned. The overall response rate for all three questionnaires was 159/400. One open-ended question on each questionnaire asked for respondents' views of class content. The response rates for this question on each questionnaire were 31.5%, 22% and 71%, respectively.

2008 update

2008 update

A rigorous Australian qualitative study conducted in 1998–99 used a grounded theory approach to describe and understand women's experience of antenatal classes, what they considered to be important and how useful they found the information provided.[686] [EL = 3] Four participant-guided interviews were undertaken, three during pregnancy and one after birth. The sample size of 13 was decided when saturation of the collected data was reached. The findings reported here relate to two of the interviews – the third-trimester interview and the postnatal interview (10–14 days following birth). All interviews lasted about 1 hour and were conducted in the woman's own home. A detailed description is given of how the grounded theory analysis was carried out and how credibility, fittingness and auditability of the analysis was achieved. This process included returning full transcripts of each interview to the woman involved a few days after the interview for her to review and comment upon, asking her to check its accuracy and make corrections where necessary.

A retrospective, national survey was conducted with a randomly selected sample of women giving birth during a particular month in 1984.[673] [EL = 3] The sample was drawn from ten regions of England stratified by county on a north to south basis. The survey included 1920 women and 1508 returned a completed questionnaire (response rate 79%). Women were asked what had been their main sources of information during pregnancy and how useful these had been. (Information received during labour and postpartum was also asked about but will not be reported here.)

A retrospective cross-sectional questionnaire survey conducted in Australia sought women's reasons for attending classes, expectations of classes and whether expectations were being met.[687] [EL = 3] A self-reported questionnaire was distributed to all women giving birth at the two study hospitals in a 1 month period in 1997. The questionnaire was handed to women while they were on the postnatal ward and returned via a collection box prior to the woman going home. There were 143 completed questionnaires, a response rate of 62% (56% of the target population). Of the respondents, 50 had attended antenatal classes (35%), 33 of whom had attended all sessions.

A Canadian cross-sectional questionnaire survey included investigation of women's reasons for not attending early (first-trimester) antenatal classes and women's interest in attending early classes.[688] [EL = 3] The questionnaire was distributed to all women attending antenatal classes in the study area during one specified week in 1990. Classes included community-based and hospital-based classes, some of which charged a registration fee. All courses included early pregnancy classes which focused on pregnancy and healthy lifestyle issues, although women could choose when to join the course. At the time the survey was undertaken, 46% of the classes were in the early pregnancy section of the course. The questionnaire was distributed, completed and returned during the antenatal class, and women were encouraged to complete the survey with their partner if he was present. There were 437 women who agreed to complete the survey, a response rate of 98.9%.

Findings
The English longitudinal study of women's views of information giving[671] identified a number of areas where women reported they would have liked more information. For all women, these included pregnancy complications and caesarean section. A quarter of nulliparous women indicated that they wanted more information about baby development. Open responses suggested that the timing of information was important to women, for example, preferring pregnancy-related information to be given as early as possible (i.e. before booking appointment), and the high value placed on information that was individually tailored.

The UK retrospective survey asked women how they preferred information to be provided.[670] Seventy percent of women stated a preference for one-to-one discussion, and a similar proportion cited leaflets as their preferred method. Only 20% indicated that taught classes or discussion groups were the preferred method of receiving information. While the majority of women reported that they understood the written information provided during pregnancy, subgroup analysis revealed an important difference. While 72% of women from professional/semi-professional groups reported that they understood all written materials, only 45.5% of women from non-professional/non-working groups reported this high level of understanding. Over 90% of women expressed that they had been given enough information and an opportunity to make decisions about screening tests. However, women's responses regarding diet, alcohol intake, exercise and smoking indicated that the information received had little or no effect on their attitude or behaviour. When asked whether information they had received influenced their decision about where to give birth, 70% said it had little or no influence. However, the only choices available in the study area were birth in the local hospital or home birth.

Findings from the UK local survey of men's and women's views of the content of antenatal classes suggested that both men and women would have preferred more information about the postnatal period to be provided by antenatal classes. This need was apparent at all phases of the survey but most prominent in the postnatal questionnaire where 95/111 (86%) participants included this topic in their response to an open-ended question. The major category within this theme was information about caring for the new baby.

Women in the Australian qualitative study[686,689] were well educated (12/13 had a degree or diploma) and 11 were in full-time employment. Twelve of the women were Caucasian and one was Australian-Chinese. All were booked for a hospital birth. When asked about their experience of antenatal classes in the third trimester, most women were satisfied with the amount of information provided about labour and pain relief. However, for some women the emphasis some antenatal teachers placed on labouring without drugs was a cause of some concern. Women were less pleased with the amount of information provided concerning breastfeeding and care of the new baby, and they contrasted this lack of information with the large amount of information given about labour and birth. Women's responses indicated that more practical advice, including practical advice on breastfeeding and what to expect when feeding, would have been welcome. During the post-birth interview women were asked to reflect on the information they had received during antenatal classes and how well they felt the classes prepared them for labour, birth and the postnatal period. The women felt classes had not prepared them for labour, with all women expressing the sentiment that nothing could prepare you for labour and birth. The preference for more practical information and advice about infant feeding (not just breastfeeding), how to handle and communicate with your baby and general baby care (e.g. bathing and playing with your baby) was also commonly expressed. Lack of information about discomfort following birth was also noted. [EL = 3]

Findings from the English national survey carried out in 1984 are reported separately for nulliparous and multiparous women.[673] [EL = 3] Almost three-quarters of nulliparous women had attended antenatal classes, but only 6% cited these as the most helpful source of information. Non-professional sources of information (own mother, husband, friends and relatives) were considered the most useful sources of information by 43% of nulliparous women, compared with 24% who reported professional sources (midwife, GP, obstetrician, health visitor) as the most useful. When asked about the amount of information given during pregnancy, 59% of all women said they felt it had been the right amount of information, 20% reported it had been too much and 20% that it had not been enough. A quarter of women felt that they had not been able to discuss all the things they had wanted to during antenatal consultations. Women who were not married, those whose social class was classified as manual and those who did not own their own homes were more likely to report dissatisfaction with this.

Findings from the Australian retrospective questionnaire survey are based upon data collected from the 33 women who attended a full course of antenatal classes.[687] All women stated that they attended classes in order to gain information. Other important reasons for attending classes were: 'to reduce anxiety or increase confidence' (94%), 'to have partner present and involved' (85%), and 'to have a more positive emotional experience' (76%). Women were also asked to rate how well the classes had met their expectations in relation to the factors listed as influencing their decision to attend classes. Findings showed that expectations had been met for the majority of women. Women were also asked to rate the level of appropriateness of the amount of information given on a range of topics. Most women reported that they felt the amount of information was right regarding normal labour (97%), pain relief in labour (91%), choices in decision making during childbirth (88%), and complications/interventions during labour and birth (91%). There were three areas where a fair proportion of women reported that the amount of information provided was too little: relaxation and breathing for labour (33%), nutrition/diet (27%), and infant care (21%).

The Canadian survey[688] investigating early pregnancy classes found that the three most common reasons women gave for not attending early pregnancy classes were insufficient knowledge about the classes (69%), early classes were not considered useful (29%), and early classes were

2008 update

not convenient (18%) (women were invited to give multiple responses if appropriate). An open-ended question asking for ideas on how to encourage women to attend early classes elicited the following responses: encourage doctors to promote early classes and using a public awareness programme to advertise the content and availability of the classes. Women reported that they would like information in early classes on how the baby develops, signs and symptoms of miscarriage, nutrition and exercise. [EL = 3]

Evidence summary for Section 3.3
The available evidence shows that, for women and their partners, knowledge regarding pregnancy, birth and parenting issues is increased following attendance at antenatal classes, and that the wish to receive this information is a strong motivator for attending classes. There is little evidence that attendance affects any birth outcomes (such as mode of birth or use of analgesia) although there is some evidence from qualitative research that women's experience of birth and parenting may be improved if they attend client-led classes compared with more traditional classes.

Evidence from well-conducted qualitative research shows that women generally view antenatal classes positively. While most women appear satisfied with the content of classes in terms of pregnancy, labour and birth information there is an expressed wish for more information regarding postnatal issues, including general baby care.

GDG interpretation of evidence for antenatal information giving
There is some evidence that breastfeeding initiation rates and breastfeeding duration can be improved by interactive antenatal breastfeeding education. One-to-one counselling and peer support antenatally are also effective.

There is some evidence that intensive antenatal dietary counselling and support is effective in increasing women's knowledge about healthy eating and can affect eating behaviours. There is no evidence linking this with improved pregnancy outcomes, however. Women should also be informed about the Healthy Start Programme (Department of Health, Social Services and Public Safety) so that those of low incomes will be aware of the availability of free supplements.

There is good-quality evidence to show that smoking cessation interventions help women reduce smoking and decrease adverse neonatal outcomes.

There is high-quality evidence that informational leaflets are effective in increasing the knowledge of pregnant women about screening tests (in general and for Down's syndrome), and that the use of a touch screen method does not improve uptake rate of screening tests compared with the leaflets but may reduce anxiety and be particularly useful for women with abnormal results. Videos can increase knowledge of prenatal diagnosis without increasing anxiety. Decision-analysis techniques can also be useful.

There is evidence from a well-conducted qualitative study showing that the process of informed decision making for prenatal screening tests is hampered by inadequate information provided to pregnant women during consultations, and the divergent approaches taken by clinicians and patients.

Evidence shows that the decision whether or not to undergo a prenatal screening test is usually made by the woman herself. However, those choosing to undergo testing report that healthcare professionals also have a strong influence on their decision. Women prefer getting information from face-to-face discussion or counselling rather than other methods.

There is evidence that both written and verbal information leads to a higher uptake of HIV screening tests in pregnant women without increasing their anxiety.

Timing of information giving was included in the scope of the guideline update but no evidence was found to inform this part of the clinical question. The GDG used their experience and expertise to decide a schedule for appropriate antenatal information and good practice around information giving, with specific recommendations being made where possible based on the available evidence.

Recommendations on antenatal information

Antenatal information should be given to pregnant women according to the following schedule.

- At the first contact with a healthcare professional:
  - folic acid supplementation
  - food hygiene, including how to reduce the risk of a food-acquired infection
  - lifestyle advice, including smoking cessation, and the implications of recreational drug use and alcohol consumption in pregnancy
  - all antenatal screening, including screening for haemoglobinopathies, the anomaly scan and screening for Down's syndrome, as well as risks and benefits of the screening tests.
- At booking (ideally by 10 weeks):
  - how the baby develops during pregnancy
  - nutrition and diet, including vitamin D supplementation for women at risk of vitamin D deficiency, and details of the 'Healthy Start' programme (www.healthystart.nhs.uk)
  - exercise, including pelvic floor exercises
  - place of birth (refer to 'Intrapartum care' [NICE clinical guideline 55], available from www.nice.org.uk/CG055)
  - pregnancy care pathway
  - breastfeeding, including workshops
  - participant-led antenatal classes
  - further discussion of all antenatal screening
  - discussion of mental health issues (refer to 'Antenatal and postnatal mental health' [NICE clinical guideline 45], available from www.nice.org.uk/CG045).
- Before or at 36 weeks:
  - breastfeeding information, including technique and good management practices that would help a woman succeed, such as detailed in the UNICEF 'Baby Friendly Initiative' (www.babyfriendly.org.uk)
  - preparation for labour and birth, including information about coping with pain in labour and the birth plan
  - recognition of active labour
  - care of the new baby
  - vitamin K prophylaxis
  - newborn screening tests
  - postnatal self-care
  - awareness of 'baby blues' and postnatal depression.
- At 38 weeks:
  - options for management of prolonged pregnancy*.

This can be supported by information such as 'The pregnancy book' (Department of Health 2007) and the use of other relevant resources such as UK National Screening Committee publications and the Midwives Information and Resource Service (MIDIRS) information leaflets (www.infochoice.org).

Information should be given in a form that is easy to understand and accessible to pregnant women with additional needs, such as physical, sensory or learning disabilities, and to pregnant women who do not speak or read English.

Information can also be given in other forms such as audiovisual or touch screen technology; this should be supported by written information.

Pregnant women should be offered information based on the current available evidence together with support to enable them to make informed decisions about their care. This information should include where they will be seen and who will undertake their care.

At each antenatal appointment, healthcare professionals should offer consistent information and clear explanations, and should provide pregnant women with an opportunity to discuss issues and ask questions.

2008 update

---

* The clinical guideline 'Induction of labour' is being updated and is expected to be published in June 2008.

Pregnant women should be offered opportunities to attend participant-led antenatal classes, including breastfeeding workshops.

Women's decisions should be respected, even when this is contrary to the views of the healthcare professional.

Pregnant women should be informed about the purpose of any test before it is performed. The healthcare professional should ensure the woman has understood this information and has sufficient time to make an informed decision. The right of a woman to accept or decline a test should be made clear.

Information about antenatal screening should be provided in a setting where discussion can take place; this may be in a group setting or on a one-to-one basis. This should be done before the booking appointment.

Information about antenatal screening should include balanced and accurate information about the condition being screened for.

Research recommendation

Alternative ways of helping healthcare professionals to support pregnant women in making informed decisions should be investigated.

Why this is important
Giving pregnant women relevant information to allow them to make an informed decision remains a challenge to all healthcare professionals. The use of media other than leaflets needs to be systematically studied, and the current available evidence is limited.

4 Provision and organisation of care

4.1 Who provides care?

One systematic review assessed the clinical effectiveness and perception of antenatal care by type of antenatal care provider, i.e. midwife and general practitioner-led managed care was compared with obstetrician and gynaecologist-led shared care.[32] Three trials were included in the study, randomising 3041 women who were considered to be low risk (i.e. no medical or obstetrical complications). The two largest trials were set in Scotland ($n = 2952$). Of these, one assessed midwifery-led care and the other assessed care led by midwives and GPs.

No differences were observed between the midwife and GP-managed care and the obstetrician and gynaecologist-led shared care for preterm birth, caesarean section, anaemia, urinary tract infections, antepartum haemorrhage and perinatal mortality. However, the midwife and GP-managed care group had a statistically significant lower rate of pregnancy-induced hypertension (Peto OR 0.56, 95% CI 0.45 to 0.70) and pre-eclampsia (Peto OR 0.37, 95% CI 0.22 to 0.64) than the standard care group. This could result from either a decreased incidence or decreased detection. [EL = 1a]

There was no significant difference in the levels of satisfaction with the types of care provided between the two groups.

Based on this meta-analysis of 3041 women from three trials, midwife-managed or midwife and GP-managed antenatal care programmes for women at 'low risk' did not increase the risk of adverse maternal or perinatal outcomes.

Recommendation

Midwife- and GP-led models of care should be offered for women with an uncomplicated pregnancy. Routine involvement of obstetricians in the care of women with an uncomplicated pregnancy at scheduled times does not appear to improve perinatal outcomes compared with involving obstetricians when complications arise. [A]

Future research

There is a lack of qualitative research on women's views regarding who provides care during pregnancy.

4.2 Continuity of care

The care of women during pregnancy, labour, and the postnatal period is often provided by many caregivers. Women may have caregivers who only work in particular settings, such as the antenatal clinic or the labour ward, and who cannot provide them with continuity of care. For the purposes of this guideline, continuity of care is defined as the provision of care by the same small team of caregivers throughout pregnancy. However, no trials investigated continuity of care solely in the antenatal period and therefore it is not possible to separate the results associated with continuity of care in the antenatal and intrapartum periods.

Two systematic reviews analysed the effects of continuous care during pregnancy and childbirth.[33,34]

One systematic review assessed the clinical effectiveness of continuity of care during pregnancy and childbirth and the postnatal period with routine care by multiple caregivers.[33] [EL = 1a] Two trials, one set in the UK, the other in Australia, were included in the review. They randomised 1815 women to continuity of care by a small group of midwives as well as consultation with an obstetrician compared with routine care provided by physicians and midwives. Women who had continuity of care by a team of midwives were less likely to:

- experience clinic waiting times greater than 15 minutes (Peto OR 0.14, 95% CI 0.10 to 0.19)
- be admitted to hospital antenatally (Peto OR 0.79, 95% CI 0.64 to 0.97)
- fail to attend antenatal classes (Peto OR 0.58, 95% CI 0.41 to 0.81)
- be unable to discuss worries in pregnancy (Peto OR 0.72, 95% CI 0.56 to 0.92)
- not feel well-prepared for labour (Peto OR 0.64, 95% CI 0.48 to 0.86).

There was no significant difference in the rates of caesarean section, induction of labour, stillbirth and neonatal death, preterm birth, admission to the neonatal unit, or birthweight less than 2500 g. Further outcomes are reported in the corresponding evidence table.

One other systematic review compared continuity of midwifery care with standard maternity services.[34] This review included seven RCTs, which randomised 9148 women. The women randomised to continuous care had significantly lower rates of many outcomes related to the intrapartum period, such as induction of labour, augmentation of labour and electronic fetal monitoring. There were no significant differences in the rates of caesarean section, admission to the neonatal unit, postnatal haemorrhage, antenatal admission to hospital or duration of labour. No maternal deaths were reported. Satisfaction with care was reported by six of the seven trials but not included in the meta-analysis due to lack of consistency between measures. However, women with continuous care were more satisfied with care during all phases of pregnancy and differences were statistically significant for each study separately. Women in the continuous care group were more pleased with information giving and communication with the caregivers and felt more involved in the decision making and more in control. [EL = 1a]

Four more recent RCTs that were not included in either of the above reviews were also located.[35–38]

Another RCT in England which compared caseload midwifery care with traditional shared care.[35] Caseload midwifery care refers to a group of midwives caring for a specific number of women where a midwife has her own group of women, with back-up support provided by another midwife when needed. This study found that although there was a significant difference between caseload and traditional care groups in terms of level of 'known carer at delivery', there were no significant differences in terms of rates of normal vaginal deliveries, operative deliveries or neonatal outcome. [EL = 1b]

An Australian RCT compared continuity of midwifery care in a community-based setting with standard care in a hospital-based antenatal clinic.[36] The latter was characterised by a lack of continuity of care as a large number of clinicians provided care. No differences in any clinical outcomes were reported except a significantly lower caesarean section rate in the midwife-led community-based care group (OR 0.6, 95% CI 0.4 to 0.9). [EL = 1b] The women in the community-based continuity of care group also reported significantly less waiting time and easier access to care and a higher perceived quality of care than the hospital-based control group.[37] [EL = 1b]

Another Australian RCT compared continuity of care provided by midwives with standard care provided by a variety of midwives and obstetric staff.[38] The women assigned to the intervention group experienced less augmentation of labour, less use of epidural analgesia and fewer episiotomies; no differences in perinatal mortality between the two groups was observed. [EL = 1b]

An RCT on satisfaction with continuity of care found that continuity of care provided by team midwifery was associated with increased satisfaction compared with standard care attended by various doctors.[39] A woman from the intervention group was twice as likely to agree with the statement, 'Overall, care during pregnancy was very good' (OR 2.22, 95% CI 1.66 to 2.95). The intervention appeared to have greatest impact on satisfaction with care during the antenatal period compared with the intrapartum and postnatal period. [EL = 1b]

In most cases, the evidence demonstrates an association between continuity of care and lower intervention rates compared with standard maternity or hospital-based care as well as beneficial effects upon various psychosocial outcomes.

> **Recommendation**
>
> Antenatal care should be provided by a small group of carers with whom the woman feels comfortable. There should be continuity of care throughout the antenatal period. [A]
>
> A system of clear referral paths should be established so that pregnant women who require additional care are managed and treated by the appropriate specialist teams when problems are identified. [D]

4.3 Where should antenatal appointments take place?

A meta-analysis of three RCTs examined whether a policy of home visits for antenatal care reduced the amount of antenatal care provided by nine hospital maternity units in France; 1410 women with pregnancy complications were assessed.[40] In the control group, women received the usual care provided by the maternity units with visits to the outpatient clinics as necessary. In the intervention group, the women received one or two home visits a week by a midwife in addition to the usual care. No difference in the rate of hospital admissions was found (pooled OR 0.9, 95% CI 0.7 to 1.2) but the average number of visits to the outpatient clinic was significantly lower in the two trials in which it was measured. [EL = 1a] Maternity care must be readily and easily accessible to all women. They should be sensitive to the needs of the local population and based primarily in the community.[9] [EL = 4]

> **Recommendation**
>
> Antenatal care should be readily and easily accessible to all women and should be sensitive to the needs of individual women and the local community. [C]
>
> The environment in which antenatal appointments take place should enable women to discuss sensitive issues such as domestic violence, sexual abuse, psychiatric illness and recreational drug use. [Good practice point]

4.4 Documentation of care

The information in antenatal records is collected for two main purposes:

- administration
- identification of maternal risk, fetal risk, and special requirements so that further management can be planned.

Beyond the management of patient care, however, antenatal records also serve as vehicles for quality assurance, legal documentation, communication and epidemiological research for deciding future public health measures.

In an RCT of three methods of taking an antenatal history, unstructured histories taken on paper by midwives, structured paper histories (incorporating a checklist) and an interactive computerised questionnaire in an antenatal clinic in England were compared.[41] The number of clinical responses to factors arising from the antenatal histories were measured and each response was weighted for clinical importance. The structured questionnaires were reported to provide more and better information and their use improved clinical response to risk factors compared with unstructured paper histories. Computerised systems offered no further advantage over structured paper histories. [EL = 1b]

Women carrying their own case notes

Three RCTs have examined the effect of giving women their own maternity case notes to carry during pregnancy.[42–44] The impact on quality of care and maternal and perinatal outcomes was assessed. In all three trials, women were randomised either to carry their own antenatal case notes or to the usual system of case notes remaining in the hospital. In the latter case, women usually carried a cooperation card.

The first study (*n* = 246) found that both the women and health professionals involved considered that giving a woman her own maternity case notes during pregnancy was a good idea and was a positive step towards improving the quality of care.[44] [EL = 1b] No reasons were found during the study to deny women carrying their own notes and no insurmountable problems arose.

In the second study (*n* = 290) specific outcomes and hypotheses were proposed.[42] [EL = 1b] The two groups of women were comparable in terms of socio-demographic characteristics. Results from the questionnaires showed that:

- women carrying their own notes were nearly 50% more likely to say they felt in control of their pregnancy (rate ratio 1.45, 95% CI 1.08 to 1.95)
- more than 70% were more likely to say they found it easier to talk to the doctors and midwives during pregnancy (rate ratio 1.73, 95% CI 1.16 to 2.59).
- there were no other significant differences between the groups in terms of any of the other outcomes predicted
- there was no difference in the availability of notes for clinic appointments but approximately 1 hour of hospital clerical time was saved per week because of not having to retrieve and refile notes.

The third study (*n* = 150) was conducted among English-speaking women in an Australian metropolitan area, using open-ended questions.[43] [EL = 1b] Parous women who carried their own notes were significantly more likely to report that the doctors and midwives explained everything in their records to them than parous women with cooperation cards or nulliparous women from either group.

- 89% of women carrying their own notes responded positively. They felt more in control, felt more informed, liked having access to their results and felt it gave them an opportunity to share information particularly with other family members and partners.
- 11% of women carrying their own notes responded negatively, as they thought the record was too bulky, the system inconvenient or were worried they would forget notes.
- No differences were noted in numbers of lost records in each group.
- 89% of women in the hand-held notes group wanted to carry their notes in a future pregnancy as well as 52% of the cooperation-card group.

Women like to carry their own maternity care records. This can lead to an increased feeling of control during pregnancy. It may facilitate communication between the pregnant woman and the health professionals involved with her care.

Recommendations

Structured maternity records should be used for antenatal care. [A]

Maternity services should have a system in place whereby women carry their own case notes. [A]

A standardised, national maternity record with an agreed minimum data set should be developed and used. This will help carers to provide the recommended evidence-based care to pregnant women. [Good practice point]

4.5 Frequency of antenatal appointments

Antenatal care programmes as currently practised originate from models developed in 1929. As advances in medicine and technology have occurred, new components have been added to antenatal care, mostly for screening purposes. However, the significance of the frequency of antenatal care appointments and the interval between appointments has not been tested scientifically.

An observational study explored the relationship between the number of antenatal visits made by 17 765 British women and adverse perinatal outcomes.[45] [EL = 3] No consistent relationship between admission to the neonatal unit or perinatal mortality and number of antenatal visits was found. A significant positive relationship between number of antenatal visits and caesarean section was found and low birthweight (less than 2500 g) was positively associated with number of visits for nulliparous but not for parous women.

Two systematic reviews of RCTs have evaluated the evidence of the effectiveness of different models of care based on a reduced number of antenatal care visits compared with the standard number of antenatal care visits.[32,46] [EL = 1a] Both reviews included the same seven trials.

Both systematic reviews assessed the clinical effectiveness and perception of care (by women) of different antenatal care programmes. Frequency of antenatal care visits was one of the components of care assessed by the reviews. Four of the trials were conducted in developed countries and three in less developed countries, with a total of 57 418 women randomised to receive either a reduced number of antenatal care visits (with or without 'goal-oriented' components) or the standard number of antenatal care visits.

Between the two reviews, outcomes assessed were: preterm delivery (less than 37 weeks), pre-eclampsia, caesarean section, induction of labour, antenatal haemorrhage, postnatal haemorrhage, low birthweight, small-for-gestational-age at birth, postpartum anaemia, admission to neonatal intensive care unit, perinatal mortality, maternal mortality, urinary tract infection and satisfaction of care. The results did not demonstrate a difference in any of the biological outcomes. Women from the developed-country trials reported less satisfaction with the frequency of visits in the reduced number group (3 RCTs, $n = 3393$, Peto OR 0.61, 95% CI 0.52 to 0.72). However, the women in these trials were being told that they had fewer visits and were therefore aware that other women had more visits than they did. It should also be noted that there was clinical and statistical heterogeneity among the three trials that looked at this outcome.

The objective of both these systematic reviews was to demonstrate equivalent efficacy of the intervention. A problem with equivalence trials is that when the two interventions are similar the outcomes are also likely to be similar. A limitation common to both of these reviews, highlighted by the authors, was protocol deviations that resulted in nonsignificant reductions in the number of visits in the intervention group. The average difference in number of visits between the two arms in the trials was approximately two in both reviews. In the context of routine antenatal care in developed countries (10–14 visits), a difference of two visits would be unlikely to demonstrate a measurable impact upon pregnancy outcomes. However, when analysing the two largest trials, which took place in less developed countries, the reduction in the number of visits is proportionately much larger (from six to four visits). Within these trials, no adverse impact on maternal or perinatal outcomes was associated with reduced visits.

A moderate reduction in the traditional number of antenatal visits is not associated with an increase in adverse maternal or perinatal outcomes. However, a reduced number of appointments may be associated with a reduction in women's satisfaction with their antenatal care. It is likely that routine antenatal care for women without risk or complications can be provided with fewer appointments. It is possible that the key issue is not more or less antenatal care, but the implementation of procedures that have been shown to be effective and which may increase women's satisfaction with care. The frequency of appointments can then be planned accordingly.

In a secondary analysis of data from an RCT comparing a traditional and a reduced schedule of antenatal appointments in London, England, women who were satisfied with reduced schedules were more likely to have a caregiver who both listened and encouraged them to ask questions than women who were not satisfied with reduced schedules.[47] [EL = 3] A survey of women's expectations on number of antenatal care appointments in Sweden found that preference for more or fewer appointments was associated with parity, marital status, age, education, obstetric history, previous birth experience and timing of pregnancy.[48] [EL = 3] Older women (over 35 years), parous women, less educated women and women with more than two children preferred fewer appointments, whereas younger women (under 25 years), single women and women with a prior adverse pregnancy history indicated a preference for more appointments than the standard schedule.

Economic considerations

The cost of antenatal appointments is determined by the number of appointments overall, and the type and grade of healthcare provider. The cost-effectiveness of the antenatal appointment schedule is determined by the primary outcomes of the antenatal care (preterm birth, low birthweight babies, maternal or infant mortality, birth complications and intensive care) and also secondary outcomes such as maternal and professional satisfaction with the package of care provided.

The evidence to date on the optimum number of antenatal appointments is inconclusive. The majority of studies have not focused on the cost-effectiveness or cost benefit of the number of antenatal appointments. The World Health Organization (WHO) Antenatal Care Trial included an assessment of quality of care and an economic evaluation. The authors concluded that the provision of routine antenatal care by the new model did not affect maternal and perinatal outcomes and therefore was more cost-effective. However, the study setting of the trial was developing countries.

Most of the existing research in industrialised countries is based on low-risk women as diagnosed at first contact. One UK-based study compared a traditional antenatal appointment schedule with a reduced schedule of appointments.[49] The estimated total cost to the NHS of the traditional schedule (around 13 appointments) was £544, of which around £250 occurred antenatally. The estimated total costs for the reduced appointment schedule (six or seven appointments) were around £560, of which £255 occurred antenatally. The authors found that any reduced costs of fewer appointments were offset by the greater number of babies requiring special or intensive care, so that the total costs were not different. Sensitivity analyses varied the unit costs of care and length of postnatal stay and found substantial overlap between schedules, leading to inconclusive results. No difference was detected in the primary outcome (caesarean section) between the two groups. The authors reported differences in the secondary outcome (maternal satisfaction and psychological outcomes) that were significantly poorer for women receiving fewer appointments than for women receiving traditional care.

A study comparing pregnancy outcomes between England and Wales and France[50] demonstrated that, although the number of appointments is lower in France, there were no differences detected in pregnancy outcomes. This suggests that fewer appointments would be more cost-effective if only these outcomes were considered.

Clearly, fewer routine antenatal appointments for low-risk pregnant women could release antenatal care resources for women who need additional support. The issue of 'satisfaction' is complex, since the long-term effects (and costs) of lower satisfaction and poorer psychosocial outcomes is not addressed in any of the studies.

Willingness-to-pay studies are one way of exploring whether one form of care is more highly valued by users of services (what they would be willing to sacrifice to have a particular form of care). This approach can incorporate the value of different forms of care and not only the final outcome. The value of information and reassurance to pregnant women is usually not included in economic evaluation.

Only one economic study has been undertaken to estimate women's valuation of antenatal care. This study did not address the number of appointments but did address the value of different providers of antenatal care. It suggested there was no significant difference in the monetary value women placed on alternatives forms of provision.[51]

Recommendations

A schedule of antenatal appointments should be determined by the function of the appointments. For a woman who is nulliparous with an uncomplicated pregnancy, a schedule of ten appointments should be adequate. For a woman who is parous with an uncomplicated pregnancy, a schedule of seven appointments should be adequate. [B]

Early in pregnancy, all women should receive appropriate written information about the likely number, timing and content of antenatal appointments associated with different options of care and be given an opportunity to discuss this schedule with their midwife or doctor. [D]

Each antenatal appointment should be structured and have focused content. Longer appointments are needed early in pregnancy to allow comprehensive assessment and discussion. Wherever possible, appointments should incorporate routine tests and investigations to minimise inconvenience to women. [D]

Future research

Alternative methods of providing antenatal information and support, such as drop in services, should be explored.

Research that explores how to ensure women's satisfaction and low morbidity and mortality with a reduced schedule of appointments should be conducted.

4.6 Gestational age assessment

Clinical question

What is the diagnostic value and effectiveness of screening methods in determining gestational age?

Previous NICE guidance (for the updated recommendations see below)

Pregnant women should be offered an early ultrasound scan to determine gestational age (in lieu of last menstrual period (LMP) for all cases) and to detect multiple pregnancies. This will ensure consistency of gestational age assessments, improve the performance of mid-trimester serum screening for Down's syndrome and reduce the need for induction of labour after 41 weeks. [A]

Ideally, scans should be performed between 10 and 13 weeks and use crown–rump length measurement to determine gestational age. Pregnant women who present at or beyond 14 weeks of gestation should be offered an ultrasound scan to estimate gestational age using head circumference or biparietal diameter. [Good practice point]

Introduction and background

Following publication of the 2003 NICE recommendations for antenatal care, virtually all pregnant women (99.5%) are offered an early ultrasound examination allows accurate dating, reduces the rate of induction in post-term deliveries, and allows identification of multiple pregnancies, so the pregnancy can be managed appropriately, and of major fetal malformations such as anencephaly. It is also necessary so that Down's syndrome screening (either first or second trimester) can be performed at the correct time.

Accuracy of screening tests

A total of 13 studies have been included in this section.

Description of included studies

A US-based retrospective study (1995)[690] [EL = II] examined the comparability of the LMP-based estimation and the clinical examination of gestational age as collected on one state's (South Carolina's) vital records. They also investigated the concordance between these measures and explored whether socio-demographic or delivery hospital characteristics influenced their agreement. A sample size of 150 898 cases that contained both clinical examination-based and LMP-based values with a range of 20 to 45 weeks were selected.

A Denmark-based study (2006)[691] [EL = II] compared the predicted date of delivery by LMP, crown–rump length (CRL) and biparietal diameter (BPD) with the actual date of delivery in a population of pregnant women divided into those with certain and those with uncertain LMP. Six hundred and fifty-seven spontaneous deliveries were used for analysis, with 339 and 318 in the certain and uncertain LMP groups, respectively. Healthy women who were enrolled at the first visit during their pregnancy underwent ultrasound examinations in the first and second trimesters.

A Finland-based study (2001)[692] [EL = II] compared different ultrasound measurements (CRL, BPD and femur length (FL)) for predicting the day of delivery at 8–16 weeks of gestation. They also compared them to prediction by certain and uncertain LMP. 17 221 non-selected singleton pregnancies at 8–16 completed weeks were scanned by ultrasound. The LMP was considered certain in 13 541 cases and uncertain in 3680 cases.

A US-based prospective cohort study (2002)[53] [EL = II] evaluated the accuracy of algorithms for the assignment of gestational age with the use of the LMP and early ultrasound information. Four algorithms were compared: LMP only; ultrasound scans only; use of LMP except when there was a disparity of 7 days or more in the estimated date of confinement, in which case ultrasound scanning was used; and the use of LMP except when there was a disparity of 14 days or more in the estimated date of confinement, in which case ultrasound scanning was used. The women were enrolled at 24–29 weeks of gestation, and 3147 women had both LMP and early ultrasound scan and were recruited and interviewed in the comparisons of pregnancy dating. There was an evaluation of digit preference in the LMP dates and a comparison of mean gestational age, preterm and post-term categories with the use of kappa statistics, difference between actual and expected delivery date, and birthweight among subgroups with discrepant assignments.

A longitudinal study (2006)[693] [EL = II] sought to determine the best method for gestational age estimation from four communities in rural Guatemala. Gestational age at birth was determined by an early second-trimester measure of BPD, LMP, the Capurro neonatal examination and symphysis–fundal height (SFH) for 171 mother–infant pairs. Regression modelling was used to determine which method provided the best estimate of gestational age using ultrasound as the reference.

A US-based retrospective study (2001)[694] [EL = II] investigated the concordance between gestational age data obtained by clinical estimate with data calculated from the date of the LMP as recorded on birth certificates. 476 034 computerised birth records from 20–44 weeks of gestation were analysed.

A prospective study in Norway (2006)[695] [EL = II] tested whether the head circumference (HC) predicts the day of confinement better than BPD. 4179 consecutive women attending the second-trimester routine ultrasound examination at 17–20 weeks of gestation were included. The difference between the time of delivery and the predicted date of delivery calculated with HC and BPD (based on pregnancy duration of 282 days) was noted.

A study in Denmark (1999)[696] [EL = II] compared the error in the predicted date of delivery using BPD with the error using the LMP. 14 805 spontaneous deliveries with a reliable LMP were included and the predicted dates of delivery were calculated using two assumptions: average length of pregnancy of 280 and of 282 days.

A UK-based prospective study (1993)[697] [EL = II] aimed to determine the most accurate predictor of the date of delivery for pregnant women in a community-based population. The two methods compared were a calculation based on LMP or a prediction based on the measurement by ultrasound scan. 106 women were included in the analysis.

A Nigerian study (1989)[698] [EL = II] assessed the accuracy of gestational age using the locally produced normogram and compared with predictors based on menstrual dates. Eight-four Nigerian women who had no complications of pregnancy and delivered infants whose birthweights were appropriate for 40 weeks were assessed. The ultrasonographer was blinded to the clinical details of the study population.

A population study (1985) in the USA[699] [EL = II] sought to determine whether a single ultrasonic measurement performed in a technician-oriented routine screening programme was more accurately predictive of gestational age than menstrual history. In addition, they determined whether a single BPD or CRL measurement was more predictive of gestational age and how the predictive accuracy of these measurements changed throughout pregnancy. 4257 consecutive pregnancies were scanned in 4246 patients as part of a routine antenatal two-tier ultrasonic screening programme. The first-tier scans were performed before the 20th week of gestation, whereas the second-tier scans were performed between 26 weeks and term. The estimated date of confinement based on ultrasound measurements was compared with menstrual history in its ability to predict the actual onset of spontaneous labour.

A US-based prospective study (1983)[700] [EL = II] compared the relative accuracy of estimated dates of confinement predicted by first-trimester CRL versus second-trimester BPD measurements in 27 women. The actual delivery date was compared with the estimated date of confinement predicted by the CRL and the BPD.

A Swedish study (1983)[701] [EL = II] evaluated the fetal CRL screening programme. Fifty-three women with regular, 28 day interval menstrual cycles were extracted consecutively from the register of the ultrasound laboratory.

Findings

The results of the US study showed that LMP-based measures produced higher percentages of preterm and post-term births. More than 60% of the LMP-based preterm births were classified as preterm by the clinical estimate. The sensitivity of the clinical estimate was 27% for post-term births. The overall concordance (the percentage of cases with the same value for both measures) was 47%, but it varied considerably by gestational age. Between 30 and 35 weeks, the clinical estimate exceeded the LMP-based value by 2 weeks or more for more than 40% of the cases. Concordance also varied by race of mother, hospital delivery size, trimester during which prenatal care began, and birthweight.

In the Danish study the median prediction errors (predicted − actual date of delivery) estimated by ultrasonography in the first and second trimesters and by corrected LMP according to cycle length were 2.32, 0.16 and 3.00 days, respectively, in women with certain LMP, and 1.71, 0.00 and 3.00 days, respectively, in women with uncertain LMP. The median gestational age at delivery estimated by ultrasonography in the first and second trimesters and by corrected LMP according to cycle length was 282, 280 and 283 days, respectively, in both groups.

The results of the Finland study showed that, at all gestational ages, ultrasound was superior to certain LMP in predicting the day of delivery to within at least 1.7 days. CRL of 15–60 mm was superior to BPD, but at a later gestation BPD (at least 21 mm) was more precise. Regression models using a combination of any two or three ultrasonic variables did not improve accuracy of prediction. When ultrasound was used instead of certain LMP, the number of post-term pregnancies decreased from 10.3% to 2.7% ($P < 0.001$).

The results of the US study showed that LMP reports showed digit preference, assign gestation 2.8 days longer on average than ultrasound scanning, yield substantially more post-term births (12.1% versus 3.4%), and predict delivery among term births less accurately. Misclassification of births as post-term was more common in younger women, those of non-optimal pre-pregnancy body weight, cigarette smokers, and women who reported LMP using preferred dates of the month.

In the Mexican study, gestational age estimated by LMP was within ±14 days of the ultrasound estimate for 94% of the sample. LMP-estimated gestational age explained 46% of the variance in gestational age estimated by ultrasound whereas the neonatal examination explained only 20%.

The US study showed an overall exact concordance of 46% between the two measurements. For +1 week it was 78% and for +2 weeks it was 87%. The incidence of preterm birth with menstrual gestational age was 16%, while it was 12% with the clinical estimate. About 47% of the LMP-based preterm births were classified as term by clinical estimate, and 83% of clinically estimated preterm births were also preterm by LMP-based gestation. The authors concluded that agreement between menstrual and clinical estimates of gestational age occurs most often close to term, with significant disagreement in preterm and post-term births.

The Norwegian study showed that for the group of women with spontaneous onset of labour ($n = 3336$), 5.6% were post-term (≥ 296 days) according to HC and 5.7% according to BPD. Preterm births (< 37 weeks) were 3.9% with HC measurement and 3.6% with the BPD method. For the entire group, the median differences between actual and predicted delivery with HC and BPD were 0.9 and 1.2 days, respectively. In the spontaneous onset of labour group the corresponding differences were 0.9 and 1.4 days. The difference between the HC and BPD methods was significant ($P < 0.0001$).

In the Denmark study the average discrepancy between predicted date of delivery from BPD and LMP and date of spontaneous delivery was 7.96 and 8.63 days, respectively ($P < 0.0001$). Adding 282 instead of 280 days to the first day of the LMP reduced the error of the LMP method from 8.63 to 8.41 days, reduced the percentage of classified post-term deliveries from 7.9% to 5.2% and increased the preterm births from 3.96% to 4.48%. It was found that none of the models of combined use of LMP and BPD were superior to the use of BPD alone.

The results of the UK study showed that, at an error of ±5 days, the scan prediction is accurate in 52% of cases and LMP in 37%, a difference of 15% (95% CI 4% to 23%). The scan accuracy is significantly better than LMP accuracy.

The Nigerian study showed that ultrasound dating was more accurate than menstrual dating as evident from the number of women who delivered on and within 1 or 2 weeks of predicted

2008 update

delivery dates. Twelve of 84 (14.3%) women delivered on the days predicted by ultrasound whereas only three of 84 (3.6%) delivered on days estimated by LMP. Sixty-nine of 84 (82.1%) ultrasound predictions were correct to within 1 week of predicted dates as compared with 42 or 84 (50%) predictions based on LMP. The difference reached statistical significance ($P < 0.05$).

In the American study 84.7% of women with optimal menstrual history delivered within ±2 weeks of the predicted date. Only 69.7% delivered within ±2 weeks of the estimate date of confinement based on suspect menstrual history. CRL measurements were as predictive (84.6%) as optimal menstrual history. BPD measurements done between 12 and 18 weeks of gestation were significantly more accurate in gestational predictions (89.4%) than those based on menstrual history ($P < .001$).

The results of the American study showed no difference between mean errors for predicting the actual date of delivery by CRL (7.73 days) and BPD (7.65 days). In both methods there was a greater tendency to overestimate the actual date of delivery.

The results of the Swedish study showed that 25% of pregnant women had a difference exceeding 7 days between menstrual age and gestational age estimated on the basis of CRL. Regular menstrual cycles and reliable menstrual history reduced this to 19%. Post-mature deliveries (> 294 days) were reduced from 1 in 15 to 1 in 300 by using CRL.

Effectiveness of screening tests

A total of six studies have been included in this section.

Description of included studies

An RCT in the USA (2004)[702] [EL = 1+] sought to determine whether application of a programme of routine first-trimester ultrasound screening to a low-risk population would result in a decreased rate of induction of labour for post-term pregnancy.

A randomised clinical trial in Australia (1999)[52] [EL = 1+] assessed the efficacy of an ultrasound scan at the first antenatal visit. The study population comprised 648 women attending for their first antenatal visit at less than 17 weeks of gestation with no previous ultrasound scan in the pregnancy, who were expected to give birth at the hospital, and for whom there was no indication for an ultrasound at their first visit. Eligible consenting women were enrolled by telephone randomisation into either the ultrasound at first visit group, who had an ultrasound at the time of their first antenatal visit, or the control group in whom no ultrasound assessment was done at their first antenatal visit.

An RCT in Sweden (1988)[703] [EL = 1+] evaluated the effectiveness of one-stage screening in the second trimester in pregnant women with no clear indication for elective scanning. 4997 women were randomised into a screening group where women had an ultrasound scan at about 15 weeks and a control/non-screening group where women did not have a scan before 19 weeks. All women in the screening group had gestational age and expected date of delivery estimation from BPD with charts derived from a Swedish population. For the control group, LMP with specially calibrated calendars was used.

A Norway-based RCT (2000)[704] [EL = 1+] evaluated the possible benefits of the routine use of ultrasound screening in pregnancy. Eight hundred and twenty-five women were allocated to an ultrasound scan between 18 and 32 weeks of gestation in addition to receiving routine antenatal care. Eight hundred and three women received standard antenatal care, but could only be referred for ultrasound examination on clinical indication.

A hospital-based cohort study in Canada (2005)[705] [EL = 2++] assessed the association between maternal and fetal characteristics, discrepancy between last normal menstrual period and early (< 20 weeks) ultrasound-based gestational age and the association between discrepancies and pregnancy outcomes. The study population comprised a total of 46 514 women with both menstrual-based and early ultrasound-based gestational age estimates.

A systematic review (1998)[57] [EL = 1+] assessed whether routine early pregnancy ultrasound influences the diagnosis of fetal malformations and of multiple pregnancies, the rate of clinical interventions, and the incidence of adverse fetal outcome compared with its selective use. Nine good-quality trials were included.

Findings

In the American study five of 104 women in the first-trimester screening group and 12 or 92 women in the second-trimester screening group had labour induced for post-term pregnancy (RR 0.37, 95% CI 0.14 to 0.96; *P* = 0.04).

In the Australian study 9% of women in the ultrasound at first visit group needed adjustment of their expected date of delivery as a result of the 18–20 week ultrasound, compared with 18% of women in the control group (RR 0.52, 95% CI 0.34–0.79; *P* = 0.002). Fewer women in the ultrasound at first visit group reported feeling worried about their pregnancy (RR 0.80, 95% CI 0.65–0.99; *P* = 0.04) or not feeling relaxed about their pregnancy (RR 0.73, 95% CI 0.56 to 0.96; *P* = 0.02) compared with women in the control group.

The results of the Swedish study showed that labour was less often induced among screened women both for all reasons (5.9% versus 9.1%; *P* < 0.0001) and for suspected post-term pregnancy (1.7% versus 3.7%; *P* < 0.0001). Among babies born to screened women, fewer had a birthweight below 2500 g (59 versus 95; *P* = 0.005) and mean birthweight was 42 g higher (*P* = 0.008).

In the Norwegian study the incidence of induced labour due to apparent post-term pregnancies was 70% lower in the ultrasound-screened group. Inductions from all causes were also less frequent among ultrasound-screened women. There were six perinatal deaths among the screened and seven among the controls after excluding three lethal malformations among the controls. The proportion of infants with Apgar score less than 8 after 5 minutes was lower among the screened group (*P* = 0.04). The need for positive pressure ventilation for more than 1 minute was lower among the screened group (*P* = 0.02).

In the Canadian study positive discrepancies between LMP and early ultrasound scan were more likely in multiparous mothers and those with diabetes, small stature or high pre-pregnancy body mass index (BMI). The proportion of women with discrepancies of +7 days or more was significantly higher among chromosomally malformed and female fetuses. With increasingly positive differences between LMP and ultrasound scan, the mean birthweight declined and the risk of low birthweight increased. Associations with fetal growth measures were more plausible with early ultrasound estimates.

The results of the systematic review showed that routine ultrasound examination significantly reduced the rates of induction of labour for post-term pregnancy (OR 0.61, 95% CI 0.52 to 0.72).

Evidence summary

Evidence suggests that ultrasound is a more accurate predictor of gestational age than date of the LMP. If only LMP is available the estimated date of delivery should be calculated as the first day of the LMP plus 282 days.

The estimated date of delivery based on LMP is subject to significant error and will be influenced by the mother's age, parity, BMI and smoking

Routine ultrasound examination significantly reduces the rates of induction of labour for prolonged pregnancy.

CRL measurement should be used in the first trimester for the estimation of gestational age. CRL > 90 mm is unreliable in estimating gestational age in second-trimester and HC measurement, which appears more reliable than the BPD, should be used instead when establishing an estimated date of birth in the second trimester.

Recommendations on gestational age assessment

Pregnant women should be offered an early ultrasound scan between 10 weeks 0 days and 13 weeks 6 days to determine gestational age and to detect multiple pregnancies. This will ensure consistency of gestational age assessment and reduce the incidence of induction of labour for prolonged pregnancy.

Crown–rump length measurement should be used to determine gestational age. If the crown–rump length is above 84 mm, the gestational age should be estimated using head circumference.

2008 update

4.7 What should happen at antenatal appointments?

The assessment of women who may or may not need additional clinical care during pregnancy is based on identifying those in whom there are any maternal or fetal conditions associated with an excess of maternal or perinatal death or morbidity. While this approach may not identify many of the women who go on to require extra care and will also categorise many women who go on to have normal uneventful births as 'high risk',[58,59] ascertainment of risk in pregnancy remains important as it may facilitate early detection to allow time to plan for appropriate management.

The needs of each pregnant woman should be assessed at the first appointment and reassessed at each appointment throughout pregnancy because new problems can arise at any time. Additional appointments should be determined by the needs of each pregnant woman, as assessed by her and her care givers, and the environment in which appointments take place should enable women to discuss sensitive issues. Reducing the number of routine appointments will enable more time per appointment for care, information giving and support for pregnant women.

The schedule below, which has been determined by the purpose of each appointment, presents the recommended number of antenatal care appointments for women who are healthy and whose pregnancies remain uncomplicated in the antenatal period; ten appointments for nulliparous women and seven for parous women. These appointments follow the woman's initial contact with a health professional when she first presents with the pregnancy and from where she is referred into the maternity care system. This initial contact should be used as an opportunity to provide women with much of the information they need for early pregnancy (see Section 3.3 for recommendations on information giving).

Booking appointment

The booking appointment needs to be earlier in pregnancy (ideally by 10 weeks) than may have traditionally occurred and, because of the large volume of information needs in early pregnancy, two appointments may be required (but if two booking appointments are made these should count as one in terms of number of appointments overall in order to ensure the woman receives the appropriate number of later appointments). At the booking antenatal appointment(s):

- give information, with an opportunity to discuss issues and ask questions; offer verbal information supported by written information (on topics such as diet and lifestyle considerations, pregnancy care services available, maternity benefits and sufficient information to enable informed decision making about screening tests). (Refer to Section 3.3 for more information about giving antenatal information.)
- identify women who may need additional care (see Care pathway and Section 1.2) and plan pattern of care for the pregnancy
- ask about mood to identify possible depression
- identify women who have had genital mutilation
- check blood group and rhesus D status
- offer screening for haemoglobinopathies, anaemia, red cell alloantibodies, hepatitis B virus, HIV, rubella susceptibility and syphilis
- inform women younger than 25 years about the high prevalence of chlamydia infection in their age group, and give details of their local National Chlamydia Screening Programme
- offer screening for asymptomatic bacteriuria
- offering screening for Down's syndrome
- offer early ultrasound scan for gestational age assessment
- offer ultrasound screening for structural anomalies (18 weeks 0 days to 20 weeks 6 days)
- measure BMI, blood pressure (BP) and test urine for proteinuria
- screen for gestational diabetes using risk factors.

At the booking appointment, for women who choose to have screening, the following tests should be arranged as appropriate:

- blood tests (for checking blood group and rhesus D status and screening for haemoglobinopathies, anaemia, red cell alloantibodies, hepatitis B virus, HIV, rubella susceptibility and syphilis) ideally before 10 weeks
- urine tests (to check for proteinuria and screen for asymptomatic bacteriuria)

2008 update

- ultrasound scan to determine gestational age using:
- – crown--rump measurement if performed at 10 weeks 0 days to 13 weeks 6 days
- – head circumference if crown–rump length above 84 mm
- Down's syndrome screening using:
- – nuchal translucency at 11 weeks 0 days to 13 weeks 6 days
- – serum screening at 15 weeks 0 days to 20 weeks 0 days.

16 weeks

The next appointment should be scheduled at 16 weeks to:

- review, discuss and record the results of all screening tests undertaken; reassess planned pattern of care for the pregnancy and identify women who need additional care (see Care pathway and Section 1.2)
- investigate a haemoglobin level of less than 11 g/100 ml and consider iron supplementation if indicated
- measure BP and test urine for proteinuria
- give information, with an opportunity to discuss issues and ask questions including discussion of the routine anomaly scan; offer verbal information supported by antenatal classes and written information.

18–20 weeks

At 18–20 weeks, if the woman chooses, an ultrasound scan should be performed for the detection of structural anomalies. For a woman whose placenta is found to extend across the internal cervical os at this time, another scan at 36 weeks should be offered and the results of this scan reviewed at the 36 week appointment.

25 weeks

At 25 weeks of gestation, another appointment should be scheduled for nulliparous women. At this appointment:

- measure and plot symphysis–fundal height
- measure BP and test urine for proteinuria
- give information, with an opportunity to discuss issues and ask questions; offer verbal information supported by antenatal classes and written information.

28 weeks

The next appointment for all pregnant women should occur at 28 weeks. At this appointment:

- offer a second screening for anaemia and atypical red cell alloantibodies
- investigate a haemoglobin level of less than 10.5 g/100 ml and consider iron supplementation, if indicated
- offer anti-D to rhesus-negative women
- measure BP and test urine for proteinuria
- measure and plot symphysis–fundal height
- give information, with an opportunity to discuss issues and ask questions; offer verbal information supported by antenatal classes and written information.

31 weeks

Nulliparous women should have an appointment scheduled at 31 weeks to:

- measure BP and test urine for proteinuria
- measure and plot symphysis–fundal height
- give information, with an opportunity to discuss issues and ask questions; offer verbal information supported by antenatal classes and written information
- review, discuss and record the results of screening tests undertaken at 28 weeks; reassess planned pattern of care for the pregnancy and identify women who need additional care (see Care pathway and Section 1.2).

34 weeks

At 34 weeks, all pregnant women should be seen in order to:

- offer a second dose of anti-D to rhesus-negative women
- measure BP and test urine for proteinuria
- measure and plot symphysis–fundal height
- give information, with an opportunity to discuss issues and ask questions on preparation for labour and birth, including the birth plan, recognising active labour and coping with pain; offer verbal information supported by antenatal classes and written information
- review, discuss and record the results of screening tests undertaken at 28 weeks; reassess planned pattern of care for the pregnancy and identify women who need additional care (see Care pathway and Section 1.2).

36 weeks

At 36 weeks, all pregnant women should be seen again to:

- measure BP and test urine for proteinuria
- measure and plot symphysis–fundal height
- check position of baby
- for women whose babies are in the breech presentation, offer external cephalic version (ECV)
- review ultrasound scan report if placenta extended over the internal cervical os at previous scan
- discuss breastfeeding technique and good management practices, refer to the UNICEF Baby Friendly Initiative (www.babyfriendly.org.uk)
- give information, including care of the new baby, newborn screening tests and vitamin K prophylaxis, postnatal self-care and postnatal depression, with an opportunity to discuss issues and ask questions; offer verbal information supported by antenatal classes and written information

38 weeks

At 38 weeks, all pregnant women should be seen again to:

- measure BP and urine testing for proteinuria
- measure and plot symphysis–fundal height
- give information, including options for management of prolonged pregnancy*, with an opportunity to discuss issues and ask questions; verbal information supported by antenatal classes and written information.

40 weeks

For nulliparous women, an appointment at 40 weeks should be scheduled to:

- measure BP and test urine for proteinuria
- measure and plot symphysis–fundal height
- give information, including further discussion about management for prolonged pregnancy, with an opportunity to discuss issues and ask questions; offer verbal information supported by antenatal classes and written information.

41 weeks

For women who have not given birth by 41 weeks:

- a membrane sweep should be offered
- induction of labour should be offered
- BP should be measured and urine tested for proteinuria
- symphysis–fundal height should be measured and plotted
- information should be given, including further discussion about management for prolonged pregnancy, with an opportunity to discuss issues and ask questions; verbal information supported by written information.

---

* The clinical guideline 'Induction of labour' is being updated and is expected to be published in June 2008.

General

Throughout the entire antenatal period, healthcare providers should remain alert to any factors, clinical and/or social, which may affect the health of the mother and fetus. For an outline of care at each appointment see the Care pathway.

5 Lifestyle considerations

5.1 Physiological, psychosocial and emotional changes in pregnancy

Many common physiological, psychosocial and emotional changes occur during pregnancy. Many of these changes may be due to the normal hormonal changes that are taking place in a pregnant woman's body or due to worries associated with pregnancy, such as concerns about the birth or the baby's wellbeing. *The Pegnancy Book*[23] has a chapter on feelings and relationships in pregnancy as well as a chapter on feelings that the father of the child may be encountering.

Some of the common changes that pregnant women might encounter include:

- bleeding gums or gingivitis (note that dental treatment is free during pregnancy and for a year after the birth of the baby) – see Section 5.2
- heartburn (indigestion) – see Section 6.2
- constipation – see Section 6.3
- vaginal discharge (thrush) – see Section 6.6
- varicose veins – see Section 6.5
- haemorrhoids (piles) – see Section 6.4
- backache – see Section 6.7
- swelling of the ankles, fingers, face and hands due to the body holding more fluid in pregnancy – a certain amount of swelling, or oedema, is normal later in pregnancy; however, more severe cases may indicate pre-eclampsia if present with other symptoms and signs (see Section 11.2).

Chapter 9 in *The Pregnancy Book*[23] addresses other common physiological problems encountered in pregnancy such as itching, feeling hot and skin and hair changes.

Not all women will experience all of the above symptoms but it is important for pregnant women to be aware that some of these changes are normal in pregnancy and to be alert to symptoms of potentially harmful complications. It is also important for pregnant women to be reassured that most symptoms of pregnancy are not putting them or their fetus in danger and to be made to feel comfortable about asking their healthcare provider about these changes.

5.2 Maternity health benefits

Prescriptions and dental treatment are free during pregnancy and for a year after the birth.

5.3 Working during pregnancy

Pregnant women want information about maternity benefits and rights. Healthcare professionals need to be aware of current UK legislation regarding employment. As of April 2007, women who work for an employer are entitled to 26 weeks of 'Ordinary Maternity Leave' and 26 weeks of 'Additional Maternity Leave' – making 1 year in total. Provided you meet certain notification requirements, you can take this no matter how long you have been with your employer, how many hours you work or how much you are paid.

Pregnant employees also have special employment rights; for example, the right to take time off work for antenatal care. Under current UK legislation:

- a woman in employment is not allowed to continue working beyond 33 weeks of gestation, unless the woman's GP or midwife informs her employer that she may continue to do so
- it is unlawful for an employer to require or allow a woman in their employment to return to work in the 2 weeks following childbirth

- employers are required to assess risks which might be posed to the health and safety of pregnant women, those who are breastfeeding or who have given birth in the past 6 months. If a significant risk is identified, steps to avoid the risk should be taken, such as:
  - use of preventative or protective behaviours
  - altering working conditions or hours
  - arranging alternative work.

As this information often changes with time, antenatal healthcare providers and pregnant women are encouraged to visit the Working Families website (www.workingfamilies.org.uk) for more comprehensive and up-to-date information. Fact sheets on maternity benefits for students, single parents and young mothers can also be downloaded from this website. Up-to-date information on maternity benefits can also be accessed at the Department for Work and Pensions website (www.dwp.gov.uk/lifeevent/famchild/fc_expecting_a_baby.asp) or the Government's interactive guidance site (www.direct.gov.uk/en/Parents/index.htm). Further information may also be obtained from the Department for Business, Enterprise and Regulatory Reform (BERR) website

Exposure to radiation and chemicals

Some workers are occupationally exposed to potentially teratogenic or toxic substances or environments. For some of these, there is evidence to support an association between exposure and adverse maternal or neonatal outcomes, e.g. exposure to x-rays for healthcare workers. For other exposures, data are inconclusive, e.g. there are inconsistent data to support an association with miscarriage in workers exposed to vapours in the dry-cleaning and painting industries.[60–62] Further information on occupational hazards can be obtained from the Health and Safety Executive website: www.hse.gov.uk/mothers/index.htm.

Physical aspects of work

One meta-analysis of 29 observational studies analysed data on 160 988 women who worked during pregnancy.[63] The outcomes it considered were preterm birth, hypertension or pre-eclampsia and small-for-gestational-age babies. Physically demanding work and prolonged standing may be associated with poor outcomes but the evidence on prolonged hours and shift working is inconclusive. Employment per se has not been associated with increased risks in pregnancy.

One further cohort study from Poland that was not included in this review was located.[64] Although heavy physical work, as reported by the woman, was shown to be significantly associated with the birth of a small-for-gestational-age baby, no significant differences were reported when heavy physical work load was evaluated by level of energy expenditure. [EL = 2b]

Recommendations

Pregnant women should be informed of their maternity rights and benefits. [C]

The majority of women can be reassured that it is safe to continue working during pregnancy. Further information about possible occupational hazards during pregnancy is available from the Health and Safety Executive (www.hse.gov.uk). [D]

A woman's occupation during pregnancy should be ascertained to identify those at increased risk through occupational exposure. [Good practice point]

5.4 Dietary information and education

In addition to the information contained in this guideline on what women should and should not eat during pregnancy, good sources of dietary information during pregnancy include *The Pregnancy Book*[23] and the publication *Eating While You Are Pregnant* from the Food Standards Agency, which may also be accessed online at www.food.gov.uk/aboutus/publications/nutritionpublications/. Further information can also be found on the following site: www.eatwell.gov.uk/agesandstages/pregnancy/whenyrpregnant/.

2008 update

In general, women should be given information about the benefits of eating a variety of foods during pregnancy including:

- plenty of fruit and vegetables
- starchy foods such as bread, pasta, rice and potatoes
- protein, such as lean meat, fish, beans and lentils
- plenty of fibre, which can be found in wholegrain breads and fruits and vegetables
- dairy foods, such as milk, yoghurt and cheese.

Pregnant women should be informed of foods that may put them or their fetus at risk including:

- soft mould ripened cheeses, such as Camembert, Brie and blue-veined cheese
- pâté (including vegetable pâté)
- liver and liver products
- uncooked or undercooked ready-prepared meals
- uncooked or cured meat, such as salami
- raw shellfish, such as oysters
- fish containing relatively high levels of methylmercury, such as shark, swordfish and marlin, which might affect the nervous system of the fetus.

The Food Standards Agency has also recently announced that pregnant women should limit their consumption of:

- tuna to no more than two medium size cans or one fresh tuna steak per week
- caffeine to 300 milligrams a day. Caffeine is present in coffee, tea and colas.

One systematic review of RCTs was located that assessed whether or not the provision of dietary information leads to improved maternal and perinatal outcomes compared with no dietary information.[65] The review was last updated in 1996, however, and although there was evidence that dietary information increased energy and protein intake, data concerning the outcome of pregnancy were available from only one trial, which was not of high quality.

5.5 Nutritional supplements

Folic acid

Neural tube defects, which comprise open spina bifida, anencephaly and encephalocele, affect 1.5/1000 pregnancies in the UK.[66] These congenital malformations, which arise from neural tube defects, are preventable through public health measures.

The effect of increased consumption of multivitamins or folic acid consumption before conception on the prevalence of neural tube defects was assessed in a systematic review of four RCTs of 6425 women.[67] In all the RCTs, folic acid was taken before conception and up to 6–12 weeks of gestation. This periconceptional folate supplementation was found to substantially reduce the prevalence of neural tube defects (RR 0.28, 95% CI 0.13 to 0.58). There was a reduction both where the mother had not had a previously affected fetus or infant (RR 0.07, 95% CI 0.00 to 1.32) and when the mother had given birth to a previously affected infant (OR 0.31, 95% CI 0.14 to 0.66). There were no significant differences found in the rates of miscarriage, ectopic pregnancy or stillbirth with folate supplementation compared with no folate supplementation. [EL = 1a] The effect of starting folic in early pregnancy has not been evaluated.

A concern raised in this review was the possible adverse effect of folate supplementation on causing an increase in the rate of twin pregnancies, with an associated increase in the rate of perinatal mortality. However, results from a large cohort study in China (n = 242 015 women) found no association between consumption of folic acid supplements in pregnancy (400 micrograms per day) and multiple births (rate ratio 0.91, 95% CI 0.82 to 1.0).[68] [EL = 2a]

It is estimated that only one-third of women take folic acid supplements before conception. As folic acid is needed at the time of embryogenesis and many women do not plan a pregnancy, folic acid-fortified foods have been advocated in the UK.[69] Folic acid-fortified foods have been found to be effective in achieving beneficial levels of red cell folate. However, increasing intake through foods naturally containing folates has not been found to be effective.[70] While other countries, such as the USA, Canada and Chile, have put the fortification of wheat flour into practice and observed resultant decreases in the birth prevalence of neural tube defects, in May 2002, the UK Foods Standards Agency decided against recommending mandatory folic acid fortification.[69]

Current advice from an Expert Advisory Group report issued by the Department of Health[71] is that women who do not have a prior history of neural tube defects should take folic acid prior to conception and daily during the first 12 weeks of pregnancy. The recommended amount is 400 micrograms/day for women who have not had a previous baby with a neural tube defect. This report was largely based on evidence from a large multicentre RCT.[72] Although the size of effect for a given dose of folic acid has been quantified and modelling has indicated that a reduced risk is associated with higher doses (i.e., 500 micrograms in lieu of 400 micrograms), the practical application of an increased dose of folic acid has not yet been investigated in studies or trials and therefore cannot be recommended.[73]

Recommendation

Pregnant women (and those intending to become pregnant) should be informed that dietary supplementation with folic acid, before conception and up to 12 weeks of gestation, reduces the risk of having a baby with neural tube defects (anencephaly, spina bifida). The recommended dose is 400 micrograms/day. [A]

Iron supplementation

A systematic review of 20 RCTs compared iron supplementation with either placebo or no iron in pregnant women ($n = 5552$) with normal haemoglobin levels (greater than 10 g/100 ml) at less than 28 weeks of gestation.[74] Routine iron supplementation raised or maintained the serum ferritin level above 10 micrograms/litre and resulted in a substantial reduction in women with a haemoglobin level below 10 or 10.5 g/100 ml in late pregnancy. There was no evidence of any beneficial or harmful effects on maternal or fetal outcomes. [EL = 1a]

The largest trial ($n = 2682$) of selective versus routine iron supplementation showed an increased likelihood of caesarean section and postpartum blood transfusion among those receiving selective supplementation, but fewer perinatal deaths.[75] [EL = 1b]

Another systematic review looked at the effects of routine iron and folate supplements on pregnant women with normal levels of haemoglobin.[76] Eight trials involving 5449 women were included. Routine supplementation with iron and folate raised or maintained the serum iron and ferritin levels and serum and red cell folate levels. It also resulted in a substantial reduction of women with a haemoglobin level below 10 or 10.5 g/100 ml in late pregnancy. However, routine supplementation with iron and folate had no detectable effects, either beneficial or harmful, on any measures of maternal or fetal outcome. [EL = 1a]

Oral iron has also been associated with gastric irritation and altered bowel habit (i.e. constipation or diarrhoea).[77]

See also Section 8.1 on anaemia.

Recommendation

Iron supplementation should not be offered routinely to all pregnant women. It does not benefit the mother's or fetus's health and may have unpleasant maternal side effects. [A]

Vitamin A

In areas of the world where vitamin A deficiency is prevalent, supplementation may be beneficial for pregnant women.[78] [EL = 1a] Vitamin A deficiency is not prevalent among pregnant women in England and Wales and therefore the results of this review were not considered relevant to this guideline.

High levels of preformed vitamin A during pregnancy are considered to be teratogenic.[79–81] From the epidemiological evidence, it is not possible to establish a clear dose–response curve or threshold above which vitamin A intake may be harmful during the first trimester (considered to be the critical period for susceptibility). A dose between 10 000 and 25 000 IU of vitamin A may pose a teratogenic risk.

The intake of vitamin A during pregnancy should be limited to the recommended daily amount, which, in Europe, is 2310 IU, equivalent to 700 micrograms. As liver and liver products contain variable and sometimes very high amounts of vitamin A (10 000–38 000 mg per typical portion size of 100 g), these foodstuffs should be avoided in pregnancy.

The consumption of liver and liver products by pregnant women (and moreover the intake of greater than 700 micrograms) is associated with an increase in the risk of certain congenital malformations.[81]

Recommendation

Pregnant women should be informed that vitamin A supplementation (intake greater than 700 micrograms) might be teratogenic and therefore it should be avoided. Pregnant women should be informed that, as liver and liver products may also contain high levels of vitamin A, consumption of these products should also be avoided. [C]

Vitamin D

Clinical question
What is the effectiveness of vitamin D supplementation during pregnancy?

The effectiveness of interventions to promote an optimal intake of vitamin D to improve the nutrition of preconceptional, pregnant and postpartum women and children was undertaken by the National Collaborating Centre for Women's and Children's Health for the NICE public health programme guidance on 'improving the nutrition of pregnant and breastfeeding mothers in low-income households'.[967] The systematic review undertaken for the public health programme development group (PDG) is reproduced here as it also forms the evidence base for recommendations made in this guideline. A section of the introduction and the evidence review relating to the effectiveness of vitamin D supplementation in pregnancy are reported here.

Previous NICE guidance (for the updated recommendations see below)
There is insufficient evidence to evaluate the effectiveness of vitamin D in pregnancy. In the absence of evidence of benefit, vitamin D supplementation should not be offered routinely to all pregnant women. [A]

Introduction
Vitamin D is essential in the maintenance of skeletal growth and bone health – vitamin D regulates calcium and phosphate absorption and metabolism. As the dietary sources of vitamin D are limited (they include oily fish, fortified margarines and some breakfast cereals, as well as smaller amounts in red meat and egg yolk) the main source is the synthesis following exposure of the skin to sunlight.[706] About 90% of vitamin D is synthesised in the skin with sunlight exposure and 10% is derived from diet. Serum 25-hydroxyvitamin D (25-OHD) reflects the vitamin D derived from both sources and is considered to be an indicator of the individual's vitamin D status. An individual is insufficient in vitamin D when serum 25-OHD falls below 25 nmol/litre.[706]

There are seasonal variations in vitamin D status in the UK (highest in July to September and lowest in January to March).[706] During the winter months, there is no ambient ultraviolet light of the appropriate wavelength at UK latitudes (the UK lies at a latitude of 50 to 58 degrees north) and the UK population relies on body stores and dietary sources to maintain vitamin D status.[706] Uptake of vitamin D supplementation in the UK is low and vitamin D deficiency has re-emerged in recent years as a public health concern, particularly for women and children from South Asian and Afro-Caribbean groups.[975, 995–1000]

Vitamin D deficiency can occur when the demand for it exceeds supply, as in period of rapid growth in fetal life, infancy, early childhood and puberty, and during pregnancy and lactation. Vitamin D status of the newborn is largely determined by the vitamin D status of the mother. Severe deficiency of vitamin D results in rickets (in children) and osteomalacia (in children and adults). Vitamin D has also been implicated in a range of other conditions, such as type 1

2008 update

diabetes, some cancers and cardiovascular disease, but the evidence is less conclusive.[706] There is also emerging evidence that improved vitamin D status of the mother during pregnancy may have a wider beneficial impact on their child's health including risk of osteoporotic fracture[995] and wheeze[996] in childhood. While concerns have been raised about very high intakes,[997] the safe upper intake for supplementary vitamin D is 25 micrograms/day[706] (i.e. considerably higher than reference nutrient intakes).

Longstanding recommendations on vitamin D intake for the UK population were established by COMA (Committee on Medical Aspects of Food Policy) in 1991.[998] More recently, SACN (Scientific Advisory Committee on Nutrition) – the independent committee which superseded COMA – published an update on vitamin D status and other related issues including a synopsis of evidence about the relationship between vitamin D status and chronic disease. SACN reiterated the recommendations of COMA on vitamin D, including the use of supplements to achieve adequate intakes.[706] In particular, SACN emphasised the advice that all pregnant and breastfeeding women should consider taking a daily supplement of vitamin D (10 micrograms) in order to ensure their own requirement is met and to build adequate fetal stores for early infancy.

The awareness of the hazards of excessive sunlight exposure in childhood and subsequent development of skin cancer resulted in public health advice from the mid to late 1990s to emphasise shielding the skin from direct sunlight from birth onwards, and the liberal use of sunscreen.[1011,1012] It has been hypothesised that there may be an association between nutritional rickets and the increasing use of sunscreen in infants and young children who have limited vitamin D intake.[1013] Although the use of sunscreen can reduce vitamin D production in the skin, a cross-sectional UK study among middle-aged adults found that sun protection was associated with slightly higher rather than lower 25-OHD concentrations, suggesting that sun protection partly reflects sun exposure and does not strongly interfere with vitamin D synthesis.[1014]

During winter at latitudes North of about 52° (the UK lies at latitudes between 50° and 60° N) there is no ambient ultraviolet light of the appropriate wavelength to support cutaneous production of previtamin D3. In Spring, Summer and Autumn, 5–15 minutes of sun exposure between 10 a.m. and 3 p.m. may be adequate for individuals with lighter coloured skin living in the UK.7[06] Consequently, there is a policy need to state clearly the length and intensity of exposure necessary to balance maintenance of vitamin D status with the risk of developing skin cancer.[706]

Factors associated with a higher prevalence of deficiency among at-risk groups include increased skin pigmentation, spending limited time outdoors, and cultural and religious practices such as extensive body covering with clothing that restrict exposure to sunlight.[968] It has also been suggested that low meat intakes[969] or a vegetarian diet[970] may increase risk of rickets or osteomalacia. However, it remains unclear whether observed associations are due to dietary, religious or cultural practices as studies have focused on particular groups of South Asian vegetarians.

Description of included studies
The search strategy identified 4691 potentially eligible reports (4647 from electronic searches and 44 from bibliographic search of reference lists of included studies), of which 207 papers were retrieved for further examination. After full text review, 22 papers reporting on 17 studies, conducted between 1976 and 2004, met the inclusion criteria and were included in this review. Fifteen of the included studies were published before 1990 and two were published after 2000.

Stand-alone vitamin D supplementation
Seven '+' quality studies were identifie®d which considered stand-alone vitamin D supplementation.[971–980] All identified studies showed that antenatal vitamin D supplementation is effective in improving the vitamin D status of South Asian and Caucasian women at delivery. Maternal serum 25-OHD concentrations were consistently higher in women supplemented with vitamin D during pregnancy compared with those with no supplementation. No adverse effects were reported.

Studies in the UK:
Six UK-based studies were identified[971–975,981–983] which assessed the effectiveness of stand-alone vitamin D supplementation in the prevention of vitamin D deficiency among South Asian and

2008 update

Caucasian populations. The evidence can be considered applicable and generalisable to the UK populations, depending on the regions, owing to the difference in latitudes and amount of sunlight hours experienced. With the exception of one intervention,[975] all identified studies were conducted in the 1970s or early 1980s. Three of the studies[981–983] were considered to be of poorer quality.

One RCT,[971–973] [EL = 1+] conducted in London (51.5° N) and which formed part of a systematic review[82] compared biochemical measurements and the mean weight gain of pregnant UK South Asian women given high-dose vitamin D supplements (25 micrograms/day) (n = 59) or placebo (n = 67) during the third trimester. Postnatal vitamin supplements were not routinely given.[972] The results suggest that vitamin D supplements to South Asian infants prenatally would improve their physical growth in terms of weight and height gains. The authors reported a significant increase in maternal plasma 25-OHD levels (nmol/litre) in the supplemented group, when compared with the placebo group at term (168 ± 96 versus 16.2 ± 22.1), and in maternal mean daily weight gain (g) in the last trimester in the supplemented group, when compared with the placebo group (63.3 ± 20.7 versus 46.4 ± 29.5). This mean weight gain in supplemented mothers was near to the quoted average weight gain for European women in their last trimester. Mean infant birthweight (g) was higher in the supplemented group than in the placebo group, but the difference was not significant (3157 ± 469 versus 3034 ± 524). There was no documented report of adverse events. The infants of these two groups were followed up for 1 year after the trial. There was a significant increase in mean weight (kg) in infants whose mothers had received antenatal vitamin D supplements (n = 53), when compared with infants whose mothers had not received antenatal vitamin D supplements (n = 64), at 3, 6, 9 and 12 months, resulting in a significant incremental increase in weight over the 12 months (6.39 ± 0.78 versus 5.92 ± 0.92).

A non-RCT[974] [EL = 2+] conducted in Edinburgh (55.7° N) suggests vitamin D supplementation (10 micrograms/day) given to women (ethnicity unknown) from the 12th week of pregnancy may be beneficial. The authors reported significant increases in maternal plasma 25-OHD concentrations (nmol/litre) between the supplemented group (n = 82) and the placebo group (n = 82) at the 24th week (39 versus 32.5; P < 0.01), 34th week (44.5 versus 38.5; P < 0.05) and at delivery (42.8 versus 32.5; P < 0.001). A significant increase in 25-OHD concentrations was also reported in infants of supplemented women (vitamin D group (n = 54) 34.5 versus placebo group (n = 86) 20.3; P < 0.001) at day 6. Formula-fed infants had significantly higher 25-OHD concentrations (P < 0.01) than breastfed infants, supplemented or unsupplemented at day 6. There was a highly significant correlation between maternal and cord values at delivery (r = 0.71). There was no documented report of adverse events.

A before–after study[975] [EL = 2+], among pregnant women from ethnic minorities (n = 160; African, African-Caribbean, South Asian, far-Eastern, Middle Eastern) living in Cardiff (51.5° N), assessed the effect of vitamin D supplementation at the first antenatal visit. Fifty percent of women were found to have low vitamin D levels (plasma 25-OHD < 20 nmol/litre) and were given vitamin D supplements (20–40 micrograms/day). At delivery, the mean level of vitamin D had increased from 15 nmol/litre at booking to 27.5 nmol/litre, suggesting that biochemical screening and subsequent supplementation would be appropriate in similar populations.

A poorer quality non-RCT[982] [EL = 2–] in Glasgow (55.9° N) compared biochemical measurements in South Asian families given vitamin D supplements (n = 18 members from four families) (75 micrograms/week) or provided with vitamin D-fortified chapatti flour (150 micrograms/kg) (n = 32 members from six families), and a control group given no vitamin D (n = 16 members from four families). There was a significant increase in serum 25-OHD concentrations in the weekly vitamin D group and in the fortified group when compared with the control group at 3 and 6 months. The number of biochemical abnormalities suggestive of rickets was also reduced (two in control group versus one in weekly vitamin D group versus 0 in fortified flour group). No adverse events were documented.

A poorer quality RCT[983] [EL = 1–] among South Asian women living in Rochdale (53.6° N) compared the effects of a single dose of vitamin D given orally (2500 micrograms) or intramuscularly (IM). The results suggest that both oral and IM vitamin D given every 6 months are equally effective as a prophylactic measure. The authors reported a significant increase in serum 25-OHD concentrations (nmol/litre) 1 month after treatment in the oral supplementation group (n = 12) when compared with the IM group (n = 12) (52.5 ± 12.0 versus 32.5 ± 13.8. No significant differences were observed between the two groups at 3 months and 5 months after treatment. Both the oral and the IM groups achieved a significantly higher serum 25-OHD concentration (nmol/litre) at 5 months than at baseline (WMD 8.00, 95% CI 2.33 to 13.67 and WMD 9.50, 95% CI 1.75 to 17.25, respectively). The range of values (nmol/litre) produced by oral vitamin D was much less than the range produced by IM vitamin D (mean 24.5, range 19.3–34.3 versus mean 23.5, range 12.8–52.3). At 1 year after the study, every patient had a serum 25-OHD level > 12.5 nmol/litre. There were no documented reports of adverse events.

A poor-quality cohort study[981] [EL = 2–] conducted in Leeds (53.5° N) compared biochemical and bone mineral measurements of babies born to South Asian women deficient in vitamin D (*n* = 45, Group 1) with South Asian women supplemented with vitamin D (25 micrograms/day) during the third trimester of pregnancy (*n* = 19, Group 2) and to white women (*n* = 12, Group 3). There was a significant difference in cord blood 25-OHD concentrations between South Asian babies who received antenatal supplementation and South Asian babies who did not. The proportion of plasma 25-OHD concentrations below 10 nmol/litre (associated with osteomalacia) was 91% in the unsupplemented group, 58% in the supplemented group and 0% in the white mothers. At term, babies born to mothers deficient in vitamin D had significantly lower cord blood 25-OHD concentrations (nmol/litre) when compared with babies born to white women (5.90 ± 0.94 versus 33.40 ± 3.60; *P* < 0.001). South Asian babies whose mothers had been supplemented with vitamin D also had significantly lower cord blood 25-OHD concentrations than babies in Group 3 (15.20 ± 3.15 versus 33.40 ± 3.60; *P* < 0.001) at term. There was no significant difference in the babies' birthweight or bone mineral content within the first 5 days after birth. There was no report of breastfeeding status of the infants studied. There were no documented reports of adverse events.

Studies in Europe:
Three RCTs were identified, conducted in Europe between 1985 and 1986, of which two were considered '+' quality[976,977] and one '–' quality.[984] The studies only included Caucasian populations and may not be applicable and generalisable to the UK populations owing to the difference in latitudes, ethnicity, sunlight hours experienced and the food fortification policy of the various countries. The dosage of vitamin D supplements recommended differed from that by COMA in the UK.

The first RCT[977] [EL = 1+] in Lyons (45.7° N), compared the effects of vitamin D supplements (25 micrograms/day) given to women (ethnicity unknown) in the third trimester (*n* = 40) with no vitamin D supplement (*n* = 40). The authors reported significantly higher serum 25-OHD concentrations (ng/ml) in the supplemented group than the control group (mean ± SD: 26 ± 7 versus 13.8 ± 8) at delivery (June), and in (breastfed) infants at day 4 (mean ± SEM: 13 ± 1 versus 5 ± 1). There was no reported difference in infant birthweights (details not presented). There were no documented reports of adverse effects.

The second RCT[976] [EL = 1+] (part of a systematic review[82]) was conducted in Rouen (49.4° N). Caucasian pregnant women were either supplemented with antenatal vitamin D (*n* = 21) (25 micrograms/day) in the third trimester, or given a single dose of vitamin D (5 mg) (*n* = 27) in the 7th month of their pregnancy, or given no vitamin D supplement (*n* = 29). The authors reported a significant increase in maternal serum 25-OHD concentrations (nmol/litre) in the daily dose group, compared with the control group (25.3 ± 7.7 versus 9.4 ± 4.9), and in the single dose group compared with the control group (26.0 ± 6.4 versus 9.4 ± 4.9) at delivery. There was a positive correlation between the maternal and cord blood 25-OHD concentrations (*r* = 9.5; *P* < 0.0001). There was no significant difference in the mean infant birthweight between the three groups.

The third, poorer quality RCT[984] [EL = 1–], conducted in Finland (61° N), considered the effects of maternal and infant vitamin D supplementation among infants who were breastfed. Around half the mother–infant pairs were studied in winter and half in summer. The 92 pairs were randomised to three groups: Group 1 where mothers were supplemented with vitamin D after delivery (25 micrograms/day) (*n* = 27); Group 2 where infants were supplemented with 10 micrograms vitamin D per day (*n* = 31); or Group 3 where infants were supplemented with 25 micrograms vitamin D per day (*n* = 29). During pregnancy, all the mothers had received vitamin supplementation (0–12.5 micrograms/day). At delivery, maternal serum 25-OHD levels were significantly higher (all absolute data presented graphically) in all three groups of women (*P* < 0.001 in Groups 1 and 2; *P* < 0.01 in Group 3). At 8 weeks after delivery (in winter), the levels were significantly higher in Group 1 than in Groups 2 and 3 (*P* < 0.001) but there was no such difference between Group 1 and Group 3 in summer. The infantile levels at delivery were similar in all three groups in winter but were significantly lower in Group 3 than in Group 1 ($P < 0.05$) in summer. In winter, at the age of 8 weeks, levels in Group 1 infants were significantly lower than those in Groups 2 and 3 ($P < 0.001$). In summer, serum 25-OHD levels of Group 1 infants were similar to those in Group 2, but were significantly lower than those in Group 3 ($P < 0.001$). Throughout the study, there was no signs of clinical or biochemical rickets seen in the infants with 25-OHD levels below the risk limit for rickets. There were no documented reports of adverse events.

Studies in the USA:
Three RCTs were identified which were conducted among predominantly Caucasian populations in the USA between 1980 and 2004, of which two[979,985] were considered '+' quality and one[986] was considered '−' quality. The evidence may not be applicable and generalisable to the UK populations owing to the difference in latitudes, ethnicity, amount of sunlight hours experienced and the food fortification policy of the two countries. The dosage of vitamin D supplements recommended differed from that by COMA in the UK.

The small RCT[985] [EL = 1+] conducted in Massachusetts (42.4° N) compared bone mineral content (BMC) and biochemical measurements in exclusively breastfed infants ($n = 46$, 13 born in summer, 33 in winter) given 10 micrograms/day vitamin D ($n = 22$, Group 1) and infants given a daily placebo ($n = 24$, Group 2) within the first week of delivery. All infants had white mothers who also received supplemental vitamin D during pregnancy. An additional convenience sample of healthy exclusively formula-fed infants ($n = 12$, Group 3) was also included as a comparison group. Maternal mean vitamin D intake (IU/day) of Groups 1 and 2 did not differ between Groups 1 and 2. Serum 25-OHD concentrations (ng/ml) did not differ at birth among the three groups. However, they were significantly higher in Group 1 than in Groups 2 and 3 at 6 weeks (30.25 ± 9.54 versus 15.76 ± 9.81 versus 30.21 ± 6.08), at 3 months (38.89 ± 10.34 versus 15.72 ± 11.25 versus 37.24 ± 6.08) and at 6 months (36.96 ± 11.86 versus $23.53 \pm 9.9.4$ versus 37.57 ± 8.54). All three groups had an increase in BMC. The measured BMC (mg/cm) in Group 2 was significantly higher than Group 1 (101 ± 17.9 versus 89.5 ± 12.5, $P < 0.05$) at 6 months. Formula-fed infants in Group 3 had a significantly higher change in measured BMC than that of combined Group 1 and 2 (38.8 ± 24.3 versus 9.2 ± 13.2 versus 18.0 ± 18.2) at 6 months. There was no significant difference in mean body weight (g) between the three groups during the study (7570 ± 858 versus 7752 ± 1182 versus 7633 ± 1002). There were no documented reports of adverse events.

A small RCT[979] [EL = 1+], conducted in Ohio (40.1° N), compared the effects of supplemental vitamin D in exclusively breastfed infants ($n = 18$, 16 born in summer and two in winter) between the first and second weeks after birth. The authors reported no significant difference in BMC between the group given 10 micrograms/day vitamin D ($n = 9$) and a placebo group ($n = 9$) at 6 weeks, but a significant increase in BMC in the supplemented group at 12 weeks ($P < 0.003$). Comparison between the supplemented infants with an additional convenience sample of formula-fed infants ($n = 12$) showed a significantly higher BMC in the supplemented group at 6 weeks ($P < 0.03$) but not at 12 weeks. Serum 25-OHD concentrations (ng/ml) were significantly higher in the supplemented group than the placebo group (38 versus 20; $P < 0.01$) at 12 weeks. Mean maternal vitamin D intakes (assessed by dietary recall) were similar in the two groups during the study. There were no documented reports of adverse events.

A poorer quality RCT[986] [EL = 1−], conducted in South Carolina (32.8° N), compared the effects of high-dose maternal vitamin D supplementation in breastfeeding women within 1 month after delivery with that in their infants, who also acted as their own control group. The authors reported a significant increase in total circulating serum 25-OHD concentrations (ng/ml) in women receiving 50 micrograms/day vitamin D (Group 1, $n = 9$ ((three African-American women)) (27.6 ± 3.3 versus 36.1 ± 2.3) and in women receiving 100 micrograms/day vitamin D (Group 2, $n = 9$ (two African-American women)) 32.9 ± 2.4 versus 44.5 ± 3.9) from baseline to 3 months. There was a significant increase in total circulating serum 25-OHD concentrations in nursing infants in both groups. There were no data on the effect of seasonal variation. There were no documented reports of adverse events.

Effectiveness of interventions to promote optimal dietary intake of vitamin D
The literature search (1990 to 2006) did not identify any studies which evaluated the effectiveness of interventions to promote optimal dietary intake of vitamin D, nor any published intervention programmes which aimed to promote optimal uptake of vitamin D, in the UK or other developed

2008 update

countries. By expanding the search back to 1966, one antenatal intervention programme was identified[971] which was carried out in the UK. The quality of reporting in the study is poor and very few details are provided.

One small quasi-RCT[971] [EL = 1–], a pilot study conducted in London (51.5° N), evaluated the effects of dietary advice to South Asian pregnant women early in their pregnancy. The intervention was delivered by a health visitor at the antenatal clinic and included advice and counselling to increase dietary vitamin D content and exposure to sunlight. Interpreters were available when required during the intervention. The authors reported a significant increase in mean dietary vitamin D intake (mg/day) in the counselled group ($n = 11$) when compared with the non-counselled group ($n = 9$) at 4 months (a mean increase from baseline of 1.5 ± 1.2 versus 0.4 ± 0.5; $P < 0.05$). However, the mean increase from baseline in serum 25-OHD levels (ng/ml) was significantly lower in the counselled group than the non-counselled group at 4 months (0.07 ± 0.06 versus 0.15 ± 0.07; P approximately 0.02). The author suggested that the unexpected results could be due to confounders such as reliability of self-reported data on dietary vitamin D intake and difference in sunlight exposure in the two groups.

Evidence statement
Evidence from seven studies (five 1+ RCTs and two 2+ studies) shows that antenatal vitamin D supplementation is effective in improving the vitamin D status of South Asian and Caucasian women.

No adverse effects were reported in any of the studies considering vitamin D supplementation to mothers or infants.

Evidence from one RCT indicates that infants of South Asian mothers who received an antenatal vitamin D supplement achieved a higher body weight during the first year after birth than infants of mothers who received no antenatal vitamin D supplement.

A 2+ study found that breastfed infants of supplemented (10 micrograms/day) mothers had higher 25-OHD levels 6 days after birth than breastfed infants of unsupplemented mothers. Vitamin D levels of all breastfed infants were lower than infants receiving infant formula.

There is 1+ evidence to suggest that supplemented breastfed infants (1000 IU/day (25 micrograms/day) during the first trimester) achieved a higher serum 25-OHD levels than un-supplemented breastfed infants, at birth and at 4 days of age.

Evidence from a 1+ study indicates that the weights of supplemented (400 IU/day (10 micrograms/day)), un-supplemented breastfed infants and formula-fed infants did not differ at 6 months.

Evidence from two 1+ RCTs indicates that the effect of vitamin D supplements on infant bone mineral content is uncertain. The results from two studies were found to be conflicting.

Antenatal Care GDG interpretation of evidence
There is no evidence that routine vitamin D supplementation of healthy pregnant women improves pregnancy outcomes.

There is good evidence that vitamin D supplementation during pregnancy improves vitamin D status and improves growth in the first year of life in South Asian babies.

It can be extrapolated from this that incidence of rickets will decrease as a result of this in groups who are at risk of vitamin D deficiency.

Based on the reviewed evidence and following discussion with the maternal and child nutrition PDG the GDG identifies the following groups as vulnerable to vitamin D deficiency:

* women in low-income households
* South Asian and black women
* women with a low intake of dietary source of vitamin D such as full-fat dairy products, eggs, animal products
* women 19–24 years of age
* women who have limited skin exposure to sunlight
* women who are obese.

Recommendations on vitamin D supplementation

All women should be informed at the booking appointment about the importance for their own and their baby's health of maintaining adequate vitamin D stores during pregnancy and whilst breastfeeding. In order to achieve this, women may choose to take 10 micrograms of vitamin D per day, as found in the Healthy Start multivitamin supplement. Particular care should be taken to enquire as to whether women at greatest risk are following advice to take this daily supplement. These include:

- women of South Asian, African, Caribbean or Middle Eastern family origin
- women who have limited exposure to sunlight, such as women who are predominantly housebound, or usually remain covered when outdoors
- women who eat a diet particularly low in vitamin D, such as women who consume no oily fish, eggs, meat, vitamin D-fortified margarine or breakfast cereal
- women with a pre-pregnancy body mass index above 30 kg/m².

Research recommendation

There is a need for research into the effectiveness of routine vitamin D supplementation for pregnant and breastfeeding women.

Why this is important
Although there is some evidence of benefit from vitamin D supplementation for pregnant women at risk of vitamin D deficiency, there is less evidence in the case of pregnant women currently regarded as being at low risk of deficiency. It is possible that there will be health gains resulting from vitamin D supplementation, but further evidence is required.

5.6   Food-acquired infections

Listeriosis

Listeriosis is an illness caused by a bacterium called *Listeria monocytogenes*, which may present with mild, flu-like symptoms. It is also associated with miscarriage, stillbirth and severe illness in the newborn baby. There is a higher incidence of listeriosis in the pregnant population (12/100 000) than in the general population 0.7/100,00).[83] Contaminated food is the usual source of infection.[83] Usual sources include unpasteurised milk, ripened soft cheeses and pâté. *L. monocytogenes* are also found in soil and in the faeces of domestic and wild animals.

Recommendation

Pregnant women should be offered information on how to reduce the risk of listeriosis by:

- drinking only pasteurised or UHT milk
- not eating ripened soft cheese such as Camembert, Brie and blue-veined cheese (there is no risk with hard cheeses such as Cheddar, or cottage cheese and processed cheese)
- not eating pate (of any sort, including vegetable)
- not eating uncooked or undercooked ready-prepared meals. [D]

Salmonella

Salmonella is a bacterium which causes food poisoning. It is usually found in poultry, eggs, unprocessed milk and in raw or undercooked meat and water. It may also be carried by pets like turtles and birds. The incidence of salmonella infection in England and Wales is at its lowest level since 1985.[84] While salmonella has not been shown to affect an unborn baby, it can cause severe diarrhoea and vomiting. Current guidelines recommend that pregnant women should avoid eating raw eggs or food that contains eggs that are raw or partially cooked. Eggs should be cooked until solid. As chicken and raw meat can also be source of salmonella, all meat should be thoroughly cooked and hands washed carefully after preparing chicken or other meat.[85]

Recommendation

Pregnant women should be offered information on how to reduce the risk of salmonella infection by:

- avoiding raw or partially cooked eggs or food that may contain them (such as mayonnaise)
- avoiding raw or partially cooked meat, especially poultry. [D]

Toxoplasmosis

See Section 10.11.

5.7 Prescribed medicines

Prescribing during pregnancy involves the balance between benefit to the mother and potential harm to the fetus. There are only a small number of drugs that have well proven safety in pregnancy and a number of drugs that were initially thought to be safe in pregnancy and later withdrawn. General principles include prescribing only well-known and tested drugs at the smallest possible doses and only when the benefit to the mother outweighs the risk to the fetus.[77]

In addition, physiological changes of pregnancy need to be considered when prescribing drugs. Drug absorption is affected due to decreased gastric emptying and delayed gut motility. Drug distribution is affected by decreased albumin and increased plasma volume of pregnancy. Drug metabolism is also affected; in particular, lipid-soluble drugs and the excretion of drugs are altered by the increased renal clearance that occurs in pregnancy. The other physiological consideration is that all the drugs that cross the placenta will also be metabolised and excreted by the fetus.[86]

Recommendation

Few medicines have been established as safe to use in pregnancy. Prescription medicines should be used as little as possible during pregnancy and should be limited to circumstances where the benefit outweighs the risk. [D]

5.8 Over-the-counter medicines

As few conventional medicines have been established as safe to take during pregnancy, a general principle of use of drugs in pregnancy is that as few should be used as possible. However, pregnancy does result in a number of symptoms and over-the-counter (OTC) medication may be used for the relief of these symptoms. In particular, the treatment of common symptoms in pregnancy, nausea and vomiting, heartburn, constipation and haemorrhoids are covered in Chapter 6.

Recommendation

Pregnant women should be informed that few over-the-counter (OTC) medicines have been established as being safe to take in pregnancy. OTC medicines should be used as little as possible during pregnancy. [D]

5.9 Complementary therapies

There is an assumption that complementary and alternative therapies are natural and therefore safe. Just as with prescription and OTC medicines, however, complementary and alternative therapies cannot be assumed to be without risk. In fact, the safety and efficacy of most complementary therapies during pregnancy has not been established.[87,88] Nevertheless, their use among pregnant women in developed countries is common and also reported to be increasing.[89–92] Although it is important for women to inform their healthcare providers about the use of complementary medicines during pregnancy, one study reported that up to one-quarter of women failed to do so.[93]

Herbal medicines

The Medicines Control Agency has responded to concerns around the safety of herbal medicines and has compiled recommendations as to their use for pregnant women. Many herbal medicines are not licensed medicines and therefore fall outside of statutory provisions for safety, quality and efficacy criteria.[94] [EL = 4] This raises the additional concern of under-reporting of adverse events.

Evidence as to the safety and efficacy of most herbal products is based on case reports, case series and retrospective surveys.[95] [EL = 4] There are few trials assessing clinical safety, notable exceptions being evening primrose oil[96] [EL = 2b], ginger (see Section 6.1 on nausea and vomiting) and raspberry leaf.[97] [EL = Ib] While neither ginger nor raspberry leaf was associated with adverse outcomes for the mother or baby, raspberry leaf was not found to confer any benefit and the results of the primrose oil trial suggested associations with negative outcomes, such as an increase in the incidence of prolonged rupture of the membranes.

A recently completed study on the use of *Echinacea* during pregnancy reported no association with increased risk for major malformations.[98] [EL = 2a] A study on the reproductive safety of St John's wort (*Hypericum perforatum*) is currently underway in Canada.[99]

Acupuncture

Acupuncture is a Chinese system of treatment and diagnosis. It is based on stimulation of certain points on the surface of the body that is thought to affect the function of specific organs. During the antenatal period, acupressure has been used for nausea and vomiting (see Section 6.1) and moxibustion for breech presentation of the fetus (see Section 13.3).

Massage therapy

Massage therapy has been found to be effective in the relief of backache during pregnancy (see Section 6.7).

Hypnosis and aromatherapy

Although studies on hypnosis and aromatherapy during childbirth were located, no studies on their effectiveness or safety for use during pregnancy were found.

Recommendation

Pregnant women should be informed that few complementary therapies have been established as being safe and effective during pregnancy. Women should not assume that such therapies are safe and they should be used as little as possible during pregnancy. [D]

5.10 Exercise in pregnancy

Exercise includes a range of physical activities and not all sports have the same impact on pregnancy. The physiological and morphological changes that occur during pregnancy may interfere with a woman's ability to engage in some forms of physical activity safely. In the absence of any obstetric or medical complications, however, most women can begin or maintain a regular exercise regimen during pregnancy without causing harm to their fetus.

In an RCT that compared babies born to women who continued regular exercise during pregnancy with women who did not exercise regularly during pregnancy, no differences in neurodevelopmental outcomes at 1 year of age were reported.[100] [EL = 1b]

One systematic review assessed the effects of advising healthy pregnant women to engage in regular (at least two to three times per week) aerobic exercise on physical fitness, ease or difficulty of childbirth and delivery, and on the course and outcome of pregnancy.[101] Ten trials randomising 688 women were included, all of which had methodological shortcomings. Five of the ten trials reported significant improvement in physical fitness in the exercise group; however, the measures used to assess fitness varied across the trials and were therefore not subject to meta-analysis. A conflicting result with no mean difference in gestational age (three RCTs, $n = 416$; WMD 0.02,

95% CI −0.4 to 0.4) and an increased risk of preterm birth in the exercise group was found (three RCTs, $n = 421$; RR 2.29, 95% CI 1.02 to 5.13). No other adverse outcomes were reported and one trial ($n = 15$) found improvement among exercising women in several aspects of self-reported body image, including muscle strength, energy level and body build.[101] [EL = 1a]

Pregnant women should avoid exercise that involves the risk of abdominal trauma, falls or excessive joint stress, as in high impact sports, contact sports and vigorous racquet sports. They are also recommended not to scuba dive, because the risk of birth defects seems to be greater among those who do, and there is a serious risk of fetal decompression disease.[102] [EL = 3]

Maternal exercise during pregnancy does not appear to have a negative effect on the fetus or on birth outcomes.

Recommendation

Pregnant women should be informed that beginning or continuing a moderate course of exercise during pregnancy is not associated with adverse outcomes. [A]

Pregnant women should be informed of the potential dangers of certain activities during pregnancy, for example, contact sports, high-impact sports and vigorous racquet sports that may involve the risk of abdominal trauma, falls or excessive joint stress, and scuba diving, which may result in fetal birth defects and fetal decompression disease. [D]

5.11 Sexual intercourse in pregnancy

Two American cohort studies of over 52 000 pregnant women reported an inverse association between the frequency of sexual intercourse at various times during pregnancy and the risk of preterm delivery.[103,104] [EL = 2a] No association between frequency of sexual intercourse and perinatal mortality was observed.[104] A study among women identified with bacterial vaginosis (BV) or *Trichomonas vaginalis* in the USA reported a similar decreased risk for preterm birth among women who reported more frequent intercourse than women who reported less frequent intercourse, but this finding applied only to women with BV and not to those with *T. vaginalis*.[105]

Recommendation

Pregnant woman should be informed that sexual intercourse in pregnancy is not known to be associated with any adverse outcomes. [B]

5.12 Alcohol and smoking in pregnancy

5.12.1 Alcohol consumption in pregnancy

Clinical question
What is the minimum level of alcohol intake associated with fetal alcohol syndrome and other baby outcomes?

Previous NICE guidance (for the updated recommendations see below)
A recent clinical guidance on antenatal care published in the UK by NICE, 2003 stated that women should limit their alcohol consumption to no more than one standard unit per day, noting that alcohol has an adverse effect on the fetus.

Introduction and background
Alcohol passes freely across the placenta to the unborn baby and, while there is general agreement that women should not drink excessively during pregnancy, it remains unclear what level of drinking is harmful to a pregnant woman and her baby. Investigating the effects of maternal drinking during pregnancy on a child's development is difficult, owing to confounding

2008 update

factors such as socio-economic status and smoking, as well as accurately measuring alcohol consumption levels and patterns both before and after birth.

Different studies have raised concerns about a variety of pregnancy outcomes which may be affected by alcohol intake during pregnancy, including growth before and after birth, miscarriage, stillbirth and preterm birth. A pregnancy outcome which has been linked to heavy alcohol intake during pregnancy is fetal alcohol syndrome, which is characterised by reduced birthweight and length, including small head size, congenital and intellectual abnormalities and certain facial features. However, not all babies of women who drink heavily during pregnancy have fetal alcohol syndrome and diagnosing the syndrome can be difficult as it requires a reliable measure of maternal alcohol intake throughout pregnancy, as well as the exclusion of other congenital syndromes with similar features.

The Department of Health now recommends that women trying to conceive should avoid drinking alcohol, and during pregnancy women should drink no more than 1 to 2 units of alcohol once or twice a week and avoid getting drunk (www.dh.gov.uk/en/Publichealth/Healthimprovement/ Alcoholmisuse/Alcoholmisusegeneralinformation/DH_4062199). However, binge drinking is more problematic. The Midwives' Information and Resource Service (2003) advises that light, infrequent drinking constitutes no risk to the baby. Although some women avoid alcohol during pregnancy, 25–50% of European women continue to drink alcohol and some drink at harmful levels for the baby (ec.europa.eu/health-eu/news_alcoholineurope_en.htm).

Description of included studies

A systematic review (2005)[707] [EL = 2++] evaluated the fetal effects of low-to-moderate prenatal alcohol exposure and binge drinking. The review sought to determine whether an intake of up to six drinks a week was associated with more risk than total abstention and whether binge drinking by low-to-moderate drinkers is associated with harm. They also aimed to evaluate a 'safe level'. Two definitions were used in the review:

- *low-to-moderate prenatal alcohol exposure* – This was defined as less than one drink per day (equivalent to maximum 1.5 UK units or 12 g of alcohol daily). This was compared with no alcohol consumption or very small amounts.
- *binge drinking* – Authors' definitions were used. These definitions varied between studies but a 'binge' was most often defined as five or more drinks on any one occasion.

This review evaluated studies concerning two measures of consumption: (1) average alcohol intake of less than seven drinks per week (or less than one drink per day); and (2) binge drinking. This review looked at a total of ten outcomes with low-to-moderate consumption of alcohol. A total of 11 separate studies examined the effect of binge drinking on the ten outcomes above.

One case–control study in Spain (2006)[708] [EL = 2+] analysed the influence of alcohol drinking during pregnancy on low birthweight. The cases (*n* = 552) were mothers delivering a single newborn weighing < 2500 g and controls (*n* = 1451) were selected randomly from all delivering women. Personal interviews, clinical charts and prenatal care records were used for obtaining information.

A case–control study in Italy (2006)[709] [EL = 2+] analysed the effect of alcohol intake on the risk of small-for gestational-age (SGA) birth, preterm or at term, and the potential interaction between alcohol consumption and risk factors for SGA birth. A total of 555 cases, women (mean age 31 years, range 16–43 years) who delivered SGA babies and 1966 controls, women (mean age 31 years, range 14–43 years) who gave birth at term (37 weeks of gestation or more) to healthy infants of normal weight at the hospitals where cases had been identified were included in the study.

Findings

The outcomes from the systematic review were as follows.

Miscarriage:

A total of eight studies looked at the effects of low-to-moderate alcohol consumption on miscarriage. Five of these reported a significant effect: two had significant limitations, one had significant results among heavy smokers and the remaining two were of borderline statistical significance. The highest reported risk was a relative risk of 3.79 (95% CI 1.18 to 12.17) associated with consuming up to 10 units (equivalent to 6.7 drinks).

Stillbirth:
Five studies examined stillbirth as the outcome and only one study reported significantly increased rates of stillbirth in babies of women who drank up to 25–60 g per week in pregnancy. Three studies reported higher rates of stillbirth in women who abstained but these were not statistically significant differences and were unadjusted for potential confounders.

Antepartum haemorrhage:
One study included antepartum haemorrhage (APH) as an outcome and found no increase in risk of APH with low-to-moderate level of alcohol consumption.

Intrauterine growth restriction:
Seven studies examined intrauterine growth restriction as an outcome and only one study found a significant association but it was unadjusted for potential confounders. Three studies found low-to-moderate alcohol consumption to be mildly protective but, although of borderline statistical significance, two may have been subject to recall bias.

Birthweight:
Twenty studies included birthweight as an outcome but only one reported a significant increase in the risk of low birthweight with consumption of < 0.1 oz alcohol per day (adjusted RR 3.20, 95% CI 1.87 to 5.46). However, at 0.1–0.25 oz per day, the RR was lower at 1.36 (95% CI 0.48 to 3.88). This result was inconsistent as higher levels were not associated with increased risk. It appeared that small amounts of alcohol exerted a mildly protective effect.

Preterm birth:
One out of a total of 16 studies that examined preterm birth as an outcome reported a significantly increased risk of preterm birth (RR 2.11 and 2.15 in women consuming < 0.1 oz and 0.1–0.25 oz, respectively, of absolute alcohol per day at 7 months of gestation). This study suffered from residual confounding as it was unadjusted for socio-economic status.

Malformation:
None of the six studies that examined malformations as the outcome reported a significant association with low-to-moderate alcohol consumption although a trend in that direction was apparent in some studies.

Head circumference and birth length:
A total of five studies looked at HC and birth length as the outcome and only one found a higher proportion of low birthweight babies among those whose mothers drank low-to-moderate amounts in pregnancy. However, this study suffered from lack of adjustment for potential confounders. None of the other studies reported any differences at these levels of consumption.

Postnatal growth:
Two studies that examined the association between alcohol exposure and postnatal growth differed in their results. One of these studies, which followed children up to age 14 years, found that children of women who drank small amounts in pregnancy were consistently lighter. However, the other study found that children of abstainers tended to be lighter. Neither of the results was significant.

Neurodevelopmental outcome:
Seven studies looked at neurodevelopmental outcomes: one was conducted at birth whereas the others were later in childhood. One study found a poorer result in children of low-to-moderate drinkers but this difference did not reach statistical significance and the analysis was not adjusted for potential confounders.

Four of the seven studies looked at neurodevelopmental outcomes and showed consistently poorer results in children exposed to binge drinking in pregnancy. The effects, although quite small, included an increase in 'disinhibited behaviour', a reduction in verbal IQ and an increase in

2008 update

delinquent behaviour, and more learning problems and poorer performance. The studies suffered from a possible overlap between binge drinkers who otherwise drink little and binge drinkers who generally drink substantial amounts. These studies represent the most consistent evidence suggesting that binge drinking in pregnancy may be associated with poor neurodevelopmental outcomes.

The results of the Spanish study showed that alcohol consumption of less than 6 g/day decreased the risk for low birthweight (adjusted OR 0.64, 95% CI 0.46 to 0.88). A similar result was obtained for moderate drinkers (< 12 g/day) on weekends only. The opposite relationship was observed between alcohol consumption on weekdays of 12 g/day or greater (adjusted OR 2.67, 95% CI 1.39 to 5.12), not observed in those drinking on weekends only.

The results of the Italian study showed that there was no increase in the risk of SGA birth observed in women drinking one or two drinks a day in pregnancy. The odds ratios of three or more drinks per day were 3.2 (95% CI 1.7 to 6.2) during the first trimester, 2.7 (95% CI 1.4 to 5.3) during the second trimester and 2.9 (95% CI 1.5 to 5.7) during the third trimester.

Evidence summary
No threshold level of alcohol consumption during pregnancy, above which alcohol is harmful to the baby and below which it is safe, was identified clearly across all studies. A systematic review of low-to-moderate alcohol during pregnancy (less than one drink or 1.5 units per day) concluded that 'there was no consistent evidence of adverse effects from low-to-moderate prenatal alcohol consumption but the evidence is probably not strong enough to rule out any risk'.

Low-to-moderate alcohol intake:
There was possibly a slight increase in miscarriage.

Studies of growth outcomes, including intrauterine growth, birthweight, head circumference and birth length, and postnatal growth are inconsistent and several report a protective effect of low-to-moderate alcohol intake compared with no alcohol during pregnancy.

Of seven studies, only one found neurodevelopmental outcomes to be poorer in babies of mothers with low-to-moderate alcohol intake and this was limited by confounding.

Most studies of preterm birth, stillbirth and miscarriage found no association with low-to-moderate alcohol intake; those studies which reported increased risk had significant limitations.

No studies found any association between low-to-moderate alcohol intake and congenital malformation but the numbers needed to exclude this possibility would need to be very large.

Binge drinking:
Binge drinking was not associated with an increased risk of stillbirth, miscarriage, preterm birth, congenital malformation, antepartum haemorrhage or prenatal or postnatal growth.

Four studies of neurodevelopmental outcomes reported poorer behavioural and intellectual results in children of mothers with low-to-moderate alcohol intake during pregnancy. However, measurement of the pattern and level of binge drinking before and after birth was very variable and conclusions about safe or harmful threshold levels could not be made.

Alcohol content of drinks is that recommended by the Office of National Statistics, 2007.

GDG interpretation of evidence
There is no evidence of a threshold level of alcohol consumption during pregnancy above which alcohol is harmful to the baby.

In the absence of clear evidence of a threshold it would appear that drinking no more than 1.5 units/day is not associated with harm to the baby but there remains a possibility that there is an increased miscarriage rate in association with alcohol consumption although the evidence is limited and of poor quality.

There is limited poor-quality evidence that binge drinking, as defined by drinking 5 or more units in a single episode, may be associated with neurodevelopmental harm to the baby.

Recommendations on alcohol consumption

Pregnant women and women planning a pregnancy should be advised to avoid drinking alcohol in the first 3 months of pregnancy if possible because it may be associated with an increased risk of miscarriage.

If women choose to drink alcohol during pregnancy they should be advised to drink no more than 1 to 2 UK units once or twice a week (1 unit equals half a pint of ordinary strength lager or beer, or one shot [25 ml] of spirits. One small [125 ml] glass of wine is equal to 1.5 UK units). Although there is uncertainty regarding a safe level of alcohol consumption in pregnancy, at this low level there is no evidence of harm to the unborn baby.

Women should be informed that getting drunk or binge drinking during pregnancy (defined as more than 5 standard drinks or 7.5 UK units on a single occasion) may be harmful to the unborn baby.

Research recommendation on alcohol consumption

Prospective research is required into the effects of alcohol consumption during pregnancy.

5.12.2 Smoking in pregnancy

Although it is estimated that up to 25% of women who smoke stop before their first antenatal appointment,[112] 27% of pregnant women in the UK report that they are current smokers at the time of the birth of the baby.[113]

Smoking is a significant modifiable cause of adverse pregnancy outcome in women and its dangers have been widely established. Meta-analyses have shown significant associations between maternal cigarette smoking in pregnancy and increased risks of perinatal mortality,[114] sudden infant death syndrome,[114] placental abruption,[115,116] preterm premature rupture of membranes,[116] ectopic pregnancies,[116] placenta praevia,[116] preterm delivery,[117] miscarriage,[114] low birthweight[114] and the development of cleft lip and cleft palate in children.[118] [all studies: EL = 2 and 3] Smoking during pregnancy has also been reported to reduce the incidence of pre-eclampsia;[116,119] however, this association should be considered in context with the many negative risks associated with smoking during pregnancy. [EL = 2 and 3]

Cohort studies have shown significant associations between maternal cigarette smoking in pregnancy and increased risks of small-for-gestational-age infant,[120] stillbirth[121] and fetal and infant mortality.[122] [EL = 2]

In addition, the link between maternal cigarette smoking and reduced birthweight has been established in over 100 publications based on studies of more than 500 000 births published between 1957 and 1986, with babies born to smokers being a consistent 175–200 g smaller than those born to similar non-smokers.[123] It has been estimated that if all pregnant women stopped smoking, a 10% reduction in infant and fetal deaths would be seen.[122] As smoking is a potentially preventable activity, it is an important public health issue in pregnancy.

Long-term effects on children born to mothers who smoked during pregnancy have been studied but report conflicting results.[124–126] [EL = 3] It is possible that effects of smoking in pregnancy resolve later in childhood.

One review of systematic reviews of RCTs found two systematic reviews and three additional RCTs that assessed the effects of smoking cessation programmes implemented during pregnancy.[127]

The first review (44 trials, $n = 16\,916$ women) found a significant reduction in smoking in late pregnancy among women who attended smoking cessation programmes compared with no programme (Peto OR 0.53, 95% CI 0.47 to 0.60)[112] [EL = 1a] The trials in this review showed substantial clinical heterogeneity; however, the effect was still present when analysis was restricted to trials in which abstinence from smoking was confirmed by means other than self-report (Peto OR 0.53, 95% CI 0.44 to 0.63). A subset of ten trials that included information on fetal outcome showed a reduction in low birthweight (Peto OR 0.8, 95% CI 0.67 to 0.95), a reduction in preterm birth (Peto OR 0.83, 95% CI 0.69 to 0.99) and an increase in mean birthweight of 28 g (95% CI 9 g to 49 g) among women who attended anti-smoking programmes. However, no differences in very low birthweight or perinatal mortality were observed.

The second review (10 RCTs, $n = 4815$ pregnant women) included a trial of physician advice, a trial of advice from a health educator, a trial of group sessions, and seven trials on behavioural therapy based on self-help manuals.[128] Cessation rates ranged from 1.9% to 16.7% among those who did not receive an intervention and from 7.1% to 36.1% among those who participated in an intervention. The review found that cessation programmes significantly increased the rate of quitting (absolute risk increase with intervention versus no intervention 7.6%, 95% CI 4.3 to 10.8). [EL = 1a]

Three additional RCTs compared nicotine patches with placebo, a brief (10–15 minutes) smoking intervention delivered by a midwife compared with usual care ($n = 1120$ pregnant women), and motivational interviewing with usual care ($n = 269$ women in their 28th week of pregnancy). Nicotine patches were not significantly associated with a difference in quit rates.[129] [EL = 1b] Furthermore, the safety of nicotine replacement therapy in pregnancy has not been established. The intervention delivered by midwives was based on a 10–15 minute session in which verbal counselling was backed up with written information and arrangements for continuing self-help support were made, if necessary. This intervention found no difference in smoking behaviour when compared with the women who received usual care.[130] [EL = 1b] The motivational interviewing trial was based on intensified, late pregnancy counselling of 3 to 5 minutes plus the distribution of self-help booklets mailed weekly, and follow-up letters and telephone calls. This trial also reported no difference in cessation rates when compared with women in their 34th week of pregnancy or at 6 months postpartum.[131] [EL = 1b]

An RCT was conducted in three NHS trusts in England.[132] The intervention consisted of giving self-help booklets on quitting smoking to pregnant women at the first opportunity, together with a booklet for partners, family members and friends. Four more booklets were sent to the woman at weekly intervals. The intervention was reported to be ineffective at increasing smoking cessation. [EL = 1b]

Pregnant women who are unable to quit during pregnancy often reduce the number of cigarettes that they smoke. Data indicate this can significantly reduce nicotine concentrations and can offer some measure of protection for the fetus, with a 50% reduction being associated with a 92 g increase in birthweight.[133,134]

The NHS pregnancy smoking telephone helpline is available at 0800 169 9 169.

Recommendations on smoking

At the first contact with the woman, discuss her smoking status, provide information about the risks of smoking to the unborn child and the hazards of exposure to secondhand smoke. Address any concerns she and her partner or family may have about stopping smoking.*

Pregnant women should be informed about the specific risks of smoking during pregnancy (such as the risk of having a baby with low birthweight and preterm birth). The benefits of quitting at any stage should be emphasised.

Offer personalised information, advice and support on how to stop smoking. Encourage pregnant women to use local NHS Stop Smoking Services and the NHS pregnancy smoking helpline, by providing details on when, where and how to access them. Consider visiting pregnant women at home if it is difficult for them to attend specialist services.*

Monitor smoking status and offer smoking cessation advice, encouragement and support throughout the pregnancy and beyond.*

Discuss the risks and benefits of nicotine replacement therapy (NRT) with pregnant women who smoke, particularly those who do not wish to accept the offer of help from the NHS Stop Smoking Service. If a woman expresses a clear wish to receive NRT, use professional judgement when deciding whether to offer a prescription.*

Advise women using nicotine patches to remove them before going to bed.*

This supersedes NICE technology appraisal guidance 39 on NRT and bupropion.*

Women who are unable to quit smoking during pregnancy should be encouraged to reduce smoking. [B]

---

* This recommendation is from the NICE public health guidance on smoking cessation (www.nice.org.uk/PH010). Following NICE protocol, the recommendations have been incorporated verbatim into this guideline.

5.13 Cannabis use in pregnancy

There is limited evidence on the impact of maternal cannabis consumption during pregnancy. Cannabis is often smoked as a mix with tobacco. One of the problems with research into cannabis consumption during pregnancy is accurately measuring the amount of cannabis consumed. Research can also be confounded by factors such as socio-economic status, alcohol use, smoking and the use of other drugs.

An estimated 5% of mothers reported smoking cannabis before and during pregnancy in England.[135] [EL = 3]

A meta-analysis of ten observational studies that were adjusted for cigarette smoking presented data on 32 483 live births.[136] Studies were examined where possible according to an arbitrarily defined dose response. Infrequent use was defined as no greater than once a week, and frequent use was defined as at least four times a week. Where possible, results were presented by gestational age at time of consumption. In the five studies that reported mean birthweight:

- any cannabis use during the first trimester of pregnancy reduced the mean birthweight by 48 g (95% CI −83 g to −14 g)
- any cannabis use during the second trimester of pregnancy reduced the mean birthweight by 39 g (95% CI −75 g to −3 g)
- any cannabis use during the third trimester of pregnancy reduced the mean birthweight by 35 g (95% CI −71 g to 1 g)
- infrequent use of cannabis resulted in an increase in mean birthweight of 62 g (95% CI 8 g to 132 g)
- frequent use of cannabis resulted in a reduction in mean birthweight of 131 g (95% CI −209 g to −52 g).

In the five studies that reported the odds ratio for low birthweight (less than 2500 g), the pooled OR was 1.09 (95% CI 0.94 to 1.27) for any cannabis use during pregnancy.

A study of over 12 000 women in England found no association between any level of cannabis use (weekly, less than weekly, or no cannabis and before, during or after the first trimester) and perinatal death, preterm delivery and admission to the neonatal unit.[135] [EL = 3] After adjustment for confounding (youth, caffeine, alcohol and illicit drug use), no statistically significant association between cannabis use and birthweight was found.

There is insufficient evidence to conclude that maternal cannabis use at the levels reported causes low birthweight. However, a study on behavioural outcomes of children at 3 years of age found increased fearfulness and poorer motor skills among those who were born to mothers who used cannabis during pregnancy.[126] [EL = 3] Taking the precautionary principle based on the positive associations between cannabis use and cigarette smoking, it is recommended that women should be discouraged from using cannabis in pregnancy.

Note
As women who use heroin, cocaine (including crack cocaine), ecstasy, ketamine, amphetamines or other drugs during pregnancy are likely to require additional care due to more adverse effects, these topics were deemed to be outside the remit of this guideline, which is intended for healthy women with uncomplicated singleton pregnancies.

Recommendation

The direct effects of cannabis on the fetus are uncertain but may be harmful. Cannabis use is associated with smoking, which is known to be harmful; therefore women should be discouraged from using cannabis during pregnancy. [C]

5.14 Air travel during pregnancy

No direct estimates of the risk of travel-related venous thromboembolism in pregnancy were located. The overall incidence of symptomatic venous thrombosis after a long-haul flight has been estimated to be around 1/400 to 1/10 000. Asymptomatic venous thrombosis is estimated to be about ten times this figure.[137] [EL = 4] Venous thromboembolism is reported to complicate 0.13/1000 to 1/1000 pregnancies,[137–140] [EL = 3] and it has been suggested that this risk is increased in pregnant women during air travel.[137] [EL = 4]

The risk of venous thromboembolism is attributed predominantly to immobility during air travel. In a trial of 231 passengers randomised to wearing below-knee elastic stockings on both legs compared with passengers who did not wear such stockings, a decreased risk of deep vein thrombosis was observed in the intervention group (OR 0.07, 95% CI 0 to 0.46).[141] [EL = 1b] No evidence on the effectiveness of compression stockings specifically in pregnant women was located. Other precautionary measures for all travellers that pregnant women should be informed about include isometric calf exercises, walking around the aircraft cabin when possible and avoiding dehydration by drinking plenty of water and by minimising alcohol and caffeine intake.[137] [EL = 4]

Commercial flights are normally safe for a pregnant woman and her fetus. However, most airlines restrict the acceptance of pregnant women. In general, uncomplicated singleton pregnancies may fly long distances until the 36th week of gestation and a letter from a doctor or midwife confirming good health, normal pregnancy and the expected date of delivery should be carried after the 28th week of pregnancy.[142] Medical clearance is required by some airlines for pregnant women if delivery is expected less than 4 weeks after the departure date or if any complications in delivery may be expected. As different airlines may have different restrictions, specific airlines should be contacted directly for more information.

Recommendation

Pregnant women should be informed that long-haul air travel is associated with an increased risk of venous thrombosis, although whether or not there is additional risk during pregnancy is unclear. In the general population, wearing correctly fitted compression stockings is effective at reducing the risk. [B]

Future research

Further research to quantify the risk of air travel and to assess the effectiveness of interventions to prevent venous thromboembolism in pregnancy is needed.

5.15 Car travel during pregnancy

From 1997 to 1999, seven pregnant women were killed in road traffic accidents.[143] [EL = 3] Irrespective of where one is sitting in the car, it has been a legal requirement in the UK to wear a seatbelt since 1991 and this law applies to pregnant women.

A 1998 survey on pregnant women's knowledge and use of seatbelts showed that, while 98% of pregnant front-seat passengers wore a seatbelt, only 68% wore one in the back of the car.[144] The survey also found that only 48% of women correctly identified the correct way to use a seatbelt, with only 37% reporting that they had received information on the correct use of seatbelts while pregnant. The women who had received information while pregnant were more likely to correctly position their seatbelts than women who had received no information (OR 0.35, 95% CI 0.17 to 0.70). [EL = 3]

An American study investigating the education of pregnant women on the correct use of seatbelts found that, even with minimal information on wearing a seatbelt, seatbelt use increased from 19.4% to 28.6%.[145] [EL = 2a]

The correct use of seatbelts is particularly important in pregnant women, as incorrect use may cause harm to the fetus and fail to protect the woman in the case of an accident. A retrospective study of 43 pregnant women involved in road traffic accidents showed an increase in adverse fetal outcome, including fetal loss, with improper maternal restraint use compared with women who used seatbelts properly: in minor crashes 33% (2/6) versus 11% (2/18); moderate crashes 100% (1/1) versus 30% (3/10); severe crashes 100% (5/5) versus 100% (3/3).[146] [EL = 3]

In an older study comparing lap-belt restraint with no seatbelt use among 208 pregnant women who were involved in severe rural car accidents, maternal mortality was 3.6% among those wearing a lap belt compared with 7.8% among those not wearing a seatbelt.[147] Total maternal injuries, including death, was 10.7% among women wearing a lap belt compared with 21.1% among those not wearing a seatbelt. Fetal mortality was 16.7% among women wearing a lap belt compared with 14.4% among women not wearing a seatbelt. [EL = 3]

No human studies on the comparison of lap belts compared with three-point seatbelts in pregnant women were located; however, a study in pregnant baboons investigating the use of three-point restraints versus lap belts found a fetal death rate of 8.3 % among animals wearing with a three-point restraint on impact compared with a 50% fetal death rate among animals impacted with lap belts only.[148] [EL = 2a]

A study on pregnancy outcomes in pregnant women drivers found that women who were not wearing seatbelts were 1.9 times more likely to have a low birthweight baby (95% CI 1.2 to 2.9) and 2.3 times more likely to give birth within 48 hours after a motor vehicle crash (95% CI 1.1 to 4.9) when compared with women drivers who were wearing seatbelts (adjusted for age and gestational age at crash).[149] Fetal death was 0.5% (7/1349) in women who did not use seatbelts and 0.2% (2/1243) in women who did use seatbelts. [EL = 3]

The Confidential Enquiry into Maternal Deaths in the United Kingdom provides information on the correct use of seatbelts in pregnancy.[143]

- Above and below the bump, not over it.
- Use three-point seatbelts with the lap strap placed as low as possible beneath the 'bump', lying across the thighs with the diagonal shoulder strap above the bump lying between the breasts.
- Adjust the fit to be as snug as comfortably possible.

Recommendation

Pregnant women should be informed about the correct use of seatbelts (that is, three-point seatbelts 'above and below the bump, not over it'). [B]

5.16   Travelling abroad during pregnancy

Vaccinations

In the event that a pregnant woman is travelling abroad, care must be taken to ensure that any vaccines that are received are not contraindicated in pregnancy. In general, killed or inactivated vaccines, toxoids and polysaccharides can be given during pregnancy, as can oral polio vaccine. Live vaccines are generally contraindicated because of largely theoretical risks to the fetus. Measles, mumps, rubella, BCG and yellow fever vaccines should be avoided in pregnancy.[150]

The risks and benefits of specific vaccines should be examined in each individual case and the advice of a travel medicine doctor should be sought for women considering travel in pregnancy. Table 5.1 summarises the WHO-compiled information on the use of various vaccines in pregnancy.

Yellow fever

Vaccination against yellow fever may be considered after the sixth month of pregnancy when the risk from exposure is deemed greater than the risk to the fetus and pregnant women. Yellow fever is transmitted by mosquitoes and fatality from yellow fever in unimmunised adults is 50%.[151] Women should be informed about the risks of yellow fever and about areas where the risk of exposure to yellow fever is high.[150]

Malaria

Malaria in a pregnant woman increases the risk of maternal death, miscarriage, stillbirth and low birthweight with associated risk of neonatal death and preterm birth.[154,155] [EL = 2a] The risks associated with malaria infection in nonimmune pregnant women include miscarriage in up to 60% of cases and maternal mortality of up to 10%.[156]

As with all travellers, taking precautions against insect bites is an important preventive measure. This includes minimising skin exposure and the use of bed nets. As pregnant women appear to attract twice as many malaria-carrying mosquitoes as women who are not pregnant,[157] [EL = 3] pregnant women should be extra diligent in using measures to protect against mosquito bites, but should take care not to exceed the recommended dosage of insect repellents as the safety of DEET (N,N-diethyl-m-toluamide, now called N,N-diethyl-3-methylbenzamide) has not been established in pregnancy.[154] [EL = 3] One case report was found of a child who was born with mental disability, impaired sensorimotor coordination and craniofacial dysmorphology to a woman who had applied DEET on a daily basis throughout pregnancy in addition to using chloroquine.[158] [EL = 3] One study on the use of permethrin bed nets in pregnancy on the Thai–Burmese border reported no adverse effects on pregnancy or infant outcome but also reported a marginal effect of bed nets on the reduction of malaria compared with no bed nets (reduction seen in one of three test sites, RR 1.67, 95% CI 1.07 to 2.61).[159] [EL = 1b]

Table 5.1 Vaccination in pregnancy[150]

Vaccine	Use in pregnancy	Comments
BCG[a]	No	
Cholera	No[151]	Safety not determined
Hepatitis A	Yes, administer if indicated	Safety not determined
Hepatitis B	Yes, administer if indicated	
Influenza	Yes, administer if indicated	In some circumstances; consult a physician
Japanese encephalitis[b]	No	Safety not determined
Measles[a]	No[c]	
Meningococcal disease	Yes, administer if indicated	Only if significant risk of infection[151]
Mumps[a]	No[c]	
Oral poliomyelitis vaccine	Yes, administer if indicated	
Inactivated poliomyelitis vaccine	Yes, administer if indicated	Normally avoided
Rabies	Yes, administer if indicated	
Rubella[a]	No[c]	
Tetanus/diphtheria	Yes, administer if indicated	
Typhoid Ty21a		Safety not determined
Smallpox	No[152]	
Varicella[a]	No	
Yellow fever[a]	Yes, administer if indicated	Avoid unless at high risk

[a] Live vaccine, to be avoided in pregnancy.

[b] Contrary to the WHO, other reports indicate that the vaccine is both contraindicated in pregnancy and may be administered in pregnancy.[152,153]

[c] Pregnancy should be delayed for 3 months after vaccine given.

The antimalarials chloroquine and proguanil may be given in usual doses in areas where *Plasmodium falciparum* strains of malaria are not resistant. In the case of proguanil, 5 mg of folic acid/day should be given. The manufacturer of mefloquine advises avoidance as a matter of principle but studies of mefloquine in pregnancy (including during the first trimester) have revealed no evidence of harm; it may therefore be considered for travel to chloroquine-resistant areas. Pyrimethamine with dapsone (Maloprim®, GSK) should not be used in pregnancy; the preparation has been discontinued in the UK. Doxycycline is contraindicated during pregnancy. Proguanil hydrochloride with atovaquone (Malarone®, GSK) should be avoided during pregnancy unless there is no suitable alternative.[77]

Travel insurance

Women who will be travelling while pregnant should obtain adequate medical and travel insurance, ensuring in advanced that complications relating to pregnancy are covered, as well as medical care in the case of birth overseas for both the mother and baby. Most insurance companies will cover up to 28 weeks and there are a few that cover to 32 weeks.[160] Insurance companies will generally cover pregnant women, providing that:

- the pregnant woman returns to this country by the time stated
- the pregnant woman has had no antenatal problems that have required treatment, especially if this has entailed a stay in hospital
- the pregnant woman is travelling with the consent of her doctor.[160]

Travel insurance agencies should be contacted directly for more comprehensive information. Pregnant women should compare various policies and read the exclusion clauses carefully before choosing. In some cases, insurance policies will terminate benefit if medical care is sought from medical facilities that are not approved[161] and some policies will cover the mother but will not extend to coverage of the baby if it is born while the woman is travelling.[162] Other policies will not cover medical expenses after a certain gestation date or for specific outcomes of pregnancy, such as miscarriage.[163]

If the pregnant woman is travelling within the European Economic Area (EEA), then she will need an E111 form. This will cover the cost of care in a hospital but it does not cover the cost of transport to get to the hospital or to bring the baby home. If the pregnant women is more than 36 weeks' pregnant or intends to have the baby within the EEA but outside the UK, she needs form E112. The Department of Health International Relations Unit can be contacted to obtain the leaflet *Health Advice for Travellers*, which gives more information. This leaflet may also be available from the local post office or health centre.[160]

Recommendation

Pregnant women should be informed that, if they are planning to travel abroad, they should discuss considerations such as flying, vaccinations and travel insurance with their midwife or doctor. [Good practice point]

6 Management of common symptoms of pregnancy

6.1 Nausea and vomiting in early pregnancy

The causes of nausea and vomiting in pregnancy are not known and, although the rise in human chorionic gonadotrophin (hCG) during pregnancy has been implicated, data about its association are conflicting.[164] Nausea and vomiting occurs more commonly in multiple pregnancies and molar pregnancies.[165] Nausea is the most common gastrointestinal symptom of pregnancy, occurring in 80–85% of all pregnancies during the first trimester, with vomiting an associated complaint in approximately 52% of women.[166,167] [EL = 3] Hyperemesis gravidarum refers to pregnant women in whom fluid and electrolyte disturbances or nutritional deficiency from intractable vomiting develops early in pregnancy. This condition is much less common with an average incidence of 3.5/1000 deliveries 168 and usually requires hospital admission.

The severity of nausea and vomiting varies greatly among pregnant women. The majority of women with nausea and vomiting report symptoms within 8 weeks of their last menstrual period (94%), with over one-third of women (34%) reporting symptoms within 4 weeks of their last menstrual period.[166,167] [EL = 3] Most women (87–91%) report cessation of symptoms by 16–20 weeks of gestation and only 11–18% of women report having nausea and vomiting confined to the mornings.[166,167] [EL = 3]

One systematic review of observational studies found a reduced risk associated with nausea and vomiting and miscarriage (OR 0.36, 95% CI 0.32 to 0.42) and conflicting data regarding reduced risk for perinatal mortality.[165] [EL = 3] No association with nausea and vomiting and teratogenicity has been reported.[169] [EL = 3]

Despite reassurance that nausea and vomiting does not have harmful effects on pregnancy outcomes, nausea and vomiting can severely impact on a pregnant woman's quality of life. Two observational studies have reported on the detrimental impact that nausea and vomiting may have on day-to-day activities, including interfering with household activities, restricting interaction with children, greater use of healthcare resources and time lost off work. [170,171] [EL = 3]

Interventions for nausea and vomiting that do not require prescription include ginger, acupressure and vitamin B. Prescribed treatments for nausea and vomiting include antihistamines and phenothiazines.

Ginger

One RCT of ginger treatment (250 mg four times daily) compared with placebo reported a significant reduction in the severity of nausea and vomiting ($P = 0.014$) and a reduction in episodes of vomiting ($P = 0.021$) after four days in the treatment group.[172] [EL = 1b] No difference in the rates of miscarriage, caesarean section or congenital anomalies was observed between the two groups.

Two systematic reviews on various treatments for nausea and vomiting in pregnancy reported on the results of one RCT of ginger which was a double-blind, placebo-controlled crossover trial of 27 women who were hospitalised for hyperemesis and used ginger (250 mg four times daily).[173,174] [EL = 1b] Both the degree of nausea and number of attacks of vomiting were reduced with the ginger treatment ($P = 0.035$).[174] [EL = 1b]

Another RCT assessed ginger syrup to alleviate nausea and vomiting in pregnancy.[175] The intervention included 1 tablespoon of ginger syrup or placebo in 4 to 8 fluid ounces of water four times daily. Higher improvement on a nausea scale was observed by women in the ginger group and vomiting resolved in 67% of the women in this group by day 6 compared with only 20% in the control group. [EL = 1b]

P6 acupressure

The P6 point (Neiguan) point is located on the volar surface of the forearm approximately three fingerbreadths proximal to the wrist.

Three systematic reviews of RCTs on P6 acupressure for the relief of nausea and vomiting were found.[173,174,176] [EL = 1a] The reviews used different inclusion criteria and each included four or more of seven RCTs. Six out of the seven trials showed a positive effect for stimulation of the P6 pressure point. The seventh trial (n = 161) showed no difference between acupressure and sham acupressure or no treatment.[174,176] [EL = 1a] This trial did not present its data in a form that could be included in a meta-analysis.[173] [EL = 1a]

The review that excluded three of the seven trials did so because they were of crossover design without separate results from the first cross over period being available. A meta-analysis of dichotomised data from two of the trials reported evidence of benefit (Peto OR 0.35, 95% CI 0.23 to 0.54) but the continuous data from a third trial did not (in contrast to the finding in the reviews above).

More recent RCTs have also reported a reduction in symptoms of nausea and vomiting among women with acupressure wristbands compared with women with dummy bands or no treatment at all.[177–180] [EL = 1b] A possible placebo effect with sham acupressure was also reported in two of the studies.[178,180]

The risk of adverse effects of acupressure on pregnancy outcome was assessed in one RCT.[181] No differences in perinatal outcome, congenital abnormalities, pregnancy complications and other infant outcomes were found between the acupressure, sham acupressure or no treatment. [EL = 1b]

Antihistamines (promethazine, prochlorperazine, metoclopramide)

In a meta-analysis of 12 RCTs that included a comparison of antiemetics (antihistamines ± pyridoxine) with placebo or no treatment, there was a significant reduction in nausea in the treated group (Peto OR 0.17, 95% CI 0.13 to 0.21).[173] [EL = 1a] Although the results suggest an increase in drowsiness associated with antihistamines (Peto OR 2.19, 95% CI 1.09 to 4.37),[173] a review of the safety of antihistamines in relation to teratogenicity found no significant increased risk (24 studies, n > 200 000; OR 0.76, 95% CI 0.60 to 0.94).[182] [EL = 2a] Metoclopramide, however, has insufficient data on safety to be recommended as a first-line agent, though no evidence of association with malformations has been reported.[183]

Phenothiazines

One systematic review of three RCTs (n = 389 women) found that phenothiazines reduced nausea or vomiting when compared with placebo (RR 0.31, 95% CI 0.24 to 0.42).[182] [EL = 1a] However, this analysis included different phenothiazines as a group and one of the RCTs recruited women after the first trimester. The bulk of evidence demonstrates no association between teratogenicity and phenothiazines (nine studies, n = 2948; RR 1.03, 95% CI 0.88 to 1.22).[171,182] [EL = 2a and 3]

Pyridoxine (vitamin B6)

RCTs in the two reviews that studied pyridoxine considered doses of 25–75 mg up to three times daily.[173,174] [EL = 1a] Although the review suggests a reduction in nausea, it was not effective in reducing vomiting (Peto OR 0.91, 95% CI 0.60 to 1.38). Although concerns about possible toxicity at high doses have not yet been resolved and it is not recommended for use, one cohort study found no association between pyridoxine and major malformations (n = 1369, RR 1.05, 95% CI 0.60 to 1.84).[182] [EL = 2a] The Committee on Toxicity of Foods has recommended a safe upper limit of 10 milligrams a day for pyridoxine in the UK.

Cyanocobalamin (vitamin B12)

Two RCTs assessed the effect of cyanocobalamin (one trial gave multivitamins containing cyanocobalamin) compared with placebo and found a significant reduction in nausea and vomiting (pooled RR 0.49, 95% CI 0.28 to 0.86).[182] [EL = 1a] No studies assessing the safety of cyanocobalamin were located but this vitamin is thought to play a role in inhibiting malformations associated with neural tube defects.

Summary

Ginger, P6 acupressure and medication with antihistamines reduce the frequency of nausea in early pregnancy. Pyridoxine (vitamin B6) also appears to be effective, although concerns about the toxicity of vitamin B6 remain. Cyanocobalamin (vitamin B12) is also effective in reducing nausea and vomiting, although no data on its safety were located.

Most cases of nausea and vomiting resolve within 16 to 20 weeks with no harm to the pregnancy, prescribed treatment in the first trimester is usually not indicated unless the symptoms are severe and debilitating.[77]

Recommendations

Women should be informed that most cases of nausea and vomiting in pregnancy will resolve spontaneously within 16 to 20 weeks of gestation and that nausea and vomiting are not usually associated with a poor pregnancy outcome. If a woman requests or would like to consider treatment, the following interventions appear to be effective in reducing symptoms [A]:

- nonpharmacological:
  - ginger
  - P6 (wrist) acupressure
- pharmacological:
  - antihistamines

Information about all forms of self-help and nonpharmacological treatments should be made available for pregnant women who have nausea and vomiting. [Good practice point]

Future research

More information on maternal and fetal safety for all interventions for nausea and vomiting in pregnancy (except antihistamines) is needed.

Further research into other nonpharmacological treatments for nausea and vomiting in pregnancy is recommended.

6.2 Heartburn

Heartburn is described as a burning sensation or discomfort felt behind the sternum or throat or both. It may be accompanied by acid regurgitation reaching the throat or the mouth, causing a bitter or sour taste in the mouth. The pathogenesis of heartburn during pregnancy is unclear but may be the consequence of the altered hormonal status interfering with gastric motility, resulting in gastro-oesophageal reflux. It is not associated with adverse outcomes of pregnancy and therefore its treatment is intended to provide relief of symptoms rather than to prevent harm to the fetus or mother. Heartburn should be distinguished from epigastric pain associated with pre-eclampsia. This may be done by checking the woman's blood pressure and urine for proteinuria.

Heartburn is a frequent complaint during pregnancy. One large study involving 607 pregnant women reported an increased frequency of heartburn with gestation, with 22% of women reporting heartburn in the first trimester, 39% in second and 72% in third trimester.[184] [EL = 3] Another study reported a weekly prevalence of 60% from the 31st week of gestation until delivery.[185] [EL = 3] An English study that separated white Europeans from Asian women reported a slightly higher prevalence of 76–87% for white Europeans and 78–81% for Asians.[186] [EL = 3]

Treatment options for heartburn include lifestyle modification, use of antacids or alkali mixtures, H_2 receptor antagonists and proton pump inhibitors, which aim to alleviate symptoms by reducing the acid reflux.

Information on lifestyle modification includes awareness of posture, maintaining upright positions, especially after meals, sleeping in a propped up position and dietary modifications such as small frequent meals, reduction of high-fat foods and gastric irritants such as caffeine. Antacids, which neutralise and bind bile acids, may also be considered for the relief of heartburn. An RCT of antacid treatment compared with placebo found that 80% of women reported relief of heartburn pain within 1 hour compared with 13% from the placebo group.[187] [EL = 1b]

Alginate preparations, such as Gaviscon® (Reckitt and Coleman), reduce reflux by inhibiting the regurgitation of gastric contents. One RCT compared alginate with magnesium trisilicate and both were found to relieve symptoms of heartburn and no differences in the effects of each treatment were reported.[188] [EL = 1b] The manufacturers of Gaviscon® state that it may be taken during pregnancy.[189]

Another RCT compared acid and alkali mixtures with placebo and reported that there was no difference in relief of heartburn symptoms when women were given either the acid or alkali mixtures but better relief was achieved using these rather than using a placebo.[190] [EL = 1b]

H_2 receptor antagonists or blockers, which reduce acid secretion and volume, have also been reported to treat heartburn effectively and safely in pregnant women. Two trials that investigated the effect of ranitidine, an H^2 receptor blocker, given once and twice daily, compared with a placebo found that there was a significant improvement in heartburn symptoms, especially when ranitidine was taken twice daily, morning and afternoon.[191,192] [EL = 1b] H_2 blockers in the first trimester have also been assessed for safety in a cohort of 178 women and no association with fetal malformations was found.[193] [EL = 2a] Nevertheless, the manufacturers of ranitidine and cimetidine advise the avoidance of these products unless essential.[77]

A meta-analysis (five cohort studies, $n = 593$ infants) of the safety of proton pump inhibitors such as omeprazole, which suppress gastric acid secretion also reported no association between exposure to proton pump inhibitors and fetal malformations.[194] [EL = 2a] However, the manufacturer of omeprazole advises caution with its use in pregnancy owing to toxicity shown in animal studies and does not advise its use unless there is no alternative.[77,189]

Recommendations

Women who present with symptoms of heartburn in pregnancy should be offered information regarding lifestyle and diet modification. [Good practice point]

Antacids may be offered to women whose heartburn remains troublesome despite lifestyle and diet modification. [A]

6.3   Constipation

Constipation is the delay in the passage of food residue, associated with painful defecation and abdominal discomfort. Constipation during pregnancy may not only be associated with poor dietary fibre intake but also with rising levels of progesterone causing a reduction in gastric motility and increased gastric transit time.

It is a commonly reported condition during pregnancy that appears to decrease with gestation. One study found that 39% of pregnant women reported symptoms of constipation at 14 weeks of gestation, 30% at 28 weeks and 20% at 36 weeks.[195] [EL = 3] The results of this study, however, may be over-estimates, as routine iron supplementation was recommended for all pregnant women in the UK at the time the study was conducted and iron consumption is associated with constipation.

One systematic review of two RCTs ($n = 215$) randomised women to fibre supplements or nothing.[196] Wheat or bran fibre supplements were significantly more effective in increasing stool frequency (Peto OR 0.18, 95% CI 0.05 to 0.67). When discomfort was not alleviated by fibre supplementation, stimulant laxatives were more effective than bulk-forming laxatives (Peto OR 0.30, 95% CI 0.14 to 0.61). However, significantly more abdominal pain and diarrhoea was observed when stimulants were used and no differences in nausea were reported. [EL = 1a]

No evidence was found for the effectiveness or safety of osmotic laxatives (e.g. lactulose) or softeners for use in pregnancy.

Recommendation

Women who present with constipation in pregnancy should be offered information regarding diet modification, such as bran or wheat fibre supplementation. [A]

6.4 Haemorrhoids

Haemorrhoids are swollen veins around the anus that are characterised by anorectal bleeding, anal pain and anal itching. This is thought to be a result of the prolapse of the anal canal cushions, which play a role in maintaining continence. A low-fibre diet and pregnancy are both precipitating factors for haemorrhoids.

One recent observational study found that 8% of pregnant women experienced haemorrhoidal disease in the last 3 months of pregnancy.[197] [EL = 3]

Treatment for haemorrhoids includes diet modification, creams (such as Anusol-HC®, Kestrel, Anacal®, Sankyo Pharma) oral medication and surgical intervention.

No evidence for the effectiveness or safety of creams used in pregnancy was found. However, the manufacturers of Anusol-HC® and Anacal® state that, 'no epidemiological evidence of adverse effects to the pregnant mother or fetus' has been reported.[189]

One RCT of oral medication or placebo for pregnant women with haemorrhoids found that 84% of women in the treatment group reported an improvement in symptoms compared with 12% in the placebo group, after two weeks. No significant differences in side effects or fetal outcome were reported.[198] [EL = 1b]

In another study of oral flavonoid therapy, 50 pregnant women were treated over three phases.[199] The majority of women reported an improvement in symptoms (bleeding, pain, rectal exudation and rectal discomfort) after 7 days, the first phase of treatment. Six women complained of nausea and vomiting, which resolved over the course of treatment. [EL = 3]

In extreme circumstances, surgical removal of haemorrhoids has been used. In a study where closed haemorrhoidectomy, under local anaesthesia, was performed on 25 women with thrombosed or gangrenous haemorrhoids in the third trimester, 24 women reported immediate pain relief with no resultant fetal complications related to the surgery.[200] [EL = 3] Surgery is rarely considered an appropriate intervention for the pregnant woman since haemorrhoids may resolve after delivery.

Recommendation

In the absence of evidence for the effectiveness of treatments for haemorrhoids in pregnancy, women should be offered information concerning diet modification. If clinical symptoms remain troublesome, standard haemorrhoid creams should be considered. [Good practice point]

6.5 Varicose veins

Varicose veins are caused by the pooling of blood in the surface veins as a result of inefficient valves that would normally prevent blood draining back down the leg. They can occur as blue swollen veins on the calves and inside of the legs, and cause itching and general discomfort. Feet and ankles can also become swollen. They are a common complaint in pregnancy.

One systematic review addressed this issue.[119] Three RCTs of three different treatments in 115 women were included. One RCT investigated external pneumatic intermittent compression and another RCT investigated immersion in water and bed rest in pregnant women with leg oedema. The outcomes studied (leg volume, diuresis, blood pressure) did not appear to be important for the women themselves. In addition, only effects immediately after treatment were studied. The third trial administered rutoside capsules or placebo for 8 weeks in the third trimester, which led to a subjective improvement of symptoms at 36 weeks of gestation (Peto OR 0.30 95% CI 0.12 to 0.77). However, no data were provided on the safety or side effects of the administration of rutosides at this stage of pregnancy.

An RCT published after this review was also located.[201] The efficacy of compression stockings (compression class I and compression class II) in preventing emergent varicose veins during pregnancy was compared with no stockings among 42 women at less then 12 weeks of gestation. Both classes of compression stockings failed to prevent the emergence of varicose veins but more treated women reported improved leg symptoms ($P = 0.045$). [EL = 1b]

Recommendation

Women should be informed that varicose veins are a common symptom of pregnancy that will not cause harm and that compression stockings can improve the symptoms but will not prevent varicose veins from emerging. [A]

6.6 Vaginal discharge

The quality and quantity of vaginal discharge often changes in pregnancy. Women usually produce more discharge during pregnancy. If the discharge has a strong or unpleasant odour, is associated with itch or soreness or associated with pain on passing urine, the woman may have bacterial vaginosis (see Section 10.2), vaginal trichomoniasis or candidiasis. However, vaginal discharge may also be caused by a range of other physiological or pathological conditions such as vulval dermatoses or allergic reactions.

Trichomoniasis, infection with the parasitic protozoan Trichomonas vaginalis, is characterised by green-yellow frothy discharge from the vagina and pain upon urination and is one of the most commonly sexually transmitted infections. A systematic review of RCTs assessed the effects of trichomoniasis and its treatment during pregnancy.[202] Two RCTs were located. Both trials used metronidazole as the treatment intervention. However, the dose used in one trial (2 g, 48 hours apart and repeated after 2 weeks), conducted in the USA, was double the dose used in the other trial, which was conducted in South Africa. Both studies demonstrated high rates of cure (two RCTs, $n = 703$, RR 0.11, 95% CI 0.08 to 0.17) but a higher risk for preterm birth was observed in the treatment group in the US study when compared with the placebo group (RR 1.78, 95% CI 1.19 to 2.66). No significant differences in low birthweight were observed between the two groups in either trial and the South African study also reported no differences in mean birthweight or gestational age when compared with the control group, who received no treatment. Therefore, although trichomoniasis is associated with adverse pregnancy outcomes,[203] the effect of metronidazole for its treatment during pregnancy remains unclear. [EL = 1a]

There is no evidence that vaginal candidiasis (also called thrush), which is caused by the yeast *Candida albicans*, harms the unborn child. One systematic review of ten RCTs assessed the effectiveness of topical treatments for vaginal candidiasis in pregnant women.[204] Meta-analysis showed that imidazoles (miconazole cream and clotrimazole pessaries) were more effective than nystatin pessaries or placebo for symptomatic relief and resolution of persistent candidiasis (five RCTs, $n = 793$, Peto OR 0.21, 95%l 0.16 to 0.29 for nystatin pessaries; one RCT, $n = 100$, Peto OR 0.14, 95% CI 0.06 to 0.31 for placebo). Two RCTs ($n = 91$) also demonstrated that treatment with miconazole or econazole for 1 week was just as effective as treatment for 2 weeks (Peto OR 0.41, 95% CI 0.16 to 1.05). However, treatment for 4 days was not as effective as treatment for 1 week (two RCTs, $n = 81$, Peto OR 11.07, 95% CI 4.21 to 29.15). One RCT ($n = 38$) found that terconazole cream was as effective as clotrimazole cream for treatment of vaginal candidiasis (Peto OR 1.41, 95% CI 0.28 to 7.10). [EL = 1a]

Although one-dose oral treatments for the treatment of vaginal candidiasis are now available, their safety or efficacy in pregnancy has not yet been evaluated.

Recommendations

Women should be informed that an increase in vaginal discharge is a common physiological change that occurs during pregnancy. If this is associated with itch, soreness, offensive smell or pain on passing urine, there maybe an infective cause and investigation should be considered. [Good practice point]

A 1 week course of a topical imidazole is an effective treatment and should be considered for vaginal candidiasis in pregnant women. [A]

The effectiveness and safety of oral treatments for vaginal candidiasis in pregnancy is uncertain and these should not be offered. [Good practice point]

6.7 Backache

The definition of back pain or back discomfort during pregnancy is subjective, due to the nature of this discomfort. The estimated prevalence of backache during pregnancy ranges between 35% and 61%.[205–210] Among these women, 47–60% reported backache first developing during the 5th to 7th months of pregnancy. It was also reported that the symptoms of backache were worse in the evenings. [EL = 3]

Back pain during pregnancy has been attributed to an altered posture due to the increasing weight in the womb and increased laxity of supporting muscles, as a result of the hormone relaxin. Back pain during pregnancy is potentially debilitating, since it can interfere with a woman's daily activities and sleep patterns, particularly during the third trimester.

A systematic review assessed three RCTs to identify the most appropriate interventions for the prevention and treatment of back pain in pregnancy.[211] The three RCTs investigated three types of interventions: water gymnastics compared with no intervention, Ozzlo pillows compared with standard pillows, and acupuncture compared with physiotherapy. [EL = 1a] Women who participated in water gymnastics took less sick leave when compared with women who had no specific intervention (OR 0.38, 95% CI 0.16 to 0.88). In the second trial, Ozzlo pillows, which are hollowed out nest-shaped pillows, were more effective in relieving back pain and improving sleep for women at more than 36 weeks of gestation compared with a standard pillow (OR 0.32, 95% CI 0.18 to 0.58 for backache relief; OR 0.35, 95% CI 0.20 to 0.62 for sleep). In the third RCT, ten acupuncture sessions were rated more helpful when compared with ten group physiotherapy sessions in pregnant women who developed back pain before 32 weeks of pregnancy (OR 6.58, 95% CI 1.00 to 43.16).

Two additional studies not included in the systematic review were identified. One RCT compared the effect of massage therapy with relaxation classes and found that back pain relief scores diminished significantly with the women who had received massage therapy when compared with the women in the relaxation group (n = 26 women, $P < 0.01$)[212] [EL = 1b]

The other study, which was excluded from the systematic review because it was quasi-randomised, was conducted in Sweden and compared three management options for backache. These were: group back-care classes, individual back-care classes and routine antenatal care (control).[213] Women who received either individual or group back-care classes reported an improvement in pelvic or back pain compared with the control group (n = 407, $P < 0.05$). Women who received individual classes also reported a significant improvement in pain relief while those in the control group and those receiving group sessions did not report any pain relief. The group receiving individual training also reported significantly less sick leave ($P < 0.05$) than those in the control group and those who had group training. [EL = 1b]

Another Swedish study compared the effects of a physiotherapy programme (five visits for teaching on anatomy, posture, vocational ergonomics, gymnastics and relaxation) and an exercise programme compared with no specific intervention on 135 pregnant women with backache.[214] This cohort study found a significantly reduced number of sick leave days taken during pregnancy by an average of 24 days per woman ($P < 0.001$). [EL = 2a]

Other interventions identified for the treatment of backache and reported to have a beneficial effect were autotraction, a chiropractic, mechanical treatment for back pain,[215] spinal manipulative therapy,[216] rotational mobilisation exercise[217] and manual joint mobilisation applied to symptomatic vertebral segments.[218] [EL = 3] However, all these studies had problems with study design or the data were derived from a small sample size.

Recommendation

Women should be informed that exercising in water, massage therapy and group or individual back care classes might help to ease backache during pregnancy. [A]

Future research

Although many treatments exist for backache in pregnancy, there is a lack of research evaluating their safety and effectiveness.

6.8 Symphysis pubis dysfunction

Symphysis pubis dysfunction has been described as a collection of signs and symptoms of discomfort and pain in the pelvic area, including pelvic pain radiating to the upper thighs and perineum. Complaints vary from mild discomfort to severe and debilitating pain that can impede mobility.

The reported incidence of symphysis pubis during pregnancy varies in the literature from 0.03% to 3%. In Leeds, a hospital survey of women (n = 248) in whom a diagnosis of symphysis pubis dysfunction had been made, estimated that 1/36 deliveries were associated with symphysis pubis dysfunction either during pregnancy or soon after delivery.[219] Among the respondents (57% response rate), 9% reported that symptoms first occurred in the first trimester, 44% reported symptoms in the second trimester, 45% in the third trimester and 2% during labour or the postnatal period. [EL = 3]

There is little evidence in the literature on which to base clinical practice. No higher levels of evidence than case reports were located on effective therapies for symphysis pubis dysfunction, although the use of elbow crutches, pelvic support and prescribed pain relief have been suggested.[220] [EL = 4] It is important to remember that many medications for pain relief for bones and joints may not be appropriate for use in pregnancy.

Future research

More research on effective treatments for symphysis pubis dysfunction is needed.

6.9 Carpal tunnel syndrome

Carpal tunnel syndrome results from compression of the median nerve within the carpal tunnel in the hand. It is characterised by tingling, burning pain, numbness and a swelling sensation in the hand that may impair sensory and motor function of the hand.

Carpal tunnel syndrome is not an uncommon complaint among pregnant women and estimates of incidence during pregnancy range from 21% to 62%.[221–223] [EL = 3]

Interventions to treat carpal tunnel syndrome include wrist splints[224,225] and wrist splints plus injections of corticosteroid and analgesia.[226] However, case series reports were the highest level of evidence identified that evaluated these therapies and the studies were not of good quality.

Future research

There is a lack of research evaluating effective interventions for carpal tunnel syndrome.

7 Clinical examination of pregnant women

7.1 Measurement of weight and body mass index

A retrospective study of 1092 pregnant women found that, after taking into account maternal gestation, age and smoking habit, weekly weight gain and maternal weight at booking were the only factors that had an association with infant birthweight.[227] Low maternal booking weight (< 51 kg) was the most effective for antenatal detection of small-for-gestational-age infants (positive predictive value 20%). Low average weekly maternal weight gain (< 0.20 kg) had a positive predictive value of 13% for detecting small-for-gestational-age infants (lower than the PPV of 16% for maternal smoking). Weight loss or failure to gain weight over a two-week interval in the third trimester was observed in 46% of all women studied.

The normal range of weight gain during pregnancy varies for each pregnant individual. Based on observational data, total weight gain ranges for healthy pregnant women giving birth to babies between 3 and 4 kg are between 7 and 18 kg.[228] A prospective observational study of 7589 women in their first pregnancy examined the differences in pattern of weight gain according to trimester for women who delivered at term versus preterm.[229] Women who delivered preterm had patterns of weight gain similar to women delivering at term. Underweight status (BMI < 19.8 kg/m²) before pregnancy increased the likelihood of delivering preterm (adjusted OR 1.98, 95% CI 1.33 to 2.98). Inadequate weight gain in the third trimester (defined as < 0.34, 0.35, 0.30 and 0.30 kg/week for underweight, normal weight, overweight and obese women, respectively) increased the risk by a similar magnitude (adjusted OR 1.91, 95% CI 1.40 to 2.61).

Body mass index (BMI) is calculated by taking a person's weight in kilograms (1 kg = 2.2 lbs) and dividing it by the square of their height (weight [kg]/height[m]², 1 in = 2.54 cm). A longitudinal study of 156 healthy pregnant women investigated whether BMI was related to energy intake during pregnancy and whether BMI, energy intake and other factors were related to net weight gain.[230] Women at the highest level of BMI were significantly less often in the high-energy intake category than women at the medium or low level of BMI. Net weight gain during pregnancy was independently influenced by BMI status and energy intake. Women at the highest level of BMI gained significantly less weight from first to third trimester compared with women at the medium or low levels of BMI. The mean birthweight in the three BMI groups did not differ and was not influenced by age, marital status, education, parity or smoking.

Routine weighing to monitor the nutrition of all pregnant women was begun in antenatal clinics in London in 1941.[227] There is a correlation between maternal weight gain and infant birthweight but this is not effective for screening for small size (low birthweight) babies. It is still important to measure maternal weight and height at least once; for example, at first contact, in order to document weight and height distributions in various subgroups of the clinic population. However, measuring maternal weight (or height) routinely during pregnancy should be abandoned as it may produce unnecessary anxiety with no added benefit. The exception is pregnant women in whom nutrition is of concern.

Recommendations

Maternal weight and height should be measured at the first antenatal appointment, and the woman's BMI calculated (weight [kg]/height[m]^2). [B]

Repeated weighing during pregnancy should be confined to circumstances where clinical management is likely to be influenced. [C]

7.2 Breast examination

Breast examination at the first antenatal appointment was traditionally used to determine whether any problems with breastfeeding could be anticipated. In particular, women were examined for the presence of flat or inverted nipples as potential obstacles to breastfeeding so that breast shields or nipple exercises could be prescribed to remedy the situation. However, an RCT examining the effectiveness of breast shields versus no breast shields or nipple exercises (Hoffman's exercises) versus no exercises found that the presence of flat or inverted nipples did not mean that women could not successfully breastfeed.[231] In fact, breast shells reduced the chances of successful breastfeeding and no differences in breastfeeding were found between the two exercise groups. [EL = 1b]

Recommendation

Routine breast examination during antenatal care is not recommended for the promotion of postnatal breastfeeding. [A]

7.3 Pelvic examination

Pelvic examination during pregnancy is used to detect a number of clinical conditions such as anatomical abnormalities and sexually transmitted infections, to evaluate the size of a woman's pelvis (pelvimetry) and to assess the uterine cervix so as to be able to detect signs of cervical incompetence (associated with recurrent mid-trimester miscarriages) or to predict preterm labour (see Section 11.3).

Pelvimetry has been used to predict the need for caesarean section in pregnant women. A systematic review of four RCTs (n = 895) assessed the effects of pelvimetry (x-ray) on method of delivery.[232] Women on whom pelvimetry was performed were more likely to be delivered by caesarean section (Peto OR 2.17, 95% CI 1.63 to 2.88). No differences in the perinatal mortality were found, but the numbers were not large enough to assess this adequately. There were also no differences in asphyxia, admission to neonatal unit, scar dehiscence or blood transfusion reported between the two groups. Although the risk of caesarean section was increased, no increased benefit of pelvimetry to the pregnant woman, fetus or neonate was found.

In an RCT that assessed the relationship between antenatal pelvic examinations and preterm rupture of the membranes (PROM), 175 women were assigned to no examinations and 174 women were assigned to routine digital pelvic examinations commencing at 37 weeks and continuing until delivery.[233] In the group of women who had no pelvic examination, ten women developed PROM (6%) compared with 32 women (18%) from the group of women who were examined weekly. This three-fold increase in the occurrence of PROM among women who had pelvic examinations was significant (P = 0.001). [EL = 1b]

With regard to ovarian cysts, the majority are benign and ovarian cancer is rare in pregnancy: 1/15 000 to 1/32 000 pregnancies.[234] [EL = 3] A study that retrospectively reviewed 11 622 antenatal records found 16 cysts, 14 of which were later detected also at ultrasound examination.[235] In total, 57 ovarian cysts were detected, but 40 were detected only by ultrasound scan. [EL = 3]

Recommendation

Routine antenatal pelvic examination does not accurately assess gestational age, nor does it accurately predict preterm birth or cephalopelvic disproportion. It is not recommended. [B]

7.4 Female genital mutilation

WHO defines female genital mutilation as, 'all procedures that involve partial or total removal of the female external genitalia or other injury to the female genital organs whether for cultural, religious or other non-therapeutic reasons'.[236] It is further classified as follows.

Type I Excision of the prepuce with or without excision of part or all of the clitoris

Type II Excision of the prepuce and clitoris, together with partial or total excision of the labia minora

Type III Excision of part or all of the external genitalia and stitching/narrowing of the vaginal opening (infibulation)

Type IV Unclassified: pricking, piercing or incision of the clitoris or labia; stretching of the clitoris or labia; cauterisation by burning of the clitoris and surrounding tissues; scraping (angury cuts) of the vaginal orifice or cutting (gishiri cuts) of the vagina; introduction of corrosive substances into the vagina to cause bleeding or herbs into the vagina with the aim of tightening or narrowing the vagina; any other procedure that falls under the definition of female genital mutilation given above.

Most of the girls and women who have undergone female genital mutilation live in 28 African countries, although some live in Asia and the Middle East. Prevalence rates at or above 90% are found in Djibouti, Guinea and Somalia, Eritrea, Mali, Sierra Leone and Sudan.[237] They are also increasingly found in Europe, Australia, Canada and the USA, primarily among immigrants from the above countries.[236]

The total number of girls and women who have undergone female genital mutilation, which is also often referred to as 'female circumcision', is estimated to be between 100 and 140 million. Each year, an estimated additional 2 million girls are at risk of undergoing genital mutilation.[236] An estimated 10 000 to 20 000 girls in the UK are thought to have undergone genital mutilation[238] and information on its prevalence among pregnant women in the UK was not located.

Ninety-four percent of referral to specialist African well-woman clinics in the UK is through midwives.[238] Twenty percent of women attending an African well-woman clinic had previously informed their GP that they had undergone genital mutilation because of underlying medical problems. However, it was also reported that some women did not want their GP to know that they had undergone this procedure.[238] In a study of women attending an African well-woman clinic, among pregnant women who required defibulation and were offered it antenatally, 8% (3 out of 39) agreed to the procedure. The rest preferred to be defibulated during the second stage of labour because they would 'rather go through a painful procedure once'.[238]

The reduced vaginal opening affects not only delivery but appears to be the main factor responsible for other obstetric problems caused by genital mutilation, making antenatal assessment, intrapartum vaginal examination or catheterisation difficult or impossible. Inadequate assessments at these times as a result of genital mutilation may compromise mother and fetus physically.[239]

Female genital mutilation type III causes a direct mechanical barrier to delivery; types I, II and IV can produce severe, although perhaps unintentional vulval and vaginal scarring that can act as an obstruction to delivery.[239] In 20 studies (one from the UK and one from the USA), where 75 cases are described, with primary data on second-stage labour, obstruction is described relating to soft-tissue dystocia and many cases of such obstruction are described as being easily overcome by episiotomies.[239]

In a series of African women with genital mutilation in Middlesex, of the 14 primigravid patients, seven had a pinhole introitus or an introitus that would require defibulation for adequate intrapartum care. In all 23 parous women, the introitus was perceived to be adequate for vaginal examination in labour; 13/14 primigravid women had normal vaginal deliveries, although all 13 had episiotomies or perinatal lacerations; 1/14 primigravid women had a caesarean section for obstetric reasons unrelated to the fact that she was infibulated; 14/23 parous women had a normal vaginal delivery, 3/23 had instrumental deliveries and 6/23 were delivered by caesarean section.[240]

Episiotomies and perineal tears are the most common complications reported, with a statistically significant increased episiotomy seen in nulliparous women with female genital mutilation compared with women with no genital mutilation (89% versus 54%).[239] There is also evidence for increased fetal distress and higher Apgar scores among women with female genital mutilation compared with women with no genital mutilation.[239] Evidence that genital mutilation leads to a higher incidence of postpartum haemorrhage, maternal death, fetal death, postpartum genital wound infection and fistulae formulation has also been reported.[239]

In 1985, the UK Parliament passed the Prohibition of Female Circumcision Act, which made female genital mutilation an illegal act punishable by a fine or imprisonment. This includes the repair of the vulva of a woman who has delivered a baby vaginally; i.e., this Act makes it illegal to repair the labia in a way that makes intercourse difficult or impossible.[241]

The management of birth in women with female genital mutilation will be covered more comprehensively in the Intrapartum Care Guideline.

Recommendation

Pregnant women who have had female genital mutilation should be identified early in antenatal care through sensitive enquiry. Antenatal examination will then allow planning of intrapartum care. [C]

7.5   Domestic violence

Domestic violence has been defined as 'Physical, sexual or emotional violence from an adult perpetrator directed towards an adult victim in the context of a close relationship'.[242] Surveys suggest a lifetime prevalence of domestic violence against women of between 25% and 30%, with an annual prevalence of 2% to 12%.[243–246] [EL = 3] Variability in these estimates has been attributed in part to differences in the definitions used.

Pregnancy is a time when abuse may start or escalate.[242,247] In pregnancy, the prevalence of domestic violence has been shown to be as high as 17% in England.[248] [EL = 3] In the last Confidential Enquiries in to Maternal Deaths for the triennia 1997–1999, eight deaths were due to domestic violence.[143] [EL = 3]

Women who experience domestic violence are at increased risk of injury and death, as well as physical, emotional and social problems. During pregnancy, domestic violence can result in direct harm to the pregnancy, such as preterm birth,[249–251] antepartum haemorrhage,[252] and perinatal death,[252] [EL = 3] and also indirect harm through a woman's inability to access antenatal care. As such, domestic violence is a major public health problem and priority. Several professional and governmental bodies recommend 'routine enquiry' about domestic violence for all women; for example, the British Medical Association,[242] the Royal College of Midwives,[253] the Royal College of Obstetricians and Gynaecologists[247] and the Royal College of Psychiatrists.[254]

Two systematic reviews have been published evaluating screening for domestic violence: the availability of screening tools, the acceptability of screening to women and healthcare professionals and the effectiveness of interventions in improving health outcomes for women.[255,256] [EL = 2] Both reviews identified valid screening tools for domestic violence. Screening with a single question was as effective as screening with multiple questions. Screening is likely to increase the number of women identified as experiencing domestic violence. Both reviews reported that screening was acceptable to the majority of women but that acceptance among health professionals was lower. A UK survey of the levels of detection, knowledge and attitudes of healthcare workers to domestic violence found that knowledge about domestic violence as a healthcare issue was poor and that this sometimes resulted in inappropriate referrals to agencies.[257]

Both reviews highlighted that there is insufficient evidence for the effectiveness of intervention in healthcare settings for women identified by screening programmes. Interventions evaluated in these studies included women staying at a shelter, counselling for women, and interventions for the male partner or couple such as counselling. Three of the studies included pregnant women. Both reviews identified the studies as of poorer quality and note that 'surrogate' outcomes rather than substantive health outcomes have been used.

There is a need for additional research to test the effectiveness of interventions on improving health outcomes before recommending routine screening. Healthcare professionals need to be alert to the possibility of domestic violence in women with symptoms or signs of domestic violence.

Further information on domestic violence is offered in the Department of Health publication, *Domestic violence: a resource manual for health care professionals*.[258]

Recommendation

Healthcare professionals need to be alert to the symptoms or signs of domestic violence and women should be given the opportunity to disclose domestic violence in an environment in which they feel secure. [D]

Future research

Although there are effective screening tools and screening for domestic violence has been shown to be acceptable to women, there is insufficient evidence on the effectiveness of interventions in improving health outcomes for women who have been identified. Therefore, evaluation of interventions for domestic violence is urgently needed.

7.6   Psychiatric screening

Depression in the childbearing years is a recognised problem, as are its associated effects on a child's behavioural and cognitive development. From 1997 to 1999, there were approximately 640 000 live births per year in England and Wales. In that same period, the Confidential Enquiries into Maternal Deaths in the UK[143] received reports of 11 deaths during pregnancy related to psychiatric causes. [EL = 3]

An association between antenatal and postnatal depression has been identified. In one systematic review,[259] a strong association between women experiencing antepartum depression and subsequently having postnatal depression was reported. [EL = 3] With regard to the effect of depression on obstetric complications, some investigators conclude that there is no relationship,[260] while others report an association between anxiety and depression with preterm labour (OR 2.1, 95% CI 1.1 to 4.1).[261] [EL = 3]

Babies of mothers who experience antenatal depression are also reported to have higher norepinephrine levels and demonstrate poorer performance on neonatal assessment tests (orientation, reflex, excitability) when compared with babies of mothers who do not experience antenatal depression.[262] [EL = 3]

While the Edinburgh Postnatal Depression Scale (EPDS) has been validated against a 30–60 minute semi-structured psychiatric interview as a tool for screening for antenatal depression.[263] No studies confirming the effective use of the EPDS as a screening tool in practice were located. [EL = 3] Using the EPDS to determine the incidence of antenatal depression, however, identified 24% of pregnant women in one survey as having clinically significant depression.[264] An association between depressive symptoms and socio-demographic status, e.g. no educational qualifications, unmarried, unemployed, was also reported. [EL = 3] In a cohort study that assessed mood during pregnancy and childbirth with the EPDS (*n* = 14 541 women), 13.5% of women scored for probable depression at 32 weeks of pregnancy while 9.1% scored for depression at 8 weeks postpartum.[265] [EL = 3]

An association between antenatal and postnatal depression has been reported in cohort and case–control studies[259] and numerous studies assessing antenatal prevention of postnatal depression have been conducted. Using antenatal screening as a predictor for postnatal depression, a systematic review of 16 studies found that the two largest studies predicted 16% and 52% of the women would develop postnatal depression but only 35% and 8% of women, respectively, actually developed depression after birth.[266] [EL = 3] In an RCT assessing the impact of an antenatal education programme on postnatal depression, no difference in reduction of depression scores was found between the intervention and control groups.[267] [EL = 1b]

In another RCT, the benefits of providing a 'preparing for parenthood' course versus routine antenatal care for the prevention of postnatal depression were investigated.[268] Among 209 women screened to be at risk of developing postnatal depression, no reduction in the rates of postnatal depression were observed when the intervention group was compared with the control group (OR 1.22, 95% CI 0.63 to 2.39). [EL = 1b] Thus, assessment of antenatal screening for the detection of postnatal depression has poor sensitivity and educational antenatal interventions do not appear to reduce postnatal depression.

However, while antenatal assessment for the detection of postnatal depression appears to have poor sensitivity in the general population, this is not the case among women with previous episodes of puerperal illness. Among these women, there is a 1/2 or 1/3 chance of recurrence and these are also the women who are at higher risk for suicide.[143] Therefore, sensitive questioning of pregnant women about previous or current mental illness is warranted for the identification of this subgroup of women. [EL = 3]

Recommendations on mental health screening

In all communications (including initial referral) with maternity services, healthcare professionals should include information on any relevant history of mental disorder.*

At a woman's first contact with services in both the antenatal and the postnatal periods, healthcare professionals (including midwives, obstetricians, health visitors and GPs) should ask about:

- past or present severe mental illness including schizophrenia, bipolar disorder, psychosis in the postnatal period and severe depression
- previous treatment by a psychiatrist/specialist mental health team, including inpatient care
- a family history of perinatal mental illness.

Other specific predictors, such as poor relationships with her partner, should not be used for the routine prediction of the development of a mental disorder.*

At a woman's first contact with primary care, at her booking visit and postnatally (usually at 4 to 6 weeks and 3 to 4 months), healthcare professionals (including midwives, obstetricians, health visitors and GPs) should ask two questions to identify possible depression.

- During the past month, have you often been bothered by feeling down, depressed or hopeless?
- During the past month, have you often been bothered by having little interest or pleasure in doing things?

A third question should be considered if the woman answers 'yes' to either of the initial questions.

- Is this something you feel you need or want help with?*

After identifying a possible mental disorder in a woman during pregnancy or the postnatal period, further assessment should be considered, in consultation with colleagues if necessary.

- If the healthcare professional or the woman has significant concerns, the woman should normally be referred for further assessment to her GP.
- If the woman has, or is suspected to have, a severe mental illness (for example, bipolar disorder or schizophrenia), she should be referred to a specialist mental health service, including, if appropriate, a specialist perinatal mental health service. This should be discussed with the woman and preferably with her GP.
- The woman's GP should be informed in all cases in which a possible current mental disorder or a history of significant mental disorder is detected, even if no further assessment or referral is made.*

---

* This recommendation is from the NICE clinical guideline on antenatal and postnatal mental health (see www.nice.org.uk/CG045). Following NICE protocol, the recommendation has been incorporated verbatim into this guideline.

2008 update

8 Screening for haematological problems

8.1 Anaemia

The most common cause of anaemia in pregnancy worldwide is iron deficiency. Maternal iron requirements increase in pregnancy because of the requirements of the fetus and placenta and the increase in maternal red cell mass. Iron absorption increases to meet this increased demand. In normal pregnancy, maternal plasma volume increases by up to 50% and the red cell mass gradually increases by about 20%. Hence, the haemoglobin (Hb) concentration drops. This normal physiological response may resemble iron deficiency anaemia.[269]

The haemoglobin level, which defines anaemia, is controversial and lacks consistency across studies, although most studies report 11 g/100 ml to 12 g/100 ml to be the mean minimum haemoglobin concentration in pregnancy. Because haemoglobin levels vary depending upon the time of gestation, it is recommended that levels are checked against a gestation-sensitive threshold. In the UK, the normal range of haemoglobin in pregnant women up to 12 weeks should be at or above 11 g/100 ml and 10.5 g/100 ml at 28 to 30 weeks of gestation.[270]

Low haemoglobin values such as those between 8.5 g/100 ml and 10.5 g/100 ml may be associated with reduced risks of low birthweight and preterm labour.[271] [EL = 3] Increased risks of poor fetal outcome are associated with particularly low and very high levels of haemoglobin.[271,272] [EL = 3]

In order to correctly diagnose iron deficiency anaemia, the impact of gestational age on the change in plasma volume must be considered. Because of the diverse pathogenesis of anaemia (e.g., iron deficiency anaemia, thalassaemia, sickle cell anaemia) the use of haemoglobin as the sole means of diagnosing anaemia is not a sensitive test although this is often used as the first indicator in clinical practice. When there is a suspicion of iron deficiency, more sensitive and specific tests should be considered. Serum ferritin is the most sensitive single screening test to detect adequate iron stores. Using a cut-off of 30 micrograms/litre a sensitivity of 90% has been reported.[273]

Routine iron supplements for women with normal haemoglobin levels

A systematic review of 20 RCTs compared iron supplementation with either placebo or no iron in pregnant women with normal haemoglobin levels (> 10 g/100 ml) at less than 28 weeks of gestation.[76] [EL = 1a] Routine iron supplementation raised or maintained the serum ferritin level above 10 micrograms/litre (Peto OR 0.12, 95% CI 0.08 to 0.17) and resulted in a substantial reduction in women with a haemoglobin level below 10 g/100 ml or 10.5 g/100 ml in late pregnancy (Peto OR 0.15, 95% CI 0.11 to 0.20). There was no evidence of any beneficial or harmful effects on maternal or fetal outcomes. One trial of routine versus selective iron supplementation included in this review showed a reduced likelihood of caesarean section and postpartum blood transfusion, but there were more perinatal deaths in the routinely supplemented group.[76] [EL = 1b]

Another systematic review looked at the effects of routine iron and folate supplements on pregnant women with normal levels of haemoglobin.[74] [EL = 1a] Eight trials involving 5449 women were included. Routine supplementation with iron and folate raised or maintained the serum iron and ferritin levels and serum and red cell folate levels. It also resulted in a substantial reduction of women with a haemoglobin level below 10 g/100 ml or 10.5 g/100 ml in late pregnancy (Peto OR 0.19, 95% CI 0.13 to 0.27). However, routine supplementation with iron and folate had no detectable effects, either beneficial or harmful, on rates of caesarean section, preterm delivery, low birthweight, admission to neonatal unit or stillbirth and neonatal deaths.

Effect of iron supplementation for iron deficiency in pregnancy

A third review assessed the effectiveness of different treatments (oral, intramuscular and intravenous) for iron deficiency anaemia in pregnancy (defined as haemoglobin less than 11 g/100 ml) on maternal and neonatal morbidity and mortality. Five trials randomising 1234 women were included. The author concluded that the evidence was inconclusive on the effects of treating iron deficiency anaemia in pregnancy because of the lack of good-quality trials. There is an absence of evidence to indicate the timing of, and who should be receiving, iron supplementation during pregnancy.[274] [EL = 1a]

Recommendations

Pregnant women should be offered screening for anaemia. Screening should take place early in pregnancy (at the booking appointment) and at 28 weeks, when other blood screening tests are being performed. This allows enough time for treatment if anaemia is detected. [B]

Haemoglobin levels outside the normal UK range for pregnancy (that is, 11 g/100 ml at first contact and 10.5 g/100 ml at 28 weeks) should be investigated and iron supplementation considered if indicated. [A]

8.2 Blood grouping and red cell alloantibodies

Identifying blood group, rhesus D status and red cell antibodies in pregnant women is important to prevent haemolytic disease of the newborn (HDN) and to identify possible transfusion problems. 15% of women are rhesus D-negative. It is important to ascertain maternal rhesus D status so that rhesus D-negative women can be offered appropriate antenatal and postnatal immunoprophylaxis with the aim of preventing rhesus D alloimmunisation in subsequent pregnancies.

The reasons for identifying other red cell antibodies in pregnant women are the prevention of haemolytic disease of the newborn, which may cause jaundice, severe anaemia, heart failure and death, and for the identification of possible transfusion problems. These can occur in rhesus D-positive and -negative women. A significant number of women will have red cell antibodies.[285] The main antibodies that can cause severe alloimmune anaemia in the fetus are anti-D, anti-c and anti-Kell. Of lesser importance but still with the potential to cause HDN are anti-e, -Ce, -Fya, -Jka and-Cw. Anti-Lea, -Leb, -Lua, -P, -N, -Xga and high-titre low-avidity antibodies such as anti-Kna have not been associated with HDN.[286] There is no value in identifying group O pregnant women with high titres of anti-A or anti-B. Antenatal testing for these antibodies has been shown to have no value in predicting the incidence of HDN caused by ABO incompatibility.[287,288]

Antibody screening should be undertaken using an indirect antiglobulin test and a red cell panel conforming to current UK guidelines.[285]

Two Swedish surveys of red cell antibody screening in similar populations used different testing schedules and both concluded that their particular schedule detected all women at risk of HDN, yet one tested once only in early pregnancy[289] and the other tested rhesus D-positive women twice in pregnancy and rhesus D-negative women three times in pregnancy.[290]

Routine antenatal serological testing has been practised throughout the UK for about 30 years. There are currently recommendations that all women should be tested as early in pregnancy as possible, usually at 8 to 12 weeks of gestation.[291] This initial testing should include ABO and rhesus D typing as well as a screening test to detect any irregular red cell antibodies. Testing should be undertaken again at 28 weeks of gestation for all women with no antibodies on initial testing to ensure that no additional antibodies have developed.[291] No RCTs of different testing schedules were found.

When an antibody is detected, the clinician responsible for the woman's antenatal care must be informed of its likely significance, with respect to both the development of HDN and transfusion problems. Management of pregnancies in which red cell antibodies are detected varies depending upon the clinical significance and titre of the antibody detected.

Guidance on the routine administration of antenatal anti-D prophylaxis for rhesus D-negative women has been recently issued, which recommends that anti-D is offered to all pregnant women who are rhesus D-negative.[292] However, in the case where a woman is rhesus D-negative, consideration should also be given to offering partner testing because, if the biological father of the fetus is negative as well, anti-D prophylaxis, which is a blood product, will not need to be administered. Other situations where antenatal anti-D prophylaxis may not be necessary include cases where a woman has opted to be sterilised after the birth of the baby or when a woman is otherwise certain that she will not have another child after the current pregnancy.

Recommendations

Women should be offered testing for blood group and rhesus D status in early pregnancy. [B]

It is recommended that routine antenatal anti-D prophylaxis is offered to all non-sensitised pregnant women who are rhesus D-negative.* [NICE 2002]

Women should be screened for atypical red cell alloantibodies in early pregnancy and again at 28 weeks, regardless of their rhesus D status. [B]

Pregnant women with clinically significant atypical red cell alloantibodies should be offered referral to a specialist centre for further investigation and advice on subsequent antenatal management. [D]

If a pregnant woman is rhesus D-negative, consideration should be given to offering partner testing to determine whether the administration of anti-D prophylaxis is necessary. [Good practice point]

8.3 Screening for haemoglobinopathies (sickle cell disease and thalassaemia)

8.3.1 Introduction and background

Haemoglobin is a substance in red blood cells which binds to oxygen, allowing oxygen to be transported in the circulation around the body and then released into body tissues that require it. Normal adult haemoglobin has four globin chains each associated with one haem part: two of these globin chains are alpha and the other two may be beta (in which case the haemoglobin type is called Hb-A; 96% of adult haemoglobin), delta (HbA$_2$; 3.5%) or gamma (Hb-F; less than 1%). In the developing baby, all haemoglobin is Hb-F type but this is slowly replaced by adult haemoglobin in the first 6 months after birth.

Sickle cell disease and thalassaemia are the two most common types of haemoglobin disorders in the UK. They are inherited as an autosomal recessive disorder, meaning that they must be inherited through both parents, who may have the disorder themselves or may be carriers.

Sickle cell disease
In the most common type of sickle cell disease in the UK, the structure of the beta globin chain is abnormal and known as sickle haemoglobin (Hb-S). A person inheriting one sickle cell gene is a carrier without the disease (sometimes known as sickle cell 'trait'). Someone who has inherited copies of the sickle cell gene from both parents has sickle cell disease.

In low oxygen environments, for example during exercise, at high altitude or during stress, the sickle haemoglobin causes red blood cells to change shape and clump, blocking small blood vessels (sickle crisis) causing tissues to be starved of oxygen. A sickle crisis is usually associated with severe pain. Effects of sickling include stroke, low immunity to infection, lung problems and chronic disorders of the hip or kidneys. Abnormal red blood cells are also removed from the circulation resulting in anaemia. Deaths occur as a result of sickle cell disease each year (0.5% of affected). There is no cure and treatment includes antibiotics, oxygen and painkillers which need to be taken for life. New treatments, such as bone marrow transplant and gene therapy, may become lower risk and available in the future.

---

* The technology appraisal guidance 'Guidance on the use of routine antenatal anti-D prophylaxis for RhD-negative women' (NICE technology appraisal 41) is being updated and is expected to be published in June 2008.

In England, there are estimated to be 240 000 healthy carriers of sickle cell[1000] and an additional 12 500 people living with sickle cell disease.[1016] Each year about 300 babies with sickle cell disease are detected by the universal screening programme for England, giving a birth prevalence of approximately 1 : 2000. In addition, 8500 newborn carriers of a sickle cell variant (S, C, D, E) are identified by the programme each year while thalassaemia carriers cannot be identified. The prevalence of sickle cell disease is highest among black African people followed by black Caribbean people.

Thalassaemia

In thalassaemia, the production of alpha and non-alpha globin chains is not balanced, causing a reduction in mean corpuscular volume (MCV) and mean corpuscular haemoglobin (MCH), and in some cases anaemia and a characteristic blood film. There are two common types of thalassaemia: alpha-thalassaemia in which too few alpha chains are produced, and beta-thalassaemia in which too few beta-chains are produced.

In alpha-thalassaemia, trait inheritance of mutations in one or two of the four alpha genes results in the production of a reduced amount of alpha globin. Carriers usually have a mild anaemia with microcytic hypochromic indices (reduced MCV and MCH) and sometimes a characteristic blood film. If three abnormal alpha genes are inherited this is known as HbH disease, which is a clinically mild disorder commonly characterised by anaemia, a characteristic blood film and splenomegaly. If an unborn child inherits no functioning alpha genes then no alpha globin is produced – this is alpha-thalassaemia major and is not compatible with life.

One beta-thalassaemia gene may be inherited, resulting in carrier (sometimes called beta-thalassaemia minor), or no beta-thalassaemia genes are inherited, resulting in a severe disease (beta-thalassaemia major). In beta-thalassaemia minor, HbA_2 comprises more than 3.5% of adult haemoglobin. A carrier does not have the disease but may pass on the abnormal gene. Beta-thalassaemia major is a severe anaemia which, without treatment, can lead to death of children between 1 and 2 years of age. The bone marrow and spleen enlarge as they try to replace damaged red blood cells but there is damage to other organs in the long term, including skeletal deformity, diabetes, heart failure and liver cirrhosis. Most patients have lifelong treatments of regular blood transfusion and then iron chelation (to bind the extra iron and remove it from the body) several times a week. An affected person may live to 50–70 years of age with such treatment. Bone marrow transplantation is an option if a suitable donor is available, and gene therapy may become an option in the future. In England, there are estimated to be 150 000 healthy carriers of beta-thalassaemia and an additional 700 people who are affected by beta-thalassaemia major. Each year, around 2800 babies are born who are carriers and 17 babies who have beta-thalassaemia major (although a greater number of pregnancies are affected). Beta-thalassaemia is most common in Cypriot, Pakistani, Bangladeshi, Indian and Chinese communities in the UK.

NHS Sickle Cell and Thalassaemia Screening Programme

The NHS Sickle Cell and Thalassaemia Screening Programme is a linked programme of newborn screening for sickle cell disease and antenatal screening for both sickle cell and thalassaemia diseases in England.

Newborn screening for sickle cell disease is now an integral part of the newborn bloodspot screening programme. The aim of newborn screening is to identify babies with sickle cell disease at an early age so that they can receive treatment to prevent or reduce the long-term effects of sickle cell disease.

Antenatal screening for sickle cell and thalassaemia has been implemented in phases by the National Screening Committee. The aim of the programme is stated as being to offer timely antenatal sickle cell and thalassaemia screening to all women (and couples) to facilitate informed decision making (the offer includes: the offer of, uptake of, and reporting of results of prenatal diagnosis and any subsequent action by the end of 12 weeks of pregnancy). Specific objectives include: to accurately diagnose women and couples with genotypes specified as requiring further investigation, and to accurately diagnose specified conditions where prenatal diagnosis is undertaken (and by implication not others which are not clinically significant). For further information see www.sickleandthal.org.uk/Documents/ProgrammeSTAN.pdf. The screening service offered varies depending on whether an area is considered to have a high prevalence

2008 update

(sickle cell affecting more than 1.5 per 10 000 pregnancies) or low prevalence (affecting less than or equal to 1.5 per 10 000 pregnancies) of these conditions. The National Screening Committee policy states that the form of screening for haemoglobin variants will depend on the prevalence of the condition. Universal laboratory screening was to be offered in those trusts identified as covering high-prevalence populations by the end of 2004/05. All other areas were to be required to offer, as a minimum, laboratory testing for variants based on an assessment of risk determined by a question to women about their family origin by the end of 2005/06. This national screening programme is being rolled out across England and Wales at present. All high-prevalence areas have implemented screening using laboratory methods. In low-prevalence areas approximately 93% or 80 of the 86 trusts have implemented the screening programme as described above, and all are expected to have implemented by the end of August 2008 (figures provided by the NHS Sickle Cell and Thalassaemia Screening Programme, March 2008; www.sickleandthal.org. uk/Documents/LowPrevTrusts.pdf).

Laboratory tests for sickle cell disease and thalassaemia
There are several tests which may be used in laboratory screening for thalassaemia or sickle cell disease and an explanation of those most commonly used in the UK are given below:

- full blood count:
  - red blood cell indices – a series of tests on red blood cells (performed as part of the full blood count which is offered to all pregnant women)
  - haemoglobin – the level of haemoglobin in the blood; this is low in anaemia owing to iron deficiency or haemoglobinopathy
  - mean corpuscular volume (MCV) – average volume of a red blood cell (measured as one of the red blood cell indices on the full blood count); this is low in thalassaemia
  - mean corpuscular haemoglobin (MCH) – average haemoglobin level per red blood cell; this is low in thalassaemia
- additional tests:
  - ferritin test – this is a test performed on blood which is low if the anaemia is due to iron deficiency
  - electrophoresis – a non-automated test which separates the haemoglobin types present in a sample of blood
  - high-performance liquid chromatography (HPLC) – an automated test which separates the haemoglobin types present in a sample of blood
  - sickle cell solubility test – a test which can be used to confirm the presence of sickle haemoglobin in the blood.

The screening process involves testing a woman for carrier status early in pregnancy and then testing her partner if she is proven to be a carrier. If both parents are confirmed as carriers, DNA analysis may be undertaken to confirm this. The unborn baby is tested using amniocentesis or chorionic villus sampling. The aim of antenatal testing for haemoglobin disorders is to inform parents and provide them with the option of pregnancy termination at an early stage of pregnancy if their child has a serious haemoglobin disorder.

8.3.2 Screening for haemoglobinopathies – health economics evidence summary

A systematic search of the literature identified 53 studies potentially related to the clinical questions. The abstracts of all papers were reviewed, and 16 articles were retrieved and critically appraised. Four papers met the inclusion criteria; one study was conducted in the USA, one in Canada and two in the UK.

A Canadian study[710] evaluated the cost-effectiveness of a thalassaemia disease prevention programme through screening and prenatal diagnosis of thalassaemia. The programme screened 80% of at-risk couples and prevented two-thirds of cases in the period of the study. The comparison between the costs of prevention versus the cost of treatment showed that the total direct cost per case prevented in the programme (carrier screening/fetoscopy: $6,754; carrier screening/DNA analysis: $6,638) is less than the cost for a single year of treatment for an individual with the disease ($7,057). Costs are in 1981 Canadian dollars.

A US study[711] was designed to evaluate the diagnostic ability of two different haemoglobinopathy screening protocols to identify at-risk pregnancies. The main comparison was between universal and selective use of Hb electrophoresis, where the selective screening involved the use of Hb electrophoresis following sickle cell solubility testing and investigation of red blood cell (RBC) indices. Using a retrospective chart review of all patients registering for prenatal care at the New York Hospital/Cornell Medical Center prenatal clinic, the study showed that the selective protocol would not diagnose four patients as carriers of a haemoglobinopathy and would save $11,384, or $18 per patient (1986 US dollars), compared with the universal protocol. In this study, universal Hb electrophoresis did not identify any additional pregnancies at risk for clinically significant haemoglobinopathy, although it did identify carriers who would not have been spotted by a selective protocol. The authors concluded that the relative costs of different screening strategies and the frequency of carriers in the population must be taken into account when instituting a protocol for haemoglobinopathy screening.

One UK study[712] compared the cost and potential benefits of universal testing for variant haemoglobins and beta-thalassaemia carrier status using HPLC and the costs and potential benefits of universal testing for beta-thalassaemia carrier status using the MCH as a screening test and less automated techniques than HPLC for definitive diagnosis. The universal testing strategy did not identify any additional cases of beta-thalassaemia carrier compared with the universal screening and selective testing strategy. Six patients were found to have an HbA_2 variant using universal testing; this can interfere in the diagnosis of beta-thalassaemia carrier status. The universal testing policy cost between £57 and £198 more than the universal screening and selective testing policy. Costs are for the year 1998. The authors argued that introducing a universal testing strategy into British laboratories could be cost neutral, though they believe that in practice this would be unlikely.

Another UK study[713] assessed the cost-effectiveness of antenatal haemoglobinopathy screening and follow-up in a community programme in terms of the costs of providing full genetic choice to women and couples, and the cost per significant haemoglobinopathy averted. The total savings to the programme as a result of cases averted, which included savings from the averted lifetime treatment costs for affected births, was estimated at £61,000. Also reported were the costs of identifying a woman with abnormal haemoglobinopathy (£209), the cost of identifying an at-risk fetus prior to prenatal diagnosis (£2,455) and the cost of providing genetic information and counselling (£109). Costs are for the year 1999. The analysis showed that antenatal screening with follow-up counselling can be self-financing at most levels of prevalence of thalassaemia.

Previous NICE guidance (for the updated recommendations see below)

Future research:
The effectiveness and costs of an ethnic question for antenatal screening for sickle cell and thalassaemia is needed.

The effectiveness and costs of laboratory methods for antenatal screening for sickle cell and thalassaemia is needed.

Health economics evidence statement
All the published economic evidence in this clinical area was focused on the cost-effectiveness of antenatal screening for haemoglobinopathies by comparing the relative costs of prevention of births affected by disease and the potential cost of treatment for an affected birth. The conclusion drawn from these studies was that screening and prevention of affected births was likely to produce cost savings in the healthcare system and would therefore be cost-effective. This result would be more pronounced in areas with a large ethnic minority population and in these areas universal antenatal screening would be cost-effective given the higher disease prevalence.

8.3.3 Thalassaemia screening

Clinical question
What is the diagnostic value and effectiveness of the following screening methods in identifying clinically significant thalassaemia and thalassaemia carrier status (trait)?

- history
- family origin
- full blood count

- Hb electrophoresis
- ferritin
- mean cell volume
- HbA_2 estimation
- mean cell haemoglobin.

Thalassaemias include: beta-thalassaemia intermedia, HbS/beta-thalassaemia.

Thalassaemia carrier status (trait) includes: beta-thalassaemia carrier status, beta-thalassaemia carrier status, HbE carrier status.

Population includes women and their partners, antenatally and preconceptionally.

Accuracy of screening for thalassaemia using red blood cell indices

Description of included studies
Six studies were identified for inclusion in this review.

A UK diagnostic case–control study (1995)[714] was conducted to compare the suitability of MCV and MCH for thalassaemia screening, and to determine the correct cut-off points for these indices. [EL = III] The study was conducted in a UK hospital where all women booking with a first pregnancy were screened for haemoglobinopathy and full blood counts (FBCs) performed to determine the MCV and MCH. The 2.5 percentiles derived from a sample of healthy non-pregnant women were used as cut-off points for MCV (85 fl) and MCH (27 pg). A diagnosis of beta-thalassaemia carrier status was made if the HbA_2 was greater than 3.5%.

Earlier work carried out in the UK (1988)[715] investigated cut-off points for MCV and MCH in screening for thalassaemia, again comparing red blood cell indices obtained at booking with Hb electrophoresis and HbA_2 estimation. [EL = III] . The cut-off points for the red blood cell indices in this study were set at MCV < 83 fl and MCH < 27.1 pg.

The accuracy of MCV in screening for thalassaemia carrier status has been tested in Thailand (2005),[716] where thalassaemia is the most common hereditary disease. [EL = III] A sample of 439 pregnant women had blood samples taken and their MCV, HbA_2 level and polymerase chain reaction (PCR) measured to test for beta-thalassaemia carrier status and the alpha-thalassaemia-1 gene respectively. A cut-off MCV < 80 fl was used.

A study carried out in Hong Kong (1985)[717] investigated the accuracy of MCV followed by HbA_2 estimation with that of MCV plus ferritin and Hb level followed by HbA_2 estimation. [EL = III] Pregnant women of < 24 weeks of gestation ($n = 299$) had blood tests performed to estimate their Hb level, MCV, HbA_2 and plasma ferritin levels. These values were compared against locally ascertained standards for women with normal haemoglobin. Women with an MCV < 80 fl level and a normal HbA_2 who were found to be iron deficient were given oral iron therapy and blood tests were repeated 4 weeks later.

An antenatal screening programme carried out in Hong Kong has also been described.[718] [EL = III] Over an 11 year period 25 834 women were screened for thalassaemia by MCV at booking. A cut-off of MCV ≤ 75 fl was used. A similar antenatal screening programme in Singapore (1994)[719] reported findings using a cut-off of MCV < 80 fl. [EL = III] Following confirmation of a low MCV, confirmatory tests for haemoglobinopathies were carried out (blood film, electrophoresis and estimation of levels of HbA_2/HbE and HbF).

Findings
Findings from the UK case–control study [714] showed that over a 2 year period 857 women were identified with either an MCV < 85 fl or an MCH < 27 pg but did not have a haemoglobinopathy. Of these women, 784 had microcytic red cells, 606 had both an MCV < 85 fl and an MCH < 27 pg, and 56 (6.5%) were beta-thalassaemia carriers. Of the remaining 251 women, none were carriers of beta-thalassaemia. Selection of the MCH rather than the MCV for screening purposes would have resulted in a 25% reduction in the number of women requiring HbA_2 estimation, and at a cut-off of MCH < 27 pg would have identified all cases of beta-thalassaemia carrier status. Further tests regarding storage of samples showed that the MCH is also more stable at room temperature compared with the MCV.

2008 update

The earlier UK case-series[715] identified 696 women with an MCV at booking of less than 83 fl. These women went on to have further screening. In 96 (13.8%) women the Hb electrophoresis showed an abnormal haemoglobin. In the other 600 women an HbA_2 estimation indicated a further 56 women with beta-thalassaemia carrier status (8% of total group screened). All MCH values for women with beta-thalassaemia carrier status fell below the cut-off point of 27.1 pg, with the highest MCH being 25.9 pg. If a cut-off of 26 pg had been chosen, all women carrying beta-thalassaemia would have been identified, with a 29% decrease in workload.

Findings from the research conducted in Thailand[716] showed that a cut-off of MCV < 80 fl as a screen for alpha- and beta-thalassaemia carrier status has a sensitivity of 92.9% (39/42) (95% CI 83.7% to 96.4%) and a specificity of 83.9% (333/397) (95% CI 80.8% to 87.6%). The positive predictive value was 37.9% (39/103) (95% CI 33.8% to 42.7%) and the negative predictive value 99.1% (333/336) (95% CI 98.2% to 99.9%). It should be noted that these figures are population-specific as prevalence affects the positive and negative predictive values of the test, and consequently their cost-effectiveness.

Findings from the control groups in the Hong Kong case–control study gave the following cut-off points for red blood cell indices: an HbA_2 > 4.5% was taken to be diagnostic of beta-thalassaemia carrier status; 8 ng/ml was taken as the lower limit for a normal ferritin level; and the MCV cut-off point was 80 fl. Eighteen of the 299 women in the study sample (6%) had HbA_2 levels > 4.5% and were diagnosed to be carrying beta-thalassaemia. All of these 18 women had an MCV < 75 fl (in 15 the MCV was < 70 fl). Forty-nine women had an MCV < 80 fl, and of these women 18 had low ferritin levels (< 8 ng/ml). Two of these women had HbA_2 levels over 4.5% and were diagnosed to be carrying beta-thalassaemia with iron deficiency. Sixteen women had low ferritin levels and normal HbA_2 estimation and were assumed to be iron deficient. Thirty-seven women were found to have Hb levels < 10 g/100 ml. They included nine beta-thalassaemia carriers, 19 women with iron deficiency and nine presumed alpha-thalassaemia carriers. The detection rate of beta-thalassaemia carriers was investigated for different cut-off levels. At a cut-off of MCV < 80 fl all beta-thalassaemia carriers were detected and the false positive rate was 63%. At a cut-off level of MCV < 75 fl the detection rate remained 100% and the false positive rate decreased to 47%. At a cut-off of < 70 fl the specificity of the test increased to 97% with a sensitivity of 83% and false negative rate of 16%. The study was repeated with a larger sample (n = 1166), with similar findings. Sixty-one beta-thalassaemia carriers were identified (5.2%), all with an MCV < 75 fl.

Findings from the large descriptive study of an antenatal screening programme in Hong Kong showed that using a cut-off of MCV < 75 fl enabled 1859 thalassaemia carriers to be identified, plus 57 women carrying other haemoglobin variants (86% of those identified by screening test). The number of false positives was 313/2229 (14%). The authors report that 'after reviewing the obstetrics and paediatrics statistics' no case of thalassaemia major was missed. This does not equate, however, to a sensitivity of 100% since it is not known how many women with carrier status were missed.

Similarly, the screening programme described in Singapore[719] identified 494/3696 (13.4%) women with an MCV < 80 fl. Of these women, 56 (11.3%) and 23 (4.7%) were confirmed to be carrying thalassaemia and HbE respectively, giving a false positive rate of 84%. Again, since only women who fell below the initial screening cut-off point went on to have further haemoglobinopathy testing, it is not possible to determine how sensitive or specific this screening test is.

Effectiveness of the UK national antenatal screening programme

Description of included studies
The UK National Confidential Enquiry into Counselling for Genetic Disorders (CEGEN) has undertaken an audit of risk detection and risk information for thalassaemia during pregnancy in order to assess at a population level the screening objective of providing informed choice.[720] [EL = 3] The antenatal records of 136 (88%) of the 156 women with a pregnancy affected by a beta-thalassaemia major (1990–94) were retrospectively reviewed and the woman's care assessed against a minimum standard. The selected standard of care was: (i) risk identification and offer of prenatal diagnosis before 23 weeks of a first pregnancy; and (ii) offer of prenatal diagnosis in the first trimester in subsequent pregnancies.

2008 update

2008 update

Findings

Findings from the CEGEN audit showed that only 50% of at-risk couples were identified and informed of their risk in time for an offer of prenatal diagnosis in the first pregnancy. Risk was identified too late in 11% of pregnancies and not at all in 38% of pregnancies. As failure to identify risk was recurrent, 28% of couples discovered their risk through the diagnosis of an affected child. A review of maternity care records identified common assumptions made by healthcare professionals that Muslim people cannot accept termination of pregnancy and that British Pakistani people 'do not want' prenatal diagnosis. However, among British Pakistani people, the CEGEN review showed that the uptake of prenatal diagnosis was over 70% when it was offered in the first trimester of pregnancy, but less than 40% when offered in the second trimester. The CEGEN concluded that current screening with routine antenatal care does not meet couples' needs for early information and access to early pregnancy diagnosis.

Views and experiences of women towards thalassaemia screening in pregnancy

Description of included studies

A descriptive qualitative study was conducted in the UK (2006)[721] to explore Pakistani women's views towards antenatal diagnosis for thalassaemia and termination of pregnancy for beta-thalassaemia major. [EL = 3] Interviews were carried out with 43 women by a female researcher. These took place in the woman's home and were conducted in the woman's chosen language. Nineteen women were identified as thalassaemia carriers, ten as possible carriers and 14 as non-carriers.

A second recent UK qualitative study (2005)[722] has also explored women's perceptions of thalassaemia screening, with particular reference to information and consent. [EL = 3] One hundred and ten Pakistani women who were thalassaemia carriers completed a questionnaire. A subsample of 14 women was later interviewed. In addition, 36 women who were identified as carriers or potential carriers also completed the questionnaire and were interviewed. The questionnaire asked women whether they were aware they had been tested for thalassaemia carrier status, whether they were asked for their consent and what information they would have liked to receive prior to the screening. Questionnaires were available in English and Urdu, and women were offered a choice of self-completion or with the aid of the researcher. All interviews were conducted by the female researcher in the woman's own home and in her chosen language.

Findings

Findings from the UK qualitative study of Pakistani women's attitudes to prenatal diagnosis revealed that most women would opt for diagnosis because they would want 'to know', not because they would consider termination of pregnancy. Some women, however, preferred not to know about the baby's status, preferring to find out after the baby was born. One woman expressed concern that knowledge that the baby was affected might lead to a negative attitude towards the baby, even though termination of pregnancy was not being considered. Women's attitudes towards termination of pregnancy for an affected baby did not seem to relate to the woman's carrier status and were influenced by, but not solely dependent upon, their religious viewpoint (all women were Muslim). Women's responses suggested that the more severe the perception of thalassaemia major, the more likely the woman was to be in favour of antenatal diagnosis and termination of pregnancy. Some women also expressed the view that termination of pregnancy was only acceptable early in pregnancy, although women's definitions of early ranged from 5–6 weeks to 'before people know you are pregnant'.

Findings from the second UK qualitative study showed that 113/146 women (77.4%) had not been told about thalassaemia carrier testing, and 97 of these (85.8%) said they would have wanted to have been told before the screening was carried out. Although some women mentioned the increased anxiety associated with receiving information prior to screening, most saw this as an inevitable part of being pregnant. Women who went on to discover they were thalassaemia carriers felt that prior information would have helped them prepare for this news. Women expressed a desire to know about the condition itself, when the results would be available, the meaning of positive and negative results and possible action following a positive result. This was not universal, however, and carrier status affected women's responses with non-carriers being less likely to say they wanted detailed pre-screening information. Some suggested the provision of a leaflet might address the issue of individual variation, and provide women who later found out they were carriers with something to refer back to for more information. All women who were carriers identified a great need for information on being told of a positive screening result. Barriers to acquiring information included not knowing enough about the condition to be able to ask pertinent questions, belief that healthcare professionals would automatically provide all the necessary information, and not being able to speak or understand English. It was also highlighted that relatives acting as interpreters do not always provide the woman with all the information she wants. While most women (88.4%) reported that they were not asked their consent for screening, they did not perceive this as a problem, accepting screening as a normal part of routine antenatal care. There was a belief and a trust that healthcare professionals will do what is best and there was no need to question. Only three women were unhappy at being tested without consent. These were articulate, professional women, two of whom stated that they would have refused screening had they been asked. Overall, the wish for information far outweighed issues of consent.

Evidence summary

There is evidence from one national audit of antenatal genetic screening that most British Pakistani women opt for prenatal diagnosis if it is offered in the first trimester of pregnancy. Findings from this audit also suggest most women are not receiving counselling and testing in time to allow reproductive choice. (This is based on evidence from 1990 to 1994, however, so the numbers may have now increased.)

There is some evidence of fair quality that screening for thalassaemias and termination of an affected pregnancy are acceptable to some Pakistani Muslim women.

Preconceptions that religion is the only determinant of views towards reproductive choice are not supported by the evidence.

MCV does not appear useful for screening for beta-thalassaemia, but may be more useful where there is a high prevalence of alpha-thalassaemia.

There is a good amount of evidence of fair quality that screening for beta-thalassaemia by MCH has high sensitivity (100%) but low specificity (31%) with a cut-off of 27 pg.

Screening for haemoglobinopathies may lead to a reduction in lifetime treatment costs through a reduction in affected births. None of the included studies estimated the benefits accruing to an individual born with a haemoglobinopathy, i.e. having a diagnosis available at birth and initiating appropriate care immediately.

HPLC is automated and therefore appears to be cost-neutral according to one economic evaluation.

Universal HPLC may be as cost-effective as a sequential screen based on MCH followed by electrophoresis.

Screening using RBC indices may be cost-effective for beta-thalassaemia even in areas of low prevalence.

8.3.4 Sickle cell disease/sickle cell carrier status

Clinical question

What is the diagnostic value and effectiveness of the following screening methods in identifying clinically important genotypes of sickle cell disease and sickle cell carrier status (trait) including:

- history
- family origin
- full blood count
- Hb electrophoresis
- ferritin
- mean cell volume
- high performance liquid chromatography
- sickle solubility testing (Sickledex)?

2008 update

Sickle cell disease includes Hb SS and Hb SC.

Carrier states include Hb AS, Hb AC, Hb AD, Hb AE.

Population includes women and their partners, antenatally and preconceptionally.

Previous NICE guidance (for the updated recommendations see below)
The previous *Antenatal Care* guideline did not make any clinical recommendations regarding screening for sickle cell disease/sickle cell carrier. Two research recommendations were made (see above).

Universal electrophoresis versus selective electrophoresis following investigation of red blood cell indices and sickle solubility testing

Description of included studies
A case–control study was identified which compared the diagnostic accuracy of universal Hb electrophoresis with selective use of Hb electrophoresis following sickle cell solubility testing and investigation of red blood cell (RBC) indices.[711] [EL = III] This US study involved retrospective review of antenatal records of 631 women. All women had RBC indices and Hb electrophoresis performed at their initial antenatal visit.

Findings
Findings from the case–control study[711] showed that there were 36 women from the sample of 631 with abnormal Hb electrophoresis. Six of these women would have had normal sickle solubility test results. In two of these cases, abnormal RBC indices would have prompted further testing with Hb electrophoresis. Thus four women in total would have remained unidentified using the selective screening model. This gives a sensitivity of 88.9% (32/36) and a specificity of 79.4% (473/595) for the selective screening model. The positive predictive value is low, however, at 20.8% compared with a high negative predictive value of 99.2%.

Views and experiences of antenatal screening for sickle cell disease/sickle cell carrier status

Description of included studies
One descriptive study was identified which aimed to examine the acceptability of prenatal diagnosis as a means of controlling the number of babies born with sickle cell disease.[723] [EL = 3] This interview survey was conducted in Nigeria, targeting well-educated, city-dwelling adults (*n* = 433).

Findings
The survey respondents were aged 15–50 years, approximately half of whom were women, and 90% of the sample had attended school up to secondary and post-secondary level and 67% were in professional occupations (e.g. medicine, law and teaching). Two-thirds of the sample knew their haemoglobin genotype. Most respondents (88%) perceived sickle cell disease as a serious disease, although 19% thought it was curable. Only 4% of those interviewed had received sickle cell counselling, although 15% reported themselves to have be sickle cell carriers. Seventy-eight percent of respondents felt prenatal sickle cell diagnosis should be available and 45% reported that they would decide to terminate a baby affected with sickle cell disease. Cross-tabulations showed that neither religion nor educational level significantly affected a person's decision whether or not to terminate an affected pregnancy.

Evidence summary
There is evidence from one study that screening for sickle cell disease and subsequent termination of an affected pregnancy is acceptable to well-educated, city-dwelling Nigerian adults.

Electrophoresis appears to be necessary for higher sensitivity and specificity compared with selective screening using sickle solubility testing and RBC indices.

Sickle cell carriers are less likely to be offered and receive screening in a timely manner.

2008 update

8.3.5 Joint screening for sickle cell disease and thalassaemia

Description of included studies

One RCT (*n* = 4559) was reviewed that compared two family origin screening questions for stability and for proportion of carriers missed.[724] [EL = 1+] The study was conducted in four hospital trusts in the UK with varying prevalence of haemoglobinopathies. The question was embedded within the antenatal booking interview. Question A was a classification question (similar to a census question) plus a 'tick all that apply' subsidiary section to record mixed heritage. Question B was in two parts. Part One contained an initial binary question to identify women with ancestors outside the British Isles. Part Two comprised five free text boxes for addition of information regarding ancestry. A laboratory test was then offered to screen all women taking part in the study for sickle cell and thalassaemia. The reliability of the screening question was tested by repeating the question at a subsequent antenatal visit. The time taken for the midwife to ask the screening question was also noted.

A UK retrospective descriptive study (1999)[725] compared unselected laboratory-based antenatal screening for sickle cell carrier status with antenatal unselected laboratory-based screening for thalassaemia carrier status. [EL = 3] All women booking at a UK hospital were screened for haemoglobinopathy (over 20 000 pregnancies) and uptake of services by women was found to be less positive for thalassaemia carrier status (*n* = 265; 1.3%) compared with uptake by women who were found to be carriers of sickle cell disease (*n* = 751; 3.7%). A similar comparison was made for a smaller sample of tertiary referrals (*n* = 95 women with 101 pregnancies).

A whole-system participatory action research project (2005)[726] was used to evaluate a system where women were screened for sickle cell and thalassaemia early in their pregnancy (prior to 12 weeks) in UK general practice. [EL = 3] The study aimed primarily to compare the gestation at screening in general practice with the more usual system of screening at first booking visit, and to investigate the feasibility of introducing such a scheme. Six general practices in North London took part in the research, reflecting different sizes of practices, relating to different hospitals and with different experiences of antenatal haemoglobinopathy screening. Two hundred and forty-one women were recruited opportunistically into the study. Two comparison groups of women were also recruited – 276 women attending their booking visit at two neighbouring hospital clinics, and 131 women attending nearby community midwife clinics. A range of workshops, public meetings and interviews were conducted throughout the research process in order to gain the views of as many stakeholders as possible.

Findings

From the UK RCT[724] involving the questionnaire the sample of 4559 women who consented to take part in the study represents a high acceptance rate of 87%. However, only 27% of women were invited by midwives to take part in the study, suggesting a level of undisclosed screening being undertaken by midwives prior to asking the ethnicity question. For Question A, 3.2% cases were missing or uninterpretable, compared with 4.7% for Question B. The test–retest error rate for reliability for Question A was 4.3% compared with 9.5% for Question B (95% C.I −8.5% to −1.8%; *P* = 0.003). For ethnicity Question A, seven of 122 (5.7%) carriers of clinically relevant haemoglobinopathies were missed at booking. Ten of 103 (9.7%) women carrying a significant haemoglobinopathy were missed using Question B. This difference is statistically different (*P* = 0.026 using a χ^2 test (χ^2 value not reported)). The mean time taken to ask the ethnicity question was very similar for each question (about 4.4 minutes for Question A and 4.5 minutes for Question B).

Comparison of utilisation of services by women found to be carriers of sickle cell disease and women found to be carriers of thalassaemia showed that there were some differences between the two groups.[725] Unselected women found to be carriers of sickle cell disease booked 2.7 weeks (95% CI 0.14 to 5.1) later in pregnancy than women who were carrying thalassaemia. Carriers of sickle cell disease were found to be less likely to choose to receive counselling (83% versus 93%, RR 0.89, 95% CI 0.85 to 0.94), their partners were less likely to be tested (77% versus 95%, RR 0.81, 95% CI 0.77 to 0.83), and they were less likely to choose prenatal diagnosis (22% versus 90%, RR 0.37, 95% CI 0.24 to 0.57), compared with women carrying thalassaemia. Uptake of neonatal diagnosis for sickle cell disease varied markedly between the first and second trimester: 80% of couples requested antenatal diagnosis in the first trimester compared with 50% after the

2008 update

first trimester. However, only 27 women (42%) who were carriers of sickle cell disease were counselled in the first trimester. Of the tertiary referrals, over 99% of women attended counselling and had their partners tested. There was no difference in acceptance of prenatal diagnosis between those at risk of sickle cell disease and those at risk of thalassaemia (55% versus 67%).

Findings from the UK action research project[726] showed that general practices that already had a screening system in place were able to screen a high proportion (63% to 86%) of women presenting in early pregnancy (prior to 12 weeks) for haemoglobinopathies. However, three practices without an existing system only managed to screen between 3% and 26% of women. Women who were screened in general practices were screened at an earlier gestation than those screened at their first hospital booking visit (mean 4.1 weeks, 95% CI 3.4 to 4.7; $P < 0.001$) or at midwifery clinics (mean 2.9 weeks, 95% CI 2.1 to 3.7; $P < 0.001$). The introduction and maintenance of a new screening system into general practice was seen as requiring more resources than initially appreciated, for example time taken for pre- and post-test counselling was much longer than had been anticipated. The overall consensus from project participants was that preconception screening would be ideal so that women of known carrier status could be fast-tracked to existing secondary services. At the end of the study period all practices involved reverted to their pre-study system of screening at hospital or by community midwives.

Evidence summary
A fixed response question for screening for family origins is supported by findings from an RCT as being a useful screening test.

A screening programme (including counselling and follow-up) based in primary care allows earlier detection of haemoglobinopathy carrier status.

GDG interpretation of evidence
There is limited evidence that antenatal screening and the offer of termination of pregnancy for sickle cell disease appears to be acceptable to women and their partners.

Screening of all pregnant women using electrophoresis has a higher sensitivity and specificity to detect sickle cell carriers compared with selection of pregnant women for electrophoresis using sickle solubility testing and red blood cell indices. HPLC is a suitable alternative to electrophoresis as a laboratory test for sickle cell disease or carrier status.

Antenatal screening and termination of pregnancy for thalassaemia is acceptable to some Pakistani Muslim women, particularly if termination can be offered during the first trimester of pregnancy. The religion of a woman or her partner is not the only factor to determine whether termination of pregnancy will be acceptable and antenatal screening to allow reproductive choice should be offered to all pregnant women regardless of religious belief.

Antenatal screening with MCH is effective as a screening test for beta-thalassaemia even in low-prevalence areas.

As universal HPLC is cost-effective, it should be the preferred method of screening for thalassaemia variants in high-prevalence areas.

If pregnant women are offered antenatal screening for thalassaemia after the first trimester of pregnancy, they are less likely to receive counselling and testing in time to facilitate reproductive choice.

Screening for family origins using a fixed response tick box question is effective in identifying pregnant mothers at risk of haemoglobinopathy. A validated family origin questionnaire has been developed for use (NHS Antenatal and Newborn Screening Programme). This is in line with National Screening Committee policy.

Screening, including counselling and follow-up, can be successfully undertaken in primary care and may allow detection of carrier status at an earlier stage of pregnancy.

Compared with thalassaemia carriers, sickle cell carriers are less likely to receive the antenatal screening programme in a timely manner and, as the timing of the offer of screening influences the choice of antenatal diagnosis, this highlights the need for provision of screening at an early stage of pregnancy to successfully offer reproductive choice.

Prevalance of sickle cell disease is used as a marker for prevalance of all haemoglobinopathies including thalassaemia. The national screening programme has now been implemented in all high prevelance areas and is expected to be fully implemented in all other areas by August 2008.

Recommendations on screening for haemoglobinopathies

Preconception counselling (supportive listening, advice giving and information) and carrier testing should be available to all women who are identified as being at higher risk of haemoglobinopathies, using the Family Origin Questionnaire from the NHS Antenatal and Newborn Screening Programme (www.sickleandthal.org.uk/Documents/F_Origin_Questionnaire.pdf) (see Appendix J).

Information about screening for sickle cell diseases and thalassaemias, including carrier status and the implications of these, should be given to pregnant women at the first contact with a healthcare professional. Refer to Section 3.3 for more information about giving antenatal information.

Screening for sickle cell diseases and thalassaemias should be offered to all women as early as possible in pregnancy (ideally by 10 weeks). The type of screening depends upon the prevalence and can be carried out in either primary or secondary care.

Where prevalence of sickle cell disease is high (fetal prevalence above 1.5 cases per 10 000 pregnancies), laboratory screening (preferably high-performance liquid chromatography) should be offered to all pregnant women to identify carriers of sickle cell disease and/or thalassaemia.

Where prevalence of sickle cell disease is low (fetal prevalence 1.5 cases per 10 000 pregnancies or below), all pregnant women should be offered screening for haemoglobinopathies using the Family Origin Questionnaire (www.sickleandthal.org.uk/Documents/F_Origin_Questionnaire.pdf).

- If the Family Origin Questionnaire indicates a high risk of sickle cell disorders, laboratory screening (preferably high-performance liquid chromatography) should be offered.
- If the mean corpuscular haemoglobin is below 27 picograms, laboratory screening (preferably high-performance liquid chromatography) should be offered.

If the woman is identified as a carrier of a clinically significant haemoglobinopathy then the father of the baby should be offered counselling and appropriate screening without delay. For more details about haemoglobinopathy variants refer to the NHS Antenatal and Newborn Screening Programme (www.sickleandthal.org.uk/Documents/ProgrammeSTAN.pdf).

2008 update

9 Screening for fetal anomalies

9.1 Screening for structural anomalies

Clinical question
What is the diagnostic value and effectiveness of the following screening methods in identifying serious structural abnormalities?

- ultrasound undertaken in first and second trimesters
- nuchal translucency measurement
- serum screening – alpha-fetoprotein (AFP).

Previous NICE guidance (for the updated recommendations see below)
Pregnant women should be offered an ultrasound scan to screen for structural anomalies, ideally between 18 to 20 weeks of gestation, by an appropriately trained sonographer and with equipment of an appropriate standard as outlined by the National Screening Committee. [A]

9.1.1 Introduction and background

Since routine ultrasonography has been introduced into antenatal care women have had the opportunity to visualise the fetus at an early stage of pregnancy. The ultrasound scan has been used by health professionals to assess gestational age more accurately, to diagnose multiple births and to detect fetal anomalies. Improvements in technology have enabled health professionals to identify fetal structures, both normal and abnormal, and also to identify minor anomalies of uncertain significance, known as 'soft markers'.

Detection of fetal anomalies on antenatal ultrasound offers women and their partners information that may help them better prepare for the birth of their child, the option of delivery in a setting that will permit rapid access to specialist surgical or medical care, and the possibility of considering pregnancy termination or palliative care in the newborn period. Routine antenatal ultrasound has therefore presented women and their partners with difficult decisions and an abnormal result on ultrasound imaging has the potential to cause great anxiety throughout the remaining weeks of pregnancy. These are important considerations with regard to the timing of routine ultrasound screening and the potential for false positive results or detection of 'soft markers'.

Since the introduction of ultrasound in the 1970s, ultrasound technology has greatly improved. Modern equipment is now far superior and obstetric ultrasound is firmly established in routine practice, allowing identification of fetal anomalies and fetal growth problems. With this technology it is essential that healthcare professionals and clinicians who perform the scans are trained correctly to perform the examination and also understand and interpret the findings of the ultrasound scan correctly.[302]

This section of the guideline highlights the areas in which ultrasound screening is thought to have a role in the prenatal diagnosis of fetal anomalies.

Aim of screening for fetal structural anomalies

The overall aim of fetal anomaly screening is to identify potential problems so that parents can make an informed choice and to improve the safety of birth.

Specifically, antenatal screening to identify fetal anomalies should allow women and their partners:

- reproductive choice (a choice about continuing with the pregnancy or choosing termination of pregnancy)
- time to prepare (for termination of pregnancy/postnatal treatment or palliative care/infant disability)
- managed delivery in specialist centre
- intrauterine therapy.

The criteria laid out by Wilson and Jungner (1968)[1020] to appraise the validity of any screening programme are that:

- disorders to be screened for should be clinically well defined
- the incidence of the conditions (individual malformations) should be known
- disorders to be screened for should be associated with significant morbidity or mortality
- effective treatment should be available, e.g. intrauterine treatment, birth managed in a specialist centre, or termination of pregnancy
- there should be a period before onset of the disorder (the antenatal period) during which intervention is possible to improve outcome or allow informed choice
- there should be an ethical, safe, simple and robust screening test, e.g. ultrasound appears safe, ethical and acceptable
- screening should be cost-effective.

However, it is important to note that many of the studies of antenatal screening for fetal anomalies evaluate ultrasound as a suitable test rather than examine the benefits for women and babies of screening for a range of fetal anomalies during pregnancy.

9.1.2 Diagnostic value of routine ultrasound in the second trimester

The diagnostic value of routine ultrasound in the second trimester, including both multi-stage and single-stage ultrasound screening, was reviewed in this section.

Description of included studies

One systematic review[297] including 11 studies, and an additional 12 studies[727–741] were identified from the search. The 12 studies were critically appraised against the same criteria applied to the systematic review. Six studies were excluded either because of incomplete data or irrelevant study populations (e.g. high-risk populations). Details of the inclusion/exclusion process are provided on the accompanying CD-ROM. A new systematic review of all identified primary 17 studies, 11 studies in the systematic review and six newly identified studies, was conducted by the NCC-WCH. [EL = II]

Data from one RCT, nine prospective cohort studies and seven retrospective cohort studies were extracted. Four studies were conducted in the UK, while four were in the USA, four in Scandinavia, two in Belgium, two in Greece and one in South Korea. Details of the included studies are shown in Table 9.1. Meta-analyses of 11 studies on positive and negative likelihood ratios are presented in Figures 9.1 to 9.4.

Findings

Overall sensitivity (detection rate), specificity and likelihood ratios:
The results of each study are presented in Table 9.1 and Figures 9.1 to 9.4. The sensitivity and specificity of detecting fetal structural anomalies before 24 weeks of gestation reported from the included studies were 24.1% (range 13.5% to 85.7%) and 99.92% (range 99.40% to 100.00%), respectively, while overall sensitivity and specificity were 35.4% (range 15.0% to 92.9%) and 99.86% (range 99.40% to 100.00%), respectively. Meta-analysis of likelihood ratios showed positive and negative likelihood ratios before 24 weeks of 541.54 (95% CI 430.80 to 680.76) and 0.56 (95% CI 0.54 to 0.58), respectively. Meta-analysis of likelihood ratios showed overall positive and negative likelihood ratios were 242.89 (95% CI 218.35 to 270.18) and 0.65 (95% CI 0.63 to 0.66), respectively.

Detection by RCOG category:
Sensitivity (detection rate) for each condition according to the RCOG category[742] was also sought, and is presented in Table 9.2. Overall sensitivity for lethal anomalies was 83.6%, that for possible

2008 update

Table 9.1 Description of included studies and detection rates of structural anomalies by antenatal ultrasound (first and second trimester)

Study	Type	Population	Ultrasound screening	Number of fetuses	Prevalence of anomalous fetuses/anomalies	Detection < 15 weeks	Detection < 24 weeks	Detection > 24 weeks	Overall detection	Termination of pregnancy	Termination of normal pregnancy
Chitty (1991)[297]	Retrospective	1988–1989 UK (Luton) Unselected District general hospital	By radiographers Number of scans not mentioned Scanned at 18–20 weeks Soft markers: yes	8785 (multiple pregnancies not mentioned)	1.50% (130 fetuses) Anomalies: not reported		93 ST: 71.5% SP: 99.98% LR+: 3095.83 LR−: 0.44		93 FP: 2 ST: 71.5% SP: 99.98%	52 (0.6%)	0
Shirley (1991)[297]	Retrospective	1989–1990 UK (Hillingdon) Unselected District general hospital	By Radiographers Number of scans not mentioned Scanned at 19 weeks Soft markers: no	6412 (73 multiple pregnancies)	1.40% (89 fetuses) Anomalies: not reported		61 ST: 57.3% SP: 99.97%		51 FP: 1 ST: 57.3% SP: 99.97%	29 (0.45%)	0
Levi (1991)[297]	Prospective	1984–1989 Belgium (Brussels) Unselected 5 hospitals	By obstetricians, technicians and sonographers Scanned at first trimester, 16–20 weeks and third trimester Soft markers: no	15 654 (240 multiple pregnancies)	2.30% (381 fetuses) Anomalies: 2.66% (417 anomalies)		(54) ST: (21.0%) SP: (100.00%) (Calculated taking only those defects exposed to scan at 12–24 weeks ($n = 259$))	(135) ST: (37.2%) SP: ? (Calculated taking only those defects exposed to scan at 12–24 weeks ($n = 259$))	154 FP: 8 ST: 40.4% SP: 99.94%	Missing value	0
Luck (1992)[297]	Prospective	1988–1991 UK (Ascot) Unselected District general hospital	By radiographers Scanned at 12–14 weeks and 19 weeks Soft markers: yes	8844	Not reported Anomalies: 1.90% (164 anomalies)		(140) ST: (85.3%) SP: 99.90% (The numbers based on number of anomalies)		(140) FP: 3 ST: 85.3% SP: 99.90% (The numbers based on number of anomalies)	19 (0.21%)	0
Crane (1994)[297]	RCT	1987–91 USA (RADIUS) Low risk Primary plus 28 laboratories	By technicians, physicians, sonologists and radiologists Scanned at 15–22 weeks and 31–35 weeks Soft markers: no	7575 (multiple pregnancies not mentioned)	2.30% (187 fetuses) Anomalies: (232 anomalies)		31 ST: 16.6% SP: 99.90%	34 ST: 18.2% SP: missing value	65 FP: 7 ST: 34.8% SP: 99.90%	9 (0.12%)	0
Levi (1995)[297]	Prospective	1990–92 Belgium (Brussels) Unselected 5 hospitals	By obstetricians, technicians, sonographers Scanned at first trimester, 16–20 weeks, and third trimester Soft markers: no	9601 (209 multiple pregnancies)	2.45% (235 fetuses) Anomalies: 2.81% (270 anomalies)		(69) ST: (25.6%) SP: Not reported (The numbers based on number of anomalies)	(109) ST: (40.4%) SP: Not reported (The numbers based on number of anomalies)	120 (178) FP: 9 ST: 51.0% (65.9%) SP: 99.90% (The numbers based on number of anomalies)	Missing value	Missing value
Skupski (1996)[297]	Retrospective	1990–94 USA (Texas) Low risk Tertiary, single centre	By experienced sonographers Scanned at 18–20 weeks Soft markers: no	860 (6 twins)	1.16% (20 fetuses) Anomalies: Not reported		3 ST: 15.0% SP: 99.90%		FP: 1 ST: 15.0% SP: 99.80%	2 (0.23%)	0

Study	Type	Population	Ultrasound screening	Number of fetuses	Prevalence of anomalous fetuses/anomalies	Detection < 15 weeks	Detection < 24 weeks	Detection > 24 weeks	Overall detection	Termination of pregnancy	Termination of normal pregnancy
Magriples (1998)[297]	Retrospective	?–18 months USA (Connecticut) Low risk Tertiary, single centre	By sonographers Scanned at 16–19 weeks and third trimester Soft markers: yes	911 (10 twins)	3.07% (28 fetuses) Anomalies: (40 anomalies)		20 ST: 71.4% SP: 99.40%		20 FP: 5 ST: 71.4% SP: 99.40%	6 (0.67%)	0
Lee (1998)[297]	Retrospective	1990–94 Korea Low risk Tertiary, single centre	By trained obstetric fellow Scanned at 18–20 weeks and 32–34 weeks Soft markers: no	3004 (twins excluded)	0.76% (23 fetuses) Anomalies: (37 anomalies)		3 (5) ST: 13.5% (13.5%) SP: 100.00% (The numbers based on number of anomalies)	5 (6) ST: 21.7% (16.2%) SP: 100.00% (The numbers based on number of anomalies)	8 (11) FP: 0 ST: 34.8% (29.7%) SP: 100.00% (The numbers based on number of anomalies)	3 (0.09%)	Missing value
Van Dorsten (1998)[297]	Prospective	1993–96 USA (South Carolina) Unselected Mixed two sites	By registered diagnostic medical sonographers Scanned at 15–22 weeks Soft markers: no	1611 (twins excluded)	1.30% (21 fetuses) Anomalies: (29 anomalies)		10 ST: 47.6% SP: 99.90%		10 FP: 1 ST: 47.6% SP: 99.90%	4 (0.25%)	0
Boyd (1998)[297]	Retrospective	1991–96 UK (Oxford) Unselected Tertiary single centre	Sonographers not mentioned Scanned at 18–22 weeks Soft markers: no	33 376 (Twins not stated)	2.17% (725 fetuses) Anomalies: not reported		298 ST: 41.1% SP: 99.90%		298 FP: 15 ST: 41.1% SP: 99.90%	169 (0.51%)	2 (1 soft marker)
Whitelow (1999)[300,743]	Prospective	Not known UK (London) Unselected Single university hospital	Sonographers: 6 different clinicians Scanned at 11–14 weeks either trasnabdominally or transvaginally Soft markers: yes	6443 (77 twins; 4 triplets)	1.4% (92 fetuses) Anomalies: not reported	37 ST: 58.7% SP: 99.90%	51 ST: 81.0%			36 (0.56%)	Missing value
Eurenius (1999)[227]	Prospective	1990–92 Sweden (Uppsala) Unselected Tertiary, single centre	By trained midwife Scanned at 15–22 weeks Soft markers: no	8324 (111 twins,3 triplets)	0.74% (145 fetuses) Anomalies: not reported		32 ST: 22.1% SP: 99.80%		32 FP: 20 ST 22.1% SP: 99.80%	16 (0.19%)	Missing value
Stefos (1999)[728]	Prospective	1990–96 Greece (Ioannina) Unselected Tertiary, single centre	By experienced obstetricians Scanned at 18–22 weeks Soft markers: no	7236 (86 twins)	2.24% (162 fetuses) Anomalies: not reported		130 ST: 80.25% SP: 99.88%		130 FP: 8 ST: 80.25% SP: 99.88%	40 (0.55%)	Missing value

2008 update

2008 update

Table 9.1 Description of included studies and detection rates of structural anomalies by antenatal ultrasound (first and second trimester) (*continued*)

Study	Type	Population	Ultrasound screening	Number of fetuses	Prevalence of anomalous fetuses/anomalies	Detection < 15 weeks	Detection < 24 weeks	Detection > 24 weeks	Overall detection	Termination of pregnancy	Termination of normal pregnancy
Taipale (2004)[729]	Prospective	1994–96 Finland (Helsinki) Low risk Tertiary, single centre	By obstetrician and trained midwives Scanned at 13–14 weeks transvaginally and 18–22 weeks transabdominally	4855 (multiples excluded)	0.7% (33 fetuses) Anomalies: not reported		16 ST: 48.5% SP: 99.96%		16 FP: 2 ST: 48.5% SP: 99.96%	Missing value	Missing value
Nakling (2005)[730]	Prospective	1989–99 Norway (Oppland), Unselected District general hospitals	By trained midwives and obstetricians Scanned at 13–24 weeks Soft markers: no	18 181 (Multiples not stated)	1.47% (267 fetuses) Anomalies: not reported		104 ST: 39.0% SP: 99.94%		104 FP: 11 ST: 39.0% SP: 99.94%	57 (0.31%)	0
Souka (2006)[731]	Prospective	2002 Greece (Athens) Unselected Tertiary, single hospital	By obstetricians Scanned at 11–14 weeks on nuchal translucency measurement and at 22–24 weeks Soft markers: yes	1148 (Multiples not stated)	1.21% (14 fetuses) Anomalies: Not reported		6 ST: 85.7%		13 FP: 3 ST: 92.9% SP: 99.74%	9 (0.78%)	Missing value
Nikkila (2006)[732]	Retrospective	1984–99 Denmark (Malmohus) Unselected 5 hospitals	Sonographers not mentioned Scanned at 18 weeks, some had scan at 33 weeks, as well Soft markers: yes	141 240	2.56% (3614 fetuses) Anomalies: not reported		503 ST: 38.9% SP: not obtained		1028 FP: 265 ST: 28.4% SP: 99.81%	386 (0.27%)	3
Total				277 638	2.19% (6074)	**ST: 58.7%** **SP: 99.90%**	**ST: 24.1%** **SP: 99.92%**		**ST: 35.4%** **SP: 99.86%**	0.36%	

FP = number of false positives; LR+ = positive likelihood ratio; LR− = negative likelihood ratio; SP = specificity; ST = sensitivity.

survival and long-term morbidity was 50.6%, that for anomalies amenable to intrauterine therapy was 100.0%, and that for anomalies associated with possible short-term/immediate morbidity was 16.1%. The sensitivity varies depending upon each condition.

Evidence summary

Second-trimester ultrasound seems to show high specificity but poor sensitivity for identifying fetal structural anomalies. Similarly, this test showed good summary value for positive likelihood ratio but poor negative likelihood ratio. However, these values ranged widely by centre and condition. The 100% detection rate for conditions amenable to intrauterine treatment is anomalous and arises from the fact that these conditions had to be identified before treatment could be considered.

9.1.3 Diagnostic value of routine ultrasound in the first trimester

The diagnostic value of routine ultrasound in the first trimester to detect fetal structural anomalies was reviewed in this section.

Review: diagnostic value of ultrasound screening during pregnancy for structural abnormalities of fetus
Comparison: 01 Likelihood ratios of antenatal ultrasound before 24 weeks
Outcome: 01 Positive likelihood ratios

Study or sub-category	Abnomalous fetuses n/N	Normal fetuses n/N	RR (fixed) 95% CI	Weight %	RR (fixed) 95% CI	Year
Chitty	93/130	2/8655		2.01	3095.83 [771.11, 12429.02]	1991
Shirley	61/89	1/6323		0.94	4333.74 [607.49, 30916.45]	1991
Crane	31/187	7/7388		11.71	174.96 [78.05, 392.22]	1994
Skupski	3/20	1/840		1.58	126.00 [13.69, 1159.31]	1996
Boyd	298/725	15/32651		22.09	894.71 [535.45, 1495.02]	1998
Lee	3/23	0/2981		0.27	869.75 [46.17, 16383.68]	1998
Magriples	20/28	5/883		10.42	126.14 [51.04, 311.78]	1998
Von Dorsten	10/21	1/1590		0.88	757.14 [101.44, 5651.03]	1998
Eurenious	32/145	20/8179		23.62	90.25 [52.91, 153.94]	1999
Stefos	130/162	8/7074		12.14	709.58 [353.51, 1424.30]	1999
Taipale	16/33	2/4822		0.92	1168.97 [279.87, 4882.58]	2004
Nakling	104/267	11/17914		10.95	634.34 [344.82, 1166.94]	2005
Souka	13/14	3/1134		2.48	351.00 [112.33, 1096.82]	2006
Total (95% CI)	**1844**	**100434**		**100.00**	**541.54 [430.80, 680.76]**	

Total events: 814 (Abnomalous fetuses), 76 (Normal fetuses)
Test for heterogeneity: Chi² = 79.13, df = 12 (P < 0.00001), I² = 84.8%
Test for overall effect: Z = 53.92 (P < 0.00001)

0.001 0.01 0.1 1 10 100 1000
Favours treatment   Favours control

Figure 9.1 Meta-analysis of positive likelihood ratios by routine ultrasound to detect fetal anomalies before 24 weeks

Review: diagnostic value of ultrasound screening during pregnancy for structural abnormalities of fetus
Comparison: 01 Likelihood ratios of antenatal ultrasound before 24 weeks
Outcome: 02 Negative likelihood ratios

Study or sub-category	Abnomalous fetuses n/N	Normal fetuses n/N	RR (fixed) 95% CI	Weight %	RR (fixed) 95% CI	Year
Chitty	57/130	8633/8655		7.07	0.44 [0.36, 0.53]	1991
Shirley	28/89	6322/6323		4.85	0.31 [0.23, 0.43]	1991
Crane	156/187	7381/7388		10.08	0.84 [0.78, 0.89]	1994
Skupski	17/20	839/840		1.08	0.85 [0.71, 1.02]	1996
Boyd	427/725	32636/32651		39.22	0.59 [0.55, 0.63]	1998
Lee	20/23	2981/2981		1.32	0.85 [0.72, 1.01]	1998
Magriples	8/28	839/840		1.50	0.29 [0.16, 0.51]	1998
Von Dorsten	11/21	1589/1590		1.15	0.52 [0.35, 0.79]	1998
Eurenious	113/145	8159/8179		7.86	0.78 [0.72, 0.85]	1999
Stefos	12/162	7069/7074		8.76	0.07 [0.04, 0.13]	1999
Taipale	17/33	4820/4822		1.81	0.52 [0.37, 0.72]	2004
Nakling	163/267	17903/17914		14.55	0.61 [0.56, 0.67]	2005
Souka	1/14	1131/1134		0.76	0.07 [0.01, 0.47]	2006
Total (95% CI)	**1844**	**100391**		**100.00**	**0.56 [0.54, 0.58]**	

Total events: 1030 (Abnomalous fetuses), 100302 (Normal fetuses)
Test for heterogeneity: Chi² = 342.55, df = 12 (P < 0.00001), I² = 96.5%
Test for overall effect: Z = 28.10 (P < 0.00001)

0.001 0.01 0.1 1 10 100 1000
Favours treatment   Favours control

Figure 9.2 Meta-analysis of negative likelihood ratios by routine ultrasound to detect fetal anomalies before 24 weeks

2008 update

Description of included studies

One review of literature included in an HTA[297] and additional four studies[300,743–746] were identified. However, only one[300,743] from the additional studies was included in this review owing to methodological weakness and incomplete data. [EL = III]

Findings

The review showed that there were relatively few data on screening an unselected or low-risk population, as most studies report results of screening in high-risk populations.[297] Results on nuchal translucency measurement are presented later in the soft markers section. The review included five studies of first-trimester anomaly screening but could not draw any conclusion because of the methodological weakness of these studies.

The additional study was published in 1999, although the study did not specify the time when it was conducted.[300,743] Details of the study are presented in Table 9.1. This was a prospective cross-sectional study at a university hospital in the UK, and included 6634 unselected women carrying 6443 fetuses. All women underwent either transabdominal or transvaginal sonography at 11–14 weeks. Nuchal translucency and an anatomical survey were performed. There were

Review: diagnostic value of ultrasound screening during pregnancy for structural abnormalities of fetus
Comparison: 02 Likelihood ratios of antenatal ultrasound (overall)
Outcome: 01 Positive likelihood ratios

Study or sub-category	Abnomalous fetuses n/N	Normal fetuses n/N	RR (fixed) 95% CI	Weight %	RR (fixed) 95% CI	Year
Chitty	93/130	2/8655		0.34	3095.83 [771.11, 12429.02]	1991
Levi	154/381	8/15273		2.25	771.67 [381.89, 1559.26]	1991
Shirley	61/89	1/6323		0.16	4333.74 [607.49, 30916.45]	1991
Crane	65/187	7/7388		1.99	366.86 [170.54, 789.20]	1994
Levi2	120/235	9/9366		2.54	531.40 [273.32, 1033.20]	1995
Skupski	3/20	1/840		0.27	126.00 [13.69, 1159.31]	1996
Boyd	298/725	15/32651		3.76	894.71 [535.45, 1495.02]	1998
Lee	8/23	0/2981		0.05	2112.25 [125.43, 35569.67]	1998
Magriples	20/28	5/883		1.77	126.14 [51.04, 311.78]	1998
Von Dorsten	10/21	1/1590		0.15	757.14 [101.44, 5651.03]	1998
Eurenious	32/145	20/8179		4.02	90.25 [52.91, 153.94]	1999
Stefos	130/162	8/7074		2.07	709.58 [353.51, 1424.30]	1999
Taipale	16/33	2/4822		0.16	1168.97 [279.87, 4882.58]	2004
Nakling	104/267	11/17914		1.86	634.34 [344.82, 1166.94]	2005
Nikkila	1028/3614	265/137626		78.20	147.73 [129.60, 168.39]	2006
Souka	13/14	3/1134		0.42	351.00 [112.33, 1096.82]	2006
Total (95% CI)	**6074**	**262699**		**100.00**	**242.89 [218.35, 270.18]**	

Total events: 2155 (Abnomalous fetuses), 358 (Normal fetuses)
Test for heterogeneity: Chi² = 160.84, df = 15 (P < 0.00001), I² = 90.7%
Test for overall effect: Z = 101.07 (P < 0.00001)

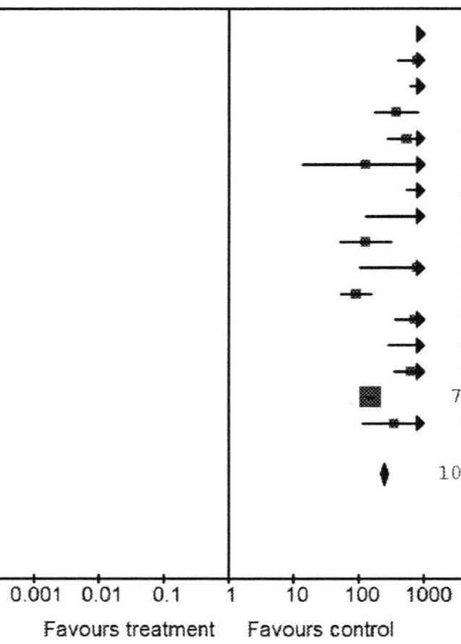

```
          0.001  0.01   0.1    1    10   100  1000
            Favours treatment   Favours control
```

Figure 9.3 Meta-analysis of overall positive likelihood ratios by routine ultrasound to detect fetal anomalies

Review: diagnostic value of ultrasound screening during pregnancy for structural abnormalities of fetus
Comparison: 02 Likelihood ratios of antenatal ultrasound (overall)
Outcome: 02 Negative likelihood ratios

Study or sub-category	Abnomalous fetuses n/N	Normal fetuses n/N	RR (fixed) 95% CI	Weight %	RR (fixed) 95% CI	Year
Chitty	57/130	8633/8655		2.16	0.44 [0.36, 0.53]	1991
Levi	227/381	15265/15273		6.27	0.60 [0.55, 0.65]	1991
Shirley	28/89	6322/6323		1.48	0.31 [0.23, 0.43]	1991
Crane	118/187	7381/7388		3.08	0.63 [0.57, 0.70]	1994
Levi2	115/235	9357/9366		3.87	0.49 [0.43, 0.56]	1995
Skupski	17/20	839/840		0.33	0.85 [0.71, 1.02]	1996
Boyd	427/725	32636/32651		11.97	0.59 [0.55, 0.63]	1998
Lee	16/23	2981/2981		0.40	0.69 [0.53, 0.90]	1998
Magriples	8/28	839/840		0.46	0.29 [0.16, 0.51]	1998
Von Dorsten	11/21	1589/1590		0.35	0.52 [0.35, 0.79]	1998
Eurenious	113/145	8159/8179		2.40	0.78 [0.72, 0.85]	1999
Stefos	12/162	7069/7074		2.67	0.07 [0.04, 0.13]	1999
Taipale	17/33	4820/4822		0.55	0.52 [0.37, 0.72]	2004
Nakling	163/267	17903/17914		4.44	0.61 [0.56, 0.67]	2005
Nikkila	2586/3614	137361/137626		59.34	0.72 [0.70, 0.73]	2006
Souka	1/14	1131/1134		0.23	0.07 [0.01, 0.47]	2006
Total (95% CI)	**6074**	**262656**		**100.00**	**0.65 [0.63, 0.66]**	

Total events: 3916 (Abnomalous fetuses), 262285 (Normal fetuses)
Test for heterogeneity: Chi² = 270.73, df = 15 (P < 0.00001), I² = 94.5%
Test for overall effect: Z = 45.93 (P < 0.00001)

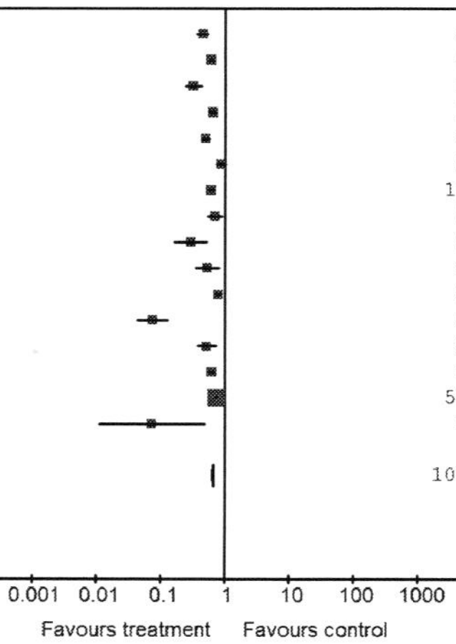

```
          0.001  0.01   0.1    1    10   100  1000
            Favours treatment   Favours control
```

Figure 9.4 Meta-analysis of overall negative likelihood ratios by routine ultrasound to detect fetal anomalies

Table 9.2 Prevalence and detection of congenital anomalies at second-trimester antenatal ultrasound according to RCOG subgroup

	Prevalence per 1000	Chi[297]	Shi[297]	Le[297]	Luc[297]	Cra[297]	Le2[297]	Sku[297]	Mar[297]	Lee[297]	Van[297]	Boy[297]	Eur[727]	Ste[728]	Tai[729]	Nak[730]	Sou[731]	Nik[732]	Total (detection rate)
Number of fetuses		8785	6412	15 654	8844	7575	9601	860	911	3004	1611	33 376	8345	7236	4855	18 181	1148	141 240	277 638
Lethal anomalies (total)	0.74	13/16	13/13	7/11	13/17	3/3	9/13		2/3	0/3			4/5	8/10	2/7	32/40	3/3	69/69	178/213 (83.6%)
Anencephaly	0.52	6/6	10/10	6/6	7/7	3/3	4/4		1/2				3/3	4/5	0/1	11/11		69/69	124/127 (97.6%)
Trisomy 18	0.30	1/1	3/3							0/2					0/1	7/10	2/2		13/19 (68.4%)
Trisomy 13	0.11	1/2																	1/2 (50.0%)
Hypoplastic left heart	0.21	1/3		1/1	4/8		3/3			0/1				2/3	2/3	4/9	1/1		18/33 (54.5%)
Bilateral renal agenesis	0.37	4/4			2/2				1/1					2/2	0/2	9/9			18/20 (90.0%)
Lethal musculo-skeletal disorders	0.08			0/4			2/6						1/1			1/1			4/12 (33.3%)
Possible survival and long-term morbidity	1.57	48/68	20/36	16/88	20/36	12/30	11/38	0/6	6/8	4/13	13/16	11/70	9/56	70/82	5/11	47/92	4/4	141/210	437/864 (50.6%)
Spina bifida	0.47	5/5	3/3	2/5	2/2	4/5	4/11				2/2		3/4	8/9	2/2	6/6		71/115	112/169 (66.3%)
Hydrocephalus	0.49	3/3	1/2	4/15			5/6			1/1	4/5		2/5	10/10	1/3	9/9	2/2		42/61 (68.9%)
Encephalocoele	0.15	2/2	1/1	2/2	1/1				1/1				1/2	2/2		2/2			10/11 (90.9%)
Holoprosencephaly	0.14	2/3		0/1	1/1				1/1	0/1				4/4					8/11 (72.7%)
Down's syndrome	0.24	1/14	3/10							0/3		11/70			1/1	2/25			18/123 (14.6%)
Complex cardiac malformations	0.35	5/6	4/8	2/44	3/14	5/19	1/5	0/1	0/1		4/5		0/26	5/10		4/16			33/155 (21.3%)
Atrioventricular septal defect	0.09			0/6			1/5	0/1		0/1			0/14	2/3			1/1		4/31 (12.9%)
Non-lethal dwarfism	0.11															2/2			2/2 (100.0%)
Anterior abdominal wall defects	0.33	4/4	2/2	4/4	4/4	1/1				1/1	1/1		2/2	4/4	1/3	4/5		49/55	77/86 (89.5%)
– Gastroschisis	0.19	3/3	1/1	2/2	2/2	1/1				1/1	1/1			2/2	0/1	3/3			16/17 (94.1%)
– Exomphalos	0.16	1/1	1/1	2/2	2/2				1/1					2/2	1/2	1/2			11/13 (84.6%)
Congenital diaphragmatic hernia	0.15	2/2	2/3	1/3	2/5	1/1	0/2			0/2	1/2		0/3	4/4	1/2	0/5	1/1		35/73 (47.9%)
Tracheo-oesophageal atresia	0.03	0/2		1/7	0/1	0/3				0/1	1/1		0/7		0/1	0/4			2/27 (7.4%)
Small bowel obstruction/atresia	0.13	0/1	0/1	0/1	1/1	1/1	0/9	0/2		0/1			0/3	11/12	0/1	0/1			13/32 (40.6%)
Congenital cystic adenomatoid malformation	0.25	4/4	1/1	1/1	1/1														6/6 (100.0%)
Renal dysplasia (bilateral)	0.77	2/3	0/1						1/1		N/A			16/20		13/13			32/38 (84.2%)
Multiple abnormality/syndrome	0.67	18/19	3/4		5/6			0/4	2/3	2/2			1/4	10/10		1/2			42/54 (77.8%)
Anomalies amenable to intrauterine therapy																3/3			3/3 (100.0%)
Obstructive uropathy																2/2			2/2 (100.0%)
Pleural effusion or hydrothorax																1/1			2/2 (100.0%)
Anomalies associated with possible short-term/immediate morbidity	0.38	12/28	4/16	4/51	8/9	5/53	3/49	1/11	2/3	0/12	0/3	27/78	0/29	15/26		1/54	0/1	21/240	103/663 (15.5%)
Non-complex cardiac anomalies																			
– Atrial/ventricular septal defect	0.09	1/1	1/1	0/26	0/1	0/19	0/25	0/6	0/1	0/4	0/3		0/19	7/15	0/1	0/23			9/144 (6.3%)
– Isolated valve anomalies	0.10	0/1		0/1	2/2	2/7	2/7		1/1	0/2			0/10		1/2				5/22 (22.7%)
Facial clefts	0.20	2/9	3/9	4/24	2/2	3/10	1/17	0/2		0/6		12/25		4/7	0/1	1/24		21/240	46/333 (13.8%)
Talipes	0.27	6/12	0/6		2/2	2/24				0/2		15/53				0/7			30/149 (20.1%)
Renal dysplasia (unilateral)	0.49	3/5		4/4	4/4				1/1	1/1	N/A			4/4					13/15 (86.7%)

2008 update

2008 update

six clinicians undertaking these examinations. The incidence of anomalous fetuses was 1.4%, and sensitivity (detection rate) was 59.0% (37/63 (95% CI 46.5% to 72.4%)). The specificity was 99.9%. Positive and negative likelihood ratios were 624.5 and 0.41. When first- and second-trimester scans were combined, the sensitivity was 81.0% (51/63 (95% CI 67.7% to 89.2%).

Evidence summary
There were only a few good-quality studies conducted which examine the diagnostic value of routine ultrasound in the first trimester. Although high specificity and positive likelihood ratio were reported, the sensitivity and negative likelihood ratio reported from a single centre in the UK were at a moderate level.

9.1.4 Effectiveness of routine ultrasound in pregnancy

The clinical effectiveness of routine use of ultrasound compared with no routine use was reviewed in this section.

Routine versus selective ultrasound before 24 weeks

Description of included studies
One systematic review that examined the effectiveness of routine ultrasound in early pregnancy (before 24 weeks), compared with selective ultrasound, was identified and included.[57] [EL = 1+] The systematic review included eight RCTs and one quasi-randomised controlled trial, involving 34 251 women. The quality of these trials was generally good.

Findings
Routine ultrasound screening for fetal anomalies showed an increase in termination of pregnancy for fetal abnormality (four trials, OR 3.19, 95% CI 1.54 to 6.60), and a reduction in the number of undiagnosed twins (at 20 weeks, one trial, OR 0.12, 95% CI 0.03 to 0.56; at 26 weeks, six trials, OR 0.08 95% CI 0.04 to 0.16) and number of inductions for 'post-term' pregnancy (six trials, OR 0.61, 95% CI 0.52 to 0.72) compared with selective ultrasound. There is borderline evidence of the effect of routine ultrasound in reducing the number of children admitted to special care (five trials, OR 0.86, 95% CI 0.74 to 1.00) and with poor spelling at school (one trial, OR 0.73, 95% CI 0.53 to 1.00), compared with selective ultrasound. There was no evidence of difference in other outcomes.

Evidence summary
There is high-level evidence that routine, rather than selective, ultrasound in early pregnancy before 24 weeks enables better gestational age assessment, earlier detection of multiple pregnancies and improved detection of fetal anomalies with resulting higher rate of termination of affected pregnancies. There is no good-quality evidence on long-term outcomes for women and their children.

Routine versus no/concealed/selective ultrasound after 24 weeks

Description of included studies
One systematic review that examined effectiveness of routine ultrasound in late pregnancy (after 24 weeks), compared with no/concealed/selective ultrasound, was identified and included.[574] [EL = 1+] The systematic review included five RCTs and one quasi-randomised controlled trial, involving 22 202 women. Among them, three trials offered routine ultrasound in the second and third trimester versus selective ultrasound. In one New Zealand trial, all women had a second-trimester scan and only the study group had a further third-trimester scan. In one UK trial, all women were offered second- and third-trimester scans but the results of the third-trimester scan were revealed only for those in the study group. In another UK trial, all women had routine second- and third-trimester scans, although placental grading at the third-trimester scans was revealed only for those in the study group. The quality of these trials was generally good.

Findings
Routine ultrasound screening for fetal anomalies after 24 weeks of gestation showed a reduction in post-term birth after 42 weeks (two trials, OR 0.69, 95% CI 0.58 to 0.81) but the timing and manner of gestational age assessment differed between the two trials. There was no difference in the overall perinatal mortality (six trials, OR 1.03, 95% CI 0.75 to 1.42), stillbirths (four trials, OR 1.15, 95% CI 0.74 to 1.79) or neonatal mortality (four trials, OR 1.04 (95% CI 0.58 to 1.86) between the two groups. After exclusion of babies with congenital anomalies, a statistically significant reduction was observed only for stillbirths (two trials, OR 0.13, (95% CI 0.04 to 0.50)), but one of the trials had incorporated placental grading into the routine third-trimester scan. There was no evidence of difference in other clinically important outcomes including obstetric and neonatal interventions.

Evidence summary
Results show a reduction in the number of post-term births and stillbirths (for normal babies) with routine third-trimester ultrasound, but the evidence is not of high quality. There is no evidence of difference for other clinically important outcomes, including obstetric and neonatal interventions and neonatal outcomes, between routine and no routine ultrasound after 24 weeks.

Routine versus no/concealed/selective Doppler ultrasound in pregnancy

Description of included studies
One systematic review that examined the effectiveness of routine Doppler ultrasound in pregnancy, compared with no/concealed/selective use of Doppler ultrasound, was identified and included.[575] [EL = 1+] The systematic review included four RCTs involving 11 504 women. In one included UK trial, two different protocols were used for high- and low-risk populations, with the high-risk group having serial Doppler examinations and the low-risk group having Doppler examination on two occasions (19–22 weeks and 32 weeks). The data for each population were not reported separately and it was not possible to analyse separately. Three included trials only studied umbilical artery Doppler and reported different parameters.

Findings
Meta-analysis of the four trials showed no evidence of difference in antenatal admissions, obstetric interventions or neonatal interventions between routine and no routine use of Doppler ultrasound during pregnancy. Although one UK trial reported significantly increased perinatal mortality in the routine Doppler group compared with the no Doppler routine group, there was no evidence of difference in overall perinatal mortality.

Evidence summary
There was no evidence of difference in antenatal admissions, obstetric interventions, neonatal interventions or overall perinatal mortality between routine and no routine use of Doppler ultrasound during pregnancy.

Serial ultrasound plus Doppler versus selective ultrasound in pregnancy

Description of included studies
Two systematic reviews[297,574] compared serial ultrasound plus Doppler with selective ultrasound. Both reviews included the same trial that compared effectiveness between serial ultrasound plus Doppler and selective ultrasound in pregnancy. [EL = 1+] This trial compared combined intensive repeated ultrasound assessment of the fetus plus Doppler study of the umbilical and uterine arteries versus selective ultrasound. The trial included 2834 women.

Findings
The included trial reported significantly more infants with intrauterine growth restriction in the routine serial and Doppler ultrasound than in the selective ultrasound group (birthweight < 10th centile, OR 1.41, 95% CI 1.11 to 1.78; birthweight < 3rd centile, OR 1.67, 95% CI 1.11 to 2.53), but otherwise no evidence of difference in antenatal and obstetric interventions, neonatal interventions or neonatal mortality/morbidity.

Evidence summary
There is little evidence on the effectiveness of routine use of combined serial and Doppler ultrasound compared with selective ultrasound and there is no evidence of difference in antenatal and obstetric interventions, neonatal interventions or neonatal mortality/morbidity.

First- versus second-trimester routine ultrasound in pregnancy

Description of included studies
One RCT was identified.[747,748] [EL = 1+] The trial compared the antenatal detection rate of malformations in chromosomally normal fetuses between the policy of offering one routine ultrasound examination at 12 weeks, including nuchal translucency measurement, and one routine ultrasound examination at 18 weeks. The trial was conducted in eight hospitals in Sweden, involving 39 572 unselected women. A repeat scan was offered in the 12 week scan group if the fetal anatomy could not be adequately seen at 12–14 weeks or if nuchal translucency thickness was 3.5 mm or greater in a fetus with normal or unknown chromosome status.

Findings
The sensitivity of detecting fetuses with a major malformation was 38% (66/176) in the 12 week scan group, while that in the 18 week scan group was 47% (72/152) ($P = 0.06$). In the 12 week scan group, 69% of fetuses with a lethal anomaly were detected at a scan at 12–14 weeks.

The sensitivity of detecting fetuses with a major heart malformation was 11% (7/61) in the 12 week scan group, while that in the 18 week scan group was 15% (9/60) ($P = 0.60$). The proportion of women whose routine ultrasound was the starting point for further investigation resulting in a prenatal diagnosis was 6.6% in the 12 week group (4/61) and 15% in the 18 week group (9/60) ($P = 0.15$).

Evidence summary
There is little evidence of the effectiveness of a routine first-trimester scan for detecting major fetal malformation compared with a routine second-trimester scan. The available evidence showed no evidence of difference in any clinical outcomes.

9.1.5   Fetal echocardiography

The diagnostic value and clinical effectiveness of fetal echocardiography to detect fetal cardiac anomalies was reviewed in this section.

Diagnostic value of fetal echocardiography

Description of included studies
Studies examining the diagnostic value of fetal echocardiography on low-risk or unselected populations were reviewed. One systematic review including five studies was identified plus two additional studies.[749–751] A description of these studies is presented in Table 9.3.

Findings
The sensitivity of detecting major cardiac anomalies from included studies ranged from 16.7% to 94.0%, and that for minor cardiac anomalies ranged from 3.6% to 82.1%. The overall sensitivity of detecting cardiac anomalies ranged from 4.5% to 86.1% and the specificity was reported as 99.9% throughout.

Evidence summary
The reported sensitivity of fetal echocardiography is widely ranged by centre and condition, although reported specificity was generally high.

Table 9.3 Diagnostic value of fetal echocardiography: description of included studies and reported sensitivity and specificity

Study and study design	Setting	Ultrasound methods	Study population and prevalence of congenital heart disease	Sensitivity	Specificity
Rustico (1995)[749] Prospective study	Italy Tertiary referral centre	20–22 weeks, four-chamber view plus outflow tracts, 5/3.5 MHz. Results confirmed by neonatal and paediatric examination, autopsy postnatally (neonatal echo and ECG, 24 month follow-up)	Low-risk women n = 7024. Prevalence of congenital heart disease: 9.3 per 1000	Major defects: 84.6% (95% CI 54.6% to 98.1%); Minor defects: 23.1% (95% CI 12.5% to 36.8%); Non-structural defects/arrhythmias: not reported; All defects: 35.4% (95% CI 23.9% to 48.2%)	Major defects: 99.9% (95% CI 99.9% to 100%); Minor defects: 99.9% (95% CI 99.9% to 100%); Non-structural defects/arrhythmias: not reported; All defects: 99.9% (95% CI 99.8% to 99.9%)
Anandakumar (2002)[749] Retrospective study	Singapore Tertiary referral centre	21–22 weeks, four-chamber view plus outflow tracts, and Doppler colour-flow mapping if suspected, 5/3.5 MHz. Results confirmed by neonatal examination (6 months follow-up)	Unselected women n = 39 808. Prevalence of congenital heart disease: 7.6 per 1000	Major defects: 94.0% (95% CI 84.4% to 98.5%); Minor defects: 82.1% (95% CI 76.5% to 86.9%); Non-structural defects/arrhythmias: 95.2% (95% CI 76.2% to 99.9%); All defects: 85.4% (95% CI 80.9% to 89.2%)	Major defects: 100.0% (95% CI 99.9% to 100%); Minor defects: 99.9% (95% CI 99.9% to 99.9%); Non-structural defects/arrhythmias: 99.9% (95% CI 99.9% to 99.9%); All defects: 99.9% (95% CI 99.9% to 99.9%)
Hafner (1998)[749] Prospective study	Austria District general hospital	22 and 34 weeks, four-chamber view plus outflow tracts, and Doppler colour-flow mapping if suspected. Results confirmed by neonatal examination (neonatal echo)	Low-risk women n = 6541. Prevalence of congenital heart disease: 13.6 per 1000	Major defects: 87.5% (95% CI 65.1% to 97.9%); Minor defects: 32.4% (95% CI 21.5% to 44.8%); Non-structural defects/arrhythmias: 83.3% (95% CI 17.7% to 19.9%); All defects: 46.1% (95% CI 35.4% to 57.0%)	Major defects: 99.9% (95% CI 99.9% to 100%); Minor defects: 99.9% (95% CI 99.9% to 100%); Non-structural defects/arrhythmias: 99.9% (95% CI 99.9% to 100%); All defects: 99.6% (95% CI 99.5% to 99.8%)
Achiron (1992)[749] Prospective study	Israel Tertiary referral centre	18–24 weeks, four-chamber view plus outflow tracts, and Doppler colour-flow mapping if suspected, 5/3.5 MHz. Results confirmed by neonatal examination and autopsy (neonatal echo)	Low-risk women n = 5347. Prevalence of congenital heart disease: 4.3 per 1000	Major defects: 83.3% (95% CI 55.6% to 97.1%); Minor defects: 50.0% (95% CI 11.8% to 88.2%); Non-structural defects/arrhythmias: 87.5% (95% CI 28.4% to 99.9%); All defects: 78.3% (95% CI 56.3% to 92.5%)	Major defects: 99.9% (95% CI 99.9% to 100%); Minor defects: 99.9% (95% CI 99.9% to 100%); Non-structural defects/arrhythmias: 99.9% (95% CI 99.9% to 100%); All defects: 99.9% (95% CI 99.9% to 100%)
Stumpflen (1996)[749] Prospective study	Austria Tertiary referral centre	18–28 weeks, four-chamber view plus outflow tracts and Doppler colour-flow mapping, 3.5 MHz. Results confirmed by neonatal examination and autopsy (diagnostic investigations)	Low-risk women n = 2181. Prevalence of congenital heart disease: 7.8 per 1000	Major defects: not reported; Minor defects: not reported; Non-structural defects/arrhythmias: not reported; All defects: 86.1% (95% CI 61.9% to 97.6%)	Major defects: not reported; Minor defects: not reported; Non-structural defects/arrhythmias: not reported; All defects: 99.9% (95% CI 99.8% to 100%)
Buskens (1996)[750] Prospective study	Netherlands Tertiary referral centre	16–24 weeks, four-chamber view plus outflow tracts, 3.5 Mhz. Results confirmed by neonatal examination and autopsy (neonatal echo)	Low-risk women n = 5319. Prevalence of congenital heart disease: 8.3 per 1000	Major defects: 16.7% (95% CI 2.1% to 48.4%); Minor defects: not reported; Non-structural defects/arrhythmias: not reported; All defects: 4.5% (95% CI 0.6% to 15.0%)	Major defects: not reported; Minor defects: not reported; Non-structural defects/arrhythmias: not reported; All defects: 99.9% (95% CI 99.8% to 100%)
Tegnander (2006)[751] Prospective study	Norway Tertiary referral centre	16–22 weeks, four-chamber view plus outflow tracts for first 5 years, then four-chamber view plus outflow tract plus venous return for next 5 years, 5/3.5 Mhz. Results confirmed by neonatal examination and autopsy (neonatal echo)	Unselected women n = 29 460. Prevalence of congenital heart disease: 14.6 per 1000	Major defects: 56.7% (95% CI 46.9% to 66.5%); Minor defects: 3.6% (95% CI 3.4 to 3.8); Non-structural defects/arrhythmias: not reported; All defects: 15.6% (95% CI 12.1 to 19.0)	Major defects: not reported; Minor defects: not reported; Non-structural defects/arrhythmias: not reported; All defects: not reported

2008 update

2008 update

Effectiveness of routine use of fetal echocardiography

Description of included studies
Neither RCTs nor quasi-randomised trials were identified to address this question. Two observational studies were identified,[752,753] neither of which controlled for the background severity of conditions.

Findings
One cohort study in France[752] compared outcome of babies between antenatally and postnatally diagnosed transposition of the great arteries (TGA). The study reported significantly lower preoperative mortality (postnatal diagnosis: 15/250 (6.0%) versus antenatal diagnosis 0/68 (0.0%); $P < 0.05$) and postoperative mortality (postnatal diagnosis: 20/235 (8.5%) versus 0/68 (0.0%); $P < 0.01$) for antenatally diagnosed TGA, although there was no evidence of difference in postoperative morbidity (postnatal diagnosis 25/235 (10.6%); antenatal diagnosis 6/68 (8.8%); $P > 0.05$). [EL = 2+]

Another population-based study in France[753] compared detection rates of TGA and mortality for babies with TGA between three study periods. Between 1983 and 1988, antenatally diagnosed TGA was 12.5% and mortality for babies with TGA was 23.5%, between 1989 and 1994 the detection rate was 48.1% and mortality 12.0%, and between 1995 and 2000 the detection rate was 72.5% and mortality 5%.

A similar trend was reported in babies with hypoplastic left heart syndrome. [EL = 3]

Evidence summary
There was low-level evidence that showed babies with antenatally diagnosed TGA had reduced mortality compared with those diagnosed after birth.

9.1.6 Soft markers

The diagnostic value and clinical effectiveness of ultrasound soft markers including nuchal translucency measurement to detect fetal cardiac anomalies was reviewed in this section. Nuchal translucency measurement to detect Down's syndrome was reviewed in Section 9.2.

Nuchal translucency measurement

Description of included studies
Studies examining the diagnostic value of nuchal translucency measurement of low-risk or unselected populations on detecting cardiac anomalies were reviewed. One systematic review including eight studies and four additional studies was identified.[754–758] Since studies used different cut-off points, meta-analysis of these twelve studies to obtain summary likelihood ratios was conducted (Table 9.4 and Figures 9.5 and 9.6) Neither RCTs nor quasi-randomised controlled trials were identified to address the effectiveness of routine use of this measurement on clinical outcomes of women and their babies.

Findings
Meta-analysis of the included 11 studies showed a positive likelihood ratio of 5.01 (95% CI 4.42 to 5.68) and a negative likelihood ratio of 0.70 (95% CI 0.65 to 0.75).

Evidence summary
The reported sensitivity and likelihood ratios of nuchal translucency measurement to detect cardiac anomalies ranged widely by centre and condition, and generally the technique seems to have poor diagnostic value.

9.1.7 Use of maternal serum alpha-fetoprotein to detect structural anomalies

The diagnostic value and clinical effectiveness of biochemical markers including maternal serum alpha-fetoprotein to detect neural tube defects was reviewed in this section.

Alpha-fetoprotein to detect neural tube defects

Description of included studies

Two studies were identified.[759,760] One study in the USA investigated the value of alpha-fetoprotein in screening for neural tube defects. The other was a case–control study in the USA comparing the ability of routine ultrasound and maternal serum alpha-fetoprotein levels to detect neural tube defects.

Findings

The first study,[759] which investigated maternal serum alpha-fetoprotein as a screening test, was conducted between 1991 and 1994 in the USA and involved 27 140 women. The prevalence of neural tube defects was reported as 1.03 per 1000. Sensitivity, specificity and positive and negative likelihood ratios were reported as 85.7%, 97.6%, 35.16 and 0.15, respectively.

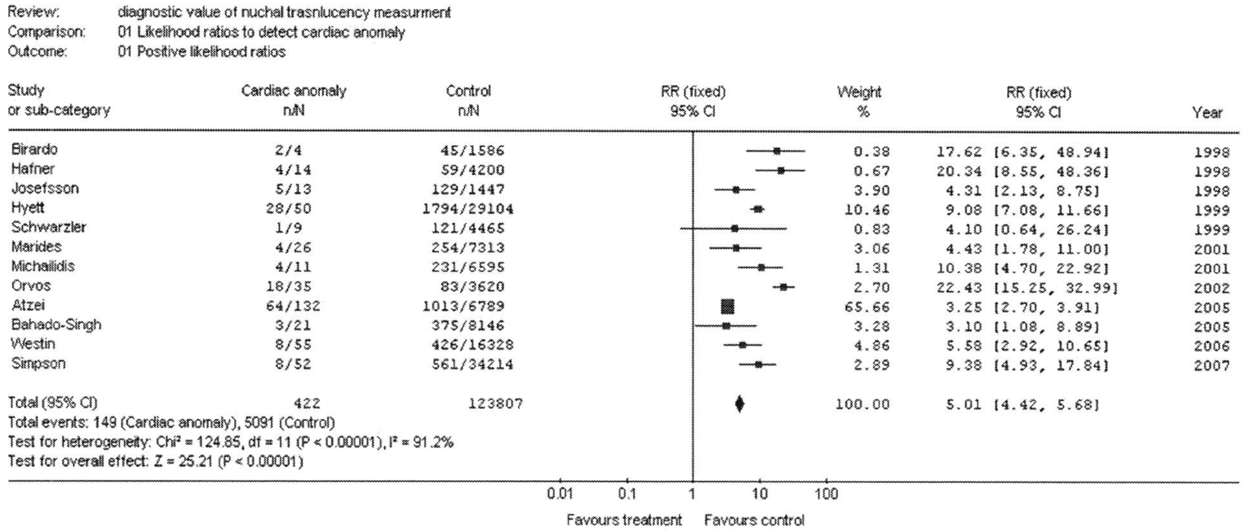

Review: diagnostic value of nuchal trasnlucency measurement
Comparison: 01 Likelihood ratios to detect cardiac anomaly
Outcome: 01 Positive likelihood ratios

Study or sub-category	Cardiac anomaly n/N	Control n/N	RR (fixed) 95% CI	Weight %	RR (fixed) 95% CI	Year
Birardo	2/4	45/1586		0.38	17.62 [6.35, 48.94]	1998
Hafner	4/14	59/4200		0.67	20.34 [8.55, 48.36]	1998
Josefsson	5/13	129/1447		3.90	4.31 [2.13, 8.75]	1998
Hyett	28/50	1794/29104		10.46	9.08 [7.08, 11.66]	1999
Schwarzler	1/9	121/4465		0.83	4.10 [0.64, 26.24]	1999
Marides	4/26	254/7313		3.06	4.43 [1.78, 11.00]	2001
Michailidis	4/11	231/6595		1.31	10.38 [4.70, 22.92]	2001
Orvos	18/35	83/3620		2.70	22.43 [15.25, 32.99]	2002
Atzei	64/132	1013/6789		65.66	3.25 [2.70, 3.91]	2005
Bahado-Singh	3/21	375/8146		3.28	3.10 [1.08, 8.89]	2005
Westin	8/55	426/16328		4.86	5.58 [2.92, 10.65]	2006
Simpson	8/52	561/34214		2.89	9.38 [4.93, 17.84]	2007
Total (95% CI)	422	123807		100.00	5.01 [4.42, 5.68]	

Total events: 149 (Cardiac anomaly), 5091 (Control)
Test for heterogeneity: Chi² = 124.85, df = 11 (P < 0.00001), I² = 91.2%
Test for overall effect: Z = 25.21 (P < 0.00001)

0.01　0.1　1　10　100
Favours treatment　Favours control

Figure 9.5 Meta-analysis of positive likelihood ratios by nuchal translucency measurement to detect fetal cardiac anomalies

Review: diagnostic value of nuchal trasnlucency measurment
Comparison: 01 Likelihood ratios to detect cardiac anomaly
Outcome: 02 Negative likelihood ratios

Study or sub-category	Cardiac anomaly n/N	Control n/N	RR (fixed) 95% CI	Weight %	RR (fixed) 95% CI	Year
Birardo	2/4	1541/1586		1.00	0.51 [0.19, 1.37]	1998
Hafner	10/14	4141/4200		3.54	0.72 [0.52, 1.01]	1998
Josefsson	8/13	1318/1447		3.02	0.68 [0.44, 1.04]	1998
Hyett	22/50	27310/29104		12.04	0.47 [0.34, 0.64]	1999
Schwarzler	8/9	4344/4465		2.25	0.91 [0.73, 1.15]	1999
Marides	22/26	7059/7313		6.43	0.88 [0.74, 1.03]	2001
Michailidis	7/11	6364/6595		2.72	0.66 [0.42, 1.03]	2001
Orvos	17/35	3537/3620		8.71	0.50 [0.35, 0.70]	2002
Atzei	68/132	5776/6789		28.32	0.61 [0.51, 0.71]	2005
Bahado-Singh	18/21	7771/8146		5.14	0.90 [0.75, 1.07]	2005
Westin	47/55	15902/16328		13.72	0.88 [0.79, 0.98]	2006
Simpson	44/52	33653/34214		13.13	0.86 [0.77, 0.97]	2007
Total (95% CI)	422	123807		100.00	0.70 [0.65, 0.75]	

Total events: 273 (Cardiac anomaly), 118716 (Control)
Test for heterogeneity: Chi² = 64.06, df = 11 (P < 0.00001), I² = 82.8%
Test for overall effect: Z = 10.16 (P < 0.00001)

0.1　0.2　0.5　1　2　5　10
Favours treatment　Favours control

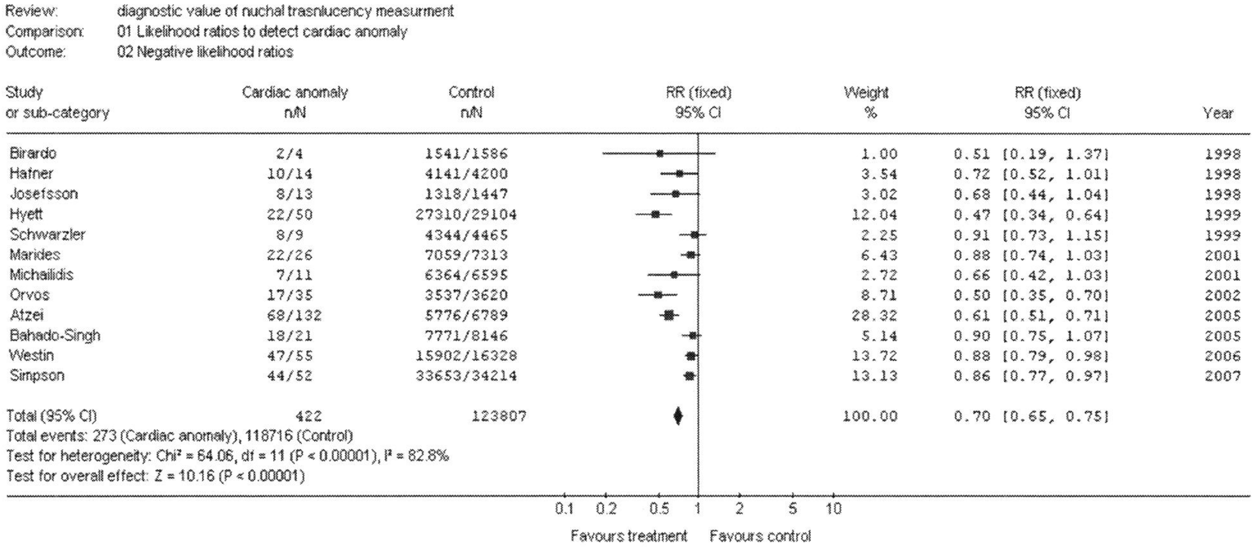

Figure 9.6 Meta-analysis of negative likelihood ratios by nuchal translucency measurement to detect fetal cardiac anomalies

2008 update

2008 update

Table 9.4 Diagnostic value of nuchal translucency measurement on fetal cardiac anomaly

Study and study design	Ultrasound measurement	Population	Cut-off	Sensitivity	Specificity	Likelihood ratios
Bilardo (1998)[754] Prospective study	10–14 weeks	n = 1590 Excluded chromosomal anomalies = 50	3.0 mm or greater	2/4 50.0%	1541/1586 97.2%	LR+ = 17.6 (95% CI 6.35 to 48.94) LR– = 0.51 (95% CI 0.19 to 1.37)
Hafner (1998)[754] Prospective study	10–13 weeks	n = 4214 Excluded chromosomal anomalies = 19	2.5 mm or greater	4/14 28.6%	4141/4200 98.6%	LR+ = 20.34 (95% CI 8.55 to 48.36) LR– = 0.72 (95% CI 0.52 to 1.01)
Josefsson (1998)[754] Prospective study	CRL 31–84 mm	n = 1460 Excluded chromosomal abnormalities = 0	2.5 mm or greater	5/13 38.5%	1318/1447 91.1%	LR+ = 4.31 (95% CI 2.13 to 8.75) LR– = 0.68 (95% CI 0.44 to 1.04)
			3.5 mm or greater	0/13 0.0%	1441/1447 99.6%	
Hyett (1999)[754,763] Retrospective study	10–14 weeks	n = 29 154 Excluded chromosomal abnormalities = 323	Greater than 95th centile	28/50 56.0%	27 310/29 104 93.8%	LR+ = 9.08 (95% CI 7.08 to 11.66) LR– = 0.47 (95% CI 0.34 to 0.64)
			Greater than 3.5 mm	20/50 40.0%	28 809/29 104 99.0%	
Schwarzler (1999)[754,764] Prospective study	10–14 weeks	n = 4474 Excluded chromosomal abnormalities = 23	2.5 mm or greater	1/9 11.1%	4344/4465 97.3%	LR+ = 4.10 (95% CI 0.64 to 26.24) LR– = 0.91 (95% CI 0.73 to 1.15)
Michailidis (2001)[754,765] Retrospective study	12–13 weeks	n = 6606 Excluded chromosomal abnormalities = 44	Greater than 95th centile	4/11 36.4%	6364/6595 96.5%	LR+ = 10.38 (95% CI 4.70 to 22.92) LR– = 0.66 (95% CI 0.42 to 1.03)
			Greater than 99th centile	3/11 27.3%	6525/6595 98.9%	
Marides (2001)[754,766] Prospective study	10–14 weeks	n = 7339 Excluded chromosomal abnormalities, not defined	2.5 mm or greater	4/26 15.4%	7059/7313 96.5%	LR+ = 4.43 (95% CI 1.78 to 11.0) LR– = 0.88 (95% CI 0.74 to 1.03)
			3.5 mm or greater	3/26 11.5%	7256/7313 99.2%	
Orvos (2002)[754] Retrospective study	10–13 weeks	n = 3655 Excluded chromosomal abnormalities = 15	3.0 mm or greater	18/35 51.4%	3537/3620 97.7%	LR+ = 22.43 (95% CI 15.25 to 32.99) LR– = 0.50 (95% CI 0.35 to 0.70)

Study and study design	Ultrasound measurement	Population	Cut-off	Sensitivity	Specificity	Likelihood ratios
Atzei (2005)[756] Prospective study	11–13 weeks	n = 6921 Chromosomal abnormalities excluded (no number obtained)	95th centile or greater	105/132 79.5%	3454/6789 50.9%	
			3.5 mm or greater	64/132 48.5%	5776/6789 85.1%	LR+ = 3.25 (95% CI 2.70 to 3.91) LR– = 0.61 (95% CI 0.51 to 0.71)
			4.5 mm or greater	41/132 31.1%	6407/6789 94.4%	
			5.5 mm or greater	28/132 21.2%	6596/6789 97.2%	
Bahado-Singh (2005)[755] Retrospective study	10–13 weeks	n = 8167 Excluded chromosomal abnormalities = 101	2.0 mm or greater	8/21 38.1%	6744/8146 82.8%	
			2.5 mm or greater	3/21 14.3%	7771/8146 95.4%	LR+ = 3.10 (95% CI 1.08 to 8.89) LR– = 0.90 (95% CI 0.75 to 1.07)
			3.5 mm or greater	1/21 4.8%	8104/8146 99.5%	
Westin (2006)[757] Retrospective study	12–14 weeks	n = 16 383 Excluded chromosomal abnormalities = 80	Greater than 95th centile	8/55 14.5%	15 902/16 328 97.4%	LR+ = 5.58 (95% CI 2.92 to 10.65) LR– = 0.88 (95% CI 0.79 to 0.98)
			3.0 mm or greater	5/55 9.0%	16 197/16 328 99.2%	
			3.5 mm or greater	3/55 5.4%	16 279/16 328 99.7%	
Simpson (2007)[758] Retrospective study	10 weeks 3 days to 13 weeks 6 days	n = 34 266 Excluded chromosomal abnormalities = 104	2.0 MoM or greater (98.3rd centile)	8/52 15.4%	33 653/34 214 98.4%	LR+ = 9.38 (95% CI 4.93 to 17.84) LR– = 0.86 (95% CI 0.77 to 0.97)
			2.5 MoM or greater (99.4th centile)	7/52 13.5%	34 012/34 214 99.4%	
			3.0 MoM or greater (99.7th centile)	5/52 9.6%	34 118/34 214 99.7%	
Total						LR+ = 5.01 (95% CI 4.42 to 5.68) LR– = 0.70 (95% CI 0.65 to 0.75)

CRL = crown–rump length.

2008 update

In the case–control study,[760] an integrated database of 219 000 consecutive pregnancies between 1995 and 2002 was used. Among 189 identified fetuses with neural tube defects, 102 had received maternal serum alpha-fetoprotein screening, and 25% of 102 cases were test negative. Of the 186 neural tube defects identified prenatally, 62% were initially detected by routine second-trimester ultrasound, 37% were detected by targeted ultrasound prompted by high maternal serum alpha-fetoprotein level, and the remaining 1% were diagnosed by pathology examination after miscarriage.

Evidence summary
There were only two studies dealing with the diagnostic value and effectiveness of maternal serum alpha-fetoprotein level as a screening test. Results from a single study indicate maternal serum alpha-fetoprotein level to have good diagnostic value in predicting and ruling out structural anomalies, but evidence from another study shows it to have less value as a screening test than routine ultrasound. There is no evidence assessing the diagnostic value and effectiveness of combining maternal serum alpha-fetoprotein and routine ultrasound.

9.1.8 Women's views on screening for structural anomalies

Three studies on women' views regarding ultrasound screening during pregnancy, their responses to detection of soft markers, and antenatal counselling by specialist staff have been included under this section.

Description of included studies
The first study was a review[297] [EL = 2++] which focused on women's views and experiences of antenatal ultrasound. As the topic was very wide, it was decided to limit the review to studies where antenatal ultrasound was used for any purpose and direct data were obtained from pregnant women. Studies and reviews about prenatal screening and diagnosis were excluded. After a broad initial search to identify material related to women's views in all screening and diagnostic tests, studies related to antenatal ultrasound use were selected after going through their abstracts. A series of six questions was prepared, targeting: (i) women's knowledge about ultrasound and what a scan can do; (ii) women's value about scans; (iii) her views about how ultrasound is conducted; (iv) impact of the result; (v) psychological impact of ultrasound; and (vi) wider impact of ultrasound on society. Studies were tabulated according to the question asked and data entered accordingly.

In the second study[761] qualitative interviews were conducted to determine women's experiences and responses to detection of a minor structural variant, the choroid plexus cyst (CPC), in their fetuses on prenatal ultrasound. Thirty-four pregnant women with isolated CPC detected during a mid-trimester scan who had already been counselled by their physicians regarding the findings at a university-based hospital in the USA were enrolled for the study. Interviews lasting approximately 15 minutes were conducted by a trained research assistant or nurse clinician at 24 weeks of pregnancy, and no information was given about CPCs by the research team. The interview included both open-ended and more specific questions, and all were audiotaped and transcribed verbatim. Common themes were identified, and several categories of responses identified for each theme. Initial validation was undertaken by an independent qualitative study consultant not involved in the research. The *t*-test was used for comparing means and χ^2 for categorical variables. The results are reported as mean ± standard deviation. [EL = 3]

The aim of the third study[762] was to evaluate parental anxiety after diagnosis of a congenital malformation and to assess whether counselling by a consultant paediatric surgeon and a neonatal nurse practitioner could decrease parents' psychological distress. Participants were all parents attending a fetal medicine unit in the UK with an antenatal diagnosis of surgical anomaly (principally abdominal wall defects and gastrointestinal and thoracic anomalies). Women unable to read English and those booked to give birth somewhere else were excluded. Anonymous questionnaires were used to gain information as well as the Spielberger State-Trait Anxiety Inventory (STAI) for measuring anxiety levels. The STAI consists of two parts – the STAI-S score measuring anxiety at the time of completing the inventory, and the STAI-T score measuring the inherent trait anxiety levels. Participants were asked to complete STAI after ultrasound at the fetal centre. Then each couple had a detailed consultation with the paediatric consultant and the clinical nurse specialist. Before leaving, the subjects were given a second STAI and asked to complete and return within 1 week. A control group comprising pregnant women with a normal ultrasound scan and uncomplicated pregnancy was recruited and asked to complete STAI as the other group. Non-parametric tests were used for comparison, and data are quoted as medians and interquartile ranges (IQRs). [EL = 3]

Findings

In the first study,[297] a total of 82 reports representing 64 studies were selected (including five studies which were added later). There was wide variation among the selected studies in terms of questions addressed, methods used, and when and where they were conducted. The studies were not graded in terms of research quality or removed because of poor quality, although many had problems of design and reporting. This was done because, in spite of poor quality, these studies gave useful information. The main findings of the review are discussed below.

Antenatal ultrasound is very attractive to pregnant women and their partners as it provides early visual confirmation of pregnancy, direct contact with their baby and reassurance about fetal wellbeing. At the same time, these features may augment the potential for feelings of anxiety, shock and disappointment when the scan shows a problem.

Recent trends in the use of ultrasound have led to more findings of uncertain clinical importance, and this is likely to have important psychological and social consequences for women.

Although it was reported in earlier studies that some women feared that ultrasound might harm their babies, there is a paucity of evidence about it from the later studies.

Reports of a reduction in anxiety after ultrasound examination are likely to reflect increased anxiety before the scan rather than a real benefit.

No reliable evidence is available for any positive health behaviour (e.g. reduced smoking) as a consequence of antenatal ultrasound.

None of the trials comparing ultrasound use with no ultrasound use has looked at its social and psychological impact on parents and babies.

In general, participants in the second study[761] were college educated (mean years of education 16.6 ± 2.5), married (85.7%), employed (100%) and had private insurance (97%). The mean maternal age was 32.2 ± 5.2 years. About 60% were primiparous and 80% had a planned pregnancy. Women's responses have been organised into categories as listed below.

- *Diagnostic situation.* Mean gestational age at CPC detection was 18.86 ± 1.29 weeks. The majority of the participants (71%) were informed about CPC by an attending or local obstetrician at the conclusion of the ultrasound examination, and 35% of women were shown the CPC on ultrasound.
- *Accuracy of knowledge.* Most of the women (79%) had never heard of CPC before the diagnosis. When asked about the significance of the CPC, 82% felt that it was probably benign, 71% expressed it is a marker for trisomy, and 53% mentioned that it could be both. Among those who expressed it as a marker for trisomy, 79% understood that other factors (maternal age, serum markers) also influenced the probability of trisomy. Women with positive serum screening results were less likely to describe CPC as benign compared with women with a normal serum screen (OR 0.04, 95% CI 0.004 to 0.36; $P < 0.001$). No statistically significant difference was observed between the older women (> 34 years) and younger ones.
- *Information seeking.* Seventy-seven percent of women reported seeking additional information about CPCs beyond that given by their provider at the original scan, with the most common source being the internet. When asked about the usefulness of this additional information, 62% found it more useful than the primary information given at the time of ultrasound screening.
- *Subsequent testing.* The majority of women (65%) already had a serum screening test before detection of CPCs. After detection of an isolated CPC and in spite of accurate counselling about low risk, three women (9%) sought diagnostic tests purely for reassurance.

- *Affective responses.* When asked in an open-ended way to describe their emotions, 88% of women described an intensely negative immediate reaction, with most (68%) reporting their initial reaction as temporary. But only half of the women with a reassuring serum screen and none with an abnormal serum screen described their reaction as temporary. Sixty-eight percent of women revealed that they continued experiencing negative emotions even after receiving the diagnostic tests results, but neither increased maternal age nor visualisation of CPC on ultrasound were associated with persistence of the initial negative response. The later emotional responses included anxiety (23.5%), shock/grief (26.5%), decreased attachment (14.7%), decreased pleasure in pregnancy (14.7%), and thoughts of abortion/miscarriage (11.8%), confusion (8.8%), guilt (2.9%) and fear (5.9%).

Fifty-six pregnant women (subjects 26, control 30) completed the questionnaire in the third study.[762] The most common congenital malformation present was gastroschisis followed by diaphragmatic hernia and cystic adenomatoid malformation. Maternal age was significantly lower in subjects (median 26.5 years) than in the control group (median 32 years) ($P = 0.006$).

No significant difference was found between STAI-T scores of subjects and controls. No correlation was found between the score and maternal age or social class, or between maternal and paternal scores.

STAI-S scores of subjects were significantly higher than those of controls before paediatric consultation ($P = 0.0004$), but not after ($P = 0.31$). There was a significant reduction in the anxiety levels of both subjects (mothers and fathers) after consultation (on comparing their scores before and after paediatric consultation) ($P = 0.01$ for mothers, $P = 0.006$ for fathers). After grouping the subjects into fetal diagnostic groups, a significant decrease in anxiety levels was found for those with anterior abdominal defects but not with cystic adenomatoid malformation. No correlation was found between the scores and maternal age.

The study showed that there was a high anxiety state in both prospective mothers and fathers of fetuses diagnosed with congenital malformations on ultrasound which is over and above that associated with pregnancy. Counselling by specialist staff reduced levels of parental anxiety significantly.

Evidence summary
Results from a well-conducted structured review show that visual confirmation of fetal wellbeing is the primary reason why women seek ultrasound during pregnancy. There is a lack of evidence regarding its other benefits and harms.

Evidence from a qualitative study indicates that detection of an isolated choroid plexus cyst on antenatal ultrasound leads to negative emotions and anxiety in the majority of women, who then seek additional information from other sources. In spite of reassurance in the form of a negative serum screening test for Down's syndrome, a few women also opt for an invasive test for confirmation.

Detection of surgically treatable congenital anomalies on antenatal ultrasound led to increased anxiety levels in the parents but counselling by specialist staff helped to alleviate it significantly.

Health economics evidence
In the NICE clinical guideline on diabetes in pregnancy[636] an economic model was developed to compare the cost-effectiveness of screening for congenital cardiac malformations using a four chamber ultrasound scan versus the four chamber plus outflow tracts view. This was considered to be important because women with diabetes are at increased risk of having a baby with a cardiac malformation. It was felt that this model was also relevant for the antenatal care guideline and therefore it was adapted for the antenatal care population. The results are summarised here; futher details are provided in Appendix E.

The baseline analysis suggested that the four chamber plus outflow tracts view has an ICER of £24,000 relative to the four chamber view alone. This falls within the borderline cost-effectiveness range of £20,000 to £30,000 per QALY used by NICE.

For the health economics evidence for the combined Down's syndrome and structural anomalies screening, please see Section 9.2 (Screening for Down's syndrome)

GDG interpretation of evidence (screening for structural anomalies)

Routine ultrasound screening:

Ultrasound appears to be acceptable to women. Prenatal ultrasound scanning for fetal anomalies is now undertaken at around 20 weeks (rather than 18 weeks). However, the screening window should be between 18 weeks 0 days and 20 weeks 6 days. Screening later than 20 weeks 6 days may delay the diagnosis of an abnormality to a point where termination of an affected pregnancy becomes problematic and may involve additional procedures such as feticide. However, it should be remembered that where women are very overweight, performing the ultrasound scan can be very difficult and time-consuming. There is also a potential for an increase in repetitive strain injury (RSI)-related problems if sonographers are expected to complete all anomaly scans by 20 weeks. For this reason, the recommendation uses the word 'normally' in recognition of these potential difficulties.

Screening for congenital cardiac anomalies using the four chamber plus outflow tracts view has been shown to have an ICER of £24,000 relative to the four chamber view alone. There are likely to be further benefits of this method for detecting congenital cardiac malformations over and above that of TGA detection (the main focus of the model).

It is noted that some of the reviewed literature is from the 1980s and 1990s when scanning equipment was less well developed. The literature on scanning for fetal heart anomalies is more recent, however. It is also important to note that detection rates very much depend on the expertise of the person scanning as well as gestation and standard of equipment. Detection rates have improved in certain areas but this is due to further training as well as to advances in technology.

The prevalence of fetal anomalies and their detection rates can be evaluated either individually or after categorising them into four groups based on the RCOG criteria – lethal anomalies, anomalies with possible survival and long-term morbidity, anomalies amenable to intrauterine therapy, and anomalies with possible short-term or immediate morbidity (Table 9.2). Ultrasound cannot reassure women that their baby is normal, as many anomalies are missed. Ultrasound may not offer improved outcomes despite antenatal diagnosis, but may offer reproductive choices and the opportunity to plan intrauterine therapy or managed delivery.

Evidence from a single study shows that a first-trimester scan with nuchal translucency measurement is equally effective as the second-trimester scan in detecting fetal malformation overall. However, this may not be true for individual conditions, for example spina bifida is more likely to be detected by the second-trimester scan, while anencephaly and anterior abdominal wall defects may be detected in the earlier scans.

There is insufficient evidence that routine ultrasound between 10 and 24 weeks improves long-term outcomes after birth.

There is no evidence to support the use of selective rather than routine ultrasound scanning for fetal anomalies, gestational age determination and the diagnosis of multiple pregnancies.

Findings from an HTA review suggest a second-trimester scan is the most cost-effective strategy for screening for fetal anomalies. However, there is also evidence that each different method of screening has its advantages and disadvantages, and these often seem to balance out. No one screening method stands out as being much more cost-effective than any other.

Diagnostic accuracy of fetal echocardiography:

The sensitivity of fetal echocardiography for detecting major malformations varies widely (from 17% to 94%) depending on gestation, skill of the operator and the equipment. However, there is some evidence that better training leads to improved performance of fetal cardiac screening and some limited evidence that antenatal diagnosis of TGA leads to better outcome for the babies.

Diagnostic accuracy of the nuchal test: soft markers:

Studies evaluating nuchal translucency as a marker of cardiac anomaly found it to have poor sensitivity. Different cut-off points across centres and for different cardiac defects affected sensitivity and false positive rates, which are important considerations for women undergoing this test.

Diagnostic accuracy of AFP:

AFP has lower diagnostic value than routine ultrasound in screening for neural tube defects. There is no evidence for effect on outcomes. However, the introduction of screening using AFP has led to a reduction in the number of affected babies born at term with neural tube defects.

2008 update

2008 update

Women's views on screening for structural anomalies:
Ultrasound screening provides reassurance if no anomaly is detected but heightens anxiety if a possible problem is identified

Recommendations on screening for fetal anomalies

Ultrasound screening for fetal anomalies should be routinely offered, normally between 18 weeks 0 days and 20 weeks 6 days.

At the first contact with a healthcare professional, women should be given information about the purpose and implications of the anomaly scan to enable them to make an informed choice as to whether or not to have the scan. The purpose of the scan is to identify fetal anomalies and allow:

- reproductive choice (termination of pregnancy)
- parents to prepare (for any treatment/disability/palliative care/termination of pregnancy)
- managed birth in a specialist centre
- intrauterine therapy.

Women should be informed of the limitations of routine ultrasound screening and that detection rates vary by the type of fetal anomaly, the woman's body mass index and the position of the unborn baby at the time of the scan.

If an anomaly is detected during the anomaly scan pregnant women should be informed of the findings to enable them to make an informed choice as to whether they wish to continue with the pregnancy or have a termination of pregnancy.

Fetal echocardiography involving the four chamber view of the fetal heart and outflow tracts is recommended as part of the routine anomaly scan.

Routine screening for cardiac anomalies using nuchal translucency is not recommended.

When routine ultrasound screening is performed to detect neural tube defects, alpha-fetoprotein testing is not required.

Participation in regional congenital anomaly registers and/or UK National Screening Committee-approved audit systems is strongly recommended to facilitate the audit of detection rates.

Research recommendation on screening for fetal anomalies

Research should be undertaken to elucidate the relationship between increased nuchal translucency and cardiac defects.

9.2 Screening for Down's syndrome

Clinical question
What is the diagnostic value and effectiveness of the following screening methods in identifying babies with Down's syndrome?

- blood tests
- nuchal translucency
- maternal age
- ultrasound – soft markers (choroid plexus cyst, thickened nuchal fold, echogenic intracardiac focus, echogenic bowel, renal pyelectasis, humeral and femoral shortening)
- ultrasound – nasal bone
- different timings include:
  - first trimester
  - second trimester
  - integrated

Previous NICE guidance (for the updated recommendations see below)
Pregnant women should be offered screening for Down's syndrome with a test that provides the current standard of a detection rate above 60% and false positive rate of less than 5%.

By April 2007, pregnant women should be offered screening for Down's syndrome with a test which provides a detection rate above 75% and false positive rate of less than 3%. These performance measures should be age standardised and based on a cut-off of 1/250 at term.

Pregnant women should be given information about the detection rates and false positive rates of any Down's syndrome screening test being offered and about further diagnostic tests that may be offered. The woman's right to accept or decline the test should be made clear.

9.2.1   Introduction and background

Down's syndrome, also termed trisomy 21, is a congenital syndrome that arises when the affected baby has an extra copy of chromosome 21. In the absence of antenatal screening, about 1 in 700 babies born would be affected. The birth incidence of Down's syndrome in England and Wales was 1.1 per 1000 live births in 2005 (represents 753 live births) (National Down's syndrome register). Down's syndrome causes learning disability, often profound, but the majority of children with the condition learn to walk, talk, read and write, although will meet these developmental milestones later than other children. It is also associated with increased incidence of congenital malformations (particularly cardiac and gastrointestinal anomalies) as well as an increased incidence of thyroid disorders, childhood leukaemias, and hearing, ophthalmic and respiratory problems. About half of children with Down's syndrome are born with cardiac defects that require surgery, but survival rates are high. Average life expectancy for someone with the condition is 50–60 years.

Screening for Down's syndrome should start with the provision of unbiased, evidence-based information about the condition, enabling women to make autonomous, informed decisions. Ideally, this information should be made available early in the pregnancy so that women have enough time to carefully consider the options and seek further information if needed. Screening for Down's syndrome is part of an integrated screening programme and all staff involved should be familiar with the care pathways and their role within them.

Screening for Down's syndrome takes place during either the first or second trimester by either ultrasound or maternal serum biochemistry, or a combination of both. Screening tests include the following:

- at 11–14 weeks:
  - nuchal translucency (NT)
  - combined test (NT + hCG + PAPP-A)
- at 15 – 20 weeks:
  - double test (hCG, uE3)
  - triple test (hCG, uE3, AFP)
  - quadruple test (hCG, uE3, AFP, inhibin A)
- at 11–14 weeks and then at 15–20 weeks:
  - integrated test (combined test at 11–14 weeks, followed by AFP, uE3 and inhibin A at 15–20 weeks)
  - serum integrated test (PAPP-A and hCG at 11–14 weeks, followed by AFP, uE3 and inhibin A at 15–20 weeks).

Once a screening test has been performed, the chance of the fetus having Down's syndrome is calculated taking into account maternal age and gestation. Results are classified as either 'screen positive' if the chance is equal to or greater than a nationally agreed cut-off level. This is often expressed numerically to indicate the likelihood that a woman has a baby with Down's syndrome when a positive screening result is returned, for example a 1/250 chance that a pregnant woman is carrying an affected baby. When a screen-positive result is returned, the woman will usually be offered a diagnostic test, either chorionic villus sampling (following a first-trimester screening test) or amniocentesis (following a second-trimester screening test). Invasive diagnostic testing and karyotyping by either chorionic villus sampling or amniocentesis is the gold standard test for confirming the diagnosis but is associated with an excess risk of fetal loss of approximately 1% compared with women with no invasive testing. When a woman is offered a diagnostic test after a positive screening result, she should be informed of the risks associated with the invasive testing and that other chromosomal abnormalities, not just Down's syndrome, may be identified and that in some cases the prognosis for the fetus may not be clear.

2008 update

9.2.2 Diagnostic accuracy

Some studies have presented data on the screening performance as observed directly, while others have estimated diagnostic accuracy based on the study results. Where possible, results have been presented using a fixed false positive rate (FPR) of 5% (wherever calculated) in order to allow comparison between the findings, but the unadjusted results are also given.

The included studies have been stratified according to:

1. the timing of the screening test, that is, conducted in the first trimester only, in the second trimester only, or both
2. the type of abnormality detected – babies with Down's syndrome only or both Down's syndrome and other chromosomal anomalies.

First-trimester studies

Description of included studies
A total of 15 studies have been included under first-trimester screening. Initially, nine studies were identified for inclusion – all prospective cohort studies, including six multicentre ones. The objectives in all studies were clearly defined. Three studies comprised an unselected population, one study included both selected and unselected, and five selected population only. Except for a single study,[767] the screening test and the quality measures used to monitor the study were adequately explained. All the studies used a validated reference test (karyotyping or postnatal assessment of babies or pregnancy records). The screening tests were performed before the reference tests in most studies, but it is difficult to ascertain blinding of the reference test operator. As the three studies on nasal bone gave conflicting results, six more studies were reviewed. All these studies were prospective cohorts but the quality of the studies was not good (all are EL III studies either owing to selected population, incomplete follow-up or inadequate quality control).

Findings
The first-trimester studies have been divided into the anomalies they looked at.

Down's syndrome and other chromosomal anomalies:
Three studies evaluated the serum combined test[768–770] and three fetal nasal bone on ultrasound.[771–773] These studies have been tabulated in Tables 9.5 and 9.6, respectively. The additional six studies on evaluation of fetal nasal bone[771,773–777] are given in Table 9.7.

Results from a good-quality cohort with large sample size[768] showed the serum combined test to have a detection rate of 92.6% at a false positive rate of 5.2% for the detection of Down's syndrome, and a slightly lower detection rate for trisomy 18 or 13 and other chromosomal anomalies. Similar results were observed in another study,[770] while the third study[769] showed a lower detection rate but higher FPR for the combined test.

Conflicting results were seen for the diagnostic accuracy of fetal nasal bone evaluation (Table 9.6). While one study[772] showed fetal nasal bone to increase the detection rate of Down's syndrome from 90% to 93% (fixed FPR 5%) compared with using the combined test only, the other study[771] showed it to have very poor diagnostic value. The third study[773] had variable diagnostic accuracy results for the selected and unselected population.

Results from the additional six studies evaluated for fetal nasal bone were also inconclusive and wide variation was observed in them (Table 9.7). In two studies[779,780] it improved the detection rate compared with using the serum combined test alone, but in one study[775] there was a reduction in the detection rate. The sensitivity and detection rate of fetal nasal bone alone in the rest of the studies varied from 32% to 70%.

From these nine included studies on nasal bone characteristics, various factors have been identified which seem to influence the finding of absent nasal bone on first-trimester ultrasound. These factors are experience and training of the ultrasound operator, gestational age at which ultrasound is conducted (ideally CRL to be more than 45 mm as ossification of nasal bone starts after this), type of population screened (low-risk or high-risk), and marker used for diagnosis (complete absence or hypoplasia of the nasal bone).

2008 update

Table 9.5 First-trimester screening for Down's syndrome and other chromosomal anomalies using the serum combined test

Study	Nicolaides et al. (2005)[768]	Wapner et al. (2003)[769]	Stenhouse et al. (2004)[770]
Type of study	Prospective cohort	Prospective cohort	Prospective cohort
Year of publication	2005	2003	2004
Period	1998–2003	Not specified	3 years
Setting	6 hospitals, 1 fetal medicine unit, UK	12 prenatal diagnostic centres, USA	ANC clinic of 1 hospital, UK
Study population	Unselected (booked for maternity care)	Selected (12 diagnostic centres) (Small sample)	Selected (75% screening uptake, 27% ≥ 35 years)
Exclusions	Adequately described	Adequately described	Adequately described
Test conducted	Combined (NT + β-hCG + PAPP-A)	Combined	Combined
Monitoring of test quality	Adequate	Adequate	Adequate
Validated reference standard	Yes (prenatal karyotype, pregnancy records)	Yes (karyotype-pre/postnatal, pregnancy records)	Yes (prenatal karyotype, pregnancy records)
Sample size (% of study population)	75 821 (96.7%)	8216 (93.2%)	5000 (98.3%)
Maternal age	Median 31 years, range 13 to 49 years	Mean 34.5 years, SD 4.6 years	Median 31.5 years, range 14 to 45 years
Number of cases (prevalence)	DS: 325 (0.43%); T 18/13: 122 (0.16%); Others: 97 (0.13%)	DS: 61 (0.74%); T 18: 11 (0.13%)	DS: 15 (0.3%); All: 26 (0.52%)
Results	Estimated detection rate for FPR 5.2%: DS: 92.6%; T 18/13: 88.5%; Others: 85.6%	Observed detection rate and FPR (with 95% CI): DS: 85.2% (73.8–93.0%), with FPR 9.4% (8.8–10.1%) T 18: 90.9% (58.7–99.8%), with FPR 2% (1.7–2.3%)	Observed detection rate: DS: 93% at FPR 5.9%; All: 96% at FPR 6.3%
Risk cut-off	≥ 1 in 300 for all	1 : 270 for DS, 1 : 150 for T 18	≥ 1 : 250 for all
Evidence level	Ib	II	II
Comments	Apart from estimating the diagnostic accuracy of the combined test, this study also evaluated the potential impact of individual risk-oriented two-stage screening using three new ultrasound markers. The population was subdivided into high risk (risk > 1 in 100), intermediate risk (1 in 101 to 1 in 1000) and low risk (< 1 in 1000). The intermediate risk group was further assessed by first-trimester ultrasound using absence of nasal bone, abnormal Doppler waveform in ductus venosus or presence of tricuspid regurgitation. Using a risk cut-off of 1 in 100, the DR and FPR were found to vary with the method used: absence of nasal bone DR 92% with FPR 2.1%, abnormal ductus venosus waveform DR 94.2% with FPR 2.7%, and tricuspid regurgitation DR 91.7% with FPR 2.7%.	For Down's syndrome, the estimated DR for a fixed FPR of 5% at the same risk was 78.7% (95% CI 66.3% to 88.1%), and for a fixed FPR of 1% was 63.9% (95% CI 50.6% to 75.8%).	This study was carried out following poor nuchal translucency measurements obtained from an earlier study[767] (discussed in Table 9.8). Efforts were made to allow more time for nuchal translucency measurement and compulsory quality control of all ultrasound operators was introduced.

DR = detection rate; DS = Down's syndrome; FPR = false positive rate; β-hCG = beta-human chorionic gonadotrophin; NT = nuchal translucency; PAPP-A = pregnancy-associated plasma protein-A; SD = standard deviation; T 18/13 = trisomy 18 or 13.

2008 update

2008 update

Table 9.6 First-trimester screening for Down's syndrome and other chromosomal anomalies using nasal bone evaluation

Study	Malone et al. (2004)[771]	Cicero et al. (2006)[772]	Prefumo et al. (2006)[773]
Type of study	Prospective cohort	Prospective cohort	Prospective cohort
Year of publication	2005	2006	2006
Period	8 months	2001–2004	2001–2003
Setting	15 specialist centres, USA	1 fetal medicine unit, UK	1 fetal medicine unit, UK
Study population	Selected (small sample)	Selected (single centre)	Both unselected and selected (routine antenatal care and referrals)
Exclusions	Adequately described	Adequately described	Adequately described
Test conducted	Fetal nasal bone (NB)	Combined with or without NB	NB
Monitoring of test quality	Adequate	Adequate	Adequate
Validated reference standard	Yes (prenatal karyotype, pregnancy records)	Yes (karyotype, pregnancy records)	Yes (prenatal karyotype, pregnancy records)
Sample size (% of study population)	6228 (98.5%)	20 418 (96.9%)	7626 *Selected* – 6.7% (100%) *Unselected* – 93.3%
Maternal age	Mean 30.1 years, SD 5.7 years, range 16–47 years	Median 35 years, range 18–50 years	Median 31.6 years, range 14.5–50.2 years
Successful NB image (% of sample size)	4801 (75.9%)	20 175 (98.8)	6872 *Selected* 91.8% (90.1%) *Unselected* 90%
Number of cases (prevalence)	DS: 11 (0.18%); T 18: 2 (0.03%); All: 13 (0.21%)	DS: 140 (0.68%); T 18: 40 (0.13%); Others: 73 (0.36%)	DS: 35 (0.5%); *Selected*: 23 (4.5%); *Unselected*: 12 (0.2%); All: 64 (0.8%)
Results	Observed detection rate and FPR (with 95% CI): DS: 0 (no case detected); All: 7.7% (0.2–36%) with FPR 0.3% (0.2–0.5)	Estimated detection rate (risk 1 : 51 to 1 : 1000) (for DS cases only): *Combined*: 90% with 5% FPR *Combined + NB*: 93.6% with 5% FPR	Observed performance (with 95% CI) (for DS cases only): *Selected*: ST 47.6% (25.7–70.2%); SP 95.3% (92.9–97.1%); PPV 33.3% (17.3–52.8%); NPV 97.4% (95.3–98.7%) *Unselected*: ST 16.7% (2.1–48.4%), SP 97.3% (96.9–97.7%); PPV 1.1% (0.1–4.1%); NPV 99.8% (99.7–99.9%)
Evidence level	II	II	II
Comments	This study was a part of a larger prospective mult-centre trial evaluating the diagnostic accuracy of both first- and second-trimester screening. NB assessment was started in the last 8 months of the trial.	The absence of NB was evaluated in all the study participants undergoing the combined test, and also in a sequential manner for women having risk between 1 in 51 to 1 in 1000 based on the combined test. The results were the same under both conditions.	The study population consisted of both selected and unselected population. Different values for these have been given above.

DS = Down's syndrome; FPR = false positive rate; NB = nasal bone; NPV = negative predictive value; PPV = positive predictive value; SD = standard deviation; SP = specificity; ST = sensitivity; T 18 = trisomy 18.

Table 9.7 First-trimester screening for Down's syndrome using nasal bone evaluation – additional studies

Study	Weingertner et al. (2006)[779]	Ramos-Corp et al. (2006)[774]	Orlandi et al. (2005)[780]
Type of study	Prospective cohort	Prospective cohort	prospective cohort
Year of publication	2006	2006	2005
Period	2002–2004	2003–2004	Not specified
Setting	1 reference centre, France	1 fetal medicine unit, Spain	1 fetal medicine unit, Italy
Study population	Both unselected and selected (single reference centre)	Selected (single centre, only 45% participated)	Selected (details not specified)
Exclusions	Adequately described	Not described	Not described
Test conducted	NT with or without NB	NB	Combined test with or without NB
Monitoring of test quality	Adequate	Adequate	Adequate
Validated reference standard	Yes (prenatal karyotype, pregnancy records)	Yes (karyotype, pregnancy records)	Yes (prenatal karyotype, pregnancy records)
Sample size (% of study population)	2044 (91.5%); *Selected – 33%; Unselected – 67%*	1800 (45%)	2411 (% not specified)
Maternal age	Median 32 years, range 16–47 years	Mean 30.09 years (SD 5.37 years), range 15–46 years	Mean 30.5 years (SD 4.115 years)
Successful NB image (% of sample size)	1260 (61.6%)	1682 (93.4%)	2411 (100%)
Number of cases (prevalence)	DS: 30 (1.47%); T 18: 14 (0.68%); others: 35 (1.71%)	DS: 7 (0.39%); others: 3 (0.17%)	DS: 15 (0.62%)
Results	(i) Observed performance for DS (risk 1 : 250 (NT), ≤ 0.60 MoM (NB)) (95% CI): *NT:* ST 88% (86–90%); FPR 23% (21–26%) *NT + NB:* ST 100%; FPR 5% (3–6%) (ii) Performance of only NB: ST 32%; FPR 10%; LR+ 4.4 (2.0–9.4)	Observed performance of NB for DS (95% CI): ST 33.3% (4.3–77.7%); FPR 1.13%; SP 98.9% (98.5–99.4%); PPV 9.5% (1.2–30.4%); NPV 99.7% (99.4–99.9%)	(i) Observed performance of NB for DS (95% CI): ST 53.3% (26.6–78.7%); SP 99.5% (99.3–99.8%); PPV 47.1% (23.3–70.8%); LR+ 142 (63–318); LR– 0.47 (0.27–0.80) (ii) Estimated performance (risk 1 : 250): *Combined:* DR 87%; FPR 4.3% *Combined + NB:* DR 90%; FPR:2.5%
Evidence level	III	III	III
Comments	The population was low-risk and mainly unselected (67%) but not representative. Feasibility of NB measurement was low (62%), but its inclusion improved the screening performance for DS detection.	The population was low-risk but not representative (only 45% opted for the test).	Details about study population (low-risk or high-risk) and exclusions were not specified. The estimated performance of adding NB into the combined test was evaluated from modelling using data from the author's previous studies.

DR = detection rate; DS = Down's syndrome; FPR = false positive rate; MoM = multiples of the median; NB = nasal bone; NPV = negative predictive value; NT = nuchal translucency; PPV = positive predictive value; SD = standard deviation; SP = specificity; ST = sensitivity; T 18 = trisomy 18.

2008 update

2008 update

Table 9.7 First-trimester screening for Down's syndrome using nasal bone evaluation – additional studies (*continued*)

Study	Kozlowski et al. (2006)[775]	Zoppi et al. (2003)[776]	Viora et al. (2003)[777]
Type of study	Prospective cohort	Prospective cohort	Prospective cohort
Year of publication	2006	2003	2003
Period	2002–2004	2001–2002	2001–2002
Setting	1 prenatal centre, Germany	1 prenatal diagnosis unit, Italy	1 prenatal diagnosis unit, Italy
Study population	Selected (single centre, 46% > 35 years)	Selected (single centre)	Selected (referred women)
Exclusions	Adequately described	Adequately described	Adequately described
Test conducted	Combined test with or without NB	NB	NB
Monitoring of test quality	Adequate	Adequate	Not described
Validated reference standard	Yes (prenatal karyotype, pregnancy records)	Incomplete info. for 35% of study population	Yes (prenatal karyotype, pregnancy records)
Sample size (% of study population)	2973 (92.4%)	3503 (64.6%)	1906 (% not specified)
Maternal age	Median 34 years, range 14–46 years	Median 32 years, range 15–48 years	Median 32.2 years, range 18–47 years
Successful NB image (% of sample size)	3194/3218 (99.3% of study population)	5525/5532 (99.8% of study population)	1752 (91.9% of sample size)
Number of cases (prevalence)	DS: 18 (0.60%); others: 22 (0.74%)	DS: 27 (0.77%); others: 13 (0.37%)	DS: 10 (0.57%); others: 9 (0.51%)
Results	Estimated performance for DS (risk cut-off 1 : 300): *Combined:* DR 94.4%; FPR 5.5% *Combined + NB:* DR 77.8%; FPR 2.8%	Observed performance of NB for DS: DR 70%; FPR missing value	Observed performance of NB for DS: DR 60% FPR: 1.4
Evidence level	III	III	III
Comments	The study population was high risk. This study compared the two algorithms of Fetal Medicine Foundation – Old algorithm using combined test vs New algorithm which allows inclusion of NB and some refinements in distribution of first-trimester parameters.	The population was low risk/unselected but follow-up was not available for 35% (1922/5532) of pregnancies. Moreover, the reported data were inadequate for calculating FPR and other screening parameters.	The population was high risk referred to the centre for chorionic villus sampling, amniocentesis or NT measurement. The results are given for absent NB. If hypoplastic NB (< 10th centile) is added, the DR becomes 80% with FPR 3.7%.

DR = detection rate; DS = Down's syndrome; FPR = false positive rate; MoM = multiples of the median; NB = nasal bone; NPV = negative predictive value; NT = nuchal translucency; PPV = positive predictive value; SD = standard deviation; SP = specificity; ST = sensitivity; T 18 = trisomy 18.

Table 9.8 First-trimester screening for Down's syndrome only

Study	Rozenberg et al. (2006)[778]	Avgidou et al. (2005)[781]	Crossley et al. (2002)[767]
Type of study	Prospective cohort	Prospective cohort	Prospective cohort
Year of publication	2006	2005	2002
Period	2001–2002	1999–2001	2 years
Setting	10 perinatal units, France	1 hospitals, 1 fetal medicine unit, UK	15 maternity units, UK
Study population	Unselected (in a health authority)	Selected (48.5 % ≥ 35 years)	Unselected (for routine antenatal care)
Exclusions	Adequately described	Adequately described	Not applicable (100% follow-up)
Test conducted	Combined	Combined	Combined
Monitoring of test quality	Adequate	Adequate	Inadequate (NT in 73% of study population) (34/45 DS cases had combined test)
Validated reference standard	Yes (prenatal karyotype, pregnancy records)	Yes (prenatal karyotype, pregnancy records)	Yes (prenatal karyotype, pregnancy records)
Sample size (% of study population)	14 380 (96.3%)	30 564 (95.8%)	17 229 (100%)
Maternal age	Median 30.7 years, 25th to 75th centile 28–33.9 years	Median 34 years, range 15–49 years	Median 29.9 years, range 15–49 years
Number of DS cases (prevalence)	51 (0.34%)	196 (0.64%)	45 (0.57%)
Results			
Diagnostic accuracy (95% CI)	Observed results: DR 79.6%; FPR 2.7%; risk cut-off 1 : 250	Estimated results: DR 90.3%; FPR 5% (fixed); risk cut-off ≥ 1 in 300	Observed results: DR 82% (95% CI 65–93%) with 34 cases; FPR 5%; risk cut-off 1 : 250
Evidence level	Ib	II	II
Comments	This study also evaluated the diagnostic value of 'first-trimester combined test followed by routine second-trimester ultrasound screening at 20–22 weeks for all the subjects' and the results showed DR of 89.7% with FPR of 4.2%. The 20–22 weeks scan was considered positive if at least one major structural malformation was present or if nuchal fold was more than 6 mm. A cost analysis was also performed.		The combined test could not be performed in all women and NT was done in 73% of the study population. 34 of 45 DS cases had completed screening. Considering the entire series of affected pregnancies, DR is reduced to 62%.

DR = detection rate; DS = Down's syndrome; FPR = false positive rate; NT = nuchal translucency.

2008 update

Down's syndrome only:

The diagnostic accuracy results of the three included studies for the serum combined test were similar (Table 9.8). While one multicentre study[778] found a detection rate of 79.6% at an FPR of 2.9%, the other two showed detection rates of 90.3% and 82% at a fixed FPR of 5%.

Second-trimester screening

Compared with the first trimester only and first and second trimester together, few studies were found relating to serum screening tests done exclusively in the second trimester. Good-quality serum marker studies comparing both the first- and second-trimester tests have been grouped under the next section on combined first- and second-trimester screening. A number of studies were identified which evaluated the use of ultrasound for identifying 'soft markers' – nuchal fold thickening, choroid plexus cyst, echogenic intracardiac foci, renal pyelectasis and shortening of femur, but the general quality was low (EL = III).

Five studies were selected for inclusion in this section – three meta-analyses, one prospective cohort study and one retrospective cohort study. As these studies were quite different from each other, their data could not be tabulated and they have been described in a narrative manner.

The second-trimester studies have been further divided into the anomalies they looked at:

(a) Down's syndrome and other chromosomal anomalies

Description of included studies

A single retrospective cohort[782] study with evaluation of maternal serum screening (MSS) using quadruple test for Down's syndrome, trisomy 18, and neural tube defects (NTD) was carried out in an Australian state using record linkage and manual follow-up. As initially the quadruple test used free alpha-hCG instead of inhibin A, data from that period were not used for analysis. The period covered was 1998 to 2000. Increased risk result was defined as > 1 : 250 for Down's syndrome, and > 1 : 200 for trisomy 18. Levels of AFP > 2.5 MoM were considered as high risk for NTD. Three databases were used for record linkage – the state's MSS database, register of births held at the Perinatal Data Collection Unit, and the Birth Defects Register. No mention was made about monitoring of test quality. An automated probabilistic record linkage technique was used to link these databases. The DR, FPR and PPV were calculated for each condition [EL = II]

Findings

In this retrospective cohort study, pregnancy outcome information was ascertained for 99.2% of all pregnancies screened during the period. The study population was 19 143 and 154 pregnancies were lost to follow-up. Mean maternal age was 30.3 years (range 14–51 years) and 20.1% were above 35 years. The sample size for analysis was 16 607 (86.7%) for Down's syndrome and trisomy 18, and 17 288 (90.3%) for NTD. The sample size for Down's syndrome and trisomy 18 was smaller owing to exclusion of pregnancies where alpha-hCG was used before inhibin A was introduced. The prevalence of Down's syndrome, trisomy 18 and NTD was 0.16%, 0.05% and 0.08%, respectively.

The observed performance of the quadruple testing was as follows:

	DR	FPR	PPV
For Down's syndrome			
Quadruple test (risk ≥ 1 : 250)	85% (95% CI 72 to 99)	6.8%	2%
Quadruple test (FPR fixed at 5%)	78%	5.0%	2.5%
For trisomy 18			
Quadruple test (risk ≥ 1 : 200)	44% (95% CI 12 to 77)	0.5%	4.7%
For NTD (AFP ≥ 2.5 MoM)			
All NTD	73%	1.1%	5.6%
Spina bifida	50%	1.1%	2.1%
Anencephaly	100%	1.1%	3.1%

(b) Down's syndrome only

Four studies (three meta-analyses and one prospective cohort study) were identified. Meta-analysis studies were related to use of ultrasonographic soft markers, effectiveness of triple marker, and evaluation of intracardiac echogenic foci. The fourth study is a good-quality prospective study evaluating the screening performance of fetal pyelectasis detected on ultrasound.

Description of included studies

A meta-analysis[315] was conducted to evaluate accuracy of second-trimester ultrasound in detecting Down's syndrome. It included all the studies of 'soft markers' – choroid plexus cyst, thickened nuchal fold, echogenic intracardiac focus, echogenic bowel, renal pyelectasis, and humeral and femoral shortening. Exclusion criteria were well defined but quality assessment of studies was not specified. Studies were independently reviewed, selected and abstracted by two reviewers. Retrospective studies were included provided that the original ultrasound interpretation was used. Sensitivity, specificity and 95% CI was calculated for each ultrasound finding individually. A summary measure (sensitivity, specificity, LR+, LR–, PPV) with 95% CI and fetal loss per case diagnosed was calculated for each marker when identified as an isolated abnormality. [EL = II]

Another meta-analysis[320] evaluated effectiveness of triple marker screen for Down's syndrome. Only cohort studies were considered. Inclusion and exclusion criteria were well defined. Quality assessment criteria included selection of study subjects, description of methods, estimates of sensitivity, screen-positive rate and FPR, cut-offs used, blinding of outcome assessors, follow-up, and accuracy estimated independently of test threshold. Studies were independently reviewed, selected and abstracted by two reviewers. Results of sensitivity and FPR from different subgroups of study sample were compared by using summary ROC analysis. [EL = III]

A third meta-analysis[783] was conducted to evaluate the diagnostic performance of intracardiac echogenic foci. Both prospective and retrospective studies (including case–control) were considered. Eligibility criteria for studies were availability of adequate information about both chromosomally normal and abnormal fetuses (so that a 2 × 2 table could be made), fetal karyotype unknown at the time of ultrasound, and chromosomal status of fetuses confirmed by either karyotyping or postnatal clinical examination. Studies were independently reviewed, selected and abstracted by two reviewers. Diagnostic performance was assessed in two different settings – 'combined' which included women regardless of whether they had other ultrasound findings, and 'isolated' where women did not have any other ultrasound finding. Weighted sensitivity and specificity values were calculated and summary ROC analysis performed using both the fixed and random effects model separately for both the settings. [EL = II]

A prospective cohort study[784] was carried out (1998–2002) in a single medical centre in Italy with the aim of determining whether isolated pyelectasis is a risk factor for Down's syndrome. The study population was low risk and the centre served the needs of a group of 30 obstetricians. Inclusion criteria were well defined and a thorough ultrasound examination was carried out for all the soft markers between 16 and 23 weeks of gestation. Monitoring of the quality of ultrasound was not specified. Complete follow-up was obtained of the study population by karyotyping, postnatal records or information from mother. The sensitivity, specificity, PPV, NPV, LR+ and LR– (with 95% CI) were calculated separately for an 'isolated' finding, and in association with other anomalies. The sample size was 12 672 (77.8%) after excluding high-risk and referred women. None of the women had a first-trimester aneuploidy screen. [EL = II]

Findings

The first meta-analysis[315] included 56 studies involving 1930 babies with Down's syndrome and 130 365 unaffected fetuses. Forty-nine studies were carried out in high-risk women. Overall prevalence of Down's syndrome was 1.5%, and outcome was assessed by karyotyping in 53 studies. There was marked heterogeneity in the results for all ultrasound findings. Two factors were found to be responsible for heterogeneity: (i) study design (retrospective or prospective); and (ii) whether the marker was seen in isolation or together with other fetal structural anomalies. The sensitivity for Down's syndrome detection with an isolated ultrasound finding was low (1% for choroid plexus cyst to a maximum of 16% for shortened femur). The specificity for each marker when seen individually was greater than 95%. Except for nuchal fold thickness (LR+ of 17), the LR+ for others was lower.

The summary measures (with 95% CI) for ultrasound markers when seen individually are given below:

Marker	Sensitivity	Specificity	LR+	LR–	Fetal loss per case
Thickened nuchal fold	0.04 (0.02–0.10)	0.99 (0.99–0.99)	17 (8–38)	0.97 (0.94–1.00)	0.6
Choroid plexus cyst	0.01 (0–0.03)	1.00 (0.97–1.00)	1.00 (0.12–9.4)	1.00 (0.97–1.00)	4.3
Femur length	0.16 (0.05–0.40)	0.96 (0.94–0.98)	2.7 (1.2–6.0)	0.87 (0.75–1.00)	1.2
Humerus length	0.09 (0–0.60)	0.97 (0.91–0.99)	7.5 (4.7–12)	0.87 (0.67–1.1)	1.9
Echogenic bowel	0.04 (0.01–0.24)	0.99 (0.97–1.00)	6.1 (3.0–12.6)	1.00 (0.98–1.00)	1.0
Echogenic intracardiac focus	0.11 (0.06–0.18)	0.96 (0.94–0.97)	2.8 (1.5–5.5)	0.95 (0.89–1.00)	2.0
Renal pyelectasis	0.02 (0.01–0.06)	0.99 (0.98–1.00)	1.9 (0.7–5.1)	1.00 (1.00–1.00)	2.6

The second meta-analysis involving the triple marker[320] included 20 cohort studies involving a total of 194 326 pregnant women. There was strong evidence of study-to-study variation, implying heterogeneity ($P < 0.001$). The cut-offs used in these studies ranged from 1 : 190 to 1 : 380. No study reported on the independence of assessment. Only four studies obtained fetal karyotypes (validated reference test) for all the women studied. In other studies, chorionic villus sampling or amniocentesis was offered to screen-positive women and the proportion of women accepting prenatal diagnostic testing ranged from 67% to 92%. Follow-up information on pregnancy outcome was incomplete in eight studies. The mean maternal age varied between 24.5 and 33.5 years. The triple marker had a high sensitivity for women older than 35 years, but did not perform well in the younger age group.

The summary sensitivity and FPR (with ranges) based on various cut-offs and maternal ages are given below:

	Sensitivity	FPR
Cut-off 1 : 190–200		
Maternal age ≥ 35 years	0.89 (0.78–1.00)	0.25 (0.20–0.29)
All ages	0.67 (0.48–0.91)	0.04 (0.03–0.07)
Cut-off 1 : 250–295		
Maternal age ≥ 35 years	0.80 (0.75–1.00)	0.21 (0.20–0.21)
Maternal age < 35 years	0.57 (0.53–0.58)	0.04 (0.03–0.06)
All ages	0.71 (0.48–0.80)	0.06 (0.04–0.07)
Cut-off 1 : 350–380		
All ages	0.73 (0.70–0.80)	0.08 (0.07–0.13)

The third meta-analysis concerning an echogenic focus in the heart[783] included 11 studies (five retrospective including two case–controls). Eight studies gave data on combined setting, while seven gave data on isolated setting independently. The data included 51 831 fetuses with 333 Down's syndrome cases ('combined': 27 360 with 321 Down's syndrome cases; 'isolated': 39 360 with 130 Down's syndrome cases). The mean age of mothers ranged between 29 and 35 years, and seven studies had high-risk women as their study population. Regarding sensitivity, there was no statistically significant heterogeneity as the confidence intervals were widely overlapping. For specificity, there was significant between-study heterogeneity ($P < 0.001$).

The weighted sensitivity and specificity estimates (with 95% CI) using the two models, random effects model (REM) and fixed effects model (FEM), are given below:

	Random effects model		Fixed effects model	
	Sensitivity	Specificity	Sensitivity	Specificity
'Combined' setting	0.26 (0.19–0.35)	0.963 (0.937–0.979)	0.30 (0.25–0.36)	0.927 (0.924–0.931)
'Isolated' setting	0.22 (0.14–0.33)	0.959 (0.910–0.982)	0.22 (0.15–0.30)	0.964 (0.961–0.966)
All	0.26 (0.19–0.34)	0.958 (0.922–0.978)	0.30 (0.25–0.36)	0.940 (0.937–0.942)

It was further estimated that the probability of Down's syndrome (assuming LR+ of 6.2) after an intracardiac echogenic foci has been detected would be 0.44% in a population with prevalence of 1 : 1400, 0.62% with prevalence of 1 : 1000, and 1.03% with prevalence of 1 : 600. The probability of a case of Down's syndrome being detected was equal to the probability of an unnecessary miscarriage caused by amniocentesis when the background prevalence of Down's syndrome was 1 : 770.

In the prospective cohort study on pyelectasis[784] the mean maternal age was 27.2 ± 5.5 years and the prevalence of Down's syndrome was 0.09% (11 cases). In the study population, the prevalence of pyelectasis was 2.9%, with 83.3% of these as an isolated finding. Only one case of Down's syndrome was identified with pyelectasis. The presence of isolated pyelectasis had sensitivity 9.1% (95% CI 1.62 to 37.4%), specificity 97.6% (95% CI 97.32 to 97.85%), PPV 0.33%, NPV 99.9%, LR+ 3.8 (95% CI 0.58 to 24.61) and LR– 0.9 (95% CI 0.77 to 112).

Among fetuses with pyelectasis and other associated markers, the sensitivity, specificity, PPV, NPV and LR+ were 9.1%, 99.5%, 1.6%, 99.9% and 19.2 (95% CI 2.91 to 126.44), respectively.

Combined first- and second-trimester studies

Description of included studies

Four good-quality studies were included: three prospective cohort studies[785–787] and one nested case–control study.[316] All the studies were multicentred with clearly defined objectives. One of the two studies with a selected population had first-trimester screen-positive and screen-negative women together in its sample population.[787] In all studies the screening test and monitoring of quality measures were adequately explained. The reference test in all was a validated one (karyotyping/postnatal assessment/pregnancy records) (Table 9.9).

Findings

All the selected studies looked at Down's syndrome only. The best-quality study[785] showed the integrated test to have the best DR of 96% at a fixed FPR of 5%, followed by the serum integrated test (DR 88%), combined test (DR 87%) and the quadruple test (DR 81%). Similar results were observed in the nested case–control study.[316] Another study[786] found the serum integrated test to have better diagnostic accuracy compared with the second-trimester serum triple and quadruple tests. In the last study,[787] sequential screening using the triple test after a first-trimester combined test had a DR of 85.7% at FPR of 8.9%.

9.2.3 | **Implementation of the integrated test**

One study[1021] was identified which evaluated the implementation of the integrated test as a new method of screening for Down's syndrome. The integrated test was conducted in a tertiary referral hospital in the UK. Prior to the introduction of the integrated test, local GPs and midwives were given information about this two-stage screening test. All women with singleton pregnancies booked before 14 weeks were offered the test, and the results of the first-trimester screening were not disclosed; however, women were offered further screening (combined test or integrated test) or invasive prenatal testing if NT was ≥ 3.5 mm. Women with NT < 3.5 mm were asked to return at 15 weeks for the second-trimester component of the integrated test, and a reminder letter was sent at 17 weeks to all those who failed to attend the second blood analysis. Women who did not have an NT measurement underwent testing by the serum integrated test, while the combined test and the quadruple test were also used depending on individual preference/timing of booking. All the data were entered in the computerised database. The cut-off values used for computing risk of Down's syndrome were ≥ 1 in 150 (at term) for the integrated test, serum integrated test and NT + quadruple test, and ≥ 1 in 250 (at term) for the combined test and the quadruple test. [EL = 3]

During the 18 month study period, the overall uptake of Down's syndrome screening was 64.4% (3417/5309) among all the pregnant women who opted for screening and NT scan at the hospital. Screening uptake was significantly higher in women booking before 14 weeks (73% versus 46%; *P* < 0.001), and the median age of the study population was 32 years (range 16–47 years). Seventy-six percent (2597/3417) of the pregnant women opting for screening had booked before 14 weeks and they were offered an integrated test – about 97% of them opted for this. Twenty-two women (0.9%) had NT ≥ 3.5 mm and the majority of these women opted for invasive testing after further counselling. For the second-trimester blood analysis, 25% of the women failed to come for the test and a reminder letter was sent to these women at 17 weeks. Overall, 5.3% of women failed to attend the second part of screening, and 78% of the women (booked before 14 weeks) were screened by the full integrated test. For various reasons, NT could not be measured in 5.9% of the women opting for the integrated test and they were screened using the serum integrated test. The observed FPR for the groups undergoing the combined test, quadruple test and the integrated test were 8.9%, 6.3% and 2.9%, respectively, but the combined test group had older women (median maternal age 35 years) and a high proportion of women with a history of aneuploidy in the previous pregnancy.

Evidence summary

Findings from a descriptive study [EL = 3] shows that the integrated test, when implemented in practice, seems to be generally acceptable to pregnant women opting for it and results in a good uptake. But 25% of these women failed to attend for the second component of the test and this required sending them reminders.

2008 update

Table 9.9 First- and second-trimester screening for Down's syndrome only

Study	Malone et al. (2005)[785]	Wald et al. (2003)[316]	Knight et al. (2005)[786]	Platt et al. (2005)[787]
Type of study	Prospective cohort	Nested case–control (within a cohort)	Prospective cohort	Prospective cohort
Year of publication	2005	2003	2005	2004
Period	1999–2002	1996–2001	2001–2003	Not specified
Setting	15 medical centres, USA	25 maternity centres, UK and Austria	229/260 prenatal care practitioners, USA	12 prenatal diagnostic centres, USA
Study population	Unselected	Unselected	Selected (61% enrolled for study)	Selected (low uptake of second-trimester screening) (small sample)
Exclusions	Adequately described	Adequately described	Adequately described	Adequately described
Test conducted	All serum tests with NT (combined, quadruple, integrated and serum integrated)	All serum and urine biochemical markers with NT	Integrated serum screening	Sequential screening using triple marker after first-trimester combined test
Monitoring of test quality	Adequate	Adequate, double blinding	Adequate	Adequate
Validated reference standard	Yes (prenatal karyotype, pregnancy records)	Yes (karyotype-pre/postnatal, pregnancy records)	Yes (prenatal karyotype, pregnancy records)	Yes (karyotype-prenatal, pregnancy records)
Sample size (% of study population)	33 547 (88.2%) with complete data from both trimesters	43 712 (92%) 98 cases, 490 controls for screening performance; 600 controls added for statistical power	8773 (78.6%)	4325 (52.7%) first-trimester screen-positive 180 first-trimester screen-negative 4145
Maternal age	Mean 30.1 years, SD 5.8 years	Not specified Median: 29 years	Mean 27.8 years, SD 5.5 years	Mean 34.5 years, SD 4.6 years
Number of cases (prevalence)	92 (0.27%)	101 (0.23%)	16 (0.18%)	13 (0.30%)
Results	Estimated detection rate at fixed FPR 5% (95% CI): combined (11 weeks): 87% (82–92%) quadruple (15–17 weeks): 81% (70–86%) serum integrated: 88% (81–92%) fully integrated: 96% (92–97%)	Estimated detection rate at fixed FPR 5%: first trimester (10–13 weeks): PAPP-A + NT 76%; combined 84%; combined + inhibin A 87% second trimester (15–20): double 71%; triple 77%; quadruple 83% Integrated screening (both first and second trimester): NT (10 weeks) + quadruple 90%; serum integrated 90%; integrated 93%	Observed screening performance with 95% CI: triple: risk 1 : 270; DR 67% (43–84%); combined 6.4% (5.9–6.9%) quadruple: risk 1 : 150; DR 56% (33–76%); FPR 3.3% (2.9–3.7%) serum integrated: risk 1 : 100; DR 79% (55–92%); FPR 3.2% (2.8–3.6%)	Observed screening performance with 95% CI among first-trimester screen-negative women: risk 1 : 270; DR 85.7% (42.1–99.6%); FPR 8.9% (8.0–9.8%)
Evidence level	Ib	II	II	II
Comments	The observed performance characteristics were: First-trimester combined screening with risk cut-off 1 : 300 – DR 82% with FPR 5.6% Second-trimester quadruple screening with risk cut-off 1 : 100 DR 85% with FPR 8.5% Sequential screening in both the trimesters – DR 94% with FPR 11% Note: The DR is subject to bias as the study excluded fetuses with hygroma which might have aborted spontaneously when most of the Down's syndrome cases were ascertained.	Screening performance was also evaluated for NT and all serum and urine markers individually. For NT – Failure to obtain satisfactory NT image was lowest (14%) at 11 weeks, and highest (19%) at 10 and 13 weeks. Success rate increased with sonographer experience – 86% with ≥ 400 images VS 81% with < 200 images experience. For urine markers – Invasive Trophoblastic Antigen (ITA) was the best marker and only discriminatory in second trimester. On combining with Quadruple Test, FPR was decreased from 6.2 to 4.2%, and with Integrated test from 0.9 to 0.6% (both tests at fixed DR of 85%). The study also evaluated the safety and cost-effectiveness of various markers. Safety will be discussed separately under effectiveness.	The study population was the same as that of Wapner et al.(2003)[769] (described in First-trimester screening for Down's syndrome and other chromosomal anomalies). After undergoing Combined test in the first trimester, risks were disclosed to the women. Triple test was offered to all screen-negative women and those screen-positive women who decided not to undergo diagnostic tests after the first-trimester positive test.	

DR = detection rate; DS = Down's syndrome; FPR = false positive rate; NT = nuchal translucency; PAPP-A = pregnancy-associated plasma protein-A; SD = standard deviation;.

9.2.4 Modelling studies

Description of included studies
Two studies were identified which used modelling as a way of comparing different screening tests for Down's syndrome detection.

To demonstrate the potential value of three-stage sequential screening for Down's syndrome, DR and FPR were estimated by multivariate Gaussian modelling using Monte Carlo simulation.[789] UK data were used for modelling. The protocol is known as 'contingent screening' and involves measuring free β-hCG and PAPP-A in all pregnant women at 10 weeks in the first stage. Those with low risk were screened negative at this stage, the remainder underwent NT measurement in the second stage and the risk was reassessed (for combined test). After the second stage, those with low risk were screened negative and those with very high risk were offered diagnostic tests. In the third stage, women with intermediate risk received a second-trimester quaduple test. Risk was reassessed according to the integrated test and high-risk women were offered diagnosis. [EL = III]

Using Monte Carlo simulation for modelling, another study[790] compared the integrated test in three policies for screening: (i) integrated screening for all women; (ii) sequential screening (based on first-trimester tests, high-risk pregnancies to be diagnosed and remaining to undergo integrated test); and (iii) contingent screening.

Detection and false positive rates were estimated based on the data from a large cohort (nested case–control study) done in the UK. [EL = III]

Findings
The first modelling study suggested that, with full adherence to a three-stage policy, an overall detection rate of nearly 90% and a false positive rate of below 2% can be achieved. About two-thirds of the women can be screened on the basis of first-trimester biochemistry alone and about 80% by the combined test. The DR for first-trimester screening is about 60%.

This protocol allows most of the Down's syndrome pregnancies to be detected in the first trimester. Furthermore, it provides an efficient way of screening for Down's syndrome where NT measurements cannot be performed in all women owing to scarcity of resources. However, it requires the selection of four different cut-offs during the three stages, each of which will affect the overall performance. Selecting a set of appropriate cut-offs is therefore complex and difficult to practise. The psychological impact of pregnant women possibly receiving four different results also needs to be evaluated.

The second modelling study concluded that integrated screening had the best screening performance. As the first-trimester test FPR was decreased, the performance of the other two policies approached that of the integrated screen. Setting the first-trimester risk cut-off to ≥ 1 in 300 with a fixed DR of 90%, sequential and contingent screening gave overall FPRs of 2.3% and 2.4%, respectively, and 66% of affected pregnancies were detected by the first-trimester tests. The integrated test on all women gave an FPR of 2.2%.

If pregnancies with a first-trimester risk of ≤ 1 in 2000 are classified screen negative and receive no further testing, then 99.5% of women with sequential screening or 30% with contingent screening would proceed to integrated screening.

9.2.5 Effectiveness studies

Five studies were identified: four related to adverse outcomes/fetal losses and one related to threshold measurement of NT. One was a multicentre RCT, one a nested case–control study, one a modelling study and one a meta-analysis to evaluate the diagnostic value of second-trimester ultrasound for Down's syndrome. The NT study analysed a database from an earlier multicentre prospective study.

Description of included studies
A multicentre RCT[791] in maternity care units affiliated to eight Swedish hospitals was carried out with an aim of comparing the effectiveness of two screening policies for detecting Down's syndrome: routine ultrasound scan at 12–14 weeks by NT (12 week policy) versus routine

ultrasound at 15–20 weeks (18 week policy). An unselected population with well-defined eligibility criteria was involved. After taking informed consent, the population was randomised block-wise at the level of maternity units using internet-based software. Appropriately trained operators carried out the ultrasound examination. Karyotyping was offered to all women with increased risk of Down's syndrome (> 1 : 250 based on NT in the first group and on maternal age in the second), detection of a structural anomaly on scan, history suggestive of increased risk, or preference/desire of the woman due to worry. Follow-up of results (karyotyping, pregnancy outcome) was adequate. Evaluation of the primary outcome (number of babies born alive at ≥ 22 weeks with Down's syndrome) and secondary outcomes (total number of babies born with Down's syndrome, number of babies born with other chromosomal abnormalities, number of pregnancy terminations for Down's syndrome, and rate of invasive tests for fetal karyotyping) was done using intention-to-treat analysis. The sample size was calculated to detect a difference of 0.1% in liveborn Down's syndrome cases between the two groups at a 5% significance level with 90% power. χ^2 tests (for proportions) and Student's two-sample test (for continuous data) were used for comparison. [EL = 1+]

The nested case–control study[316] has been discussed in the combined first- and second-trimester screening section above. Apart from evaluating the screening performance of various tests, it also examined their safety in terms of number of unaffected fetal losses per 100 000 women screened, and number of Down's syndrome pregnancies detected for each procedure-related unaffected fetal loss. Both calculations were done at different detection rates. [EL = 2+]

A decision-analysis model[792] was used to compare five screening strategies: (i) first-trimester combined screen; (ii) second-trimester quadruple screen; (iii) second-trimester triple screen; (iv) integrated screen; and (v) sequential screen. A hypothetical cohort of 1 000 000 women below 35 years was analysed assuming the entire cohort would present for antenatal care before 10 weeks and accept prenatal screening for Down's syndrome. After a positive triple or quadruple test, genetic sonogram would be performed and then prenatal diagnosis would be available. Four separate outcomes were examined: (i) overall cost-effectiveness; (ii) Down's syndrome cases detected; (iii) Down's syndrome live births averted; and (iv) euploid losses from invasive procedures. [EL = 3]

Clinical parameters used for modelling were synthesised from review of published data (mainly UK data). The prevalence of Down's syndrome at 10 weeks of gestation was estimated as 1 in 595 pregnancies, with a baseline live birth rate of 1 in 1030. Seventy percent of women were estimated to opt for invasive diagnostic techniques after a positive screening test, and 90% to opt for termination of affected pregnancies. Baseline fetal loss after amniocentesis and chorionic villus sampling were estimated to be 0.9% and 1.6%, respectively, but this was also varied over a range. Spontaneous fetal loss of euploid pregnancies was estimated at 1% between 10 and 14 weeks, and an additional 1% between 15 weeks and delivery. The screening performance of various tests was derived from published data. [EL = 3]

Details of the fourth study[315] have already been discussed in the second-trimester screening section above.

The last study[793] analysed the database from the FASTER trial (a multicentre prospective trial in the USA) to determine whether there is an NT measurement above which immediate invasive testing should be offered, without waiting for serum testing and computerised aneuploidy risk assessment. Pregnant women were eligible for inclusion if they were above 16 years of age, had a singleton pregnancy and a CRL of 36–79 mm (gestation 10 weeks 3 days to 13 weeks 6 days) at the time of first-trimester sonography for NT. Cases with cystic hygroma were excluded. NT was measured in the first trimester using a standardised protocol by specially trained ultrasonographers at the same time as when serum levels of PAPP-A and β-hCG were obtained. At 15–18 weeks, a quadruple serum screening test was also obtained, but the present study used only the risks as assessed from the first-trimester tests. A formal quality control programme was used throughout the study. [EL = 2+]

Findings

In the multicentre RCT a total of 39 572 women were randomised in the two groups (19 796 in the 12 week group, 19 776 in the 18 week group). Demographically the two groups did not differ in mean age, mean parity or other characteristics. In the 12 week group, NT measurement

2008 update

could not be carried out in 9% of the population owing to increased CRL or fetal demise, but was successfully measured in 96% of the remaining population. The prevalence of Down's syndrome during the study period was 0.25% (98/39 572). The results are as follows:

Outcome	12 week group	18 week group	P value
Prevalence rate	55/19 796 (0.28%)	43/19 776 (0.22%)	0.18
Rate of liveborn babies with DS (at ≥ 22 weeks)	10/19 796 (0.05%)	16/19 776 (0.08%)	0.25
Antenatal detection rate (< 22 weeks in living fetus)	42/55 (76%)	25/41[a] (61%)	0.12
Antenatal detection rate (if karyotyping performed only for defined policy)	39/55 (71%)	21/41[a] (51%)	0.06
Detection rate (other chromosomal anomalies)	20/35 (57%)	25/35 (71%)	0.32
Terminations done for DS	39/19 796 (0.20%)	24/19 776 (0.12%)	0.08
Fetal loss rate in fetuses with DS (terminations and miscarriages)	45/19 796 (0.23%)	27/19 776 (0.14%)	0.04
Rate of invasive tests (for karyotyping)	1593/19 796 (8%)	2118/19 776 (0.14%)	< 0.001
Spontaneous fetal loss rate after invasive tests in normal fetuses	14/1507 (0.9%)	15/2041 (0.7%)	0.58
No. of invasive tests per one case of DS detected (< 22 weeks) (if karyotyping performed only for defined policy)	16	89	

[a] Of the 43 cases of DS, diagnosis was made in one case by amniocentesis at < 22 weeks but pregnancy continued, and in other diagnosis made at 35 weeks – leaving 41 cases for calculating DR.

In the second study, the safety of various tests was evaluated at a fixed DR of 85%. The integrated test had about one-fifth the number of fetal losses when compared with the combined and quadruple test, and half that of the serum integrated test. The number of cases of Down's syndrome detected for each fetal loss was almost three times higher with the integrated test when compared with the combined and quadruple test.

Test	FPR	Unaffected fetal losses per 100 000 women	Cases of DS detected for each procedure-related fetal loss
Combined	6.1%	44	3.9
Double	13.1%	94	1.8
Triple	9.3%	67	2.6
Quadruple	6.2%	45	3.8
Serum integrated	2.7%	19	9.1
Integrated	1.2%	9	19.2

The modelling study found sequential screening to be the most cost-effective. Compared with other screens, it was shown to detect antenatally most cases of Down's syndrome and avert most live births of affected fetuses. But it also had the highest number of euploid losses due to diagnostic procedure. From the point of view of safety, the integrated screen performed the best with the lowest euploid losses. The addition of a genetic sonogram to the triple and quadruple screens increased the cost but brought the euploid losses down to very low levels.

Strategy	Cost of programme (2002 prices, million US$)	Cases of DS detected (n)	DS live births averted (n)	Euploid losses due to procedure (n)
No screening	662	0	0	0
Triple screen				
No sonogram	497	529	366	311
With sonogram	566	365	253	25
Quadruple screen				
No sonogram	472	618	427	311
With sonogram	554	426	295	25
Combined screen	486	941	490	559
Integrated screen	521	750	520	62
Sequential screen	455	1213	678	859

2008 update

The meta-analysis concluded that the number of fetal losses per case diagnosed when identified as an isolated 'soft marker' abnormality on ultrasound was highest with choroid plexus cysts (4.3) and lowest with thickened nuchal fold (0.6).

For others the values were femur length (1.2), humerus length (1.9), echogenic bowel (1.0), echogenic cardiac foci (2.0) and renal pyelectasis (2.6)

In the NT study, the sample population included 36 120 pregnancies with complete first-trimester results. The mean and median NT measurements increased from 10 through 13 weeks and there was considerable variation in the proportion of cases with NT ≥ 2.0 mm at each gestational week, but there was minimal gestational age variation in NT once a threshold of 3.0 mm was passed.

	≥ 2 mm	≥ 3 mm	≥ 4 mm	≥ 5 mm
10 weeks	2.0%	0.4%	0.16%	0%
11 weeks	1.5%	0.5%	0.1%	0.04%
12 weeks	2.5%	0.3%	0.1%	0.09%
13 weeks	5.1%	0.4%	0.05%	0%
Total	**3.0%**	**0.4%**	**0.09%**	**0.05%**

On comparison of outcome of pregnancies based on the various NT cut-offs, the following results were observed:

Outcome	≥ 2 mm	≥ 3 mm	≥ 4 mm
Number	1081 (3.0%)	128 (0.4%)	32 (0.09%)
Aneuploidy	51	22	10
T 21	39	17	6
T 18	5	4	4
Others	7	1	0
ST for DS/T 21	42%	19%	7%
FPR for DS/T 21	3%	0.3%	0.06%
Final risk of DS less than 1 : 200 with the combined test	533 (49.0%)	10 (8.0%)	0 (0%)

There were 32 women with NT ≥ 4 mm, and the addition of first-trimester serum markers to NT measurements did not reduce the final risk in any patients. In contrast, for patients with NT ≥ 3 mm, subsequent addition of serum markers reduced the final risk to less than 1 : 200 in only 8% of cases (ten women). For women with NT ≥ 2 mm, a large number of women (49%) had their risk reduced to less than 1 : 200 by the addition of first-trimester test results.

The authors concluded that the use of 4.0 and 3.0 mm cut-off of NT measurement for estimating pregnancies at risk of Down's syndrome would lead to just 0.09% and 0.4%, respectively, of the population being subjected to invasive testing based on the two cut-offs. By waiting for serum assays and computerised risk assessment, no benefit (0%) was observed in the women with NT ≥ 4 mm and only a minimal benefit (8.0%) in women with NT ≥ 3 mm, that is, who had their final risk reduced to less than 1 in 200. This will increase the screen-positive rate for the whole population by a very small proportion, but will be beneficial in providing immediate results to the healthcare providers and reducing anxiety for the pregnant women.

Evidence summary
Reported evidence shows that the combined test in the first trimester has good diagnostic accuracy for Down's syndrome and other chromosomal anomalies.

Among the currently available second-trimester serum tests, the quadruple test seems to have the best screening performance.

There is high-quality evidence to indicate that combining results of first- and second-trimester screening tests improves the diagnostic performance for Down's syndrome and other chromosomal anomalies and is better than when either of them is used alone.

The integrated test seems to have a higher detection rate and a lower FPR compared with other currently used combined screening tests.

2008 update

There is little evidence on the diagnostic value of other policies of combining first- and second-trimester results.

There is conflicting evidence regarding the performance of nasal bone ultrasound assessment as a screening tool for Down's syndrome.

'Soft markers' on ultrasound have low sensitivity and LR+ when seen individually, except for nuchal fold thickening. When found in association with other anomalies, they seem to improve the diagnostic value but the evidence is not strong.

Retrospective analysis of a database from a high-quality prospective study shows that an NT measurement of 3 mm or more in the first trimester (any gestational age) identified the majority of pregnant women with Down's syndrome, and increased the screen-positive rate/risk of invasive testing by only a small fraction compared with first-trimester risk evaluated by the combined test.

9.2.6 Women's views and psychosocial aspects

Seven studies have been included in this section: two systematic reviews, three cross-sectional surveys and two prospective observational studies. Although the systematic reviews have been well conducted, as the principal question involved women's views/preferences/experiences/feelings, which is quite subjective and difficult to interpret, other descriptive studies (even with poorer quality) were included so that important information was not missed. Grading the two systematic reviews according to the NICE quality criteria is difficult – they are well-conducted systematic reviews but with a definite risk of confounding or bias as individually the included studies were not assessed for quality.

Description of included studies

A systematic review[794] was carried out to understand the psychosocial aspects of genetic screening of pregnant women and newborns. The review aimed to address five broad questions concerned with: (i) knowledge; (ii) anxiety; (iii) other emotional aspects; (iv) factors associated with participation in the programmes; and (v) long-term sequelae of the results. Any genetic screening programme aimed at pregnant women or newborn babies was included. Both comparative and descriptive studies which reported data collected directly from pregnant women or parents were included. There were no geographical or methodological limits except that studies asking hypothetical questions, case reviews and those where ultrasound was done to detect structural anomalies only (and did not include chromosomal anomalies) were excluded. Five electronic databases and two journals were hand searched. The retrieved articles were equally divided among the five authors for quality assessment and data extraction, and these processes were completed using well-defined criteria and validated forms. A new quality score was devised for quality assessment which was not found to be useful later on. Literature on 'other emotional aspects' and 'long-term sequelae' was too fragmented (except in neonatal screening programmes) for useful conclusions to be drawn. [EL = 2++]

A prospective cohort study[795] was carried out in four antenatal clinics in Australia to assess informed choice in pregnant women to participate in second-trimester serum screening using a validated measure, and to compare anxiety levels in women who are well informed compared with those who are poorly informed. Participants included pregnant women at between 8 and 14 weeks of gestation attending at their first prenatal visit and with sufficient English to complete a written questionnaire. Written and oral information was provided to all participants as per the existing hospital policy. Informed choice was measured by Multidimensional Measure of Informed Choice (MMIC), a validated measure of informed choice which assesses knowledge and attitude dimensions and also confirms whether a woman's participation in a screening test matches her expressed attitude towards it. The Hospital Anxiety and Depression Scale (HADS) was used to measure anxiety and this scale specifically distinguishes between anxiety and depression. Both the scales were administered at the booking visit and HADS was repeated at 20 weeks (after participation in the test) and at 30 weeks using postal questionnaires. [EL = 2+]

In the third study, a smaller sample drawn from the RCT described above[791] was used to study the effect of screening on women's anxiety during pregnancy and after birth, with a specific focus on worries about the health of the baby.[796] The 12 week group was the intervention group and the 18 week group acted as the control. The principal outcome of women's worries about the 'possibility of something being wrong with the baby' was measured by the Swedish version

2008 update

of the Cambridge Worry Scale questionnaire including 16 items of common concerns during pregnancy. The State-Trait Anxiety Inventory (a validated tool for evaluating general anxiety) and the Edinburgh Postnatal Depression Scale (validated for evaluating anxiety in the antenatal/postnatal period) were also used. Information was collected at three different timings – the first questionnaire was filled at the antenatal clinic, the second was sent at 24 weeks of gestation (mid-pregnancy), and the last was posted 2 months after delivery. The same instruments were used for all three questionnaires. [EL = 3]

A cross-sectional survey[797] was carried out in three Canadian cities to investigate the relationship between MSS use and maternal attachment to pregnancy following the receipt of a favourable result (i.e lowered risk ratio). Building on the preliminary evidence that MSS results are not reassuring to women, it was predicated that favourable MSS results would not be sufficient to allow women to move beyond tentative pregnancy stage. Hence it was hypothesised that:

- there would be no difference in prenatal attachment between women receiving favourable amniocentesis results (amniocentesis group) and who opt against testing (no testing group)
- there would be a lower level of attachment among women who receive favourable MSS results and did not undergo amniocentesis (MSS group) compared with the other two testing groups, and this difference would be evident in the second and third trimesters.

Participants included high-risk pregnant women (maternal age > 35 years) who opted for MSS or amniocentesis or did not opt for any testing. Informational posters were placed at various places (physician offices, laboratories, maternity stores), and interested women who met the eligibility criteria were enrolled. The instrument used to collect information was a self-administered questionnaire by mail, and prenatal attachment was measured by a 21-item Prenatal Attachment Inventory (PAI) score (construct validity and reliability of this scale were established). The three groups were compared using ANOVA and ANCOVA for statistical analysis. [EL = 3]

To address the question of whether there are social and ethnic inequalities in the offer and uptake of prenatal screening and diagnosis in the UK, a systematic review[798] was carried out employing a broad search strategy. In order to address the review question, studies were assessed in terms of:

- utilisation – number of women screened as a proportion of those eligible
- offer – number of women offered screening as a proportion of those eligible
- uptake – number of women screened as a proportion of those offered screening.

Studies were reviewed and summarised by one reviewer. Two key aspects of the studies were assessed independently by two reviewers and summarised as indicators of quality – non-participation rate and whether the distinction between utilisation, offer and uptake was recognised in the study. Owing to heterogeneity, meta-analysis could not be performed. [EL = 2+]

A prospective descriptive study[799] was carried out in two UK district hospitals to find out reasons for lower uptake of screening tests in women from minority ethnic groups and socio-economically disadvantaged sections of society. Screening uptake was evaluated from hospital records. Attitudes towards undergoing the test were assessed by women's responses to a structured question with four items. Knowledge about the test was assessed using an eight-item questionnaire deemed important in professional guidelines for informed consent in screening. Choices were classified as 'informed' depending on the consistency between test uptake, women's attitude towards the test, and their knowledge about it. [EL = 3]

Another cross-sectional survey[800] was carried out in six UK maternity units (three in Scotland, three in England) to ascertain by means of a structured questionnaire women's preference for type of screening test. Pregnant women attending antenatal clinics were asked to put in order of preference four different approaches for screening (all with FPR of 5%):

- first-trimester testing – 90% detection with results available in 1 hour
- first-trimester testing – 90% detection with results within 2–3 days (combined test)
- first-trimester plus second-trimester detection – 93% detection and results within 2–3 days of second test (integrated test)
- second-trimester testing – 75% detection and results available within 2–3 days. [EL = 3]

Findings

In the first systematic review 106 out of 288 identified studies met the eligibility criteria – 78 concerned with antenatal screening and 28 with neonatal screening. Only results pertaining to antenatal screening programmes are discussed below. Findings from antenatal carrier testing for cystic fibrosis and other diseases prevalent in minority ethnic groups are similarly also not discussed here.

Most of the antenatal studies were descriptive and only 33% (26/78) were RCTs or comparative. A questionnaire was the most common instrument used to collect data (in 79% of studies), either alone or together with other methods. Only 16 studies (20%) included both women who were tested and those who were not. Fifty-four studies were concerned with screening for Down's syndrome and other chromosomal anomalies. The sample size of studies varied from ten to 6442 participants. Data were collected after the test results in 40 studies, and in just three studies was it collected at three different times – before test, after test and after test results. A large number of studies assessed knowledge (64.6%), anxiety (46.8%) or attitudes/beliefs (46.2%). Thirty-four antenatal studies (43.6%) had an apparent input from a psychologist or a social scientist. The various findings have been divided into three sections.

1. Knowledge and understanding of screening for Down's syndrome:

Thirty studies were selected: seven used pre-test measures only, six employed both before- and after-test measures (ideal for comparing), and 17 employed after-test measures only. Eight areas of information as specified in RCOG 1993 professional guidelines were used as a 'validated/gold standard questionnaire' for evaluating knowledge in the selected studies. Thirty studies relating to knowledge were reviewed but owing to disparate research aims, poorly operationalised measures for evaluation and variation in timing of assessment, it was concluded that none of them evaluated all the eight areas and hence knowledge was inadequately assessed by all of them. The broad conclusions drawn from these studies were:

- compared with the RCOG list, only limited aspects of knowledge have been the subject of intervention studies
- levels of knowledge adequate for decision making are not being achieved
- leaflets giving information about tests improve knowledge, but substantial gaps in understanding of the written information still remain, especially concerning risk calculations
- substantial social and cultural inequalities exist in knowledge about testing
- other findings that emerged were:
  – pre-screening information can increase knowledge scores but does not necessarily mean that concept of risk is understood
  – women seem to value personally delivered information rather than group-based
  – videos may be slightly more effective in communicating certain types of information than leaflets.

2. Influence on anxiety in prenatal screening for Down's syndrome:

Of the 24 studies measuring anxiety, 13 used a validated scale (mainly the State-Trait Anxiety Inventory). Most studies were carried out in the UK. As knowledge influences anxiety and attitudes, the findings from studies represents the feelings and views of many people who are in fact not well informed about the topic under discussion. Owing to a number of methodological concerns (as with knowledge), robust conclusions could not be drawn. The main findings were as follows:

- increasing women's knowledge by providing more information prior to testing does not raise post-test anxiety
- there is unconvincing data to suggest that knowledge has a moderating role on anxiety in the period after screening but before receipt of test results
- receipt of a screen-positive result raises women's anxiety score, but this returns to normal levels if no abnormality is detected upon diagnostic testing.

Owing to application of inappropriate theoretical frameworks in these studies, two basic misconceptions about knowledge and anxiety were noted:

- information that increases knowledge is the same as that which reduces anxiety
- increased anxiety is inappropriate, abnormal and undesirable as most studies assume that increased anxiety is an abnormal response and/or an iatrogenic consequence of prenatal testing.

2008 update

3. Understanding decision making about screening:

Of the 52 studies included, 34 were concerned with Down's syndrome screening and 11 of them compared differences in those screened with those not screened. Most studies employed questionnaire or interview survey methods. The principal findings were:

- most women evaluate screening programmes positively but some are concerned about their usefulness and impact on pregnancy
- the reasons as to why women had a screening test were:
  - information to help avoid nasty surprises (range 11–82%)
  - need to know for certain whether or not the child had abnormality (8–73%)
  - reassurance that everything was OK (17–88%)
  - following the recommendation of a health professional or spouse (6–24%)
  - could think of no reason (16–26%)
- the reasons as to why women chose not to have a test were:
  - not wanting to act on or worry about the test results (17–71%)
  - not wanting to have an abortion (32–100%)
  - the test results were unreliable and did not provide a definite answer (10–55%)
  - not perceiving themselves at high risk and/or the abnormality to be serious (21–64%), and their own or others' poor screening experience (1–32%)
- most women are not making informed choices about screening although they want to do so; there is evidence to suggest a gap between women's desire to make informed choices with their awareness of what constitutes an informed decision, and the skills with which to achieve it
- informed decision making results in better post-decision outcomes.

Of the initial 134 recruited women completing the first assessment in the second study, 63.9% returned the second questionnaire and 57.8% the third. The mean age of women in the sample was 29.1 ± 4.7 years and 89.6% were married. Using MMIC, 48.1% of women were classified as having 'good knowledge' and 87.2% as having a 'positive attitude' to screening. Overall, only 37.3% of decisions to participate in screening were informed: those who participated in screening were more than twice as likely to have made an informed choice than those who did not participate (47% versus 20%; $P = 0.01$). Informed decisions were not significantly associated with participants' age, parity, country of birth or whether pregnancy was unwelcome or unexpected. No significant association was found between the knowledge levels and attitude to the test ($P = 0.27$). Some important misconceptions were revealed about further testing: 31% did not know that miscarriage was a possible consequence of diagnostic testing subsequent to an increased risk screening result, and only 62% correctly identified that termination of pregnancy would be offered if Down's syndrome was diagnosed. Regarding anxiety, no significant difference was found between the informed and not informed group in psychological outcomes at any of the three assessments, even after adjusting for repeated measures on individual participants. It was concluded that many women participating in prenatal genetic screening are inadequately informed regarding aspects of testing, including the management of pregnancy in the event of increased risk.

A total of 2026 women were enrolled for the third study. Analysis was carried out in 82.7% (854/1030) women in the 12 week group and 84.1% (837/996) in the 18 week group who responded to all three questionnaires. The demographic characteristics of the two groups were similar. Emotional wellbeing at baseline in early pregnancy was also similar. In early pregnancy, 39.1% of women in the 12 week group and 36.0% in the 18 week group were worried about something being wrong with the baby, but the difference was not statistically significant. The prevalence decreased to 29.2% versus 27.8% during mid-pregnancy, and finally to 5.2% versus 6.6% at 2 months after delivery in the two groups. No statistically significant differences were found between the two groups during these periods either.

Within both trial groups, there was a statistically significant decrease in the levels of major worry about the baby's health from early to mid-pregnancy ($P < 0.001$) and from mid-pregnancy to 2 months after delivery ($P < 0.001$).

In the fourth study, a cross-sectional survey, 101 women formed the study group which comprised 31 women in the amniocentesis group, 32 in the MSS group and 38 in the no-test group. The mean gestational age at the time of participation was 28.3 ± 7.0 weeks. The mean maternal age in the amniocentesis group was higher than in the other two groups ($P = 0.005$), while no statistically significant differences were found between the three groups with respect to gestational age, number of previous pregnancies or previous miscarriages. A significant difference was found between the amniocentesis and no-test group regarding attitude towards abortion.

One-way ANOVA indicated that mean attachment scores nfor the MSS group (mean 51.7, SD 9.4) were significantly lower than those reported by the amniocentesis group (mean 58.5, SD 10.7) and no-test group (mean 57.0, SD 8.3) ($t(68) = 0.68$; $P = 0.02$). Furthermore, the amniocentesis group did not differ in bonding levels compared with the no-test group ($t(67) = 0.66$; $P = 0.51$), thereby proving the hypothesis. This difference persisted even after removing the influence of maternal age and attitude towards abortion. There was no significant interaction between testing status of the three groups and timing of conducting the survey (second or third trimester) when they were used as independent variables with PAI score as the dependent variable.

The results suggest that MSS may disrupt the developmental trajectory of the maternal–fetal bond even after favourable results are known. This may be due to the probabilistic nature of MSS results, which creates confusion rather than reassurance.

For the second systematic review, 600 studies were identified and 19 met the inclusion criteria. Ten related to screening/diagnosis for Down's syndrome and NTD, three for haemoglobin disorders and six studies for HIV. Several studies were limited by small sample size and poor reporting of data and statistical analysis. Only findings from ten studies of Down's syndrome and NTD are discussed below.

Nine studies reported on utilisation and/or uptake of prenatal screening or diagnosis. One of these suggested that, compared with white women, utilisation of testing was lower in South Asian women, two others indicated that both utilisation and uptake was lower, and a fourth study found both acceptance and uptake of amniocentesis lower in women from South Asia. In the remaining five studies, no statistically significant association was found between socio-demographic factors and test utilisation.

Four studies reported on the offer of screening or diagnosis for Down's syndrome. Two of these suggested that South Asian women were less likely to be offered amniocentesis, while in the third study fewer Bangladeshi than white women were offered screening, although this result was not statistically significant. The fourth study did not analyse the results according to the social class or ethnic group.

It was concluded that there is evidence that women from some ethnic groups, particularly South Asian women, may be less likely to receive prenatal diagnosis for Down's syndrome. A significant proportion of these women will take up prenatal testing if offered, but these women may be less likely to be offered testing. This points to the need to identify the factors associated with the offer and uptake of prenatal screening, barriers to offering screening at institutional and professional levels, and reasons for failure to take up screening when offered.

In the sixth study 2059 women were included and 1791 (89%) returned questionnaires but only 84% of these were completed on time. The results were:

- screening uptake – the overall uptake was 49% (95% CI 47% to 52%); uptake was higher in white and socio-economically advantaged women
- knowledge – overall, the mean knowledge score was above the midpoint of the scale; knowledge was higher for white, socio-economically advantaged and older women
- attitudes towards test – the mean overall score was above the scale midpoint, that is, overall women had a positive attitude towards the test; no difference in attitudes was found relating to ethnicity, socio-economic status or parity, but older women had a more positive attitude than younger ones
- uptake–attitude consistency – in women with positive attitudes, white and socio-economically advantaged women were more likely to act in line with their attitudes (76% of white women had the test compared with 45% of South Asian women; $P < 0.001$, and 78% of socio-economically advantaged women had the test compared with 63% of socio-economically disadvantaged women; $P < 0.001$); in women with a negative attitude, no difference was found between ethnic or social groups

2008 update

2008 update

- informed choice – the rates of informed choice were higher for white women (56% versus 20% of South Asian women; $P < 0.001$) and for socio-economically advantaged women (59% versus 14% for socio-economically disadvantaged women; $P < 0.001$).

After controlling for confounding variables (ethnicity, age, socio-economic status and hospital attended), it was found that both South Asian women and socio-economically disadvantaged women with positive attitudes were less likely to act consistently with their attitudes compared with white and socio-economically advantaged women (OR 0.22, 95% CI 0.10 to 0.45 for South Asian versus white women; and OR 0.62, 95% CI 0.41 to 0.93 for social groups).

The study was not able to determine the cause of lower consistency between positive attitudes and behaviour of these women.

In the last study, 1127 women returned the questionnaire. A total of 75% of women selected first-trimester screening (option 1 or option 2) as their first choice, with 68.2 % preferring results within 1 hour (option 1) and 6.8% preferring a combined test. Twenty-four percent opted for the integrated test and just 1% opted for second-trimester testing as their first choice.

Evidence summary
There is high-quality evidence to indicate that pregnant women do not have sufficient knowledge to make the informed decisions that need to be made regarding Down's syndrome screening and they find the concept of risk calculation particularly difficult to understand. Providing them with more information does not lead to an increase in their anxiety level.

Good evidence from a cohort study shows that women taking part in prenatal screening programme are inadequately informed regarding aspects of testing and the further pathway of management when an increased risk is identified.

Results from a cross-sectional study indicate that women undergoing a serum screening test for Down's syndrome develop less attachment for the baby owing to the uncertainty surrounding interpretation of the test result.

Evidence from a review of literature shows that pregnant women from South Asia have a lower rate of uptake, acceptance and utilisation of screening tests.

For the screening tests in general, white women and women from socio-economically advantaged sections of society have a higher uptake, better knowledge, more consistency of actions related to positive attitude, and a higher rate of informed decision making when compared with women from South Asia and socio-economically disadvantaged sections of society.

9.2.7   Health economics evidence

Antenatal screening for Down's syndrome
A systematic search of the literature was conducted to identify economic evaluations of screening for Down's syndrome. The search identified 132 abstracts, of which 40 full papers were retrieved for further consideration. Six studies are included in the review.

One study[801] was conducted to examine the performance of integrated Down's syndrome screening (first- and second-trimester measurements integrated into a single screening test) when ratios of the levels of the same serum markers measured in both these trimesters (cross-trimester ratios) are added as new screening markers. The addition of cross-trimester ratios to an integrated test significantly improves the efficacy and safety of prenatal screening for Down's syndrome. So, the addition of cross-trimester ratios is cost-effective and could be usefully introduced into screening programmes.

Another UK study[802] was conducted to compare the effects, safety and cost-effectiveness of antenatal screening strategies. The main outcomes of the study were the number of liveborn babies with Down's syndrome, miscarriages due to chorionic villus sampling or amniocentesis, healthcare costs of the screening programme, and additional costs and additional miscarriages per additional affected live birth prevented by adopting a more effective strategy. Compared with no screening, the additional cost per additional liveborn baby with Down's syndrome prevented was £22,000 for measurement of NT. The cost of the integrated test was £51,000 compared with the measurement of NT. All other strategies were more costly and less effective, or cost more per additional affected baby prevented. Depending on the cost of the screening test, the first-trimester combined test and the quadruple test would also be cost-effective options. The main conclusions of the study were that the choice of screening strategy should be between the integrated test, first-trimester combined test, quadruple test or NT measurement depending on how much service providers are willing to pay, the total budget available and values on safety. Screening based on maternal age, the second-trimester double test and the first-trimester serum test was less effective, less safe and more costly than these four options.

One HTA study[316] was conducted to identify the most effective, safe and cost-effective method of antenatal screening for Down's syndrome using NT, maternal serum and urine markers in the first and second trimesters of pregnancy and maternal age in various combinations. The cost-effectiveness analysis showed that the screening using the integrated test is less costly than might be expected because the extra screening costs tend to be offset by savings in the cost of diagnosis arising from the low FPR. It was estimated that to achieve an 85% detection rate the cost to the UK NHS would be £15,300 per Down's syndrome pregnancy detected. The corresponding cost of using the second-trimester quadruple test would be £16,800 and using the first-trimester combined test it would be £19,000.

Antenatal screening for Down's syndrome + structural anomalies

One HTA[297] study was conducted and one of the aims of this study was to refine and update a decision model of cost-effectiveness of options for routine scanning for fetal anomalies. The initial eight options considered were reduced to three dominating options: one second-trimester scan alone, one third-trimester scan alone and a combination of the one second-trimester scan followed by one third-trimester scan. More representative cost data are required before precise estimates of the additional costs and benefits of alternative options can be determined. Also, it is clear from the analysis that one second-trimester analysis scan emerged as a clear reference case, being one of the cheapest options yet still detecting a significant number of anomalies. When termination is acceptable and available, a third-trimester scan alone or the combination of one second- with one third-trimester scan, although comparable in economic terms, may be impractical because of the delay in identifying anomalies.

Another study[803] was conducted to compare the cost-effectiveness of different programmes of routine antenatal ultrasound screening to detect four key fetal anomalies: serious cardiac anomalies, spina bifida, Down's syndrome and lethal anomalies. The study showed that there was a substantial overlap between the cost ranges of each screening programme demonstrating considerable uncertainty about the relative economic efficiency of alternative screening programmes consisting of one second-trimester ultrasound scan. The cost per target anomaly detected (cost-effectiveness) for this programme was in the range £5,000–109,000, but in any 1000 women it would also fail to detect between 3.6 and 4.7 target anomalies. The model highlighted the weakness of the available evidence and demonstrated the need for more information both about current practice and costs.

Finally, a study[804] was conducted in the UK to determine the most clinically and cost-effective policy of scanning and screening for fetal anomalies in early pregnancy. The number of anomalies detected and missed, the number of iatrogenic losses resulting from invasive tests, the total cost of strategies and the cost per abnormality detected were compared between strategies. First-trimester screening for chromosomal anomalies costs more than the second-trimester screening but results in fewer iatrogenic losses. Strategies which include a second-trimester ultrasound scan result in more anomalies being detected and have lower costs per anomaly detected.

GDG interpretation of evidence

Accuracy and effectiveness of screening:
The integrated test was found to be cost-effective and resulted in the fewest losses of normal fetuses. However, there are concerns regarding the practicality of screening by this method. There is also evidence that women prefer a one-stage test to the integrated test.

Evidence shows that the combined test in the first trimester is also cost-effective and has good diagnostic value for detection of Down's syndrome and other chromosomal anomalies.

Among the currently used second-trimester tests, the quadruple test seems to have the best screening performance but the measurement of inhibin A (the fourth analyte) is not generally available in the UK.

Although isolated 'soft markers' on second-trimester ultrasound (18–23 weeks) with the exception of thickened nuchal fold have limited effectiveness in screening for Down's syndrome, two or more soft markers should prompt referral for fetal medicine opinion.

Other than the presence of increased nuchal fold thickening, isolated soft markers noted on the second-trimester scan should not be used to adjust the risk for Down's syndrome which has been derived from an established, nationally approved screening programme.

Women's views:

Levels of knowledge among women are not currently adequate for informed decision making about whether or not to undergo screening.

The biggest gap in knowledge is in understanding risk.

Increasing pre-screen knowledge does not raise anxiety levels.

Fewer South Asian women than white women are offered screening and fewer of those who are offered it choose to go ahead with it. Some healthcare professionals appear to have misconceptions regarding the likely attitudes of South Asian women to screening and termination of pregnancy.

The knowledge of those women opting out of screening seems to be better than that of those who are screened (16–26% don't know why they are being screened).

Serum screening can have a detrimental effect on women's attachment to pregnancy even with a low-risk result, owing to the uncertainty created by the probabilistic nature of the way the result is presented.

Recommendations on screening for Down's syndrome

All pregnant women should be offered screening for Down's syndrome. Women should understand that it is their choice to embark on screening for Down's syndrome.

Screening for Down's syndrome should be performed by the end of the first trimester (13 weeks 6 days), but provision should be made to allow later screening (which could be as late as 20 weeks 0 days) for women booking later in pregnancy.

The 'combined test' (nuchal translucency, beta-human chorionic gonadotrophin, pregnancy-associated plasma protein-A) should be offered to screen for Down's syndrome between 11 weeks 0 days and 13 weeks 6 days. For women who book later in pregnancy the most clinically and cost-effective serum screening test (triple or quadruple test) should be offered between 15 weeks 0 days and 20 weeks 0 days.

When it is not possible to measure nuchal translucency, owing to fetal position or raised body mass index, women should be offered serum screening (triple or quadruple test) between 15 weeks 0 days and 20 weeks 0 days.

Information about screening for Down's syndrome should be given to pregnant women at the first contact with a healthcare professional. This will provide the opportunity for further discussion before embarking on screening. (Refer to Section 3.3 for more information about giving antenatal information). Specific information should include:

- the screening pathway for both screen-positive and screen-negative results
- the decisions that need to be made at each point along the pathway and their consequences
- the fact that screening does not provide a definitive diagnosis and a full explanation of the risk score obtained following testing
- information about chorionic villus sampling and amniocentesis
- balanced and accurate information about Down's syndrome.

If a woman receives a screen-positive result for Down's syndrome, she should have rapid access to appropriate counselling by trained staff.

The routine anomaly scan (at 18 weeks 0 days to 20 weeks 6 days) should not be routinely used for Down's syndrome screening using soft markers

The presence of an isolated soft marker, with an exception of increased nuchal fold, on the routine anomaly scan, should not be used to adjust the a priori risk for Down's syndrome.

The presence of an increased nuchal fold (6 mm or above) or two or more soft markers on the routine anomaly scan should prompt the offer of a referral to a fetal medicine specialist or an appropriate healthcare professional with a special interest in fetal medicine.

Research recommendations on screening for Down's syndrome

There should be multicentred studies to evaluate the practicality, cost-effectiveness and acceptability of a two-stage test for Down's syndrome and other screening contingencies including the integrated test.

Further research should be undertaken into the views and understanding of women going through the screening process.

2008 update

10 Screening for infections

10.1 Asymptomatic bacteriuria

Asymptomatic bacteriuria (ASB) is defined as persistent bacterial colonisation of the urinary tract without urinary tract symptoms. Its incidence has been quoted as being 2–10% in studies conducted in the USA, with the higher incidence among women of lower socio-economic status.[328] Studies in the UK have shown that it occurs in 2–5% of pregnant women.[329-331] [EL = 3]

Evidence from RCTs that were conducted to show the benefit of treatment among women with ASB indicate an increased risk between ASB and maternal and fetal outcomes, such as preterm birth and pyelonephritis, among untreated women compared with women without bacteriuria.[329,331-337] [EL = 1b] The reported increased risk of pyelonephritis among pregnant women with ASB ranges from a risk difference of 1.8% to 28%.[329,331-333,335,338] [EL = 2a and 1b]

These trials also indicate an increased risk of preterm birth in women who have untreated ASB compared with women who do not have ASB. The risk difference ranges from 2.1% to 12.8%.[329,332,333,338] [EL = 1b] The large range in risk difference may be due to variation in effect size over time because earlier studies reported larger effects than more recent studies. Also, with regards to randomisation, many of the older studies did not specify the method of randomisation or were open to bias because of quasi-random allocation to treatment versus control groups.

Urine culture (midstream) has been used as the reference standard for diagnosis of ASB. In studies of ASB, a growth of 105 organisms of a single uropathogen per millilitre in a single midstream sample of urine is considered significant,[339,340] although some tests have used figures such as 104 and 108.[330] When urine culture is used in screening for ASB, the drawbacks include the time lag: results are not usually available for at least 24 hours,[341] and the cost: £1.40 in a 1993 UK study[342] compared with the maximum cost of a reagent strip test of £0.14. Its advantages are in being able to identify causative organisms and determine antibiotic sensitivities.

A number of rapid tests have been evaluated against urine culture in test evaluation studies. These include:

- reagent strip tests which test for one or more of the following:
  - nitrite
  - protein
  - blood
  - leucocyte esterase
- microscopic urinalysis
- Gram stain with or without centrifugation
- urinary interleukin
- rapid enzymatic screening test (detection of catalase activity)
- bioluminescence assay.

Reagent strip testing

This has the advantage of being rapid and inexpensive and requiring little technical expertise. Reagent strips have panels that have nitrites and leucocyte esterase,[343-346] and in which the presence of either nitrites or leucocyte esterase is considered positive.[345,347] Other strips have protein, blood, nitrite and leucocyte esterase.[348] In test evaluation studies with all four panels, a positive test result is defined as a strip showing any of the following:

- more than a trace of protein
- more than a trace of blood
- any positive result for nitrite
- any positive result for leucocyte esterase.[348]

The sensitivity of reagent strip testing, using two or four panels in combination (all tests positive) ranges from 8.18% to 50.0%.[342,343,345,347,348] [EL = 2a] With either test positive, in the case of the nitrite and leucocyte esterase test, two studies from the USA conducted in 2001 and 1993, respectively, showed sensitivities of 45% and 50%,[343,347] [EL = 2a] whereas a 1988 study, also from the USA, showed a sensitivity of 92%.[346] [EL = 2a] These findings are confirmed in another study, where the reported sensitivity of testing for protein alone for ASB was 57% with a specificity of 93.2%.[342] [EL = 2a] This implies that, at best, reagent strip testing will detect 50% of women with ASB.

Microscopic urinalysis

This test consists of microscopic analysis of urinary sediment and pyuria is deemed significant with ten cells per high-power field.[345,347] [EL = 2a] A study that examined a population of women attending an antenatal clinic found a sensitivity of 25%, which means that 75% of women with ASB will be missed using this test.[347] Two other studies report higher sensitivities but the population in one of the studies was a mixture of women attending an antenatal clinic and women in preterm labour and the second study used a wide range of pyuria of between one and eight per high-power field.[345,349]

Gram stain

Two American studies were identified in which Gram staining was compared with urine culture. In one study, a specificity of 7.7% was reported when urine was centrifuged and considered positive if the same morphotype of bacteria was seen in more than 6 of 12 high-power fields.[345] [EL = 2a] In the other study, urine was not centrifuged and a positive smear was defined as more than two organisms per high-power field. This yielded a specificity of 89.2%.[347] [EL = 2a] With the low specificity in the more rigorous estimation, more than 90% of women who do not have ASB will be incorrectly identified as cases.[345] [EL = 2a]

Other tests

Other tests identified include the urinary interleukin-8 test[343] and the rapid enzymatic test,[344] both of which have a sensitivity of 70% and will potentially miss 30% of women with ASB. [EL = 2a] A bioluminescence test has been described, with a sensitivity of 93% and a specificity of 78 %.[350] [EL = 2a]

Treatment

A systematic review of 14 RCTs compared antibiotic treatment with no treatment or placebo. Antibiotic treatment reduced persistent bacteriuria during pregnancy (Peto OR 0.07, 95% CI 0.05 to 0.10), reduced risk of preterm delivery or low-birthweight babies (OR 0.60, 95% CI 0.45 to 0.80), and reduced the risk of development of pyelonephritis (OR 0.24, 95% CI 0.19 to 0.32, NNT 7).[351] [EL = 1a]

A systematic review that compared single-dose antibiotic treatment with a 4 to 7 day course of antibiotic treatment for asymptomatic bacteriuria showed no difference in the prevention of preterm birth (RR 0.81, 95% CI 0.26 to 2.57) or pyelonephritis (RR 3.09, 95% CI 0.54 to 17.55). Longer duration of treatment, however, was associated with increased reports of adverse effects (RR 0.53, 95% CI 0.31 to 9.91).[352] [EL = 1a]

Economic considerations (see Appendix B)

Screening antenatally for asymptomatic bacteriuria can have important healthcare resource consequences associated with the reduction of maternal and infant morbidity. Using resources to screen women antenatally could save the future costs of treating pyelonephritis (which can have severe symptoms in pregnant women) and preterm birth and the consequent lifetime costs of disability associated with preterm birth. Screening and treating pregnant women can lead to healthier mothers and infants and does not lead to a choice to end a pregnancy. Therefore, screening and consequent treatment has only positive benefits for pregnant women and their children.

Implementing either of the screening strategies is more cost-effective than a policy of no screening. There is controversy around whether to use a dipstick or a culture test for screening. The culture test is relatively more expensive but has a higher sensitivity and specificity. One economic study concluded that the urine culture, which is regarded as the gold standard, is not cost beneficial when compared with the dipstick strategy.[600] However, this study did not consider the cost consequences of preterm birth in their analysis. Since these costs may be quite high (considering the lifetime costs of an infant born with disability), it was decided to try and model the alternative screening programmes and include these costs.

For that reason, a decision analytic model was created to compare the two strategies:

1. screening with urine culture
2. screening with leukocyte esterase-nitrite dipstick.

The economic data used in the model were extracted from five papers that met the criteria for high-quality economic evaluation (see Appendix B). The clinical effectiveness data were extrapolated from the evidence tables of the present guideline document.

The model indicated the difference in costs and benefits of adopting a dipstick method when compared with the culture method (the current gold standard). The unit of effectiveness was defined as cases of pyelonephritis averted and cases of preterm birth averted. The value and non-resource consequences of averting these cases could not be explored as data were not available.

The costs were expressed in three different ways:

1. the cost of screening only
2. the cost of screening and treatment (of ASB and pyelonephritis)
3. the cost of screening, treatment and the cost of preterm birth.

The model showed that the mean cost per case of pyelonephritis averted for the dipstick method was £4,300 when preterm birth was excluded and £115,000 when preterm birth was included. The mean cost per case averted for the culture method was £82,500 with and £36,500 without preterm birth. The results of the models indicate that it would cost an extra £32,400 for an extra case of preterm birth prevented if the dipstick method was followed instead of the culture.

The analysis supports the conclusion that the culture method is favourable, taking into account the wider cost consequences of ASB. The model indicated that if the policy of using a dipstick test led to only one additional case of preterm birth, then this is no longer the more favourable screening option, relative to the urine culture method.

Threshold analysis was also undertaken to explore the circumstances under which the screening options would have similar costs. The analysis indicated that for the two screening strategies to have equal overall costs (including the cost of preterm birth), the sensitivity of the dipstick method would have to be equal to or greater than 0.912, which is very high for this method of screening. Any sensitivity below this makes the culture method more cost-effective in comparison with the dipstick method.

This result has not yet been fully explored in primary cost-effectiveness studies and should be considered a priority for future research.

GDG interpretation of evidence

The evidence for screening for preterm birth was re-reviewed for this guideline update. In examining this evidence the GDG noted that the previous recommendation advising screening for bacteriuria in order to reduce the risk of preterm birth was no longer valid since an update of the Cochrane review which underpinned the recommendation no longer showed an association between treating asymptomatic bacteriuria and reducing the incidence of preterm birth. In order to bring this updated guideline in line with the current evidence base the updated Cochrane review[987] has been included in this section of the guideline and the recommendation amended accordingly.

Relevant findings from the Cochrane review are as follows: 14 controlled trials were included. Overall the study quality was poor. Antibiotic treatment compared with placebo or no treatment was effective in clearing asymptomatic bacteriuria (risk ratio 0.25 [95% CI 0.14 to 0.48]). The incidence of pyelonephritis was reduced (risk ratio 0.23 [95% CI 0.13 to 0.41]). Antibiotic treatment was also associated with a reduction in the incidence of low birthweight babies (risk ratio 0.66 [95% CI 0.49 to 0.89]) but a difference in preterm delivery was not seen. However, due to poor reporting of low birthweight in the original studies it is not possible to be confident in this finding.

Recommendation

Women should be offered routine screening for asymptomatic bacteriuria by midstream urine culture early in pregnancy. Identification and treatment of asymptomatic bacteriuria reduces the risk of pyelonephritis.

Future research

Randomised controlled trials are needed to confirm the beneficial effect of screening for asymptomatic bacteriuria.

10.2 Asymptomatic bacterial vaginosis

Bacterial vaginosis results from the relative deficiency of normal *Lactobacillus* species in the vagina and relative overgrowth of anaerobic bacteria. These may include *Mobiluncus* species, *Gardnerella vaginalis*, *Prevotella* species and *Mycoplasma hominis*. This results in a reduction of the normal acidity of the vagina. It is the most common cause of vaginal discharge and malodour,[353] although 50% of women with bacterial vaginosis infection during pregnancy will be asymptomatic.[354] Why these organisms, many of which are present in small numbers in the vagina normally, multiply is not well understood. The condition is not sexually transmitted, although it is associated with sexual activity.

The presence of bacterial vaginosis during pregnancy varies according to ethnicity and how often a population is screened. In a cross-sectional study of 13 747 pregnant women in the USA, 8.8% of white women had bacterial vaginosis compared with 22.7% in black women ($P < 0.05$), 15.9% in Hispanic women ($P < 0.05$) and 6.1% in Asian-Pacific Islander women.[355] [EL = 3] In a northwest area of London, screening before 28 weeks of gestation found a prevalence of 12%.[356] [EL = 3]

Bacterial vaginosis is associated with preterm birth. In a review of case–control and cohort studies, women with bacterial vaginosis infection were found to be 1.85 times more likely (95% CI 1.62 to 2.11) to deliver preterm than women without bacterial vaginosis.[357] [EL = 2 and 3] The higher risk of preterm birth remains in women diagnosed with bacterial vaginosis early in pregnancy even if the bacterial vaginosis spontaneously recovers later in pregnancy.[358] [EL = 3]

Bacterial vaginosis may be diagnosed by either Amsel's criteria (thin white-grey homogenous discharge, pH greater than 4.5, release of 'fishy odour' on adding alkali, clue cells present on direct microscopy)[359] or Nugent's criteria (Gram-stained vaginal smear to identify proportions of bacterial morphotypes with a score of less than 4 normal, 4–6 intermediate, and greater than 6 bacterial vaginosis).[360] Culture of *G. vaginalis* is not recommended as a diagnostic tool because it is not specific. Cervical Papanicolaou tests have limited clinical utility for the diagnosis of bacterial vaginosis because of low sensitivity.

One RCT was located which investigated the efficacy of yoghurt in treating bacterial vaginosis compared with vaginal metronidazole and vaginal placebo.[361] Although metronidazole was the most effective treatment against persistence of infection (relative risk reduction 62%, 95% CI 50 to 72%), yoghurt was two-thirds as effective as metronidazole when compared with the placebo group (relative risk reduction 46%, 95% CI 31 to 58%). [EL = 1b]

A systematic review of ten RCTs ($n = 4249$) found oral or vaginal antibiotics to be highly effective in the eradication of bacterial vaginosis in pregnancy when compared with placebo or no treatment (Peto OR 0.21, 95% CI 0.18 to 0.24)[362] [EL = 1a] Antibiotics used in the interventions included oral metronidazole (four RCTs), oral metronidazole plus erythromycin (one RCT), amoxicillin (one RCT), vaginal metronidazole cream (one RCT) and intravaginal clindamycin cream (three RCTs). No significant differences in the rates of preterm birth (birth before 37, 34 or 32 weeks) or perinatal death were observed between the two groups. However, a reduction in risk of preterm premature rupture of membranes was associated with antibiotics (three RCTs, $n = 562$ women, Peto OR 0.32, 95% CI 0.15 to 0.67). There were no differences in maternal side effects due to treatment found between the treated and non-treated or placebo groups. There was also no evidence of the effect of treatment on the subsequent risk of preterm birth among women with a prior preterm birth (five RCTs, $n = 622$ women, OR 0.83, 95% CI 0.59 to 1.17). Most women in these trials did not have symptoms of bacterial vaginosis because symptomatic women were treated and therefore excluded.

One trial that was not included in the above systematic review was located.[363] This study identified women between 12 to 22 weeks of gestation with bacterial vaginosis ($n = 485$) using Nugent's criteria. The study was double blind and women in the intervention group ($n = 244$) took 300 mg oral clindamycin twice daily for 5 days, while women in the control group ($n = 241$) took placebos. Women receiving clindamycin had significantly fewer spontaneous preterm deliveries, which were defined as birth occurring between 24 and 37 weeks of gestation, than women in the control group (11 (5%) versus 28 (12%), $P = 0.001$). [EL = 1b] When analysed with the ten trials from the systematic review, the effect of treatment for bacterial vaginosis on preterm birth was not statistically significant (Peto OR 0.93, 95% CI 0.76 to 1.13).

In addition, although oral clindamycin is not known to be harmful in pregnancy, its use as a general antibiotic is limited because of serious adverse effects.[77] In particular, antibiotic-associated colitis may arise and this can be fatal.

Evidence from RCTs indicates that screening and treating healthy pregnant women (i.e. low risk for preterm birth) for asymptomatic bacterial vaginosis does not lower the risk for preterm birth nor for other adverse reproductive outcomes.

Recommendation

Pregnant women should not be offered routine screening for bacterial vaginosis because the evidence suggests that the identification and treatment of asymptomatic bacterial vaginosis does not lower the risk for preterm birth and other adverse reproductive outcomes. [A]

10.3 *Chlamydia trachomatis*

Clinical question
What is the diagnostic value and effectiveness of the following screening methods in identifying genital chlamydia?

- age
- urine testing
- endocervical swabs
- serum antibody testing
- history.

Previous NICE guidance (for the updated recommendations see below)
Pregnant women should not be offered routine screening for asymptomatic chlamydia because there is insufficient evidence on its effectiveness and cost-effectiveness. However, this policy is likely to change with the implementation of the national opportunistic chlamydia screening programme. [C]

Future research:
Further investigation into the benefits of screening for chlamydia in pregnancy is needed.

10.3.1 Introduction and background

Genital chlamydia is the most common sexually transmitted infection in England, with a high disease burden of 1 in 10 positives among men and women aged 16–25 years.[999] The National Chlamydia Screening Programme annual report for 2005/06 states that 8.5% of all tests undertaken among women under 25 years of age in obstetrics and gynaecology, antenatal, infertility and colposcopy clinics were positive.[999]

2008 update

The majority of people infected with *Chlamydia trachomatis* are not aware of their infection because they do not have symptoms that would prompt them to seek medical care. Untreated infections in women can lead to serious complications such as pelvic inflammatory disease, infertility, ectopic pregnancy and chronic pelvic pain. During pregnancy, chlamydia infection can lead to neonatal conjunctivitis and pneumonia, and maternal postpartum endometritis (www.cdc.gov/std/Chlamydia/STDFact-Chlamydia.htm#complications).

The traditional reference test for determining whether chlamydial infection is present is the growth of chlamydiae in cell culture. However, it is an inadequate 'gold standard' owing to the necessity of maintaining the viability of chlamydiae in patient samples prior to inoculation and the effects of many potential variables that can affect the culture process. Discrepant analysis is an attempt to identify the true positive cases of infection that cell culture misses. Apparent 'false positives' (culture negative, test positive) are subjected to a battery of further tests. If any of these are positive, the original positive result is considered a true positive and, conversely, the original cell culture negative is considered a false negative. It is advocated that the discrepant analysis-based estimates of sensitivity and specificity are typically less biased than those based on culture, but its use has also been criticised for being biased in favour of the new tests (subjecting only the new test-positive tests to a battery of further test).

Nineteen studies have been included in this review – 13 for diagnostic value and six for effectiveness of treatment. The review has been divided into two sections – the first section deals with diagnostic accuracy of the various tests while the second deals with effectiveness of treatment.

10.3.2   Diagnostic accuracy

Thirteen studies are included in this section and all are prospective cohort studies with mostly EL = II owing to absence of blinding. The study population in some of the publications included non-pregnant symptomatic women and symptomatic men in addition to asymptomatic pregnant women, but the results of predictive accuracy have been calculated for asymptomatic pregnant women only. This review was limited to include tests carried out on urine and endocervical specimens only. The screening tests covered under this section are:

- antigen detection tests – enzyme immunoassay (EIA) or direct fluorescent antibody test (DFA)
- nucleic acid amplification tests (NAAT) – polymerase chain reaction (PCR) or ligase chain reaction (LCR) test
- nucleic acid hybridisation test – DNA probe test
- Gram staining or Pap smear
- culture.

Antigen detection tests (EIA or DFA)

Description of included studies
A prospective cohort study[805] was carried out in an obstetric and gynaecology clinic in a county hospital in the USA. The study population included both pregnant (*n* = 231) and non-pregnant women under the age of 35 years (*n* = 827). Excluded were women suspected of having a sexually transmitted infection, those desiring abortion, and those with acute salpingitis. EIA and DFA were compared with culture (with blind passage) as the reference test, and specimens were collected in a random sequence from the endocervix for the three tests. All the tests were described in detail. Each test was performed independently without knowledge on the part of technicians of the results of other tests. Specimens which were not positive in all three of the tests but were positive by at least one of the tests were re-evaluated by all the three systems. The threshold of a positive DFA test was ≥ 10 elementary bodies (EB) per slide, while for EIA it was optical density 0.100 greater than mean optical density of three negative controls. Specimens were considered to be 'true positive' if they were positive by initial culture or repeat culture. [EL = Ib]

A study in Canada[805] compared EIA and DFA with tissue culture in a cohort of consecutive pregnant women opting for abortion. Excluded were women with lower genital tract infection, those who declined to give detailed sexual history, or where laboratory specimens were lost. Separate specimens were collected for the three tests but details of testing were not described. Blinding of technicians was not specified. Thresholds for positive DFA and EIA results were not clearly explained. Tissue culture without blind passage was used as the reference test to define 'true positives'. Diagnostic accuracy was also compared separately by defining 'true positive' as positive results for any two of the three tests. [EL = II]

Another prospective cohort study [806] was carried out in a regional medical centre in the USA comparing EIA (Chlamydiazyme) and DFA (MicroTrak, Syva) with cell culture. The study comprised 255 indigent pregnant women from a population showing a chlamydia isolation rate consistently above 20%. Exclusion criteria were not specified, but the tests were described in detail. Specimens were sequentially collected from the cervix and technicians performing the tests were unaware of the results of other tests. Positive EIA was defined as absorbance greater than the mean value of negative controls plus 0.1, while for DFA it was the presence of one or more typical inclusion bodies. Isolation of chlamydia in cell culture was taken as the 'reference test' and a single positive test defined as 'true positive'. [EL = II]

A multicentre cohort study[807] was carried out in the USA recruiting symptomatic men and women from sexually transmitted disease clinics, and asymptomatic pregnant women attending abortion clinic or prenatal clinic. Exclusion criteria were not specified. Pregnant women were selected from two centres and cervical specimens collected for DFA and culture. The tests performed were described adequately and laboratory personnel were blinded from other test results. Smears showing two or more elementary bodies were considered positive for DFA. Culture was performed twice and a 'true positive' was taken as isolation of chlamydia on either culture. [EL = Ib]

Findings

Of the 231 pregnant women in the first study, 28 were true positive (prevalence 12.1%). Given below are the results for diagnostic accuracy of the tests when compared with 'true positive' results.

Test	Sensitivity	Specificity	PPV	NPV
EIA (n = 231)	85.7%	95.6%	72.7%	98.0%
DFA (n = 144)	84.6%	96.6%	84.6%	96.6%
First culture with blind passage	82.1%	–	–	98.8%
First culture without blind passage	60.7%	–	–	94.7%

In the second study, cultures were positive for 56 women out of an initial sample of 531 (prevalence 10.8%), while results of all the three tests were available for 462 women only. Women with chlamydial infection were more likely to be ≤ 20 years (P = 0.0009) and have a prior history of gonorrhoea (P = 0.013). No difference was observed for number of lifetime sex partners or more than one sexual partner in the 6 months before study. The results with two different definitions of 'true positive' are as follows:

(a) isolation in cell culture defined as 'true positive'

Test	Sensitivity	Specificity	PPV	NPV
DFA	89%	99%	78%	99%
EIA	96%	95%	69%	99.5%

(b) any two positive test results defined as 'true positive'

Test	Sensitivity	Specificity	PPV	NPV
Culture	80%	99.8%	98%	97%
DFA	93%	100%	100%	99%
EIA	98	98	87	99.8

Fifty-four culture-confirmed infections were detected (prevalence 21.2%) in the third study. For a comparison of diagnostic accuracy, the sample size was 247 for DFA and 250 for EIA owing to non-interpretable culture results (four) and loss of slides or assays (four slides for DFA and one assay for EIA). Compared with cell culture as the reference tests, the results are as follows:

Test	Sensitivity	Specificity	PPV	NPV
DFA	98.1%	95.4%	85.0%	99.5%
EIA	96.3%	92.9%	78.8%	98.9%

In the last study, the sample size was 1396 including 225 pregnant women. The prevalence of chlamydia infection was 13%. The results are as follows:

Test	Sensitivity	Specificity	PPV	NPV
DFA	86.2%	99.0%	92.6%	98.0%

Nucleic acid amplification tests (PCR, LCR)

Description of included studies

In the first study,[808] consecutive pregnant women going for legal termination of pregnancy were enrolled at a tertiary hospital in Australia over a 12 month period. Women refusing to participate and those with incomplete test results were excluded from the final analysis. The specimens collected were first-catch urine and self-inserted tampon for both PCR and LCR testing, and endocervical swabs for testing by PCR and culture. The methods for collecting specimens and the tests were described in detail. All assays on clinical samples were performed blinded to the results of one another. A women was considered 'true positive' if the endocervical specimen was positive by culture and/or at least one of first-catch urine, tampon, or endocervical swab was positive by PCR and LCR. [EL = Ib]

The other study was a prospective cohort study[809] carried out in the USA, which recruited predominantly unmarried, publicly funded pregnant women, with many having risk factors for chlamydia genital tract infection (young age, history of sexually transmitted disease, reported drug use, education level less than 12 years). The tests employed were LCR for the voided urine sample, and LCR and culture of endocervical swabs. The method of specimen collection and the tests were described in detail, but blinding was not been specified. A 'true positive' result was defined as a positive culture result or negative culture with positive LCR test confirmed by supplementary testing with DFA or MOMP-LCR. If either of these supplementary tests gave a positive result, then the original positive LCR was considered a 'true positive' and the negative culture as a false negative result. [EL = II]

Findings

In the first study, the initial population was 1245 but 70 had incomplete specimens, leaving a sample size of 1175 women for determining diagnostic accuracy. The overall prevalence of chlamydia infection was 2.8% (33/1175). The breakdown of true positive results according to the site and test used is as follow:

Specimen	PCR	LCR	Culture
First-catch urine	34	31	Not done
Tampon	31	29	Not done
Endocervical swab	27	29	15

No statistically significant difference was observed between the diagnostic value of PCR and LCR test from the three specimens – urine ($P = 0.25$), tampon ($P = 0.5$) or endocervical swab ($P = 0.5$). On comparing the diagnostic value of PCR/LCR with culture for endocervical swabs, detection by PCR/LCR was significantly better ($P = 0.0005$). With 'true positive' as the reference standard, sensitivities of the three tests for endocervical specimens were 45.5% (15/33) for culture, 81.8% (27/33) for PCR and 87.9% (29/33) for the LCR test.

The study population in the second study consisted of 478 women and the mean maternal age of the cohort was 22.9 ± 5.6 years. Sixteen women were excluded from the final analysis owing to non-availability of specimens. The prevalence of infection was 20.1% (93/462). Compared with the reference standard, the diagnostic accuracy of the three tests was:

Test	Sensitivity	Specificity
Culture endocervix	30.1%	100%
LCR endocervix	90.3%	100%
LCR urine	83.9%	99.5%

2008 update

Comparison of EIA/DFA versus PCR/LCR or/and culture

Description of included studies

A multicentre prospective cohort study[810] carried out in Sweden at three hospitals recruited consecutive pregnant women seeking abortion during a 6 month period. No exclusion criteria were described. This study evaluated the diagnostic efficacy of culture, DFA, EIA and PCR tests performed on specimens from the endocervical region. The method for collecting specimens and the procedures of the various tests were adequately described, but blinding of laboratory personnel to the results was not specified. When the initial culture was negative, the specimen was recultured using multiple passages. For the reference standard, 'true positive' was defined as a positive culture in any passage (first time or on reculturing) or at least two positive non-culture tests. The threshold of a positive test for DFA was taken as ≥ 10 elementary bodies per slide, but the diagnostic value of DFA was also calculated for ≥ 1 elementary body. [EL = II]

Four methods of screening were compared in a prospective cohort study[811] in the UK: EIA of endocervical swab and LCRs for first-void urine sample, vaginal swab and endocervical swab. The study sample comprised consecutive women less than 25 years of age attending abortion, family planning, and antenatal clinics. Women with symptoms of pelvic infection and ruptured membranes were excluded. The method of specimen collection and the test performed were described adequately, but blinding was not specified. All positive EIA results were confirmed by DFA (another antigen detection test), while LCR-positive results were confirmed by another LCR test coding for major outer membrane protein (MOMP-LCR). Any discrepancy in test results was resolved by supplementary testing – DFA performed for negative EIA but positive LCR from any site, and MOMP-LCR performed for LCR negative but EIA positive result. For calculating diagnostic accuracy, 'true positive' was defined as one or more specimens from any site confirmed positive by two independent tests, i.e. EIA confirmed by DFA or negative EIA but positive LCR confirmed by MOMP-LCR. [EL = II]

Another prospective cohort study in the UK[812] recruited women presenting for termination of pregnancy at a family planning clinic. Criteria for study exclusion were not defined but specimen collection and test were adequately described. LCR and DFA tests were performed separately on cervical, vaginal and urine specimens obtained from each participant. Blinding of laboratory personnel was not specified. The 'reference test' was taken as a positive result for any test at any site. [EL = II]

Findings

The results of culture, EIA and DFA were available for 419 women in the multicentre Swedish study, and PCR test results were missing for a further 38 women. Of the participants, 175 women (41.8%) were below 24 years of age. Using the reference standard, prevalence was 4.3% (18/419). Below are the results for diagnostic accuracy of the various tests:

Test	Sensitivity	Specificity	PPV	NPV
Culture	66.7%	100%	100%	98.5%
DFA (≥ 10 EB)	61.1%	99.8%	91.7%	98.3%
DFA (≥ 1 EB)	77.8%	99.5%	87.5%	99.0%
EIA	64.7%	100%	100%	98.5%
PCR (*n* = 381)	71.4%	100%	100%	98.9%

In the first UK study, the mean maternal age of 303 women was 20 years (SD 2.7 years) and 67% of the study population was pregnant (204/303) – 104 at the abortion clinic and 100 at antenatal clinic. One patient from the antenatal population was excluded from the final analysis as her positive LCR was not available for confirmation. The overall prevalence of chlamydia infection was 9.9% (30/302) while it was 10.8% (22/203) among the pregnant women. The results of diagnostic accuracy of the four tests in pregnant women are as follows:

Test	Sensitivity (95% CI)	Specificity (95% CI)
EIA	82% (62–93%)	100% (98–100%)
LCR endocervix	82% (62–93%)	100% (98–100%)
LCR vagina	100% (85–100%)	100% (98–100%)
LCR urine	91% (72–98%)	100% (98–100%)

Of the 863 women recruited in the second UK study, 74 were infected by chlamydia (prevalence 8.5%). The median age of infected women was significantly lower than that of the uninfected group ($P < 0.0001$). Compared with the reference standard, the sensitivities of the various tests were:

Site	Sensitivity for LCR (95% CI)	Sensitivity for DFA (95% CI)
Cervical swab	97% (93–99%)	93% (87–99%)
Vaginal swab	94% (88–99%)	92% (86–99%)
Urine	83% (75–92%)	78% (68–88%)

The sensitivity and specificity of the DFA test was also compared with LCR test as the reference test using results from the same test site:

Site	Sensitivity (95% CI)	Specificity (95% CI)
Cervical swab	93.8% (93.2–94.4%)	99.9% (99.8–100%)
Vaginal swab	92.1% (92.0–93.2%)	99.5% (99.2–99.9%)
Urine	89.3% (81.2–97.4%)	99.7% (99.4–99.9%)

Nucleic acid hybridisation tests (DNA probe test)

Description of included studies

A prospective cohort study[813] in the USA compared the diagnostic value of DNA probe tests with that of culture for both chlamydia and gonorrhoea. The study population comprised consecutive low-income pregnant women attending a university medical centre, but no exclusions were specified. Endocervical specimens were collected during the first prenatal examination, and the methods and test performed were adequately described. Technologists performing the tests were blinded to other test results. The presence of one or more fluorescing inclusion was considered a positive DFA test, and isolation of chlamydia on culture was taken as the 'reference standard'. [EL = II]

Another US-based prospective cohort study[814] compared a DNA probe test with the standard tissue culture method for the detection of endocervical chlamydia infection. The study population comprised both asymptomatic pregnant women attending for routine prenatal care and women with symptoms of lower genital tract infection or history of sexually transmitted disease. Excluded were women receiving antibiotics within 4 weeks of specimen collection. The method of collecting specimens and the tests were described in detail, but blinding of laboratory personnel to the results was not specified. In cases of discrepant results, 'probe competition assays' were performed. The cut-off range for a positive DNA probe test was calculated on the basis of the difference between the response in relative light units of the specimen and mean of three negative reference values. 'True positive' results were defined as those specimens positive by culture or positive by two non-culture tests (i.e. DNA probe test and probe competition assay) if the culture was negative. [EL = II]

Findings

In the first study, there were 322 women overall with a median age of 21 years and an average gestational age of 22 weeks at the time of testing. The results for both tests for chlamydia were available for 246 women only (76.4% of the study population) and 33 were positive by culture (prevalence 13.4%). The DNA probe test for chlamydia had a sensitivity of 93.9%, specificity of 99.1%, PPV of 93.9% and NPV of 99.1%.

The study population in the second US study was 426 women, consisting of 257 asymptomatic pregnant women and 169 symptomatic women. The prevalence of infection among pregnant women was 8.6% (22/257). The diagnostic accuracy results for pregnant women are as follows:

Test	Sensitivity (95% CI)	Specificity	PPV	NPV
DNA probe test	86.4% (75–100%)	100%	100%	98.7%
Culture	95.4% (87–100%)	100%	100%	99.6%

When culture alone was taken as the reference standard, the sensitivity, specificity, PPV and NPV of the DNA probe test was 85.7%, 99.6%, 94.7% and 98.7%, respectively.

2008 update

2008 update

Gram staining/Pap smear

Description of included studies

A prospective cohort study in the USA[815] compared the diagnostic accuracy of a Gram stain of cervical mucus with that of a DNA probe test and PCR for the detection of chlamydia and gonorrhoea. Pregnant women examined at their initial visit to the obstetric clinic or at 36 weeks of gestation were enrolled. No specific exclusion criterion were mentioned. The procedure for specimen collection and methodology of the tests was adequately described. The examiners for Gram stain were masked to other tests results. A positive Gram stain was defined as having ≥ 10 polymorphonuclear leucocytes per high power field and a positive DNA probe test was taken as the reference standard. [EL = Ib]

Another prospective study of unselected pregnant women seeking first- or second-trimester termination of pregnancy was conducted at a tertiary hospital in the USA[816] to compare Pap smear with culture. Women who had received tetracycline or erythromycin within 2 weeks of the procedure were excluded. Specimens were collected 2–10 days prior to abortion and the tests were described in detail. Pap smear findings were grouped into inflammation, consistent with chlamydia infection, others and negative. The reference test employed was a positive growth on culture. [EL = II]

Findings

The study population included 519 pregnant women in the first study, and DNA probe results were unavailable for one. Sixty-three percent of the sample population was less than 24 years of age. The prevalence of chlamydia identified by DNA probe test was 6.8% (35/518). Age less than 20 years ($P < 0.0001$) and unmarried status ($P = 0.005$) were found to be significant predictors of the disease by logistic regression.

Compared with the DNA probe test as the 'reference standard', values for diagnostic accuracy of Gram staining were sensitivity 91%, specificity 18%, PPV 7.5% and NPV 96.7%.

In the second study, the mean age of the sample population of 300 women was 21.4 years and the majority of them (80.3%) were single. Chlamydia was isolated in 43 women (prevalence 14.3%).

When a Pap smear consistent with chlamydia infection was used as the threshold, the sensitivity and specificity were 2.3% and 98.1%, respectively. When the threshold was increased to include smear findings of inflammation, sensitivity was 60.5% and specificity was 56.4%.

Evidence summary

There is high-quality evidence to show that both antigen detection and nucleic acid amplification tests have high sensitivity and specificity for detecting chlamydia infection [EL = Ib]

Evidence indicates that the diagnostic accuracy of both antigen detection and nucleic acid amplification tests is better than that of tissue culture method for endocervical specimens. [EL = II]

There is some evidence that nucleic acid amplification tests (PCR, LCR) carried out on first-void urine and endocervical specimens might have better diagnostic ability in detecting chlamydial infection compared with the antigen detection tests. [EL = II]

The DNA probe test has high sensitivity and specificity for detecting chlamydia infection, but the evidence is of moderate quality and is also limited. [EL = II]

Evidence from a single study shows that Gram staining has high sensitivity but poor specificity for detecting chlamydia infection. [EL = Ib]

10.3.3 Effectiveness studies

Six papers have been included in this review: one RCT and five cohort studies (four prospective and one retrospective).

Description of included studies

A randomised placebo-controlled double-blinded trial[817] was carried out in the USA to determine whether treatment of pregnant women with chlamydia infection would lower the incidence of preterm delivery and/or low birthweight. This study was part of a large multicentre trial known as the Vaginal Infection and Prematurity (VIP) study. Pregnant women at 23–29 weeks of pregnancy and with chlamydia isolated from endocervical specimens by culture were enrolled for the trial if they successfully completed a 1 week placebo run-in. Women were randomised to the treatment group (erythromycin base 333 g TDS for 7 days, n = 205) or the placebo group (n = 209) using computer randomisation and method of allocation was concealed. At the mid-study stage (2–4 weeks after starting study), random samples for culture were obtained to ensure quality control and drug efficacy. Baseline characteristics of the two groups were similar. When data from all the study sites were combined using intention-to-treat analysis, the treatment group showed fewer low birthweight (LBW) infants (8% versus 11%), fewer preterm deliveries < 37 weeks (13% versus 15%), and fewer instances of PROM (3% versus 4%) compared with the placebo group but the difference was not statistically significant for all the outcomes. No difference was observed for stillbirth or neonatal deaths. The results from the mid-study culture showed two centres having low culture positive recovery rates in the placebo group (high-clearance group) which could not be explained even after controlling for factors such as quality and use of antibiotics outside the trial. The trial outcome was then stratified into two groups: data from study sites with high clearance versus low clearance of chlamydia infection in the placebo-treated women. At sites with low clearance, LBW occurred in 8% of the treatment group versus 17% in the placebo group (P = 0.04), while preterm delivery occurred in 13% versus 17% (P = 0.4). In the high-clearance group, no statistically significant difference was seen for the two outcomes although no reason was given as to why some women cleared infection better. [EL = 1++]

A US-based prospective study (1990)[818] sought to determine whether treatment of chlamydia infection during pregnancy could reduce the effect of the infection on adverse pregnancy outcomes. Endocervical cultures for chlamydia were obtained from 11 544 consecutive new obstetric patients – 9111 were negative and 2433 were culture positive. No treatment was recommended for women with positive culture during the first 16 months of the study but, after reviewing the high rate of chlamydia infection among the cohort, a treatment protocol was instituted (with erythromycin 500/250 mg QID for 7 days or sulfisoxazole 1 g QID for 7 days) for women with positive culture for the remaining study period of 20 months. Baseline characteristics of the three groups were not compared and all the information was collected from the computerised database. Of the 2433 initial culture-positive pregnant women, 1323 were successfully treated and 1110 were untreated. The results showed a 21.1% prevalence of chlamydia that was inversely related to age and parity. The prevalence was 32% in women under the age of 17 years and 20% in the 20- to 24-year-old group. The treated group as compared with the untreated group showed a significantly lower frequency of PROM (2.9% versus 5.2%) and LBW (11% versus 19.6%) (P < 0.001 for both). The newborn survival was significantly higher (P < 0.001) in the treated group (99.4% versus 97.6%). Similar results were observed when the culture-negative group was compared with the untreated group. Multiple logistic regression analysis was then used to control for confounding variables. The incidence of PROM was significantly higher in the untreated group compared with the treated group (P < 0.01). Perinatal mortality was also observed to be higher in the untreated group but the difference was not statistically significant (P = 0.08). On comparing outcomes between the treated group and negative culture group, infants born to mothers in the treated group were more likely to survive (P < 0.01) but no difference was seen for PROM as an outcome. It was concluded that screening of populations at high risk of chlamydia is recommended and treatment may improve pregnancy outcomes. [EL = 2+]

A US-based retrospective study[819] compared the clinical outcome in pregnant women whose cervical chlamydial infection was successfully treated with erythromycin 500 mg QID for 7 days (Group 1, n = 244) with the outcome of pregnant women who remained chlamydia-positive throughout pregnancy, at the end of pregnancy (Group 2, n = 79), as well as to a group of chlamydia-free matched control patients (Group 3, n = 244). These three groups were selected from a cohort of low-income, indigent, and urban pregnant women considered at high risk for infection with *Chlamydia trachomatis*. The demographic characteristics of the three groups were similar. On comparing pregnancy outcomes between the groups, Group 1 was associated with significantly lower frequency of PROM (7.4% versus 20.3%), preterm contractions (4.1% versus 24.1%) and SGA babies (13.1% versus 25.3%) when compared with Group 2, but no such differences were observed between Groups 1 and 3. The frequency of preterm delivery was significantly lower in Group 1 than either Group 2 (2.9% versus 13.9%) or Group 3 (2.9% versus

2008 update

11.9%). No difference was found between the three groups regarding other pregnancy outcomes – frequency of vaginal deliveries, caesarean sections, postpartum endometritis, antepartum haemorrhage or stillbirth. The authors concluded that there can be a significant reduction in certain adverse outcomes in a pregnant population at high risk for infection with chlamydia with repeated prenatal chlamydial testing plus successful erythromycin treatment. [EL = 2–]

A US-based prospective study (1990)[820] sought to determine whether a rapid EIA antigen detection system (Chlamydiazyme) can be used reliably in a screening programme to identify and treat chlamydial infections in pregnant women to prevent perinatal transmission of the organism to their infants. Chlamydiazyme was used to screen 199 asymptomatic pregnant women in the third trimester. Fifty-two were Chlamydiazyme-positive (prevalence 26%) and were treated with erythromycin 500 mg QID for 7 days whereas 128 were Chlamydiazyme-negative. The results showed no significant differences in the incidence of respiratory tract illnesses or conjunctivitis in infants born among the two groups (n = 50 study group, n = 48 control group). There were no significant differences in the incidence of rupture of membranes, preterm birth, caesarean section or postpartum endometritis among the erythromycin-treated Chlamydiazyme-positive and Chlamydiazyme-negative group. It was concluded that Chlamydiazyme can be used in a screening programme to identify and treat third-trimester women infected with *Chlamydia trachomatis*. [EL = 2–]

A prospective study in the USA (1997)[821] compared maternal, neonatal and infant outcomes between two groups of pregnant women with chlamydial cervicitis – one group correctly identified by antigen detection tests and treated with erythromycin 800 mg QID for 7 days (n = 23), and the second group missed by antigen detection tests (positive by culture) and which did not receive any treatment (n = 58). The two groups in this study were formed as a result of an earlier study done to evaluate the diagnostic value of antigen detection tests and their demographic characteristics were similar. The clinicians were blinded to culture results but not antigen detection tests results. Maternal complications including abortion, PROM, preterm delivery and chorioamnionitis were similar in the two groups. Similarly, no difference was observed for neonatal (stillbirth, preterm birth, respiratory distress syndrome (RDS), tachypnoea, sepsis) and infant complications (conjunctivitis, pneumonia, otitis, bronchitis, diarrhoea). The authors concluded that further prospective, controlled, culture-based studies are needed before recommending routine screening for chlamydia. [EL = 2+]

A US-based prospective cohort study (1985)[822] compared the clinical outcome of chlamydia infection treated mothers and infants with that of untreated ones. Routine cervical cultures for chlamydia were obtained during the third trimester to identify infected mothers (n = 85) whose infants may also be infected and 38 were treated with erythromycin 500 mg BD for 10 days. A total of 16 culture-positive infants born to treated mothers were compared with 21 culture-positive infants from untreated mothers. The baseline characteristics of the two groups were not compared and blinding was not specified. The results showed that in the culture-positive treated group, none of the infants developed infection with chlamydia, while five of 21 infants of untreated mothers (P < 0.04) were culture positive and symptomatic (four with conjunctivitis, one with pneumonia). The follow-up of infants born to chlamydia-positive mothers showed no evidence of more frequent episodes of upper respiratory infection and otitis media during the first 6 months of life. The authors concluded that diagnosis and treatment of cervical chlamydia infection during the third trimester provides a practical approach to the prevention of infection in the newborn. [EL = 2–]

Evidence summary

There is limited evidence to indicate that treatment of chlamydia infection during pregnancy is effective in reducing the incidence of PROM, preterm delivery and LBW babies, but the studies are not of good quality.

There is no significant evidence to show that treating chlamydia infection during pregnancy leads to decreased incidence of adverse neonatal outcomes (conjunctivitis, pneumonia).

GDG interpretation of evidence

There is no good-quality evidence which would support routine antenatal screening for genital chlamydia. Asymptomatic chlamydia infection during pregnancy has been associated with adverse outcomes of pregnancy (LBW, preterm delivery, PROM) and neonatal morbidities (respiratory tract infection and conjunctivitis). However, a causal link between the organism and adverse outcomes of pregnancy has not been established and the evidence remains difficult to evaluate in relation to neonatal morbidities. Where a causal link between organism and outcome has been established, rapid identification and good management of affected neonates is thought to be a clinical and cost-effective alternative to screening.

There are concerns regarding the practicality of undertaking adequate counselling, contact tracing, partner testing and follow-up in the antenatal period.

In addition, it seems likely that the implementation of the National Chlamydia Screening Programme should itself lead to a reduction in the prevalence of chlamydia infection in women under the age of 25 years. In order to support this, pregnant women under 25 years should be informed of the screening programme. Where antenatal services are already undertaking, or planning to undertake, chlamydia screening as part of the national programme, this can be continued.

Recommendations on screening for chlamydia

At the booking appointment, healthcare professionals should inform pregnant women younger than 25 years about the high prevalence of chlamydia infection in their age group, and give details of their local National Chlamydia Screening Programme (www.chlamydiascreening.nhs.uk).

Chlamydia screening should not be offered as part of routine antenatal care.

Research recommendation on screening for chlamydia

Further research needs to be undertaken to assess the effectiveness, practicality and acceptability of chlamydia screening in an antenatal setting.

Why this is important
Chlamydia is a significant healthcare issue, especially among the young, but the current level of evidence provides an insufficient basis for a recommendation. Of particular importance is the possibility that treatment might reduce the incidence of preterm birth and neonatal complications, and studies should be directed to these areas.

10.4   Cytomegalovirus

Cytomegalovirus (CMV) is a member of the herpesvirus family. It remains latent in the host after primary infection and may become active again, particularly during times of compromised immunity.

In England and Wales in 1992 and 1993 ($n = 1.36$ million live births) there were 47 reported cases of CMV infections in pregnant women with 22 resulting in intrauterine death or stillbirth.[374] [EL = 3] Congenital infection is thought to occur in 3/1000 live births[375,376] [EL = 3] This is likely to be an underestimate, as women who suffer a stillbirth or intrauterine death are more likely to be investigated for CMV infection.

At present, antenatal screening for this condition is thought to be inappropriate, as it is not currently possible accurately to determine which pregnancies are likely to result in the birth of an infected infant,[376] [EL = 3] there is no way to determine which infected infants will have serious sequelae, there is no currently available vaccines or prophylactic therapy for the prevention of transmission and no way to determine whether intrauterine transmission has occurred.[377,378] [EL = 4]

Recommendation

The available evidence does not support routine cytomegalovirus screening in pregnant women and it should not be offered. [B]

10.5 Hepatitis B virus

Hepatitis B is a virus that infects the liver and many people with hepatitis B viral infection have no symptoms. The hepatitis B virus has an incubation period of 6 weeks to 6 months, it is excreted in various body fluids including blood, saliva, vaginal fluid and breast milk; these fluids may be highly infectious.

The prevalence of hepatitis B surface antigen (HBsAg) in pregnant women in the UK has been found to range from 0.5% to 1%.[379-381] [EL = 3] An older study of the prevalence of hepatitis B virus in pregnant women in the West Midlands from 1974–1977 reported a lower rate of 0.1%.[382] [EL = 3] The range in prevalence rates is most likely due to wide variation in prevalence among different ethnic groups, as Asian women in particular appear to have a higher prevalence of HBsAg.[379] [EL = III] Consequently, Asian babies also have higher rates of mother-to-child transmission of HBsAg.[382] [EL = 3]

As many as 85% of babies born to mothers who are positive for the hepatitis e antigen (eAg) will become HBsAg carriers and subsequently become chronic carriers, compared with 31% of babies who are born to mothers who are eAg negative (RR2.8, 95% CI 1.69 to 4.47).[383] [EL = 3] It has been estimated that chronic carriers of HBsAg are 22 times more likely to die from hepatocellular carcinoma or cirrhosis than noncarriers (95% CI 11.5 to 43.2).[384] [EL = 2b]

Approximately 21% of hepatitis B viral infections reported in England and Wales among children under the age of 15 years is due to mother-to-child transmission.[385] [EL = 3] Mother-to-child transmission of the hepatitis B virus is approximately 95% preventable through administration of vaccine and immunoglobulin to the baby at birth.[386-392] [EL = 1b]

To prevent mother-to-child transmission, all pregnant women who are carriers of hepatitis B virus need to be identified. Screening of blood samples is the accepted standard for antenatal screening for hepatitis B virus. Screening consists of three stages: screening for HBsAg, confirmatory testing with a new sample upon a positive result and, where infection is confirmed, testing for hepatitis B e-markers in order to determine whether the baby will need immunoglobulin in addition to vaccine.[393] Using risk factors to identify 'high-risk' women for HBsAg screening would miss about half of all pregnant women with HBsAg infection.[394] [EL = 3] Screening for HBsAg in saliva samples found a sensitivity of 92% (95% CI 84.5% to 99.5%) and a specificity of 86.8% (95% CI 76.0% to 97.6%) when compared with serum samples.[395] [EL = 3] Because of the high proportion of cases of mother-to-child transmission that can be prevented through vaccination and immunisation and because risk factor screening fails to identify carriers, the UK National Screening Committee recommends that all pregnant women be screened for hepatitis B virus (Health Services Circular 1998/127).

Recommendation

Serological screening for hepatitis B virus should be offered to pregnant women so that effective postnatal intervention can be offered to infected women to decrease the risk of mother-to-child transmission. [A]

10.6 Hepatitis C virus

As one of the major causes of liver cirrhosis, hepatocellular carcinoma and liver failure, hepatitis C virus (HCV) is a major public health concern.[396] Acquisition of the virus can occur through infected blood transfusions (pre-1992 blood screening), injection of drugs, tattooing, body piercing and mother-to-child transmission. HCV prevalence observed in studies of antenatal populations in England ranges from 0.14 in the West Midlands (95% CI 0.05 to 0.33) to 0.8 in London (95% CI 0.55 to 1.0).[397] Based on estimates from other European countries, the risk of mother-to-child transmission in the UK is estimated to lie between 3% and 5%.[397] Another study estimated that 70 births each year are infected with HCV as a result of mother-to-child transmission in the UK, which represents an overall antenatal prevalence of 0.16% (95% CI 0.09 to 0.25).[398] [EL = 3]

Although there is consistent evidence that the risk of mother-to-child transmission of HCV increases with increasing maternal viral load,[399,400] whether a threshold level for transmission exists remains unknown. [EL = 3]

A higher proportion of infected babies has been observed among those delivered vaginally compared with those delivered by caesarean section but only one study has demonstrated a statistically significant difference.[401] [EL = 3]

The clinical course of HCV in infants who have acquired the disease through mother-to-child transmission is unclear. Among 104 children studied who were infected through mother-to-child transmission, two developed hepatomegaly with no other clinical symptoms related to HCV infection reported.[402] [EL = 3] It has also been suggested that a proportion of infected children subsequently become HCV-RNA negative. In one study of 23 infants, five infants tested HCV-RNA positive 48 hours after birth. All five infants became HCV-RNA negative and lost HCV antibodies by 6 months after birth.[403] [EL = 3] Although HCV infection in infants may be benign in the short to medium term, given that HCV infection in adults has a long latency period, it is possible that infected children may develop long-term clinical outcomes.

Screening for HCV in the UK involves detection of anti-HCV antibodies in serum by enzyme immunoassays (EIAs) or enzyme-linked immunosorbent assays (ELISA). Upon a positive result, a second ELISA or a confirmatory recombinant immunoblot assay (RIBA) is performed on the same sample. If the second test is positive, the woman is informed and a second sample is taken to confirm the diagnosis. Using polymerase chain reaction (PCR) as the gold standard, the sensitivity and specificity of third-generation assays are reported to be 100% and 66%, respectively.[404] [EL = 3] Other estimates of specificities from studies of blood donors using ELISA and RIBA report ranges between 96% and 99%.[405,406] Upon confirmation of a positive screening test, a woman should be offered post-test counselling and referral to a hepatologist for management and treatment of her infection.

Recommendation

Pregnant women should not be offered routine screening for hepatitis C virus because there is insufficient evidence to support its effectiveness and cost-effectiveness.[C]

10.7 HIV

Infection with human immunodeficiency virus (HIV) begins with an asymptomatic stage with gradual compromise of immune function eventually leading to acquired immunodeficiency syndrome (AIDS). The time between HIV infection and development of AIDS ranges from a few months to as long as 17 years in untreated patients.[353]

The prevalence of HIV infection in pregnant women in London in 2001 was about 1/286 (0.35%), a 22% increase from the year 2000 (1/349 or 0.29%). Elsewhere in England, the prevalence of HIV infection is reported to be around one in 2256 (0.044%).[407,408] [EL = 3]

In the absence of intervention, mother-to-child transmission was reported to occur in 25.5% of deliveries and was reduced to 8% with antiretroviral treatment with zidovudine.[409] [EL = 1b] The combination of interventions (i.e. combination antiretroviral therapy, caesarean section and avoidance of breastfeeding) can further reduce the risk of transmission to 1%.[410] In the UK, mother-to-child transmission rates were 19.6% (95% CI 8.0% to 32%) in 1993 and declined to 2.2% (95% CI 0% to 7.8%) in 1998.[411]

By the end of January 2001, a total of 1036 HIV-infected children had been reported in the UK (excluding Scotland). Mother-to-child transmission of HIV accounted for about 70% of the cases.[412] [EL = 3] Some 1885 children have been born in the UK (excluding Scotland) to HIV-positive mothers, of which 712 were known to be HIV positive (457 indeterminate, 716 not infected) by the end of January 2001.[412] [EL = 3]

In the year 1999, there were 621 872 live births in England and Wales (ONS Birth Statistics, 2000). In the same year, 404 babies were born to HIV infected mothers resulting in 66 HIV-positive babies, 244 not infected and 94 as yet undetermined.[412] [EL = 3]

The most common way to diagnose HIV infection is by a test for antibodies against HIV-1 and HIV-2. HIV antibody is detectable in at least 95% of patients within 3 months of infection.[353] Early HIV diagnosis improves outcomes for the mother and can reduce the rate of disease progression.

Currently available HIV tests are more than 99% sensitive and specific for the detection of HIV antibodies.[413] The sensitivities and specificities of various commercial HIV screening assays can be found at the Medicines and Healthcare products Regulatory Agency website at www.mhra.gov.uk. Available tests for HIV diagnosis in pregnant women include the EIA and Western blot protocol, which is at least 99% and 99.99% sensitive and specific,[413] and the 'two-ELISA approach' protocol.[414] [EL = 3]

In both protocols, an EIA is initially used and if the results are unreactive, a negative report may be generated.[415] [EL = 4]

If the reaction is positive, further testing with different assays (if EIA, then at least one of which is based on a different principle from the first) is warranted. If both confirmatory tests are nonreactive, a negative report may be issued. If the confirmatory tests are reactive, one more test with a new specimen should be obtained in order to ensure no procedural errors have occurred.

Mother-to-child transmission of HIV infection can be greatly reduced through diagnosis of the mother before the baby's birth so that appropriate antenatal interventions can be recommended.[416] [EL = 1a] [417] [EL = 1b] Interventions to reduce mother-to child transmission of HIV during the antenatal period include antiretroviral therapy, elective caesarean section delivery and advice on avoidance of breastfeeding after delivery (see evidence table).

The risk of infant mortality and maternal death was found to be reduced with zidovudine treatment compared with treatment with placebo (infant mortality: OR 0.57, 95% CI 0.38 to 0.85, maternal death: OR 0.30, 95% CI 0.13 to 0.68). All other outcomes measured (i.e. incidence of stillbirth, preterm delivery, low birthweight, side effects in child, side effects in mother) did not show a significant difference between the treated and untreated groups.[416] [EL = 1a] Similarly, nevirapine compared with zidovudine did not show any significant difference in the above-mentioned outcomes.[416] [EL = 1a] There were also no significant adverse effects reported when caesarean section was compared with vaginal delivery.[418] [EL = 1b] Newer antiretrovirals, which are likely to be in use in developed countries, exist. However, these treatments have not yet been evaluated in RCTs.

The use of antiretrovirals to reduce mother-to-child transmission has resulted in resistant mutations. This has raised concerns about the efficacy of antiretroviral treatment decreasing with time.[419,420] [EL = 3] In a substudy to the Pediatric AIDS Clinical Trials Group Protocol, 15% of the women (95% CI 8 to 23%) developed nevirapine resistant mutations by 6 weeks' postpartum.[419] [EL = 3] In another study, although 17.3% of the women and 8.3% of the HIV infected infants developed zidovudine- or nucleotide reverse-transcriptase inhibitor-resistant mutations, respectively, there was no significant association detected between perinatal transmission and the presence of any resistant mutations.[420] [EL = 3]

Since 1999, the NHS has recommended that all pregnant women (i.e., not just in areas of higher prevalence as recommended in 1992) be offered and recommended an HIV test as an integral part of antenatal care, and that the offer be recorded (Health Service Circular 1999/183). The Expert Advisory Group on AIDS (www.advisorybodies.doh.gov.uk/eaga/index.htm) and the UK National Screening Committee (www.nsc.nhs.uk/) websites can be checked periodically for updates on HIV screening information.

Recommendations

Pregnant women should be offered screening for HIV infection early in antenatal care because appropriate antenatal interventions can reduce mother-to-child transmission of HIV infection. [A]

A system of clear referral paths should be established in each unit or department so that pregnant women who are diagnosed with an HIV infection are managed and treated by the appropriate specialist teams. [D]

10.8 Rubella

The aim of screening for rubella in pregnancy is to identify susceptible women so that postpartum vaccination may protect future pregnancies against rubella infection and its consequences. Hence, rubella screening does not attempt to identify current affected pregnancies.

Rubella infection is characterised by a febrile rash but may be asymptomatic in 20% to 50% of cases.[421] There is no treatment to prevent or reduce mother-to-child transmission of rubella for the current pregnancy.[422] [EL = 4] Detection of susceptibility during pregnancy, however, enables postpartum vaccination to occur to protect future pregnancies.

Surveillance in England and Wales by the National Congenital Rubella Surveillance Programme (NCRSP) indicates that susceptibility in the antenatal population varies with parity as well as with ethnicity. Susceptibility is slightly higher in nulliparous women (2%) than in parous women (1.2%).[423] [EL = 3] Certain ethnic groups also appear to have higher susceptibility, such as women from the Mediterranean region (4%), Asian and black women (5%) and Oriental women (8%), compared with less than 2% in white women, with an overall susceptibility of about 2.5% reported for pregnant women.[424] [EL = 3]

In 1995, the incidence of rubella in susceptible nulliparous women was 2/431 (risk/1000 = 4.6) and 0/547 in parous women, resulting in an overall risk of 2/1000 susceptible women.[423] [EL = 3]

From 1976 to 1978, among 966 pregnant women in England and Wales with confirmed rubella infection, 523 (54%) had elective abortions, 36 (4%) had a miscarriage, 9 women had stillbirths (4 of which had severe anomalies) and 5 infants died in the neonatal period.[425] [EL = 2b]

Since the introduction of the measles, mumps and rubella vaccine, an average of three births affected by congenital rubella a year and four rubella-associated terminations were registered with the NCRSP (births) and Office for National Statistics (terminations) from 1996 to 2000.[422] [EL = 4]

For pregnant women who are offered a rubella susceptibility test, the protective level of antibodies was originally set at 15 international units (IU). However, newer, more sensitive screening tests[426] [EL = 2a] have resulted in the detection of women with low but protective levels of antibodies being reported as rubella susceptible and therefore a lower cut-off of 10 IU is the level recommended in the National Screening Committee draft document for the UK in 2002.[422] [EL = 4] Results of rubella screening should be reported as rubella antibody detected or not detected as opposed to reports of 'immune' or 'susceptible', to avoid misinterpretation.[422] [EL = 4] If rubella antibody is **not** detected, rubella vaccination after pregnancy should be advised.[427]

A Public Health Laboratory service (PHLS) guideline offers an algorithm for the management of pregnant women who present with rash illness.[427]

Detection of rubella does not protect against mother-to-child transmission in the current pregnancy. However, protection of subsequent pregnancies against the rubella virus will prevent future mother-to-child transmission of rubella and reduce the risk of stillbirth and miscarriage due to rubella infection.

In a cohort study of pregnant women with confirmed rubella infection at different stages of pregnancy, a follow-up of nearly 70% of the surviving infants (n = 269) found that 43% (n = 117) of infants were congenitally infected.[425] [EL = 2b] Congenital infection in the first 12 weeks of pregnancy among mothers with symptoms was over 80% and reduced to 25% at the end of the second trimester. 100% of infants infected during the first 11 weeks of pregnancy had rubella defects.[425] [EL = 2b]

In another study, a decline in the rate of infection was seen from weeks 9 to 16 of gestation (rate of infection 57% to 70%) compared with weeks 17 to 20 (22%) and weeks 21 to 24 (17%) and a minimal risk of deafness only was observed in the children who were born to mothers infected during the 17th to 24th weeks of gestation.[428] [EL = 2b]

About 10% of congenital rubella cases reported since 1990 are associated with maternal reinfection[422] [EL = 4] and maternal reinfection is usually diagnosed through changes in antibody concentration only.[427] In a study of seven asymptomatic rubella reinfections in early pregnancy, six pregnant women went to term and the infants showed no evidence of intrauterine infection. One pregnancy was terminated and the rubella virus was not identified in the products of conception.[429] [EL = 3] Symptomatic maternal reinfection is very rare and risk of fetal damage, which is presumed to be significant, has not been quantified.[427]

Vaccination during pregnancy is contraindicated because of fears that the vaccine could be teratogenic.[422] [EL = 4] However, in an evaluation of surveillance data from the USA, UK, Sweden and Germany of 680 live births to susceptible women who were inadvertently vaccinated during or within 3 months of pregnancy (with HPV-77, Cendehill or RA27/3), none of the children was born with congenital rubella syndrome.[430] [EL = 3]

Screening for the rubella antibody in pregnancy helps to identify susceptible women so that rubella vaccination can be offered postpartum to protect future pregnancies.

Recommendation

Rubella susceptibility screening should be offered early in antenatal care to identify women at risk of contracting rubella infection and to enable vaccination in the postnatal period for the protection of future pregnancies. [B]

10.9   Streptococcus group B

Group B streptococcus (GBS), *Streptococcus agalactiae*, is the leading cause of serious neonatal infection in the UK.[431] Although GBS can affect a pregnant woman or her fetus or both, it may exist in the genital and gastrointestinal tract of pregnant women with no symptoms and may also exist without causing harm.

It is estimated that GBS can be recovered from 6.6% to 20% of mothers in the USA.[432,433] [EL = 3] In the UK, the prevalence has been estimated at 28%, with no association to maternal age or parity.[434] [EL = 3] Maternal intrapartum GBS colonisation is a risk factor for early-onset disease in infants.[435] [EL = 3] Early-onset GBS disease (occurring in infants within the first week of life) can result in many conditions, including sepsis, pneumonia and meningitis.[436] The prevalence of early-onset GBS disease in England and Wales is estimated to range from 0.4/1000 to 1.4/1000 live births,[435,437,438] [EL = 3] which is equivalent to approximately 340 babies per annum. A 2001 UK surveillance study identified 376 cases of early-onset GBS (prevalence in England 0.5, 95% CI 0.5 to 0.6), among which 39 infants died.[431] [EL = 3] In 2000, there were 2519 neonatal deaths from all causes in the UK.

The collection of cultures between 35 and 37 weeks of gestation appears to achieve the best sensitivity and specificity for detection of women who are colonised at the time of delivery.[439] [EL = 3] Swabs of both the vagina and rectum provide the highest predictive value for identification of women colonised by GBS.[440] [EL = 3] Studies have also indicated that women who obtain their own screening specimen, with appropriate instruction, have comparable sensitivity to specimens collected by a physician. With any positive culture used as the reference standard, self-collected sensitivity ranged from 79% to 97% and physician sensitivity was 82% to 83%.[441,442] [EL = 3] When asked about preference, 75% of women either preferred to collect their own specimen or were indifferent as to who collected their swab.[441] [EL = 3]

A comparison of screening methods (obtaining cultures from all pregnant women or identifying women for intrapartum treatment through clinical risk factor assessment) in a large interstate study in the USA found that the risk of early-onset disease was more than 50% lower in the universally screened group compared with those screened by assessment of clinical risk factors to identify candidates for intrapartum antibiotics (adjusted relative risk 0.46, 95% CI 0.36 to 0.60).[443] [EL = 2b]

However, a systematic review of RCTs of intrapartum antibiotics for the reduction of perinatal GBS infection have not yet demonstrated an effect on neonatal deaths from infection (Peto OR 0.12, 95% CI 0.01 to 2.0), although a reduction in infant colonisation rate (Peto OR 0.10, 95% CI 0.07 to 0.14), as well as a reduction in early-onset neonatal infection with GBS, was observed (Peto OR 0.17, 95% CI 0.07 to 0.39).[444] [EL = 1a] A review of trials of antibiotics administered in the antenatal period found that two of four studies reported a reduction in maternal colonisation at delivery and that results from five other trials showed a reduction of 80% in early-onset GBS with intrapartum treatment.[445] [EL = 2a] In a trial that compared 5 ml 2% clindamycin cream intravaginally with no treatment in women admitted in labour who had had a positive culture for GBS at 26 to 28 weeks of gestation, no difference was found in the reduction of colonisation.[446] [EL = 1b]

With an assumption of 80% effectiveness for the prevention of early-onset GBS disease in infants with intrapartum antibiotics, the number of babies affected each year will decrease from an estimated 340 to 68. This means that for every 1000 women treated with intrapartum antibiotics for GBS, 1.4 cases of early-onset disease may be prevented. However, this estimate assumes that screening will identify all GBS carriers and therefore, in practice, the number of women treated to prevent one case is most likely higher.

No trials comparing antenatal screening with no antenatal screening have been conducted, nor have any trials comparing different screening strategies been identified. Therefore, estimates of efficacy of screening strategies are based only on observational studies. In the USA, an analysis of the incidence of early-onset GBS disease from 1993 to 1998 found a decline from 1.7/1000 live births in 1993 to 0.6/1000 live births in 1998 (65% decrease, $P < 0.001$),[447] [EL = 3] which is the incidence observed in the UK in 2001.[431] [EL = 3] This 65% decrease in early-onset GBS disease coincided with efforts in the USA to promote the wider use of intrapartum antibiotics for the prevention of GBS disease in infants less than 7 days old. An Australian study that determined the incidence of GBS in the population before implementing a screening programme found a significant decrease from 4.9/1000 to 0.8/1000 live births after the intervention.[448] [EL = 3]

Further information on GBS, such as guidance for when GBS is incidentally detected during pregnancy, can be found in the RCOG guideline on the prevention of early-onset neonatal Group B streptococcal disease (www.rcog.org.uk/index.asp?PageID=520).

Economic considerations (see Appendix C)

The review of the economic literature on GBS found 26 articles including the guideline published by the Royal College of Obstetrics and Gynaecology on the prevention of early-onset neonatal Group B streptococcal disease. Of these studies, 25 were relevant to the topic and were examined in detail. However, almost all the economic studies were conducted in the US setting (one was from Australia). The extrapolation and generalisability of the results of the US studies was limited also because the prevalence of the disease used was not comparable with a UK setting. Four of the US studies were of sufficient quality to extrapolate data for the economic model.

An economic model was constructed to estimate the number of early-onset GBS cases in infants averted due to screening and treatment. The model also took into consideration how many cases of early-onset GBS were missed following each screening method and how many cases of early-onset GBS were prevented through the screening and subsequent treatment of the pregnant women. The benefit or harm to the pregnant women and infants over and above the financial costs to the NHS were not included in the model because of the lack of data. The only unit of benefit included in the model was 'case of early-onset GBS averted'. This is a limitation of the model.

The model set out to calculate the following outcomes:

- the number of pregnant women treated per case of early-onset GBS averted
- the number of cases of early-onset GBS averted by screening and subsequent treatment
- an estimate of the total financial cost to the health service provider of the different screening methods
- the average cost per case prevented and the incremental cost-effectiveness of the two screening methods.

During the course of developing this model, it became clear that data on a number of crucial parameters in the model were not available in the clinical literature. These were:

- the prevalence of early-onset GBS in infants of women who have been screened positively using the universal (bacteriological) screening strategy
- the number of women screened as falsely negative (who have the disease but are screened as negative) in the universal screening strategy
- the prevalence of GBS among the women with the risk factors (the proportion of 'true positive' women who have risk factors for GBS).

The true prevalence of GBS among women with risk factors would indicate the proportion of women treated unnecessarily for GBS (who have risk factors but do not have the disease). This would probably give an idea of the avoidable cases of severe anaphylaxis due to treatment of women in the risk factor group.

Without good estimates of the prevalence of disease, it was not possible to calculate the overall number of cases of early-onset BGS avoided and costs of implementing each screening strategy. Early-onset GBS is a severe disease and the treatment has very high costs for the NHS. Therefore, missing even one case could presumably change the cost-effectiveness of the two methods. More clinical evidence is required in order to undertake an economic model of different screening methods for GBS.

Recommendations

Pregnant women should not be offered routine antenatal screening for group B streptococcus because evidence of its clinical and cost-effectiveness remains uncertain. [C]

Future research

Further research into the effectiveness and cost-effectiveness of antenatal screening for streptococcus group B is needed.

10.10 Syphilis

Syphilis is a sexually acquired infection caused by *Treponema pallidum*. The body's immune response to syphilis is the production non-specific and specific treponemal antibodies. The first notable response to infection is the production of specific anti-treponemal immunoglobulin M (IgM), which is detectable towards the end of the second week of infection. By the time symptoms appear, most people infected with syphilis have detectable levels of immunoglobulin G (IgG) and IgM.[449] [EL = 4] However, syphilis may also be asymptomatic and latent for many years.[353]

The incidence of infectious syphilis in England and Wales is low, but four outbreaks of infectious syphilis occurred in England from 1997 to 2000.[450] In the USA, an epidemic of syphilis translated into an epidemic of congenital syphilis with rates increasing from 4.3/100 000 live births in 1982 to 94.7/100 000 in 1992.[451]

The prevalence of syphilis in pregnant women as estimated by reports from genitourinary medicine clinics in England and Wales was 0.068/1000 live births (95% CI 0.057 to 0.080) from 1994 to 1997, ranging from zero in East Anglia to 0.3/1000 live births in the North East Thames region.[452] [EL = 3] [453] [EL = 4] Thirty-four cases of early congenital syphilis (under age 2 years) were reported by genitourinary medicine clinics in England and Wales between 1988 and 1995,[453] [EL = 4] and 35 cases were reported from 1995 to 2000,[454] [EL = 3] giving an incidence of 0.92/100 000 live births per year (calculated with livebirth rates from ONS Birth Statistics, 2000).

In pregnant women with early untreated syphilis, 70% to 100% of infants will be infected and one-third will be stillborn.[455] [EL = 3] [456,457] [EL = 4]

Mother-to-child transmission of syphilis in pregnancy is associated with neonatal death, congenital syphilis (which may cause long-term disability), stillbirth and preterm birth. However, because penicillin became widely available in the 1950s, no data from recent prospective observational studies in developed countries are available. Data from two observational studies in the USA in the 1950s and, more recently, from developing countries, provide a picture of the effects of untreated syphilis compared with women who did not have syphilis or who had been treated for syphilis. Among pregnancies in women with early untreated syphilis, 25% resulted in stillbirth compared with 3% among women without syphilis; 14% died in the neonatal period compared with 2.2% among women without syphilis and 41% resulted in a congenitally infected infant (compared with 0% among women without syphilis).[455] [EL = 3] These findings were reported to be significant, but the level of significance was not specified in the study. In the other US study, 25% of babies were born preterm to mothers with syphilis compared with 11.5% among women without syphilis. The sample size was small and this finding was not reported to be significant.[458] [EL = 3] The risk of congenital transmission declines with increasing duration of maternal syphilis prior to pregnancy.

Among 142 pregnant women in South Africa who tested positive for syphilis, 99 were 'adequately' treated with at least two doses of 2.4 mega-units of benzathine penicillin and 43 received 'inadequate' treatment of less than two doses. Among inadequately treated women, perinatal death occurred in 11 (26%) cases compared with 4 (4%) cases among adequately treated women ($P < 0.0001$).[459] [EL = 3]

There are two main classifications of serological tests for syphilis: non-treponemal and treponemal. Non-treponemal tests detect non-specific treponemal antibodies and include the Venereal Diseases Research Laboratory (VDRL) and rapid plasma reagin (RPR) tests. Treponemal tests detect specific treponemal antibodies and include EIAs, *T. pallidum* haemagglutination assay (TPHA) and the fluorescent treponemal antibody-absorbed test (FTA-abs).

EIA tests that detect IgG or IgG and IgM are rapidly replacing the VDRL and TPHA combination for syphilis screening in the UK.[449] [EL = 4] Screening with a treponemal IgG EIA is useful for detecting syphilis antibodies in patients who are infected with HIV and is comparable to the VDRL and TPHA combination in terms of sensitivity and specificity.[460,461]

EIAs are over 98% sensitive and over 99% specific. Non-treponemal tests, on the other hand, may result in false negatives, particularly in very early or late syphilis, in patients with reinfection or those who are HIV positive. The positive predictive value of non-treponemal tests is poor when used alone in low prevalence populations. In general, treponemal tests are 98% sensitive at all stages of syphilis (except early primary syphilis) and more specific (98% to 99%) than non-treponemal tests. None of these serological tests will detect syphilis in its incubation stage, which may last for an average of 25 days.[453] [EL = 3]

A reactive result on screening requires confirmatory testing with a different treponemal test of equal sensitivity to the one initially used and, preferably, one with greater specificity. A discrepant result on confirmatory testing needs further testing, which is provided by Birmingham Public Health Laboratory (PHL), Bristol PHL, Manchester PHL, Newcastle PHL and Sheffield PHL.[449] [EL = 4]

Following confirmation of a reactive specimen, testing of a second specimen to verify the results and ensure correct identification of the person should be done. Whether or not the pregnant woman should then be referred for expert assessment and diagnosis in a genitourinary medicine clinic should be considered. To assess the stage of the infection or to monitor the efficacy of treatment, a quantitative non-treponemal or a specific test for treponemal IgM should be performed.[449] [EL = 4]

Not all women who test positive will have syphilis, as these serological tests cannot distinguish between different treponematoses (e.g. syphilis, yaws, pinta and bejel). Therefore, positive results should be interpreted with caution.

In the UK, the Clinical Effectiveness Group of the Association for Genitourinary Medicine and the Medical Society for the Study of Venereal Disease recommend screening for syphilis at the first antenatal appointment.[456] [EL = 4]

Parenteral penicillin effectively prevents mother-to-child transmission of syphilis, although available evidence is insufficient to determine whether or not the current treatment regimens in use in the UK are optimal.[462] [EL = 1a] In a US study of the effectiveness of treatment with penicillin, a 98.2% success rate for preventing congenital syphilis was observed.[463] [EL = 2b] Treatment of syphilis in pregnancy with penicillin has not shown any difference in adverse pregnancy outcomes when compared with untreated seronegative women.[464] [EL = 2a] Although erythromycin is useful in the treatment of syphilis for non-pregnant women who are allergic to penicillin, treatment of pregnant women with erythromycin has been shown to be ineffective in some cases.[465] [EL = 3] The European and UK guidelines on the management of syphilis in pregnant women with penicillin allergy suggest desensitisation to penicillin followed by treatment with penicillin as an alternative.[456,457] All women testing positive for syphilis should be referred to a specialist for treatment.

Economic considerations (see Appendix D)

An economic model was constructed to consider three screening options: no screening, universal screening and selective, ethnicity-based screening. Clearly, the prevalence of syphilis in each strategy was assumed to be different, higher for the ethnicity-based strategy than for the universal strategy. The ethnicity-based approach will be associated with varying levels of prevalence depending upon how the strategy is constructed, based on geographical location (and proportion of women of specific ethnic origins in each group) or on screening for ethnicity during antenatal check-ups.

The costs incorporated in the model were only the costs incurred by the health service. A societal perspective would increase the overall costs of providing screening and would be greater for the universal group but data do not exist on whether these costs would differ by screening method. If more couples were subject to the test using a universal approach, there would be potentially more harm incurred by undertaking unnecessary tests.

The benefits and harm of syphilis screening (to the couples undertaking the screening test) has not been explored in the literature. The test is not associated with a choice to end the pregnancy and the treatment for syphilis is not associated with adverse effects that should be incorporated into the analysis. However, the psychological cost and benefit of undergoing the test have not been estimated in the model, since these data were unavailable.

The model also incorporated the costs of the economic consequences of syphilis cases missed due to the different screening methods. The economic consequences of syphilis were considered to be preterm birth, miscarriage and fetal death and the lifetime treatment costs of the cases of congenital syphilis.

Recommendations

Screening for syphilis should be offered to all pregnant women at an early stage in antenatal care because treatment of syphilis is beneficial to the mother and baby. [B]

Because syphilis is a rare condition in the UK and a positive result does not necessarily mean that a woman has syphilis, clear paths of referral for the management of pregnant women testing positive for syphilis should be established. [Good practice point]

10.11 Toxoplasmosis

Caused by the parasite *Toxoplasma gondii*, primary toxoplasmosis infection is usually asymptomatic in healthy women. Once infected, a lifelong antibody response provides immunity from further infection.

A total of 423 cases of toxoplasmosis related to pregnancy were reported to the PHLS, Communicable Disease Surveillance Centre (PHLS CDSC) in England and Wales from 1981 to 1992, during which time there was an average of 667 000 live births per year (ONS, Population Trends). A systematic review from 1996 identified 15 studies that reported toxoplasmosis incidence among susceptible (i.e., antibody negative) women in Europe.[466] [EL = 3] Although no data specific to England or Wales were found, incidence rates for other countries ranged from 2.4/1000 women in Finland to 16/1000 women in France. Approximately 75% to 90% of pregnant women in the UK are estimated to be susceptible to toxoplasmosis.[467,468] The prevalence of congenital toxoplasma infection was recently reported to be approximately 0.3/1000 live births in Denmark.[469] [EL = 3]

Toxoplasmosis infection is acquired via four routes in humans:

- ingestion of viable tissue cysts in undercooked or uncooked meat (e.g., salami, which is cured) or tachyzoites in the milk of infected intermediate hosts
- ingestion of oocytes excreted by cats and contaminating soil or water (e.g., unwashed fruit or vegetables contaminated by cat faeces)
- transplanted organs or blood products from other humans infected with toxoplasmosis
- mother-to-child transmission when primary infection occurs during pregnancy.

A study in six European centres identified undercooked meat and cured meat products as the principal factor contributing to toxoplasma infection in pregnant women.[470] [EL = 3] Contact with soil contributed to a substantial minority of infections.

When primary infection with *T. gondii* occurs during pregnancy, the risk of mother-to-child transmission increases with gestation at acquisition of maternal infection.[471–473] [EL = 3] The reported overall risk of congenital toxoplasmosis ranges from 18% to 44%. The risk is low in early pregnancy at 6% to 26% from 7 to 15 weeks of gestation and rising to 32% to 93% at 29 to 34 weeks of gestation.[471–473] [EL = 3]

Clinical manifestations of congenital toxoplasmosis include inflammatory lesions in the brain and retina and choroids that may lead to permanent neurological damage or visual impairment. Reported overall rates of clinical manifestations range from 14% to 27% among infants born to infected mothers.[472,473] [EL = 3] In contrast to the risk of transmission, the risk of an infected infant developing clinical signs of disease (hydrocephalus, intracranial calcification, retinochoroiditis) is highest when infection occurs early in pregnancy, declining from an estimated 61% (95% CI 34 to 85%) at 13 weeks to 9% (95% CI 4% to 17%) at 36 weeks.[472] [EL = 3]

As primary toxoplasma infection is usually asymptomatic, infected women can only reliably be detected by serological testing. Antenatal screening for toxoplasma infection involves initial testing to determine IgG and IgM positivity. Subsequently, in women in whom antibodies are not detected (i.e., susceptible), monthly or 3 monthly re-testing to determine seroconversion is necessary. Positive results should then be confirmed by multiple tests.[474] [EL = 3] However, available screening tests to determine seroconversion cannot distinguish between infection acquired during pregnancy or up to 12 months beforehand and women who have acquired the infection before conception are not at risk of fetal infection.[475]

For pregnant women with a diagnosis of primary toxoplasma infection, an informed decision as to whether or not to undergo prenatal diagnosis needs to be made. To calculate the risk of clinical signs in a fetus born to an infected woman, it is possible to multiply the risk of congenital infection by the risk of signs among congenitally infected children. For example, at 26 weeks of gestation the risk of maternal–fetal transmission is 40% and the risk of clinical signs in an infected fetus is 25%. The overall risk is therefore 10% (0.4 x 0.25). If this calculation is repeated for all gestational ages, a positively skewed curve results that reaches a maximum of 10% at 24 to 30 weeks of gestation. In the second and third trimesters, the risk never falls below 5% and is 6% just before delivery.

Knowledge of these risks allows women to balance the risks of harm and benefit when deciding about treatment, amniocentesis or ending the pregnancy. The possible reduction in this risk that might be achieved by prenatal treatment must be balanced against the risk of fetal loss of 1% associated with amniocentesis.[307] Most importantly, they need to know the risk of disability due to neurological damage or visual impairment. Unfortunately, information on these latter outcomes is less reliable and the effect of gestation is not known.

Primary prevention of toxoplasmosis with the provision of information about how to avoid toxoplasma infection before or early in pregnancy should be given. Women should be informed about the risks of not cooking meat thoroughly, possible contact with cat faeces, not washing their hands after touching soil, not washing vegetables thoroughly and eating cured meat products.

Of two systematic reviews on the effects of antiparasitic treatment on women who acquire primary toxoplasmosis infection during pregnancy, the first identified no RCTs.[476] The second identified nine cohort studies that compared treatment (spiramycin alone, pyrimethaminesulphonamides or a combination of the two) with no treatment.[477] [EL = 2a] Five of the studies reported a treatment effect and four reported no treatment effect and none of the studies accounted for the rise in the risk of transmission with gestation at maternal infection.

Treatment with spiramycin and pyrimethamine-sulphonamides is reported to be well tolerated and non-teratogenic, although sulpha drugs may carry a risk of kernicterus in infants and also of bone marrow suppression in the mother and infant.[478]

In a comparison of antenatal screening strategies for toxoplasmosis in pregnancy, although universal screening with antenatal treatment reduced the number of cases of congenital toxoplasmosis, an additional 18.5 pregnancies were lost for each case avoided.[479] [EL = 3] Other costs include the unnecessary treatment or termination of uninfected or unaffected fetuses and the distress and discomfort of repeated examinations and investigations, both antenatal and postnatal. A further problem is that, even when antenatal diagnostic tests are negative, absence of congenital toxoplasmosis cannot be confirmed until the child is 12 months old. Finally, children with confirmed congenital toxoplasmosis, most of whom are asymptomatic, are labelled as at risk of sudden blindness, or even mental impairment, throughout childhood and adolescence.

An alternative to antenatal screening for toxoplasmosis is neonatal screening. Neonatal screening aims to identify neonates with congenital toxoplasmosis in order to offer treatment and clinical follow up. The vast majority of congenitally infected infants are asymptomatic in early infancy and would be missed by routine paediatric examinations. Neonatal screening is based on the detection of toxoplasma-specific IgM on Guthrie-card blood spots and has been found to detect 85% of infected infants. There are no published studies that have determined the effect of postnatal treatment compared with no treatment, or treatment of short duration compared with 1 year or more on the risk of clinical signs or impairment in children with congenital toxoplasmosis in the long term.

The UK National Screening Committee recently reported that screening for toxoplasmosis should not be offered routinely.[475] There is a lack of evidence that antenatal screening and treatment reduces mother-to-child transmission or the complications associated with toxoplasma infection.

There are also important and common adverse effects associated with antenatal screening, treatment and follow up for mother and child. Antenatal screening based on monthly or 3-monthly re-testing of susceptible women would be labour intensive and would require substantial investment without any proven benefit. Primary prevention of toxoplasmosis through avoidance of undercooked or cured meat may prove a good alternative to antenatal screening, which cannot currently be recommended.

Recommendation

Routine antenatal serological screening for toxoplasmosis should not be offered because the risks of screening may outweigh the potential benefits. [B]

Pregnant women should be informed of primary prevention measures to avoid toxoplasmosis infection such as:

- washing hands before handling food
- thoroughly washing all fruit and vegetables, including ready-prepared salads, before eating
- thoroughly cooking raw meats and ready-prepared chilled meals
- wearing gloves and thoroughly washing hands after handling soil and gardening
- avoiding cat faeces in cat litter or in soil. [C]

11 Screening for clinical problems

11.1 Gestational diabetes

Clinical question
What is the diagnostic value and effectiveness of screening tests to identify women at risk of diabetes in pregnancy?

Previous NICE guidance (for the updated recommendations see below)
The evidence does not support routine screening for gestational diabetes and therefore it should not be offered. [B]

11.1.1 Introduction and background

Gestational diabetes is defined as carbohydrate intolerance resulting in hyperglycaemia of variable severity with onset or first recognition during pregnancy and with a return to normal after birth.[823] It includes women who have both diabetes and impaired glucose tolerance (IGT). Definitions and diagnosis in pregnancy are blurred by the fact that blood glucose levels are higher in pregnancy and there is an overlap between women who are clearly diabetic (and at increased risk) and women who are technically diabetic but are actually not at increased risk. Women who develop gestational diabetes are at increased risk of developing type 2 diabetes in later life[823] and the escalating rise in the incidence of this in the population at large creates a compelling argument for screening healthy women in pregnancy, whose subsequent health may benefit from education about diet and lifestyle. However, a decision to implement screening of healthy women in pregnancy has to be made on a judgement of the contribution of each of the following:

- the potential reduction in perinatal morbidity and mortality
- the possible reduction in maternal morbidity remembering that increased obstetric intervention may bring about an iatrogenic increase in maternal morbidity
- the increase in health service expenditure
- the potential long-term health benefits for the woman.

There has been uncertainty about the value of screening for gestational diabetes for many years and indeed this uncertainty was reflected in the previous antenatal care guideline. However, the recent Australian Carbohydrate Intolerance Study in Pregnant Women (ACHOIS) trial[824] group showed that women treated for gestational diabetes had a significantly lower rate of serious perinatal complications compared with women with routine care. These women had a higher rate of induction of labour than the women in the routine care group.

Not only has there been uncertainty about the value of screening but there is little agreement about a suitable screening method. A UK survey of obstetric units in 1999[825] indicated that, of the blood tests, 43% used the random blood glucose (RBG) test, 11% used random plasma glucose (RPG), and 10% used a 50 g glucose challenge test (GCT). Sixty-seven percent used a risk factor assessment. An earlier survey in 1994[826] involving one district health authority in England found a variety of screening practices for gestational diabetes and in fact only eight out of 18 hospitals operated a screening policy. Six undertook RBG, one undertook fasting blood glucose and one a GCT. They noted that GCT was the most thoroughly evaluated method of screening for gestational diabetes. A survey of gynaecologists in Italy[827] reported that 53% (151/283) carried out screening with a glucose load. Of these, 36% gave a 50 g GCT to all women, 17% a 100 g GCT to all women and 40% restricted the test to women with risk factors. In an American survey,[828] 98.5% of clinicians used the 50 g GCT.

2008 update

205

A well-conducted RCT (the ACHOIS trial) has provided evidence for the effectiveness of treating mild gestational diabetes.[988] [EL = 1++] The trial allocated 490 women with IGT (2 hour 75 g oral glucose tolerance test (OGTT) fasting level< 7.8 mmol/litre and 2 hour level of 7.8–11.0 mmol/litre) to treatment and 510 women with IGT to routine care. The rate of serious perinatal outcomes (prospectively defined for the purpose of the study as a compound outcome including shoulder dystocia and perinatal mortality) among babies was significantly lower in the intervention group (1% versus 4%; $P = 0.01$). The number needed to treat to prevent a serious outcome in a baby was 34. There was no significant difference between groups in maternal quality of life.

11.1.2 Risk factors

The use of risk factors such as obesity, country of family origin and the birth of a previous macrosomic baby have been used by healthcare practitioners for many years and indeed often appear as alerts on antenatal care notes.

Description of included studies and findings
A Health Technology Assessment (HTA) in 2002[483] [EL = 2+] conducted a systematic review on screening for gestational diabetes. The results showed that the risk factors for gestational diabetes included obesity, advanced maternal age, family history of diabetes, minority ethnic background, increased weight gain in early adulthood and current smoker.

The HTA review included a retrospective analysis in the UK (1992)[829] [EL = 2−] aimed at determining the frequency of gestational diabetes according age, BMI, parity and ethnic origin in women without known pre-existing diabetes and to analyse the influence of risk factors separately for each ethnic group. 170/11 205 (1.5%) women were diagnosed with gestational diabetes. Women with gestational diabetes were significantly older (32.3 versus 28.3 years; $P < 0.001$), had higher BMI (27.7 versus 23.8 kg/m²; $P < 0.001$) and more likely to be from an ethnic minority (55.4% versus 15.3%; $P < 0.0001$). Rates of gestational diabetes by ethnicity were white 0.4% (26/6135), black 1.5% (29/1977), South East Asian 3.5% (20/572) and Indian 4.4% (54/1218). After adjusting for age, BMI and parity, the RR (with white as the reference category) was as follows: black 3.1 (95% CI 1.8 to 5.5), South East Asian 7.6 (95% CI 4.1 to 14.1), and Indian 11.3 (95% CI 6.8 to 18.8).

An observational study in Australia (1995)[830] [EL = 3] sought to determine the proportion of women with gestational diabetes missed if testing was confined to risk factors. The results showed that women without gestational diabetes were significantly younger (26.4 versus 28.1 years; $P < 0.02$) and had a lower BMI (24.2 versus 25.9 kg/m²; $P < 0.05$) than women with gestational diabetes. Thirty-one women (39.2%) with gestational diabetes had no historical risk factors and would have been missed if only selective testing had been undertaken.

A case–control study in Australia (2001)[831] [EL = 2+] assessed risk factor screening as a practical alternative to universal screening. The results were as follows: for age ≥ 25 years OR 1.9 (95% CI 1.3 to 2.7), for BMI ≥ 27 kg/m² OR 2.3 (95% CI 1.6 to 3.3), for high-risk racial heritage OR 2.5 (95% CI 2.0 to 3.2), and for family history of diabetes OR 7.1 (95% CI 5.6 to 8.9). It was found that, by using these four criteria for screening, 313 cases (0.6%) would have been missed and could have saved screening up to 1025 women without gestational diabetes (17%).

A US RCT (2000)[832] [EL = 2+] compared a risk factor-based screening programme with a universally based one. The risk factor group were given a 3 hour 100 g OGTT at 32 weeks of gestation if any risk factor was present. The universal screening group was given a 50 g GCT and then a 3 hour 100 g OGTT if the plasma glucose at 1 hour was ≥ 7.8 mmol/litre. The results showed that the PPVs of risk factors were as follows: first-degree relative with type 2 diabetes 6.7%, first-degree relative with type 1 diabetes 15%, previous baby > 4.5 kg 12.2%, glycosuria in current pregnancy 50%, macrosomia in current pregnancy 40%, and polyhydramnios in current pregnancy 40%. The detection rate using the universal screening was significantly higher than for risk factor screening, at 2.7% versus 1.45%.

A study in Denmark (2004)[833] [EL = 2−] retrospectively investigated the power of pre-screening to identify gestational diabetes and screening to predict adverse clinical outcomes. Risk factors for developing gestational diabetes were used for pre-screening. Pregnant women with at least one risk factor were offered capillary fasting blood glucose (cFBG) in weeks 20 and 32. If the cFBG measurements were ≥ 4.1 mmol/litre and < 6.7 mmol/litre, then a 3 hour 75 g OGTT was offered. If cFBG values were ≥ 6.7 mmol/litre, the woman was diagnosed as having gestational diabetes. The most frequent pre-screening risk factors were BMI ≥ 27 kg/m² (present in 65% of cases) and age ≥ 35 years (present in 16% of cases). No single factor seemed the best indicator for gestational diabetes. The highest OR for developing gestational diabetes was 9.04 (95% CI 2.6 to 63.7) for glycosuria.

A cross-sectional 5 year investigation in the Netherlands (2006)[834] [EL = 2–] examined the clinical usefulness of antepartum clinical characteristics, along with measures of glucose tolerance, in Dutch multi-ethnic women with gestational diabetes for their ability to predict type 2 diabetes within 6 months of delivery (early postpartum diabetes). The following risk factors were assessed for all women: age and gestational age at entry into the study; pre-pregnancy BMI; ethnicity; obstetric and clinical history, including the onset of early postpartum diabetes; and pregnancy outcome. The results showed that apart from family history of diabetes no other risk factor showed an association with the development of early postpartum diabetes.

A prospective population-based study in Sweden [EL = 2+] offered all non-diabetic pregnant women a 75 g OGTT at 28–32 weeks of gestation.[835] Traditional risk factors used were family history of diabetes (first-degree relative), obesity (≥ 90 kg), prior LGA baby (≥ 4500 g) or prior gestational diabetes. The results showed that women who did not take the OGTT were more likely to be multiparous and of non-Nordic origin but were less likely to have a family history of diabetes, prior macrosomic baby or prior gestational diabetes. Of the women who were given OGTT, 1.7% were diagnosed with gestational diabetes. The risk factors with the strongest association were prior gestational diabetes (12/61, OR 23.6, 95% CI 11.6 to 48.0) and prior macrosomic baby (9/61, OR 5.59, 95% CI 2.68 to 11.7). Other risk factors were family history of diabetes (13/61, OR 2.74, 95% CI 1.47 to 5.11), non-Nordic origin (13/61, OR 2.19, 95% CI 1.18 to 4.08), weight ≥ 90 kg (8/61, OR 3.33, 95% CI 1.56 to 7.13), BMI ≥ 30 kg/m² (11/61, OR 2.65, 95% CI 1.36 to 5.14) and age ≥ 25 years (55/61, OR 3.37, 95% CI 1.45 to 7.85).

A systematic review published in the USA in 2007[836] [EL = 2++] examined the rates and factors associated with recurrence of gestational diabetes among women with a history of gestational diabetes. A total of 13 studies were included. The results showed the recurrence rate of glucose intolerance during subsequent pregnancies varied markedly across studies. The most consistent predictor of future recurrence appeared to be nonwhite race/ethnicity, although the racial breakdowns within a study were not always clearly described. The recurrence rates varied between 30% and 84% after the index pregnancy. The recurrence rates were higher in the minority populations (52–69%) as compared with lower rates found in non-Hispanic white populations (30–37%). No other risk factors were consistently associated with recurrence of gestational diabetes across studies. Other risk factors, such as maternal age, parity, BMI, OGTT levels and insulin use, inconsistently predicted development of recurrent gestational diabetes across studies.

Evidence summary

Evidence shows that risk factors for developing gestational diabetes are pre-pregnancy obesity, advanced maternal age, prior gestational diabetes, family history of diabetes, minority ethnic background, prior macrosomic baby ≥ 4.5 kg, increased maternal weight gain in early adulthood and being a current smoker. The recurrence rates for gestational diabetes varied between 30% and 84% after the index pregnancy.

The alternative to the use of risk factors is the use of some form of biochemical test, either of urine or blood.

11.1.3 Accuracy of biochemical screening tests

Urine test for glucose

Two studies have been identified in this section.

Description of included studies

A US-based retrospective observational study (3217 women) (1995)[494] [EL = II] assessed the ability of urine testing for glucose to predict gestational diabetes or pregnancy outcomes. For this review, only the prediction of gestational diabetes has been taken into consideration. Study participants had complete urinalysis at the first prenatal visit and dipstick at each subsequent visit together with a screening 50 g GCT at 24–28 weeks. Women with at least two urinalysis tests during the first two trimesters were included. 2965 women were categorised into two groups, negative or positive for glycosuria. Those with positive GCT screens (cut-off 7.78 mmol/litre (140 mg/100 ml)) started a 3 day carbohydrate load, and had a 100 g glucose tolerance test (GTT).

A German study (1990)[493] [EL = II] compared urine and blood screening tests to detect gestational diabetes. Random urine glucose screening values from each antenatal visit of 500 consecutive pregnant women were compared with a serum glucose test done at 28 weeks of gestation after ingestion of a 50 g glucose-containing beverage. A positive test of a serum glucose level of 7.78 mmol/litre (140 mg/100 ml) or more was followed by a 100 g 3 hour OGTT. Glycosuria was considered present if a trace or greater values were found on at least two prenatal visits. Severe glycosuria was defined as a 2+ (13.9 mmol/litre (250 mg/100 ml)) level or greater on urine screening on at least two prenatal visits.

Findings

The US study found a higher incidence of gestational diabetes in women with positive glycosuria in the first two trimesters (12.8% versus 2.9% for negative screens). The sensitivity of glycosuria in the first trimester as a predictor of gestational diabetes was 7.1%, specificity was 98.5%, PPV was 12.8% and NPV was 97.1%.

In the German study any degree of glycosuria had a sensitivity of 27.3%, specificity of 83.5%, efficiency of 81% and PPV of 7.1%. Severe glycosuria had sensitivity of 18.2%, specificity of 96.9%, and PPV of 21.1%. The incidence of glycosuria was not increased in gestational diabetics when compared with pregnant women with normal glucose tolerance. Severe glycosuria occurred in only 18% of these patients.

Random blood glucose (RBG) test

Two studies have been identified in this section (Table 11.1)

Description of included studies

A prospective population-based study conducted in Sweden (2004)[837] [EL = II] aimed to find out whether repeated RBG, with different cut-off levels, with or without anamnestic factors, could be an effective universal screening test method for identifying high-risk women for the OGTT as the second step. All pregnant women without diabetes (*n* = 4918) visiting the maternal healthcare clinics over a 2 year period were offered a 75 g OGTT between 28–32 weeks of gestation. RBG was proposed every 4–6 weeks.

A study in Kuwait (1988)[838] [EL = II] tested the predictability of an RPG test in women who had their last meal within 2 hours and those who had their last meal more than 2 hours previously. Two hundred and seventy-six unselected pregnant women had RPG followed by 75 g OGTT at 28–32 weeks of gestation.

Table 11.1 Random blood glucose test

Author, year, country, evidence level, study design	Study population, weeks of gestation	Screening test(s), cut-off value for giving diagnosis, diagnostic test, prevalence/incidence	Threshold, sensitivity, specificity, PPV, NPV	Comments and conclusion
Ostlund (2004)[837] Sweden, EL II, prospective population-based study	3616 28–32 weeks	RBG, risk factors, All were offered diagnostic test, 75 g OGTT, 61/3616 or 1.7%	≥ 8 mmol/litre ST 47.5%, SP 97%	Traditional risk factors have poor sensitivity for gestational diabetes.
Nasrat (1988)[838] Kuwait, EL II, prospective study	250 28–32 weeks	RPG, Lind and Anderson threshold used 7.0 mmol/litre < 2 hour 6.4 mmol/litre > 2 hour, 75 g OGTT, 3/250 or 1.2%	7.0 mmol/litre < 2 hour 6.4 mmol/litre > 2 hour ST 16%, SP 96%, PPV 47% 90th percentile cut-off ST 29%, SP 89%, PPV 38%	RPG has limited predictive value

Findings

In the Swedish study traditional risk factors and values of repeated RBG measurements were registered as well as results of the OGTT in terms of fasting blood glucose and 2 hour blood glucose. A total of 3616 women had an OGTT. Results showed that an RBG cut-off level ≥ 8.0 mmol/litre as the only indicator for an OGTT was optimal for detecting gestational diabetes with regard to sensitivity (47.5%) and specificity (97.0%). It had the same sensitivity for detecting gestational diabetes as using traditional risk factors, but reduced the need to carry out the OGTT from 15.8% to 3.8% of the population.

The Kuwait study used the Lind and Anderson threshold,[839] 7.0 mmol/litre if eaten within 2 hours, 6.4 if eaten after 2 hours. This gave a sensitivity of 16%, specificity of 96% and PPV of 47%. Using the 90th percentile of study group sensitivity of 29%, specificity of 89% and PPV of 38% were reported.

50 g glucose challenge test (GCT)

Description of included studies

A total of four studies tested the diagnostic value of 50 g GCT (Table 11.2). All studies had an evidence level of II.

Table 11.2   Glucose challenge test

Author, year, country, evidence level, study design	Study population, weeks of gestation	Screening test(s), cut-off value for giving diagnosis, diagnostic test, prevalence/incidence	Threshold, sensitivity, specificity, PPV, NPV	Comments and conclusion
Seshiah (2004)[840] India, II, prospective consecutive population-based study	1251 891 positive screens, Second or third trimester	1 hour 50 g GCT, 2 hour 75 g OGTT, given to all, 168/891 or 18.9%	No threshold used, ST 79.8%, SP 42.7%, PPV: 24.5%, NPV: 90.1%	Using 2 hour plasma glucose ≥ 7.78 mmol/litre (140 mg/100 ml) as one step procedure is simple and economical for countries more prone to gestational diabetes
Perucchini (1999)[499], Switzerland, II, prospective population-based observational study	772 eligible 558 consented 520 completed study, 24–28 weeks	FPG, 50 g GCT, 3 hour 100 g OGTT, given to all, 52/520 or 10.2%	FPG 4.8 mmol/litre, 50 g GCT 7.8 mmol/litre ST FPG 81%, 50 g GCT 59%, SP FPG 76%, 50 g GCT 91%	Sample representative of general population. Measuring FPG is easier than 50 g GCT and allows 70% of women to avoid the GCT.
Cetin and Cetin (1997)[841], Turkey, II, prospective study	291/344 eligible, 274/291 completed study, 24–28 weeks	1 hour 50 g GCT, 100 g OGTT, given to all, 17/274 or 6.2%	ST: < 2 hour cut-off 7.78 mmol/litre (140 mg/100 ml) 75%, cut-off 8.22 mmol/litre (148 mg/100 ml) 63% 2–3 hour cut-off 7.78 mmol/litre (140 mg/100 ml) 60%, cut-off 7.89 mmol/litre (142 mg/100 ml) 60% > 3 hour cut-off 7.78 mmol/litre (140 mg/100 ml) 50%, cut-off 8.33 mmol/litre (150 mg/100 ml) 50% SP: < 2 hour cut-off 7.78 mmol/litre (140 mg/100 ml) 86%, cut-off 8.22 mmol/litre (148 mg/100 ml) 91% 2–3 hour cut-off 7.78 mmol/litre (140 mg/100 ml) 89% cut-off 7.89 mmol/litre (142 mg/100 ml) 92% > 3 hour cut-off 7.78 mmol/litre (140 mg/100 ml) 89%, cut-off 8.33 mmol/litre (150 mg/100 ml) 92% PPV: < 2 hour cut-off 7.78 mmol/litre (140 mg/100 ml) 27%, cut-off 8.22 mmol/litre (148 mg/100 ml) 33% 2–3 hour cut-off 7.78 mmol/litre (140 mg/100 ml) 30% cut-off 7.89 mmol/litre (142 mg/100 ml) 30% > 3 hour cut-off 7.78 mmol/litre (140 mg/100 ml) 25%, cut-off 8.33 mmol/litre (150 mg/100 ml) 33%	Sample too small. Standard cut-off 7.78 mmol/litre (140 mg/100 ml) Sens 65% Spec 88% PPV 27% Suggested cut-off ST 59%, SP 92%, PPV 32%
O'Sullivan (1973)[842], USA, III, cohort study	752/ 986 (76%) eligible, weeks of gestation not mentioned	1 hour 50 g GCT, 3 hour OGTT given to all, 15/752 or 2%	1 hour 50 g GCT ≥ 130 mg/100 ml cut-off ST 78.9%, SP 87.2%, PPV 13.8%, NPV 99.4%	Timing of testing in relation to stage of pregnancy not reported. No quantity of glucose stated for GTT. Sample collected between 1956 and 1957.

2008 update

Findings

Four studies[499,840–842] in which a diagnostic test was performed on all participants showed sensitivities of 79.8%, 59%, 59% and 78.9% and specificities of 42.7%, 91%, 92%, and 87.2%, respectively. The PPVs were 24.5%, not reported, 32% and 13.8%, respectively.

Comparison studies

Three studies were identified in this section (Table 11.3).

Description of included studies

A prospective study in Germany (2003)[843] [EL = II] tested the usefulness of glucose meters in screening pregnant women for gestational diabetes. One hundred and ninety-three pregnant women were administered the 50 g GCT and their blood glucose levels were simultaneously measured with five portable meters and a HemoCue. The results were compared with a standard hexokinase method. A cut-off value of 7.8 mmol/litre was used. The six portable meters used were Accu-Chek, EuroFlash, GlucoTouch, HemoCue, OneTouch and Precision Plus.

A US-based randomised trial with no control (1992)[844] [EL = II] compared three carbohydrate sources: 50 g glucose polymer, 50 g standard glucose solution and 50 g milk chocolate bar. A New Zealand-based RCT (1985)[845] [EL = II] compared the 100 g glucose screening test with 100 g glucose polymer test.

Findings

All meters showed an excellent correlation ($r > 0.9$; $P < 0.01$). The various sensitivities were as follows: Accu-Chek 84%, EuroFlash 100%, GlucoTouch 98%, HemoCue 57%, OneTouch 92%, Precision Plus 90%. The specificities were Accu-Chek 98%, EuroFlash 79%, GlucoTouch 86%, HemoCue 100%, OneTouch 92%, Precision Plus 91%.

The overall sensitivity in the American study was 60%, for standard glucose 33.3% and for polymer 100%. The specificities for overall, standard glucose and polymer were 84%, 73.6% and 92.8%, respectively, and PPVs were 16%, 9% and 49%, respectively.

In the New Zealand-based study the sensitivity of the glucose polymer test was 89%, the specificity was 81% and the PPV was 29%.

Table 11.3 Comparison studies

Author, year, country, evidence level, study design	Study population, weeks of gestation	Screening test(s), cut-off value for giving diagnosis, diagnostic test, prevalence/incidence	Threshold, sensitivity, specificity, PPV, NPV	Comments and conclusion
Buhling (2003)[343] Germany, II, prospective study	193 weeks of gestation not mentioned	Comparison of 50 g GCT with five portable meters, 7.8 mmol/litre, hexokinase method, prevalence not calculated	ST: Accu-check 84%, EuroFlash 100%, GlucoTouch 98%, HemoCue 57%, OneTouch 92%, Precision Plus 90% SP: Accu-check 98%, EuroFlash 79%, GlucoTouch 86%, HemoCue 100%, OneTouch 92% Precision Plus 91%	The accuracy of Accu-check, GlucoTouch, OneTouch and Precision Plus was acceptable for use in gestational diabetes screening.
Murphy (1992)[344] USA, II, randomised trial, no control	124 women randomly assigned to 1 of 3 CHO sources, 24–28 weeks	Comparison of 3 CHO sources 50 g glucose polymer, 50 g standard glucose solution and 50 g milk chocolate bar, No cut-off used, 3 hour 100 g OGTT, 5/108 or 4.6%	Glucose ≥ 7.5 mmol/litre ST: overall 60, standard glucose 33.3%, polymer 100% SP: overall 84%, standard glucose 73.6%, polymer 92.8% PPV: overall 16%, standard glucose 9%, polymer 49%	The polymer is an inexpensive and well tolerated but the use of candy bar needs further research.
Court (1985)[345] New Zealand, II, RCT	100 women randomised to glucose screening test (48) and glucose polymer test (52) glucose polymer test given to additional 178 women so total 230 women received polymer test. 28 weeks	100 g glucose screening test and 100 g glucose polymer screening test, No cut-off value used, 3 hour 100 g OGTT, 12/230 or 5.2%	8 mmol/litre or 144 mg/100 ml, For glucose polymer ST 89%, SP 81%, PPV 29%	The glucose polymer is preferable to glucose for CHO loading in pregnancy because of lower rates of nausea and better reproducibility of test results.

2008 update

Fasting plasma glucose (FPG)

Two studies were identified that tested the diagnostic value of FPG (Table 11.4).

Description of included studies

A Brazilian study (1998)[498] [EL = II] used baseline data from a cohort study of consecutive pregnant women to evaluate the performance of FPG as a screening test for gestational diabetes as defined by WHO in an unselected group of pregnant Brazilian women. The study included 5579 women aged ≥ 20 years with gestational ages of 24–28 weeks at the time of testing and no previous diagnosis of diabetes. A standardised 2 hour 75 g OGTT was performed in 5010 women.

A cross-sectional, population-based study in Sweden (2006)[846] [EL = II] evaluated the diagnostic properties of cFBG as a screening test in an unselected low-risk Swedish population (*n* = 3616). They compared cFBG (measured at 28–32 weeks of gestation) with traditional risk factors (registered) and repeated (4–6 times during pregnancy) random capillary glucose measurements as screening models for gestational diabetes. A 75 g OGTT was used to diagnose gestational diabetes.

Findings

The Brazilian study showed that for the detection of gestational diabetes an FPG of 4.94 mmol/litre (89 mg/100 ml) jointly maximises sensitivity (88%) and specificity (78%), identifying 22% of the women as test-positive. Lowering the cut-off point to 4.5 mmol/litre (81 mg/100 ml) increases sensitivity (94%), decreases specificity (51%) and identifies 49% of women as test-positive. For detection of IGT, a value of 4.72 mmol/litre (85 mg/100 ml) jointly maximises sensitivity and specificity (68%), identifying 35% of women as test-positive. A cut-off point of 4.72 mmol/litre (85 mg/100 ml) for the detection of gestational diabetes gives sensitivity of 94% and specificity of 66%.

The Swedish study found that 1.52% (55/3616) of women were diagnosed before 34 weeks of gestation. For cFBG cut-off values between 4.0 and 5.0 mmol/litre, the sensitivity ranged between 87% and 47% and specificity between 51% and 96%. The LR+ and LR− were best at ≥ 5.0 mmol/litre. The combination of traditional risk factors with cFBG only slightly increased the sensitivity as compared with the use of cFBG alone.

Jelly beans

Two studies were identified in this section (Table 11.5).

Description of included studies

A US study (1999)[847] [EL = II] tested the hypothesis that a standardised dose of jelly beans could be used as an alternative sugar source to the 50 g glucose beverage to screen for gestational diabetes. This prospective study recruited 160 pregnant women at 24 to 28 weeks of gestation to compare two sugar sources for serum glucose response, side effects, preference, and ability to detect gestational diabetes. Patients were randomly given 50 g glucose beverage or 28 jelly beans (50 g simple carbohydrate) and serum glucose values were determined 1 hour later. A 100 g 3 hour OGTT was performed finally.

Table 11.4 Fasting plasma glucose test

Author, year, country, evidence level, study design	Study population, weeks of gestation	Screening test(s), cut-off value for giving diagnosis, diagnostic test, prevalence/incidence	Threshold, sensitivity, specificity, PPV, NPV	Comments and conclusion
Reichelt (1998)[498] Brazil, II, cohort study	5,579, 5,010 remaining in the study 24–28 weeks	FPG Diagnostic test given to all, 2 hour 75 g OGTT, 379/5,010 or 7.6%	81 mg/100 ml or 4.5 mmol/litre: ST 94%, SP 51%, PPV 0.6, NPV 100% 85 mg/100 ml or 4.7 mmol/litre: ST 94%, SP 66%, PPV 0.9, NPV 100% 89 mg/100 ml or 4.9 mmol/litre: ST 88%, SP 78%, PPV 1.3, NPV 100%	FPG is a useful screening test for gestational diabetes, a threshold of 4.94 mmol/litre or 89 mg/100 ml maximises sensitivity and specificity.
Fadl (2006)[846] Sweden, II, cross-sectional population-based study	3616 28–32 weeks for cFBG	cFBG Diagnostic given to all, 2 hour 75 g OGTT, 55/3616 or 1.52%	cFBG Cut-off values between 4.0 and 5.0 mmol/litre, ST 87% to 47%, SP 51% and 96%. LR+ and LR− best at ≥ 5.0 mmol/litre	

Another American study (1995)[848] [EL = II] tested the diagnostic value and patient tolerance of jelly beans as an alternative to a 50 g glucose solution. Pregnant women between 26 and 30 weeks of gestation were recruited to participate in the study. Each participant was given cola beverage containing 50 g of glucose and blood glucose was tested 1 hour later. Within 2 weeks of this test, each patient ate 18 jelly beans and had glucose level tested within 1 hour. Within 2 weeks of the jelly bean test, all participants were given a 3 hour 100 g OGTT.

Findings

In the US study 136 participants completed the study and a comparison of efficacies of jelly beans and 50 g glucose beverage as sugar sources in detection of gestational diabetes was made. There was not much difference between serum glucose values after ingestion of jelly beans (6.49 ± 1.31 mmol/litre (116.9 ± 23.6 mg/100 ml)) and of 50 g glucose beverage 6.47 ± 1.5 mmol/litre (116.5 ± 27.0 mg/100 ml). There was a significantly lower incidence of side effects after consumption of the jelly beans (20%) as compared with 50 g glucose beverage (38%). Seventy-six percent of the participants preferred jelly beans and 24% preferred the 50 g glucose beverage.

In the second study the sensitivity, specificity and PPV of the cola beverage using 7.78 mmol/litre (140 mg/100 ml) as the threshold were 46%, 81% and 18%, respectively. The sensitivity, specificity and PPV of jelly beans using a threshold of 6.67 mmol/litre (120 mg/100 ml) were 54%, 81%, and 20%, respectively. Participants tolerated jelly beans better than the cola beverage.

In order to compare the various blood tests for screening gestational diabetes, likelihood ratios were calculated (Table 11.6).

Effectiveness of screening tests

Description of included studies

A US-based RCT[832] [EL = 2+] compared a risk factor-based screening programme with a universally based one. The risk factor group had a 3 hour 100 g OGTT at 32 weeks if any risk factor for gestational diabetes was present. The universal group had a 50 g GCT and if the plasma glucose at 1 hour was ≥ 7.8 mmol/litre, a formal 3 hour 100 g OGTT was then performed.

Table 11.5 Jelly bean studies

Author, year, country, evidence level, study design	Study population, weeks of gestation	Screening test(s), cut-off value for giving diagnosis, diagnostic test, prevalence/incidence	Threshold, sensitivity, specificity, PPV, NPV	Comments and conclusion
Lamar (1999)[847] USA, II, prospective study	160, 136 completed the study 24–28 weeks	Jelly beans vs standard glucose (randomisation done), Blood glucose ≥ 7.78 mmol/litre (140 mg/100 ml), 3 hour 100 g fasting GTT, 5/136 or 3.7%	7.78 mmol/litre (140 mg/100 ml), standard glucose: ST 80%, SP 82%, PPV 15%, NPV 99% Jelly beans: ST 40%, SP 85%, PPV 9%, NPV 97%	There is no significant difference in screening performance for jelly beans and the standard glucose. Patients report fewer side effects after a jelly bean challenge than after a 50 g glucose beverage test. So jelly beans may be used an alternative to the 50 g glucose beverage test.
Boyd (1995)[848] USA, II, prospective study	157 26–30 weeks	Cola beverage vs jelly beans, Diagnostic test given to all participants, 3 hour 100 g GTT, 13/157 or 8.3%	7.78 mmol/litre (140 mg/100 ml) for cola beverage: ST 46%, SP 81%, PPV 18% 6.67 mmol/litre (120 mg/100 ml) for jelly beans: ST 54%, SP 81%, PPV 20%	Patient tolerance was greater for jelly beans as compared with the 50 g cola beverage. Jelly beans may serve as an alternative to a cola beverage containing 50 g of glucose.

Table 11.6 Likelihood ratios for three blood tests

Test	No. of studies/population	Heterogeneity for LR+ (I2)	LR+ (95% CI)	Heterogeneity for LR− (I2)	LR− (95% CI)
RBG	2 studies, 5168 women	0%	15.49 (11.44–20.99)	0%	0.55 (0.44–0.69)
FPG	3 studies, 9146 women	94.8%	4.77 (3.16–7.21)	97.4%	0.27 (0.10–0.78)
50 g GCT	4 studies, 2437 women	98%	4.34 (1.53–12.26)	0%	0.42 (0.33–0.55)

A study in Denmark (2004)[833] [EL = 2−] retrospectively investigated in 1 year the clinical outcome of pregnant women in relation to separate components of the pre-screening procedure, presence of gestational diabetes and the capillary blood glucose 120 minutes after glucose load ($cBG_{120\,min}$) concentration after a 75 g glucose load. The aim was to investigate the power of the pre-screening to identify gestational diabetes and for the screening to predict adverse clinical outcomes.

A cross-sectional 5 year investigation in the Netherlands (2006)[834] [EL = 2−] examined the clinical usefulness of antepartum clinical characteristics, along with measures of glucose tolerance, in Dutch multi-ethnic women with gestational diabetes for their ability to predict type 2 diabetes within 6 months of delivery (early postpartum diabetes). The following data were collected for all women: age and gestational age at entry into the study; pre-pregnancy BMI; ethnicity; obstetric and clinical history, including the onset of early postpartum diabetes; pregnancy outcome; level of fasting C-peptide; and glycaemic parameters of 50 g 1 hour GCT and 100 g 3 hour OGTT (diagnostic OGTT). Eleven of 168 or 6.6% of women developed early postpartum diabetes.

A prospective cohort study (1998)[849] [EL = 2+] in the United Arab Emirates compared the outcome of pregnancy in women with GCT screening levels ≥ 7.7 mmol/litre and ≥ 8.3 mmol/litre. Pregnancy outcomes were compared for the following groups:

A. GCT ≥ 7.7 and < 8.3 mmol/litre (194 women)
B. GCT ≥ 8.3 mmol/litre (194 women)
C. GCT < 7.7 mmol/litre (194 women matched for age, parity and weight with Group B)

The screening test used was blood glucose 1 hour after a 50 g glucose load (GCT) given in fasting state between 28 and 32 weeks. If the blood glucose was ≥ 7.7 mmol/litre then 3 hour GTT was given.

A prospective cohort study of 6854 participants (2005)[850] [EL = 2+] in the USA evaluated the association between obesity, GCT and pregnancy outcome. A 50 g GCT was performed at 24–28 weeks of gestation and a screening value of ≥ 7.22 mmol/litre (130 mg/100 ml) was followed by a 100 g OGTT. For the purpose of analysis, women were categorised by pre-pregnancy BMI and by different GCT thresholds. Maternal outcome was defined by the rate of pre-eclampsia, gestational age at delivery, caesarean section rate and the need for labour induction. Neonatal outcome was defined by fetal size (macrosomia/LGA), arterial cord pH, respiratory complications and neonatal intensive care unit (NICU) admission.

A prospective study (1987)[851] [EL = 2+] in a midwestern US population compared the value of routine versus selective diabetes screening in a group of predominantly middle-class, healthy, Caucasian pregnant women. 2000 women were divided into two groups (they were otherwise similar):

1. those to undergo routine screening between 24 and 28 weeks of gestation
2. those to be tested selectively in the presence of standard risk factors.

The screening test involved a 50 g GCT followed by a 3 hour OGTT if necessary.

A prospective randomised study (1995)[852] [EL = 2+] in China was conducted to determine the relationship between the 50 g GCT and pregnancy outcomes. In this study, 622 pregnant women underwent a 50 g GCT and a 75 g OGTT was performed if the screening test value was ≥ 7.8 mmol/litre.

Findings
The American study showed that universal screening detected a gestational diabetes prevalence of 2.7%, 1.45% more than in the risk factor-screened group. Universal screening for gestational diabetes was found to be superior to risk factor-based screening as it detected more cases, facilitated early diagnosis and is associated with improved pregnancy outcomes.

The results of the Danish study showed that screening using a cFBG of 4.1 mmol/litre was unable to predict gestational diabetes and adverse outcome. The best predictor of complicated delivery was a high BMI. The best predictor of fetal adverse outcome was $cBG_{120\,min}$ ≥ 9.0 mmol/litre after a 75 g glucose load. Identical pregnancy complications were present in gestational diabetes and non-gestational diabetes.

The Netherlands study showed that only a family history of diabetes showed an association with early postpartum diabetes. ROC curve analysis identified all three GCT parameters, including

2008 update

fasting glucose concentration, as poor diagnostic tests, with a PPV of 22%, whereas PPV associated with the area under the diagnostic OGTT curve increased progressively over the duration of the test from 20.6% to 100%. Using a 3 hour OGTT glucose area threshold of 35.7 mmol·h/litre resulted in 100% sensitivity and 100% specificity, identifying the 11 women who developed early postpartum diabetes.

In the UAE study, 197/3400 or 5.8% of women were considered to have abnormal GTT plus 199/3400 or 5.8% had IGT. There was no significant difference in pregnancy-induced hypertension between groups. Preterm delivery was significantly higher in Group B. Birthweight above 4.5 kg was 4% in group C, 6% in group A and 9% in group B. The Apgar score > 6 at 1 minute found no significant differences between groups.

In the US-based study, a positive GCT result (GCT ≥ 7.22 mmol/litre (130 mg/100 ml)) was identified in 2541/6854 or 37% of women. In this study, 464/6854 or 6.8% of women were diagnosed with gestational diabetes. In both groups of screening results (> 7.22 mmol/litre (130 mg/100 ml) and < 7.22 mmol/litre (130 mg/100 ml)), the women who were obese were significantly older, gained more weight during pregnancy and had a lower rate of nulliparity in comparison with the women who were not obese. The women who were obese had higher rates of macrosomia, LGA and induction of labour. No difference was found in mean birthweight, the total rate of ceasarean section, preterm delivery, 5 minute Apgar score ≤ 7, mean arterial cord pH, NICU admission or a need for respiratory support in comparison with non-obese women in both groups of screening results. A gradual increase in the rate of macrosomia, LGA and ceasarean section was identified in both obese and non-obese women in relation to increasing GCT severity categories.

The midwestern American study showed that the incidence of gestational diabetes in the selectively screened group was twice (19/453, 4.2%) that in the routinely screened group (21/1000, 2.1%). Glucose intolerance without a risk factor was found in only one case (1/1000, 0.1%) in the routinely screened group.

In the Chinese study, 103/622 or 16.6% of women underwent the diagnostic test, among whom 32 were identified as having gestational impaired glucose tolerance (GIGT) and 12 as having gestational diabetes. The sensitivity of 50 g GCT was 42.7% (44/103). The incidences of oedema–proteinuria–hypertension syndrome (EPH syndrome), PROM, fetal macrosomia, operative deliveries and perinatal morbidity were higher in women with GIGT/gestational diabetes than in women without GIGT/gestational diabetes.

11.1.4 Women's views on screening for gestational diabetes

Description of included studies

A prospective survey (2002)[853] [EL = 2–] in Australia surveyed women on their experiences of being screened for gestational diabetes in a hospital that screens all women in pregnancy. They tested the hypothesis that women with a positive result on the screen test will experience a reduction in quality of life, their health and that of their baby when compared with women with a normal screening result. The study took place at a level III teaching hospital with a high-risk pregnancy service and NICU. A Spielberger State-Trait Anxiety Inventory, Edinburgh Postnatal Depression Scale and Short Form 36 Item Health Survey were used to study the main outcome measures: anxiety, depression, health status, concerns about the health of the baby and perceived health. Prior to being screened, a total of 158 women participated in the study whereas 51 women participated after being screened.

A prospective cohort study (1997)[854] [EL = 2+] in Canada investigated whether false positive results of 50 g GCT for gestational diabetes were associated with adverse psychological effects. Women between 12 and 14 weeks of gestation with no previous history of diabetes or gestational diabetes were included. In this study, 897 women had complete data both at enrolment and at 32 weeks, including 88 who had false positive GCT results. A total of 809 women completed questionnaires at baseline, 32 weeks and 36 weeks of gestation.

Findings

The Australian study found no differences in the levels of anxiety, depression or the women's concerns about the health of their babies. When women positively screened for gestational diabetes were compared with negatively screened women, the positively screened group had significantly lower health perceptions, were significantly less likely to rate their health as 'much better than one year ago' and were significantly more likely to rate their health as 'fair' rather than 'very good' or 'excellent'.

The Canadian study showed that, at 32 weeks, 20% of women with false positive GCT results significantly perceived their health as excellent as compared with 38% of women with negative results or not tested. These results were sustained at 36 weeks. The study showed no significant association between false positive test result and anxiety levels, depression or woman's concern for health of baby. These results were neither significant between baseline and 32 weeks nor at 36 weeks.

11.1.5 Clinical characteristics and screening

Description of included studies

A Canada-based prospective study (1997)[855] [EL = 2+] tested the hypothesis that using clinical characteristics for assessing women's risks of gestational diabetes could enhance the efficiency of screening. In this study, 3131 women were randomly divided into two groups – a derivation group and a validation group. The screening strategies were derived from the derivation group data which were then tested in the validation group by comparing the effectiveness and efficiency with those with usual care. The strategies used were: no screening for low-risk women, usual care for intermediate-risk women, and universal screening with lower thresholds (plasma glucose values of 130 mg/100 ml (7.2 mmol/litre) or 128 mg/100 ml (7.1 mmol/litre) for high-risk women.

Findings

In the Canadian study there was a 34.6% reduction (95% CI 32.3% to 37.0%) in the number of screening tests performed after using the new strategies. The detection rate of gestational diabetes with new strategies was 81.2–82.6 % compared with the 78.3% detected through usual care. There was a significant reduction in the percentage of false positive screening tests, from 17.9% with usual care to 16.0% or 15.4% ($P< 0.001$) with the new strategies, depending on the threshold values for high-risk women.

Evidence summary for Section 11.1

Owing to the heterogeneity among studies for different screening tests there is no obvious best test available to screen for gestational diabetes. The evidence for the accuracy of these tests is further undermined by the fact that the thresholds for sensitivity and specificity are determined by the individual researchers rather than with reference to an agreed standard.

There is low-grade evidence from the effectiveness studies that IGT in pregnancy or frank gestational diabetes is associated with macrosomia, and possible increases in the incidence of pre-eclampsia and preterm delivery. On the other hand obesity was the factor most likely to be associated with complicated delivery and family history seemed to relate to post-delivery diabetic risk.

The ACHOIS study seems to suggest that treating women who have mild gestational diabetes in pregnancy is likely to be effective in reducing the risk of complications.

There is some evidence suggesting that receiving a positive screen result reduces women's health perceptions and makes them more likely to rate their health as 'fair' rather than 'very good' or 'excellent'.

Health economics – screening, diagnosis and treatment of gestational diabetes:
The effectiveness of screening, diagnosis and treatment (including monitoring) for gestational diabetes was identified by the GDG as a priority for health economic analysis. The analysis of cost-effectiveness was addressed through joint work with the GDG for the NICE *Diabetes in Pregnancy* guideline.[636] The methods and results from the health economic modelling are summarised here; further details are provided in Appendix F.

A systematic search of the literature identified 337 studies potentially related to the clinical question. After reviewing the abstracts, 33 articles were retrieved for further appraisal and eight have been included in this section of the review. Two papers were identified in the literature that

2008 update

examined the cost-effectiveness of screening for and treating gestational diabetes, six papers were identified that examined the cost-effectiveness of screening only for gestational diabetes and one paper was found that examined the cost-effectiveness of treating gestational diabetes. None of these papers was suitable for answering the question addressed in the guideline. The results of the systematic review are reported in Appendix F.

The recently published ACHOIS trial[972] demonstrated potential benefit of treatment for mild gestational diabetes. Evidence of clinical effectiveness is not always sufficient for a treatment to be considered cost-effective – often the people that would benefit from treatment must be identified from a group of people who do not require treatment. This is the case with gestational diabetes; the cost-effectiveness of screening and treatment for gestational diabetes are highly interdependent. As a result, a single decision-analytic health economic model was developed to help the combined GDGs make recommendations in relation to screening and treatment for gestational diabetes (see Appendix F for a full description of the model structure, data inputs and results).

The health economic model considered screening based on risk factors (age, ethnicity, BMI and family history of gestational diabetes) and/or blood tests (RBG, FPG and a 1 hour 50 g GCT) followed by a diagnostic test (2 hour 75 g OGTT). The possibility of universal diagnostic testing was also considered. The treatment alternatives considered in the model were diet, oral hypoglycaemic agents (glibenclamide and metformin) and insulin. All women diagnosed with gestational diabetes were assumed to undertake self-monitoring of blood glucose, regardless of which form of treatment they were using.

Under the baseline assumptions of the health economic model, two screening strategies were not dominated by other strategies. A strategy of offering an OGTT to women from high-risk ethnic backgrounds had an ICER of £3,678 compared with no screening or treatment (strategy 2). A strategy of offering an OGTT to all women defined by the American Diabetes Association (ADA) as being at high risk of gestational diabetes (i.e. women older than 25 years or BMI above 27 kg/m² or family history of diabetes or high-risk ethnic background; strategy 6) had an ICER of £21,739 compared with screening based on ethnicity alone. However, the combined GDGs expressed concern over the number of women that would undergo an OGTT if the ADA screening strategy were recommended because a large proportion of women would be tested based on age criteria alone. Using age as a risk factor for screening has a high sensitivity (i.e. it will identify the majority of women with gestational diabetes). Owing to data limitations it was not possible to evaluate the cost-effectiveness of using a combination of the individual risk factors considered in the model (see Appendix F). In the absence of this possibility, an analysis of the cost-effectiveness of each individual risk factor followed by an OGTT was conducted, with each strategy being compared with a strategy of no screening or treatment. The results are presented in Table 11.7.

Table 11.7 ICER for single risk factor strategies followed by a diagnostic test when compared with a strategy of no screening or treatment.

Strategy	Incremental QALY	Incremental cost	ICER
Ethnicity	9.55	£66,226	£6,935
BMI	6.29	£80,109	£12,736
Family history	15.73	£81,915	£5,208

All of these ICERs are below the £20,000 per QALY threshold used by NICE as a willingness to pay for cost-effectiveness, and so each one could be regarded as being cost-effective.

GDG interpretation of evidence
Currently an unselected pregnant population will have the risk of gestational diabetes assessed using risk factors such as:

- BMI > 30 kg/m²
- previous macrosomic baby ≥ 4.5 kg for Caucasian and black women, ≥ 4.0 kg for other women
- previous gestational diabetes (see *Diabetes in Pregnancy* guideline[636])
- family history of diabetes (first-degree relative with type 1 or type 2 diabetes)

- women from a high-risk ethnic group, which would include:[856]
  - South Asian (Indian, Pakistani, Bangladeshi)
  - black Caribbean
  - Middle Eastern (Saudi Arabia, United Arab Emirates, Iraq, Jordan, Syria, Oman, Qatar, Kuwait, Lebanon or Egypt).

This last group of women has been identified from the Diabetes Atlas (third edition) 2006 using prevalance of type 2 diabetes as a surrogate for gestational diabetes.

Approximately 20–50% of women will have a positive screen using these risk factors, with proportions varying considerably from one area to another.

According to a 1999 survey,[825] 67% of UK maternity service providers currently screen using a combination of these factors.

Evidence from health economic modelling carried out by the NCC-WCH shows that screening and treating gestational diabetes is cost-effective using identification of risk factors as the screening method followed by an OGTT.

While screening using risk factors is less sensitive than performing a glucose challenge or glucose tolerance test, it is more practical and less disruptive for women. The biochemical tests considered (GCT, FPG, RBG and urine testing) perform only moderately well in terms of diagnostic value.

Approximately 10–20% of women diagnosed as having gestational diabetes will go on to need oral hypoglycaemic agents or insulin therapy where diet and exercise have not afforded adequate control of blood glucose levels (refer to *Diabetes in Pregnancy* (NICE clinical guideline 63)[636] for further details).

Evidence from one large trial (the ACHOIS study) has shown treatment of gestational diabetes to be effective in reducing poor outcomes (refer to *Diabetes in Pregnancy* (NICE clinical guideline 63)[636] for further details).

Recommendations on screening for gestational diabetes

Screening for gestational diabetes using risk factors is recommended in a healthy population. At the booking appointment, the following risk factors for gestational diabetes should be determined:

- body mass index above 30 kg/m²
- previous macrosomic baby weighing 4.5 kg or above
- previous gestational diabetes (refer to 'Diabetes in pregnancy' [NICE clinical guideline 63], available from www.nice.org.uk/CG063)
- family history of diabetes (first-degree relative with diabetes)
- family origin with a high prevalence of diabetes:
  - South Asian (specifically women whose country of family origin is India, Pakistan or Bangladesh)
  - black Caribbean
  - Middle Eastern (specifically women whose country of family origin is Saudi Arabia, United Arab Emirates, Iraq, Jordan, Syria, Oman, Qatar, Kuwait, Lebanon or Egypt).

Women with any one of these risk factors should be offered testing for gestational diabetes (refer to 'Diabetes in pregnancy' [NICE clinical guideline 63], available from www.nice.org.uk/CG063).

In order to make an informed decision about screening and testing for gestational diabetes, women should be informed that:

- in most women, gestational diabetes will respond to changes in diet and exercise
- some women (between 10% and 20%) will need oral hypoglycaemic agents or insulin therapy if diet and exercise are not effective in controlling gestational diabetes
- if gestational diabetes is not detected and controlled there is a small risk of birth complications such as shoulder dystocia
- a diagnosis of gestational diabetes may lead to increased monitoring and interventions during both pregnancy and labour.

Screening for gestational diabetes using fasting plasma glucose, random blood glucose, glucose challenge test and urinalysis for glucose should not be undertaken.

2008 update

Research recommendation on screening for gestational diabetes

Is screening for gestational diabetes based on expected local prevalence, with or without modification by risk factors, clinically effective and cost-effective?

11.2 Pre-eclampsia

Clinical question
What is the diagnostic value of different screening methods in identifying women at risk of developing pre-eclampsia?

Previous NICE guidance (for the updated recommendations see below)
At first contact, a woman's level of risk for pre-eclampsia should be evaluated so that a plan for her subsequent schedule of antenatal appointments can be formulated. The likelihood of developing pre-eclampsia during a pregnancy is increased in women who:

- are nulliparous
- are age 40 years or older
- have a family history of pre-eclampsia (e.g., pre-eclampsia in a mother or sister)
- have a prior history of pre-eclampsia
- have a BMI at or above 35 kg/m² at first contact
- have a multiple pregnancy or pre-existing vascular disease (for example, hypertension or diabetes). [C]

Whenever blood pressure is measured in pregnancy, a urine sample should be tested at the same time for proteinuria. [C]

Standardised equipment, techniques and conditions for blood-pressure measurement should be used by all personnel whenever blood pressure is measured in the antenatal period, so that valid comparisons can be made. [C]

Pregnant women should be informed of the symptoms of advanced pre-eclampsia because these may be associated with poorer pregnancy outcomes for the mother or baby. Symptoms include headache, problems with vision, such as blurring or flashing before the eyes, bad pain just below the ribs, vomiting, and sudden swelling of face, hands or feet. [D]

Future research:
Research is needed to determine the optimal frequency and timing of blood pressure measurement and on the role of screening for proteinuria.

11.2.1 Introduction and background

Pre-eclampsia is a condition usually associated with hypertension and proteinuria, and occurring in the second half of pregnancy. Hypertension is defined as a single diastolic blood pressure of 110 mmHg or any consecutive readings of 90 mmHg on more than one occasion at least 4 hours apart. Proteinuria is defined as 300 mg excretion of protein in a 24 hour collected urine, two clean catch urine specimens at least 4 hours apart with 2+ proteinuria by dipstick.[535]

Pre-eclampsia and eclampsia remain among the major causes of maternal mortality in the UK (CEMACH 2004) although the reduction in the number of deaths since the 1950s may have been at least in part due to the monitoring of blood pressure during pregnancy. Current knowledge on the pathophysiology of pre-eclampsia has identified that it is a complex disorder with widespread endothelial damage which can involve every organ of the body. Therefore presenting signs and symptoms may be more varied than a rising blood pressure and proteinuria. However, the antenatal care of all pregnant women is an opportunity to screen for rising blood pressure, especially in groups who are at increased risk, and to educate them about the symptoms which might signal fulminating disease.

11.2.2   Accuracy of screening tests

The quality of studies included in this review was variable, with deficiencies in many areas of methodology. In particular, studies suffered from a lack of blinding and relatively small sample sizes. There was heterogeneity regarding the reference standard used in each study.

Only a few tests reached specificity above 90%. These were AFP, β-hCG and uterine artery Doppler (bilateral notching). The sensitivities of these tests were variable and generally low.

It was often not possible to be certain about the definition of pre-eclampsia used in studies. There was a lack of information on the exact technique of blood pressure measurement and Korotkoff threshold for abnormality, whether the proteinuria was in the absence of urinary tract infection and pre-existing renal disease, or whether there was normalisation of blood pressure within 6 weeks of giving birth.

Alpha-fetoprotein (AFP)

Two studies have been identified in this section (Table 11.8).

Description of included studies

An American prospective cohort study (1999)[857] [EL = II] evaluated the value of AFP as a predictor of pregnancy outcomes. Maternal serum markers were analysed over a 5 year period (March 1991 to May 1996) from 60 040 women who underwent serum marker screening at 14–22 weeks of gestation. All women had maternal serum AFP measurements. A value of at least 2.5 MoM was used for calculation.

A population-based cohort study in Finland (1998)[858] [EL = II] sought to determine whether maternal mid-trimester AFP can predict pre-eclampsia. 1037 nulliparous women were included, of whom 637 were analysed. Measurement of AFP was made from maternal serum collected at 15–19 weeks of gestation. Sensitivity, specificity and predictive values were calculated for elevated AFP (at least 2.0 MoM).

Findings

The American study gave a very low sensitivity of 4.3% but a high specificity of 97.4% for AFP measurement. The overall incidence of pre-eclampsia was 3.2%.

The Finland-based study calculated a poor sensitivity of 3% and a specificity of 98%. The incidence of pre-eclampsia was reported as 5.3%.

Both these studies used slightly different reference standards.

Fetal DNA

A total of two studies were included in this section (Table 11.9).

Table 11.8   Alpha-fetoprotein (AFP)

Author, year, country, EL, study design	No. of women analysed, inclusion/exclusion criteria, age, gestational age at test	Reference standard used, incidence of PE	Index test cut-off	Results	Comments and conclusion
Yaron (1999)[857] USA, EL II, prospective cohort study	60 040, EX: structural or chromosomal anomalies Age n.r. 14–22 weeks	SBP ≥ 140 mmHg or DBP ≥ 90 mmHg; presence of proteinuria, 3.2%	Competitive RIA (Sanofi Diagnostics) 2.5 MoM	ST 4.3%, SP 97.4%	Multiple marker screening can be used for the detection of not only fetal anomalies and aneuploidy but also for detection of high-risk pregnancy
Pouta (1998)[858] Finland, EL II, population-based cohort study	637, IN: nulliparas EX: multiple pregnancies, fetal defects 27.7 ± 4.5 years 15–19 weeks	BP ≥ 140/90 mmHg 6 hours apart or rise 30/15 mmHg; Prot. ≥ 300 mg/24 hours, 5.3%	Time-resolved FIA (Wallac) 2.0 MoM	ST 3%, SP 98%	AFP not helpful in predicting pre-eclampsia

2008 update

Description of included studies

A case–control study in Ireland (2004)[859] [EL = II] investigated whether the presence of fetal DNA in the maternal circulation in early pregnancy might be a marker for the prediction of pre-eclampsia. A total of 264 women (88 cases and 176 controls) were analysed in the study. Blood was obtained from women attending for a first antenatal clinic. Cases were asymptomatic women who subsequently developed pre-eclampsia matched to control women for parity and gestational age. Fetal DNA was quantified by real-time PCR using TaqMan primers and probes directed against SRY gene sequences.

A Hong Kong-based case–control study (2001)[860] [EL = II] aimed to test whether the abnormal increase in circulating DNA concentrations could be detected in susceptible subjects before onset of the clinical disease. A total of 51 women (18 cases and 33 controls) were analysed in this study. The gestational age at testing was 11–22 weeks.

Findings

The Ireland study found that the presence of fetal DNA in the maternal circulation is associated with an eight-fold increased risk of developing pre-eclampsia. In this study, SRY copies/ml < 10 000 gave a sensitivity of 94.32% and specificity of 32.39%. SRY copies/ml < 50 000 gave a sensitivity of 81.82% and specificity 64.77%. SRY copies/ml > 50 000 gave a sensitivity of 38.64% and a specificity of 90.34%.

In the Hong Kong-based study an SRY value of ≥ 33.5 Genome equivalents/ml was found to be significant and this gave a sensitivity of 67% and a specificity of 82%.

β-hCG

A total of three studies were included (Table 11.10).

Description of included studies

A US-based prospective cohort study (1999)[857] [EL = II] evaluated the value of β-hCG as predictor of pregnancy outcomes. Maternal serum markers were analysed over a 5 year period (March 1991 to May 1996) from 60 040 women who underwent serum marker screening at 14–22 weeks of gestation. 45 565 women had maternal serum β-hCG measurements. A value of at least 2.5 MoM was used for calculation.

A US-based case–control study (2000)[861] [EL = II] sought to determine whether second-trimester (15–21 weeks) serum levels of human chorionic gonadotrophin is predictive of the later onset of pre-eclampsia in pregnancy. A total of 359 women (60 cases and 299 controls) were included. Levels of each analyte were compared in women with pre-eclampsia and controls using matched rank analysis.

A prospective cohort study (1997)[862] [EL = II] in the USA investigated the association of elevated second-trimester (15–22 weeks) β-hCG with the subsequent development of hypertension in

Table 11.9 Fetal DNA

Author, year, country, EL, study design	No. of women analysed, inclusion/exclusion criteria, age, gestational age at test	Reference standard used, incidence of PE	Index test cut-off	Results		Comments and conclusion
Cotter (2004)[859] Ireland, EL II, case–control study (nested and matched)	264 (88 cases and 176 controls) IN: normotensive non-proteinuric women, male fetuses EX: aneuploid fetuses 26.1 ± 5.9 years, 15.7 ± 3.6 weeks	BP ≥ 140/90 mmHg; Prot. ≥ 0.3 g/ 24 hours or 1+/2+ dipstick, Incidence n.r.	fDNA Real-time PCR TaqMan SRY < 10 000 copies/ml < 50 000 > 50 000	SRY copies/ml < 10 000: ST 94.32%, SP 32.39%, LR+ 1.39 < 50 000: ST 81.82%, SP 64.77%, LR+ 2.32 > 50 000: ST 38.64%, SP 90.34%, LR+ 4.00		Increased fetal DNA is present in the maternal circulation in early pregnancy in women who subsequently develop pre-eclampsia and there appears to be a graded response between the quantity of fetal DNA and the risk of developing pre-eclampsia.
Leung (2001)[860] Hong Kong, EL II, case–control study (nested and matched)	51 (18 cases and 33 controls), IN: singleton pregnancies, male fetuses Age n.r. 11–22 weeks	DBP ≥ 90 mmHg 2x ≥ 4 hours apart or DBP ≥ 110 mmHg; Prot. ≥ 0.3 g/ 24 hours or 2+ dipstick 2x ≥ 4 hours apart, Incidence n.r.	fDNA Real-time PCR TaqMan SRY ≥ 33.5 Geq/ml	SRY ≥ 33.5 Geq/ml: ST 67%, SP 82% (can't calculate LRs)		Maternal plasma fetal DNA might be used as a marker for predicting pre-eclampsia.

pregnancy and evaluated its utility as a screening test for later development of pre-eclampsia. A total of 6138 women were analysed in the study. A value of 2.0 MoM was used as the cut-off for the index test.

Findings
The first study found a 3% incidence of pre-eclampsia. The sensitivity at 2.5 MoM cut-off was found to be 5.5% and specificity was 96%.

The second study used 2.0 MoM cut-off and found a 3.2% incidence of pre-eclampsia. With 95% specificity, a modelled sensitivity of 15% was found.

The third study found a 3.2% incidence of pre-eclampsia. The sensitivity was 17.5% whereas the specificity was 89.8%.

Urinary calcium excretion

Two studies were included in this section (Table 11.11).

Description of included studies
A US-based prospective longitudinal study (1991)[863] [EL = II] was designed to determine whether an alteration in calcium excretion precedes the signs and symptoms of pre-eclampsia and therefore would be a useful early marker for this disease. A total of 99 women were analysed in this study. The index test was administered at between 10 and 24 weeks of gestation and a value of ≤ 195 mg/24 hours was considered significant.

A UK-based prospective non-interventional study (1994)[864] [EL = II] assessed the potential of urinary calcium/creatinine as screening tests for pregnancy-induced hypertension in a white population. A total of 500 women were included in the study who provided a urine sample at 19 weeks of gestation.

Findings
The American study found am 8.1% incidence of pre-eclampsia. The index cut-off found a sensitivity of 86%, specificity of 84%, PPV of 46% and NPV of 98%.

The UK study found a sensitivity of 31% and a specificity of 72%. The overall incidence of pre-eclampsia was 2.6%.

Calcium/creatinine ratio

A total of four studies were included (Table 11.12).

Table 11.10 β-hCG

Author, year, country, EL, study design	No. of women analysed, inclusion/exclusion criteria, age, gestational age at test	Reference standard used, incidence of PE	Index test cut-off	Results	Comments and conclusion
Yaron (1999)[857] USA, EL II, prospective cohort study	45 565, EX: structural or chromosomal anomalies Age n.r. 14–22 weeks	SBP ≥ 140 mmHg or DBP ≥ 90 mmHg; presence of proteinuria, 3.0%	β-hCG IRMA 2.5 MoM	ST 5.5%, SP 96%	Multiple marker screening can be used for the detection of not only fetal anomalies and aneuploidy but also for detection of high-risk pregnancy
Lambert-Messerlian (2000)[861] USA, EL II, case–control study	359 (60 cases, 299 controls) IN: singleton pregnancies EX: chronic hypertension, diabetes; 26.9 ± 7.3 years 15–21 weeks	BP> 140/90 mmHg; Prot. > 300 mg/24 hours or ≥ 2+ dipstick, 16.7%	Total hCG (Serono MAIO Clone) 2.3 MoM	With 95% SP a modeled ST of 15% (cant calculate LRs)	Second-trimester serum levels of hCG is a modest predictor of later onset pre-eclampsia.
Ashour (1997)[862] USA, EL II, prospective cohort study	6138, IN: singleton pregnancies EX: fetal/ chromosomal abnormalities, diabetes, chronic hypertension 28.1 ± 5.3 years 15–22 weeks	SBP ≥ 140 mmHg or DBP ≥ 90 mmHg 2x 6 hours apart; Prot. > 300 mg/24 hours or ≥ 1+ dipstick 2x 6 hours apart, 3.2%	β-hCG (IMx Abbott) 2.0 MoM	ST 17.5%, SP 89.8%, PPV 5.3%	The utility of an elevated second-trimester β-hCG level as a screening test for pre-eclampsia is limited.

2008 update

Description of included studies

A Hong Kong-based cohort study (1994)[865] [EL = II] attempted to clarify some of the changes that occur in enzyme and electrolyte excretion in pregnancy, before onset of clinical signs, and to relate these changes to the antenatal development of pre-eclampsia or gestational hypertension. A total of 199 women were included and the gestational age at test was in the range 18–26 weeks. A cut-off value of 0.3 was used.

One Argentina-based prospective cohort study (1994)[866] [EL = II] investigated the usefulness of calcium/creatinine ratio and other laboratory tests as predictors in the development of hypertensive disorders of pregnancy. The study included 387 women and the test was administered at 20 weeks of gestation. A value of 0.07 was considered significant.

A prospective cross-sectional study (2003)[867] [EL = II] in Iran determined the relationship between pre-eclampsia and calcium/creatinine ratio. A total of 102 women were included and the test was administered at 20–24 weeks of gestation. A value of ≤ 0.229 was found to be significant.

A UK-based prospective non-interventional study (1994)[864] [EL = II] assessed the potential of urinary calcium/creatinine as screening tests for pregnancy-induced hypertension in a white population. A total of 500 women were included in the study who provided a urine sample at 19 weeks of gestation.

Findings

The Hong Kong study found a sensitivity of 49% and specificity of 90%. The overall incidence was 4%.

The Argentina study found an overall incidence of 3.4%. The study gave a sensitivity of 33%, specificity of 78%, PPV of 5% and NPV of 97%.

The Iran study found an incidence of 7.8%. The test showed a sensitivity of 75%, specificity of 77.7%, PPV of 20.7%, and NPV of 97%.

The UK study reported an incidence of 2.6%. The test sensitivity was 31% and specificity was 55%.

Bilateral uterine artery notching

A total of four studies were included (Table 11.13).

Description of included studies

A multicentre cohort study (2001)[868] [EL = II] conducted in the UK examined the value of transvaginal uterine artery Doppler velocimetry at 23 weeks of gestation in the prediction of pre-eclampsia in singleton pregnancies. A total of 7851 women were analysed at 22–24 weeks of gestation. The presence of an early diastolic notch in the waveform was noted, and the mean pulsatility index of the two arteries was calculated. Screening characteristics in the prediction of pre-eclampsia were calculated.

Table 11.11 Urinary calcium excretion

Author, year, country, EL, study design	No. of women analysed, inclusion/exclusion criteria, age, gestational age at test	Reference standard used, incidence of PE	Index test cut-off	Results	Comments and conclusion
Sanchez-Ramos (1991)[863] USA, EL II, prospective longitudinal study	99, IN: normotensive nulliparas EX: diabetes mellitus, renal disease, chronic hypertension, other chronic medical illnesses 18.7 ± 0.5 years, 10–24 weeks	BP ≥ 140/90 mmHg twice ≥ 6 hours apart or rise SBP ≥ 30 mmHg or DBP ≥ 15 mmHg Prot. ≥ 0.3 g/ 24 hours or ≥ 1+ dipstick, 8.1%	Colorimetric/ colorimetric autoanalyser ≤ 195 mg/24 hours	ST 86%, SP 84%, PPV 46%, NPV 98%	The study suggests a pathophysiologic role for altered urinary calcium excretion in women with pre-eclampsia that may contribute to early identification of patients at risk for the disease.
Baker (1994)[864] UK, EL II, A prospective, non-interventional study	500, IN: normotensive nulliparas EX: renal disease, chronic hypertension Median 27 years (range 24–31), 18–19 weeks	DBP ≥ 90 mmHg twice ≥ 4 hours apart Prot. ≥ 0.3 g/ 24 hours, 2.6%	Perspective analyser (colorimetric)/ Monarch centrifugal analyser (kinetic) n.r.	ST 31%, SP 72% (correctly predicted 71%)	

Table 11.12 Calcium/creatinine ratio

Author, year, country, EL, study design	No. of women analysed, inclusion/exclusion criteria, age, gestational age at test	Reference standard used, incidence of PE	Index test cut-off	Results	Comments and conclusion
Rogers (1994)[865] Hong Kong, EL II, cohort study	199, IN: normotensive primigravidas, singleton pregnancies EX: congenital malformations 27.1 ± 3.8 years, 18–26 weeks	BP ≥ 140/90 mmHg ≥ twice Prot. ≥ 0.3 g/litre, 4.0%	Cresolphtalein method (American Monitor)/ Beckman Astra-8 analyser 0.3	ST 49%, SP 90%	
Conde (1994)[866] Argentina, EL II, prospective cohort study	387 women, IN: normotensive nulliparas, singleton pregnancies EX: diabetes mellitus, renal disease, proteinuria, chronic hypertension, other chronic medical illnesses 23.8 ± 5.7 years, 20 weeks	SBP ≥ 140 or DBP ≥ 90 mmHg twice ≥ 6 hours apart Prot. ≥ 0.3 g/litre, 3.4%	Colorimetric (direct)/ picrato alcalino method 0.07	ST 33%, SP 78%, PPV 5%, NPV 97%	Poor predictive values suggest that changes in the biochemical and haematologic tests occur only when pre-eclampsia has been established.
Kazerooni (2003)[867] Iran, EL II, Prospective cross-sectional study	102, IN: nulliparas (18–35 years) EX: renal disease, diabetes mellitus, proteinuria, chronic hypertension, other chronic medical illnesses 22.8 ± 4.5 years, 20–24 weeks	BP ≥ 140/90 mmHg or rise SBP ≥ 30 mmHg or DBP ≥ 15 mmHg twice ≥ 6 hours apart Prot. ≥ 0.3 g/ 24 hours or ≥ 1+ dipstick, 7.8%	n.r. ≤ 0.001 mmol/litre (0.229 mg/100 ml: mg/100 ml)	ST 75%, SP 77.7%, PPV 20.7%, NPV 97%	Single urine calcium to creatinine ratio may be an effective method for screening women at the greatest risk of pre-eclampsia.
Baker (1994)[864] UK, EL II, A prospective, non-interventional study	500, IN: Normotensive nulliparas EX: renal disease, chronic hypertension Median 27 years (range 24–31), 18–19 weeks	DBP ≥ 90 mmHg twice ≥ 4 hours apart Prot. ≥ 0.3 g/ 24 hours, 2.6%	Perspective analyser (colorimetric)/ Monarch centrifugal analyser (kinetic) n.r.	ST 31%, SP 55% (correctly predicted 71%)	

Table 11.13 Bilateral uterine artery notching

Author, year, country, EL, study design	No. of women analysed, inclusion/exclusion criteria, age, gestational age at test	Reference standard used, incidence of PE	Index test cut-off	Results	Comments and conclusion
Papageorghiou (2001)[868] UK, EL II, cohort study	7851, IN: singleton pregnancies, routine antenatal care. EX: fetal anomalies 29.7 (16–47) years, 22–24 weeks	DBP ≥ 90 mmHg twice > 4 hours apart, prot. ≥ 0.3 g/24 hours or ≥ 2+ dipstick twice if no 24 hour collection available, 1.4%	CD+PW, transvaginal Acuson SP-10, Aloka 5000, Aloka 17000, ATL HDI 3000, ATL Hdi 3500, Hitachi, Toshiba, Siemens	ST 25.4%, SP 90.9%, PPV 2.5%, NPV 99.3% LR+: 8.87 LR−: 0.62	
Harrington (1997)[869] UK, EL II, cohort study	626, IN: singleton pregnancies, unselected 15–49 years, 12–16 weeks	SBP ≥ 140 or DBP ≥ 90 mmHg, prot > 0.3 g/24 hours, 4.8%	CD+PW, transvaginal Acuson 128	ST 92.9%, SP 85.1%, PPV 23.6%, NPV 99.5%	
Marchesoni (2003)[870] UK, EL II, case–control study	895 (177 cases and 718 controls) Unselected women 31.7 ± 5.3 years, 20 weeks, 24 weeks	BP > 140/90 mmHg, prot. > 0.3 g/24 hours, 2.9%	CD Acuson Sequoia	ST 72%, SP 94%, PPV 26%, NPV 99%	
Schwarze (2005)[871] Germany, EL II, prospective study	346 women (19–22 weeks: 215 women) (23–26 weeks-131 women), EX: essential hypertension, diabetes, autoimmune disorders, history of PE, FGR, IUD, placental abruption; multiple pregnancies, fetal anomalies 31.4 (17–46) years, 19–22 weeks, 23–26 weeks	RR ≥ 140/90 mmHg, prot. ≥ 0.3 g/24 hours, no UTI, 4.9%	CD Elegra (Siemens), Acuson 128 XP10	19–22 weeks vs 23–26 weeks ST 40% vs 67%, SP 82% vs 84%, PPV 10% vs 17%, NPV 97% vs 98%	The predictive value of uterine artery Doppler for adverse pregnancy outcome in a low-risk population is of limited diagnostic value. Performing uterine artery Doppler studies at 23–26 weeks of gestation increases the predictive value for adverse pregnancy outcomes.

2008 update

223

A cohort study conducted in the UK (1997)[869] [EL = II] aimed to establish the predictive value of transvaginal uterine artery Doppler studies in early pregnancy for the prediction of pre-eclampsia. A total of 626 women were included and the test was administered at between 12 and 16 weeks of gestation.

A case–control study in the UK (2003)[870] [EL = II] aimed to evaluate the clinical usefulness of the Doppler velocimetry test used to screen pre-eclampsia in the period 2000–2001. A total of 895 women were included and the test was conducted at 20 weeks of gestation and then at 24 weeks.

A prospective study conducted in Germany (2005)[871] [EL = II] examined the use of uterine artery Doppler at 19–22 weeks and 23–26 weeks of gestation in a low-risk population as a screening test for the prediction of pre-eclampsia. A total of 346 women were included.

Findings

The first study found a sensitivity of 25.4%, specificity of 90.9%, PPV of 2.5% and NPV of 99.3%. The overall incidence reported was 1.4%.

The second study reported an incidence of 4.8%. The sensitivity of the test was 92.9%, specificity was 85.1%, PPV was 23.6% and NPV was 99.5%.

An incidence of 2.9% was reported in the third study. The test sensitivity was 72%, specificity 94%, PPV 26% and NPV 99%.

The German study compared the results at 19–22 weeks versus 23–26 weeks of gestation. A sensitivity of 40% versus 67%, specificity of 82% versus 84%, PPV of 10% versus 17% and NPV of 97% versus 98% was reported for the two periods of gestation, respectively.

Integrated Doppler test with serum markers

A total of two studies were identified (Table 11.14).

Description of included studies

A prospective study in Turkey (2005)[872] [EL = II] aimed to analyse the predictive power of maternal serum inhibin A, activin A, hCG, uE$_3$, AFP levels and uterine artery Doppler, either alone or in combination, in the second trimester of pregnancy in screening for pre-eclampsia. A total of 178 women were included in whom serum samples were collected at between 16 and 18 weeks of gestation and Doppler investigation was performed at between 24 and 26 weeks of gestation.

Table 11.14 Integrated Doppler test with serum markers

Author, year, country, EL, study design	No. of women analysed, inclusion/exclusion criteria, age, gestational age at test	Reference standard used, incidence of PE	Index test cut-off	Results	Comments and conclusion
Ay (2005)[872] Turkey, EL II, prospective study	178, EX: multiple pregnancies, hypertension before 26 weeks, diabetes or pregnancy with prenatal and postnatal diagnosis of a chromosomal/ structural abnormality, previous pregnancy complicated by pre-eclampsia, 28.8 ± 5.1 years 30.6 ± 4.3 years, 16–18 weeks 24–26 weeks	BP≥ 140/ 90 mmHg and first diagnosis after 20 weeks, proteinuria ≥ 300 mg/24 hour 7.9%	Two site enzyme immunoassays, immunometric assays, two site chemiluminescent immunometric assay, ultrasound machines	Bilateral notch: ST 85.7%, SP 97.6% Bilateral notch + serum activin: ST 78.6%, SP 100% Bilateral notch+ serum inhibin A: ST 71.4%, SP 100% Bilateral notch or serum activin: ST 100%, SP 86%	Maternal serum inhibin A and activin A levels and uterine artery Doppler appear to be useful screening tests during the second trimester for pre-eclampsia. However, the addition of these hormonal markers to Doppler velocimetry only slightly improves the predictive efficacy.
Audibert (2005)[873] France, EL II, cohort study	2615, EX: multiple pregnancies, without ultrasound between 10–14 weeks, women refered for NT, structural anomalies, chromosomal anomalies, 30.9 ± 4.5 years, 14–18 weeks 18–26 weeks	SBP ≥ 140 mmHg or a DBP ≥ 90 mmHg twice, proteinuria > 0.3 g/24 hour or at least 2+ protein on urine dipstick, Prevalence of PE 1.95%	Amerlite kit,	Bilateral notch: ST 21.56%, SP 95.94% History of pre-eclampsia or bilateral notch or hCG > 2.5 MoM: ST 41.17%, SP 91.61%	Combination of serum markers and abnormal uterine Doppler ultrasound improves the identification of women at risk for subsequent pregnancy complications. The care providers should be encouraged to perform a uterine Doppler ultrasound when serum markers are abnormal. However, the sensitivity of these tests is too low to provide an efficient generalised screening.

2008 update

A cohort study in France (2005)[873] [EL = II] assessed the performance of early screening for pre-eclampsia and fetal growth restriction (FGR) by combining MSS with uterine Doppler ultrasound. A total of 2615 women were analysed in whom both a double test at between 14 and 18 weeks of gestation (by maternal serum AFP and total serum hCG assay) and a uterine Doppler ultrasound at between 18 and 26 weeks were performed.

Findings

The Turkish study found a 7.9% incidence of pre-eclampsia. The presence of a notch on Doppler investigation reported a sensitivity of 85.7% and specificity of 97.6%. The addition of high serum activin to the presence of a notch decreased the sensitivity to 78.6% and increased the specificity to 100%. The addition of high serum inhibin to the presence of a notch decreased the sensitivity to 71.4% and increased the specificity to 100%. The integrated test of presence of a notch or high serum activin increased the sensitivity to 100% and decreased the specificity to 86%.

In the French study, the bilateral notch test reported a sensitivity of 21.6% whereas the specificity was 95.9%. An integrated test-history of pre-eclampsia or bilateral notch or hCG > 2.5 MoM increased the sensitivity to 41.1% and reduced the specificity to 91.6%.

Time interval between pregnancies

Description of included studies

A Norwegian study (2002)[531] [EL = 2+] used a large registry in Norway to evaluate the effects on the risk of pre-eclampsia of both the interbirth interval and a change of partner. A total of 551 478 women who had two or more singleton deliveries and 209 423 women who had three or more singleton deliveries were studied.

A retrospective cross-sectional study from Uruguay (2000)[874] [EL = 3] studied the impact of interpregnancy interval on maternal morbidity and mortality. A total of 456 889 parous women delivering singleton infants were studied.

A Danish cohort study (2001)[875] [EL = 2+] evaluated whether the interpregnancy interval may confound or modify the paternal effect on pre-eclampsia. The outcome of the second birth in a cohort of Danish women with pre-eclampsia in the previous birth (8401 women) and in all women with pre-eclampsia in second (but not first) birth together with a sample of women with two births (26 596 women) was studied.

Findings

The results from the Norwegian study showed that the risk in a second or third pregnancy was directly related to the time elapsed since the previous delivery. The association between risk of pre-eclampsia and interval was more significant than the association between risk and change of partner. When the interval was 10 years or more the risk of pre-eclampsia was about the same as that in nulliparous women. After adjustment for the presence or absence of a change of partner, maternal age and year of delivery, the probability of pre-eclampsia was increased by 1.12 for each year increase in the interval (OR 1.12, 95% CI 1.11 to 1.13).

The Uruguay study showed that women with more than 59 months between pregnancies had significantly increased risks of pre-eclampsia (RR 1.83, 95% CI 1.72 to 1.94) compared with women with intervals of 18–23 months. The authors concluded that interpregnancy intervals below 6 months and above 59 months are associated with an increased risk of adverse maternal outcomes.

The Danish study found that a long interval between pregnancies was associated with a significantly higher risk of pre-eclampsia in a second pregnancy when pre-eclampsia had not been present in the first pregnancy and paternity had not changed.

Blood pressure at booking

Description of included studies

A US-based study (1987)[876] [EL = 2−] reviewed the outpatient charts of all patients with pre-eclampsia who received prenatal care at their clinics during the past 3 years. Thirty patients met

2008 update

2008 update

their criteria for pre-eclampsia and were matched for age, race and parity with normotensive control subjects.

A US-based large clinical trial (1995)[877] [EL = 1+] sought to determine whether any maternal demographic or clinical characteristics are predictive of pre-eclampsia. A total of 2947 healthy women with a single fetus were prospectively followed up from randomisation at 13–27 weeks of gestation to the end of pregnancy.

A population-based nested case–control Norwegian study (2000)[878] [EL = 2+] studied the associations between established risk factors for pre-eclampsia and different clinical manifestations of the disease. A total of 323 cases of pre-eclampsia and 650 healthy controls were selected.

A US-based retrospective cohort study (2000)[530] [EL = 2−] was undertaken to develop a clinical prediction rule for severe pre-eclampsia that was based on clinical risk factors and biochemical factors. Cases with severe pre-eclampsia were compared with control subjects with respect to clinical data and multiple-marker screening test results. Women were assigned a predictive score according to the presence or absence of predictive factors.

Findings
The first study found that both systolic and diastolic blood pressures were significantly higher ($P < 0.05$) in the first trimester for women with pre-eclampsia than for normal control subjects beginning in the first trimester. This difference persisted throughout pregnancy and was also present at the 6 week postpartum visit ($P < 0.025$).

The second study showed that higher systolic and diastolic blood pressures at the first visit were associated with an increased incidence of pre-eclampsia (3.8% in women with diastolic blood pressure of < 55 mmHg, 7.4% in those with diastolic blood pressure 70–84 mmHg). However, their recruitment was limited to women with a first blood pressure reading of ≤ 135/85 mmHg.

The third Norwegian study found that a systolic blood pressure ≥ 130 mmHg compared with < 110 mmHg at the first visit before 18 weeks was significantly associated with the development of pre-eclampsia later in pregnancy (adjusted OR 3.6, 95% CI 2.0 to 6.6). The association with a diastolic pressure ≥ 80 mmHg compared with < 60 mmHg was similar but not significant (adjusted OR 1.8, 95% CI 0.7 to 4.6).

The fourth study results showed that the only variables that remained significantly associated with severe pre-eclampsia were nulliparity (RR 3.8, 95% CI 1.7 to 8.3), history of pre-eclampsia (RR 5.0, 95% CI 1.7 to 17.2), elevated screening mean arterial pressure (RR 3.5, 95% CI 1.7 to 7.2), and low unconjugated estriol concentration (RR 1.7, 95% CI 0.9 to 3.4). This predictive model for severe pre-eclampsia, which included only these four variables, had a sensitivity of 76% and a specificity of 46%.

Proteinuria

Description of included studies
A US-based retrospective study (1992)[879] [EL = 2−] evaluated varying degrees of chronic proteinuria as a predictor of pregnancy outcome. Their purpose was to determine the significance of otherwise 'asymptomatic' proteinuria identified during pregnancy. Perinatal outcomes of 65 pregnancies in 53 women with the following criteria were studied: proteinuria exceeding 500 mg per day, no previously known renal disease, no reversible renal dysfunction, and no evidence for pre-eclampsia at discovery.

Findings
The results showed that 58% of the women with proteinuria combined with renal insufficiency developed pre-eclampsia. 100% of women with proteinuria combined with chronic hypertension developed pre-eclampsia whereas 77% of women with with all three together developed pre-eclampsia.

Evidence summary for Section 11.2
Given the quality, level and precision of the evidence, no single test has emerged as a front runner in the quest to predict and prevent pre-eclampsia. Tests that offer high specificity, such

as AFP, β-hCG and uterine artery Doppler (bilateral notching), have the potential to minimise unwarranted inconvenience, expense and morbidity associated with false positive results. There is evidence to show that when the interval between two pregnancies is 10 years or more the risk of pre-eclampsia is about the same as that in nulliparous women.

GDG interpretation of evidence

None of the current screening tests offer a high enough diagnostic value, all being EL II, to be used in routine care. In addition, the purpose of screening for pre-eclampsia is only to identify those women who require additional care since there is no effective intervention. However, the following risk factors for the development of pre-eclampsia should be noted:

- age 40 years or over
- nulliparity
- pregnancy interval of more than 10 years
- family history of pre-eclampsia
- previous history of pre-eclampsia
- BMI of 30 kg/m² or over
- pre-existing vascular disease such as hypertension
- pre-existing renal disease
- multiple pregnancy.

The routine measurement of blood pressure and of proteinuria should be undertaken on the schedule outlined in the algorithm.

Recommendations on screening for pre-eclampsia

Blood pressure measurement and urinalysis for protein should be carried out at each antenatal visit to screen for pre-eclampsia.

At the booking appointment, the following risk factors for pre-eclampsia should be determined:

- age 40 years or older
- nulliparity
- pregnancy interval of more than 10 years
- family history of pre-eclampsia
- previous history of pre-eclampsia
- body mass index 30 kg/m² or above
- pre-existing vascular disease such as hypertension
- pre-existing renal disease
- multiple pregnancy.

More frequent blood pressure measurements should be considered for pregnant women who have any of the above risk factors.

The presence of significant hypertension and/or proteinuria should alert the healthcare professional to the need for increased surveillance.

Blood pressure should be measured as outlined below:

- remove tight clothing, ensure arm is relaxed and supported at heart level
- use cuff of appropriate size
- inflate cuff to 20–30 mmHg above palpated systolic blood pressure
- lower column slowly, by 2 mmHg per second or per beat
- read blood pressure to the nearest 2 mmHg
- measure diastolic blood pressure as disappearance of sounds (phase V).

Hypertension in which there is a single diastolic blood pressure of 110 mmHg or two consecutive readings of 90 mmHg at least 4 hours apart and/or significant proteinuria (1+) should prompt increased surveillance.

If the systolic blood pressure is above 160 mmHg on two consecutive readings at least 4 hours apart, treatment should be considered.

2008 update

All pregnant women should be made aware of the need to seek immediate advice from a healthcare professional if they experience symptoms of pre-eclampsia. Symptoms include:

- severe headache
- problems with vision, such as blurring or flashing before the eyes
- severe pain just below the ribs
- vomiting
- sudden swelling of the face, hands or feet.

Although there is a great deal of material published on alternative screening methods for pre-eclampsia, none of these has satisfactory sensitivity and specificity, and therefore they are not recommended.

Research recommendation on screening for pre-eclampsia

Further research using large prospective studies should be conducted into the effectiveness and cost-effectiveness of using alpha-fetoprotein, beta-human chorionic gonadotrophin, fetal DNA in maternal blood and uterine artery Dopplers, or potentially a combination of these, to detect women at risk of developing pre-eclampsia. Testing should focus particularly on the prediction of early-onset pre-eclampsia, with priority given to blood tests.

11.3   Preterm birth

Clinical question
What is the diagnostic value of the following screening methods in identifying women at risk of preterm labour?

- history
- vaginal examinations
- ulrasound scan – cervical length up to 22 weeks of pregnancy
- oral health/dental health
- swabs for bacterial vaginosis.

Previous NICE guidance (for the updated recommendations see below)
Routine vaginal examination to assess the cervix is not an effective method of predicting preterm birth and should not be offered. [A]

Although cervical shortening identified by transvaginal sonography (TVS) and increased levels of fetal fibronectin (FFN) are associated with an increased risk of preterm birth, the evidence does not indicate that this information improves outcomes; therefore neither TVS nor FFN should be used to predict preterm birth in healthy pregnant women. [B]

11.3.1   Introduction and background information

In the UK approximately 7% of births occur prior to 36 completed weeks of gestation and 1.4% prior to 31 completed weeks (figures for England, NHS Maternity Statistics 2003–2004). According to CEMACH, more than 70% of all neonatal deaths occur in preterm babies, that is, birth of a baby before 37 weeks of completed gestational age (Perinatal mortality surveillance, 2004, England, Wales and Northern Ireland, CEMACH, www.cemach.org.uk/publications. aspx). It is an important cause of major and minor morbidity such as necrotising enterocolitis, bronchopulmonary dysplasia, intraventricular haemorrhage, cerebral palsy and cognitive impairment during the early years of life. Even after infancy, these babies are at increased risk of developing chronic diseases in adult life.

Forty-four papers from 38 studies have been included in this review for evaluating diagnostic accuracy of the following twelve screening tests:

1. previous history of spontaneous preterm birth (SPTB)
2. clinical/digital examination
3. cervico-vaginal fetal fibronectin (FFN) levels

4. cervico-vaginal interleukin-6 (IL-6) levels
5. cervico-vaginal interleukin-8 (IL-8) levels
6. maternal serum alpha-fetoprotein (MSAFP) levels
7. maternal serum beta-human chorionic gonadotrophin (MSHCG) levels
8. maternal serum C-reactive protein (CRP) levels
9. asymptomatic bacteriuria
10. bacterial vaginosis (BV)
11. transvaginal sonography (TVS) for cervical length
12. transvaginal sonography for funnelling of cervix.

Most of the studies included for this review are prospective cohort studies. High-quality studies with EL 1 were identified and included for evaluating diagnostic accuracy of the following screening tests: previous history of SPTB, cervico-vaginal FFN levels, BV using Nugent's criteria for Gram staining, and TVS for cervical length and funnelling. For other screening tests, the evidence level of included studies was predominantly 2 or 3 owing to two main reasons: absence of blinding and/or study population not being representative of the reference population. Only studies conducted on asymptomatic women (with no signs and symptoms of preterm labour) were considered for this review. Since most of the studies identified for cervico-vaginal IL-6 and IL-8 and serum CRP tests were conducted in symptomatic women (with threatened preterm labour), only a few quality studies remained for these tests for asymptomatic women.

Details of the screening tests including timing, frequency and thresholds have been specified where possible. The outcome assessed was spontaneous preterm delivery at less than 37 weeks (SPTB < 37 weeks), and efforts were made to calculate the diagnostic value of the tests after excluding cases of induced preterm delivery (PTD). Many studies had evaluated screening performance of various tests for outcome with different gestational age (for example < 32, 33 or 35 weeks), but for the sake of comparison results have been provided for commonly used thresholds and SPTB < 37 weeks as the outcome. Wherever possible, the incidence of SPTB and prevalence of test positive have also been calculated.

Studies included in the review of each screening test have been tabulated in decreasing order of their evidence level. In case of those with similar evidence levels, priority is given to the study with a larger sample size.

11.3.2 History of previous spontaneous preterm birth (SPTB)

Description of included studies
Three studies were included – two prospective cohort [EL = Ib] and one retrospective cohort. [EL = II] All were multicentre studies with good sample sizes. Although the thresholds of the screening tests were different in these studies and outcomes other than SPTB < 37 weeks were also evaluated, the results have been given for history of previous SPTB > 20 weeks as the screening test and outcome SPTB < 37 weeks only (Table 11.15).

Findings
In the three studies sensitivity and specificity ranged from 19% to 67% and 73% to 97%, respectively. The test had high LR+ of 5.78 (95% CI 4.47 to 7.46) in one study,[882] but LR– was 0.84 (95% CI 0.80 to 0.89) and it was a study with EL 2. For the studies with EL 1, values of LR+ ranged from 2.26 to 2.74 and LR– from 0.45 to 0.77. On meta-analysis, significant statistical heterogeneity ($P < 0.00001$) was observed for both the positive and negative LR. The summary LR+ was 2.83 (95% CI 2.53 to 3.16) and summary LR– was 0.76 (95% CI 0.72 to 0.80) (Figure 11.1).

Evidence summary
Evidence indicates that history of previous SPTB does not seem to have high diagnostic value in predicting and ruling out SPTB in the current pregnancy.

11.3.3 Clinical examination

Description of included studies
Five prospective cohort studies were included – one with EL Ib and four with EL II, the reason being absence of blinding in these studies. In the study with EL Ib, Bishop score was used for

2008 update

2008 update

Table 11.15 Characteristics of included studies on diagnostic value of maternal history of previous SPTB

Study and EL	Study characteristics	Population characteristics	Sample size (% of study population)	Timing of screening test with threshold (prevalence of test positive)	Outcome in weeks (incidence of SPTB)	Diagnostic value with 95% CI
Goldenberg (1998)[880] (USA) EL 1b	Prospective cohort, multicentre.	Singleton pregnancies. *Exclusions*: multiple gestations, cervical cerclage, placenta previa, major fetal anomaly.	1711 (58.4% – rest were primiparas)	History of previous SPTB (20–37 weeks) at 22–24 weeks visit (21.2% in study population)	< 32, < 35, and < 37 (11.9% at < 37)	For SPTB < 37 weeks: ST 0.42 (0.35–0.49), SP 0.82 (0.80–0.83)
Iams (1998)[881] (USA) EL lb	Prospective cohort, multicentre.	Singleton pregnancies. (secondary analysis of data from Goldenberg study to measure risk of recurrent SPTB – lower limit of gest. age for SPTB reduced from 20 to 18 weeks)	1282	History of previous SPTB at 18–26, 27–31, and 32–36 weeks.	History of previous SPTB < 35	History of previous SPTB at 27–31 weeks: ST 0.33 (0.23–0.44), SP 0.88 (0.86–0.89) History of previous SPTB at 32–36 weeks: ST 0.67 (0.56–0.77), SP 0.73 (0.70–0.76)
Kristensen (1995)[882] (Denmark) EL II	Retrospective cohort, multicentre. (records from National Health Registers used	All women with permanent address in Denmark who gave birth to their first singleton infant in 1982 and a second in 1982–87	13 967 (99.5%)	History of previous SPTB at < 37 weeks (3.5% in study population)	History of previous SPTB < 37 (2.2% – SPTB, 3.5% all PTD)	For SPTB < 37 weeks: ST 0.19 (0.14–0.23), SP 0.97 (0.96–0.97)

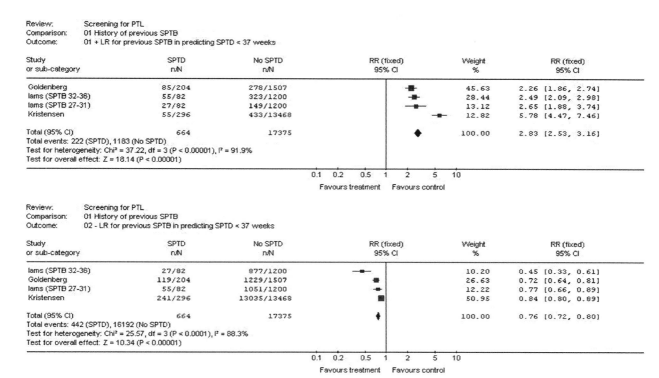

Figure 11.1 Likelihood ratios for history of previous SPTB for screening for preterm birth

screening and clinical examination carried out four times in each woman. In studies with EL II, difference was observed in the frequency, timing and threshold of the screening test used. Owing to existing heterogeneity, meta-analysis was not performed. Values for positive and negative LR have been presented separately for the two most commonly used signs at clinical examination – cervical dilatation (in four studies) and short cervix (in two studies) (Table 11.16).

Findings

For cervical dilatation, sensitivity and specificity ranged from 13% to 57% and 57% to 98%, respectively. The study by Leveno et al.[887] had a high LR+ of 9.25 (95% CI 3.91 to 21.85), but LR− was 0.46 (95% CI 0.19 to 1.08). Chambers et al.[885] had moderate values for LR+ and LR− of 2.16 and 0.76, respectively. LRs for the other two studies were not as good as those of the two studies just mentioned (Figure 11.2).

Sensitivity for a short cervix diagnosed clinically ranged from 11% to 21% and specificity from 89% to 95%. Chambers et al.[885] had a better LR− of 0.88 (95% CI 0.81 to 0.97) among the included studies, but LR+ was 1.96 (95% CI 1.41 to 2.74) (Figure 11.3).

Evidence summary

A wide variation in results of screening accuracy is observed for different clinical methods for predicting SPTB. Evidence shows that clinical examination has poor diagnostic value in predicting and ruling out SPTB.

11.3.4 Cervico-vaginal fetal fibronectin levels

Description of included studies

The six studies concerning this test were prospective cohort studies and blinding was specified in all. In two EL II studies the dropout rate was more than 40% while the rest were classified EL Ib. The population was low-risk singleton pregnancies in all studies. A single swab in the second trimester at different gestational ages was taken usually from the posterior vaginal fornix, and the threshold used for a positive test was FFN levels ≥ 50 ng/ml. Meta-analysis was performed for

2008 update

Table 11.16 Characteristics of included studies on diagnostic value of vaginal digital examination

Study and EL	Study characteristics	Population characteristics (low risk or high risk)	Sample size (% of study population)	Timing and frequency of screening test (with threshold)	Outcome in wks (incidence of SPTB)	Diagnostic value with 95% CI
Iams (2001)[883] (USA) EL Ib	Prospective cohort, multicentre, blinded	Nulliparous women and multiparous with no history of previous SPTB or abortion. (low risk)	2107 (71.9%)	Digital examination 4 times before 35 weeks (Bishop score≥ 4)	< 35 (3.0% in sample population)	ST 0.23 (O.13–0.33), SP 0.93 (0.91–0.94)
Blondel (1990)[884] (France) EL II	Prospective cohort, in 2 centres, not blinded	Singleton pregnancies attending two outpatient clinics (both low and high risk)	6909 (90.4%) nulliparous 4025 and parous 2884	Clinical examination at 25–28 and 29–31 weeks for 5 signs – (1 cm internal os dilatation, short cervix ≤ 1 cm, mid position of cervix, soft or firm cervix, expansion of lower uterine segment)	< 37 (For nullipara at 25–28 weeks 5.0%, 29–31 weeks 4.4%. For multipara at 25–28 weeks 5.3%, 29–31 weeks 4.1%)	*Examination at 25–28 weeks:* 1) Cervical dilatation: ST nulli – 0.13 (0.08–0.19) ST multi – 0.15 (0.09–0.23), SP nulli – 0.98 (0.98–0.99), SP multi – 0.97 (0.96–0.98) 2) Short cervix: ST nulli – 0.14 (0.09–0.20) ST multi – 0.11 (0.06–0.17), SP nulli – 0.95 (0.94–0.96), SP multi – 0.95 (0.94–0.96)
Chambers (1990)[885] (France) EL II	Prospective cohort, in 2 centres, not blinded	Pregnant women with at least 2 visits at < 28 weeks (both low and high risk)	5758 (study population not specified)	Once in 2 weeks (Length ≤ 1 cm before 28 weeks for short cervix, dilatation ≥ 1 cm before 37 weeks for open cervix)	< 37 (4.04%)	For cervical dilatation: ST 0.37 (0.30–0.45), SP 0.83 (0.82–0.84) For short cervix: ST 0.21 (0.15–0.28), SP 0.89 (0.88–0.90)
Parikh (1961)[886] (India) EL II	Prospective cohort, single centre, not blinded	Singleton pregnancies attending antenatal clinic of a government hospital (both low and high risk)	463 (70.7%)	Twice / week at 21–36 weeks (admit digit at internal os for cervical dilatation)	< 37 (12.3% in sample population)	ST 0.49 (0.36–0.63), SP 0.57 (0.52–0.62)
Leveno (1986)[887] (USA) EL II	Prospective cohort, single centre, blinded	Consecutively enrolled singleton pregnancies (low risk)	185 (no exclusions specified)	Single examination at 26–30 weeks. (> 2cm dilated)	< 37 (3.8% in sample population)	ST 0.57 (0.18–0.90), SP 0.94 (0.89–0.98)

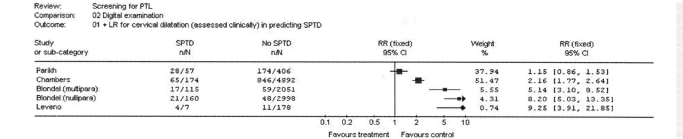

Review: Screening for PTL
Comparison: 02 Digital examination
Outcome: 01 + LR for cervical dilatation (assessed clinically) in predicting SPTD

Study or sub-category	SPTD n/N	No SPTD n/N	RR (fixed) 95% CI	Weight %	RR (fixed) 95% CI
Parikh	28/57	174/406		37.94	1.15 [0.86, 1.53]
Chambers	65/174	846/4892		51.47	2.16 [1.77, 2.64]
Blondel (multipara)	17/115	59/2051		5.55	5.14 [3.10, 8.52]
Blondel (nullipara)	21/160	48/2998		4.31	8.20 [5.03, 13.35]
Leveno	4/7	11/178		0.74	9.25 [3.91, 21.85]

0.1 0.2 0.5 1 2 5 10
Favours treatment   Favours control

Review: Screening for PTL
Comparison: 02 Digital examination
Outcome: 02 - LR for cervical dilatation (assessed clinically) in predicting SPTD

Study or sub-category	SPTD n/N	No SPTD n/N	RR (fixed) 95% CI	Weight %	RR (fixed) 95% CI
Leveno	3/7	167/178		1.47	0.46 [0.19, 1.08]
Chambers	109/174	4046/4892		32.39	0.76 [0.67, 0.85]
Blondel (nullipara)	139/160	2950/2998		34.83	0.88 [0.83, 0.94]
Blondel (multipara)	98/115	1992/2051		24.65	0.88 [0.81, 0.95]
Parikh	29/57	232/406		6.66	0.89 [0.68, 1.16]

0.1 0.2 0.5 1 2 5 10
Favours treatment   Favours control

Figure 11.2   Likelihood ratios for cervical dilatation for screening for preterm birth

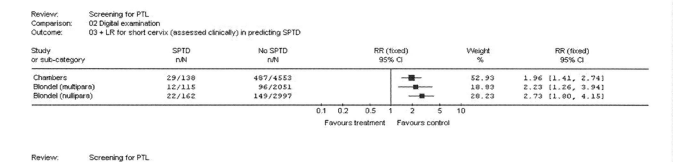

Review: Screening for PTL
Comparison: 02 Digital examination
Outcome: 03 + LR for short cervix (assessed clinically) in predicting SPTD

Study or sub-category	SPTD n/N	No SPTD n/N	RR (fixed) 95% CI	Weight %	RR (fixed) 95% CI
Chambers	29/138	487/4553		52.93	1.96 [1.41, 2.74]
Blondel (multipara)	12/115	96/2051		18.83	2.23 [1.26, 3.94]
Blondel (nullipara)	22/162	149/2997		28.23	2.73 [1.80, 4.15]

0.1 0.2 0.5 1 2 5 10
Favours treatment   Favours control

Review: Screening for PTL
Comparison: 02 Digital examination
Outcome: 04 - LR for short cervix (assessed clinically) in predicting SPTD

Study or sub-category	SPTD n/N	No SPTD n/N	RR (fixed) 95% CI	Weight %	RR (fixed) 95% CI
Chambers	109/138	4046/4533		32.36	0.88 [0.81, 0.97]
Blondel (nullipara)	140/162	2848/2997		39.54	0.91 [0.86, 0.97]
Blondel (multipara)	103/115	1955/2051		28.10	0.94 [0.88, 1.00]

0.1 0.2 0.5 1 2 5 10
Favours treatment   Favours control

Figure 11.3   Likelihood ratios for length of cervix for screening for preterm birth

the predictive accuracy of a single test in the second trimester with outcome SPTB < 37 weeks. One good-quality study was excluded from meta-analysis as it evaluated SPTB < 33 weeks as the outcome (Table 11.17).

Findings
Sensitivity ranged from 13% to 55% and specificity from 83% to 99% for the test in predicting SPTB < 37 weeks. In the study that used < 33 weeks as the time for the outcome, sensitivity and specificity were 33% and 97%, respectively.

For the individual studies, LR+ ranged from 2.19 (95% CI 1.08 to 4.47) to as high as 18.00 (95% CI 3.21 to 100.86), and LR− from 0.92 (95% CI 0.83 to 1.02) to a low of 0.53 (95% CI 0.26

Table 11.17 Characteristics of included studies on diagnostic value of cervico-vaginal fetal fibronectin levels

Study and EL	Study characteristics	Population characteristics (low or high risk)	Sample size (% of study population)	Timing of screening test with threshold (prevalence of test positive)	Outcome in weeks (incidence of SPTB)	Diagnostic value with 95% CI
Heath (2000)[888] (UK) EL Ib	Prospective cohort, single fetal medicine unit, blinded.	Singleton pregnancies for routine anomaly US scan at 23 weeks. *Exclusions:* multiple gestations, fetal anomaly, cervical cerclage, previous SPTB < 33 weeks (low risk)	5058 (98.5%)	Single swab from posterior fornix at 22–24 weeks, threshold ≥ 50 ng/ml. (3.5% in sample population)	< 33 (0.85% in sample population)	ST 0.33 (0.20–0.49), SP 0.97 (0.96–0.97)
Goldenberg (1998)[880] (USA) EL Ib	Prospective cohort, multicentre, blinded.	Singleton pregnancies. *Exclusions:* multiple gestations, cervical cerclage, placenta praevia, fetal anomaly. (low risk)	2929 (95.3%)	Single swab from posterior fornix at 24–26 weeks, threshold ≥ 50 ng/ml. (6.6% in sample population)	< 35 (4.4%) < 37 (10.3%)	For SPTB < 37 weeks: ST 0.19 (0.14–0.23), SP 0.95 (0.94–0.95)
Chang (1997)[889] (Singapore) EL Ib	Prospective cohort, single centre, blinded.	Singleton pregnancies with no risk factor for PTL. *Exclusions:* active vaginal bleeding, uncertain gestational age, hypertensive disease, PROM (low risk)	234 (97.5%)	Single swab from posterior fornix at 22–25 weeks, threshold ≥ 50 ng/ml. (2.1% in sample population)	< 34 (2.4%) < 37 (7.7%)	For SPTB < 37 weeks: ST 0.17 (0.04–0.41), SP 0.99 (0.97–1.00)
Faron (1997)[890] (Belgium) EL Ib	Prospective cohort, single centre, blinded	Pregnant women attending ANC for routine care with known gestation *Exclusions:* vaginal bleeding (low risk)	155 (91.2%)	Single swab from endocervix at 24–33 weeks, threshold ≥ 50 ng/ml. (6.5% in sample population)	< 37 (9.7% in sample population)	ST 0.27 (0.04–0.49), SP 0.96 (0.92–1.00)
Daskalakis (2006)[891] (Greece) EL II	Prospective cohort, single centre, blinded	Singleton pregnancies having anomaly scan at 22–25 weeks *Exclusions:* previous SPTB, multiple gestation, placenta praevia, fetal anomalies, cervical incompetence or cerclage (low risk)	718 (55.8%)	Single swab from posterior fornix at 22–25 weeks, threshold ≥ 50 ng/ml. (6.7% in sample population)	< 37 (8.3% in study population)	ST 0.13 (0.05–0.23), SP 0.94 (0.92–0.96)
Crane (1999)[892] (Canada) EL II	Prospective cohort, single centre, blinded	Singleton pregnancies at 20–24 weeks *Exclusions:* ruptured membrane, placenta praevia, active bleeding, multiple gestations, cervical cerclage, fetal anomalies (low risk)	140 (59.7%)	Swabs from both posterior fornix and cervix at 20–24 weeks, threshold ≥ 50 ng/ml. (19.2% for vaginal FFN, 25% for cervical FFN)	< 37 (6.4% in study population)	For vaginal FFN: ST 0.55 (0.24–0.84), SP 0.83 (0.76–0.89)

to 1.11). The study with the highest LR+ (Chang et al.[889]) had an LR– of 0.84, but the confidence interval (CI) crossed unity. Similarly, Crane et al.[892] had the best value for LR– but again the CI crossed unity.

No statistically significant heterogeneity was observed for either LR+ and LR– on performing meta-analysis. The summary LR values for a positive test was 3.53 (95% CI 2.78 to 4.49) and for the negative test was 0.86 (95% CI 0.82 to 0.90) (Figure 11.4).

Evidence summary
There is high-quality evidence to show that a single second-trimester cervico-vaginal swab with a positive result for fibronectin levels has moderate value in predicting SPTB < 37 weeks, but a negative result decreases the probability of SPTB only minimally.

11.3.5   Cervico-vaginal IL-6 levels

Description of included studies
There were three studies included for this test, all with EL II – a prospective cohort study and two nested case–control studies. All had a small sample size. The timing and frequency of screening tests, thresholds used for a positive test, and outcomes assessed were different in all the three studies. Meta-analysis was not conducted and results have been presented separately for each study (Table 11.18).

Findings
In the three studies, sensitivity ranged from 9% to 50% while specificity ranged from 84% to 90%. Best values for the LRs were obtained for the prospective cohort study (Lockwood et al.[893]). For the threshold > 250 pg/ml, it showed an LR+ of 3.34 (95% CI 1.96 to 5.70) and LR– of 0.59 (95% CI 0.42 to 0.83). Results from the other prospective cohort study (Inglis et al.[894]) were in complete contrast. Values obtained in the study for LR+ and LR– were poor: 0.56 (95% CI 0.08

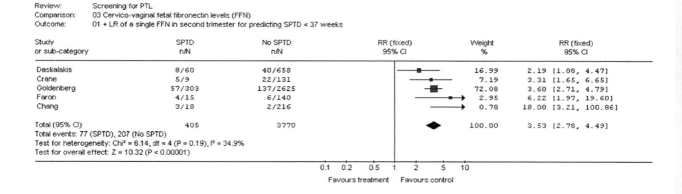

Figure 11.4   Likelihood ratios for fetal fibronectin for screening for preterm birth

2008 update

Table 11.18 Characteristics of included studies on diagnostic value of cervico-vaginal IL-6 levels

Study and EL	Study characteristics	Population characteristics (low or high risk)	Sample size (% of study population)	Timing of screening test with threshold (prevalence of test positive)	Outcome in weeks (incidence of SPTB)	Diagnostic value with 95% CI
Lockwood (1994)[893] (USA) EL II	Nested case–control, single centre, blinded	Pregnant women attending single obstetric clinic *Exclusions*: placenta praevia, unknown dates, hydatidiform mole, major congenital anomaly, serious maternal complications.	161 (not specified)	Serial testing every 3–4 weeks from 24–36 weeks Threshold 125 and 250 pg/ml from ROC curve.	< 37 (26.8% in sample population)	For threshold > 250 pg/ml at 24–36 weeks: ST 0.50 (0.33–0.67), SP 0.85 (0.79–0.91)
Inglis (1994)[894] (USA) EL III	Prospective cohort, single centre, blinded	Singleton pregnancies (15 to 40 years) at < 37 weeks with intact membranes. *Exclusions*: congenital anomalies, placenta praevia, known genital or urinary infection, use of antibiotics within 7 days prior to entry to study. (low risk)	73 (65.8%) after excluding women with threatened preterm labour.	Single test at 20–36 weeks, Threshold 50 pg/ml. (15.06% in sample population)	< 37 (16.4% in sample population)	ST 0.09 (0.00–0.41), SP 0.84 (0.72–0.92)
Goepfert (2001)[895] (USA) EL III	Retrospective case–control nested within a multicentre cohort study, blinded	*Cases*: women with SPTB < 35 weeks and cervical specimen available for IL-6 assay. *Controls*: women with term deliveries pregnancies matched for race, parity and centre.	250 (cases 125, controls 125)	Single test at 22–24 weeks. Threshold 305 pg/ml	< 32 < 35	For SPTB < 35 weeks: ST 0.20 (0.13–0.28), SP 0.90 (0.84–0.95)

to 3.97) for LR+ and 1.08 (95% CI 0.87 to 1.35) for the LR−. In the nested case–control study, LR for a positive test was 2.08 (95% CI 1.10 to 3.96) and for a negative test was 0.88 (95% CI 0.80 to 0.98) (Figure 11.5).

Evidence summary

Although studies on diagnostic performance of cervico-vaginal IL-6 levels in asymptomatic women are limited, the available evidence shows that it has poor screening accuracy for SPTB.

11.3.6 Cervico-vaginal IL-8 levels

Description of included studies

Two prospective cohorts were included – both with EL II and carried out by the same principal author in Japan. Blinding was not specified in either study. In the study with a bigger sample size, IL-8 was measured serially in the cervico-vaginal fluid – initially once at 20–23 weeks and then biweekly at 24–28 weeks. The threshold for a positive test was also different in the two studies. Owing to heterogeneity of the test timing, frequency and threshold values, meta-analysis was not performed (Table 11.19).

Findings

The larger study with serial testing showed sensitivity and specificity of 27% and 80%, respectively. It had an LR+ of 1.38 (95% CI 1.04 to 1.82) and LR− of 0.91 (95% CI 0.82 to 1.01) for predicting SPTB < 37 weeks. Another study with a smaller sample size showed better results for all values. Sensitivity was 42%, specificity 85%, LR+ 2.75 (95% CI 1.68 to 4.52) and LR− 0.67 (95% CI 0.30 to 1.15). In both studies, the confidence interval for the LR− crossed unity (Figure 11.6).

Evidence summary

Although the evidence is limited, it shows that the likelihood of SPTB < 37 weeks is increased minimally with a positive test for cervico-vaginal IL-8 levels.

11.3.7 Maternal serum alpha-fetoprotein (MSAFP) levels

Description of included studies

Three prospective cohort studies were included for this test but there was no blinding in two studies [EL = II] where retrospective analysis of data was done. In all studies, the screening test was performed at 15–20 weeks as part of routine screening for Down's syndrome and NTD. AFP levels ≥ 2.0 MoM was the threshold used in two studies. In two studies outcome was defined as

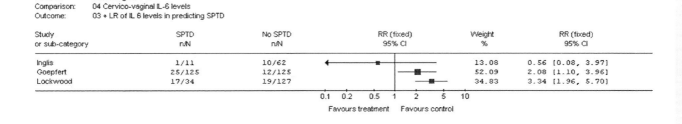

Figure 11.5 Likelihood ratios for cervico-vaginal IL-6 levels for screening for preterm birth

2008 update

2008 update

Table 11.19 Characteristics of included studies on diagnostic value of cervico-vaginal IL-8 levels

Study and EL	Study characteristics	Population characteristics (low or high risk)	Sample size (% of study population)	Timing and site of screening test with threshold	Outcome in weeks (incidence of SPTB)	Diagnostic value with 95% CI
Sakai (2004)[896] (Japan) EL II	Prospective cohort, multicentre, not blinded.	Singleton pregnancies *Exclusions*: preterm labour at < 20 weeks, PROM, genital bleeding, abruptio placentae, placenta praevia, pre-eclampsia, fetal anomalies.	4203 (95.4%)	Serial testing – once a month in 20–23 weeks and then once biweekly in 24–28 weeks. Threshold 360 ng/ml (IL-8 positivity once in 19.1%)	< 32 (0.43%) < 34 (0.64%) 37 (3.3%)	*For SPTB < 37 weeks* ST 0.27 (0.20–0.36), SP 0.80 (0.79–0.81)
Sakai (2004)[897] (Japan) EL II	Prospective cohort, single centre, not blinded.	Singleton pregnancies *Exclusions*: preterm births caused by fetal asphyxia, abruptio placentae, placenta praevia, pre-eclampsia.	501 (study population not specified)	Single test at 20–24 weeks. (377 ng/ml)	< 37 (5.2% in sample population)	ST 0.42 (0.23–0.63), SP 0.85 (0.81–0.88)

SPTB < 37 weeks while the third looked at SPTB < 32 weeks. As studies had different thresholds and outcome, they were not combined and the results are presented individually (Table 11.20).

Findings

The range of sensitivity was from 2% to 19% and for specificity from 80% to 99%. The study with the highest level of evidence had poor values for both LR+ (0.97 (95% CI 0.51 to 1.85)) and LR– (1.01 (95% CI 0.86 to 1.17)). The study by Dugoff *et al.*[899] had a high LR+ of 6.80 (95% CI 4.75 to 9.74) but the LR– was only 0.91 (95% CI 0.87 to 0.95) for outcome SPTB < 32 weeks (Figure 11.7).

Evidence summary

Positive and negative results of MSAFP at 15–20 weeks seem to have poor predictive accuracy for SPTB, although the evidence is limited.

11.3.8 Maternal serum beta-human chorionic gonadotrophin (MSHCG) levels

Description of included studies

The three studies included were prospective cohort studies [EL = II] without blinding. Data were analysed retrospectively in two studies. In two studies the screening test was performed in the first

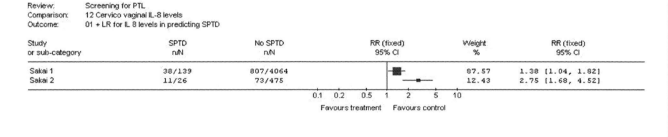

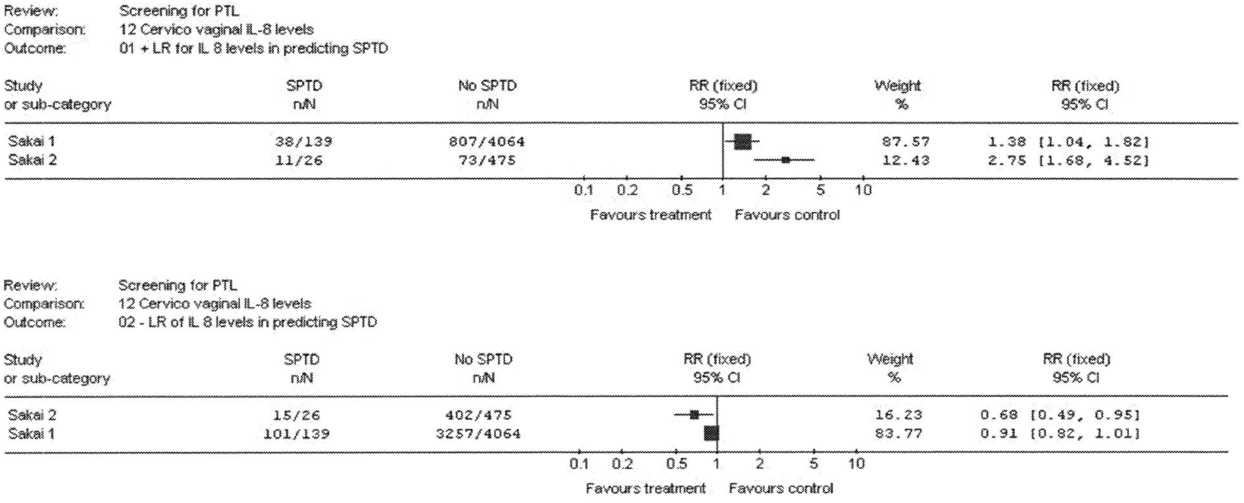

Figure 11.6 Likelihood ratios for cervico-vaginal IL-8 levels for screening for preterm birth

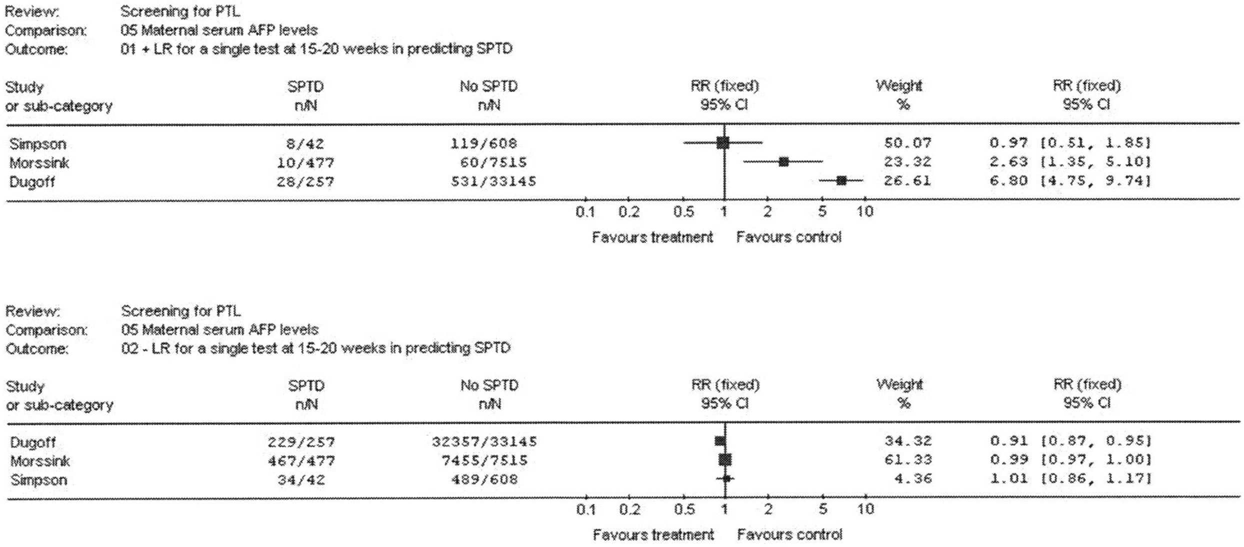

Figure 11.7 Likelihood ratios for maternal serum alpha-fetoprotein levels for screening for preterm birth

2008 update

Table 11.20 Characteristics of included studies on diagnostic value of maternal serum AFP levels

Study and EL	Study characteristics	Population characteristics (low or high risk)	Sample size (% of study population)	Timing of screening test with threshold (prevalence of test positive)	Outcome in weeks (incidence of SPTB)	Diagnostic value with 95% CI
Simpson (1995)[898] (USA) EL Ib	Prospective cohort, single centre, blinded.	Singleton pregnancies attending regional medical centre who provided both samples. *Exclusions*: multiple gestations, neural tube defects, other malformations (low risk)	650 (86.3%)	Testing done twice – at 15–20 weeks and 24–36 weeks, threshold ≥ 2.0 MoM. (19.5% of sample population)	< 37 (6.5% in sample population)	For sampling at 15–20 weeks: ST 0.19 (0.05–0.34), SP 0.80 (0.77–0.84)
Dugoff (2005)[899] (USA) EL II	Prospective cohort, multicentre, not blinded (retrospective analysis of data)	Women ≥ 16 years age confirmed to have singleton pregnancies between 10–14 weeks *Exclusions*: Fetal chromosomal and structural anomalies (low risk)	33 145 (98.0%)	Single test at 15–19 weeks, threshold ≥ 2.0 MoM (1.7% in sample population)	< 32 (0.77% in sample population)	ST 0.11 (0.07–0.115), SP 0.98 (0.98–0.99)
Morssink (1995)[900] (Netherlands) EL II	Prospective cohort, multicentre, not blinded (retrospective analysis of data)	Singleton pregnancies who underwent screening for Down's syndrome or neural tube defects *Exclusions*: pregnancies with diabetes, congenital anomaly, SPTB < 25 weeks	7992 (87.6%)	Single test at 15–20 weeks, threshold ≥ 2.5 MoM (1.1% of study population)	< 37 but excluding infants with weight < 10th centile (6.0% in sample population)	ST 0.02 (0.01–0.02), SP 0.99 (0.99–0.99)

trimester, while in the third it was done in the second trimester. The study population was low risk in all. The threshold of a positive test and outcome were different in all studies (Table 11.21).

Findings

In the study with the largest sample size (Dugoff *et al.*[899]), carried out in the second trimester for predicting SPTB < 32 weeks, values for sensitivity, specificity, LR+ and LR− were 17%, 94%, 2.87 (95% CI 2.18 to 3.78) and 0.89 (95% CI 0.84 to 0.94), respectively. In the other two first-trimester studies, wide variation was observed in all the results. Sensitivity and specificity ranged from 5% to 73% and from 21% to 95%, respectively. The confidence intervals of both the LR+ and LR− included value of 1 and gave poor probability for the test results (Figure 11.8).

Evidence summary

A positive test for a second-trimester MSHCG is more useful in predicting SPTB < 32 weeks than a negative test in ruling it out, but the evidence is poor. The screening performance of a first-trimester MSHCG test is poor.

11.3.9 Maternal serum C-reactive protein (CRP) levels

Description of included studies

Two nested case–control studies without blinding [EL = III] were identified. One study was conducted in the first trimester and used CRP levels greater than 4.3 ng/ml as the threshold for a positive test, while the other carried out in the second trimester used 7.6 ng/ml as the cut-off. Both evaluated SPTB < 37 weeks as outcome (Table 11.22).

Findings

The first-trimester study showed sensitivity of 35% and specificity of 78%. LR+ was 1.55 (95% CI 1.12 to 2.13) and LR− was 0.84 (95% CI 0.73 to 0.98). In the second-trimester study sensitivity and specificity was 26% and 86%, and values for LR+ and LR− were 1.81 (95% CI 1.12 to 2.13) and 0.86 (95% CI 0.76 to 0.99), respectively (Figure 11.9).

Evidence summary

There is a lack of good-quality studies on the diagnostic value of maternal serum CRP levels. Evidence from level III studies shows that positive and negative results of maternal serum CRP have poor predictive accuracy for SPTB < 37 weeks.

2008 update

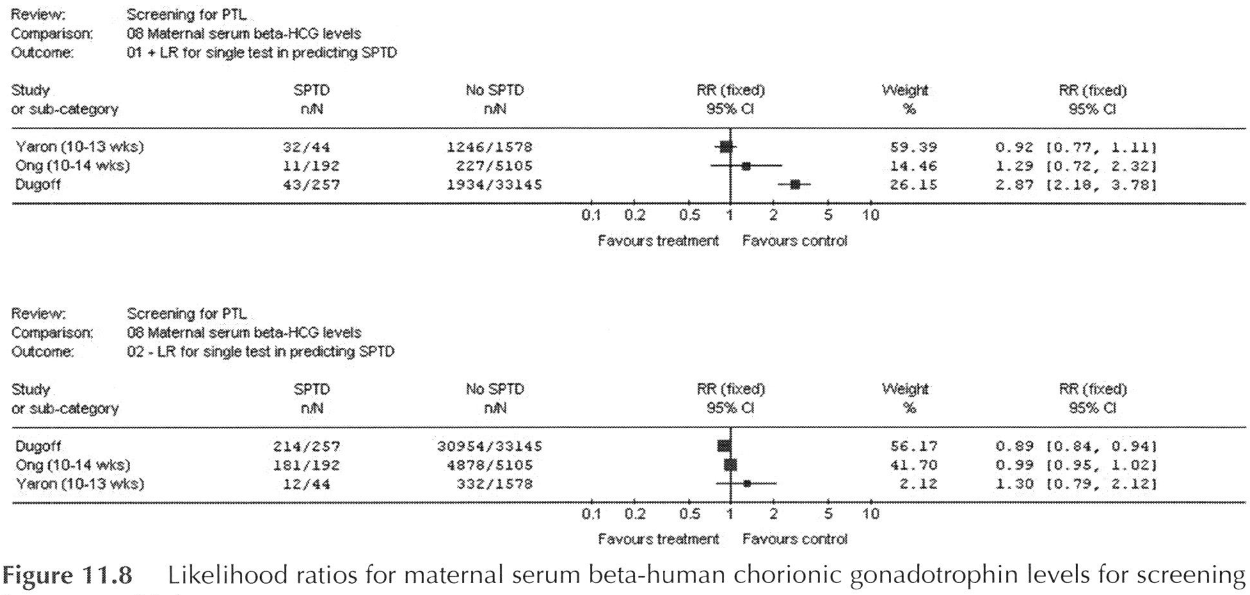

Review: Screening for PTL
Comparison: 08 Maternal serum beta-HCG levels
Outcome: 01 + LR for single test in predicting SPTD

Study or sub-category	SPTD n/N	No SPTD n/N	RR (fixed) 95% CI	Weight %	RR (fixed) 95% CI
Yaron (10-13 wks)	32/44	1246/1578		59.39	0.92 [0.77, 1.11]
Ong (10-14 wks)	11/192	227/5105		14.46	1.29 [0.72, 2.32]
Dugoff	43/257	1934/33145		26.15	2.87 [2.18, 3.78]

0.1   0.2   0.5   1   2   5   10
Favours treatment   Favours control

Review: Screening for PTL
Comparison: 08 Maternal serum beta-HCG levels
Outcome: 02 - LR for single test in predicting SPTD

Study or sub-category	SPTD n/N	No SPTD n/N	RR (fixed) 95% CI	Weight %	RR (fixed) 95% CI
Dugoff	214/257	30954/33145		56.17	0.89 [0.84, 0.94]
Ong (10-14 wks)	181/192	4878/5105		41.70	0.99 [0.95, 1.02]
Yaron (10-13 wks)	12/44	332/1578		2.12	1.30 [0.79, 2.12]

0.1   0.2   0.5   1   2   5   10
Favours treatment   Favours control

Figure 11.8   Likelihood ratios for maternal serum beta-human chorionic gonadotrophin levels for screening for preterm birth

2008 update

Table 11.21 Characteristics of included studies on diagnostic value of maternal serum beta-hCG levels

Study and EL	Study characteristics	Population characteristics (low or high risk)	Sample size (% of study population)	Timing of screening test with threshold (prevalence of test positive)	Outcome in weeks (incidence of SPTB)	Diagnostic value with 95% CI
Dugoff (2005)[899] (USA) EL II	Prospective cohort, multicentre, not blinded (retrospective analysis of data)	Women ≥ 16 years age confirmed to have singleton pregnancies between 10–14 weeks. *Exclusions:* Fetal chromosomal and structural anomalies (low risk)	33 145 (98.0%)	Single test at 15–19 weeks, threshold ≥ 2.0 MoM (6.0% in sample population)	< 32 (0.77% in sample population)	For threshold ≥ 2.0 MoM: ST 0.17 (0.13–0.21), SP 0.94 (0.94–0.94)
Ong (2000)[901] (UK) EL II	Prospective cohort, two centres, not blinded (retrospective analysis of data)	Singleton pregnancies without fetal and chromosomal anomalies (low risk)	5297 (94.9%)	Single test at 10–14 weeks, threshold < 5th and 10th centile (4.5% in sample population)	< 37 (3.6%) < 34 (0.9%)	For threshold < 5th centile: ST 0.05 (0.02–0.09), SP 0.95 (0.95–0.96)
Yaron (2002)[902] (Israel) EL II	Prospective cohort, single centre, not blinded	Singleton pregnancies undergoing first-trimester screening for Down's syndrome. *Exclusions:* Fetal and chromosomal anomalies (low risk)	1622 (91.5%)	Single test at 10–13 weeks, different thresholds – < 1.0, 1.01–2.0, 2.01–3.0, 3.01–4.0, 4.01–5.0, and > 5.01 MoM.	< 37 (2.7% of sample population)	For threshold ≤ 2.0 MoM: ST 0.73 (0.60–0.85), SP 0.21 (0.19–0.23)

Table 11.22 Characteristics of included studies on diagnostic value of maternal serum CRP levels

Study and EL	Study characteristics	Population characteristics	Sample size (% of study population)	Timing of screening test with threshold	Outcome in weeks	Diagnostic value with 95% CI
Hvilsom (2002)[903] (Denmark) EL III	Nested case–control study, single centre, not blinded.	*Cases:* women having idiopathic SPTB < 37 weeks. *Controls:* randomly selected women who had term delivery	484 (84 cases, 400 controls) from a cohort of 2846 singleton pregnancies	Single test at 14–19 weeks (median 16.3 weeks). Threshold 7.6 ng/ml	< 37	ST 0.26 (0.17–0.36), SP 0.86 (0.82–0.89)
Karinen (2005)[904] (Finland) EL III	Nested case–control study, from population-based birth cohort, not blinded	*Cases:* women having idiopathic SPTB < 37 weeks *Controls:* randomly selected women who had term delivery matched on age and parity	506 (104 cases, 402 controls) from a cohort of 2309 singleton pregnancies.	Single test in first trimester (mean age 10.4 weeks) Threshold – 4.3 ng/ml	< 37	ST 0.35 (0.26–0.45), SP 0.78 (0.73–0.82)

11.3.10 Asymptomatic bacteriuria

Description of included studies

All the four prospective cohort studies with EL II included for this test did not specify blinding as a study criterion. Three of these studies were conducted in the 1960s. All of them used culture of midstream urine sample (MSU) as the screening test, and in two studies it was repeated after the first positive test to confirm asymptomatic bacteriuria. The outcome evaluated was SPTB < 37 weeks in all. In two studies the sample size was very small compared with the study population as treatment was started later during the study and that population was excluded. Meta-analysis was performed to calculate summary LRs for a positive and negative test taking results from the firstly performed urine analysis only where possible (Table 11.23).

Findings

Sensitivity ranged from 7% to 30% and specificity from 65% to 97%. Statistically no significant heterogeneity was observed for either the LR+ or the LR−. The summary value of LR+ was 1.97 (95% CI 1.45 to 2.68) and the range in individual studies was from 0.89 to 2.63. LR− had a summary value of 0.46 (95% CI 0.31 to 0.67) and range of 1.19 to 0.31 (Figure 11.10).

Evidence summary

A negative result for an MSU sample for asymptomatic bacteriuria has good diagnostic value in ruling out SPTB < 37 weeks compared with a positive result for predicting it, but the evidence is not of high quality.

11.3.11 Bacterial vaginosis

Description of included studies

Five studies were included – all prospective cohort studies with EL Ib and II were conducted in more than one centre. The study population was low risk in four studies and risk status was not specified in the last study. In all studies, swab (usually single) was taken from the posterior vaginal fornix in the late first or second trimester, and Gram staining with Nugent's criterion was used to diagnose BV. In one study (Hillier et al.[910]) results were calculated only for those women who did not receive antibiotics. All the studies used SPTB < 37 weeks as the outcome. Meta-analysis was performed for LR of a single test in the second trimester for predicting SPTB < 37 weeks (Table 11.24).

Review findings

In the studies, BV had a sensitivity ranging from 15% to 44% and specificity from 76% to 93%. For the LRs of individual studies, Purwar et al.[911] had the best results, with a high LR+ value of 5.31 (95% CI 3.84 to 7.33) and a low LR− of 0.54 (95% CI 0.42 to 0.71). When the results of all

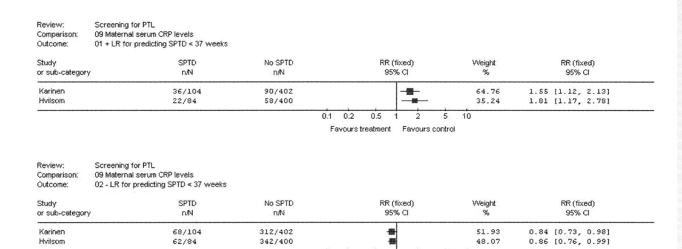

Figure 11.9 Likelihood ratios for maternal serum CRP levels for screening for preterm birth

2008 update

Table 11.23 Characteristics of included studies on diagnostic value of asymptomatic bacteriuria by midstream urine testing

Study and EL	Study characteristics	Population characteristics (low or high risk)	Sample size (% of study population)	Timing and site of screening test (prevalence of test positive)	Outcome in weeks (incidence of SPTB)	Diagnostic value with 95% CI
Wren (1969)[905] (Australia) EL II	Prospective cohort, single centre, not blinded.	All pregnant women booking at antenatal clinic. *Exclusions:* twin pregnancies, women who moved hospital (both low and high risk)	3009 (83.5%) This is after excluding women who were treated.	MSU at first booking visit, repeated if positive. (4.9% in study population for both positive test)	< 37 (7.1% in sample population)	For both test positive: ST 0.07 (0.04–0.11), SP 0.97 (0.97–0.98)
Robertson (1968)[906] (UK) EL II	Prospective cohort, single centre, not blinded.	All pregnant women attending the booking antenatal clinic *Exclusions:* twin pregnancies, abortions, symptomatic at first visit, women who moved hospital. (both low and high risk)	2184 (26.4%) Later in the study women were given treatment, hence small sample for untreated.	Single MSU at booking visit. (6.2% in study population)	< 36 (3.4% in sample population)	ST 0.17 (0.08–0.26), SP 0.91 (0.90–0.92)
Uncu (2001)[907] (Turkey) EL II	Prospective cohort, single centre, not blinded.	All pregnant women < 32 weeks seen at outpatient ANC clinic. *Exclusions:* existing renal disease or bacteriuria, on antibiotics.	186 (68.9%)	Single MSU at < 32 weeks (9.3% in study population)	< 37 (11.8% in sample population)	ST 0.27 (0.09–0.46), SP 0.90 (0.86–0.95)
Layton (1964)[908] (UK) EL II	Prospective cohort, single centre, not blinded	All pregnant women attending antenatal clinic < 32 weeks	169	MSU at < 32 weeks, repeated if positive. (8.8% in sample population)	< 37 (7.7% in sample population)	ST 0.30 (0.05–0.55), SP 0.65 (0.58–0.73)

the included studies were combined, significant statistical heterogeneity was observed for both LR+ and LR−, and the summary values obtained were not as good as those for individual studies. The summary LR+ was 1.70 (95% CI 1.49 to 1.94) and the summary LR− was 0.88 (95% CI 0.85 to 0.92) (Figure 11.11).

Evidence summary
There is high-quality evidence that a single second-trimester vaginal swab for BV (using Nugent's criterion on Gram staining) has poor diagnostic value as a screening test for SPTB < 37 weeks.

11.3.12 Transvaginal sonography (TVS) for cervical length

Description of included studies
Of the five prospective cohort studies included for reviewing this test, four had EL Ib and one EL II because blinding was not a study criterion. In three studies the population was made up of both low- and high-risk pregnant women, while the other two studies had only a low-risk population. TVS for measuring cervical length was carried out in all studies in the second trimester. The critical length used for labelling a cervix as 'short' was calculated by ROC curve in two studies, while in others the length varied. However, all studies used a cervical length of ≤ 20 or 25 mm, and this length was used to conduct the meta-analysis. The outcome evaluated was SPTB < 37 weeks for all but one study which assessed SPTB < 34 weeks (Table 11.25).

Findings
Sensitivity ranged from 5% to 26% and specificity from 93% to 100%. Fukami et al.[914] had the best LRs for positive and negative test results compared with other studies, but it was a study with EL II. Its LR+ was 34.34 (95% CI 16.18 to 72.88) and LR− was 0.51 (95% CI 0.25 to 1.01). On conducting meta-analysis of studies using data for common thresholds, significant statistical heterogeneity was observed for both LR+ and LR−. The summary LR+ was 3.84 (95% CI 3.12 to 4.17) and LR− was 0.85 (95% CI 0.82 to 0.89) (Figure 11.12).

Evidence summary
High-quality evidence shows that a shortened cervix (length ≤ 25 mm) on TVS in the second trimester increases the likelihood of SPTB < 37 weeks by a moderate value, but a cervical length of greater than 25 mm is poor at ruling it out.

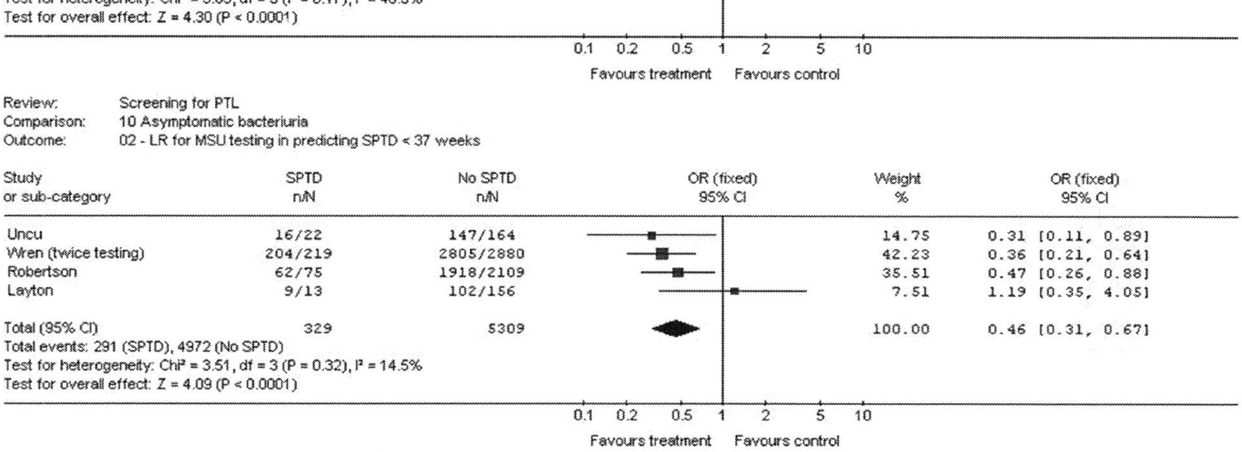

Figure 11.10   Likelihood ratios for midstream urine testing for screening for preterm birth

Table 11.24 Characteristics of included studies on diagnostic value of Gram staining (Nugent's criteria) for bacterial vaginosis

Study and EL	Study characteristics	Population characteristics (low or high risk)	Sample size (% of study population)	Timing and site of screening test (prevalence of BV)	Outcome in weeks (incidence of SPTB)	Diagnostic value with 95% CI
Klebanoff (2005)[909] (USA) EL Ib	Prospective cohort, multicentre, blinded.	Pregnant women with no major medical or obstetric complications, no symptoms of UTI, and not received any antibiotics within past 14 days. (Low risk)	12 937 (81.5%)	Single vaginal swab at < 13, 13–14, 15–16, 17–18, 19–20, or 21–22 weeks. (34.4% in study population)	< 37 (11.4%)	For vaginal swab at 21–22 weeks: ST 0.28 (0.21–0.35), SP 0.76 (0.74–0.78)
Hillier (1995)[910] (USA) EL Ib	Prospective cohort, multicentre, blinded.	Singleton pregnancies during routine prenatal visits after 23–26 weeks. (Low risk)	10 397 (74.7%)	Single posterior fornix swab at 23–26 weeks (16% in study population)	< 37 and birthweight < 2500 g (4.8%)	For women who did not receive antibiotics (n = 8196): ST 0.21 (0.17–0.25), SP 0.84 (0.83–0.85)
Purwar (2001)[911] (India) EL Ib	Prospective cohort, single centre, blinded.	Randomly selected asymptomatic singleton pregnancies without vaginal discharge. (Low risk)	938 (93.2%)	Single vaginal swab at 16–28 weeks (11.5% in study population)	< 37 (7.7% for PTD, 6.3% for SPTB)	For SPTB: ST 0.44 (0.33–0.55), SP 0.90 (0.88–0.92)
Daskalakis (2006)[891] (Greece) EL Ib	Prospective cohort, single centre, blinded	Singleton pregnancies having anomaly scan at 22–25 weeks (Low risk)	1197 (93.0%)	Single vaginal swab at 22–25 weeks (7.9% in sample population)	< 37 (8.7%)	ST 0.15 (0.08–0.22), SP 0.93 (0.91–0.94)
Gratacos (1998)[358] (Spain) EL Ib	Prospective cohort, single centre, blinded	Singleton pregnancies at hospital clinic < 35 weeks (risk not specified)	635 (92.3%)	Twice sampling from posterior fornix – at < 24 and < 35 weeks. (19.6% in study population)	< 37 (7.2%)	For sampling < 24 weeks: ST 0.43 (0.29–0.57), SP 0.82 (0.79–0.85)

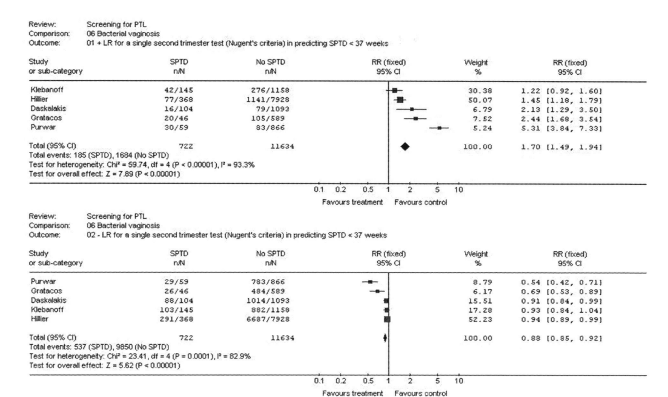

Figure 11.11 Likelihood ratios for swabbing for bacterial vaginosis for screening for preterm birth

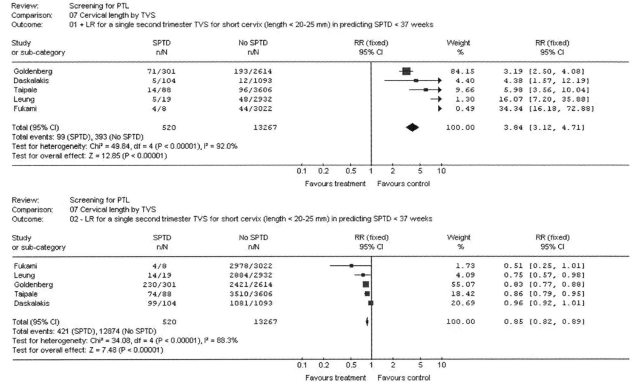

Figure 11.12 Likelihood ratios for TVS for cervical length for screening for preterm birth

2008 update

Table 11.25 Characteristics of included studies on diagnostic value of cervical length by TVS

Study and EL	Study characteristics	Population characteristics (low or high risk)	Sample size (% of study population)	Timing of screening test with threshold in mm (prevalence of test positive)	Outcome in weeks (incidence of SPTB)	Diagnostic value with 95% CI
Taipale (1998)[912] (Finland) EL Ib	Prospective cohort, single centre, blinded	Singleton pregnancies at 18–22 weeks for routine US anomaly scan. *Exclusions*: fetal anomalies, induced PTB, length of gestation beyond pre-specified limits. (low and high risk)	3694 (87.8%)	Single TVS at 18–22 weeks, Different thresholds but ≤ 29 mm best from ROC curve of study findings (3.0% in sample population)	< 37 (2.4% in sample population)	Threshold ≤ 29 mm: ST 0.16 (0.09–0.25), SP 0.97 (0.97–0.98) Threshold ≤ 25 mm: ST 0.06 (0.02–0.13), SP 1.00 (0.99–1.00)
Leung (2005)[913] (Hong Kong) EL Ib	Prospective cohort, single centre, blinded	Ethnic Chinese women with singleton pregnancies at 18–22 weeks *Exclusions*: fetal anomalies (both low and high risk)	2880 (97.6%)	Single TVS at 18–22 weeks. Different thresholds but ≤ 27 mm best from ROC curve of study findings	< 34 (0.7% in sample population)	Threshold ≤ 27 mm: ST 0.37 (0.15–0.58), SP 0.96 (0.95–0.97) Threshold ≤ 25 mm: ST 0.26 (0.06–0.46), SP 0.98 (0.98–0.99)
Goldenberg (1998)[880] (USA) EL Ib	Prospective cohort, multicentre, blinded	Singleton pregnancies. *Exclusions*: multiple gestations, cervical cerclage, placenta praevia, fetal anomaly. (both low and high risk)	2929 (95.3%)	Single TVS at 24 and 28 weeks Threshold ≤ 25, 26–35, > 35 mm	< 32 < 35 < 37 (10.3%)	For SPTB < 37 weeks and threshold ≤ 25 mm: ST 0.24 (0.19–0.28), SP 0.93 (0.92–0.94)
Daskalakis (2006)[891] (Greece) EL Ib	Prospective cohort, single centre, blinded.	Singleton pregnancies having anomaly scan at 22–25 weeks *Exclusions*: History of previous SPTB or abortion, fetus with anomalies, placenta praevia, cervical cerclage or incompetence. (low risk)	1197 (93.0%)	Single TVS at 22 to 25 weeks Threshold < 20 mm (1.4% in sample population)	< 37 (8.7% in sample population)	ST 0.05 (0.01–0.09), SP 0.99 (0.98–0.99)
Fukami (2003)[914] (Japan) EL II	Prospective cohort, single centre, not blinded	Singleton pregnancies scanned between 16–19 weeks. *Exclusions*: chronic medical or obstetric problems that might lead to PTB, uterine or fetal anomalies, cervical cerclage. (low risk)	3030 (90.0%)	Single TVS at 16 to 19 weeks Threshold ≤ 30 mm (1.6% in sample population)	< 32 and 32–36 weeks (2.9% in sample population)	For 32–36 weeks outcome: ST 0.18 (0.10–0.26), SP 0.99 (0.99–0.99)

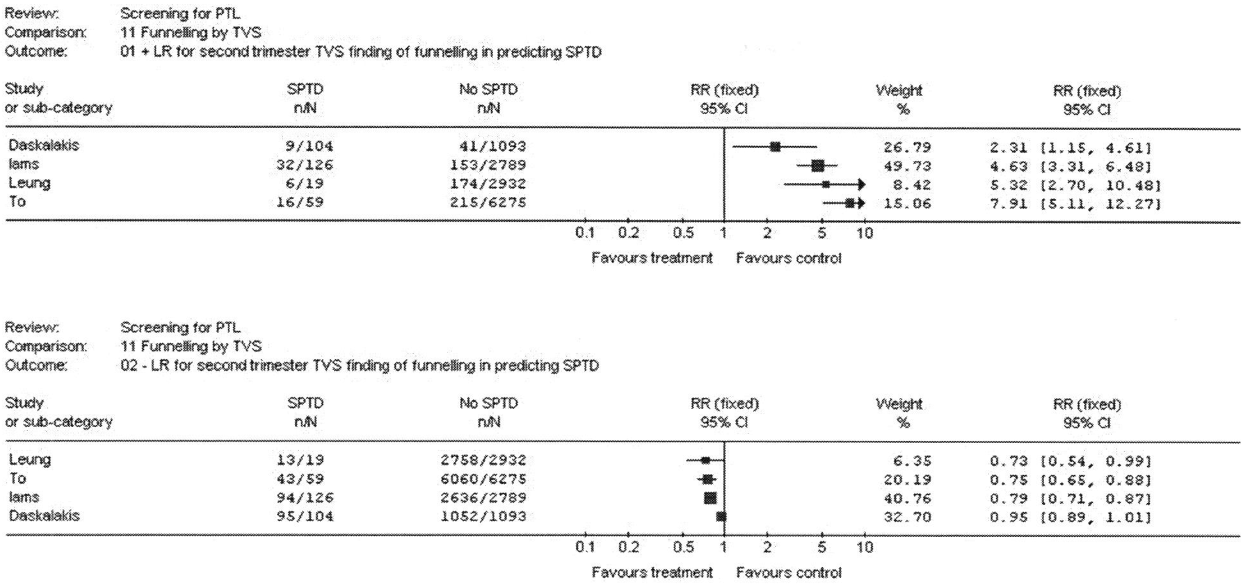

2008 update

Review: Screening for PTL
Comparison: 11 Funnelling by TVS
Outcome: 01 + LR for second trimester TVS finding of funnelling in predicting SPTD

Study or sub-category	SPTD n/N	No SPTD n/N	RR (fixed) 95% CI	Weight %	RR (fixed) 95% CI
Daskalakis	9/104	41/1093		26.79	2.31 [1.15, 4.61]
Iams	32/126	153/2789		49.73	4.63 [3.31, 6.48]
Leung	6/19	174/2932		8.42	5.32 [2.70, 10.48]
To	16/59	215/6275		15.06	7.91 [5.11, 12.27]

```
         0.1   0.2   0.5   1    2     5    10
              Favours treatment   Favours control
```

Review: Screening for PTL
Comparison: 11 Funnelling by TVS
Outcome: 02 - LR for second trimester TVS finding of funnelling in predicting SPTD

Study or sub-category	SPTD n/N	No SPTD n/N	RR (fixed) 95% CI	Weight %	RR (fixed) 95% CI
Leung	13/19	2758/2932		6.35	0.73 [0.54, 0.99]
To	43/59	6060/6275		20.19	0.75 [0.65, 0.88]
Iams	94/126	2636/2789		40.76	0.79 [0.71, 0.87]
Daskalakis	95/104	1052/1093		32.70	0.95 [0.89, 1.01]

```
         0.1   0.2   0.5   1    2     5    10
              Favours treatment   Favours control
```

Figure 11.13   Likelihood ratios for funnelling by transvaginal sonography for screening for preterm birth

11.3.13   Funnelling by TVS

Description of included studies
All the included studies were prospective cohorts (three with EL Ib, one with EL II). The population was low risk in one study, both low and high risk in two studies, and not specified in the fourth one. TVS was carried out in all studies in the second trimester, but different thresholds were used to define 'funnelling'. The outcome evaluated was not the same in all studies. Owing to heterogeneity in thresholds and outcome, meta-analysis was not performed (Table 11.26).

Findings
For the EL Ib studies, sensitivity ranged from 9% to 32% and specificity from 94% to 96%. The only study with EL II had a sensitivity of 27% and specificity of 97%. On calculating the LR for positive and negative test results, all the studies showed better results for LR+ than for LR−. Among EL I studies, Leung et al.[913] had the best results, with an LR+ of 5.32 (95% CI 2.70 to 10.48) and LR− of 0.73 (95% CI 0.54 to 0.99). The other two studies with EL I had lower LR+ and higher LR− values than the Leung study. In the To et al. study[915] [EL = II], values for LR+ and LR− were 7.91 (95% CI 5.11 to 12.27) and 0.75 (95% CI 0.65 to 0.88), respectively (Figure 11.13).

Evidence summary
Funnelling detected by TVS in the second trimester seems to have moderate diagnostic value in predicting SPTB, but interpretation of the evidence is made difficult by variation in thresholds and outcome.

GDG interpretation of evidence for Section 11.3
The evidence does not justify the routine screening of low-risk women for preterm labour with clinical examination, asymptomatic bacteriuria, vaginal swabs or ultrasound to assess cervical change. The evidence shows possible moderate specificity but very poor sensitivity.

Recommendation on screening for preterm birth

Routine screening for preterm labour should not be offered.

Table 11.26 Characteristics of included studies on diagnostic value of cervical funnelling by TVS

Study and EL	Study characteristics	Population characteristics (low or high risk)	Sample size (% of study population)	Timing of screening, test with threshold in mm (prevalence of test positive)	Outcome in weeks (incidence of SPTB)	Diagnostic value with 95% CI
Leung (2005)[913] (Hong Kong) EL Ib	Prospective cohort, single centre, blinded.	Ethnic Chinese women with singleton pregnancies at 18–22 weeks Exclusions: fetal anomalies (both low and high risk)	2880 (97.6%)	Single TVS at 18–22 weeks. Threshold – protrusion of amniotic memb. length > 5 mm into the cervical canal.	< 34 (0.7% in sample population)	ST 0.32 (0.11–0.52), SP 0.94 (0.93–0.95)
Iams (1996)[543] (USA) EL Ib	Prospective cohort, multicentre, blinded	Singleton pregnancies. Exclusions: multiple gestations, cervical cerclage, placenta praevia, fetal anomaly. (both low and high risk)	2915 (94.8) for 24 weeks visit, 2531 (82.4) for 28 weeks visit	Twice testing – at 24 and 28 weeks Threshold – protrusion of amniotic memb. length > 3 mm into internal cervical os.	< 35 (4.3% in sample examined at 24 weeks)	For testing at 24 weeks: ST 0.25 (0.18–0.33), SP 0.94 (0.94–0.95)
Daskalakis (2006)[891] (Greece) EL Ib	Prospective cohort, single centre, blinded.	Singleton pregnancies having anomaly scan at 22–25 weeks Exclusions: History of previous SPTB or abortion, fetus with anomalies, placenta praevia, cervical cerclage or incompetence. (low risk)	1197 (93.0%)	Single TVS at 22 to 25 weeks Threshold not defined	< 37 (8.7% in sample population)	ST 0.09 (0.03–0.14), SP 0.96 (0.95–0.97)
To (2001)[915] (UK) EL II	Prospective cohort, single centre, not blinded.	Singleton pregnancies attending for routine ANC and undergoing 22–24 week cervical assessment using ultrasound scan. Exclusions: not described	6334 (92.9%)	Single TVS at 22–24 weeks. Threshold – dilatation of internal os ≥ 5 mm in width. (4.3% of sample population)	< 33 (0.9% in sample population)	ST 0.27 (0.16–0.39), SP 0.97 (0.96–0.98)

Research recommendation on screening for preterm birth

There is need for future research investigating the value of tests that are cheap and easy to perform such as maternal serum human chorionic gonadotrophin (MSHCG), serum C-reactive protein (CRP) and cervico-vaginal fetal fibrinonectin levels. The diagnostic accuracy and cost-effectiveness of transvaginal ultrasound to measure cervical length and funnelling to identify women at risk of preterm labour should also be investigated.

2008 update

11.4 Placenta praevia

Placenta praevia occurs when the placenta covers the internal os and obstructs vaginal delivery of the fetus. A higher rate of pregnancy complications, including abruption placenta, antepartum haemorrhage and intrauterine growth restriction has been reported in women with low-lying placentas identified in the second trimester, despite apparent 'resolution' by the time of delivery.[547] [EL = 3]

Evaluation of transvaginal sonography for placental localisation has been shown to be safe in observational studies[549–550] [EL = 3] and more accurate than transabdominal sonography in one RCT.[551] [EL = 1b] Reported sensitivities range from 88% to 100% and false positives and false negatives are rare.[549,552] [EL = 3]

Using ultrasonography, placenta praevia may be detected early in pregnancy. However, many placentas that appear to cover the cervical os in the second trimester will not cover the os at term. In one cohort study (n = 6428 women), 4.5% of women were identified with a placenta extending over the internal os at 12 to 16 weeks of gestation with transvaginal sonographic screening and only 0.16% (10/6428) of these women had placenta praevia at birth. Eight of the ten women with placenta praevia had been identified prior to delivery and, in all eight of these women, the placenta extended 15 mm or more over the internal os at the initial scan.[553] [EL = 2b]

In another cohort study, among women scanned transvaginally at 18 to 23 weeks of gestation (n = 3696 women), 1.5% had a placenta extending over the internal os.[554] At delivery, 0.14% of women had placenta praevia and, again, the placenta covered the internal os by 15 mm or more at the time of the first scan for all five of the women. With a cut-off of 15 mm, 0.7% (27/3696) of women would have screened 'positive' and all five cases of praevia at delivery would have been identified (i.e., positive predictive value 19% and sensitivity 100%). [EL = 2b]

Similarly, a cross-sectional study which examined 1252 women who underwent ultrasound examination from 9 to 13 weeks of gestation found that although 6.2% (77/1252) of women had a placenta extending over the internal cervical os at initial examination, only 0.32% (4/1252) of the cases persisted to delivery.[555] In all four cases, the edge of the placenta extended over the os by more than 15 mm during the first-trimester ultrasound examination. [EL = 3]

With regard to gestational age at the time of detection, later detection appears to be related to likelihood of persisting until delivery. A retrospective study demonstrated that, among women with placenta praevia at 15 to 19 weeks of gestation, 12% persisted until delivery compared with 73% among women in whom placenta praevia was identified at 32 to 35 weeks of gestation.[556] [EL = 3]

Symptomatic placenta praevia is associated with the sudden onset of painless bleeding in the second or third trimester. Women with placenta praevia are reported to be 14 times more likely to bleed in the antenatal period compared with women without placenta praevia.[557] Risk factors for symptomatic placenta praevia include prior history of placenta praevia, advancing maternal age, increasing parity, smoking, cocaine use, previous caesarean section and prior spontaneous or induced abortion.[558,559] [EL = 2a]

In the case of symptomatic placenta praevia, inpatient management has been recommended[560] [EL = 4] and no conclusive evidence contrary to this recommendation was located. A Cochrane review of interventions for the management of placenta praevia compared home with hospitalisation and cervical cerclage with no cerclage.[561] Only three trials with a total of 114 women were identified and although a reduction of length of stay in hospital was observed no other significant differences were found to support inpatient or outpatient management. [EL = 1a] Three trials of such small size were considered insufficient evidence to support a change in practice.

GDG interpretation of evidence

There is evidence that detection of a placenta extending over the internal os early in pregnancy (studies range from 9–19 weeks) is associated with persistent placenta praevia in 6–12% of women. If a placenta is found to extend over the internal cervical os at 32 to 35 weeks this persists until birth in 73% of women. The GDG noted that in clinical practice a number of women were presenting with vaginal bleeding between 32 and 36 weeks. The GDG expressed concern that the previous (2003) recommendation of repeating an ultrasound scan at 36 weeks following earlier detection of placenta praevia was too late in pregnancy and that the number of women experiencing antepartum haemorrhage would be reduced by bringing forward the timing of the repeat scan to 32 weeks. For this reason the following recommendation has been updated.

Recommendation on screening for placenta praevia

Because most low-lying placentas detected at the routine anomaly scan will have resolved by the time the baby is born, only a woman whose placenta extends over the internal cervical os should be offered another transabdominal scan at 32 weeks. If the transabdominal scan is unclear, a transvaginal scan should be offered.

12 Fetal growth and wellbeing

Clinical question

What is the diagnostic value and effectiveness of the following methods for determining fetal growth?

- symphysis–fundal height measurement (SFH)
- ultrasound scanning (US)
- use of customised growth charts with SFH measurement
- use of customised growth charts with US scanning
- clinical judgement/abdominal palpation
- frequency

Previous NICE guidance (for the updated recommendations see below)

The use of umbilical artery Doppler ultrasound for the prediction of fetal growth restriction should not be offered routinely. [A]

The use of uterine artery Doppler ultrasound for the prediction of pre-eclampsia should not be offered routinely. [B]

The evidence does not support the routine use of ultrasound scanning after 24 weeks of gestation and therefore it should not be offered. [A]

The evidence does not support the routine use of antenatal electronic fetal heart rate monitoring (cardiotocography) for fetal assessment in women with an uncomplicated pregnancy and therefore it should not be offered. [A]

Auscultation of the fetal heart may confirm that the fetus is alive but is unlikely to have any predictive value and routine listening is therefore not recommended. However, when requested by the mother, auscultation of the fetal heart may provide reassurance. [D]

Routine formal fetal-movement counting should not be offered. [A]

Pregnant women should be offered estimation of fetal size at each antenatal appointment to detect small- or large-for-gestational-age infants. [A]

Symphysis–fundal height should be measured and plotted at each antenatal appointment. [Good practice point]

Future research:

Further research on more effective ways to detect and manage small- and large-for-gestational age fetuses is needed.

Fetal presentation should be assessed by abdominal palpation at 36 weeks or later, when presentation is likely to influence the plans for the birth. Routine assessment of presentation by abdominal palpation should not be offered before 36 weeks because it is not always accurate and may be uncomfortable. [C]

Suspected fetal malpresentation should be confirmed by an ultrasound assessment. [Good practice point]

12.1 Introduction and background

The average duration of a full term pregnancy is 282 days from the first day of the last menstrual period and during this time the fetus passes through various stages of growth and development. Monitoring the growth of the fetus is of vital importance in identifying small- and large-for-

2008 update

253

2008 update

Table 12.1 Characteristics of included studies on diagnostic value of clinical examination

Study and EL	Study characteristics	Population characteristics	Sample size (% of study population)	Timing of screening test with threshold(s) (prevalence of test positive)	Outcome in weeks (incidence of SPTB)	Diagnostic value with 95% CI
Bais (2004)[916] (Netherlands) EL II	Retrospective analysis of a geographical cohort, blinding not specified.	All low-risk singleton pregnancies with confirmed GA by US at 20 weeks Exclusions: women who delivered between 16–20 weeks, gave birth to infant < 500 g, multiple pregnancies	6318 (93.9)	Abdominal palpation by midwives after 20 weeks till referral or delivery (frequency not specified) Threshold: clinical judgement	BW < 10th centile for SGA and < 2.3rd centile for severe SGA (8.5% SGA, 1.5% severe SGA)	For SGA: ST 0.21 (0.18–0.24), SP 0.96 (0.95–0.96), LR+ 5.19 (4.23–6.37), LR− 0.82 (0.79–0.86)
Secher (1990)[917] (Denmark) EL III	Retrospective cohort, single centre, blinding not specified.	Randomly selected singleton pregnancies with confirmed GA by US at 16–18 weeks. Exclusions: pregnancies complicated by diabetes or severe blood group incompatibilities.	199 (Not specified)	Once a week from 33–36 weeks, study sample with more than 3 measurements. EFW calculated and EFW curve generated using modelling. Threshold: Last EFW value < 10th centile, and EFW curve < 10th centile.	BW < 85% of expected for GA (or < 9.4th centile for GA).	For EFW value < 10th centile: ST 0.45 (0.32–0.58), SP 0.91 (0.87–0.95), LR+ 4.82 (2.69–8.78), LR− 0.61 (0.48–0.77) For EFW curve< 10th centile: ST 0.38 (0.26–0.50), SP 0.92 (0.88–0.96)

gestational age babies, both of whom are at an increased risk of associated morbidity and mortality. The methods currently used to screen fetal growth are abdominal palpation, symphysis–fundal height (SFH) measurements, ultrasound scanning and fetal biometry, and customised growth charts. But the challenge is to identify these high-risk pregnancies using the most effective screening methods. There is currently no agreed UK population standard to define normal ranges for estimated fetal weight, fetal growth or birthweight.

12.2 Diagnostic value for predicting SGA babies

Twenty one studies have been reviewed under this section. Most of them are prospective cohort studies. Blinding has not been specified in most studies and these have been assigned [EL = II] except for Doppler US of Umbilical Artery where all the included studies are of EL Ib.

The population in these studies was either a low-risk group of women with singleton pregnancies or an unselected group. Exclusions and number of women in the study population have been specified where information was available. Details of screening tests including timing, frequency and thresholds have been described if recorded. Many studies have evaluated screening performance of various tests at different thresholds and used different criteria for defining SGA. For the sake of comparison efforts have been made to calculate diagnostic value for commonly used thresholds (< 2SD or < 10th centile of reference curve/value) and outcome as birthweight < 10th centile for gestational age.

12.2.1 Clinical examination/abdominal palpation

Description of included studies
Two retrospective studies were identified – one using a database of a large geographical cohort,[916] [EL = II] and the other random selection of hospital records.[917] [EL = III] Low-risk singleton pregnancies with confirmed gestational age were included in both the studies, but blinding was not specified. Women were examined regularly after the 20th week in the first study and the diagnostic value of abdominal palpation calculated for SGA defined as birthweight < 10th centile. In the other study with a much smaller sample size, examination was done once a week from 33 to 36 weeks, and the last value of estimated fetal weight (EFW) taken. Based on three or more measurements, an EFW curve was also generated. Predictive accuracy was calculated for threshold < 10th centile in both parameters with birthweight < 9.4th centile as the outcome (Table 12.1).

Findings
In the larger study (Bais et al.[916]) abdominal palpation had a sensitivity of 0.21 and specificity of 0.96 for predicting SGA babies. It had an LR+ value of 5.19 (4.23–6.37) and an LR– value of 0.82 (0.79–0.86).

In the second study,[917] the diagnostic value of both the EFW value (single) and EFW curve was similar. EFW had sensitivity of 0.45 and specificity of 0.91, while EFW curve had sensitivity of 0.38 and specificity of 0.92. Wide variation was observed in confidence intervals owing to the small sample size. The LR for a positive test was 4.82 (2.69–8.78), while that for a negative test was 0.61 (0.48–0.77).

Evidence summary
There is a lack of good-quality evidence on the diagnostic value of clinical examination/abdominal palpation. The available evidence indicates that clinical examination/abdominal palpation does not have good diagnostic value for predicting SGA babies.

12.2.2 Symphysis–fundal height measurement

Description of included studies
All the five studies included under this heading had EL = II. Blinding was not specified in most of the studies. One was a retrospective cohort[918] and the other four were prospective cohort studies.[919–922] In one study the population was made up of a cohort of singleton pregnancies

2008 update

Table 12.2 Characteristics of included studies on diagnostic value of SFH measurement

Study and EL	Study characteristics	Population characteristics	Sample size (% of study population)	Timing of screening test with threshold(s) (prevalence of test positive)	Outcome(s) and its threshold (incidence in %)	Diagnostic value with 95% CI
Persson (1986)[919] (Sweden) EL II	Prospective cohort, multicentre, blinding not specified.	Singleton pregnancies with regular menstrual cycles and known LMP. *Inclusions:* multiple gestation, mothers with more than 1 infant during study period or lack of registration in Medical Register.	2919 (91.3%)	15 times approx. during the entire pregnancy. *Threshold:* SFH value < 2 SD of Reference Curve generated from 1350 healthy pregnant women.	BW < 10th centile for GA and sex (9.0% in sample population)	ST 0.27 (0.22–0.32), SP 0.88 (0.87–0.89)
Harding (1995)[920] (Australia) EL II	Prospective cohort, single centre, single blinded. (cohort was a group of women in one arm of RCT)	Randomly selected pregnant women who had approx. 5 scans between 18–38 weeks. *Exclusions:* multiple pregnancies, pre-existing HT, diabetes, maternal renal disease, fetal anomalies	747 at 28 weeks, 913 at 34 weeks. (65.8% at 28 weeks and 80.4% at 34 weeks)	5 times at 18–20, 24, 28, 34, and 38 weeks. *Threshold:* Single SFH value < 10th centile for sample population and best cut-off from ROC curve.	BW < 10th centile for GA. (12.3% at 28 weeks, 11.8% at 34 weeks)	Threshold < 10th centile (28 weeks): ST 0.32 (0.23–0.40), SP 0.88 (0.86–0.90) Threshold < 10th centile (34 weeks): ST 0.31 (0.22–0.40), SP 0.87 (0.85–0.89)
Rosenberg (1982)[918] (UK) EL II	Retrospective cohort, single centre, blinding not specified.	Singleton pregnancies with known GA at < 26 weeks gestational age. *Exclusions:* multiple pregnancies, uncertain GA	753 (98.9%)	From 20 weeks till delivery. *Threshold:* Two consecutive or three isolated SFH values < 10th centile of Reference Curve generated from 478 healthy pregnant women.	BW < 10th centile for GA (6.6% in sample population)	ST 0.56 (0.42–0.70), SP 0.85 (0.82–0.87)
Grover (1991)[921] (India) EL II	Prospective cohort, single centre, blinding not specified	Singleton pregnancies with known GA attending ANC. *Exclusions:* Not defined	350 (87.5%)	SFH recording fortnightly till 30 weeks then weekly till term. *Threshold:* SFH value < 1 SD of Reference Curve generated from 200 healthy pregnant women	BW < 10th centile for GA (29.7% in sample population)	ST 0.81 (0.73–0.88), SP 0.94 (0.91–0.97)
Rogers (1985)[922] (UK) EL II	Prospective cohort, single centre, blinding not specified.	Randomly selected pregnant women attending ANC of a hospital. Exclusions: not well defined	250 (study population not specified)	SFH measurements in the third trimester. *Threshold:* Single SFH value < 3 cm below mean of sample or 3 consecutive static or declining values.	BW < 10th centile for GA (10.4% in sample population)	ST 0.73 (0.56–0.90), SP 0.92 (0.88–0.96)

included in one arm of an RCT.[920] Two studies did not have well-defined exclusion criteria. SFH was measured in all studies from 20 weeks onward till term, but the exact timing, frequency and threshold of a positive test were different. All studies evaluated birthweight < 10th centile as the outcome. Meta-analysis was not performed owing to existing heterogeneity (Table 12.2).

Findings
There was wide variation in the results. Results from the two studies with smaller sample size showed better values of LR+ and LR− compared with the other studies. The best results were seen in the Grover study,[921] with an LR+ of 12.42 (95% CI 7.66 to 20.13) and an LR− of 0.21 (95% CI 0.14 to 0.31). However, the study with largest sample size (Persson *et al.*[919]) showed poor values for LR+ at 2.22 (95% CI 1.77 to 2.78) and LR− at 0.83 (95% CI 0.77 to 0.90) (Figure 12.1).

Evidence summary
A wide variation in the results was observed for predictive accuracy of SFH measurement during pregnancy. The results from a multicentre study show that it does not have good diagnostic value for predicting and ruling out SGA babies.

12.2.3   Fetal biometry

Description of included studies
Four of the included studies were prospective cohort studies[923–926] and one was a retrospective[927] – all with EL II and well-defined exclusion criteria. Ultrasound was conducted in the third trimester and the diagnostic value calculated for a single measurement. All studies had used abdominal circumference (AC) as a parameter, two had also used EFW based on Shepard's formula (using AC, BPD), and one used head circumference (HC). The threshold for a positive test was similar in all (< 10th centile) and the outcome assessed was birthweight < 10th centile for gestational age. Meta-analysis was performed for diagnostic accuracy of a single AC measurement in the third trimester (Table 12.3).

Findings
With AC as the only parameter used and threshold < 10th centile, sensitivity ranged from 48% to 87% while specificity ranged from 69% to 96%. Threshold values were not properly defined in the study by Hedriana *et al.*[926] On combining results of all the five studies, strong evidence of statistical heterogeneity was observed ($P < 0.00001$). The summary LR+ was 6.25 (95% CI 5.60

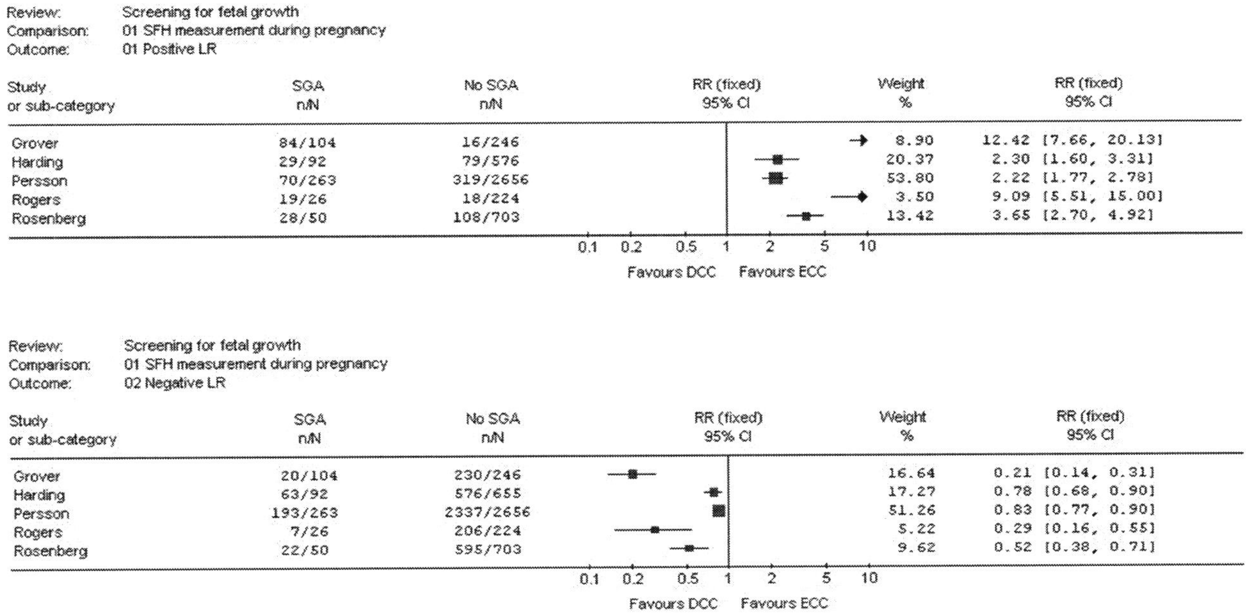

2008 update

Review: Screening for fetal growth
Comparison: 01 SFH measurement during pregnancy
Outcome: 01 Positive LR

Study or sub-category	SGA n/N	No SGA n/N	RR (fixed) 95% CI	Weight %	RR (fixed) 95% CI
Grover	84/104	16/246		8.90	12.42 [7.66, 20.13]
Harding	29/92	79/576		20.37	2.30 [1.60, 3.31]
Persson	70/263	319/2656		53.80	2.22 [1.77, 2.78]
Rogers	19/26	18/224		3.50	9.09 [5.51, 15.00]
Rosenberg	28/50	108/703		13.42	3.65 [2.70, 4.92]

0.1   0.2   0.5   1   2   5   10
Favours DCC   Favours ECC

Review: Screening for fetal growth
Comparison: 01 SFH measurement during pregnancy
Outcome: 02 Negative LR

Study or sub-category	SGA n/N	No SGA n/N	RR (fixed) 95% CI	Weight %	RR (fixed) 95% CI
Grover	20/104	230/246		16.64	0.21 [0.14, 0.31]
Harding	63/92	576/655		17.27	0.78 [0.68, 0.90]
Persson	193/263	2337/2656		51.26	0.83 [0.77, 0.90]
Rogers	7/26	206/224		5.22	0.29 [0.16, 0.55]
Rosenberg	22/50	595/703		9.62	0.52 [0.38, 0.71]

0.1   0.2   0.5   1   2   5   10
Favours DCC   Favours ECC

Figure 12.1   SFH measurement

2008 update

Table 12.3 Characteristics of included studies on diagnostic value of fetal biometry

Study and EL	Study characteristics	Population characteristics	Sample size (% of study population)	Timing of screening test with threshold(s) (prevalence of test positive)	Outcome(s) and its threshold (incidence in %)	Diagnostic value with 95% CI
Warsof (1986)[923] (UK) EL II	Prospective cohort, single centre, blinding not specified.	Ultrasonically confirmed singleton pregnancies before 24 weeks. *Exclusions*: lack of dating scan before 24 weeks.	3616 (79.9%)	Once in third trimester at 28, 30, 32, 34 or 36 weeks. *Threshold*: BPD, HC and AC values < 25th centile or < 10th centile for GA.	BW < 10th centile for GA. (12.4% in sample population)	Threshold < 25th centile: For AC: ST 0.79 (0.76–0.82), SP 0.80 (0.79–0.81); For HC: ST 0.54 (0.50–0.58), SP 0.78 (0.77–0.80) Threshold < 10th centile: For AC: ST 0.48 (0.45–0.51), SP 0.93 (0.93–0.94); For HC: ST 0.35 (0.32–0.39) SP 0.91 (0.90–0.92)
Skovron (1991)[924] (USA) EL II	Prospective cohort, single centre, blinding not specified.	Singleton pregnancies *Exclusions*: gestational diabetes, placenta praevia, preterm labour, Rh sensitisation, fetal anomalies.	768 (77.1%)	Once between 26 and 34 weeks. *Threshold*: AC and EFW (Shepard's formula) at < 10th and < 25th centile for GA.	BW < 10th centile for GA and sex (9.9% in sample population)	Threshold < 25th centile: For AC: ST 0.83 (0.74–0.92), SP 0.56 (0.52–0.60); For EFW: ST 0.51 (0.40–0.62), SP 0.80 (0.77–0.83) Threshold < 10th centile: For AC: ST 0.72 (0.62–0.83), SP 0.69 (0.66–0.72); For EFW: ST 0.25 (0.15–0.35), SP 0.97 (0.96–0.98)
Newnham (1990)[925] (Australia) EL II	Prospective cohort, single centre, not blinded for AC.	Singleton pregnancies with known GA at < 18 weeks gestational age. *Exclusions*: multiple pregnancies, gestational age > 20 weeks, language difficulties, not pregnant, major fetal anomaly.	535 (87.0%)	At 28 and 34 weeks. *Threshold*: AC < 5th centile for GA in the study population.	BW < 10th centile for GA (9.5% in sample population)	At 28 weeks: ST 0.27 (0.14–0.40), SP 0.96 (0.94–0.98) At 34 weeks: ST 0.49 (0.33–0.65), SP 0.94 (0.92–0.96)
Lin (1990)[927] (USA) EL II	Retrospective cohort, single centre, blinding not specified	Singleton pregnancies undergoing obstetric US at a tertiary hospital. *Exclusions*: multiple gestation, ruptured membranes, uncertain dates, fetal anomalies.	463 (study population not specified)	Twice in third trimester at interval of 2–4 weeks. *Threshold*: AC < 10th centile for GA in the study population.	BW < 10th centile for GA (13.8% in sample population)	ST 0.87 (0.78–0.96), SP 0.77 (0.73–0.81)
Hedriana (1994)[926] (USA) EL II	Prospective cohort, single centre, blinding not specified.	Ultrasonically confirmed singleton pregnancies. *Exclusions*: multiple gestation, maternal complications associated with severe intrauterine growth retardation, fetuses with anatomic defects.	249 (94.3%)	Single and serial third-trimester scans between 28 and 42 weeks. *Threshold*: Slope ± SD calculated for AC and EFW (Shepard's formula) centile using regression analysis. Exact values not specified.	BW < 10th centile for GA (7.6% in sample population)	For single scan: For AC: ST 0.68 (0.47–0.89), SP 0.88 (0.84–0.92); For EFW: ST 1.00 (1.00–1.00), SP 0.76 (0.71–0.82)

to 6.97) and summary LR– was 0.55 (95% CI 0.52 to 0.58). Values for LR+ ranged from 3.84 to 8.20 and those for LR– from 0.16 to 0.78 (Figure 12.2).

Evidence summary
There is some evidence to indicate that a single measurement of fetal AC in the third trimester has some diagnostic value in predicting the birth of SGA babies but the studies show statistical heterogeneity.

12.2.4　Reduced amniotic fluid volume by ultrasound

Description of included studies
Three studies have been included – two cohort studies[920,927] with EL II (one prospective and the other retrospective) and one case–control study[928] with EL III. Blinding was not specified in any but exclusions were well defined. Timing, frequency and threshold of a positive test were all different in the three studies. In one study (Lin *et al.*[927]) the diagnostic performance of AC and reduced amniotic fluid volume was calculated as a single test (Table 12.4).

Findings
Values for LR+ and LR– in the prospective cohort study (Harding *et al.*[920]) were poor at 1.02 (95% CI 0.58 to 1.79) and 1.00 (95% CI 0.93 to 1.07), respectively. The Lin *et al.* study[927] showed a high LR+ of 12.47 and LR– of 0.77, but results from the third study were not consistent (Figure 12.3).

Evidence summary
Evidence from three studies shows that reduced amniotic fluid volume diagnosed by ultrasound during pregnancy has poor diagnostic value in predicting and ruling out SGA babies.

12.2.5　Umbilical artery Doppler examination

Description of included studies
All of the five included studies were prospective cohort studies [EL = Ib] with blinding[925,929–932] and one was conducted in more than one centre. The exclusion criteria were well defined in

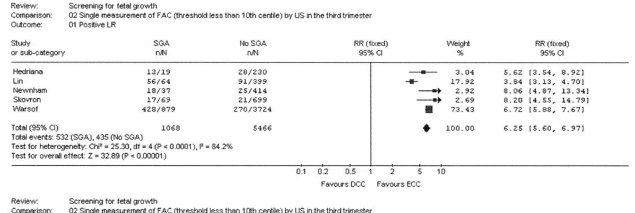

Figure 12.2　Fetal abdominal circumference by ultrasound

2008 update

Table 12.4 Characteristics of included studies on diagnostic value of reduced amniotic fluid volume (AFI) by ultrasound

Study and EL	Study characteristics	Population characteristics	Sample size (% of study population)	Timing of screening test with threshold(s) (prevalence of test positive)	Outcome(s) and its threshold (incidence in %)	Diagnostic value with 95% CI
Harding (1995)[920] (Australia) EL II	Prospective cohort, single centre, not blinded for US measurements. (cohort was a group of women in one arm of RCT)	Randomly selected pregnant women who had approx. 5 scans between 18–38 weeks. *Exclusions*: multiple pregnancies, pre-existing HT, diabetes, maternal renal disease, fetal anomalies.	760 at 28 weeks, 914 at 34 weeks. (67.0% at 28 weeks and 80.5% at 34 weeks)	5 times at 18–20, 24, 28, 34, and 38 weeks. *Threshold*: Single AFI value < 10th centile for sample population.	BW < 10th centile for GA. (12.6% at 28 weeks, 11.7% at 34 weeks)	Threshold < 10th centile (28 weeks): ST 0.21 (0.13–0.29), SP 0.93 (0.91–0.95) Threshold < 10th centile (34 weeks): ST 0.11 (0.05–0.17), SP 0.89 (0.87–0.91)
Lin (1990)[927] (USA) EL II	Retrospective cohort, single centre, blinding not specified	Singleton pregnancies undergoing obstetric US at a tertiary hospital. *Exclusions*: multiple gestation, ruptured membranes, uncertain dates, fetal anomalies.	463 (study population not specified)	Twice in third trimester at interval of 2–4 weeks. *Threshold*: AC < 10th centile for GA in the study population and vertical diameter < 2 cm in largest pocket of amniotic fluid for oligohydramnios.	BW < 10th centile for GA (13.8% in sample population)	For AC < 10TH centile and oligohydramnios: ST 0.25 (0.15–0.36), SP 0.98 (0.97–0.99)
Chauhan (1999)[928] (USA) EL III	Retrospective case–control, single centre, blinding not specified.	*Cases*: Singleton pregnancies, AFI ≤ 5 cm, reliable GA and no known anomalies. *Controls*: Next pregnancy with same GA and AFI between 5.1 to 23.9 cm.	324 (Cases – 162 Controls – 162)	Third-trimester US for AFI within 72 hours of delivery. Threshold: AFI ≤ 5 cm	BW < 10th centile for GA (13.6% in sample population)	ST 0.66 (0.52–0.80), SP 0.53 (0.47–0.58)

AFI = amniotic fluid index.

four studies. Doppler ultrasound was conducted in either the late second or the third trimester. Three studies evaluated the systolic/diastolic (S/D) ratio as a screening parameter, one study used pulsatility index (PI) and the fifth study evaluated both of them. Meta-analysis was performed for two different timings – 26–31 weeks (four studies) and 32–36 weeks (three studies) without taking into account the parameter used. One study was not included for meta-analysis as it did not provide data for calculation of their confidence intervals (Table 12.5).

Findings

Sensitivity at both 26–31 weeks and 32–36 weeks ranged between 17% and 43% while specificity at both times was as high as 96%. There was not much variation in the values of positive and negative LR for individual studies.

At 26–31 weeks, LR+ ranged from 2.20 to 4.18 while LR– ranged from 0.71 to 0.87. No evidence of statistical heterogeneity was observed for wither positive or negative LRs. The summary values for LR+ and LR– were 2.67 (95% CI 2.02 to 3.53) and 0.84 (95% CI 0.78 to 0.90), respectively (Figure 12.4).

At 32–36 weeks there was also no evidence of heterogeneity for either LR. The summary LR+ was 3.34 (95% CI 2.27 to 4.93) and LR+ ranged from 2.74 to 3.92 in individual studies. The LR– ranged from 0.83 to 0.88 and its summary value was 0.85 (95% CI 0.79 to 0.92) (Figure 12.5).

Evidence summary

High-quality evidence indicates that umbilical artery Doppler ultrasound examination in the third trimester (at 26–31 weeks and 32–36 weeks) has poor diagnostic value in predicting SGA births in a low-risk population.

12.2.6 Customised fetal growth charts

No study was identified that provided sufficient data to calculate the predictive accuracy of SFH measurements using customised fetal growth charts (CFGC).

Evidence summary

There is no good-quality evidence on the predictive performance of SFH measurements using customised fetal growth charts.

Review: Fetal growth
Comparison: 04 Oligohydramnios by US (AFI or AFV)
Outcome: 01 Positive LR

Study or sub-category	SGA n/N	No SGA n/N	RR (fixed) 95% CI	Weight %	RR (fixed) 95% CI
Lin	16/64	8/399		3.74	12.47 [5.57, 27.93]
Harding	12/107	89/807		35.22	1.02 [0.58, 1.79]
Chauhan	29/44	133/280		61.05	1.39 [1.09, 1.77]

0.1   0.2   0.5   1   2   5   10
Favours treatment   Favours control

Review: Fetal growth
Comparison: 04 Oligohydramnios by US (AFI or AFV)
Outcome: 02 Negative LR

Study or sub-category	SGA n/N	No SGA n/N	RR (fixed) 95% CI	Weight %	RR (fixed) 95% CI
Lin	48/64	391/399		34.19	0.77 [0.66, 0.88]
Harding	95/107	718/807		53.18	1.00 [0.93, 1.07]
Chauhan	15/44	147/280		12.63	0.65 [0.42, 0.99]

0.1   0.2   0.5   1   2   5   10
Favours treatment   Favours control

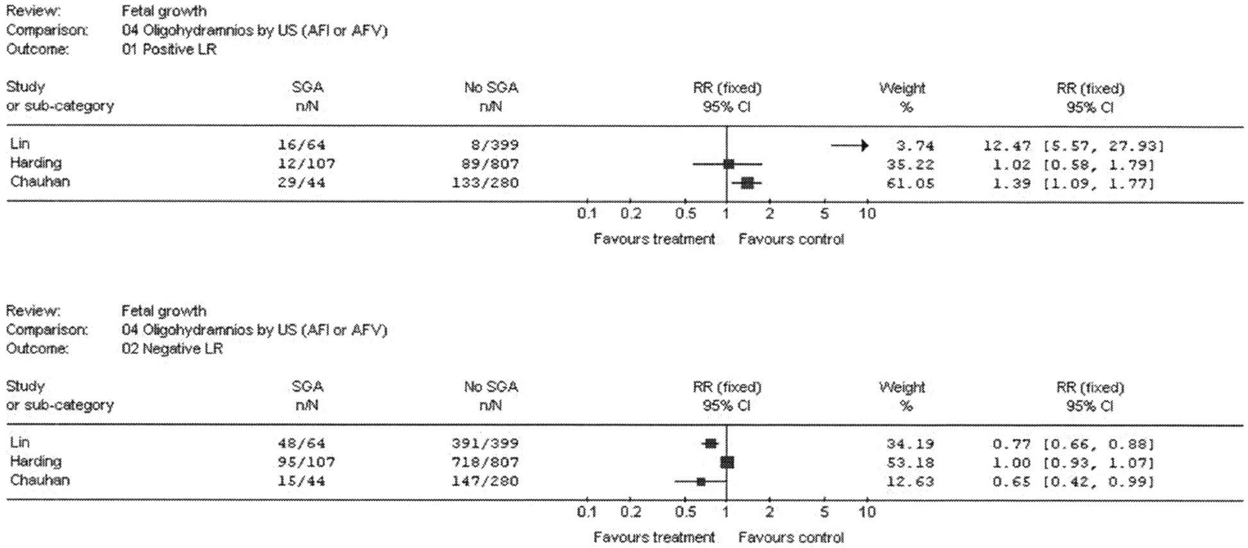

Figure 12.3   Reduced amniotic fluid volume by ultrasound

2008 update

Table 12.5 Characteristics of included studies on diagnostic value of Doppler ultrasound (umbilical artery)

Study and EL	Study characteristics	Population characteristics	Sample size (% of study population)	Timing of screening test(s) with threshold(s) (prevalence of test positive)	Outcome(s) and its threshold (incidence in %)	Diagnostic value with 95% CI
Beattie (1989)[929] (UK) EL Ib	Prospective cohort, single centre, blinded.	Ultrasonically dated singleton pregnancies attending within 7 days of their 28th gest. week. *Exclusions*: private patients, late bookings, with altered dates who attended after 29 weeks, late referrals.	2097 (62.0%)	At 28, 34 and 38 weeks. Thresholds: Pulsatility index (PI), Systolic/diastolic (S/D) ratio and Resistance parameter – all > 90th centile for GA in the study population.	BW < 5th centile for GA. (values not given)	At 28 weeks: For PI: ST 28%, SP 89%; For S/D ratio: ST 31%, SP 90% At 34 weeks: For PI: ST 32%, SP 89%; For S/D ratio: ST 40, SP 84%
Todros (1995)[930] (Italy) EL Ib	Prospective cohort, multicentre, blinded.	Singleton pregnancies with no obstetrical risk, pre-pegnancy pathologic condition or anomaly. *Exclusions*: women delivered at other hospitals	916 (95.2%)	At 19–24 and 26–31 weeks Threshold: S/D ratio of 4.5 (at 19–24 weeks) and 3.5 (at 26–31 weeks) derived from ROC curve.	BW < 10th centile for GA (4.6% in sample population)	At 19–24 weeks: ST 0.45 (0.30–0.60), SP 0.74 (0.71–0.77) At 26–31 weeks: ST 0.43 (0.28–0.58), SP 0.80 (0.78–0.83)
Newnham (1990)[925] (Australia) EL Ib	Prospective cohort, single centre, blinded.	Singleton pregnancies with known GA at < 18 weeks gestational age. *Exclusions*: multiple pregnancies, gestational age > 20 weeks, language difficulties, not pregnant, major fetal anomaly.	535 (87.0%)	At 18, 24, 28 and 34 weeks. Threshold: S/D ratio > 95th centile for GA in study population.	BW < 10th centile for GA (9.5% in sample population)	At 28 weeks: ST 0.19 (0.07–0.30), SP 0.96 (0.94–0.97) At 34 weeks: ST 0.17 (0.04–0.29), SP 0.95 (0.93–0.97)
Sijmons (1989)[931] (Netherlands) EL Ib	Prospective cohort, single centre, blinded.	Randomly selected singleton pregnancies from a tertiary referral centre.	339 to 394 (84.5 to 98.5%) for different timing and outcomes	At 28 and 34 weeks Threshold: PI > 95th centile for GA in the study population.	1) BW < 10th centile for GA (22% in study population) 2) Ponderal index < 10th centile for GA	At 28 weeks: 1) ST 0.17 (0.09–0.25), SP 0.95 (0.93–0.97); (2) ST 0.19 (0.06–0.32), SP 0.95 (0.93–0.97) At 34 weeks: 1) ST 0.22 (0.13–0.31), SP 0.94 (0.92–0.97); (2) ST 0.24 (0.09–0.39), SP 0.93 (0.90–0.96)
Atkinson (1994)[932] (USA) EL Ib	Prospective cohort, single centre, blinded. (part of RCT for pre-eclampsia prevention)	Low-risk nulliparaous women with singleton pregnancies. *Exclusions*: multiple gestation, history of renal disease, collagen vascular disease, diabetes, hypertension.	475 (84.0) at 27–31 weeks, 439 (77.7) at 32–36 weeks	At 20–26, 27–31, 32–36 and 37–42 weeks Threshold: S/D ratio > 90th centile for GA in study population.	BW < 10th centile for GA (7.8% in study population)	At 27–31 weeks: ST 0.20, SP 0.91 At 32–36 weeks: ST 0.24, SP 0.91

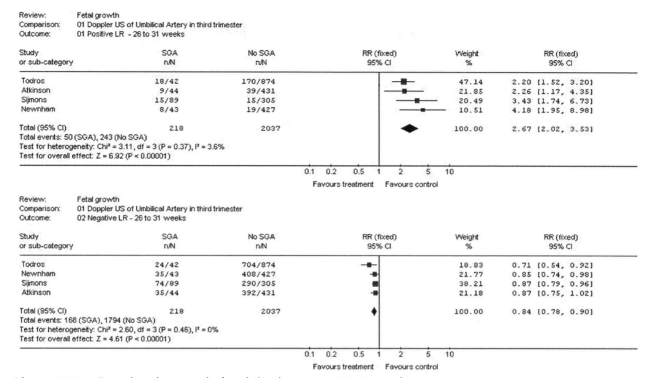

Figure 12.4   Doppler ultrasound of umbilical artery at 26–31 weeks

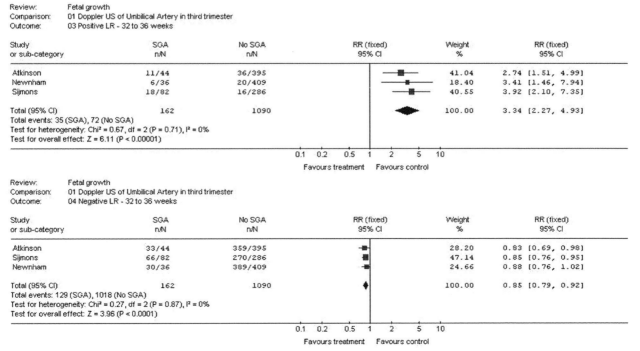

Figure 12.5   Doppler ultrasound of umbilical artery at 32–36 weeks

2008 update

Table 12.6 Characteristics of included studies on diagnostic value of SFH measurement for LGA babies

Study and EL	Study characteristics	Population characteristics	Sample size (% of study population)	Timing of screening test with threshold(s) (prevalence of test positive)	Outcome(s) and its threshold (incidence in %)	Diagnostic value with 95% CI
Persson (1986)[919] (Sweden) EL II	Prospective cohort, multicentre, blinding not specified.	Singleton pregnancies with regular menstrual cycles and known LMP. *Inclusions*: multiple gestation, mothers with more than 1 infant during study period or lack of registration in Medical Register.	2919 (91.3%)	15 times approx. during the entire pregnancy. *Threshold*: SFH value > 2 SD of Reference Curve generated from 1350 healthy pregnant women.	BW > 90th centile for GA and sex (9.5% in sample population.	ST 0.38 (0.33–0.43), SP 0.88 (0.87–0.89), LR+ 3.09 (2.57–3.71), LR– 0.71 (0.65–0.78)
Grover (1991)[921] (India) EL II	Prospective cohort, single centre, blinding not specified	Singleton pregnancies with known GA attending ANC. *Exclusions*: Not defined	350 (87.5%)	SFH recording fortnightly till 30 weeks and then weekly till term. *Threshold*: SFH value > 1 SD of Reference Curve generated from 200 healthy pregnant women	BW > 1SD according to national BW chart (13.7% in sample population)	ST 0.79 (0.68–0.90), SP 0.95 (0.93–0.98), LR+ 16.63 (9.39–29.42), LR– 0.22 (0.13–0.38)
Okonofua (1986)[934] (UK) EL III	Prospective cohort, single centre, blinding not specified.	Singleton uncomplicated pregnancies attending a hospital ANC clinic and who were sure of their LMP. *Exclusions*: Not defined	100 (study population not specified)	SFH measurements and US biometry after 20 weeks in the third trimester. *Threshold*: Two consecutive SFH values > 90th centile of Reference curve generated from a sample of 30 healthy uncomplicated singleton pregnancies.	BW > 90th centile for GA (6.0% in sample population)	ST 0.33, SP 0.85

12.3 Diagnostic value for predicting LGA babies

No study was identified for diagnostic accuracy of four screening tests – clinical examination, amniotic fluid volume or polyhydramnios by ultrasound, Doppler ultrasound of umbilical artery and customised fetal growth charts. For the two remaining screening tests – SFH measurement and ultrasound biometry – all the six studies included are cohort studies with EL II (blinding not specified). Details of these studies have been tabulated. Meta-analysis could not be performed for either screening test owing to heterogeneity in timing, thresholds and outcome assessed.

12.3.1 Symphysis–fundal height measurement for LGA babies

Description of included studies
All the three studies included were prospective cohort studies.[919,921,934] Two of them also assessed the diagnostic value of SFH in SGA babies. [EL = II] None of the studies specified blinding, and two did not specify the exclusion criteria. In all studies, SFH measurements were made in the third trimester and plotted on a reference curve generated from a normal population of healthy pregnant women. One study did not specify exact values for diagnostic accuracy results,[934] [EL = III] and thus its diagnostic value is given as published without the corresponding confidence intervals (Table 12.6).

Findings
The prospective cohort study with the largest sample size[919] did not show good values for sensitivity (38%), specificity (88%), LR+ (3.09, 95% CI 2.57 to 3.71) or LR− (0.71, 95% CI 0.65 to 0.78). The other prospective cohort study[921] showed a very high LR+ of 16.63 (95% CI 9.39 to 29.42) and a low LR− or 0.22 (95% CI 0.13 to 0.38). However, this was a single centre unblinded study with a small sample size.

Evidence summary
There is wide variation in the results for the diagnostic accuracy of SFH measurements in the prediction of LGA babies. Results from the largest study show that this measurement has poor diagnostic value in predicting and ruling out LGA babies.

12.3.2 Fetal biometry for LGA babies

Description of included studies
Three studies were included – two prospective cohorts[926,934] [EL = II and EL = III, respectively] and one retrospective cohort.[935] [EL = III] Exclusions were not defined in one study. Wide variation was seen in the timing, frequency, parameters employed and the threshold used for a positive test, but all studies used birthweight > 90th centile as the outcome for defining LGA (Table 12.7).

Findings
Two studies employing EFW by Shepard's formula showed sensitivity of 48% and 74%, and similar specificity values of 94%. LR+ in one was 12.87 (95% CI 8.22 to 20.15) while it was 8.09 (95% CI 4.32 to 15.14) in the other. Values for LR− were 0.28 (95% CI 0.18 to 0.45) and 0.55 (95% CI 0.42 to 0.73), respectively. Positive and negative LR values for AC measured in one study were 5.01 (95% CI 3.12 to 8.07) and 0.51 (95% CI 0.37 to 0.70), respectively.

Evidence summary
There is a lack of good-quality studies for the diagnostic value of fetal biometry for detecting LGA babies. Results from one small study show that it might have some value in predicting and ruling out birth of LGA babies.

2008 update

2008 update

Table 12.7 Characteristics of included studies on diagnostic value of fetal biometry for LGA babies

Study and EL	Study characteristics	Population characteristics	Sample size (% of study population)	Timing of screening test with threshold(s) (prevalence of test positive)	Outcome(s) and its threshold (incidence in %)	Diagnostic value with 95% CI
Hedriana (1994)[926] (USA) EL II	Prospective cohort, single centre, blinding not specified.	Ultrasonically confirmed singleton pregnancies. *Exclusions*: multiple gestations, maternal complications associated with severe intrauterine growth retardation, fetuses with anatomic defects.	249 (94.3%)	Single and serial third-trimester scans between 28 and 42 weeks. *Threshold*: Slope ± SD calculated for AC and EFW (Shepard's formula) centile using regression analysis. Exact values not specified.	BW > 90th centile for GA. (18.5% in sample population)	For single scan: For AC: ST 0.54 (0.40–0.68), SP 0.89 (0.85–0.93), LR+ 5.01 (3.12–8.07), LR– 0.51 (0.37–0.70) For EFW: ST 0.48 (0.34–0.62), SP 0.94 (0.91–0.97), LR+ 8.09 (4.32–15.14), LR– 0.55 (0.42–0.73)
Okonofua (1986)[934] (UK) EL III	Prospective cohort, single centre, blinding not specified.	Singleton uncomplicated pregnancies attending a hospital ANC clinic and who were sure of their LMP. *Exclusions*: Not defined	100 (study population not specified)	SFH measurements and US biometry after 20 weeks in the third trimester. *Threshold*: Two consecutive values > 90th centile of BPD and AC reference curve generated from a sample of 30 healthy uncomplicated singleton pregnancies.	BW > 90th centile for GA (6.0% in sample population)	ST 0.66, SP 0.95
Ott (1984)[935] (USA) EL III	Retrospective cohort, single centre, blinding not specified.	Pregnant women undergoing US examination within 72 hours of delivery. *Exclusions*: not defined.	595 (study population not specified)	BPD and AC measured within 72 hours of delivery and EFW (Shepard's formula) calculated. *Threshold*: EFW > 1.5 SD for the reference curve.	BW > 90th centile for GA (8.2% in sample population)	ST 0.74 (0.62–0.86), SP 0.94 (0.92–0.96), LR+ 12.87 (8.22–20.15), LR– 0.28 (0.18–0.45)

12.4 Effectiveness studies

Nine studies were included – two Cochrane reviews, one controlled trial, four retrospective and one prospective cohort study, and one nested case–control study. Apart from three studies (two Cochrane reviews and one controlled trial) which compared the effectiveness of screening tests, the rest of the studies compared the risk of adverse perinatal outcomes between pregnant women with positive test results and those with negative tests results.

The two Cochrane reviews were on effectiveness of SFH measurement and Doppler ultrasound, respectively. Two cohort studies were selected for ultrasound biometry, and two studies (one cohort and one nested case–control) for amniotic fluid volume. No effectiveness study was identified for clinical examination of fetal growth. Three studies (one controlled trial and two retrospective cohorts) were identified for customised fetal growth charts, and the two retrospective cohort studies had analysed the same Swedish birth cohort database but in a different manner.

12.4.1 Symphysis–fundal height measurement

Description of included studies

A Cochrane review[566] was conducted to assess whether routine use of SFH measurement during antenatal care improves pregnancy outcome compared with abdominal examination. [EL = 1+] It included all controlled trials of tape measurement of SFH during pregnancy compared with an abdominal palpation method alone. Studies were identified using the Pregnancy and Childbirth search strategy of the Cochrane group. One reviewer assessed the quality of included studies and extracted data. Analysis was done using Review Manager software. The primary outcomes were:

- complications associated with FGR – intrauterine death, intrapartum asphyxia and neonatal hypoglycaemia
- complications associated with fetal macrosomia – cephalopelvic disproportion, caesarean section for failure to progress, shoulder dystocia
- complications associated with multiple pregnancy – preterm delivery, perinatal mortality.

The secondary outcomes were other indices of maternal and perinatal mortality and morbidity, and indices of obstetric care including admission to hospital.

Findings

A single trial enrolling 1639 participants was included. Pregnant women at around 14 weeks of gestation were randomly allocated to the experimental or control group using sealed, opaque and unnumbered envelopes. Twenty-one women with twin pregnancies, 13 with uncertain dates and 60 with antenatal care somewhere else were excluded from the study. SFH was routinely measured after 28 weeks and the results plotted on a locally derived centile chart. Women in the control group had observations made with a fabric strip.

The Peto OR for the main outcomes was:

- perinatal mortality – 1.25 (95% CI 0.38 to 4.08)
- labour induction for FGR – 0.84 (95% CI 0.44 to 1.59)
- caesarean section for FGR – 0.72 (95% CI 0.31 to 1.67)
- birthweight < 10th centile – 1.34 (95% CI 0.91 to 1.98)
- admission to neonatal unit – 1.07 (95% CI 0.69 to 1.65).

No statistically significant difference was found for other outcomes (Apgar score < 4 at 1 minute and 5 minutes, umbilical artery pH < 7.15 or antepartum hospitalisation for suspected FGR).

Evidence summary

The results from the single trial in the Cochrane review show no evidence of improved outcome from SFH measurements.

12.4.2 Ultrasound biometry

Description of included studies

A retrospective cohort study[936] was carried out in a tertiary care hospital in the USA to determine whether fetal growth measured at serial ultrasound examinations can predict neonatal morbidity

2008 update

independently of whether gestational age is known. [EL = 2+] The study population (n = 321) was selected from a cohort of 1836 singleton pregnancies and included all those women who underwent two or more ultrasound examinations 2–17 weeks apart during the study period (July 1994 to March 1997). Excluded were women with five or more ultrasound examinations, twin pregnancies reduced to singleton, those who had undergone fetal surgery, those transferred for delivery, and fetuses with major congenital and chromosomal anomalies. Results of ultrasound including fetal biometry measurements were obtained from the computerised database and EFW calculated using HC, AC and FL. Data from 236 women were used to construct a reference growth chart for EFW, and fetal growth < 10th centile was defined as FGR while that between the 20th and 80th centile was defined as normal fetal growth (NFG). Information from the obstetric and neonatal database was collected for the following outcomes: low birthweight (birthweight < 2500 g, < 2000 g, < 1500 g, < 5th centile and < 3rd centile for gestational age) and poor neonatal outcomes: preterm birth (< 37 weeks), long hospital stay (> 4 days), admission to NICU, and assisted ventilation required at birth. The risk of each outcome for the FGR and NFG groups was calculated in women with known gestational age only (n = 236), and relative risk (RR) with 95% CI computed. Multivariate analysis was then performed after adjusting for potential confounders (maternal age, height, weight, race, BMI, parity, fetal sex, history of substance abuse and EFW). In the end, gestational age was simulated for those with unknown gestational age and RR calculated for the whole sample. Blinding of investigators was not specified.

A prospective cohort study in Ireland[937] aimed to identify fetuses with ultrasound evidence of inadequate growth but born with birthweight > 10th centile for gestational age, and to determine whether these infants have high risk of obstetric interventions, intrapartum complications and neonatal morbidity compared with a group with normal ultrasound for fetal growth. [EL = 2–] The study population was 285 unselected mothers with singleton pregnancies and confirmed gestational age by a second-trimester scan referred for third-trimester ultrasound examination. Cases with multiple pregnancies and fetal anomalies incompatible with life were excluded. Two scans were performed – in the early third trimester and later at an average interval of 6 weeks. The Hadlock formula using HC, AC and FL was used to calculate EFW and its reference chart was drawn using data from 40 004 singleton healthy pregnancies. Inadequate fetal growth (IFG) was defined as a fall in EFW centile > 20 between the two scans, and this group was compared with the group not showing evidence of inadequate fetal growth (adequate fetal growth (AFG)) for the following complications: abnormal Doppler, induction of labour, meconium staining, need for intrapartum fetal blood sampling, operative vaginal delivery, caesarean section, Apgar score < 7 at 5 minutes and need for admission to NICU.

Findings

In the first study[936] there was no statistically significant difference in age, racial distribution, parity or substance abuse between the study population (n = 321) and the total cohort (n = 1836). 71.9% of the study population underwent two second- or third-trimester ultrasound examinations while others had more than two.

The relative risk in women with fetuses of known gestational age is shown in Table 12.8.

Table 12.8 Summary of findings from a retrospective cohort study[936] to determine the predictive value of fetal growth restriction detected by serial ultrasound

Outcome	FGR (n = 24)	NFG (n = 212)	RR
Low birthweight			
BW < 2500 g	63%	16%	3.9 (95% CI 2.5 to 6.0)
BW < 1500 g	25%	3%	8.8 (95% CI 3.1 to 25.2)
BW < 5th centile	25%	1%	17.7 (95% CI 4.7 to 66.1)
Poor neonatal outcome			
Preterm birth	50%	22%	2.3 (95% CI 1.4 to 3.7)
Long neonatal hospital stay	50%	19%	2.6 (95% CI 1.6 to 4.2)
NICU admission	46%	13%	3.6 (95% CI 2.1 to 6.3)
Assisted ventilation required	21%	5%	4.0 (95% CI 1.5 to 10.6)

Fetuses with FGR had significantly increased risk of being low birthweight or having poor neonatal outcome compared with the NFG group. In multivariate analysis after adjusting for potential confounding variables, fetal growth remained an independent predictor of low birthweight and poor neonatal outcomes, with adjusted odd ratios ranging from 4.1 to 36.1. The risks of poor neonatal outcomes were very similar when analysis was done for the whole group using simulated gestational age.

In the second study[937] 89 women were excluded from the study population because their birthweight was either < 10th centile ($n = 60$) or > 90th centile ($n = 29$). Infants with birthweight < 10th centile had significantly increased incidence of intrapartum fetal blood sampling and admission to NICU ($P < 0.05$ for both with χ^2 analysis) compared with infants with birthweight between the 10th and 90th centile. Infants having birthweight > 90th centile had increased incidence of caesarean section ($P < 0.05$).

Of the remaining 196 fetuses, 75 showed evidence of inadequate growth (IFG group) while the remaining 121 formed the comparator group (AFG group). Babies in the IFG group had a significantly higher incidence of admission to the NICU (OR 3.1, 95% CI 1.19 to 8.52; $P < 0.05$), and higher incidence of meconium staining but this was not statistically significant (OR 1.40, 95% CI 0.64 to 3.03; $P = 0.36$). No difference was observed between the two groups regarding all other outcomes.

Evidence summary
Inadequate fetal growth detected by ultrasound is associated with an increased risk of low birthweight and poor neonatal outcome.

There is no difference in the risk of obstetric and neonatal complications between fetuses with evidence of inadequate growth on ultrasound but with birthweight appropriate for gestational age, and fetuses with adequate growth.

12.4.3   Ultrasound for amniotic fluid volume

Description of included studies
The first cohort study conducted in the USA[938] examined fetal growth and perinatal outcomes in pregnancies with isolated oligohydramnios (OH) by using data from the multicentre clinical trial of Routine Antenatal Diagnostic Imaging with Ultrasound (RADIUS trial). [EL = 2+] The study population for this cohort ($n = 7549$) included English-speaking women at least than 18 years of age with singleton pregnancy, known LMP and gestational age below 18 weeks in the screening arm of trial only, that is, those who underwent ultrasound screening twice at 15–22 and 31–35 weeks. Oligohydramnios was defined as AFI ≤ 5 cm and clinicians were blinded to the results. This cohort was use to describe the incidence and conditions associated with OH. To examine perinatal outcomes further, women with OH were compared with those having normal AFI (Normal/N group, $n = 7215$). This comparison was made in both groups: Group 1 with associated maternal/fetal conditions (PROM, congenital malformations, hypertension (HT), diabetes, FGR, post-term) and Group 2 without any such condition. Isolated OH was defined as OH in women without any associated maternal/fetal condition. The χ^2 test was used for comparison and RR with 95% CI calculated wherever appropriate.

The other study was a nested case–control study from the USA[939] carried out to determine whether hydramnios is associated with increased risk of adverse perinatal outcomes. [EL = 2+] Computerised records of all ultrasound examinations carried out from 1986 to 1996 were reviewed to identify singleton pregnancies in which AF volume was assessed. Cases were defined as pregnancies complicated by hydramnios after 20 weeks of gestation and controls included all singleton pregnancies having normal AF volume on ultrasound after 20 weeks. Hydramnios was taken as AFI ≥ 25 cm or depth more than 8 cm measured in a single vertical pocket or sonographer's subjective impression. Multiple gestations and OH cases were excluded. Blinding was not specified. Comparison was made for adverse perinatal outcomes using χ^2 test/Fischer exact test for dichotomous variables and Student's t test for continuous variables. Confounding variables known to influence perinatal outcomes were analysed in a multiple logistic regression model.

2008 update

Findings

In the cohort study OH was diagnosed in 113/7549 of the study cohort and among these 47% had certain associated maternal/fetal conditions, leaving 60 cases with isolated OH. To compare perinatal outcomes, all cases of OH including those from the other arm of the trial (*n* = 164) were used. OH in pregnancies associated with unfavourable maternal/fetal conditions (Group 1) had higher risk of adverse perinatal outcomes, but isolated OH (in Group 2) had perinatal outcomes similar to those with normal AFI (Table 12.9).

Table 12.9 Summary of findings comparing labour and neonatal outcomes for women with oligohydramnios plus coexisting pregnancy complications and those with isolated oligohydramnios[938]

Outcome	Group 1			Group 2		
	OH (n = 78)	N (n = 644)	RR (95% CI)	OH (n = 86)	N (n = 6571)	RR (95% CI)
Preterm delivery	24.4%	13.2%	1.9 (1.2–3.1)	3.5%	4.1%	0.9 (0.3–2.7)
Caesarean section	24%	29%	0.9 (0.6–1.3)	19%	14%	1.4 (0.8–2.4)
Apgar < 7 (5 minutes)	7.7%	3.1%	2.2 (1.1–4.7)	1.2%	1.2%	1.0 (0.1–7.0)
Perinatal mortality	5.1%	1.2%	4.1 (1.3–13.4)	0%	0.5%	0
Severe morbidity	7.7%	5.3%	1.5 (0.5–3.8)	1.2%	0.8%	1.4 (0.2–10.3)
Moderate morbidity	6.4%	5.9%	1.1 (0.3–2.9)	1.2%	2.2%	0.5 (0.1–3.8)

Severe morbidity included grade IV retinopathy of prematurity (ROP), bronchopulmonary dysplasia (BPD), ventilation more than 48 hours, intestinal perforation due to necrotising enterocolists, grade III or IV intraventricular haemorrhage, subdural/cerebral haemorrage, neonatal seizures, chest tube insertion, documented neonatal sepsis, and special care nursery stay ≥ 30 days.

Moderate morbidity included presumed neonatal sepsis, oxygen requirement > 48 hours, NEC without perforation, intraventricular haemorrhage grade I or II, fracture of clavicle or other bone, facial nerve or brachial plexus injury, and special care nursery stay ≥ 5 days.

In the nested case–control study,[939] ultrasound examinations were done in 40 065 women during the study period. After exclusion, 370 cases with hydramnios and 36 426 controls with normal AF volume were identified. The perinatal mortality rate was more than 3 times higher, fetal anomalies 25 times higher, rate of caesarean section 3 times higher and diabetes 6 times higher in cases compared with women with normal AF volume (Table 12.10).

After controlling for confounding variables in a regression model, women with hydramnios still had increased risk of perinatal mortality (RR 3.8, 95% CI 1.9 to 7.3) and fetal anomalies (RR 18.2, 95% CI 8.7 to 38.2).

Table 12.10 Summary of findings comparing labour and neonatal outcomes for women with hydramnios and those with normal volume of amniotic fluid[939]

Outcome	Cases	Controls	RR (95% CI)
Perinatal mortality rate (per 1000 births)	49	14	3.4 (2.2–5.4)
Fetal anomalies	8.4%	0.3%	25.4 (17.4–37.2)
FGR	3.8%	6.7%	0.6 (0.3–0.9)
Caesarean section	47%	16.4%	2.9 (2.6–3.2)
Diabetes	19.5%	3.2%	6.0 (4.9–7.5)

Evidence summary

Pregnancies with reduced amniotic fluid volume and no associated maternal or fetal conditions do not show an increased incidence of obstetric interventions or adverse perinatal outcomes. However, oligohydramnios in the presence of pregnancy complications is associated with an increased risk of preterm delivery and perinatal death.

Increased amniotic fluid volume in pregnancies is associated with increased risk of maternal diabetes, fetal anomalies and perinatal mortality.

12.4.4 Doppler ultrasound

Description of included studies

A Cochrane review[575] was carried out to assess the effectiveness of routine Doppler ultrasound in obstetric practice and pregnancy outcomes in unselected and low-risk pregnancies. [EL = 1++] It included all randomised and quasi-randomised controlled trials where routine Doppler ultrasound of umbilical artery and/or uterine artery was done in both unselected and low-risk pregnant women. Primary outcome measures were induction of labour, caesarean section, preterm delivery < 28 and < 34 weeks, all deaths (perinatal, neonatal and infant), neurodevelopment at 2 years of age, and maternal psychological effects. The Cochrane Pregnancy and Childbirth Group Specialized Register and Cochrane Controlled Trial Register were searched. Two independent reviewers evaluated the trials for methodological quality and inclusion criteria. Additional information was sought from the authors of two trials by personal communication. Data were extracted by both reviewers independently and double-checked for discrepancies. Statistical analysis was performed using RevMan software and stratified analysis was planned for single, multiple and Doppler in all versus no Doppler/selective Doppler.

Findings

Five trials were included – two studied unselected population and three only low-risk populations. A total of 14 338 pregnant women were recruited. Three trials evaluated umbilical artery Doppler only and used sealed envelopes for randomisation. The other two evaluated both umbilical and uterine artery waveforms and in addition used serial ultrasound or serial Doppler for the population. The methodological quality of all included studies was generally good. No data were available for prespecified outcomes of acute neonatal problems, long-term neurodevelopment or maternal psychological effects. Owing to the small number of included trials, no stratified analysis was performed.

Routine Doppler ultrasound (umbilical and/or uterine) versus no/concealed/selective Doppler ultrasound:
Meta-analysis of four trials showed no differences between the two groups in antenatal admissions or other tests of fetal wellbeing, induction of labour, instrumental deliveries, caesarean section, neonatal interventions or overall perinatal mortality. Three trials reported perinatal mortality for fetuses/neonates without congenital anomalies, but there was heterogeneity of results (χ^2 10.44; $P < 0.025$) with one trial finding increased perinatal mortality in the screened group (OR 3.31, 95% CI 1.37 to 2.53).

Serial ultrasound and Doppler ultrasound versus selective ultrasound:
A single trial compared the two groups and no difference was found between them for all the primary outcomes. More babies in the screened group were of birthweight < 10th and < 3rd centile.

Evidence summary

Existing evidence shows that routine use of Doppler ultrasound (umbilical and/or uterine) in low-risk or unselected populations does not seem to be beneficial for either mother or baby.

12.4.5 Customised fetal growth charts

The customised fetal growth chart (CFGC) is the term used for an individually adjusted standard for fundal height, EFW and birthweight which takes into consideration maternal characteristics such as height, country of family origin, cigarette smoking and diabetes.

Description of included studies

A prospective non-RCT in the UK[567] was carried out to evaluate the effect of a policy of using serial SFH measurements plotted on CFGC compared with a routine antenatal care policy of recording SFH against women's gestational age. Two similar catchment areas (in terms of distance from hospital, ethnicity and socio-economic background of population, and number of referrals per year) of a tertiary level hospital served by separate and non-overlapping groups of community midwives and GPs were selected as the study and control group. The study commenced in May 1994 and ended in March 1995. The study group comprised all singleton pregnancies (n = 734) booked before 22 weeks gestational age and issued CFGC, but 67 were excluded owing to miscarriage or migration to other areas before delivery. The control group included 605 consecutive singleton pregnancies booked before 22 weeks and delivered in the hospital. Primary outcomes measured were the number of SGA (< 10th centile) and LGA (> 90th centile) babies detected antenatally in each group. Secondary outcomes were the total number of investigations performed in each group, including referrals to ultrasound department/pregnancy assessment unit, and admissions to the ward. Sample size was calculated to detect an increase of 25% detection of SGA at a significance level of 5% and power of 80%. Blinding of outcome investigator and concealment of allocation was not possible owing to the study design. [EL = 1−]

The second study was a population-based cohort study[940] using the Swedish Birth Register. Two standards for estimating birthweight were constructed from the database – a fixed population one based on gender and gestational length, and an individually customised one with further adjustment for maternal height, weight, parity and ethnic group. SGA determined by the population standard was termed SGA (pop.), by the customised standard as SGA (cust.), and by both standards as SGA (both). In both the groups, SGA was defined as the lowest 10%, 5% or 2.5% of birthweights in the population. Risks of stillbirth, neonatal death and Apgar score < 4 at 5 minutes were then compared in infants classified as SGA by the two standards with that of non-SGA infants (classified using both standards). The cohort included all recorded births from 1992 to 1995 and the study sample excluded multiple births and those with congenital malformations, unknown gestation and missing values for the required parameters. All the outcomes were adequately defined, but confounding factors were not controlled for. [EL = 2 +]

In the third study[941] the same Swedish database as the one used in the second study was analysed retrospectively to examine the potential biases underlying the use of customised standards of birthweight for gestational age. It included all recorded births with complete data for a period of 10 years (1992–2001). Apart from using the same exclusion criteria as the other study, this study also excluded births with gestational age < 28 weeks in order to ensure comparability between the two groups. After classifying the births as non-SGA (both standards), SGA (cust.), SGA (pop.), and SGA (both), the same outcomes as used in the earlier study were compared. In addition, logistic regression models were used to examine the association between the two standards and different outcomes taking into account the effect of potential confounding variables. [EL = 2+]

Another multicentre study from France (Ref ID 38842) used the same methodology as that followed by the Swedish study above to determine the association between customised standards and adverse pregnancy outcomes. Data sets from five maternity hospitals were analysed retrospectively to identify SGA babies using both the population-based standard and the customised standard, and the risk of adverse perinatal outcomes was compared between these two group of babies using non-SGA babies (classified by both standards) as the reference group. About 25% of the data could not be analysed because of missing values, and the study did not make any adjustment for confounding variables. [EL = 2+]

In the last study from Spain (Ref ID 38840), a database of a tertiary hospital was analysed retrospectively and SGA babies identified with the two standards using the same methodology as in the above-mentioned three studies. The risk of perinatal mortality and neonatal morbidity (neurological and non-neurological) was then compared between the two groups of SGA babies after adjusting for gestational age at delivery by means of logistic regression. [EL = 2+]

2008 update

Findings

The baseline characteristics including those related to pregnancy were similar in the two groups in the controlled trial.[567] 96.3% of the issued CFGC were retrieved after birth and most of them had from three to seven measurements plotted.

A significantly higher proportion of SGA infants in the study group were suspected antenatally compared with the control group (47.9% versus 29.2%; OR 2.23, 95% CI 1.12 to 4.45). Furthermore, higher numbers of LGA babies were detected before birth in the study group (45.7% versus 24.2%; OR 2.63, 95% CI 1.27 to 5.45). However, no data were collected to allow determination of specificity.

No difference was observed between the two groups for obstetric interventions (induction of labour, caesarean section, and instrumental delivery), preterm delivery, admission to special care baby unit, fetal abnormality or resuscitation at birth.

There were significantly fewer referrals from the study group to a pregnancy assessment centre, both in numbers of women referred and total number of visits. The number of women admitted to antenatal ward was also significantly lower in the study group.

The study sample in the second study[940] was 326 377, and the rates of adverse outcomes were similar between the study group and the excluded group.

Based on the population standard, maternal age < 19 years, primiparity, BMI < 19.9 kg/m² and maternal height < 154 cm were found to be the risk factors for SGA babies while BMI > 30 kg/m² and maternal age more than 35 years were the risk factors found with a customised standard.

Table 12.11 presents the risks (odds ratio) between the two groups using births that are non-SGA by both standards as the reference category.

Table 12.11   Comparison of risks for poor neonatal outcomes for babies that are non-SGA defined by population standard and customised standard as the reference category

	Stillbirth OR	Neonatal death OR	Apgar < 4 OR
SGA (pop.) vs non-SGA (cust.)	1.2 (95% CI 0.8 to 1.9)	0.9 (95% CI 0.3 to 2.3)	1.2 (95% CI 0.9 to 1.5)
SGA (cust.) vs non-SGA (pop.)	6.1 (95% CI 5.0 to 7.5)	4.1(95% CI 2.5 to 6.6)	2.2 (95% CI 1.9 to 2.7)
SGA (cust.) vs SGA (pop.)	5.1 (95% CI 4.3 to 5.9)	3.4 (95% CI 2.4 to 4.8)	2.0 (95% CI 1.7 to 2.3)

cust. = customised; pop. = population.

Compared with births that were non-SGA by both standards, births classified as SGA (cust.) had 5–6 times higher risk of stillbirth regardless of whether they were also small by the population standard. In contrast, SGA classified by population standard only did not show an elevated risk. For the other two adverse outcomes a similar pattern of increased risk was seen among babies classified as SGA by the customised standard. They had an increased risk of neonatal death (OR 3.4, 95% CI 2.4 to 4.8) and low Apgar score < 4 (OR 2.0, 95% CI 1.7 to 2.3) compared with SGA babies classified by the population standard.

In the third study,[941] a total of 782 303 singleton pregnancies at ≥ 28 weeks were included. There was substantial agreement in the classification by the two standards, with 95% of births classified as SGA or non-SGA by both standards. Analysis of the database showed increased risks of stillbirths (crude OR 7.8) and neonatal death (crude OR 6.7) among the SGA (cust.) babies, compared with marginally increased risks for SGA (pop.) births (crude OR 1.4 and 1.3, respectively). The risk among SGA (cust.) babies was even higher than that of SGA classified by both standards (crude OR 5.7 for both outcomes). These results were similar to those of the previous study.

However, after controlling for gestational age as the potential confounder, the risk of adverse outcomes in SGA (cust.) babies (adjusted OR 2.4 and 2.1) became less than that of SGA by both standards (adjusted OR 4.8 and 4.9), and slightly higher than that of SGA (pop.) babies (adjusted OR 1.6 and 1.5). A substantial number of babies classified as SGA (cust.) were born at < 37 weeks compared with the other groups (16.6% versus 7.0% for SGA both standards, 3.4% for SGA (pop.), and 4.2% for non-SGA). Among the stillbirths and neonatal deaths, the mean gestational age among SGA (cust.) births was 234 days and 239 days, respectively. This is much lower than that of SGA (both) at 257 and 258 days, and SGA (pop.) births at 273 days for both groups. Similar results were seen after controlling for another confounding variable – maternal pre-pregnancy BMI.

There were 75 306 recorded singleton births in the French multicentre study between 1997 and 2002, but for 18 700 births the information was insufficient to calculate the customised birthweight and hence these were excluded from the final analysis. This group of excluded births had a much higher rate of stillbirths and neonatal deaths compared with the population included for the study ($n = 56 606$). In 95.5% of cases, there was complete agreement between the two standards for classification of either SGA or non-SGA babies, while 1.8% of all infants were reclassified as non-SGA and 2.7% as newly identified SGA by using the customised standard. Compared with non-SGA babies with both standards as the reference group, risk of stillbirth (OR 4.5, 95% CI 2.5 to 8.1) and perinatal mortality (OR 2.6, 95% CI 1.6 to 4.1) was higher in the SGA (cust.) babies compared with the SGA (pop.) babies where the odds ratio contained the null value for both these outcomes. No statistically significant difference was found between the two groups for the other adverse outcomes – caesarean section before onset of labour, Apgar score < 7, admission to NICU or neonatal death.

In the last study from Spain, the final sample of 13 661 cases excluded the 1803 cases with one or more missing data, and the rates of stillbirth and neonatal death were significantly higher among the excluded cases than the included cases (stillbirth 1.3% versus 0.6%, $P = 0.001$; neonatal death 0.5% versus 0.1%, $P < 0.001$). The unadjusted odds ratios for perinatal mortality and neurological and non-neurological morbidity was higher for SGA babies identified by a customised standard compared with SGA babies identified using the population-based standard (perinatal mortality OR 3.2 versus 1.8; neurological morbidity OR 3.2 versus 1.6; non-neurological morbidity OR 8.0 versus 1.1). After adjusting for gestational age at the time of delivery, the odds ratios for neurological and non-neurological morbidity were 1.6 (95% CI 1.0 to 2.6) and 2.1 (95% CI 1.2 to 3.6), respectively, for SGA (cust.) cases and 1.4 (95% CI 0.8 to 2.3) and 1.5 (95% CI 0.7 to 2.9), respectively, for SGA (pop.) cases.

Evidence summary
One prospective study has been conducted to evaluate the effectiveness of CFGC, plus four retrospective studies. Findings from the single prospective study suggest that customised fetal growth charts lead to antenatal detection of a higher proportion of SGA and LGA babies compared with routine SFH charts and a decrease in referrals to obstetricians and referrals to the antenatal ward, but do not decrease obstetric interventions such as caesarean section or adverse perinatal outcomes such as admission to neonatal intensive care. However, there is variable evidence on the effectiveness of CFGC in identifying SGA babies at increased risk of perinatal mortality. Data from the prospective study were insufficient to allow calculation of predictive accuracy. Results from four studies with retrospective analysis of the data set have indicated that babies with a higher risk of stillbirths and perinatal mortality are more likely to be categorised as SGA on a CFGC compared with a population-based standard. Two of these studies did not control for confounding variables. In the remaining two studies, the increased risk of adverse perinatal outcomes in SGA babies identified using the customised standard was lowered after adjusting for confounding variables (substantial reduction in the study with a larger sample size). No study was identified where the CFGC was prospectively used to evaluate its effectiveness in improving the outcome in identified SGA babies.

12.5   Health economics evidence

A systematic review of the evidence found no studies concerned with the cost-effectiveness of fetal growth monitoring and so it was decided that a decision-analysis model would be developed. For full details of the review and the model, please refer to Appendix G. The GDG felt that through the identification of babies that are SGA, approximately 185–225 perinatal deaths could be prevented. Cost-effectiveness analysis showed that if this were the case then SFH measurement followed by ultrasound monitoring of fetal growth would be a cost-effective intervention.

GDG interpretation of evidence for Sections 12.1 to 12.13

SGA babies:
Abdominal palpation is not useful in identifying fetuses at risk.

SFH measurement may have limited use in identifying SGA babies but good-quality evidence is lacking and the GDG felt it was not appropriate to recommend a change in current practice. There is no evidence to suggest that there is any benefit in measuring SFH prior to 24 weeks.

Measurement of fetal abdominal circumference has some diagnostic value in identifying SGA babies but the studies show statistical heterogeneity.

AFI is a poor predictor of SGA babies.

Doppler examination has limited diagnostic value in the low-risk population.

There is a lack of good-quality prospective evidence for plotting SFH on customised growth charts to identify SGA babies, but the GDG is aware they are in use in some maternity units.

There is no good-quality prospective evidence that the use of customised fetal growth charts improves perinatal outcomes.

LGA babies:
Evidence suggests SFH measurements are not good at predicting LGA babies.

There is lack of good-quality evidence for the diagnostic value of fetal biometry for LGA. One small study suggested that fetal biometry may be of some value in identifying LGA babies.

Recommendations on determining fetal growth

Symphysis–fundal height should be measured and recorded at each antenatal appointment from 24 weeks.

Ultrasound estimation of fetal size for suspected large-for-gestational-age unborn babies should not be undertaken in a low-risk population.

Routine Doppler ultrasound in low-risk pregnancies should not be used.

Research recommendations on determining fetal growth

Further prospective research is required to evaluate the diagnostic value and effectiveness (both clinical and cost-effectiveness) of predicting small-for-gestational-age babies using:

- customised fetal growth charts to plot symphysis–fundal height measurements
- routine ultrasound in the third trimester.

Why this is important
Poor fetal growth is undoubtedly a cause of serious perinatal mortality and morbidity. Unfortunately, the methods by which the condition can be identified antenatally are poorly developed or not tested by rigorous methodology. However, existing evidence suggests that there may be ways in which babies at risk can be identified and appropriately managed to improve outcome, and this should form the basis of the study.

12.6 Fetal wellbeing

12.6.1 Abdominal palpation for fetal presentation

A study of clinicians using Leopold manoeuvres to assess presentation and engagement if the presenting part found that 53% of all malpresentations were detected and that there was a definite correlation with years of clinical experience and better results.[562] [EL = 3] This finding was supported by another study which looked specifically detection of breech presentation.[563]

2008 update

[EL = 3] The sensitivity and specificity of Leopold manoeuvres is reported to be about 28% and 94%, respectively.[564] [EL = 3]

One descriptive study reported that women do not enjoy being palpated, finding it uncomfortable and not reassuring or informative.[565] [EL = 3]

Recommendations

Fetal presentation should be assessed by abdominal palpation at 36 weeks or later, when presentation is likely to influence the plans for the birth. Routine assessment of presentation by abdominal palpation should not be offered before 36 weeks because it is not always accurate and may be uncomfortable. [C]

Suspected fetal malpresentation should be confirmed by an ultrasound assessment. [Good practice point]

12.6.2 Routine monitoring of fetal movements

There is often no obvious cause of late fetal death of normally formed singleton births. Many of these deaths are unpredictable and occur in women who are healthy and who have had otherwise uncomplicated pregnancies.

Maternal recognition of decreased fetal movement has long been used during antenatal care in an attempt to identify the jeopardised fetus and intervene to prevent death. Given the low prevalence of fetal compromise and an estimated specificity of 90% to 95%, the positive predictive value of the maternal perception of reduced fetal movements for fetal compromise is low, 2% to 7%.[568]

One RCT was found that assessed the ability of the 'count to ten' method to reduce the prevalence of antenatal fetal death.[569] [EL = 1b] The method records on a chart the time interval each day required to feel ten fetal movements. This cluster RCT randomised 68 000 women to either routine formal fetal-movement counting or to standard care. It found that there was no decrease in perinatal mortality in the test group and this policy would have to be used by about 1250 women to prevent one unexplained death.

Following a reduction in fetal movements women should be advised to contact their midwife or hospital for further assessment.

The evidence does not support the routine use of formal fetal movement counting to prevent late fetal death.

Recommendation

Routine formal fetal-movement counting should not be offered. [A]

12.6.3 Auscultation of fetal heart

Auscultation of the fetal heart is a component of the abdominal examination and forms an integral part of a standard antenatal examination. Although hearing the fetal heart confirms that the fetus is alive there appears to be no other clinical or predictive value.[570,571] [EL = 3] This is because it is unlikely that detailed information on the fetal heart such as decelerations or variability can be heard on auscultation.

There is a perception among doctors and midwives that fetal heart rate auscultation is enjoyable and reassuring for pregnant women and therefore worthwhile. This is not based on published evidence and may not be a correct assumption. Research done on attitudes of women towards auscultation compared with electronic fetal monitoring in labour revealed that many women found the abdominal pressure from auscultation uncomfortable,[572] [EL = 3] so perhaps their attitudes to antenatal auscultation cannot be presumed.

Recommendation

Auscultation of the fetal heart may confirm that the fetus is alive but is unlikely to have any predictive value and routine listening is therefore not recommended. However, when requested by the mother, auscultation of the fetal heart may provide reassurance. [D]

12.6.4 Cardiotocography

There is no evidence to evaluate the use of antenatal cardiotocography (CTG) for routine fetal assessment in normal pregnancies. RCTs which included women who were healthy and who had uncomplicated pregnancies were not found.

A systematic review of RCTs assessed the effects of antenatal CTG monitoring on perinatal morbidity and mortality and maternal morbidity.[573] [EL = 1a] Four trials were included randomising 1588 woman who satisfied the inclusion criteria. In these trials, carried out on high- or intermediate-risk women, antenatal CTG appeared to have no significant effect on perinatal morbidity or mortality. There was no increase in the incidence of interventions such as elective caesarean section or induction of labour.

Recommendation

The evidence does not support the routine use of antenatal electronic fetal heart rate monitoring (cardiotocography) for fetal assessment in women with an uncomplicated pregnancy and therefore it should not be offered. [A]

12.6.5 Ultrasound assessment in the third trimester

One systematic review of seven RCTs examined the use of routine ultrasound after 24 weeks in an unselected and designated low-risk population. There was a wide variation in the provision of ultrasound within the studies. The main comparison group of six studies compared routine ultrasound after 24 weeks with no, selective or concealed ultrasound after 24 weeks.[574] [EL = 1a]

There were no differences between preterm delivery, birthweight or perinatal mortality. The screened group was less likely to deliver post-term (over 42 weeks), although this may be a result of more accurate dating prior to 24 weeks, as outlined above. Similarly, there were no differences in other outcomes of antenatal, obstetric or neonatal interventions.[574]

Recommendation

The evidence does not support the routine use of ultrasound scanning after 24 weeks of gestation and therefore it should not be offered. [A]

13 Management of specific clinical conditions

13.1 Pregnancy after 41 weeks

2008

Note: This section is being updated by the NICE Induction of Labour clinical guideline due to be published in June 2008. Following its publication, the relevant section in that guideline will supersede the text and recommendations contained here.

Data from one cohort[577] [EL = 2a] revealed that, at 40 weeks of gestation, only 58% of women had delivered. This increased to 74% by 41 weeks and to 82% by 42 weeks. Population studies indicate that in women who are healthy and have otherwise uncomplicated pregnancies perinatal mortality and morbidity is increased in pregnancies of longer duration than 42 weeks. The risk of stillbirth increases from 1/3000 ongoing pregnancies at 37 weeks to 3/3000 ongoing pregnancies at 42 weeks to 6/3000 ongoing pregnancies at 43 weeks.[577] [EL = 2a] A similar increase in neonatal mortality is also reported.

Ultrasound assessment of fetal size is associated with a reduction in rates of intervention for post-term pregnancies. One systematic review of nine RCTs found routine ultrasound scanning before 24 weeks to be associated with a reduction in the rate of induced labour for post-term pregnancy when compared with selective use of ultrasound (Peto OR 0.61, 95% CI 0.52 to 0.72). A systematic review evaluated interventions aimed at prevention or improvement of outcomes of delivery beyond term.[578] [EL = 1a]

Membrane sweeping

Sweeping the membranes in women at term reduced the delay between randomisation and spontaneous onset of labour, or between randomisation and birth, by a mean of 3 days. Sweeping the membranes increased the likelihood of both spontaneous labour within 48 hours (63.8% versus 83.0%; RR 0.77, 95% CI 0.70 to 0.84; NNT 5) and of birth within 1 week (48.0% versus 66.0%; RR 0.73, 95% CI 0.66 to 0.80; NNT 5). Sweeping the membranes performed as a general policy from 38 to 40 weeks onwards decreased the frequency of prolonged pregnancy: more than 42 weeks: 3.4% versus 12.9%; RR 0.27, 95% CI 0.15 to 0.49; NNT: 11; more than 41 weeks: 18.6% versus 29.87%, RR 0.62, 95% CI 0.49 to 0.79; NNT: 8.[579] [EL = 1a]

Membrane sweeping reduced the frequency of using other methods to induce labour ('formal induction of labour'). The overall risk reduction in the available trials was 15%. This risk reduction of a formal induction of labour was 21.3% versus 36.3% (RR 0.59, CI 0.50 to 0.70; NNT 7). The risk of operative delivery is not changed by the intervention. There was no difference in other measures of effectiveness or adverse maternal outcomes. Sweeping the membranes was not associated with an increase in maternal infection or fever rates (4.4% versus 4.5%; RR 0.97, 95% CI 0.60 to 1.57), Similarly, there was no increase in neonatal infection (1.4% versus 1.3%; RR 0.92, 95% CI 0.30 to 2.82). No major maternal side effects were reported in the trials.[579] [EL = 1a]

A trial that systematically assessed minor side effects and women's discomfort during the procedure, found women in the 'sweeping' group reported more discomfort during vaginal examination. Median pain scores were higher this group. (Pain was assessed by the Short Form of the McGill Pain Questionnaire, that included three scales: a visual analogue scale (0–10 cm), the present pain index (0–5) and a set of 15 descriptors of pain scoring 0–3). In addition, more women allocated to sweeping experienced vaginal bleeding and painful contractions not leading to onset of labour during the 24 hours following the intervention.[580]

There was no difference in any fetal outcome between the membrane sweeping and the non-membrane sweeping groups. These results must be interpreted with caution due to the presence of heterogeneity. The trials included in this review did not report in relevant clinical subgroups.

Induction of labour after 41 weeks

The benefit of active induction of labour compared with expectant management is derived from trials of routine induction of labour after 41 weeks. With routine induction, perinatal death was reduced (Peto OR 0.23, 95% CI 0.06 to 0.90) and the rate of caesarean section was reduced (Peto OR 0.87, 95% CI 0.77 to 0.99).[578] [EL = 1a] There was no effect on instrumental delivery rates, use of epidural analgesia or fetal heart rate abnormalities during labour with a routine policy of induction of labour.[578] [EL = 1a] There was a reduction in meconium staining of the amniotic fluid with routine induction (Peto OR 0.74, 95% CI 0.65 to 0.84). However, this finding is probably related to the increase in meconium-stained liquor seen with increasing gestation in the conservative management arm of these trials.[578] [EL = 1a] No difference in maternal satisfaction as measured by one trial with either active management or expectant management was found (Peto OR 0.84, 95% CI 0.57 to 1.24).[578] [EL = 1a]

Recommendations

Prior to formal induction of labour,* women should be offered a vaginal examination for membrane sweeping. [A]

Women with uncomplicated pregnancies should be offered induction of labour* beyond 41 weeks. [A]

13.2 Pregnancy after 42 weeks

The systematic review included data on one trial comparing complex antenatal fetal monitoring (computerised cardiotocography, amniotic fluid index and assessment of fetal breathing, tone and gross body movements) to simpler monitoring (standard cardiotocography and ultrasound measurement of maximum pool depth) for identification of high-risk pregnancies from 42 weeks. There was no difference between the two policies with respect to perinatal mortality or caesarean section. However, the number of pregnant women included in this trial was small (n = 145) and, hence, the trial was underpowered to detect any significant differences in perinatal mortality.[578] [EL = 1a]

Offering routine early pregnancy ultrasound reduces the incidence of induction for perceived prolonged pregnancy. A policy of offering routine induction of labour after 41 weeks reduces perinatal mortality without an increase in caesarean section rates. The type of antenatal monitoring in the identification of high-risk pregnancies beyond 42 weeks is uncertain (but the simpler modalities used have been as effective as the more complex). There has been no detectable difference in effect of simpler modalities compared with more complex modalities.

Comprehensive information on the induction of labour can be found in the NICE Induction of Labour guideline (to be published June 2008).

Recommendation

From 42 weeks, women who decline induction of labour should be offered increased antenatal monitoring consisting of at least twice-weekly cardiotocography and ultrasound estimation of maximum amniotic pool depth. [Good practice point]

See also Section 4.6 Gestational age assessment.

---

* The clinical guideline 'Induction of labour' is being updated and is expected to be published in June 2008.

13.3 Breech presentation at term

Evidence from the National Sentinel Caesarean Section Audit indicates that about 4% of singleton pregnancies are breech presentation: 3% of term infants, 9% of those born at 33 to 36 weeks of gestation, 18% of those born at 28 to 32 weeks and 30% of those born at less than 28 weeks.[581]

Breech presentation, but not breech delivery, has been associated with cerebral palsy and handicap, due principally to the association with preterm birth and congenital malformations.[582,583]

Interventions to promote cephalic version of babies in the breech position include external cephalic version (ECV), moxibustion and postural management.

ECV involves applying pressure to the pregnant woman's abdomen to turn the fetus in either a forward or backward somersault to achieve a vertex presentation. Recognised complications of ECV attributable to the procedure (and incidence) include:

- fetal heart rate abnormalities: the most common is transient bradycardia (1.1% to 16%)[584–587]
- placental abruption (0.4% to 1%)[584,586]
- painless vaginal bleeding (1.1%)[586]
- admission for induction of labour (3%).[587]

Success rates for cephalic presentation at delivery following ECV in nulliparous women range from 35% to 57% and from 52% to 84% in parous women.[584–586,588] Caesarean section rates as a complication resulting from the procedure range from 0.4% to 4%.[584,588]

Two systematic reviews identified nine RCTs that examined the effect of ECV for breech at term and before term.[589,590] The trials excluded women with uterine scars or abnormalities, multiple gestations, fetal compromise, ruptured membranes, vaginal bleeding or medical conditions, and those in labour.

ECV before 37 weeks of gestation did not make a significant difference to the incidence of noncephalic births at term (three RCTs, $n = 889$ women, RR 1.02, 95% CI 0.89 to 1.17) nor to the rate of caesarean section (two RCTs, $n = 742$, RR 1.10, 95% CI 0.78 to 1.54).[589] [EL = 1a] Performing ECV at term (defined as 37 weeks of gestation or more in three RCTs, at least 36 weeks of gestation in two RCTs and between 33 and 40 weeks in one RCT) reduced the number of noncephalic births by 60% when compared with no ECV (six RCTs, $n = 612$ women, RR 0.42, 95% CI 0.35 to 0.50).[590] [EL = 1a] A significant reduction in caesarean section was also observed in the ECV group when compared with no ECV (six RCTs, $n = 612$, RR 0.52, 95% CI 0.39 to 0.71). Five of the trials used tocolysis routinely or selectively[585,588,591–593] and in one of them,[586] no tocolysis had been used. [EL = 1a]

Various interventions have been tried to increase the success rates of ECV. These include the routine or selective use of tocolysis, the use of regional analgesia, the use of vibroacoustic stimulation and amnioinfusion. A systematic review of six randomised and quasi-randomised trials comprising 617 women with a breech presentation at term was identified.[594] Routine tocolysis with betamimetic drugs was associated with a 30% increase in the chances of successful ECV (RR 0.74, 95% CI 0.64 to 0.87). This review also showed that the rate of caesarean section was reduced in the group of women who had tocolysis (RR 0.85, 95% CI 0.72 to 0.99). No differences, however, were reported in rates of noncephalic births at term (RR 0.80, 95% CI 0.60, 1.07). [EL = 1a] None of the RCTs used newer tocolytics and the effectiveness of these is uncertain. There is also not enough evidence to evaluate the use of fetal acoustic stimulation in midline fetal spine positions, or epidural or spinal analgesia.

An RCT[595] conducted in the USA evaluated the value of performing pelvimetry in predicting who would deliver vaginally compared with using clinical examination.[235] Women with a breech presentation at term were studied. In the first group, pelvimetry results were revealed to the obstetricians and used as a basis for the decision on mode of delivery. In the second group, pelvimetry results were not disclosed and mode of delivery was decided clinically. Main outcome measures (a priori) were the rates of elective and emergency caesarean section and the early neonatal condition. There was no effect of pelvimetry on the vaginal delivery rate or the overall caesarean section rate but use of pelvimetry lowered the emergency caesarean section rate by half (RR 0.53, 95% CI 0.34 to 0.83). [EL = 1b]

It is not certain from this evidence whether magnetic resonance imaging pelvimetry selects cases accurately for vaginal delivery or whether knowledge of pelvic adequacy gives the obstetrician confidence in allowing a trial of vaginal delivery.[596]

ECV at term for women with a singleton breech presentation reduces the number of noncephalic births. When ECV is carried out, tocolysis reduces the chances of failed external cephalic version. ECV is associated with adverse maternal and fetal outcomes, which can be minimised by fetal monitoring during the procedure.

Postural management to promote cephalic version entails relaxation with the pelvis in an elevated position. This is usually achieved either in a knee-to-chest position or in a supine position with the pelvis elevated by a wedge-shaped cushion. Maternal postural techniques have been assessed in a systematic review of RCTs.[597] The size of all the trials was small and no effect on the rate of noncephalic births from postural management was detected between the intervention and control groups (five RCTs, $n = 392$, RR 0.95, 95% CI 0.81 to 1.11). Nor were any differences detected for caesarean section (four RCTs, $n = 292$, RR 1.07, 95% CI 0.85 to 1.33). [EL = 1a]

Further guidance on ECV and postural management may be found in the RCOG guideline on the management of breech presentation.[631]

Moxibustion refers to the burning of herbs to stimulate the acupuncture points beside the outer corner of the fifth toenail (acupoint BL 67). Two RCTs on moxibustion were located. One trial assessed the efficacy and safety of moxibustion.[598] The other trial assessed efficacy only.[599] In the first trial,[598] primigravidae in the 33rd week of gestation with breech presentation were identified by ultrasound. In the intervention group ($n = 130$), women were treated with moxibustion for one week and an additional week for those in whom ECV had not yet occurred. Women in the control group ($n = 130$) received no interventions for breech presentation. All women with persistent breech presentation after 35 weeks of gestation could undergo ECV. At an ultrasound check at the 35th week of gestation, 75% of babies were cephalic in the intervention group compared with 48% in the control group (RR 1.58, 95% CI 1.29 to 1.94). One woman in the intervention group and 24 in the control group underwent ECV after the 35th week of gestation. Version was not obtained in the woman from the intervention group but was obtained in 19 of the women from the control group. Nevertheless, babies in the moxibustion group were still significantly more likely to be cephalic at delivery compared with babies in the control group (RR 1.21, 95% CI 1.02 to 1.43). [EL = 1b]

Recommendations

All women who have an uncomplicated singleton breech pregnancy at 36 weeks should be offered external cephalic version. Exceptions include women in labour and women with a uterine scar or abnormality, fetal compromise, ruptured membranes, vaginal bleeding and medical conditions. [A]

Where it is not possible to schedule an appointment for external cephalic version at 37 weeks, it should be scheduled at 36 weeks. [Good practice point]

Future research

Further research is necessary to determine whether tocolysis improves the success rate of external cephalic version.

14 Antenatal assessment tool

14.1 Introduction and background

The CEMACH *Why Mothers Die 2000–2002* report[942] suggested that a 'national guideline for a booking clinic "risk assessment" chart should be developed to identify those pregnant women for whom midwifery-led antenatal care and birth can be advised, and those for whom specialist or joint care is more appropriate'. The report recommended that every woman should be 'offered the type of care that most suits her own particular requirements'.

This view was supported by the National Service Framework's guidance on maternity services,[943] which sets the standard of giving women '… easy access to supportive high-quality maternity services designed around their individual needs and those of their babies'.

The National Collaborating Centre for Women's and Children's Health (NCC-WCH) was commissioned by the National Institute for Health and Clinical Excellence (NICE) as part of the update of this guideline to develop an antenatal assessment tool for midwives to use at a first antenatal booking appointment.

14.2 Systematic review of the evidence

Introduction

While there exists an extensive literature on antenatal screening, including prevalence of risk factors, screening for medical and obstetric complications and screening for psychosocial problems, very few studies have been conducted to investigate the effectiveness of comprehensive antenatal assessment.

Interventions for antenatal assessment (often referred to as risk assessment) identified for this systematic review are all questionnaires, meant either for self-completion by the woman or as an interview guide for healthcare professionals. Some assessments are intended simply to identify factors which are known to be associated with increased risk of poor outcome such as low birthweight;[1001] others include a more complex weighted scoring system.[1002,1003] Five papers were identified for this systematic review which examined the usefulness of screening for psychosocial risk factors,[1004–1008] although none of these evaluated the impact of such assessment on pregnancy outcomes. Four papers investigated the usefulness of comprehensive antenatal assessment tools including medical, obstetric and psychosocial factors in predicting adverse outcomes such as perinatal outcomes,[1003] preterm labour,[1001] very low birthweight[1002] and maternal outcomes.[1009] Finally, one study examined the effect of risk scoring and the subsequent 'labelling' of women as being at high risk on women's psychological wellbeing.[1010]

Antenatal psychosocial assessment

Description of included studies

A systematic review of screening women and elderly adults for intimate partner violence (IPV) has been undertaken by the US Preventive Services Task Force (USPSTF).[1004] [EL = III] Screening was defined as an assessment of current harm or risk from family and IPV in asymptomatic persons in a healthcare setting. The quality of the included studies was rated as good, fair or poor. Within this review, one study was identified which compared scores obtained using different screening assessments when used with a sample of pregnant women (*n* = 691; quality rating good), two studies were identified which compared performance of a screening instrument with social services interview (*n* = 224 and *n* = 334; quality rating both poor), and one study which compared methods of administration of a screening questionnaire (*n* = 777; quality rating fair).

None of the identified studies evaluated the performance of a screening instrument using verified abuse outcomes.

An RCT conducted in Canada compared detection of psychosocial risk factors using the Antenatal Psychosocial Health Assessment (ALPHA) with detection through usual antenatal consultations.[1008] [EL = 1−] Midwives, obstetricians and family health physicians involved in providing antenatal care were randomly assigned to the intervention (ALPHA) group (*n* = 21) or the control group (usual antenatal care) (*n* = 27). Providers allocated to the intervention group were invited to attend a 1 hour workshop on using the ALPHA form which included role play to practice asking the questions, discussion of management strategies for partner violence and information regarding community resources for psychosocial problems. Providers were asked to enrol five consecutive women into the study, excluding women identified as being at high obstetric risk based on identified medical factors. Following the woman's consent, providers in the intervention group were asked to complete the ALPHA form with women at one antenatal visit of their choice between 20 and 32 weeks of pregnancy. The questionnaire contained 15 items, each one rated for the 'level of concern' raised as 'low', 'some' or 'high'. For the purposes of the study, issues rated as causing 'some' or a 'high' level of concern were considered as being of concern (i.e. screen positive).

A US cross-sectional descriptive study[1006] examined the relationship between routine/usual information given at first contact and responses to the three-item Abuse Assessment Screen. [EL = III] The study was carried out in an inner city primary healthcare setting serving a population of mostly Hispanic and non-Hispanic white women living in poverty, many with no or poor understanding of English. All women booking in a 6 month period (*n* = 109) were included in the study. The three-item Abuse Assessment Screen was administered by one of two bilingual medical assistants, well known to the clients of the clinic and trained in the use of the tool. The three-item Abuse Assessment Screen contains the following questions:

1. Within the last year have you been hit, slapped, kicked or otherwise physically hurt by someone?
2. Since you've been pregnant have you been hit, slapped, kicked or otherwise physically hurt by someone?
3. Within the last year has anyone forced you to have sexual activities?

A positive response to any item on the questionnaire is categorised as a positive screen for IPV.

A cross-sectional survey conducted in Eire has investigated the acceptability of routine enquiry during antenatal visits regarding intimate partner abuse.[1005] [EL = 3] When alone with the obstetrician at the first antenatal visit, women (*n* = 478) were asked four direct questions about their experience of verbal, physical, emotional and sexual abuse in the preceding year. The women were then asked by the obstetrician whether they found the questions acceptable and whether they felt the questions should be asked during antenatal visits.

A retrospective audit of medical records conducted in Australia compared the performance of a self-completion six-item Maternity Social Support Scale checklist ('I have good friends who support me', 'My family is always there for me', 'My husband/partner helps me a lot', 'There is conflict with my husband/partner', 'I feel controlled by my husband/partner', 'I feel loved by my husband/partner') with responses obtained from four items relating to partner violence asked directly during the initial booking interview (The Domestic Violence Initiative form – 'Are you ever afraid of your partner?', 'In the last year, has anyone at home kicked, punched or otherwise hurt you?', 'In the last year, has anyone at home often put you down, humiliated you or tried to control what you can do?', 'In the last year, has anyone at home threatened to hurt you?').[1007] [EL = III] Medical records for 937 (58.7%) women were found to have responses to both screening instruments during the 2 month study period.

Findings

The study reported in the USPSTF systematic review[1004] which compared four screening assessments for IPV found that pregnant women (95% of whom were identified as being below the poverty level) who were identified as abused by the three-item Abuse Assessment Screen also scored significantly higher than non-abused women on three other validated screening tools (the 30-item Index of Spouse Abuse, 19-item Conflict Tactic Scale and the Domestic Abuse Screen). The

2008 update

2008 update

accuracy of the screening tools in identifying women suffering from IPV is not reported, however. When the detection rate of IPV using the five-item Abuse Assessment Screen was compared with that of using a social services interview, the screening instrument was found to be better at detecting IPV (41% versus 14%). A further US study reported within the systematic review found that a higher prevalence of abuse was detected by nurse-conducted interview (29%) compared with self-completion of the same four-item questionnaire (7%).

The Canadian RCT assessing the performance of the ALPHA[1008] had a low response rate, with only 44% of healthcare providers in the intervention group and 56% in the control group included in the analysis, thus all findings need to be interpreted with caution. ALPHA group providers identified 115 psychosocial problems in their subsample of 98 women. Providers in the control group identified 96 psychosocial concerns in their subsample of 129 women (OR 1.8, 95% CI 1.1 to 3.0). ALPHA group providers identified at least one concern in 39% of women, compared with providers in the control group who identified at least one concern in 29% of women (this difference is not statistically significant). Providers in the ALPHA group were significantly more likely to indicate a high level of concern about psychosocial issues (11.2% versus 2.3%; $P = 0.006$). Women with providers in the ALPHA group were almost 5 times as likely as women in the control group to be identified as having risk factors associated with family violence. This difference remained after adjusting for confounding variables (marital status and level of education). When asked for their views of care involving the ALPHA screening tool, 72.7% of women reported that they felt comfortable discussing personal issues in an antenatal consultation, with 76.3% stating that they felt this was part of the providers' role. Of the 67% of providers who reported on use of the ALPHA form, 64% said they had found it easy to use and 86% reported that they would recommend it for routine use.

Findings from the US cross-sectional study investigating the usefulness of the three-item Abuse Assessment Screen identified eight women as suffering abuse.[1006] All abused women identified only friends as their sources of support whereas all non-abused women identified only family, including their intimate partner, as sources of support. Lack of an intimate partner, fear of the partner, childhood sexual abuse, self-reported depression, anxiety and a stressful life situation were reported significantly more frequently in the abused group based on findings of χ^2 analysis ($P = 0.05$).

The survey of acceptability of screening for intimate partner abuse during antenatal consultations found that the majority of women did report that they found the direct questioning acceptable (99.4%) and considered that all women should be asked these questions.[1005] During the survey, 12.9% of women ($n = 61$) reported experiencing at least one form of intimate partner abuse during the previous year.

Findings from the Australian retrospective survey of antenatal medical records found that women reported more abuse when they completed the six-item Maternity Social Support Scale.[1007] On 107 occasions, items associated with abuse were answered positively on the self-completion scale (defined as responses 'some of the time', 'most of the time' and 'always' on a five-point scale) and not on the interview-based form. This included seven women who reported being in conflict with their partner 'all of the time' and 21 women who responded that they felt controlled in their relationship at least some of the time. On the other hand, the direct questioning using the Domestic Violence Initiative form identified 22 women who screened positive for abuse who were not picked up by the self-completion questionnaire, including seven women who were suffering physical abuse.

Antenatal assessment of obstetric and medical risk factors

A systematic review was identified which investigated the effectiveness of antenatal risk assessment, health promotion and medical and psychosocial interventions aimed at preventing low birthweight (i.e. preterm birth and IUGR).[1001] [EL = III] The risk assessment interventions reviewed included both identification of risk factors and risk scoring in order to predict preterm birth. Risk factors included maternal characteristics (e.g. age, socio-economic status, cigarette smoking), medical conditions (e.g. hypertension, presence of infection) and obstetric history (e.g. previous preterm birth). Fifteen studies were included in the review (12 from a previous systematic review plus three individual studies). The quality of evidence was rated as 'fair' for both risk assessment and risk scoring.

A second systematic review was identified for inclusion which examined the evidence of the effectiveness of antenatal care interventions in relation to maternal mortality and serious morbidity.[1009] [EL = III] The focus of the review was mainly on care provided in developing countries. The review states that the rationale behind risk assessment in developed countries is to limit medical interference and to give women informed choice, while attempting to ensure all women have access to antenatal care of a high standard. This is compared to risk assessment in developing countries where risk assessment is used to help allocate resources according to need. Seven studies are included in the review, which describe risk assessment systems and their ability to correctly identify women at risk of poor maternal outcomes. Two of these included studies involved complex scoring systems involving large numbers of variables.

A retrospective cross-sectional US study has evaluated a weighted risk scoring system developed to predict very low birthweight.[1002] [EL = III] The work was undertaken in the US state of Florida. The risk scoring system was developed using a statistical modelling technique applied to potential risk factors identified through review of medical records ($n = 166\ 372$). The final model comprised 13 items, including three items which examined interactions of risk factors (e.g. marital status × moved more than three times in past year). Six of the items in the scoring system related to social factors while only one related to medical history (illness requiring continuing care) and one related to obstetric history (previous pregnancy experience: no previous pregnancy/pregnancy resulting in a live birth/pregnancy not resulting in a live birth). Performance of the new scoring system in predicting very low birthweight babies was compared with the risk assessment used at the time, the Healthy Start screening test, a system developed through professional judgement by an expert panel.

Another US risk scoring system has been developed for use throughout pregnancy.[1003] [EL = III]. The assessment tool includes 63 variables, with weights based upon assessment of clinical severity. The variables relate to previous obstetric history, social factors, medical conditions and the woman's current pregnancy. There is no reference to family history or psychological factors. A prospective evaluation of the tool was conducted with a sample of 782 pregnant women. The risk assessment was carried out at each antenatal visit and at the onset of labour. Following birth, maternal and neonatal outcomes were recorded and correlated with the risk score.

Findings
The systematic review of 15 studies investigating risk assessment for predicting preterm birth found that none of the risk assessment methods investigated were able to predict more than two-thirds of women who went on to give birth preterm, with most predicting less than 50% of preterm births.[1001] One of the most comprehensive risk assessment tools developed, reported by the Preterm Prediction Study (Cardiff, Wales), included a graded risk assessment using over 100 clinical risk factors. Despite its comprehensiveness, the risk assessment demonstrated sensitivities of 24% and 18% for nulliparous women and multiparous women, respectively, and PPVs of just 29% and 33%, respectively.

The systematic review of antenatal assessment aimed at identifying risk factors associated with poor maternal outcomes concluded that formal risk scoring systems were poor at discriminating between women at high and low risk.[1009] A review of five studies of individual risk scoring found that only 10–30% of women allocated to high-risk groups experienced the adverse outcome for which the risk assessment had identified them to be at risk. Two studies which described more complex scoring systems based on a larger number of variables failed to provide sufficient data regarding women's risk factors and outcomes and thus it was not possible to calculate the positive and negative likelihood ratios of the assessment tools.

The retrospective evaluation of a weighted risk scoring system reported that the new system was better at predicting very low birthweight babies than the existing risk assessment being used.[1002] The ROC curve for the newly developed tool showed its sensitivity to be approximately 10% higher than the Healthy Start screening tool. Specificity was similar for the two tests. However, the LR+ values for the risk scoring system ranged from 1.34 to 2.95 for all cut-off points examined, suggesting that the tool is not a very good predictor of very low birthweight.

The weighted risk assessment used throughout pregnancy, the Risk Index, was found to correlate inversely with birthweight. Using a cut-off score of 6 (range 1–29), the incidence of low birthweight was found to be 13% in the high-risk group compared with 4.9% in the low-risk group (RR 2.27,

95% CI 1.57 to 4.59). The risk score of 6 identified babies of low birthweight with a sensitivity of 40% and a specificity of 81% (PPV 51%, NPV 95%). The incidence of caesarean birth was 28.6% for the study sample. Women scored as high risk had an incidence of caesarean birth of 51% compared with 23% incidence in the low-risk group (RR 2.2, 95% CI 1.77 to 2.70). The sensitivity was 35%, specificity 86%, PPV 51% and NPV 77%. The incidence of Apgar score < 7 at 5 minutes was 1.3% for the study sample. The difference between the high-risk and low-risk groups of women for low 5 minute Apgar was statistically significant (RR 4.1, 95% CI 1.2 to 13.9). The sensitivity was 50%, specificity 81%, PPV 3% and NPV 99%. Thus for all three outcome variables tested, the Risk Index was good at identifying true negatives (i.e. good at defining low risk) but much less good at detecting true positives (i.e. correctly identifying women and/or babies who went on to have adverse outcomes), with many false positives.

Antenatal assessment and its effect on women's psychological state in pregnancy

Description of included studies

One prospective cross-sectional study conducted in Germany was reviewed which investigated the effect of being labelled at 'high risk' on women's psychological state during pregnancy.[1010] [EL = 3] A convenience sample of pregnant women (n = 111; response rate 76%) were divided into two groups. Group 1 (n = 57) consisted of women who were identified on their handheld antenatal records as having risk factors requiring them to be labelled as 'high risk' on their hospital medical records in Germany but who would be classified as low risk or suitable for midwife-led care in Scotland or the Netherlands using risk assessments of those countries. Group 2 (n = 54) consisted of women who had no risk factors identified on their handheld antenatal records that required the label 'high risk' to be applied to their hospital records. All women were given a previously validated psychometric questionnaire to complete in order to gauge their psychological state during pregnancy.

Findings

The group of women labelled as 'high risk' were significantly older than the 'low risk' group. The two groups were similar for other variables relating to maternal characteristics. The mean week of pregnancy was 34.1 (SD 3.7 weeks). The most common risk factor in the group labelled 'high risk' was age over 35 years. Women who were labelled as 'high risk' were found to have significantly poorer scores compared with women of 'low risk' after adjusting for age (analysis of covariance: $R^2 = 0.07$, $F = 7.592$, 1 df; $P = 0.007$). However, all scores but one appear in the moderate–good or good sections of the psychometric scale thus making it difficult to interpret the meaning of this difference in scores.

Evidence summary

There is some evidence of fair to low quality that the use of a simple screening tool improves identification of intimate partner/family abuse compared with usual clinical or social services consultation. The evidence is contradictory when considering self-assessment versus interview. There is evidence that women find questioning about intimate partner/family violence acceptable in an antenatal consultation.

There is a good amount of fair- to low-quality evidence that antenatal risk assessment tools have high specificity but low sensitivity in predicting poor pregnancy outcomes, i.e. they are good at identifying true negatives (low risk) but there are many false positive results.

There is no evidence of the effectiveness of carrying out antenatal assessment with respect to maternal and neonatal outcomes.

14.3 Developing an antenatal assessment tool

Method

The aim was to highlight those items which would identify women as requiring obstetric input into their antenatal care. Given the lack of good-quality clinical evidence in this area, it was felt that consensus methodology should be undertaken to decide the content of the assessment tool. The approach adopted was that of a modified Delphi technique. Delphi participants are generally specifically chosen for their expertise in a particular area; in the NCC-WCH survey they were self-selecting, although it was specified that all respondents to the original survey should have an involvement with maternity care. Individual specialists were not selected.

Developing an online survey

Drawing up the questions

The possible topics for inclusion were drawn from three sources. Firstly, expert opinion was sought from the GDG. Further topics were identified through a systematic review of the literature. Additional topics were then taken from a sample of antenatal booking notes ($n = 16$). In total, 203 topics for possible inclusion in the tool were drawn up. These topics were then subdivided into six areas:

- previous pregnancies ($n = 61$)
- family medical history ($n = 21$)
- past and existing medical problems ($n = 45$)
- current pregnancy ($n = 18$)
- social factors ($n = 35$)
- personal factors ($n = 23$).

First consensus round

The first round of consensus work consisted of an anonymous online survey accessible from the NCC-WCH website. The online software from www.surveyconsole.com was used. The survey was aimed at all relevant stakeholder groups. This included midwives, obstetricians, service user representatives, paediatricians and health visitors.

Publicity

The survey was publicised to the stakeholder groups through various channels:

- letters to all of the guideline stakeholders
- letters to some heads of midwifery along with all of the board members of the NCC-WCH
- advertisements in *BJOG*, the RCOG newsletter and the RCM journal (*Midwives*)
- online advertisements on the corresponding websites to the journals, as well as on the RCN, NCC-WCH and NICE websites
- through NICE's Patient and Public Involvement Programme (PPIP).

Online survey

The survey was accessible online for 4 weeks. Respondents to the survey were asked to rate each of the topics on a scale from 1 to 9 in terms of relative importance in deciding whether a woman required obstetric- or midwife-led care, and thus whether the item ought to be included in an antenatal assessment tool. A score of 1 indicated that the respondent considered the topic 'not at all important' while a score of 9 was 'very important'. If a respondent felt unsure about a question or unable to answer, they were asked to move on to the next question. To avoid exhaustion bias, the question order was randomised daily.

All respondents to the survey were given the chance to apply online to attend the second round of consensus work. In this way, it was ensured that the second consensus sample was a subsample of the first.

Before conducting the survey, it had been decided that an overall median score of 1–3 for a topic would indicate consensus that it should not be included, a score of 7–9 that it should be included, and a score of 4–6 that there was no overall consensus. However, analysis of the frequency distribution of the median scores from the survey showed a skew towards higher scores and so it was decided that a score of 8–9 would indicate consensus on inclusion, 1–3 would indicate consensus on exclusion, 5–7 would indicate no overall consensus and a score of 4 would be taken to an advisory panel.

The topics with median score 4 ($n = 14$) were taken to the GDG, a panel of nine members. Each was asked to rate the topics in the same manner as the survey. It had been decided previously that a median score of 1–3 would indicate consensus that the tool should not be included while any other score would indicate that the question should be taken to the second round of consensus work. Eight topics were excluded and six were taken forward to be voted on in the second round.

Results from the first consensus round

A total of 731 online questionnaires were received that were at least partially complete, of which 566 were fully complete. Forty-eight percent of the respondents were midwives, 19% healthcare consumers/consumer representatives, 16% medical staff including obstetricians (8.6% of total) and 17% other (which includes health visitors, antenatal teachers, etc.) The overall completion to started rate was 48.1%.

Consensus on inclusion was reached on 78 of the topics and consensus on exclusion was reached on 19 of the topics. This left 106 topics to take forward to the consensus conference.

Second/third round

The second and third round of consensus voting took place during a one-day conference consisting of survey respondents who had applied to attend (120 applied, 56 attended).

Selection procedure

Applicants who wished to apply to attend the conference were asked to complete an online application form. As well as providing contact details, applicants were asked to provide a supporting statement detailing their current involvement with maternity care. Participants were selected both on the basis of their supporting statement and their geographical location to ensure that as many regions of England and Wales as possible were represented. Originally, it was felt that the delegates should be made up of an equal number of midwives, obstetricians and healthcare consumers. However, after conducting subgroup analysis on the responses to the first round of voting, there was no statistical difference in median scores between the three groups. To confirm this, a randomised sample of the median scores of obstetricians and midwives was compared with the median scores from healthcare consumers. By inspection, there was no statistical difference between the results for the different groups. As a result, more midwives were invited (as many more midwives applied to attend than the other groups).

Voting procedure

At the conference, delegates were presented with those topics where consensus had not been reached in the first round and asked to vote on each in turn using an electronic voting system (supplied by Group Dynamics – www.groupdynamics.co.uk). After the questions were displayed and read out, delegates were given 8 seconds to record their vote. As well as voting electronically, participants were also asked to vote on a paper version so that they could compare their own score with the median for the group. The results of the vote on each question were displayed along with the median score. After each topic had been voted on, a frequency distribution of the median scores was analysed. It showed a skew towards lower scores and so it was decided that a median score of 7–9 indicated consensus on inclusion, 1–2 indicated consensus on exclusion and 3–6 indicated no overall consensus. The delegates were then asked to vote on those remaining topics where no consensus had been reached ($n = 39$). In this round, each vote was preceded by a discussion amongst the delegates in an attempt to achieve consensus.

Results from the second/third round

Consensus was reached for inclusion on 14 topics, consensus for exclusion on 83 topics and no overall consensus on ten topics. From the discussion which followed, it became apparent that further work should be conducted into further developing the tool in order to define a care pathway for women with social risk factors who may benefit from the input of specialists other than an obstetrician.

Evidence statement

This approach showed that it was possible to gain consensus on a range of potential risk factors derived from a number of sources, including systematic reviews, to allow the development of an antenatal assessment tool.

Interpretation of evidence

Although it has been possible to agree the basis of an antenatal assessment tool it requires further refinement and validation before it can be applied in practice.

Research recommendation on antenatal assessment

Multicentred validation studies are required in the UK to validate and evaluate the use of the 'Antenatal assessment tool'. Using structured questions, the tool aims to support the routine antenatal care of all women by identifying women who may require additional care. The tool identifies women who:

- can remain within or return to the routine antenatal pathway of care
- may need additional obstetric care for medical reasons
- may need social support and/or medical care for a variety of socially complex reasons.

Why this is important
The idea of some form of assessment tool to help group pregnant women into low-risk (midwifery-only care) and increased-risk (midwifery and obstetric care) categories is not new. The 'Antenatal assessment tool' has been developed using a consensus approach. Once developed, it will be essential to subject the tool to a multicentred validation study. The validated tool should have the potential to identify a third group of women who are particularly vulnerable and at increased risk of maternal and perinatal death.

2008 update

Appendix A

Declarations of interest

A.1 Guideline development group members

Jane Anderson
No interests declared

Chris Barry
No interests declared

Marie Benton
No interests declared

Jennifer Elliott
No interests declared

Rhona Hughes
No interests declared

Nina Khazaezadeh
No interests declared

Rachel Knowles
No interests declared

Anne Longton
No interests declared

Tim Overton
Personal specific: Treasurer to the British Maternal and Fetal Medicine Society

Katie Yiannouzis
No interests declared

A.2 NCC-WCH staff and contractors

Rupert Franklin
No interests declared

Eva Gautam-Aitken
No interests declared

Paul Jacklin
No interests declared

Rajesh Khanna
No interests declared

Rintaro Mori
Personal specific: Part-time lecturer (since July 2005) – School of Public Health, Kyoto University, £125 per day of work. External Supervisor (Seasonal June–November every year) London School

of Hygiene and Tropical Medicine, £300 per project plus expenses. Non-pecuniary: Director of CRIPH: Collaboration for Research in International Perinatal Health; Overseas Advisor: Health Policy Unity, the Japan Pediatric Society.

Personal non-specific: Personal family interests: Dr Kyoko Mori (wife), Chief Investigator for Research Fund – Promoting welfare of disabled children: Parental stress of autistic spectrum disorder. £1,240 – T&D Holdings inc.

Non-personal specific: Supervisor (Principal Investigator: Dr Shuko Nagai) Research Educational Fund. Promoting Neonatal Survival in Developing Countries: a randomised control trial of early skin-to-skin contact between low birthweight infants and their mothers in Madagascar. January 2007 to December 2007. £20,700, Foundation for Advances Studies on International Development.

Co-investigator (Chief Investigator: Professor Takeo Nakayama) Research Fund.

Patient Involvement in Guideline Development. April 2007 to March 2010. £124,400. Ministry of Health, Labour and Welfare – the Japanese Government.

Co-investigator (Chief Investigator: Dr Masanori Fujimura) Research Fund. Development of perinatal healthcare network: A comparative study of healthcare professionals' attitudes towards care of extremely premature babies between UK and Japan. April 2007 to March 2010. £165,000. Ministry of Health, Labour and Welfare – the Japanese Government.

Francesco Moscone
No interests declared

Debbie Pledge
No interests declared

Jeff Round
No interests declared

Anuradha Sekhri
No interests declared

Roz Ullman
No interests declared

Martin Whittle
Personal specific: Non-pecuniary: Chair of Steering Group on Ultrasound Screening

A.3 External advisers

Fiona Ford
No interests declared

Jane Hawdon
Personal specific: Non-pecuniary: *Ad hoc* advice and invited lecturer for BFI
Personal non-specific: Non-pecuniary: *Ad hoc* advice and host of visits to the UCLH neonatal unit – Bliss

Anne Longton
No interests declared

Guy Rooney
Personal specific: Pecuniary: Contacted to speak on behalf of Johnson & Johnson about their new anti-HIV drug 'PREZISTA'. The fee includes training/education expenses on presentation. Fee £1000.
Contacted to speak on a new vaccine to prevent human papillomavirus infection – 'GARDASIL'. Fee – £265. Merck.

2008 update

Appendix B

Economic model: asymptomatic bacteriuria screening programme

The purpose of the model was to compare the cost-effectiveness and cost consequences of two different methods for detecting the presence of asymptomatic bacteriuria (ASB). A decision analytic model was created to compare the two strategies:

1. screening with urine culture
2. screening with leucocyte esterase-nitrite dipstick.

These methods have different sensitivities and specificities and associated costs. Untreated ASB can lead to pyelonephritis, which can lead to increased rate of preterm birth. Screening for ASB can lead to the treatment of women for ABS, prevent cases of pyelonephritis and prevent the costs and consequences of preterm birth. The cost consequences of preterm birth by missing one case of ASB have not yet been included in other economic evaluations and may be extremely high. Therefore a model was constructed to include this parameter.

Literature review

Thirteen papers were identified by the search strategy and the abstracts were reviewed. All the papers were retrieved and reviewed using the standard economic evaluation checklist. Of the 13, four papers contained data that were relevant for the economic model. One study[45] considered the cost consequences of preterm birth.

Designing the model

The clinical effectiveness data needed to construct the model were obtained from the guideline. Additional data that had to be collected to construct the model were the prevalence of pyelonephritis and the prevalence of preterm birth. Data on these parameters were derived from a review showing a range of values that were used in the model and subjected to sensitivity analysis.[351] A meta-analysis was also undertaken by the systematic reviewer on the guideline to provide relevant estimates used in the model.

The cost data included in the model were reported for three levels of analysis:

- screening and treatment for asymptomatic bacteriuria
- screening and treatment for asymptomatic bacteriuria and for treatment for pyelonephritis
- screening and treatment for asymptomatic bacteriuria, treatment for pyelonephritis and the cost of preterm birth.

The model reported the cost-effectiveness of the two screening options in the following ratios:

- average cost of screening and treating for asymptomatic bacteriuria per person screened
- average cost of screening and treating for asymptomatic bacteriuria and pyelonephritis per person screened
- average cost of screening and treating for asymptomatic bacteriuria, pyelonephritis and the cases of preterm birth per person screened
- total cost per case of pyelonephritis averted
- total cost per case of preterm birth averted
- incremental cost of moving from dipstick test to a culture test screening programme.

Cost data

The cost data used are shown in Table B.1. All costs apart from the costs of preterm birth were originally reported in US dollars and transformed to UK pounds sterling at the year 2002, using the Purchasing Power Parity Index taken from the website: www.oecd.fr/dsti/sti/it/stats/ppp.htm, and were inflated to year 2002 prices using the Retail Price Index for Health Services.

Table B.1   Cost data used in the ASB model

Cost item	Range of values used in the model (£)
Cost of screening[600]	1,242 (sensitivity analysis ± 10% of this value)
Cost of pyelonephritis[600]	1,930 sensitivity analysis (± 10% of this value)
Cost of preterm birth[45]	14,000 to 21,000

The baseline model

The sensitivity of the dipstick was assumed to be 0.72 and the sensitivity of the culture method was assumed to be close to 100%. The value used for the prevalence of pyelonephritis in the treatment was 0.04, while the value used for the prevalence of pyelonephritis without treatment was 0.19. The prevalence of preterm birth for the treatment group was 0.088 and for the untreated group 0.155.

The cost of preterm birth was taken from a UK study[601] and was estimated to be around £14,200. This value was subjected to sensitivity analysis. The incremental cost-effectiveness analysis shows that, when taking the cost of treating the cases of preterm birth into account, the dipstick screening method would cost an extra £32,357 for each case of preterm birth averted.

Sensitivity analysis

The parameters examined in the model were the sensitivity of the dipstick method, the prevalence of pyelonephritis among women who are treated for ASB, the cost of preterm birth and the prevalence of preterm birth. Increasing the sensitivity of the dipstick by 10% (from 0.72 to 0.82) led to a reduction in the overall difference in costs between the screening tests (savings reduced to £4 to £5 per test). Threshold sensitivity analysis was undertaken to establish the sensitivity of the dipstick test that would have to be reached in order for both the culture and the dipstick test to have equivalent overall costs when taking all costs (screening, treatment and preterm birth) into account. The threshold was 0.91. A greater sensitivity than this for the dipstick test would make it the preferred method of screening. In reality, such sensitivity is considered to be extremely high and reported only in one study (see Section 10.1).

Overall, preterm birth should be included in the analysis, since the relative cost-effectiveness of the tests is sensitive to even one additional case of preterm birth at the higher and lower value of the baseline cost. This has not been explored in economic models published in the literature to date and should be explored further in future studies, alongside more robust UK-based estimates of the long-term costs of preterm birth. Increasing and decreasing the cost estimates of preterm birth by as much as 50% did not change the overall results (favouring the culture method).

Appendix C

Economic model: streptococcus group B screening programme

The purpose of the model was to compare the cost-effectiveness and cost consequences of two screening programmes, namely bacteriological screening compared with risk factor screening.

Literature review

Forty-three papers were identified by the search strategy and the abstracts were reviewed. Of these, 19 full papers were retrieved and reviewed using the Drummond checklist. Two unauthored reports were also reviewed.

None of the identified economic studies were undertaken in the UK setting and the majority of them were from a US setting. Sources of effectiveness data and the evidence for the clinical outcomes and all the ranges of their values were based on the clinical effectiveness data of the guideline using the best available data from the literature and expert opinion.

The lack of some definitive effectiveness data, such as the prevalence of early-onset group B streptococcus among positively screened women makes the completeness of the model problematic and therefore no conclusion can be reached from this model as far as the two screening procedures are concerned.

Future cost-effectiveness research should include these parameters in order for a model to be estimated.

Appendix D

Economic model: syphilis screening programme

The purpose of the model was to compare the cost-effectiveness and cost consequences of two screening programmes, namely universal screening versus selective screening. The reason for this specific comparison was to consider a change in policy from the current practice of universal screening towards a more limited and potentially more cost-effective approach. This is because the prevalence of syphilis is the UK is very low and, in addition, there maybe identifiable groups of women who are at higher risk of contracting syphilis. A programme of selective screening could significantly reduce the number of women screened,[602] while at the same time identifying a relatively high proportion of carriers of the disease (100% for universal versus 70% to 78% for selective).

Literature review

In all, 47 papers were identified by the search strategy and the abstracts were reviewed. Of these, 25 full papers were retrieved and reviewed using the Drummond checklist. All the papers had some useful background information and contributed to the general structure of the model.

Data were extracted from one paper only, as it used UK-based cost data, post-1995, and UK effectiveness data, and considered the same screening alternatives.[602] This study identified possible screening strategy for the programme to compare their effectiveness and cost-effectiveness to assess whether screening for syphilis is still necessary. Three possible strategic options for antenatal screening were examined:

- to continue the current universal screening programme
- to target the screening programme to pregnant women in high-risk groups
- to stop the screening programme entirely.

The study population comprised pregnant women in the UK, from which three high-risk groups were identified when considering screening strategy options: pregnant women in the Thames region, women from non-white ethnic groups and women born outside the UK.

Although the incremental cost per case detected of universal screening was high and although selectively screening groups by country of birth or by ethnic group could detect at least 70% of cases, this could be politically and practically difficult. Targeting by region would also be effective but difficult to implement.

The published evidence from this study is not ideal because the validity of estimate of measure of effectiveness was not reported. Also, the analysis did not include any cost to pregnant women such as anxiety or time taken to attend clinics and to set up partner notification services. Furthermore, the cost for the treatment of a woman's sexual partner was not calculated.

Designing the model

Because of the lack of data on the parameters discussed above, a model approach similar to the above study was adopted in this guideline. The model set out to estimate the total costs of screening and cost of syphilis treatment in pregnant women positively screened, cost of preterm birth, lifetime cost of congenital syphilis, and cost of spontaneous fetal loss.

Cost data

The cost data used are shown in Table D.1.

Table D.1 Cost data used in the syphilis model

Cost item	Range of values used in the model (£)
Cost of screening[602]	0.9 to 2.85
Cost of preterm birth[601]	14,000 to 145,000
Lifetime cost of congenital syphilis	Arbitrary value due to lack of literature data (arrived at through consensus with the Guideline Development Group)
Cost of treatment[602]	519 to 1,364

The evidence for the clinical outcomes and all the ranges of their values were based on the clinical effectiveness data of the guideline using the best available data from the literature and expert opinion.

Baseline results of the model

The model indicated that selective screening could detect from 70% (worse case scenario) to 78% of women affected by syphilis and that it is more cost-effective even if preterm birth and lifetime costs of congenital syphilis cases are included. This model did not consider the value forgone of a programme that results in more cases of preventable congenital syphilis. This may be very high and therefore the selective screening programme may not be acceptable because of these losses.

Sensitivity analysis

Parameters examined in the sensitivity analysis were rate of transmission of congenital syphilis from the mother to the fetus (5%, 10%, 15%, 20%, 30%). Keeping all parameters constant, a rate of transmission more than 20% made the universal screening a more cost-effective option in comparison with selective screening. The results are found to be insensitive to the sensitivity of the screening test.

Appendix E

Economic model: screening for congenital cardiac malformations

E.1 Introduction

As part of the guideline on diabetes in pregnancy,[636] a decision tree model was developed in Microsoft Excel® to assess the cost-effectiveness of mid-trimester screening for congenital cardiac malformations in pregnant women. It was felt that this model was of relevance within the context of the antenatal care guideline and therefore the model has been adapted for use with the antenatal population. Current UK practice is to screen pregnant women using a four chamber ultrasound scan at a gestational age of 20 weeks but using a four chamber view plus outflow tracts (also sometimes known as the four chamber plus outflow tracts view) may allow the detection of some abnormalities, such as transposition of the great arteries (TGA) and tetralogy of Fallot, which are not usually visible with a four chamber view.

There are two principal reasons why it may be beneficial to screen for congenital cardiac malformations:

- it allows the mother to consider termination of pregnancy, and
- improved maternal and neonatal outcomes.

There are difficulties in considering the cost-effectiveness of screening using termination as a 'desirable outcome' and the evidence that screening produces a survival advantage is limited.[944] Nevertheless, there is some evidence suggesting that an antenatal diagnosis of TGA may reduce mortality. This is important for this analysis because TGA is an anomaly that would not normally be identifiable with a four chamber view but can be with an additional outflow tracts view and, therefore, the model particularly focuses on the cost-effectiveness of antenatal diagnosis of TGA.

The basic decision tree structure is illustrated in Figure E.1. At 20 weeks of gestation women receive either a four chamber view ultrasound scan or a four chamber plus outflow tracts view ultrasound scan. Women with a positive result on either scan will then be referred for fetal echocardiography to confirm diagnosis and guide subsequent treatment. If the diagnosis is confirmed then the woman has the option to either terminate or proceed with the pregnancy. If the woman chooses to continue with the pregnancy then she will either give birth to a live baby or suffer a pregnancy loss. A proportion of babies born with cardiac malformations will have TGA and they may either survive or die.

E.2 Model parameters

The parameter values used in the baseline model are shown in Tables E.1 to E.4.

E.3 Results

With baseline results, the four chamber view is the cheapest strategy for screening for cardiac malformations owing to the higher cost of the four chamber plus outflow tracts view (Table E.5). However, the higher sensitivity of the four chamber plus outflow tracts view results in 0.334 more live births per 1000 pregnancies with antenatally detected cardiac malformations (Table E.6). A proportion of these (36% at baseline) would be TGA and given the baseline assumption about lower mortality for TGA with an antenatal diagnosis, this leads to a concomitant 1.8 neonatal deaths averted per 100 000 pregnancies (Table E.7). Following on from these cost and effects the estimated incremental cost-effectiveness ratio (ICER) for the four chamber plus outflow tracts view is £24,125 per QALY.

2008 update

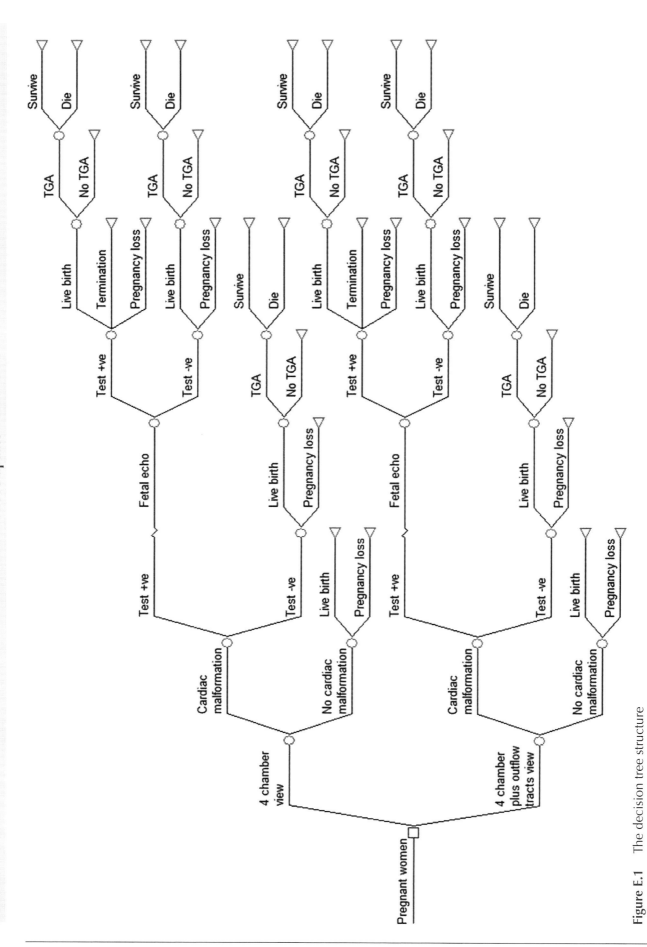

Figure E.1   The decision tree structure

Table E.1   Population characteristics

Characteristic	Value	Source	Notes
Population	1000		Event data is often given as a rate per 1000 and the ICER from the model is not affected by population size.
Prevalence of cardiac malformations at 20 weeks of gestation	0.0056	Wren et al. (2000)[1024]	Value is for prevalence at birth.[a]
Proportion of cardiac malformations that are TGA	0.043	Wren et al. (2003)[945]	
Pregnancy loss post 20 weeks (no cardiac malformations present)	0.0115	Ritchie et al. (2004)[804] www.nhshealthquality.org/ nhsqis/files/Ultrasound%20CAR. pdf	Derived from survival probability from second trimester to birth.
Pregnancy loss post 20 weeks (cardiac malformations present)	0.0405	Ritchie et al. (2004)[804]	Derived from survival probability from second trimester to birth.

ICER = incremental cost-effectiveness ratio; TGA = transposition of the great arteries.

[a] The prevalence of cardiac malformations at 20 weeks of gestation may be slightly higher than at birth if we consider that terminations and fetal death are higher in affected pregnancies than non-affected. This is likely to represent a small bias in the model against the four chamber plus outflow tracts view but this is not important if the four chamber plus outflow tracts view is shown to be cost-effective.

Table E.2   Costs

Characteristic	Cost	Source	Notes
Four chamber view ultrasound scan	£34	NHS Reference Costs 2005–06	Mean value for a maternity ultrasound
Four chamber plus outflow tracts view ultrasound scan	£46	GDG estimate	Based on estimate that appointment slots would be 20 minutes, compared with 15 minutes for a four chamber view.[a]
Fetal echocardiography	£62	NHS Reference Costs 2005–06	Mean value for an echocardiogram
Termination of pregnancy	£492	NHS Tariff 2006/07	Cost of a surgical termination
Birth	£3,000	NHS Reference Costs 2003; NHS General Medical Services Revised Fees and Allowances 2003–04	A weighted average including birth, GP fees, other maternity events, outpatient visits, neonatal care, tests

[a] The cost of the four chamber plus outflow tracts view does not take into account the fact that the number of equivocal scans is likely to increase.

Table E.3   Test characteristics

Characteristic	Value	Source	Notes
Four chamber view sensitivity	0.73	Smith RS et al. (1997)[946] (see www.d4pro.com/IDM/site/ idm4cr.pdf)	
Four chamber view specificity	1.00	Smith RS et al. (1997)[946]	
Four chamber plus outflow tracts view sensitivity	0.82	Smith RS et al. (1997)[946]	
Four chamber plus outflow tracts view specificity	1.00	Smith RS et al. (1997)[946]	
TGA proportion of defects only detectable on four chamber plus outflow tracts view	0.36	Ogge G et al. (2006)[947]	In 58 cases of congenital cardiac defects, 14 were only usually diagnosable with outflow-tract view. Of these, 5 were TGA.[a]
Fetal echocardiography sensitivity	0.92	www.unepsa.org/china/ab/1327. HTM – accessed 30/08/2006	
Fetal echocardiography specificity	0.95	Pan et al.[1015]	
Termination of pregnancy rate for diagnosis of cardiac malformation	0.25	Ritchie et al. (2004)[804]	

TGA = transposition of the great arteries.

[a] Only one TGA was actually detected, giving the four chamber plus outflow tracts view a sensitivity for detecting TGA of only 20%.

2008 update

Table E.4 Outcomes and QALYs

Characteristic	Value	Source	Notes
Life expectancy if TGA successfully treated (years)	76	Office of National Statistics (2006)	UK life expectancy at birth (2003–05) is 76.6 years for males and 81.0 years for females.
TGA mortality detected antenatally	0.018	Wessex UK (1994–2005), EUROCAT, Bonnet 1998–97,[1016] Bonnet 1998–2002,[1017] Kumar 1988–96[1018]	Results reported in presentation by Wellesley et al. (4/226).
TGA mortality detected postnatally	0.166	Wessex UK (1994–2005), EUROCAT, Bonnet 1998–97[1016]	Results reported in presentation by Wellesley et al. (70/422).
QALY weight successful TGA treatment	1.0		Assumes no long-term morbidity associated with successful TGA treatment.
Annual discount rate	3.5%	NICE guidelines technical manual	

QALY = quality-adjusted life year; TGA = transposition of the great arteries.

Table E.5 Costs of four chamber and four chamber plus outflow tracts view strategies

Screening method	Cardiac scan	Fetal echo	Termination of pregnancy	Birth	Total cost	Cost per patient
Four chamber view	£34,000	£253	£463	£2,962,306	£2,997,022	£2,997
Four chamber plus outflow tracts view	£46,000	£285	£520	£2,691,973	£3,008,777	£3,009

Table E.6 Outcomes of four chamber and four chamber plus outflow tracts view strategies

Screening method	Pregnancy loss	Termination of pregnancy	Healthy live birth	Live birth, cardiac malformation detected	Live birth, cardiac malformation not detected
Four chamber view	11.62	0.94	982.96	2.706	1.765
Four chamber plus outflow tracts view	11.62	1.06	982.96	3.040	1.320

Table E.7 Incremental cost-effectiveness of four chamber plus outflow tracts view

Screening method	Incremental values					
	Costs	Antenatal diagnosis of cardiac malformations	Antenatal diagnosis of TGA	Neonatal deaths averted	QALYs	ICER
Four chamber plus outflow tracts view	£11,755	0.33	0.12	0.018	0.487	£24,125 per QALY

ICER = incremental cost-effectiveness ratio; QALY = quality-adjusted life year; TGA = transposition of the great arteries.

E.4 Sensitivity analysis

A number of one-way sensitivity analyses were undertaken to assess to what extent uncertainty over certain parameter values was likely to be important in interpreting the baseline results. The results of the sensitivity analyses are shown in Figures E.2 to E.7. A £30,000 cost per QALY threshold is indicated in each of the figures.

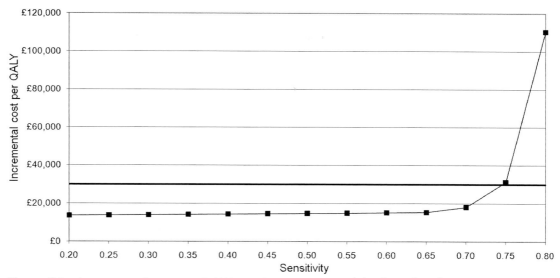

Figure E.2   Incremental cost per QALY, varying sensitivity of the four chamber view

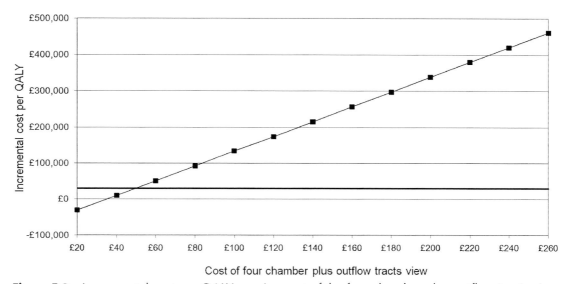

Figure E.3   Incremental cost per QALY, varying cost of the four chamber plus outflow tracts view

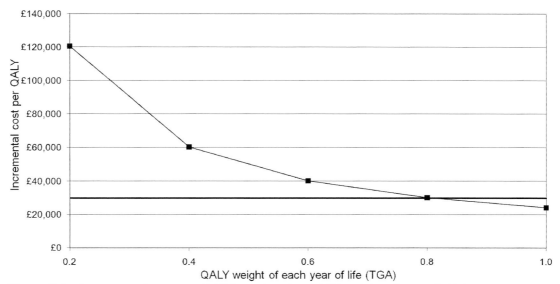

Figure E.4   Incremental cost per QALY, varying the QALY weight of treated TGA

E.5 Discussion

With baseline values this model suggests that the four chamber plus outflow tracts view is borderline cost-effective for screening for cardiac malformations in pregnant women compared with the four chamber view. The higher costs of the four chamber plus outflow tracts view make it the more expensive option and the ICER of £24,125 is just above the £20,000 per QALY threshold used by NICE as a willingness to pay benchmark for cost-effectiveness. (NICE states that interventions with a cost per QALY of less than £20,000 should be considered cost-effective but there must be 'strong reasons' for accepting anything with a cost per QALY of greater than £30,000 per QALY as cost-effective.) However, it is likely that there are benefits of the four chamber plus outflow tracts view over and above those measured by the antenatal diagnosis of TGA.

The model assumes that TGA is the only cardiac malformation where an antenatal diagnosis confers a benefit in terms of improved health outcomes for infant and/or mother. The model's baseline parameter values give a TGA prevalence of approximately 0.24 per 1000 pregnancies. With the model's baseline assumptions for TGA mortality detected and not detected antenatally, one neonatal death would be averted for every seven TGA malformations detected. If a four chamber plus outflow tracts view screen detected all TGA malformations then the number of pregnancies needed to screen with four chamber plus outflow tracts view to avert one neonatal death compared with four chamber view would be approximately 28 000.

The literature does not generally provide test sensitivity and specificity for individual cardiac malformations; instead, it gives a value for detecting any cardiac malformation. Hence, the improved sensitivity of the four chamber plus outflow tracts view compared with four chamber view arises because it detects additional malformations that cannot be usually observed with the four chamber view (the sensitivity of detecting TGA with the four chamber view is 0%). The model follows the literature in using overall sensitivities and specificities and it is this which generates the additional 0.33 antenatal diagnoses of cardiac malformations using the four chamber plus outflow tracts view. The model assumption is that these additional diagnoses are for malformations that would not normally be detectable with a four chamber view but would be detectable with a view of the outflow tracts. However, as TGA is not the only malformation falling into this category, the model does not assume that all additional antenatal diagnoses are TGA. It uses data presented by Ogge et al. (2006)[947] to estimate that 36% of these additional diagnoses would be TGA, which leads to the model result that a four chamber plus outflow tracts view would identify 0.12 TGA malformations per 1000 pregnancies. This is approximately 50% of the total TGA malformations present in the population, and four chamber plus outflow tracts view screening is still borderline cost-effective with this relatively low detection rate. However, it may be appropriate to assume a relatively low detection rate as the study by Ogge et al. (2006)[947] detected only one out of five TGA malformations with a four chamber plus outflow tracts view. With the model's baseline detection rate it would be necessary to screen approximately 56 000 women with a four chamber plus outflow tracts view to avert one neonatal death.

The model's baseline result suggests that the detection rate threshold for TGA for four chamber plus outflow tracts view to achieve cost-effectiveness is quite low. The one-way sensitivity analyses indicate thresholds for cost-effectiveness for other parameter values. Figure E.2 suggests that the test sensitivity for the four chamber view would have to be greater than 75% for the ICER for the four chamber plus outflow tracts view to exceed £30,000 per QALY. Such test sensitivity would suggest there was only a very limited added value in terms of cardiac malformations detected by using the four chamber plus outflow tracts view. The key point is the difference in test sensitivity between the four chamber and four chamber plus outflow tracts view rather than the absolute value. The one-way sensitivity analysis of the four chamber view sensitivity is undertaken holding the four chamber plus outflow tracts view sensitivity constant at 82%. The sensitivity analysis suggests that the four chamber plus outflow tracts view requires a sensitivity that is at least four percentage points better than the four chamber view in order to achieve cost-effectiveness.

Figure E.3 shows that the cost-effectiveness of four chamber plus outflow tracts view screening compared with four chamber is highly sensitive to the costs of screening. Again it is the difference between screening costs using the four chamber and the four chamber plus outflow tracts view that is important, rather than the absolute amount of one of the screening tests. The four chamber plus outflow tracts view screening ceases to be cost-effective at screening costs of greater than £49, a cost only slightly higher than the baseline value.

2008 update

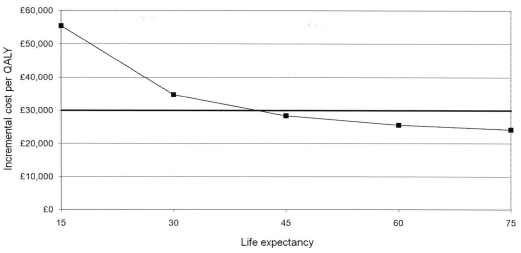

Figure E.5   Incremental cost per QALY, varying life expectancy of treated TGA

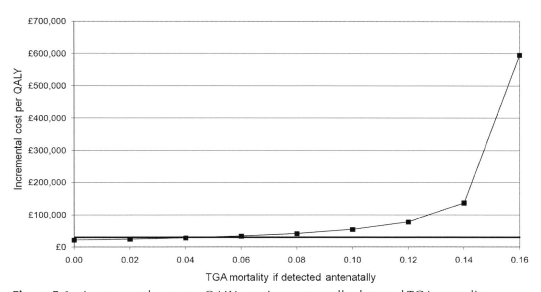

Figure E.6   Incremental cost per QALY, varying antenatally detected TGA mortality

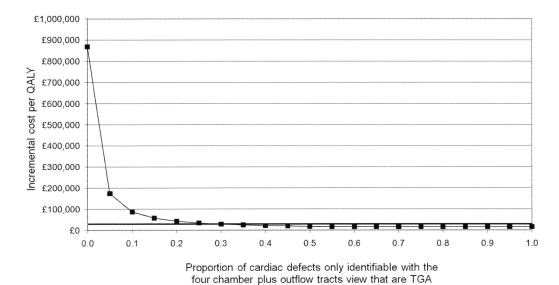

Figure E.7   Incremental cost per QALY, varying the proportion of cardiac malformations only identifiable with four chamber plus outflow tracts view that are TGA

2008 update

Figures E.4 and E.5 generally show that the cost-effectiveness of four chamber plus outflow tracts view screening is not that sensitive to assumptions about QALYs or life expectancy within plausible ranges. Baseline values suggest that the incremental costs of four chamber plus outflow tracts view screening are £11,755 in a population of 1000 pregnant women. Therefore, only 0.39 incremental QALYs are needed to generate a cost per QALY of £30,000. With baseline values this is approximately 21.7 QALYs per neonatal death averted. Life expectancy would have to be less than 40 years in order for the four chamber plus outflow tracts view to generate a cost per QALY of greater than £30,000. A QALY weight of less than 0.8 for TGA treatment would be necessary to produce a cost per QALY of £30,000 or more. Given the good outcomes and low morbidity from successfully treated TGA, these threshold values seem lower than what is plausible.

Figure E.6 does show that the model's results are very sensitive to the assumptions made about the positive impact an antenatal diagnosis of TGA has on mortality. Antenatally detected TGA mortality must be lower than 5% (with antenatally undetected TGA mortality being 16.6% – i.e. a difference of 11.1 percentage points*) to yield a cost per QALY of less than £30,000.

Finally, Figure E.7 shows that cost-effectiveness is also sensitive to the proportion of additional cardiac malformations detected with the four chamber plus outflow tracts view that are assumed to be TGA. However, this also relates to the earlier discussion about the overall detection rate of TGA as, given the way the model is constructed, a lower proportion implies a lower detection rate. Here, TGA would have to account for less than 15% of the additional cardiac malformations detected for the four chamber plus outflow tracts screen ICER to exceed £30,000 per QALY.

The results of these sensitivity analyses suggest that considerable uncertainty remains regarding the cost-effectiveness of screening using the four chamber plus outflow tracts view. However, the model only addresses cost-effectiveness of screening for cardiac malformations in terms of the impact an antenatal diagnosis of TGA has on improved health outcomes; it does not address the cost-effectiveness of such screening in providing information to inform decision making about termination of pregnancy.

---

* The 95% confidence intervals for the reduction in percentage points mortality with antenatally detected TGA is 10.9% to 17.0%.

Appendix F

Economic model: screening and treatment of gestational diabetes

F.1 Systematic review of screening

A systematic search of the literature identified 337 studies potentially related to the clinical question. After reviewing the abstracts, 33 articles were retrieved for further appraisal and eight have been included in this section of the review. Six papers were identified that examined the cost-effectiveness of screening for gestational diabetes. Two additional papers were identified that considered the cost-effectiveness of screening for and treatment of gestational diabetes.

F.1.1 Screening and treatment of gestational diabetes

A study conducted in France[948] examined three strategies for screening for gestational diabetes using a decisionanalysis model. Under strategy one, women deemed to be at higher risk of gestational diabetes based on a series of risk factors (family history of diabetes in a first-degree relative, age over 35 years, BMI greater than 27 kg/m², previous history of gestational diabetes, pre-eclampsia, fetal death after 3 months of gestation or previous macrosomia) were given a non-fasting 50 g oral glucose tolerance test (OGTT). In strategy two all women were given the 50 g OGTT and in strategy three all women were given a 75 g OGTT. Data on costs were collected through a prospective study of 120 pregnancies and clinical data were taken from a review of published literature. Incremental analysis was reported in terms of cost per additional case prevented of macrosomia, prematurity, perinatal mortality or hypertensive disorder. All strategies were compared with a baseline of no screening for each outcome. The authors recommended strategy one, screening the population of high-risk pregnant women using the 50 g OGTT, based on its favourable incremental cost-effectiveness ratio (ICER) for preventing perinatal mortality (€7,870*, compared with €8,660 and €29,400 for strategies two and three, respectively).

A retrospective study conducted in Italy[949] examined the costs and outcomes for two groups of women. The first group had universal screening using a 50 g glucose challenge test (GCT) while the second were screened based on the presence of given risk factors (history of gestational diabetes, previous macrosomia, family history of diabetes mellitus, age over 30 years and body mass). All women that tested positive in either screening group underwent a 100 g OGTT. Universal screening was found to be more costly than the selective screening approach per case of gestational diabetes diagnosed (€424 and €406, respectively) and that treatment cost €366. No incremental analysis was reported. The authors concluded that, based on the savings from downstream interventions associated with untreated gestational diabetes, such as caesarean section, screening in some form was justified.

F.1.2 Screening for gestational diabetes

A cost–utility analysis[950] examined four screening strategies for gestational diabetes. The strategies were no screening, a 75 g OGTT, a 100 g OGTT and a sequential test (50 g GCT followed by a 100 g OGTT). The authors concluded that the sequential testing strategy was cost-effective, although in a high-prevalence population the 100 g OGTT may be an alternative cost-effective screening strategy. The study was conducted from a societal perspective, which could limit its applicability for decision making in an NHS setting, as this may overestimate costs. References were given for clinical and cost parameters but no specific details of these were reported. No detail was provided on what components comprised the total cost of each strategy and no unit

---

* Exchange rate of £1 = €1.31, from markets.ft.com/ft/markets/currencies.asp on 28 February 2008.

2008 update

costs were reported. Incremental analysis was undertaken and outcomes reported in quality-adjusted life years (QALYs), with maternal and infant outcomes reported separately. Sources for utility estimates were not provided. Given these drawbacks, the results of this study cannot be generalised to an NHS setting.

One study from the UK[951] examined the cost per case of gestational diabetes detected. Six screening strategies were considered: universal fasting plasma glucose (FPG), universal GCT with 7.8 mmol/litre cut-off, universal GCT with 8.2 mmol/litre cut-off, GCT with 8.2 mmol/litre cut-off in women aged over 25 years, GCT with 8.2 mmol/litre cut-off in women aged over 25 years and risk factors, and universal OGTT. The authors recommended the use of a universal FPG or giving a GCT to those over age 25 years and with risk factors. The FPG detected an additional 6009 cases at a cost of £489 per additional case detected when compared with GCT. A strategy of universal OGTT was predicted to detect an additional 1493 cases compared with the universal FPG, at a cost per additional case detected of £4,665.

Four studies reported in US dollars estimated the cost per case detected of gestational diabetes.[952–955] One study[952] examined the cost per case diagnosed of six different strategies. Incremental analysis was not reported. The authors recommended screening women aged over 25 years using a 50 g 1 hour glucose screening test. In a second study[953] the authors examined the cost per case diagnosed using different thresholds for the diagnosis of gestational diabetes in a high-risk population. The cost per case of gestational diabetes identified by a 50 g oral glucose screening test was $114* at a cut-off of 7.2 mmol/litre and $106 at a cut-off of 8.3 mmol/litre. The authors made no conclusion on the cost-effectiveness of either approach. A third study[954] examined the cost per case diagnosed of gestational diabetes in two groups of women. Group 1 had historical or clinical risk factors for gestational diabetes and Group 2 were offered routine screening. Screening was with a 50 g GCT followed by a OGTT for women with greater than 150 mg/100 ml. The number of cases of gestational diabetes diagnosed did not differ between groups. The cost per case diagnosed of the testing programme was $329. A fourth study[955] was conducted in Iran and reported in US dollars. Women were stratified into high-, intermediate- and low-risk groups based on American Diabetes Association (ADA) criteria. The authors recommended universal screening in a high-prevalence population such as theirs, with a cost per case diagnosed of $80.56. No incremental analysis was reported.

F.2 Introduction to the model

The recently published Australian Carbohydrate Intolerance Study in Pregnant Women (ACHOIS) demonstrated potential benefit of treatment for mild gestational diabetes.[824] However, while clinical effectiveness is a necessary condition for cost-effectiveness it is not sufficient. Resources have competing uses and showing that resources yield a benefit does not demonstrate that an even greater benefit could not be produced if those resources were deployed in an alternative use. Furthermore, treatment requires identification of those affected by gestational diabetes using some screening/diagnostic strategy which further reduces scarce resources available to other NHS patients. Therefore, the cost-effectiveness of treatment will partly be determined by the ability to identify patients for treatment via screening in a cost-effective fashion. Similarly, the cost-effectiveness of screening is predicated on an efficacious treatment which gives an acceptable cost per effect given the finite resources available.

Therefore, the cost-effectiveness of screening, diagnosis and treatment for gestational diabetes are highly interdependent. As a result, a single cost-effectiveness model addressing screening, diagnosis and treatment for gestational diabetes was developed jointly by the diabetes in pregnancy and antenatal care GDGs to enable them to make recommendations on this area of care for pregnant women.

However, in addition to this single model incorporating both screening and treatment, a separate cost-minimisation analysis of the various treatment options is also presented. This better illustrates the cost-effectiveness of different treatment alternatives, under the assumption of equivalent effectiveness, where the decision to screen for cases and treat has been accepted on economic grounds.

---

* Exchange rate of £1 = $1.98, from markets.ft.com/ft/markets/currencies.asp on 28 February 2008.

F.2.1 The decision tree

The model utilises a decision-analytic approach. In this approach, competing alternatives represent the decisions. Then, by considering the probabilities of different scenarios under each decision, drawing on best available evidence, the expected costs and effects of each decision can be computed and compared.

At its most basic, this cost-effectiveness model can be represented as the decision to screen and treat patients identified with gestational diabetes versus no screening, which was the recommendation of the previous antenatal care guideline (Figure F.1).

Data from the ACHOIS intervention group were used to estimate the outcomes and associated costs of treating true positives. As ACHOIS was limited to those with 'mild' gestational diabetes, the costs and effects may be an underestimate of the true costs and effects in the population under consideration. The outcomes and associated costs of false negatives were estimated from the routine care group in ACHOIS. It is also necessary to consider the cost of providing treatment to women falsely diagnosed with gestational diabetes (false positives). The outcomes for women without gestational diabetes (true negatives and false positives) in the screening arms were not considered as the perinatal outcomes for these pregnancies do not differ from those in the population of otherwise healthy pregnant women.

In Figure F.1 the decision, for diagrammatic simplicity, is depicted as screen versus no screen. However, given an initial decision to screen there is then the decision of how to screen. The various screening options that have been considered in this model are described in the next section.

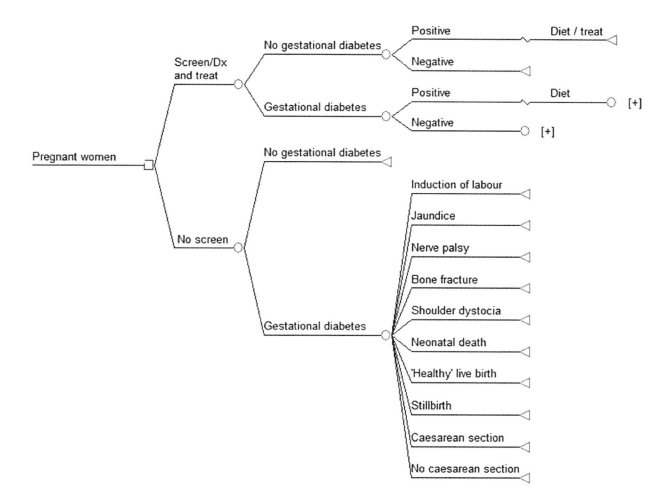

Figure F.1 The basic decision tree structure; [+] denotes that the tree is truncated – see Figure F.3 for the treatment sub-tree; the sub-tree for those with gestational diabetes who are undetected on screening is the same as the sub-tree for women with gestational diabetes who are not screened; Dx = diagnose

The key outputs of each screening strategy are the costs of screening and treating women and the number of women accurately diagnosed with gestational diabetes. There are four possible outcomes when applying a diagnostic test:

- true positive – the patient is diagnosed as positive and has the condition/disease
- false positive – the patient is diagnosed as positive but does not have the condition/disease
- true negative – the patient is not diagnosed with the condition/disease and does not have it
- false negative – the patient is not diagnosed with the condition/disease but does in fact have it.

The number of individuals diagnosed correctly is determined by the accuracy of the diagnostic test applied (sensitivity and specificity) and by the prevalence of the condition in the population being tested. The treatment and outcome sub-trees are identical for each screening strategy in this model but the costs and effects will vary according to the numbers diagnosed as having gestational diabetes or not.

F.3   Screening strategies

Table F.1 contains a list of the various strategies that have been considered as screening strategies for gestational diabetes. All screening methods, including risk factor screening, screening blood tests and universal diagnostic tests, have been considered in isolation. Combinations of these tests have then been considered.

Not all possible strategies have been considered – particularly where they are clinically inappropriate, for example treating patients based on the presence of a risk factor alone. Some strategies have been excluded from further analysis after preliminary analysis showed them to be dominated by alternative strategies. Limitations in the data are discussed in greater detail later in this appendix.

Table F.1   List of screening strategies

Strategy number	Risk factor	Screening blood test	Screening diagnostic test
1	–	–	OGTT
2	ADA criteria[a]	FPG	OGTT
3	ADA criteria[a]	RBG	OGTT
4	ADA criteria[a]	GCT	OGTT
5	ADA criteria[a]	FPG	–
6	ADA criteria[a]	–	OGTT
7	ADA criteria[a]	GCT	–
8	–	FPG	–
9	–	RBG	–
10	–	GCT	–
11	–	FPG	OGTT
12	–	GCT	OGTT
13	Age ≥ 30 years	FPG	OGTT
14	Age ≥ 30 years	GCT	OGTT
15	Age ≥ 25 years	FPG	OGTT
16	Age ≥ 25 years	GCT	OGTT
17	Age ≥ 30 years	–	OGTT
18	Age ≥ 25 years	–	OGTT
19	High-risk ethnicity	FPG	OGTT
20	High-risk ethnicity	GCT	OGTT
21	High-risk ethnicity	–	OGTT

[a] Having one or more of the following risk factors: age > 25 years; BMI > 27 kg/m²; family history of diabetes; high-risk ethnic group.

Risk factors that have been considered:

- age ≥ 30 years
- age ≥ 25 years
- high-risk ethnic background (ethnicity; see Table F.5)
- BMI ≥ 27 kg/m² (high BMI)
- family history of diabetes.

Screening blood tests considered:

- FPG
- RBG
- 1 hour 50 g GCT.

Diagnostic blood test considered:

- 2 hour 75 g OGTT.

F.3.1 Screening strategy assumptions

Decision analysis is used to help us make decisions about the best treatment or intervention to use, based on grounds of cost and clinical effectiveness. When developing a decision-analysis model it is necessary to make simplifying assumptions to highlight what the important elements of the model might be and to reduce the complexity of the model. It is not possible to consider every possible potential outcome in a model and it is important to focus on those with the greatest relevance in answering the question at hand. The assumptions used in the model of screening strategies are given below:

- A 2 hour 75 g OGTT is used as the gold standard diagnostic test (refer to Section 4.2 in the *Diabetes in Pregnancy* guideline[636] for details) and is assumed to be 100% sensitive and specific.
- It has not been possible to establish an accurate fertility rate in some population subgroups. It is therefore assumed that the fertility rate among women with a high BMI is the same as the rate among women with a BMI in the normal range. This may overestimate the number of pregnancies in this group, as high BMI is associated with fertility problems.[956]
- The available data on BMI are not consistent. Population level data on BMI from the Office of National Statistics or the Health Survey for England is presented as overweight and obese with a BMI greater than or equal to 25 kg/m², whereas the data presented in the literature[831] used a BMI greater than or equal to 27 kg/m² to define some at risk of gestational diabetes based on BMI. It is assumed initially that the risk of those with a BMI greater than 25 kg/m² is equal to that of those with a BMI greater than 27 kg/m², although this assumption can be relaxed in sensitivity analysis. If there is a genuine difference in the subpopulation (BMI 25–217 kg/m²), this assumption may overestimate the number of cases of gestational diabetes in the at-risk population and lead to a greater number of false positive diagnoses of gestational diabetes.

F.3.2 Screening strategy input parameters

The parameters used to populate the model have been chosen based on the best available evidence, and those relating to screening are listed in Tables F.2 to F.5.

After some initial modelling, the GDG expressed concern that test acceptability might be an additional important consideration. Some women may find the tests inconvenient and unpleasant, especially where they are required to fast for a period beforehand. Table F.6 lists the input parameters relating to test acceptability.

The model assumes that women are more likely to accept a test if they have already been identified as being at higher risk, either by risk factor or a previous screening test. The baseline values reflected the views of the GDG, but clearly considerable uncertainty surrounds the actual test acceptance, and thus sensitivity analysis was undertaken to determine to what extent test acceptance determines the cost-effectiveness conclusions of the model.

2008 update

Table F.2   Accuracy of screening and diagnostic blood tests

Test	Sensitivity	Specificity	Source
FPG	0.88	0.78	Reichelt *et al.* (1998)[498]
RBG	0.48	0.97	Ostlund and Hanson (2004)[837]
1 hour 50 g GCT	0.80	0.43	Seshiah *et al.* (2004)[840]
2 hour 75 g OGTT	1.0	1.0	Gold standard

Table F.3   Cost of screening and diagnostic blood tests

Variable	Cost	Source
Risk factor screening	£2	GDG estimate
FPG	£5.39	Updated from Scott *et al.* (2002)[483]
RBG	£5.39	Updated from Scott *et al.* (2002)[483]
1 hour 50 g GCT	£10.61	Updated from Scott *et al.* (2002)[483]
2 hour 75 g OGTT	£28.58	Updated from Scott *et al.* (2002)[483]

Table F.4   Risk factors for gestational diabetes – age

Risk factor	% of population (Source)	% of women with gestational diabetes (source)	PPV (%)
Age ≥ 30 years	48.7 (ONS, 2005)	0.65 (Coustan, 1993)[957]	4.7
Age ≥ 25 years	74.2 (ONS, 2005)	0.85 (Coustan, 1993)[957]	4.0

Table F.5   Risk factors for gestational diabetes other than age

Risk factor	% of population (Source)	% of women with gestational diabetes (source)	PPV (%)
Gestational diabetes in a previous pregnancy	3.5 (HES, 2005)	30 (Weeks *et al.*, 1994)[958]	10.5
Family history of diabetes	10.0 (Davey and Hamblin, 2001)[831]	39.9 (Davey and Hamblin, 2001)[831]	14.0
High-risk ethnic group	8.5 (ONS, 2001)	68.7 (Davey and Hamblin, 2001)[831]	28.1
BMI ≥ 27 kg/m²	35.8 (ONS, 2001)	36.2 (Davey and Hamblin, 2001)[831]	3.5

Table F.6   Test acceptance

Test	Initial test acceptance	Test acceptance if identified as 'at risk'	Source
FPG	0.50	0.90	GDG estimate
RBG	0.90	1.00	GDG estimate
1 hour 50 g GCT	0.70	1.00	GDG estimate
2 hour 75 g OGTT	0.40	0.90	GDG estimate

2008 update

F.3.3   Incorporating risk factors within the model

General overview

In terms of the decision tree for the gestational diabetes screening/treatment model, risk factors can be thought of analogously to diagnostic tests (Figure F.2).

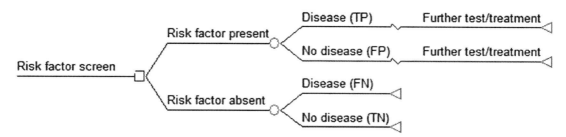

Figure F.2   Decision tree for risk factors; TP = true positive; FP = false positive; FN = false negative; TN = true negative

Positives from a risk factor screen or screen/diagnostic test progress to the next stage of testing or treatment. Negatives do not progress.

The detection rate of a risk factor screen is given by the true positive rate*. This detection rate is an important component of the model, as treatment costs and effects are predicated on it. Its flip-side (false negatives) is also important because there may be 'downstream' costs associated with missed cases.

In the economic model of screening we are also concerned with the unnecessary costs of screening which are caused by false negatives. The screening does not lead to improved outcomes in women with gestational diabetes and the scarce resources used in screening have an opportunity cost in terms of the benefit they could have achieved if used elsewhere in the healthcare system[†].

Therefore, the screening strategy with the highest detection rate is not necessarily the most cost-effective. There may be some desirable trade-off between detection and unnecessary testing and treatment.

The methodological problem

The data requirements for the model for any risk factor screening strategy are conceptually straightforward:

- what is the disease prevalence?
- what proportion of the population meets the risk criteria[‡]?
- what proportion of cases is detected in the population who meet the criteria?

With answers to these questions the true positive, false positive, true negative and false negative branches of the decision tree can be completed.

The literature tends to focus on the detection rates of a particular risk factor (or more rarely combination of risk factors). Using ONS data in combination with the literature it is possible to estimate the true positive, false positive, true negative and false negative rates for a single risk factor screen at baseline prevalence. However, given data limitations, it is much more difficult to derive these estimates for screening strategies based on combinations of risk factors.

Prevalence varies across the country and this is potentially important in the cost-effectiveness of screening as it influences the trade-off between detection and false positives. Therefore, the model has been developed to explore how the conclusion may vary at different disease prevalence. To

---

* In our gestational diabetes model, this is complicated by assumptions made about test acceptance.

† It is not explicitly addressed in the model, but an undesirable consequence of screening may be the unnecessary inconvenience and worry associated with false positives.

‡ This information obviously also gives the proportion who do not meet the criteria.

do this required that we model a relationship between changes in disease prevalence and the proportion classed at 'high risk'. This poses further methodological difficulties because of the complex and interdependent relationship between risk factors.

With sufficient individual level data, it is possible to envisage a multiple regression equation which would predict the change in prevalence arising from a change in the proportions with different risk factor (RF) combinations.

$$\text{Prevalence} = a + b_1 RF_1 + b_2 RF_2 + b_3 RF_3 + \ldots + b_n RF_n$$

Such a model could be used to predict individual risk of disease.

However, in this model, risk factor proportion would be the dependent variable. As a result any model change in gestational diabetes prevalence would lead to a change in risk factor proportion. However, in reality, it is likely that different combinations of risk factors are consistent with the same overall disease prevalence. So, for example, a relatively young pregnant population may have the same gestational diabetes prevalence as an older pregnant population, if the younger population has a higher proportion in high-risk ethnic groups. This means that the most cost-effective screening strategy may be determined by the demographic characteristics of a particular population rather than prevalence *per se* (although the latter is a function of the former).

Our approach to modelling risk factor screening
Owing to data limitations and methodological complexity, our approach involved certain simplifying assumptions and the accuracy of the model may ultimately depend on whether these give a sufficiently good approximation to the real world.

Each risk factor screening strategy involves dividing the population in two – those at 'high' risk and those at 'low' risk[*]. Logically, the disease prevalence is the weighted average of the respective prevalence in these two groups. The weights are the proportions in each of the groups.

Prevalence = (proportion high risk × high-risk prevalence) + (proportion low risk × low-risk prevalence)

The first step is to estimate a positive predictive value (PPV) for each risk factor screen, i.e. what proportion of the high-risk group had gestational diabetes? This gives the gestational diabetes prevalence for the high-risk group. Next, a negative predictive value (NPV) is calculated, i.e. what proportion of the low-risk group did not have gestational diabetes. The prevalence in the low-risk group is given by 1 − NPV. These estimates use a combination of the literature and ONS data and they are probably reasonably good at baseline because they are not based on a simplified model extrapolation[†].

We then assume that the PPV and NPV are independent of prevalence. In a hypothetical scenario where there was just one risk factor for a disease, this would be correct. However, this linear relationship between risk factor proportion and prevalence is clearly a simplifying assumption in this case.

The model does not capture the impact and interdependence of multiple risk factors. As the proportion with a risk factor (e.g. age) increases, there would be concomitant increases in the proportion with multiple risk factors, which would change the PPV in those of 'at risk' age. This would exert an upward pressure on prevalence over and above that arising from the change in a single risk factor. In practice, changes in gestational diabetes prevalence are likely to lead to a smaller change in risk factor proportion than that implied by the model. This is even true for the ADA strategy, as clearly there is no reason why the proportion with multiple risk factors should be constant with respect to prevalence. Similarly, if the low-risk group have some risk factors then their disease prevalence (1 − NPV) is also likely to change with the demographic differences associated with changing disease prevalence.

Recognising these simplifying assumptions as a limitation, it should also be noted that the software developed for modelling included an option to override the relationship between prevalence and risk factors. If this option were chosen, the user of the software would themselves select the 'at risk' proportion and the proportion of cases that would exist in this population. This can be used to reflect better local data, if known, or to conduct sensitivity analysis. Such sensitivity analysis may indicate to what extent the simplifying assumptions drive the cost-effectiveness conclusions.

---

[*] 'High' and 'low' risk should be interpreted as a comparison of two groups, where one has a higher level of risk than the other.

[†] ADA may be a slight exception because the paper used to derive PPV and NPV values was based on a US population with a lower prevalence than our baseline model.

Below we outline in more detail the assumptions that were made for each risk factor screening strategy used in the model.

ADA criteria:
ADA selective screening criteria exclude women who are:

- age < 25 years
- BMI < 27 kg/m²
- low-prevalence ethnic group
- no first-degree relative with history of diabetes.

The PPV and NPV for the ADA criteria were calculated as follows, using a retrospective study by Danilenko-Dixon et al.[991] which compared selective screening (using ADA criteria) with universal screening. The authors estimated that only 10% would be exempt from screening in their population (of which 17.8% were under 25 years), i.e. having none of the ADA risk factors. They found that 3% (17/564) of gestational diabetes cases were missed using ADA criteria[*]. The prevalence of gestational diabetes in their population was 3% (564/18 504) (see Table F.7).

Table F.7 Calculating PPV and NPV using ADA criteria as a risk factor screen

Parameter	Value
n	18 504
Prevalence = 564/18 504	3.05%
High risk = 0.9 × 18 504	16 654
Gestational diabetes cases in high risk = 564 − 17	547
PPV = 547/ 16 654	3.28%
Low risk = 0.1 × 18 504	1,850
Gestational diabetes cases in low risk	17
NPV = 1833/1850	99.1%

In this case, we needed to model the relationship between ADA parameters and prevalence even for our baseline analysis, because the calculations are taken from a population having different disease prevalence.

The key assumption in modelling this was to assume that the PPV and NPV were independent of disease prevalence. The PPV is essentially the disease prevalence in the high-risk group. The gestational diabetes prevalence in the low-risk group is given by 1 − NPV (0.92%).

The overall prevalence can then be seen as a weighted average of the high-risk and low-risk groups. For a given population gestational diabetes prevalence, it is therefore possible to estimate the proportions in the high-risk and low-risk categories. The PPV in conjunction with the high-risk proportion gives the detection rate.

What this modelled relationship implies is that for prevalence of 3.28% or more, all the population would be high risk as defined by ADA and therefore this is what our model assumes for the baseline prevalence (3.5%). This would not be the case in reality for reasons outlined in the preceding section[†].

Ethnicity:
Here 'high risk' is defined as women in a 'high' prevalence ethnic group and 'low risk' is defined as women in a 'low' prevalence ethnic group.

---

[*] Another study by Williams et al.[992] suggested 4% of gestational diabetes cases would be missed by ADA criteria.

[†] However, given the study on which our calculations were based, > 90% proportion 'high risk' and > 97% gestational diabetes detection might be considered 'realistic' .

2008 update

The approach we used was similar to that used for the ADA criteria and is described in Table F.8.

Table F.8 Calculating PPV and NPV in using high-risk ethnicity as a risk factor screen

Parameter	Value	Source
Proportion of high risk	8.5%	ONS
Proportion of gestational diabetes high-risk ethnic group	68.7%	Weeks *et al.* (1994)[958]
Births	645 835	ONS
Births high-risk ethnic groups	54 896	Calculated
Gestational diabetes prevalence	3.5%	GDG estimate
Gestational diabetes births	22 604	Calculated
Gestational diabetes births high-risk ethnic groups	15 529	Calculated
PPV (15 529/54 896)	28.1%	Calculated
NPV (583 864/590 939)	98.8%	Calculated

Again it was assumed that PPV and NPV were independent of disease prevalence. As with the ADA criteria, these provide prevalence in the high-risk and low-risk group with the overall population prevalence being a weighted average of the two*. Therefore, it is possible to estimate the high-risk ethnic group proportion from any given population gestational diabetes prevalence.

The model suggests that at a population prevalence of 2%, the high-risk ethnic proportion would be 2.98%. At a gestational diabetes prevalence of 10% it predicts 32.6%. On the face of it, these seem fairly plausible estimates but with the caveat that they are derived from a high-risk prevalence which is much higher than the literature would suggest.

BMI of 27 kg/m² or more:
This strategy identifies high-risk women as having a BMI of 27 kg/m² or more and low-risk women has having a BMI of less than 27 kg/m². The proportion of high-risk women in this strategy at baseline was calculated as shown in Table F.9.

Table F.9 Calculating PPV and NPV using a BMI of 27 kg/m² or more as a risk factor screen

Parameter	Value	Source
High-risk BMI proportion	0.358	ONS[a]
Proportion of gestational diabetes high-risk BMI	0.362	Davey and Hamblin (2001)[831]
Births	645 835	ONS
High-risk BMI births	231 209	Calculated
Low-risk BMI births	414 624	Calculated
Gestational diabetes prevalence	0.035	GDG estimate
Gestational diabetes births	22 604	Calculated
High-risk BMI gestational diabetes births	8 183	Calculated
Low-risk BMI gestational diabetes births	14 421	Calculated
PPV (8183/231 209)	3.5%	Calculated
NPV (400 203/414 624)	96.5%	Calculated

[a] ONS data are based on proportions with BMI > 25 kg/m² (see earlier discussion).

---

* A prevalence of 28.1% for 'high-risk' ethnic groups seems considerably higher than values quoted in the literature.

Family history of diabetes:
This strategy identifies high-risk women as having a first-degree relative with a history of diabetes and low-risk women has having no first-degree relative with a history of diabetes. The proportion of high-risk women in this strategy at baseline was calculated as shown in Table F.10.

Table F.10   Calculating PPV and NPV using a first-degree relative with a history of diabetes as a risk factor screen

Parameter	Value	Source
High-risk family history proportion	0.10	Davey and Hamblin (2001)[831]
Proportion of gestational diabetes high-risk history	0.399	Davey and Hamblin (2001)[831]
Births	645 835	ONS
Low-risk family history births	581 252	Calculated
High-risk family history births	64 584	Calculated
Gestational diabetes prevalence	0.035	GDG estimate
Gestational diabetes births	22 604.	Calculated
High-risk family history gestational diabetes births	9,018	Calculated
Low-risk family history gestational diabetes births	13 586	Calculated
PPV (9018/64 584)	14.0%	Calculated
NPV (567 666/581 252)	97.6%	Calculated

Age ≥ 25 years:
This strategy identifies high-risk women as 25 years of age or older and low-risk women being 24 years of age or less. At baseline this gives a high-risk proportion of 74.2% and low-risk proportion of 25.8% (source: ONS).

The detection rate is then derived using a PPV, which is again assumed not to change with disease prevalence. The proportion of high-risk women in this strategy at baseline was calculated as shown in Table F.11.

Table F.11   Calculating PPV and NPV using age 25 years or older as a risk factor screen

Parameter	Value	Source
Total births	645 835	ONS
Total births ≥ 25 years	478 860	ONS
Gestational diabetes prevalence	3.5%	GDG estimate
Gestational diabetes births (0.035 × 645 835)	22 604	Calculated
Proportion detected ≥ 25 years	85%	Coustan (1993)[957]
Gestational diabetes detected (0.85 × 22 604)	19 214	Calculated
PPV (19 214/478 860)	4.01%	Calculated
NPV (163 585/166 975)	98.0%	Calculated

It should be noted that the model assumes that all the population is in the high-risk category for prevalence values of 4.01% and above.

Age ≥ 30 years:
The method is the same as for age ≥ 25 years, but using an older age threshold to define the high-risk and low-risk proportion. At baseline this gives a high-risk proportion of 48.7% and low-risk proportion of 51.3% (source: ONS).

The detection rate is then derived using a PPV, which is again assumed not to change with disease prevalence (Table F.12).

Table F.12 Calculating PPV and NPV using aged 30 years or older as a risk factor screen

Parameter	Value	Source
Total births	645 835	ONS
Total births ≥ 30 years	314 512	ONS
Gestational diabetes prevalence	3.5%	GDG estimate
Gestational diabetes births (0.035 × 645 835)	22 604	Calculated
Proportion detected ≥ 30 years	65%	Coustan (1993)[957]
Gestational diabetes detected (0.65 × 22 604)	14 693	Calculated
PPV (14 693/314 512)	4.7%	Calculated
NPV (323 412/331 323)	97.6%	Calculated

It should be noted that the model assumes that all the population is in the high-risk category for prevalence values of 4.7% and above.

F.4 Treatment

F.4.1 Treatment decision tree

The basic decision tree for treatment is depicted in Figure F.3.

The screening part of the model produces an output of true positives, false negatives, false positives and true negatives and these numbers then inform the probabilities attached to given patient treatment pathways following a positive or negative diagnosis of gestational diabetes.

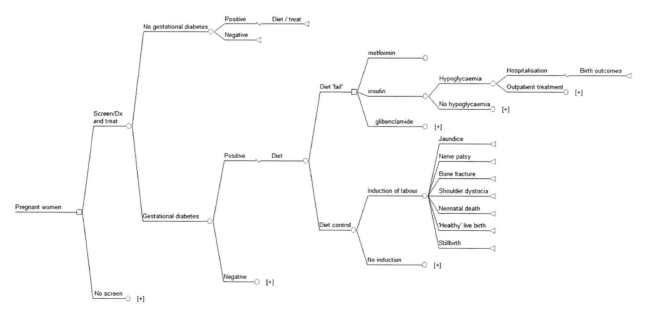

Figure F.3 The basic treatment sub-tree

2008 update

As far as possible, treatment was modelled according to the ACHOIS protocol, as this is what the effectiveness data were based upon. It is assumed that women with gestational diabetes would start treatment at a gestational age of 27 weeks and that this would continue for 90 days.

The treatment protocol used in the model is outlined below.

Diet
Initial treatment aims to control blood glucose using diet. This part of treatment consists of:

- 30 minutes of individualised dietary advice from a qualified dietitian
- 30 minutes of instruction on self-monitoring of blood glucose (SMBG) provided by a specialist nurse (band 5/6)
- SMBG, four times daily (costing of SMBG includes one monitor, and assumes one lancet and one test strip per reading)
- 5 minutes of assessment of control after 10 days on diet by a specialist nurse.

At this 10 day assessment, women with gestational diabetes are judged to have achieved adequate control with diet or not. If they have achieved adequate control, they remain on dietary control until the end of their pregnancy, with SMBG reduced to twice daily.

If women are deemed not to have achieved adequate control with diet, medical treatment (insulin analogue, glibenclamide, metformin) is then initiated.

Insulin analogue
- 45 minutes of instruction from a diabetes specialist nurse
- daily insulin dose: 20 units
- pre-filled disposable injection device
- twice-daily injections (two needles per day of treatment)
- a proportion of women will experience hypoglycaemia and a small proportion of these will be severe cases requiring an inpatient admission
- SMBG, two times daily.

Glibenclamide and metformin, two alternative oral hypoglycaemic treatments to analogue insulin, were also included in the model. An RCT of glyburide (glibenclamide) versus insulin for gestational diabetes showed no statistically significant differences in outcomes. The effectiveness of metformin is currently being investigated as part of the ongoing Metformin in Gestational Diabetes (MIG) trial and is therefore a potential treatment option. The basic tree structure for an oral hypoglycaemic treatment, such as glibenclamide, would be as illustrated in Figure F.4.

Glibenclamide
- daily dose: 15 mg.

Metformin
- daily dose: 1.5 g.

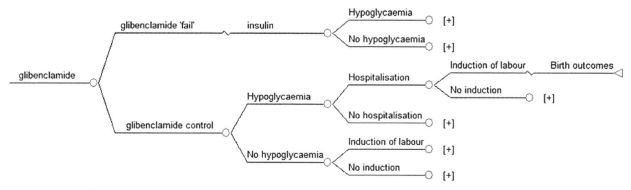

Figure F.4   Glibenclamide treatment sub-tree

2008 update

F.4.2 Outcomes and downstream costs

The model uses the following outcomes presented in the ACHOIS study to estimate the incremental QALY gain associated with screening, diagnosis and treatment of gestational diabetes:

- stillbirth
- neonatal death
- maternal health state utility.

Furthermore, the following outcomes from ACHOIS are assumed to have downstream cost implications. Costs are assigned to these outcomes and included in the evaluation of incremental costs:

- neonatal death
- shoulder dystocia
- bone fracture
- admission to neonatal unit
- jaundice requiring phototherapy
- induction of labour
- caesarean section.

We used the outcome data of ACHOIS for 'serious perinatal complications' as the measure of the effectiveness in the model. The trial data allow this to be easily done for deterministic sensitivity analysis, with the different event rates giving well-defined relative risks. In order to reflect the individual components of the composite measure, a weighted cost and QALY was calculated for a serious perinatal complication based on the QALY and costs associated with each of the individual components. In order to calculate the weights, it was assumed, based on the lack of statistical significance for any difference, that the proportion of serious perinatal complications accounted for by individual components did not differ according to whether the women were treated for gestational diabetes or not. Therefore, the data on individual events were pooled across both arms of the trial in order to estimate the weighting for individual components (Table F.13).

Table F.13 ACHOIS trial outcome data for serious perinatal complications combined across control and intervention groups

Outcome	Total	Weight
All serious perinatal complications	32	1.00
Stillbirth	3	0.09
Neonatal death	2	0.06
Shoulder dystocia	23	0.72
Bone fracture	1	0.03
Nerve palsy	3	0.09

F.4.3 Treatment model parameters

The baseline parameter values for all model treatment inputs are shown in Tables F.14 to F.20.

Table F.14 Treatment timeframe

Variable	Value (days)	Source	Notes
Treatment duration	90	Diabetes in pregnancy GDG	The diabetes in pregnancy GDG consensus was that treatment would usually commence between 26 and 28 weeks of gestation. Taking the midpoint of 27 weeks, 90 days is a reasonable approximation of the typical time to term.
Exclusive diet	10	Diabetes in pregnancy GDG	The diabetes in pregnancy GDG suggested that diet alone would be given 7–14 days to achieve adequate control.
4 × daily SMBG	10	ACHOIS[824]	The ACHOIS protocol suggested that SMBG be done 4 × daily until glucose levels had been in the recommended range for 2 weeks.

SMBG = self-monitoring of blood glucose.

Table F.15   Cost of healthcare professionals' time

Variable	Time (minutes)	Cost per hour	Source	Notes
Dietary advice	30	£28	Curtis and Netten (2006)[959]	Unit costs of a dietitian for an hour of client contact
SMBG instruction	30	£63	Curtis and Netten (2006)[959] GDG estimate	Unit cost of a nurse specialist (community) for an hour of client contact
Control with diet; assessment/review	5	£63	Curtis and Netten (2006)[959] GDG estimate	Unit cost of a nurse specialist (community) for an hour of client contact
Insulin instruction	45	£63	Curtis and Netten (2006)[959] GDG estimate	Unit cost of a nurse specialist (community) for an hour of client contact
Risk factor screening questions	2	£63	Curtis and Netten (2006)[959] GDG estimate	Unit cost of a nurse specialist (community) for an hour of client contact

SMBG = self-monitoring of blood glucose.

Table F.16   Self-monitoring of blood glucose and treatment costs

Variable	Cost	Source	Notes
Blood glucose monitor	£7.79	BNF 52 (2006)[989]	
Test strips	£0.31 each	BNF 52 (2006)[989]	Many makes, all similarly priced. £15.55 for a pack of 50 was the cheapest found from a small sample.
Lancets	£0.03 each	BNF 52 (2006)[989]	
Needles	£0.09 each	BNF 52 (2006)[989]	£8.57 for a pack of 100 needles
Insulin analogue (Humalog®)	£0.39 per day	BNF 52 (2006)[989]	This is based on a dose of 20 units per day. A pre-filled disposable pen has 1500 units and costs £29.46.
Glibenclamide	£0.16	BNF 52 (2006)[989]	Based on 15 mg daily. A 5 mg 28 tablet pack costs £1.50.
Metformin	£0.10	BNF 52 (2006)[989]	Based on 1.5 g daily. A 500 mg 84 tablet pack costs £2.85.
Treatment of severe hypoglycaemia	£403	Curtis and Netten (2006)[959] NHS Reference Costs 2005–06	Average cost per patient journey for paramedic ambulance: £323. A&E admission with low-cost investigation: £80.

Table F.17   'Downstream' outcome costs

Variable	Cost	Source	Notes
Admission to neonatal unit	£1,676	NHS Reference Costs 2004	Assume 2 days of neonatal intensive care at £838 per day.
Induction of labour	£20	Davies and Drummond (1991)[960] and (1993)[993]	Updated to 2006 prices using Retail Price Index published by Office of National Statistics.
Neonatal death	£2,568	NHS Tariff 2006 NHS Reference Costs 2004	From NHS Reference Costs 2004 FCE (finished consultant episode) data assume that 25% of neonatal deaths are < 2 days (n = 974). NHS Reference Costs for this is £527. For remaining 75% assume 2 days of neonatal intensive care (£838 × 2) and neonate with one major diagnosis which has an NHS Tariff of £1,572. £1,676 + £1,572 = £3,248
Shoulder dystocia	£629	NHS Tariff 2006	Cost for neonate with one minor diagnosis (HRG N03)
Bone fracture	£629	NHS Tariff 2006	Cost for neonate with one minor diagnosis (HRG N03)
Nerve palsy	£629	NHS Tariff 2006	Cost for neonate with one minor diagnosis (HRG N03)
Phototherapy	£629	NHS Tariff 2006	Cost for neonate with one minor diagnosis (HRG N03)
Emergency caesarean section	£1,205	NHS Reference Costs 2004	Incremental cost over and above that of a normal vaginal birth
Elective caesarean section	£822	NHS Reference costs 2004	Incremental cost over and above that of a normal vaginal birth

HRG = Health Resource Group.

2008 update

Table F.18 Treatment pathway probabilities

Variable	Value	Source	Notes
Control with diet	0.86	Persson *et al.* (1985)[505]	–
Control with glibenclamide	0.96	Langer *et al.* (2000)[961]	GDG member suggested that data from Southampton (their local practice) indicate a higher failure rate (23%).
Control with metformin	0.96	–	Assumed the same as for glibenclamide.
Hypoglycaemia on insulin therapy	0.20	Langer *et al.* (2000)[961]	–
Hypoglycaemia on insulin analogue	0.20	–	Assumed the same as for insulin.
Hypoglycaemia on glibenclamide	0.02	Langer *et al.* (2000)[961]	–
Hypoglycaemia on metformin	0.02	–	Assumed the same as for glibenclamide.
Severe hypoglycaemia requiring hospitalisation	0.05	GDG estimate	–

Table F.19 ACHOIS outcome probabilities

Variable	Treatment value	No treatment value	Source
Serious perinatal complications	0.014	0.044	ACHOIS[824]
Admission to neonatal unit	0.706	0.613	ACHOIS[824]
Induction of labour	0.374	0.286	ACHOIS[824]
Elective caesarean section	0.142	0.116	ACHOIS[824]
Emergency caesarean section	0.158	0.197	ACHOIS[824]
Jaundice (phototherapy)	0.087	0.092	ACHOIS[824]

Table F.20 QALYs

Variable	QALY	Source	Notes
Averted death (stillbirth/neonatal)	25		This is the approximate lifetime QALYs from 75 years lived in perfect health with QALYS discounted at 3.5% per annum.
Maternal QALY – treatment (during pregnancy)	0.72	ACHOIS[824]	It is assumed that this QALY gain persists throughout treatment.
Maternal QALY – no treatment (during pregnancy)	0.70	ACHOIS[824]	It is assumed that this QALY gain persists throughout treatment.
Maternal QALY – treatment (3 months postpartum)	0.79	ACHOIS[824]	It is assumed that this QALY gain covers the entire 3 months postpartum period.
Maternal QALY – no treatment (3 months postpartum)	0.78	ACHOIS[824]	It is assumed that this QALY gain covers the entire 3 months postpartum period.

F.5　Baseline results

The baseline results from the modelling exercise are given based on a population of 10 000 pregnant women and assume a baseline prevalence of gestational diabetes of 3.5%. The total cost and QALYs generated for each strategy under the baseline assumptions are presented in Table F.21 and are plotted on a cost-effectiveness plane in Figure F.5. The origin represents the no screening/no treatment option and all costs and QALYs are measured relative to this.

Table F.21 Total QALYs and cost for each screening strategy

Screening strategy[a]	QALYs	Cost
11	16.63	£146,188
1	17.48	£212,816
8	18.48	£304,753
9	18.70	£145,419
3	18.70	£126,929
13	19.46	£119,940
14	20.39	£191,529
19	20.56	£77,465
20	21.55	£89,758
12	21.96	£259,791
10	24.40	£838,561
15	25.45	£160,670
17	25.56	£203,902
16	26.66	£269,731
21	27.01	£99,341
2	29.94	£198,769
4	31.37	£345,932
5	33.26	£489,580
18	33.43	£286,763
7	34.85	£1,172,747
6	39.33	£367,009

[a] Ranked in order of effectiveness (from fewest to most QALYs).

As can be seen from Figure F.5, a number of strategies are more expensive than the two circled and yet offer a lower QALY gain. Such strategies can unambiguously be excluded (they are said to be (strictly) dominated). Once these strategies are excluded the remainder are again ranked in order of effectiveness. Moving down the list, it is possible to calculate the incremental costs and incremental QALYs of selecting a given strategy relative to the next best strategy. From this, the

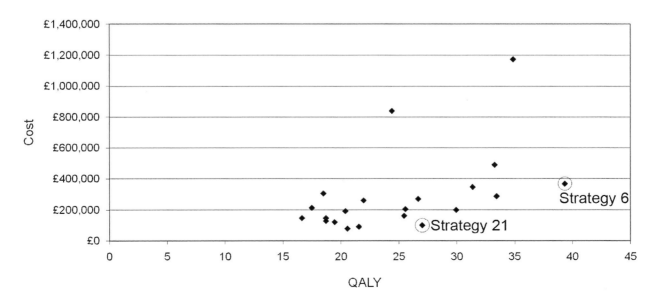

Figure F. 5 The cost-effectiveness plane for the baseline analysis

ICER is derived which effectively shows the cost of 'buying' QALYs. It is then possible to exclude certain further strategies on the grounds of 'extended dominance'. Extended dominance occurs when a strategy has a higher ICER than a more effective strategy. If the decision maker was willing to buy QALYs at the cost implied by the ICER of the less effective strategy, they would logically be willing to buy (and prefer) strategies where additional QALYs could be obtained at a lower cost.

In Table F.22 all but two of the strategies are excluded on these dominance grounds. The ICER for strategy 21 is calculated relative to no screening/treatment and the ICER for strategy 6 is calculated relative to strategy 21. The cost-effective option is the most effective strategy which falls within the willingness to pay threshold set by the decision maker.

Table F.22 ICER for non-dominated strategies

Strategy	QALYs	Cost	Incremental QALYs	Incremental cost	ICER
21	27.01	£99,341	27.01	£99,341	£3,677
6	39.33	£367,009	12.31	£267,668	£21,738

The baseline analysis suggests that a strategy of offering women from a high-risk ethnic background a diagnostic test (Strategy 21) would be cost-effective when compared with not offering a screening, with an ICER of £3,677. The strategy of offering a diagnostic test to those women who are deemed to be at increased risk according to the ADA criteria (Strategy 6) has an ICER of £21,738 when compared with Strategy 21. Although it is higher than the £20,000 per QALY threshold suggested by NICE, it is comfortably under the maximum willingness to pay per QALY of £30,000 and may be considered cost-effective under certain circumstances, for example if it is believed some salient piece of information falls outside the model such as the identification of women at higher risk of developing type 2 diabetes in the future. Thus it is possible that Strategy 6 could reasonably be argued to be cost-effective.

F.6 Sensitivity analysis

All decision-analysis models are subject to uncertainty[962] and there are two common approaches to dealing with this uncertainty – making use of a reference case (that is, a standard of good practice) and sensitivity analysis. This model takes as its reference case the NICE guidelines manual standards for conducting economic evaluations. The methods and assumptions used in the model are highlighted above in detail and were tested using a second method of examining uncertainty, sensitivity analysis. In the following analyses we primarily used a series of one-way and multi-way sensitivity analyses to explore what happened when the value of one or more parameters is changed. This allows us to see what happens to the model results when these values are changed, and thus the implications for our baseline results. The analyses that follow explore the uncertainty in a number of key areas, including:

- the reliability of the trial data on which the likelihood of an event occurring was based
- the prevalence of gestational diabetes in the population
- the proportion of women that would undergo a screening or diagnostic blood test if it were offered as a first-line test or based on identification of a potentially high-risk population
- treatment options
- the efficacy of using risk factors to define high- and low-risk populations, based on the presence of one or more of the risk factors highlighted in the ADA criteria (age over 25 years, BMI greater than 27 kg/m², family history of diabetes or from a high-risk ethnic background).

Tables F.23 to F.27 give the sensitivity analysis ICER for strategies which have not been excluded on the grounds of strict or extended dominance.

Table F.23 Effect on ICER of varying the number of perinatal deaths attributable to gestational diabetes

Strategy	QALYs	Cost	Incremental QALYs	Incremental cost	ICER
Four deaths					
21	21.26	£99,490	21.26	£99,490	£4,680
6	30.95	£367,227	9.69	£267,737	£27,633
Three deaths					
21	15.80	£100,136	15.80	£100,136	£6,336
6	23.01	£368,167	7.20	£268,031	£37,209
Two deaths					
21	10.69	£100,287	10.69	£100,287	£9,385
6	15.56	£368,386	4.87	£268,100	£55,042
One death					
21	5.94	£100,473	5.94	£100,473	£16,913
6	8.65	£368,657	2.71	£268,184	£99,045
No deaths					
21	1.61	£101,069	1.61	£101,069	£62,854
6	2.34	£369,525	0.73	£268,456	£366,272

Table F.24 Gestational diabetes prevalence of 2%

Strategy	QALYs	Cost	Incremental QALYs	Incremental cost	ICER
21	9.41	£48,856	9.41	£48,856	£5,192
2	12.84	£100,583	3.43	£51,727	£15,085
6	16.87	£177,118	4.03	£76,536	£19,005

Table F.25 Gestational diabetes prevalence of 5%

Strategy	QALYs	Cost	Incremental QALYs	Incremental cost	ICER
19	33.97	£113,694	33.97	£113,694	£3,347
21	44.62	£149,825	10.65	£36,131	£3,392
6	56.18	£401,205	11.56	£251,379	£21,738
18	56.18	£401,205	11.56	£251,379	£21,738

Table F.26 Gestational diabetes prevalence of 2% and 100% test acceptance

Strategy	QALY	Cost	Incremental QALY	Incremental cost	ICER
21	10.46	£51,385	10.46	£51,385	£4,915
11	21.12	£163,434	10.66	£112,049	£10,507
1	24.97	£336,113	3.85	£172,679	£44,852

Table F.27 Gestational diabetes prevalence of 5% and 100% test acceptance

Strategy	QALY	Cost	Incremental QALY	Incremental cost	ICER
19	41.93	£130,634	41.93	£130,634	£3,115
21	49.58	£161,816	7.64	£31,183	£4,079
1	62.43	£411,583	12.85	£249,766	£19,439

F.6.1 Outcomes

The outcome that had the greatest influence on the model results was the number of perinatal deaths (stillbirths and neonatal deaths). This is because of the non-negligible weight given to this outcome as a proportion of all serious perinatal complications and the significant gain in QALYs to be made by preventing a perinatal death. In the ACHOIS trial there were five perinatal deaths recorded in those who received no treatment (n = 524) while in the treatment arm there were none (n = 506). This difference was not statistically significant. The number of deaths in the control group was similar to the number of perinatal deaths that would be expected in the general population according to ONS data on perinatal mortality (in 2005 there were 5.4 stillbirths, 2.6 early neonatal deaths and 3.4 late neonatal deaths per 1000 total births in England and Wales). The authors of the ACHOIS study highlight that at least one death in the control group was unrelated to gestational diabetes.

Table F.23 shows the results of the models when the number of perinatal deaths in each group was assumed to be different to that reported in the ACHOIS trial. As the number of perinatal deaths decreases, the cost-effectiveness of the various strategies changes. When only four deaths in the trial group are attributed to gestational diabetes, the ICERs of both Strategy 21 and Strategy 6 become less favourable and this continues until only one perinatal death is attributed to gestational diabetes. Even when there is only a single death assumed, there is still a screening, diagnosis and treatment strategy that would be considered cost-effective – in this case Strategy 21. However, if no perinatal deaths are attributed to gestational diabetes, then there is no strategy for screening, diagnosis and treatment that could be considered cost-effective.

This result demonstrates that the model is highly sensitive to the potential QALYs gained by preventing even a single perinatal death. The model also potentially underestimates the QALYs to be gained by preventing other adverse outcomes, such as shoulder dystocia or nerve palsy, and may therefore underestimate the cost-effectiveness of screening. However, the ICERs when no deaths are assumed are sufficiently large to suggest that the potential QALY gain from preventing some of these events would not be adequate for these strategies to be cost-effective.

What is clear from this analysis is that the potential benefits to the NHS with respect to QALYs gained from intervention are likely to be felt in the form of preventing perinatal deaths, and the cost-effectiveness of screening, diagnosis and treatment strategies are highly influenced in the model by this particular adverse outcome.

F.6.2 Gestational diabetes prevalence

The prevalence of a disease can often be a very important determinant of the cost-effectiveness of screening. Tables F.24 and F.25 show how the results of the model varied for different prevalences of gestational diabetes. The results suggest that varying the prevalence over a range of 3 percentage points has little impact on the cost-effectiveness conclusions of the model, but it should be remembered that the simplified model relationship between risk factor proportions and gestational diabetes prevalence has a bearing on these results.

F.6.3 Test acceptance

As noted earlier, test acceptance rates are potentially an important source of uncertainty within the model, especially as with default assumptions there is an inverse relationship between test accuracy and test acceptance. Tables F.26 and F.27 show how the results varied when it was assumed that all women were tested in populations with a relatively low and relatively high disease prevalence, respectively.

The results show that a universal screening strategy using the gold standard diagnostic test becomes more cost-effective as disease prevalence increases. This is because of its advantages over other test options in terms of its detection rate. However, its advantages in terms of detection rate are negated if it is assumed that the test has a low level of acceptance.

A threshold analysis, with all other model parameters at their baseline values, showed that, even if test acceptance for FPG/OGTT in women identified as 'at risk' fell from 90% at baseline to 52%, Strategy 6 would remain the preferred option up to a willingness to pay threshold of £20,000 per QALY.

F.6.4   Treatment option

The model also allowed the ICERs for different strategies to be calculated for different treatment options (analogue insulin, glibenclamide and metformin). Table F.28 shows that the choice of treatment option in the model made little difference to the ICERs for the screening strategies. This is because treatment represents a relatively small proportion of the total costs, and because all the incremental analysis is undertaken with treatment cost as a given. For example, a lower treatment cost will reduce the cost of each strategy but may have relatively little impact on the incremental costs.

Table F.28   ICER for Strategy 6 for different treatment options in the baseline model

Treatment	ICER
Analogue insulin	£21,738
Glibenclamide	£21,647
Metformin	£21,642

F.6.5   Single risk factors

The baseline analysis suggested that Strategy 6 was a borderline cost-effective strategy using a willingness to pay threshold of £20,000 per QALY. However, the GDG expressed concerns over the number of women that would have to undergo a OGTT if Strategy 6 were adopted. A large proportion of women tested would be tested based on age criteria alone – under the baseline assumptions as many as 90% might be offered the diagnostic test. This would be a considerable inconvenience to a large number of women, only a small minority of whom would ultimately benefit from the testing process, as well as putting a strain on local services. As a result it was decided that the use of screening based on risk factors other than age should be considered.

The PPVs and NPVs of different risk factor combinations are not accurately known which means that the relative cost-effectiveness of different combinations of any of the single risk factors could not be calculated. However, it may be the case that where single risk factors are cost-effective on their own, then any combination of these is also likely to be cost-effective. Therefore an analysis of the cost-effectiveness of each single risk factor, followed by an OGTT, has been performed, with each risk factor plus OGTT combination compared with a strategy of no screening or treatment. The results are presented in Table F.29.

Table F.29   ICER for single risk factor strategies followed by a diagnostic test when compared with a strategy of no screening or treatment

Strategy	QALY	Cost	ICER
Ethnicity	9.55	£66,226	£6,935
BMI	6.29	£80,109	£12,736
Family history	15.73	£81,915	£5,208

Any strategy where a single risk factor from the ADA criteria other than age is applied alone, followed by a diagnostic test, has an ICER that is below the threshold of £20,000 and could in each case be considered cost-effective on its own.

The above analysis established that screening, diagnosis and treatment of gestational diabetes is generally cost-effective in some populations. Below we consider the cost-effectiveness of the various treatment options for gestational diabetes.

F.7   Cost analysis of different treatment options for gestational diabetes

A systematic review of the literature, targeted at the guideline question on what is cost-effective treatment for gestational diabetes, identified a single paper for inclusion.[963] This paper described a cost model to compare the costs of an oral hypoglycaemic, glyburide (glibenclamide), with those of insulin for the treatment of gestational diabetes. The paper justifies what is essentially a cost minimisation approach on the basis that glyburide and insulin confer similar glycaemic control.[961] Their model, based in a US setting, excluded resource items that were identical in both treatments. Included in the costs for insulin were drug costs, costs of the consumables needed to administer the insulin and the cost of instructing women with gestational diabetes on how to draw up the insulin and inject themselves. The cost of glyburide was based on the average wholesale cost of a milligram of drug multiplied by the weekly dose expected to be necessary for glycaemic control. In addition, it was assumed that 4% of patients would not achieve control with glyburide and would have to switch to insulin. Therefore, the model also incorporated a cost for glyburide treatment failure. Women switching to insulin also incurred the educational costs associated with insulin treatment. Finally, the model also included the downstream costs of hypoglycaemia, which was assumed to be more common in insulin-treated women. In the baseline analysis, glyburide produced an average cost saving of $166 per woman. The authors reported that most sensitivity analyses did not alter the direction of this finding. A threshold analysis suggested that insulin was only less costly than glyburide at the highest wholesale cost of $18.24 per week in conjunction with a daily dose of 18.9 g, which is considerably higher than what is believed to be necessary to achieve good glycaemic control. A similar cost model was developed to compare the cost of insulin analogue (lispro) with that of two oral hypoglycaemics (glibenclamide and metformin) in a UK context.

F.7.1   Introduction

A cost minimisation analysis can be considered to be a special case of cost-effectiveness analysis when the interventions being compared are equally efficacious. In such a scenario, the cheapest option is unambiguously cost-effective as it dominates the alternatives, being cheaper and equally effective. A randomised study[961] failed to find significant differences in outcomes (maternal and neonatal) between glyburide and insulin treatment in women with gestational diabetes. It is on this basis, and in the absence of any conflicting evidence, that such a cost minimisation analysis might be justifiable to determine the cost-effectiveness of various gestational diabetes treatments. Of course, no evidence of a difference is not the same as evidence of no difference, but the *P* values in this study were particularly large and the inference of no difference does not arise as a result of some outcomes being just the wrong side of an arbitrary 5% cut-off point for statistical significance.

Insulin analogue was used in this cost comparison rather than insulin, as this is what would be offered to women with gestational diabetes in the UK. Implicit in this is an assumption that outcomes with an insulin analogue would be equivalent to those with insulin. Metformin was additionally added into this analysis as the ongoing MIG study is assessing its use in women with gestational diabetes and it could potentially be an important treatment option in the UK.

F.7.2   Method

The basic structure of the cost analysis is shown in Figure F.6. It is assumed that a diagnosis of gestational diabetes would be made at a gestational age of 27 weeks. As described in the screening, diagnosis and treatment model, women with gestational diabetes would start with dietary treatment. In women who do not achieve adequate glycaemic control after 10 days, pharmacological therapy would be started and this is the starting point for the cost comparison.

Costs which are common to all treatments, such as those associated with self-monitoring of blood glucose, are not included in the analysis. The costs for a woman taking insulin analogue include the time of a diabetes specialist nurse in providing instruction on how to administer the drug. Women with gestational diabetes are assumed to use a pre-filled disposable injection pen (e.g. Humalog® Mix50) and to be on a daily dose of 20 units administered in twice-daily injections. Therefore, they require two needles per day for their injection pen. The cost of glibenclamide is the drug cost based on a daily dose of 15 mg. Similarly, the cost of metformin is based on a daily dose of 1.5 g.

2008 update

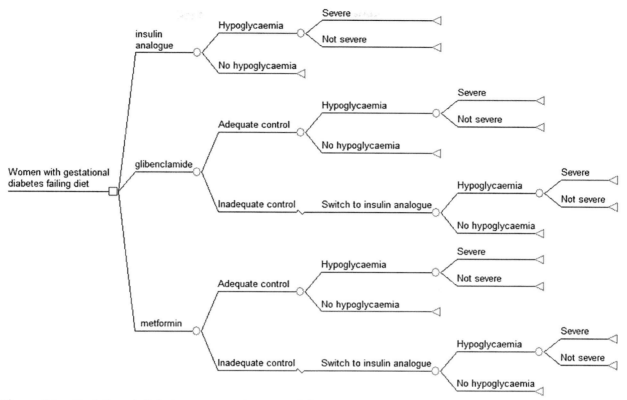

Figure F.6 Gestational diabetes treatment cost model

In addition to the cost of treatment it is important also to consider downstream costs. Overall outcomes are assumed not to differ, but following the Langer study the model addresses a possible differential in the hypoglycaemia risk between the different treatments. It is additionally assumed at baseline that 5% of hypoglycaemic events will be 'severe' and it is these for which there will typically be an NHS resource implication. The cost of a 'severe' hypoglycaemic event is assumed to be the cost of a paramedic ambulance journey and an A&E admission.

The complete list of model parameters is given in Tables F.30 to F.32.

F.7.3   Results

Table F.33 lists the cost per patient of each of the three treatment options. These show the oral hypoglycaemics to be considerably cheaper than analogue insulin. Of the oral hypoglycamics, metformin is the cheapest and, with the assumption of equal clinical effectiveness, the most cost-effective treatment.

F.7.4   Sensitivity analysis

A number of sensitivity analyses were undertaken to determine how robust the conclusion of the baseline result was to changes in model parameters where some uncertainty exists as to their 'true' value. For ease of exposition, most sensitivity analyses focus on a comparison of glibenclamide and insulin analogue on the basis that, apart from a small difference in costs, these are assumed to be identical treatments in terms of both outcomes and downstream costs.

However, threshold analyses were also undertaken which showed that, holding all other factors constant, metformin remained cheapest as long as control on metformin was at least 90.3% (with control on glibenclamide 96%) or control on metformin was at least 72.3% (with control on glibenclamide 77%).

Figure F.7 shows how the incremental cost of insulin analogue varies with different assumptions about the proportion of women with gestational diabetes who achieve adequate glycaemic

2008 update

Table F.30   Treatment timeframe (days)

Variable	Value (days)	Source	Notes
Treatment duration	80	Diabetes in pregnancy GDG	It is assumed a gestational diabetes diagnosis would be made at 27 weeks of gestation. Women with gestational diabetes would be given approximately 10 days to achieve control with diet and 80 days is a reasonable approximation of the typical time to term at the commencement of pharmacological treatment.
Oral hypoglycaemic trial period	14	ACHOIS[824]	

Table F.31   Costs

Variable	Cost	Source	Notes
Insulin instruction	£47.25	Curtis and Netten (2006)[959] GDG estimate	This is based on an instruction time of 45 minutes with instruction provided by a specialist nurse.
Insulin analogue	£0.57 per day	BNF 52 (2006)[989]	This is based on a dose of 20 units per day. A pre-filled disposable pen has 1500 units and costs £29.46. It is further assumed that injections are twice daily, requiring two needles at £0.09 each.
Glibenclamide	£0.16	BNF 52 (2006)[989]	Based on 15 mg daily. A 5 mg 28 tablet pack costs £1.50.
Metformin	£0.10	BNF 52 (2006)[989]	Based on 1.5 g daily. A 500 mg 84 tablet pack costs £2.85.
Switching cost of oral hypoglycaemia failure	£0.00	GDG estimate	It is assumed there is no additional cost over and above those incurred by all women with gestational diabetes starting insulin analogue treatment.
Treatment of severe hypoglycaemia	£403	Curtis and Netten (2006)[959] NHS Reference Costs 2005–06	Average cost per patient journey for paramedic ambulance: £323. A&E admission with low-cost investigation: £80.

Table F.32   Probabilities

Variable	Probability	Source	Notes
Control with glibenclamide	0.96	Langer et al. (2000)[961] GDG estimate	A GDG member reported 0.77 for this parameter in his clinical practice.
Control with metformin	0.96	Langer et al. (2000)[961]	Assumed identical to glibenclamide.
Hypoglycaemia on insulin analogue	0.20	Langer et al. (2000)[961]	Assumed to be the same as Langer found for insulin.
Hypoglycaemia on glibenclamide	0.02	Langer et al. (2000)[961]	–
Hypoglycaemia on metformin	0.02	Langer et al. (2000)[961]	Assumed identical to glibenclamide.
Proportion of hypoglycaemia that is 'severe'	0.05	GDG estimate	–

Table F.33   Cost per women with gestational diabetes

Treatment	Average cost per woman with gestational diabetes
Insulin analogue	£96.92
Glibenclamide	£16.32
Metformin	£11.68

2008 update

control with glibenclamide. Although the differential in cost declines with reduced glibenclamide clinical effectiveness, insulin analogue continues to be the more costly option even if only 40% of women achieve adequate glycaemic control with glibenclamide. Figure F.8 shows that the cost analysis is not sensitive to the risk of hypoglycaemia in women taking glibenclamide. Similarly, Figure F.9 shows that the costs of treating hypoglycaemia are not an important determinant of the additional costs of insulin analogue.

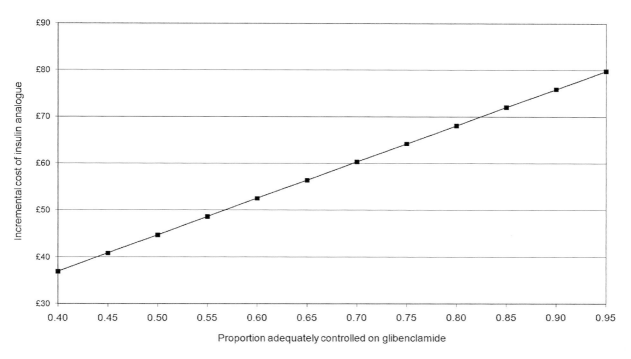

Figure F.7   Incremental cost of insulin analogue as control on glibenclamide varies

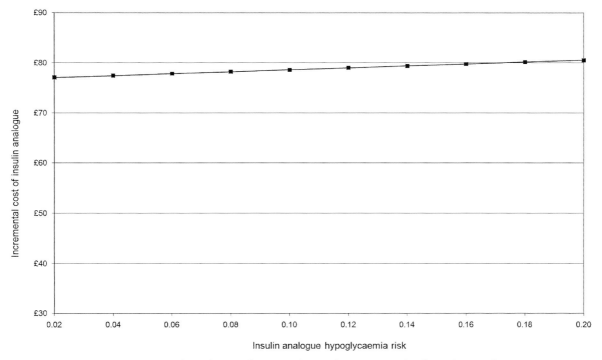

Figure F.8   Incremental cost of insulin analogue as hypoglycaemia risk of insulin analogue varies

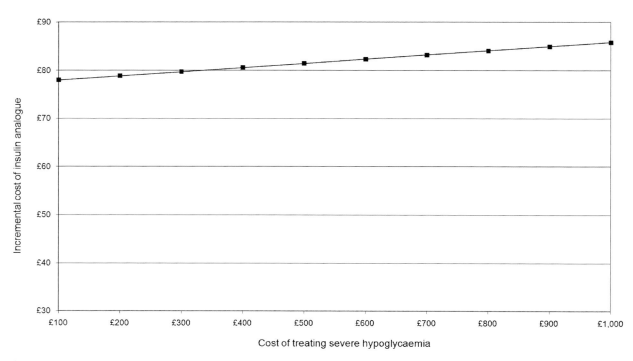

Figure F.9 Incremental cost of insulin analogue as cost of treating severe hypoglycaemia varies

F.7.5 Discussion

Using the data from ACHOIS, this guideline has demonstrated that screening, diagnosis and treatment of gestational diabetes is cost-effective and that this finding is not contingent on the type of pharmacological treatment used (insulin analogue or oral hypoglycaemic agent). However, given that the treatments have different resource implications for the NHS, it does not follow that all treatments are equally cost-effective. One study[961] suggested that 'among women with gestational diabetes, the degree of glycaemic control and the perinatal outcomes were essentially the same for those treated with glyburide (glibenclamide) and those treated with insulin. The lack of differences between the infants born to mothers in the two treatment groups corroborated the results in the mothers'. Therefore, if it is argued on the basis of this study that glibenclamide is equally effective as insulin analogue and would have achieved similar outcomes to those observed with diet and insulin treatment in ACHOIS, then we can say that the results presented here suggest that glibenclamide is a more cost-effective treatment for gestational diabetes than insulin analogue. Sensitivity analysis suggested that this conclusion was robust when model parameters were changed in a one-way fashion. The diabetes in pregnancy GDG has suggested that the proportion of women with gestational diabetes achieving control with glibenclamide may be lower in clinical practice than that observed by Langer et al.[961] However, as the sensitivity analysis shows, glibenclamide continues to be cost-saving compared with insulin analogue even with a much smaller proportion achieving adequate control.

As yet, there is no evidence to justify a cost minimisation approach with metformin. However, if it too was shown to be as effective as insulin analogue then it would be the most cost-effective treatment of all.

One caveat to these findings is the assumption that there is no cost to the NHS in switching women with gestational diabetes from an oral hypoglycaemic agent to insulin analogue, other than those ordinarily incurred for patients taking insulin analogue. If there were a 'switching cost', then the cost-effectiveness of the oral hypoglycaemic agents would be less than that implied here.

Appendix G

Economic model: monitoring fetal growth

G.1 Health economics evidence summary

A systematic search of the literature identified 42 articles potentially related to the economic evaluation of the measurement of fetal growth. The abstracts of all 42 papers were reviewed, but none met the inclusion criteria. All of the published economic evidence focused on the clinical aspects of fetal growth; few mentioned the importance of conducting a cost-effectiveness analysis. The lack of empirical evidence on economic evaluation is due, at least in part, to the paucity of robust clinical studies apart from the use of Doppler ultrasound of the umbilical artery and poor evidence of effectiveness of fetal biometry by ultrasound, as shown in the review of clinical evidence. Furthermore, as ultrasound scanning is among the most common screening tests used in clinical practice, there is no clear alternative to compare ultrasound screening with and an economic evaluation requires a comparator (which can be 'do nothing') to examine alternative strategies.

G.2 Exploring the economic perspective of fetal growth

The lack of health economics studies in the area means that it is necessary to begin with a very general health economic framework. The objective is to conduct a cost-effectiveness analysis of specific clinical strategies to identify and monitor babies that are small for gestational age (SGA). The aim is to help the GDG members to make a recommendation, on the basis of clinical and economic evidence, on what is the best strategy, if any, for monitoring fetal growth and identifying the SGA fetus, within the context of enabling the NHS to redistribute resources more efficiently across healthcare services.

The model focuses on a hypothetical population of pregnant women. The decision tree (Figure G.1), depicts the decision pathway of the hypothetical cohort of patients (here pregnant women). The pathway starts with the decision whether to offer one of three strategies:

1. no measurement or monitoring of fetal growth
2. measure and monitor fetal growth by ultrasound alone
3. measure and monitor fetal growth by symphysis–fundal height (SFH) measurement and ultrasound.

Patient flow from this decision proceeds from left to right, with the branches indicating all feasible pathways. The pathway of each pregnant woman is determined by the probability of an event occurring and these are represented in the model by chance nodes. Branches that originate from chance nodes (denoted by circles) indicate all possibilities that exist at that point in the pathway. The outcome of each terminal node (or endpoint) in the tree is birth by either caesarean section or by normal delivery.

G.3 Assumptions underlying the model

- The model that is presented here does not conform to the standard model of decision analysis. Under ideal circumstances, an economic model of a healthcare intervention would be based on robust clinical data with an outcome that allows comparisons between alternative interventions, for example the quality-adjusted life year (QALY). The approach taken towards answering this question is different, owing to the lack of reliable clinical data, as highlighted above and in the systematic review of the clinical evidence (Chapter 12). In this instance we look at what number of perinatal deaths attributable to being SGA would need to be prevented in order for the measurement and monitoring of fetal growth to be cost-effective.

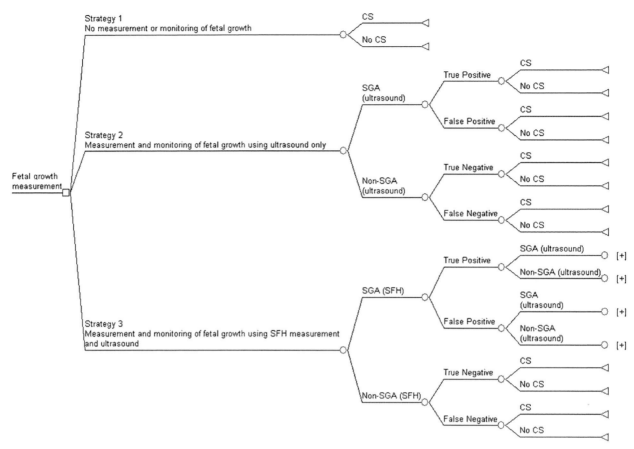

Figure G.1   The decision tree for measuring and monitoring fetal growth; CS = caesarean section; SFH = symphysis–fundal height; SGA = small for gestational age

- In the absence of any reliable data on the accuracy of ultrasound scanning for the measurement of fetal growth, the initial assumption made in the analysis is that ultrasound scanning is 100% sensitive and 100% specific, giving perfect information on the size of the fetus and enabling healthcare professionals the opportunity to intervene where action will be of the greatest benefit. If this intervention (Strategy 2, ultrasound screening) is not cost-effective when there is perfect information, then it would be unlikely to be cost-effective if we relax the assumption of perfect information with less accurate estimates of sensitivity and specificity. In any case, this strategy can act as a benchmark for comparison with other strategies (no fetal growth monitoring or monitoring using SFH measurement and ultrasound scanning).
- Also assumed with the model is that fetal growth rates and SGA fetuses are well defined. There exist different definitions for normal fetal growth. Within the model, normal fetal growth is defined as those fetuses falling within the 10th and 90th percentiles.
- A number of parameter values used in the model are based on the expert opinion of the members of the GDG, drawing on the clinical experience of doctors, midwives, health visitors and patient representatives. However, this approach to populating the decision model introduces a great deal of uncertainty and this uncertainty is examined in sensitivity analysis.
- An assumption has been made by the GDG that for every 1000 known SGA fetuses, approximately 40 perinatal deaths can be prevented. This is based on the following assumptions:
  - there are approximately 60 000 SGA age babies each year
  - just under one-third of these (18 050) will have intrauterine growth restriction
  - of these, roughly 50% will not survive, regardless of any intervention
  - 20–25% (approximately 1850–2250) of the remaining number could benefit from intervention in the form of a perinatal death prevented.

G.4 Model description

There are three main branches on the decision tree, representing the three different strategies for measuring and monitoring fetal growth. The tree is designed to highlight the differences in cost and effects of each strategy and to provide a basis for comparison.

Strategy 1: No measurement of fetal growth

In this strategy, fetal growth is not measured by any means and there is no subsequent monitoring. As with all strategies considered, there are two key maternal outcomes considered, caesarean section and normal birth. Rates of caesarean section and the costs associated with each outcome are given in Tables G.1 and G.2. The key perinatal outcome is death.

Strategy 2: Measuring fetal growth by ultrasound

Under this strategy, all women will be offered an ultrasound scan and at present we have assumed that all women will accept the offer, although there may be instances where a woman chooses not to undergo any fetal growth monitoring. Following the ultrasound, there are four possible diagnoses that the woman could receive:

1. true positive – the fetus is correctly identified as SGA following the ultrasound scan
2. true negative – the fetus is correctly identified as not being SGA following the ultrasound scan
3. false positive – the fetus is incorrectly identified as SGA following the ultrasound scan when it is within the normal size range
4. false negative – the fetus is incorrectly identified as not being SGA following the ultrasound scan when it is in fact in the bottom decile of fetal size.

Strategy 3: Measuring fetal growth by symphysis–fundal height and ultrasound

Under this strategy, all women will be offered symphysis–fundal height (SFH) measurement to estimate the size of the baby. Where SFH measurement indicates that the fetus may be SGA, ultrasound scan monitoring of fetal growth is offered. The group offered further monitoring includes the true and false positive cases; the true and false negative cases will undergo no further monitoring. As in Strategy 2, at each stage of measurement there is a chance that the fetus will be correctly or incorrectly diagnosed as SGA or not, that is there is a probability that the diagnosis is a true or false positive or true or false negative.

G.4.1 Clinical and cost data used in the model

Clinical data

The clinical parameters used in the model were agreed with the GDG members and are shown in Table G.1. These include the probability of a baby being SGA or non-SGA, the accuracy with which SFH measurement and ultrasound scanning can identify an SGA fetus and the probability of having a caesarean section or normal birth dependent on whether or not the fetus is considered SGA.

Table G.1 Clinical parameters

Probability of key events and outcomes	Value	Range	Source
Probability of non-SGA	0.9	–	
Probability of SGA	0.1	–	
Probability of CS (non-SGA)	0.25	–	Hospital Episode Statistics (HES) 2005/06
Probability of CS (SGA)	0.5	0.4–0.6	GDG opinion
Sensitivity of SFH measurement	0.27	0.1–1	Persson *et al.* (1986)[919]
Specificity of SFH measurement	0.9	0.1–1	Persson *et al.* (1986)[919]
Sensitivity of ultrasound scan of fetal size	0.48	0.1–1	Warsof *et al.* (1986)[923]
Specificity of ultrasound scan of fetal size	0.93	0.1–1	Warsof *et al.* (1986)[923]

2008 update

Costs of fetal growth monitoring and birth

The perspective adopted for the economic evaluation conforms to that of the NHS, in line with NICE guidance on economic evaluations for guidelines. The cost parameters used in the model are shown in Table G.2. These include the cost of ultrasound monitoring, cost of monitoring appointments and the cost of a normal birth or birth by caesarean section.

Table G.2 Cost parameters

Cost of key events	Value	Source
Hospital birth (without complications)	£753	2007/08 NHS Tariff
Hospital birth (with complications)	£1,124	2007/08 NHS Tariff
Caesarean section (without complications)	£1,404	2007/08 NHS Tariff
Caesarean section (with complications)	£1,926	2007/08 NHS Tariff
SFH measurement	£3.67	PSSRU (2006)[959]
Ultrasound fetal growth scan	£34	NHS Reference Costs 2006

G.5   Results

G.5.1   Comparing strategies

Having illustrated how the costs and benefits of the two strategies are generated, the next step is to compare them. The difference between the total cost of each strategy when compared with another gives the incremental cost. In this analysis, the incremental cost is then divided by the NICE willingness to pay per QALY to obtain the incremental effect needed to be achieved in order for the intervention to be considered cost-effective. In line with the NICE guidelines manual, the maximum willingness to pay is assumed to be £20,000 per additional QALY. The number of QALYs per infant saved is assumed to be 25, based on the average life span of 76 years in the UK, discounted at 3.5% per annum and assuming a life lived in perfect health. Thus the additional effectiveness as measured in perinatal deaths required to be prevented by adopting any given strategy compared with any other strategy is obtained by dividing the incremental effect in QALYs by 25.

If the model assumptions concerning the benefit of identifying SGA fetuses are correct then there will be a cost-effective strategy for measuring and monitoring fetal growth, based on the results presented below.

G.5.2   Perfect information

When the assumption about perfect information on fetal growth is held, the following results are obtained.

Strategy 1 compared with Strategy 2

The additional cost of Strategy 2 compared with Strategy 1 is £40.2 million, with an incremental effect (QALYs) to be cost-effective of 2011. The additional neonatal deaths needed to be averted to be cost-effective are 80.

Strategy 1 compared with Strategy 3

The additional cost of Strategy 3 compared with Strategy 1 is £20.7 million, with an incremental gain of at least 1037 QALYs necessary for cost-effectiveness. The additional neonatal deaths needed to be averted to be cost-effective are 41.

Strategy 2 compared with Strategy 3

The additional cost of Strategy 3 compared with Strategy 2 is £19.5 million, with an incremantal gain of at least 974 QALYs necessary for cost-effectiveness. The additional neonatal deaths needed to be averted to be cost-effective are 39.

G.5.3   Imperfect information

In the above results, the absence of reliable data on the accuracy of ultrasound scanning for identifying SGA led to a base-case analysis where all forms of fetal growth measurement were assumed to be 100% sensitive and 100% specific. In line with the GDG assumptions about the number of perinatal deaths that could be avoided given the knowledge that the fetus was SGA, it would be cost-effective to choose either Strategy 2 or Strategy 3 for fetal growth monitoring. However, in practice it is known that both SFH and ultrasound scanning are much less accurate than this. An estimate of the sensitivity and specificity of each method is estimated from the clinical data and the results are presented here.

Strategy 1 compared with Strategy 2

The additional cost of Strategy 2 compared with Strategy 1 is £45.7 million, with an incremantal gain of at least 2286 QALYs necessary for cost-effectiveness. The additional neonatal deaths needed to be averted to be cost-effective are 91.

Strategy 1 compared with Strategy 3

Implementing Strategy 3 would lead to additional costs of £4.9 million when compared with Strategy 1, with an incremantal gain of at least 262 QALYs necessary for cost-effectiveness. Ten additional perinatal deaths would need to be averted for Strategy 3 to be cost-effective when compared with Strategy 1.

Strategy 2 compared with Strategy 3

The additional cost of Strategy 2 compared with Strategy 3 is £40.7 million, with an incremental effect (QALYs) to be cost-effective of 2039. Furthermore, Strategy 2 correctly diagnoses 35 more SGA babies than Strategy 3 per 1000 births. The additional neonatal deaths needed to be averted for Strategy 2 to be cost-effective is 84.

G.6   Discussion

The measurement and monitoring of fetal growth is necessarily difficult and current technologies are limited in the accuracy with which they can predict the size of the fetus. It is believed that a proportion of fetal deaths that occur each year could be prevented if the size of the fetus at a given gestational age could be determined accurately. The results of this analysis show that, given current technology and the estimates of the GDG, the measurement and monitoring of fetal growth may be considered cost-effective when the health service is willing to pay £20,000 per QALY. There are large numbers of both false positive and false negative diagnoses made using the strategies tested here and there are significant potential health gains to be made if more accurate forms of measurement could be introduced. Any new method of measurement would be likely to prove cost-effective if it could be shown to be more accurate than the currently available techniques without significant increase in costs.

2008 update

Appendix H

Training and equipment standards for ultrasound screening in pregnancy

Sonography is not recognised as a speciality by the Health Act 1999, so there is no obligation for sonographers to be registered to practise. There is currently no statutory requirement for ultrasound practitioners to receive accredited training.

Many sonographers will have achieved a postgraduate certificate or diploma in clinical ultrasound. Well-established programmes leading to these qualifications are available in a number of universities in the UK and courses are accredited by the Consortium for the Accreditation of Sonographic Education (CASE). Members of the consortium include the British Medical Ultrasound Society, the Royal College of Radiographers (RCR), the Royal College of Midwives and the United Kingdom Association of Sonographers.

To achieve and attain CASE accreditation, an individual course must demonstrate that both its academic and clinical teaching programmes and its assessment methods are sufficiently rigorous to ensure that successful students are safe to practise in the ultrasound areas for which they have studied. Current postgraduate education certificates and diploma training programmes in obstetric ultrasound are designed with the provision of a safe, accurate and efficient screening service for fetal anomaly in mind.

With regard to the implementation of the National Down's Syndrome Screening Programme for England, all professionals involved in providing antenatal screening information and services should have received the appropriate education for their roles and responsibilities and any specific tasks required.

All health professionals undertaking an ultrasound scan must have an accredited certificate in obstetric ultrasound or equivalent and also attend an appropriate communication/counselling course.

(Extracted from Antenatal screening – working standards, National Down's Syndrome Screening Programme for England, (March 2004))[964]

There is a need for practical competence tests at NHS trust level. The RCOG Working Party recommends that local departments monitor standards and keep checks on them.

Trusts should have a process for retraining and updating as required but at present there is little provision for this in trust budgets. Clinical governance provides a facilitating mechanism.

The RCOG is in the process of implementing Advanced Training Skills Modules (ATSMs) and all medical staff who undertake fetal anomaly scanning should hold the relevant ATSM. Skills should be maintained by performing detailed scans in at least one and preferably two sessions per week.

Medical and midwifery staff should not undertake scans of any sort if they have not been specifically trained.

A scan to perform a fetal structural survey demands the use of modern equipment (not more than 5 years old) of modest sophistication. The scanner must be capable of performing the necessary measurements and should provide good image quality. As always, regards for safety in the use of ultrasound is paramount and minimum output should be used in accordance with the ALARA principle: as low as reasonably attainable.

(Extracted from the recommendations of the Royal College of Obstetricians and Gynaecologists Working Party on Ultrasound Screening for Fetal Anomalies.[302])

Appendix I

Further information

During the review process of this guideline, various topics were suggested by stakeholders and peer reviewers for inclusion in the guideline. The inclusion or exclusion of any subject not already contained in the guideline was carefully considered by the Guideline Development Group.

Topics that were not originally included in the scope of this guideline and for which guidance already exists are listed in this Appendix, with information on where further information can be obtained. All other topics raised by stakeholders or peer reviewers have been addressed in the main text of the guideline.

Cystic fibrosis UK National Screening Committee
www.nsc.nhs.uk/

Herpes *Management of Genital Herpes in Pregnancy* (RCOG Guideline No. 30, September 2007).
www.rcog.org.uk/resources/Public/pdf/greentop30_genital_herpes0907.pdf

HTLV 1 The UK National Screening Committee position on HTLV1 (human T lymphocyte virus 1) is that screening should not be offered for pregnant women.
www.library.nhs.uk/screening/ViewResource.aspx?resID=51538&tabID=288&catID=2000

Thrombophilia The UK National Screening Committee position on thrombophilia is that there is no evidence to support screening to identify those deemed at increased risk of venous thrombosis in pregnancy.
www.library.nhs.uk/screening/ViewResource.aspx?resID=32586&tabID=288&catID=1989

Varicella *Chickenpox in Pregnancy* (RCOG Guideline No. 13, September 2007).
www.rcog.org.uk/resources/Public/pdf/greentop13_chickenpox0907.pdf

Note

RCOG Guidelines (also known as Green-top guidelines) are clinical guidelines produced by the Guidelines and Audit Committee of the Royal College of Obstetricians and Gynaecologists. Guidelines can be accessed online at: www.rcog.org.uk/index.asp?PageID=1042.

Appendix J

Family origin questionnaire*

Family Origin Questionnaire

If using a pre-printed label please attach one to each copy

Hospital Name . . . .
Hospital No . . . .
NHS No . . . .
Estimated Delivery Date . . . .
Surname . . . .
Forename . . . .
Date of Birth . . . .
Add1 . . . .
Add2 . . . .
Post Code . . . .

Screening test declined ☐
Do you want to give a reason
why declined?

Yes . . . .
. . . .
. . . .
No ☐

DESTINATION (eg Community Midwife, GP, Antenatal Clinic, Obstetrician) . . . .
. . . .

What are your family origins?

Please tick all boxes in ALL sections that apply to the woman and the baby's father

	Woman	Baby's father
A. AFRICAN OR AFRICAN-CARIBBEAN (BLACK)		
Caribbean Islands	☐	☐
Africa (excluding North Africa)	☐	☐
Any other African or African-Caribbean family origins (please write in...)		
B. SOUTH ASIAN (ASIAN)	Woman	Baby's father
India or African-Indian	☐	☐
Pakistan	☐	☐
Bangladesh	☐	☐
C. SOUTH EAST ASIAN (ASIAN)	Woman	Baby's father
China	☐	☐
Thailand	☐	☐
Malaysia, Vietnam, Philippines etc	☐	☐
Any other Asian family origins (please write in...) (e.g. Caribbean-Asian)		
D. OTHER NON-EUROPEAN (OTHER)	Woman	Baby's father
North Africa, South America etc	☐	☐
Middle East (Saudi Arabia, Iran etc)	☐	☐
Any other Non-European family origins (please write in...)		
E. SOUTHERN & OTHER EUROPEAN (WHITE)	Woman	Baby's father
Cyprus	☐	☐
Greece, Turkey	☐	☐
Italy, Portugal, Spain	☐	☐
Any other Mediterranean country	☐	☐
Albania, Czech Republic, Poland, Romania, Russia etc	☐	☐
F. **UNITED KINGDOM** (WHITE) *refer to chart*	Woman	Baby's father
England, Scotland, N Ireland, Wales	☐	☐
G. **NORTHERN EUROPEAN** (WHITE) *refer to chart*	Woman	Baby's father
Austria, Belgium, Ireland, France, Germany, Netherlands	☐	☐
Scandinavia, Switzerland etc	☐	☐
Any other European family origins, *refer to chart* (please write in) (e.g. Australia, N America, S Africa)		
*Hb Variant Screening Requested by (F) and/ or (G)	☐	☐
	Woman	Baby's father
H. DON'T KNOW (incl. pregnancies with donor egg/sperm)	☐	☐
I. DECLINED TO ANSWER	☐	☐
J. ESTIMATED DELIVERY DATE (please write in if not above)		

Any other relevant information . . . .
. . . .

All women need to be informed that routine analysis of blood may identify them as a thalassaemia carrier. In *low* prevalence areas OFFER haemoglobin variant screening to all women if they or the baby's father have answers in any yellow box. In *high* prevalence areas OFFER haemoglobin variant screening to all women irrespective of answers, ie. if they or the baby's father have answers in white and yellow boxes A - I.

Signed . . . . Print Name . . . . Job Title . . . . Date . . . .
(By Health Care Professional Completing the Form)

July 2007

* This form can be downloaded from www.sickleandthal.org.uk/Documents/F_Origin_Questionnaire.pdf.

Appendix K

Deleted material from the 2003 version

2.1 Summary of recommendations

Chapter 3 Woman-centred care and informed decision making

3.2 Antenatal education
Pregnant women should be offered opportunities to attend antenatal classes and have written information about antenatal care. [A]

Pregnant women should be offered evidence-based information and support to enable them to make informed decisions regarding their care. Information should include details of where they will be seen and who will undertake their care. Addressing women's choices should be recognised as being integral to the decision-making process. [C]

At the first contact, pregnant women should be offered information about the pregnancy care services and options available, lifestyle considerations, including dietary information, and screening tests. [C]

Pregnant women should be informed about the purpose of any screening test before it is performed. The right of a woman to accept or decline a test should be made clear. [D]

At each antenatal appointment, midwives and doctors should offer consistent information and clear explanations and should provide pregnant women with an opportunity to discuss issues and ask questions. [D]

Communication and information should be provided in a form that is accessible to pregnant women who have additional needs, such as those with physical, cognitive or sensory disabilities and those who do not speak or read English. [Good practice point]

4.6 Gestational age assessment: LMP and ultrasound
Pregnant women should be offered an early ultrasound scan to determine gestational age (in lieu of last menstrual period (LMP) for all cases) and to detect multiple pregnancies. This will ensure consistency of gestational age assessments, improve the performance of mid-trimester serum screening for Down's syndrome and reduce the need for induction of labour after 41 weeks. [A]

Ideally, scans should be performed between 10 and 13 weeks and use crown–rump length measurement to determine gestational age. Pregnant women who present at or beyond 14 weeks of gestation should be offered an ultrasound scan to estimate gestational age using head circumference or biparietal diameter. [Good practice point]

Chapter 5 Lifestyle considerations

5.5 Nutritional supplements
There is insufficient evidence to evaluate the effectiveness of vitamin D in pregnancy. In the absence of evidence of benefit, vitamin D supplementation should not be offered routinely to all pregnant women. [A]

5.12 Alcohol and smoking in pregnancy
Excess alcohol has an adverse effect on the fetus. Therefore it is suggested that women limit alcohol consumption to no more than one standard unit per day. Each of the following constitutes one 'unit' of alcohol: a single measure of spirits, one small glass of wine, and a half pint of ordinary strength beer, lager or cider. [C]

Chapter 9 Screening for fetal anomalies

9.1 Screening for structural anomalies

Pregnant women should be offered an ultrasound scan to screen for structural anomalies, ideally between 18 and 20 weeks of gestation, by an appropriately trained sonographer and with equipment of an appropriate standard as outlined by the National Screening Committee. [A]

9.2 Screening for Down's syndrome

Pregnant women should be offered screening for Down's syndrome with a test that provides the current standard of a detection rate above 60% and a false positive rate of less than 5%. The following tests meet this standard:

- From 11 to 14 weeks:
  - nuchal translucency (NT)
  - the combined test (NT, hCG and PAPP-A)
  - From 14 to 20 weeks:
  - the triple test (hCG, AFP and uE_3)
  - the quadruple test (hCG, AFP, uE_3, inhibin A)
- From 11 to 14 weeks AND 14 to 20 weeks:
  - the integrated test (NT, PAPP-A + hCG, AFP, uE_3, inhibin A)
  - the serum integrated test (PAPP-A + hCG, AFP, uE_3, inhibin A). [B]

By April 2007, pregnant women should be offered screening for Down's syndrome with a test which provides a detection rate above 75% and a false positive rate of less than 3%. These performance measures should be age standardised and based on a cut-off of 1/250 at term. The following tests currently meet this standard:

- From 11 to 14 weeks:
  - the combined test (NT, hCG and PAPP-A)
- From 14 to 20 weeks:
  - the quadruple test (hCG, AFP, uE_3, inhibin A)
- From 11 to 14 weeks AND 14 to 20 weeks:
  - the integrated test (NT, PAPP-A + hCG, AFP, uE_3, inhibin A)
  - the serum integrated test (PAPP-A + hCG, AFP, uE_3, inhibin A). [B]

Pregnant women should be given information about the detection rates and false positive rates of any Down's syndrome screening test being offered and about further diagnostic tests that may be offered. The woman's right to accept or decline the test should be made clear. [D]

10.3 Chlamydia trachomatis

Pregnant women should not be offered routine screening for asymptomatic chlamydia because there is insufficient evidence on its effectiveness and cost-effectiveness. However, this policy is likely to change with the implementation of the national opportunistic chlamydia screening programme. [C]

Chapter 11 Screening for clinical conditions

11.1 Gestational diabetes mellitus

The evidence does not support routine screening for gestational diabetes mellitus (GDM) and therefore it should not be offered. [B]

11.2 Pre-eclampsia

At first contact a woman's level of risk for pre-eclampsia should be evaluated so that a plan for her subsequent schedule of antenatal appointments can be formulated. The likelihood of developing pre-eclampsia during a pregnancy is increased in women who:

- are nulliparous
- are age 40 or older
- have a family history of pre-eclampsia (e.g., pre-eclampsia in a mother or sister)
- have a prior history of pre-eclampsia

- have a body mass index (BMI) at or above 35 at first contact
- have a multiple pregnancy or pre-existing vascular disease (for example, hypertension or diabetes). [C]

Whenever blood pressure is measured in pregnancy, a urine sample should be tested at the same time for proteinuria. [C]

Standardised equipment, techniques and conditions for blood-pressure measurement should be used by all personnel whenever blood pressure is measured in the antenatal period so that valid comparisons can be made. [C]

Pregnant women should be informed of the symptoms of advanced pre-eclampsia because these may be associated with poorer pregnancy outcomes for the mother or baby. Symptoms include headache, problems with vision, such as blurring or flashing before the eyes, bad pain just below the ribs, vomiting and sudden swelling of face, hands or feet. [D]

11.3 Preterm birth

Routine vaginal examination to assess the cervix is not an effective method of predicting preterm birth and should not be offered. [A]

Although cervical shortening identified by transvaginal ultrasound examination and increased levels of fetal fibronectin are associated with an increased risk for preterm birth, the evidence does not indicate that this information improves outcomes, therefore, neither routine antenatal cervical assessment by transvaginal ultrasound nor the measurement of fetal fibronectin should be used to predict preterm birth in healthy pregnant women. [B]

Chapter 12 Fetal growth and wellbeing

12.2 Measurement of symphysis–fundal distance

Pregnant women should be offered estimation of fetal size at each antenatal appointment to detect small- or large-for-gestational-age infants. [A]

Symphysis–fundal height should be measured and plotted at each antenatal appointment. [Good practice point]

12.7 Umbilical and uterine artery Doppler ultrasound

The use of umbilical artery Doppler ultrasound for the prediction of fetal growth restriction should not be offered routinely. [A]

The use of uterine artery Doppler ultrasound for the prediction of pre-eclampsia should not be offered routinely. [B]

2.3 Algorithm

Antenatal care: routine care for the healthy pregnant woman

[see overleaf]

Antenatal care: routine care fo

The needs of each pregnant woman should be reassessed at each appointment throughout pregnancy

At each appointment, women should be given information with an opportunity to discuss issues and ask questions.

Women should usually carry their own case notes.

Women should be informed of the results of all tests and systems in place to communicate results to women.

Verbal information should be supported by classes and written information that is evidence based.

Nulliparous (1st pregnancy)   **Parous**

Identify women who may need additional care.

Give information on diet and lifestyle considerations, pregn___ ___re services, maternity benefits and screening tests.

Inform women about the benefits of folic acid supplem___ion (400 micrograms per day for up to 12 weeks).

⮕ Offer screening tests. The purpose of all tests sh___ld b___ understood before they are undertaken.

Measure body mass index and blood pressure ___ test urin___ or proteinuria.

Support women who smoke or who have re___ntly ___t by offering anti-smoking interventions.

Review, discuss and record ___ult___ of all screening tests undertaken.
Measure BP and ___ ___rine ___or proteinuria.

Measure symphysis fundal heig___ BP.
Urinalysis for protein___ia.

Meas___ ___F___ + BP. Urinalysis for proteinuria.
⮕ Offer repeat screening___ ___ ___emia and atypical red cell alloantibodies.
___ 1st d___se anti-D if rhesus negative.

SFH + BP + pro___inuria urin___ysis.
Review, discuss and ___ ___d res___ts of all
screening tests un___ ___en.

Measure SFH + BP. Urinalysis for proteinuria. Offer 2nd dose anti-D if rhesus negative.
For parous women, review, discuss and record results of all screening tests undertaken.

Measure SFH + BP. Urinalysis for proteinuria. Check presentation: ⮕ Offer ECV if breech

SFH + BP + urinalysis for proteinuria.

SFH + BP + urinalysis for proteinuria.

Measure SFH + BP + urinalysis for proteinuria.
⮕ Offer membrane sweep.
⮕ Offer induction after 41 weeks.

G E S T A T I O N A L   A G E

| Prior to 12 weeks (may be 2 appts) |
| 16 |
| 25 |
| 28 |
| 31 |
| 34 |
| 36 |
| 38 |
| 40 |
| 41 |

Total appointments for nulliparous women: 10   **Total appointments for parous women: 7**

Key: ECV external cephalic version • EPDS Edinburgh Postnatal Depression Scale • HELLP haemolysis, elevated
LGA large for gestational age • SFH symphysis–fundal height • SGA small for gestational age • USS ultrasound

r the healthy pregnant woman

Antenatal care should be provided by a small group of carers with whom the woman feels comfortable. There should be continuity of care throughout the antenatal period.

Healthcare professionals should be alert to the symptoms or signs of domestic violence and women should be given the opportunity to disclose domestic violence.

Women who may need additional care

Pregnant women should be informed about the purpose of any screening test before it is performed. The right of a woman to accept or decline a test should be made clear.

Planning care: assessment

Are any of the following present?

- Conditions such as hypertension, cardiac or renal disease, endocrine, psychiatric or haematological disorders, epilepsy, diabetes, autoimmune diseases, cancer, HIV
- Factors that make the woman vulnerable such as those who lack social support
- Age 40 years and older or 18 years and younger
- BMI greater than or equal to 35 or less than 18
- Previous caesarean section
- Severe pre-eclampsia, HELLP or eclampsia
- Previous pre-eclampsia or eclampsia
- 3 or more miscarriages
- Previous preterm birth or mid trimester loss
- Previous psychiatric illness or puerperal psychosis
- Previous neonatal death or stillbirth
- Previous baby with congenital abnormality
- Previous SGA or LGA infant
- Family history of genetic disorder

To be arranged early in pregnancy (before 16 weeks of gestation)

Blood tests to screen for:
- blood group, rhesus status and red cell antibodies
- haemoglobin (to screen for anaemia)
- hepatitis B virus
- HIV
- rubella susceptibility
- syphilis serology.

Urine test to screen for asymptomatic bacteriuria.

Ultrasound scan to determine gestational age.

Down's syndrome screening:
- Nuchal translucency at 11–14 weeks
- Serum screening at 14–20 weeks.

These women are likely to need additional care which is outside the scope of this guideline. The care outlined here is the *'baseline care'*.

The following interventions are *NOT* recommended components of *routine* antenatal care:
- repeated maternal weighing
- Breast examination
- Pelvic examination
- Screening for post natal depression using EPDS
- iron supplementation
- Vitamin D supplementation
- Screening for the following infections
  o *Chlamydia trachomatis*
  o cytomegalovirus
  o hepatitis C virus
  o group B streptococcus
  o toxoplasmosis
  o bacterial vaginosis
- Screening for gestational diabetes mellitus (including dipstick testing for glycosuria)
- Screening for preterm birth by assessment of cervical length (either by USS or VE) or using fetal fibronectin
- Formal fetal movement counting
- Antenatal electronic cardiotocography
- Ultrasound scanning after 24 weeks
- Umbilical artery Doppler USS
- Uterine artery Doppler USS to predict pre-eclampsia

To be arranged between 18 to 20 weeks of gestation

Ultrasound scan for detection of structural anomalies.

If the placenta is found to extend across the internal cervical os at this time, another scan at 36 weeks should be offered and the results of this scan reviewed at the 36-week appointment.

This algorithm should, where necessary, be interpreted with reference to the full guideline.

d liver enzymes and low platelet count •
scan • VE vaginal examination

3.1 Provision of information

Informed decision making has been described as 'a reasoned choice made by a reasonable individual using relevant information about the advantages and disadvantages of all the possible courses of action, in accord with the individual's beliefs'.[8]

In 1993, the Expert Maternity Group from the Department of Health released the *Changing Childbirth* report, which made explicit the right of women to be involved in decisions regarding all aspects of their antenatal care.[9] One of the priorities of antenatal care is to enable women to be able to make informed decisions about their care, such as where they will be seen, who will undertake their care, which screening tests they will undertake and where they plan to give birth. To do so, women require access to evidence-based information to take part in discussions with caregivers about these decisions. In practice however, it is reported that women feel that they have less say over some aspects of care than others and a substantial number of women would like to have more information about their options for care and services.[10] [EL = 3]

In a survey of maternity services in the NHS, just over 30% of recent mothers reported that they felt they had the option to choose where they received their pregnancy care. With screening tests, however, 60% of mothers reported feeling that they had been offered a choice. Women's assessment of information and communication in antenatal care indicated that 32–40% felt that they had not received enough spoken or written information about the risks and benefits of having different screening tests during pregnancy.[10] [EL = 3] Before making a decision about whether or not to have a test a woman needs to have information about what the test is looking for, what the test involves and any risks of the test itself to herself and her pregnancy, the type of result that will be reported (such as a probability or risk, the false positive and false negative rate) and the decisions she might face as a result of the test. However, it is not clear how this information should be given and how much information is optimal, as this is likely to vary among individual women.

In one survey, 1188 pregnant women's point of view on information needs were explored by means of self-completed postal questionnaires.[3] Half of the women reported that they would have liked additional information to be provided at their first antenatal appointment, with first time mothers most likely to believe that they had been provided with too little information. Written sources of information were also highly valued. [EL = 3]

In order to meet individual women's needs, it is likely that a variety of ways of giving information will be required. Written information varies widely in quality. A study of 81 leaflets used in antenatal screening programmes in England and Wales found that only 11 (14%) included comprehensive information on all aspects of screening.[11] [EL = 3]

An RCT that compared three methods of giving information about antenatal screening tests randomised pregnant women into three groups. In the first group, extra information was delivered to women on an individual basis. In the second group, women received extra information in classes and the third group (the control group), received routine antenatal clinic information. The study reported no differences between the groups in the uptake of screening for Down's syndrome and other fetal anomalies, haemoglobinopathies or cystic fibrosis. Anxiety, however, was reported to be higher by 20 weeks of gestation among women who were not offered extra information compared with women who received individual information.[12] [EL = 1b]

Another RCT assessed the impact of evidence-based leaflets to promote informed decision making among pregnant women compared with no leaflets.[13] The leaflets were designed to be used in a conscious and controlled way (i.e., not left in a rack at an antenatal clinic or GP office) and the information provided in them was the result of systematic review of the best available evidence and they were peer reviewed. No differences were detected in the proportion of women who reported that they had exercised informed choice or among those who reported an 'active' decision making role during antenatal care between the groups. Satisfaction with the amount of information between the two groups, however, was higher in the group that received the leaflets. [EL = 1b] Qualitative assessment within the trial of the use of the leaflets found that their potential as decision aids was greatly reduced due to competing demands within the clinical environment.[14] Time pressures limited discussion and hierarchical power structures resulted in defined norms, which dictated which 'choices' were available. This meant that women complied with their carers' choice rather than making an informed decision. [EL = 3]

Much of the responsibility for providing information, which should be unbiased and evidence-based, falls upon the healthcare provider. Although users of antenatal care services report that they place high value on quality information that will allow them to make an informed decision about antenatal screening tests,[15,16] [EL = 3] a study that recorded consultations in the USA and UK found that the information provided on antenatal screening tests was insufficient for informed decision making and occasionally misleading or inaccurate.[17] This may be explained by a lack of knowledge on the part of the carer,[18] [EL = 3] a lack of training on how to present information in an understandable way[19] or a lack of time and resources to present the information.[20] A comparison of those who completed and those who did not complete training to improve information providing skills in an RCT[19] found that those who dropped out were the ones who had poorer communication skills at baseline, suggesting that those most likely to need training in effective communication are the ones least likely to avail themselves of it.[21] [EL = 3]

Beyond the issue of poor understanding of tests undergone or declined, additional issues reported to be associated with antenatal screening programmes include anxiety following false positive results and false negative reassurance in those receiving negative test results.[22] This highlights the importance of the need for information on the outcomes of testing in order to make informed decisions. Although more is known about antenatal screening than other aspects of antenatal care, more research is needed to help ascertain how best to help parents make informed decisions about choices around antenatal testing. In addition, although the provision of information is perhaps a necessary condition for informed decision making, it is not sufficient. Other factors are necessary to achieve informed decision making and this may be difficult in the context of health care as, historically, pregnant women are not expected to make decisions themselves.

Available information

All first time pregnant women in England and Wales should be offered *The pregnancy book* (published by health departments in England and Wales)[23] by their carer. This book provides information on many aspects of pregnancy including: how the fetus develops; deciding where to have a baby; feelings and relationships during pregnancy; antenatal care and classes; a section for expectant fathers; problems in pregnancy; when pregnancy goes wrong; rights and benefits information and a list of useful organisations.

The Cochrane Database of Systematic Reviews (www.update-software.com/clibng/cliblogon. htm) provides the best available evidence on safe and effective antenatal care.

The MIDIRS Informed Choice initiative has produced 15 leaflets to assist women in making informed objective decisions during pregnancy. Each leaflet has a corresponding leaflet for professionals, aiming to help them guide pregnant women through decisions. Access to this resource is available online at www.nelh.nhs.uk/maternity.

A leaflet entitled *Tests for you and your baby during pregnancy* provides information to assist women in making informed decisions about the screening tests that are offered in pregnancy. It is published by Bro Taf Health Authority and may be tailored for specific health authorities.[24]

3.2   Antenatal education

There are many different ways of providing antenatal classes and antenatal education. There is variation in the underlying aims of antenatal education, in the number of classes offered, whether classes are offered individually or in groups, when during the course of pregnancy the classes are offered and the content of the classes. These factors may impact on the effectiveness of antenatal education programmes.

Antenatal classes are often used to give information regarding a woman's pregnancy, childbirth and parenting to expectant parents. However, antenatal education can encompass a broader concept of educational and supportive measures that help parents and prospective parents to understand and explore their own social, emotional, psychological and physical needs during pregnancy, labour and parenthood and enable them to be confident in their abilities to give birth and to parent successfully. In a study of three groups of childbirth teachers working in different organisations in the UK who were asked to identify the aims of antenatal education, the need to build women's confidence in their ability to give birth and care for their babies was reported as the most important aim.[25]

The scope of this guideline covers antenatal education relating to pregnancy, and does not cover important aspects of antenatal education that relate to childbirth or parenthood, although it is recognised that antenatal education is often considered the first step in the pathway of becoming a parent. Although women who experience fear of childbirth are not necessarily more likely to have interventions during labour such as emergency caesarean section, it is possible that building up a woman's confidence during pregnancy in her ability to give birth has the potential to influence her choices for the birth of her baby and the interventions she receives during birth.[26]

A systematic review based on six RCTs involving 1443 women assessed the effects of antenatal education on knowledge acquisition, anxiety, sense of control, pain, support, breastfeeding, infant care abilities, and psychological and social adjustment. The largest study ($n = 1275$) examined an educational intervention to increase vaginal birth after caesarean section only. The remaining five trials (combined $n = 168$, range $n = 10–67$) included more general educational interventions; however, the methodological quality of these trials is uncertain, as they do not report randomisation procedures, allocation concealment or accrual and loss of participants. None of the trials included labour and birth outcomes, anxiety, breastfeeding success or general social support. The effects on knowledge acquisition and infant care competencies were measured but interpretation is difficult because of the size and methodological quality of the trials.[27] [EL = 1b] The findings of observational studies are also inconsistent.[28–30] [EL = 3] One survey found acquisition of knowledge was increased among all women who attended antenatal education classes compared with women who did not attend, although antenatal classes appear to have stronger effects on women from higher socio-economic classes.[28] [EL = 3] Women who attended antenatal classes were also less anxious than women who did not attend antenatal classes. The inconsistency across the observational studies maybe explained by confounding factors for which it is not possible to control in an analysis.

A survey of what women would like to learn in antenatal classes found that information on physical and psychological changes during pregnancy, fetal development, what will happen during labour and childbirth, their emotions during labour and childbirth and how to care for themselves during this time, possible complications and how to care for the baby after birth were the main issues.[31] [EL = 3] Evidence for the best method to deliver antenatal education is lacking. Ideally, the aims of antenatal education might include facilitating pregnant women to make informed decisions and to communicate more effectively with their carers, thus enabling them to contribute to the design of future antenatal education, to convey the issues they feel are most important to learn about and to feel empowered by their pregnancy and birth experience.

Recommendations

Pregnant women should be offered opportunities to attend antenatal classes and have written information about antenatal care. [A]

Pregnant women should be offered evidence-based information and support to enable them to make informed decisions regarding their care. Information should include details of where they will be seen and who will undertake their care. Addressing women's choices should be recognised as being integral to the decision-making process. [C]

At the first contact, pregnant women should be offered information about the pregnancy care services and options available, lifestyle considerations, including dietary information, and screening tests. [C]

Pregnant women should be informed about the purpose of any screening test before it is performed. The right of a woman to accept or decline a test should be made clear. [D]

At each antenatal appointment, midwives and doctors should offer consistent information and clear explanations and should provide pregnant women with an opportunity to discuss issues and ask questions. [D]

Communication and information should be provided in a form that is accessible to pregnant women who have additional needs, such as those with physical, cognitive or sensory disabilities and those who do not speak or read English. [Good practice point]

4.6 Gestational age assessment: LMP and ultrasound

Estimates of gestational duration based on the timing of the last normal menstrual period (LMP) are dependent upon a woman's ability to recall the dates accurately, the regularity or irregularity of her menstrual cycles and variations in the interval between bleeding and anovulation. Between 11% and 42% of gestational age estimates from LMP are reported as inaccurate.[52] However, there is thought to be little variation in fetal growth rate up to mid-pregnancy and therefore, estimates of fetal size by ultrasound scan provides estimates of gestational age which are not subject to the same human error as LMP.

Ultrasound assessment of gestational age at 10–13 weeks is usually calculated by measurement of the crown–rump length. For pregnant women who present in the second trimester, gestational age can be assessed with ultrasound measurement of biparietal diameter or head circumference. Ultrasound measurement of biparietal diameter is reported to provide a better estimate of date of delivery for term births than first day of the LMP.[53-55] [EL = 2a] Gestational age assessment with ultrasound occurs routinely prior to 24 weeks and where discrepancies between ultrasound and LMP exist, choosing to use the ultrasound dating reduces the number of births considered to be post-term.[53-56] [EL = 2a]

Routine ultrasound before 24 weeks is also associated with a reduction in rates of intervention for post-term pregnancies. One systematic review of nine RCTs found ultrasound scanning before 24 weeks to be associated with a reduction in the rate of induced labour for post-term pregnancy when compared to selective use of ultrasound (Peto OR 0.61, 95% CI 0.52 to 0.72). This may have consequences when pregnancies are misclassified as pre- or post-term and inappropriate action is taken. Earlier detection of multiple pregnancy was also reported, although this did not have a significant affect on perinatal mortality (twins undiagnosed at 26 weeks: Peto OR 0.08, 95% CI 0.04 to 0.16). No adverse influence on school performance or neurobehavioural function as a consequence of antenatal exposure to ultrasound was observed.[57] [EL = 1a]

Accurate assessment of gestational age also permits optimal timing of antenatal screening for Down's syndrome and fetal structural anomalies. Reliable dating is important when interpreting Down's syndrome serum results as it may reduce the number of false positives for a given detection rate. An RCT evaluating ultrasound assessment at the first antenatal appointment at less than 17 weeks of gestation compared with no ultrasound found that fewer women needed adjustment of the date of delivery in mid-gestation (9% versus 18%; RR 0.52, 95% CI 0.34 to 0.79) and that women who had an ultrasound at their first appointment reported more positive feelings about their pregnancy.[52] [EL = 1b]

Recommendations

Pregnant women should be offered an early ultrasound scan to determine gestational age (in lieu of LMP for all cases) and to detect multiple pregnancies. This will ensure consistency of gestational age assessments, improve the performance of mid-trimester serum screening for Down's syndrome and reduce the need for induction of labour after 41 weeks. [A]

Ideally, scans should be performed between 10 and 13 weeks and use crown–rump length measurement to determine gestational age. Pregnant women who present at or beyond 14 weeks of gestation should be offered an ultrasound scan to estimate gestational age using head circumference or biparietal diameter. [Good practice point]

5.5   Nutritional supplements

Vitamin D

Vitamin D requirements are thought to increase during pregnancy to aid calcium absorption. The main sources of vitamin D are sunlight and oily fish. Daily exposure to sunlight should avoid vitamin D deficiency. Maternal deficiency in vitamin D is purported to be associated with neonatal rickets although this is a theoretical risk as we were unable to find evidence to quantify it.

Women from the Indian subcontinent living in England and Wales are thought to be particularly vulnerable to vitamin D deficiency. Those women who remain indoors, whose clothing leaves little exposed skin, who live in a sunless climate and who are vegetarian are also thought to be at higher risk of vitamin D deficiency.

One systematic review assessed the effects of vitamin D supplementation on pregnancy outcome.[82] Only two small RCTs were included (*n* = 232). Neonatal hypocalcaemia was less common in the supplemented group (OR 0.13, 95% CI 0.02 to 0.65). However, there were no other significant findings and there was not enough evidence to evaluate the effects of vitamin D supplementation during pregnancy. [EL = 1a]

Although the Food Standards Agency recommends vitamin D supplementation during pregnancy, there is no indication of what evidence this recommendation is based on.

Recommendation

There is insufficient evidence to evaluate the effectiveness of vitamin D in pregnancy. In the absence of evidence of benefit, vitamin D supplementation should not be offered routinely to pregnant women. [A]

5.12   Alcohol and smoking in pregnancy

Alcohol consumption in pregnancy

Alcohol passes freely across the placenta to the fetus and, while there is general agreement that women should not drink excessively during pregnancy, it remains unclear what level of drinking is harmful to a pregnant woman and her fetus. Investigating the effects of maternal drinking on fetal development is difficult due to confounding factors such as socio-economic status and smoking.

Research evidence is consistent in finding no evidence of fetal harm among women who drink one or two units of alcohol per week.[106] There is also little or no evidence of harm in women who drink up to ten units per week. However, binge drinking or otherwise heavy consumption of alcohol is associated with adverse baby outcomes such as low birthweight[107,108] and behavioural and intellectual difficulties later in life.[109] [EL = 3] Binge drinking is also associated with fetal alcohol syndrome and the incidence in Europe is reported to be 0.4 cases/1000.[110]

As a safe low level of alcohol consumption has yet to be ascertained and associations with fetal alcohol syndrome exist only with binge or heavy drinking, guidance from professional bodies is slightly inconsistent. One guideline recommends that while there is no conclusive evidence that consumption levels below 15 units/week have an adverse effect on fetal growth or childhood IQ levels, pregnant women should be careful about the amount of alcohol they consume and limit it to no more than one standard unit of alcohol per day.[111] [EL = 4] Other guidance (e.g. MIDIRS Informed Choice and Foods Standards Agency) recommends one to two units once or twice a week. [EL = 4]

Recommendation

Excess alcohol has an adverse effect on the fetus. Therefore it is suggested that women limit alcohol consumption to no more than one standard unit per day. Each of the following constitutes one 'unit' of alcohol: a single measure of spirits, one small glass of wine, and a half pint of ordinary strength beer, lager or cider. [C]

8.2 Screening for sickle cell disorders and thalassaemia

Haemoglobin (Hb) disorders are autosomal recessive; however, it is possible to inherit more than one haemoglobin disorder. Sickle cell disease include a variety of haemoglobin variants, the most common of which are haemoglobins SS, Hb SC, Hb SD Punjab, HbS B thalassaemia and HbS O Arab. Hb SS causes anaemia, increased susceptibility to infection and infarction of various organs, including the brain. It is characterised by sickle-shaped red blood cells, resulting in their premature removal from the circulation. The prevalence of sickle cell trait in Northern European populations is 0.05% compared with 4% to 11% in black Caribbean populations, 20% (range 10% to 28%) in black African populations, 1% (range 0% to 1%) in Indians and 0.75% (range 0.5% to 10%) in Cypriot populations.[275] It is estimated 160 babies are born each year with sickle cell disorder in England. Implementation of the national universal screening of newborn babies for sickle cell disorders began in April 2003 in England and Wales.

Beta thalassaemia major causes severe anaemia from infancy, which is usually fatal within ten years if not treated. It is most common in people of Mediterranean origin and across the Middle and Far East. Prevalence estimates for thalassaemia trait are 0.9% among black Caribbean populations and black African populations, 3.5% (range 2.55 to 4.5%) among Indian populations, 4.5% (range 3.5% to 5.5%) among Pakistani populations, 3.0% among Bangladeshi populations (range 2.0% to 4.0%) and Chinese populations (range 1.0% to 4.0%) and 16% among Cypriot populations, compared with 0.1% among Northern Europeans.[275] Seventeen babies are born each year with thalassaemia, but there may be two to three times this number of pregnancies affected.[275] [EL = 3]

The aim of antenatal screening for sickle cell disorders and thalassaemia is to identify women at risk early in pregnancy, so that genetic counselling can be provided and women may make timely and informed reproductive choices. An audit of current practice in the UK indicated that about 50% of thalassaemia-affected pregnancies in England were not offered prenatal diagnosis, although a risk was recognised in 43–55% of pregnancies,[276] [EL = 3] while an audit of prenatal diagnosis found that only 50% and 13% of couples at risk for thalassaemia and sickle cell disorder, respectively, actually have a prenatal diagnosis.[277] [EL = 3]

Screening may be based on an ethnic question used to identify pregnant women at higher risk, who are then investigated for haemoglobin variants, or on offering laboratory screening to all pregnant women. Irrespective of which method is used, information on ethnicity (ancestry) needs to be collected for interpretation of screening results.

In 1993, the UK Standing Medical Advisory Committee recommended screening using laboratory methods in districts where 15% or more of the antenatal population were from ethnic minorities.[278] [EL = 4] More recently, two Health Technology Assessment (HTA) reports have evaluated the effectiveness of screening in the antenatal, neonatal or preconceptional period and have addressed the question of screening using an ethnic question or using laboratory methods.[275,279]

Screening using an ethnic question is based on questions to identify ethnic origin of the pregnant woman. Ethnic origin is an important issue in screening, as sickle cell trait is found predominantly in people of African-Caribbean and sub-Saharan African origin, and thalassaemia trait is found predominantly in people of Arab, Mediterranean and Indian origin. The effectiveness and suitability of questions about ethnic origin is uncertain.[280] It is reported that data from the Department of Health showed that ethnic origin information was missing from 43% of records in London and 37% in England although the collection of this information is mandatory.[281] Substantial variability in practice and in the quality of data collected has also been reported, with up to 20% of high-risk ethnic origins being misclassified.[281] Further evaluation of using an ethnic question as the basis for screening is currently underway.

Screening antenatal women using laboratory methods involves both screening to detect haemoglobin variants and the interpretation of red cell indices with investigation of those identified as screen positive. If the pregnant woman has confirmed sickle cell or thalassaemia trait (or any other genetic mutation of haemoglobin), the father of the fetus should be offered testing. If both parents have the trait, counselling should be offered. Prenatal diagnosis usually involves chorionic villus sampling. Parents who would like to consider prenatal diagnosis of the fetus must be referred to a specialist centre.[282] More information on screening for thalassaemia and abnormal haemoglobins is available from the NHS sickle cell and thalassaemia website (www.kcl-phs.org.uk/haemscreening/).

Issues around the psychological impact of screening for haemoglobinopathies also exist as ending the pregnancy may be considered if the fetus is affected. For this reason, women at risk should be identified as soon as possible. Among couples counselled in the first trimester, one study reported that 85–95% of couples at risk request prenatal diagnosis for thalassaemias and 50–80% request prenatal diagnosis for sickle cell disorders.[282,283] A UK audit reported that the uptake of prenatal diagnosis for thalassaemia trait is sensitive to gestational age and that when offered, uptake ranged from 70% to 95% in the first trimester, depending upon ethnic origin with 11 of 12 affected pregnancies being terminated among British Pakistani women.[276] [EL = 3] In a study of the response of Muslim communities in Pakistan to antenatal diagnosis and termination of pregnancies due to thalassaemia, 89% of woman carrying an affected fetus chose to terminate their pregnancy.[284] [EL = 3]

Economic considerations

The search for economic papers on this topic found 13 studies including two HTA reports. The first HTA examined the total costs of screening programmes in high and low prevalence areas of people of specific ethnic origins.[279] The report indicated that the relative cost-effectiveness of the strategies were highly sensitive to:

* the uptake of screening
* the presumed fetal prevalence of sickle cell disease
* the ethnic composition
* the inter-ethnic union rates.

The second HTA report included a systematic review of published studies.[275] No studies reporting the full benefits of screening and no good-quality UK-based cost data were found. A cost study based on one hospital estimated that the cost of identification of an at-risk fetus was £2455 per woman, including follow-up costs. The cost of treatment was estimated to be around £5000 per annum. The question of whether a universal or selective programme should be adopted was not directly addressed but it was suggested that a screening programme would be cost-effective in areas with haemoglobinopathy traits at or above 2.5%.

It was first envisaged that a model could be constructed for this guideline, using census data to assess which areas of the UK might benefit from a more selective approach to screening. However, despite efforts to obtain these data, it was not possible in the end to construct the model due to the inadequacy of the data that could be obtained.

The parameters that they suggest may be important in deciding whether to adopt a selective screening strategy are the ethnic composition of geographical area and the number of inter-ethnic unions resulting in a pregnancy. Since these rates may change quickly in any given population, this policy may not be effective or equitable to implement in practice.

Future research

The effectiveness and costs of an ethnic question for antenatal screening for sickle cell and thalassaemia is needed.

The effectiveness and costs of laboratory methods for antenatal screening for sickle cell and thalassaemia is needed.

9   Screening for fetal anomalies

Screening tests that aim to detect structural and chromosomal anomalies include ultrasound scan assessment and maternal serum screening (for open neural tube defects and Down's syndrome) early in pregnancy. The objectives of fetal anomaly screening include the identification of:[293]

* anomalies that are not compatible with life
* anomalies associated with high morbidity and long-term disability

- fetal conditions with the potential for intrauterine therapy
- fetal conditions that will require postnatal investigation or treatment.

The scope of any screening test for fetal anomalies should be made clear to women when the screening is offered. Although results from RCTs have not yet demonstrated whether informed decision making in screening affects uptake,[294] the UK National Screening Committee has adopted the principle that screening programmes should offer choice to individuals and that each person should make an informed decision about screening based upon appreciation of the risks and benefits.[295] Although the amount of information needed to make choices about antenatal screening varies from person to person, a report from the RCOG outlines the topics that should be discussed with a woman before screening.[296] Written information should be provided on details of the nature and purpose of the screening (i.e. for ultrasound scans, explanation of the structures examined), the screening procedure, details of detection rates for defined common conditions, the meaning of a positive and negative screening result, and actions to be taken if a test is reported as 'normal' or 'abnormal'.

9.1 Screening for structural anomalies

The aim of screening for fetal anomalies is to identify specific structural malformations. This allows the parents to plan appropriate care during pregnancy and childbirth or for the parents to be offered other reproductive choices. The detection of fetal anomalies varies, depending upon the anatomical system being examined, the gestational age at assessment, the skill of the operator and the quality of the equipment.

Ultrasound scanning for structural anomalies

A systematic review, based on 11 studies (one RCT, six retrospective cohorts and four prospective cohorts) was undertaken to examine the use of routine ultrasound to detect fetal anomalies.[297] The studies, which included 96 633 babies, were performed in Europe, the USA and Korea between 1988 and 1996. The overall prevalence of fetal anomaly was 2.09%, ranging from 0.76% to 2.45% in individual studies and including major and minor anomalies. [EL = IIa]

None of the studies conducted screening for anomalies at less than 15 weeks of gestation. Detection rates at less than 24 weeks was 41.3%, and 18.6% at greater than 24 weeks. Overall, detection of fetal anomaly was 44.7%, with a range of 15.0% to 85.3%, as different anomalies are more or less likely to be correctly identified. For example, anomaly scanning at 14 to 22 weeks for anencephaly can detect nearly 100% of cases.[298] [EL = 3]

Detection rates of ultrasound in the studies from the review may be inflated, as some studies reported the number of anomalies detected rather than the number of babies with structural anomalies. However, the authors also only included studies that reported adequate methods of postnatal ascertainment of anomalies to verify their presence and allow a more accurate calculation of test performance. Variation in detection rate occurs with:

- the type of anomaly being screened (see Table 9.1)
- the gestational age at scanning
- the skill of the operator
- the quality of the equipment being used•
- the time allocated for the scan.

Table 9.1 Percentage of fetal anomalies detected by routine ultrasound screening in the second trimester according to anatomical system.[297] [EL = IIa]

Anatomical systems	Percentage detected (%)
Central nervous system	76
Urinary tract	67
Pulmonary	50
Gastrointestinal	42
Skeletal	24
Cardiac	17

The use of ultrasound to detect fetal anomalies reduces perinatal mortality only if the parents choose to end the pregnancy following the detection of those anomalies.[297] [EL = 1b and 2a]

Another RCT that was not included in the above review compared routine ultrasound scanning with selective ultrasound.[299] [EL = 1b] A better detection rate for major malformations was reported for routine ultrasound than for selective ultrasound (40% versus 28%). A significantly lower perinatal mortality rate in the routine ultrasound group was also reported and was mainly attributed to differences in termination of pregnancy after detection. There was more than a two-fold difference in the detection rates between the two hospitals that participated in this trial (75% versus 35%), which reinforces the need to ensure a high skill level among those performing the scan.

As detection rates vary, those providing ultrasound scanning need to monitor the quality of their service. This requires the collection of follow-up information on all babies scanned during pregnancy. As detection rates are influenced both by the skill of the operator and the quality of the ultrasound scanning equipment, the RCOG working party report outlined standards for training and equipment (Appendix 3).

The detection rate of fetal structural anomalies also varies with gestational age at the time of ultrasound. An observational study on the detection of major structural anomalies with a scan at 12 to 13 weeks reported an 84% detection rate for anencephaly.[300] [EL = 3] The potential benefit of scanning for structural anomalies in the first trimester is that gestational age assessment (see Section 4.6) and Down's syndrome screening (i.e. nuchal translucency) could be performed concurrently.

In Wales, 100% of maternity units currently offer a routine 18–20 week anomaly scan.[301] A UK recommended minimum standard for the 20 week anomaly scan is provided by the RCOG (Box 9.1). The standards for an 'optimal scan' include additional features to improve the detection of cardiac anomalies and facial cleft defects.[302] [EL = 4] Although many maternity units may not currently be able to afford the additional scanning time or scans required, these have been included as a standard that maternity units may aspire to achieve.

Box 9.1   Minimum standards for the 20 week anomaly scan, derived from the RCOG[302]

Fetal normality:
- Head shape and size and internal structures (cavum pellucidum, cerebellum, ventricular size at atrium < 10 mm)
- Spine: longitudinal and transverse
- Abdominal shape and content at level of stomach
- Abdominal shape and content at level of kidneys and umbilicus
- Renal pelvis < 5 mm anterior–posterior measurement
- Longitudinal axis abdominal–thoracic appearance (diaphragm and bladder)
- Thorax at level of a four-chamber cardiac view
- Arms: three bones and hand (not counting fingers)
- Legs: three bones and foot (not counting toes)

Optimal standard for a 20 week anomaly scan:
- Cardiac outflow tracts
- Face and lips

When a screening result for structural anomalies suggests a malformation, all women should be offered a more detailed ultrasound scan, if necessary at a regional centre, for a definitive diagnosis.

Recommendation

Pregnant women should be offered an ultrasound scan to screen for structural anomalies, ideally between 18 to 20 weeks of gestation, by an appropriately trained sonographer and with equipment of an appropriate standard as outlined by the National Screening Committee. [A]

9.2 Screening for Down's syndrome

Down's syndrome, also termed Trisomy 21, is a congenital syndrome that arises when the affected baby has an extra copy of chromosome 21. The birth incidence of Down's syndrome in England and Wales was 6.2/10 000 live and stillbirths in 1998.[303] [EL = 3] The main clinical feature of this disorder is intellectual impairment, although it is also associated with excess mortality due to congenital malformations (of which cardiac anomalies are the most common), leukaemia and increased incidence of thyroid disorders, epilepsy and Alzheimer's disease. An estimated 80% of children affected with Down's syndrome will have profound or severe intellectual disability and 20% will have mild or no intellectual disability. About 46% of children with Down's syndrome are born with a congenital heart defect that may require surgery.[304]

Principles of screening for Down's syndrome

The first step of any screening for congenital anomalies should include the provision of unbiased, evidence-based information so that the pregnant woman will be able to make autonomous informed decisions. This should include information on Down's syndrome, the characteristics of the screening test the woman is being offered and the implications of the test results.[305] The results of a cross-sectional study have shown, however, that although many women understand practical aspects of the test (e.g. that serum screening occurs at 16 to 18 weeks of gestation and that blood would be needed for the test), they lack knowledge about the likelihood and implications of possible results.[306] Women were surveyed after consultation with a midwife or obstetrician during which serum screening for Down's syndrome was offered and only 36% of women answered correctly the question, 'Negative results do not guarantee that everything is all right with the baby'. [EL = 3] Women should be made aware that they could opt out of the screening process at any time. However, knowing about a problem that the baby may have will allow for reproductive choice and also the opportunity for doctors and midwives to provide optimal care during pregnancy and childbirth.

Antenatal screening for Down's syndrome can take place during the first or second trimester of pregnancy and a variety of screening tests can be used. In the first trimester, nuchal translucency (NT), which is the measurement of the normal subcutaneous space between the skin and the cervical spine in the fetus early in pregnancy, can be used to identify women at increased risk of carrying a Down's syndrome baby at around 10 to 14 weeks. Nuchal translucency may be used with or without two first-trimester maternal serum markers, human chorionic gonadotrophin (hCG) and pregnancy-associated plasma protein A (PAPP-A): i.e., the combined test, or as part of the integrated test. In the early second trimester, screening techniques include biochemical marker screening at around 15 to 16 weeks.

Once a screening test is performed, the risk of Down's syndrome is calculated, taking into account maternal age, gestational age and the levels of biochemical markers. Results are 'positive' or classified as 'high risk' if the risk is equal to or greater than a locally agreed cut-off level. This is often expressed numerically to indicate the likelihood that a woman has a baby with Down's syndrome when a positive screening result is returned; e.g., a 1/250 chance that a pregnant woman is carrying an affected baby. When a high-risk screening result is returned, a woman will usually be offered a diagnostic test, such as amniocentesis, which has an excess fetal loss rate of 1%.[307] [EL = 1b]

It should be made clear to the woman that the nature of screening tests is such that a number of 'false positives' and 'false negatives' will result from a screening programme. The effectiveness of Down's syndrome screening tests are often reported with a 'false positive rate', which indicates the proportion of positive screening tests that indicate there may be a problem when there is not.

Differences in the performance of screening tests between studies may occur for a number of reasons:

- variation in statistical models of both prior age-related maternal risk and risk calculation from biochemical markers
- variation in biochemical assays used
- variation in the test thresholds, i.e. cut-off levels
- methodological quality of studies leading to both under- or over-ascertainment of cases in cohort studies or the use of case–control designs leading to biased estimates of test performance.[308,309]
- chance variation.

An associated increase in miscarriage throughout pregnancy has been reported among pregnant women known to have a fetus affected by Down's syndrome compared with pregnant women with unaffected fetuses.310 [EL = 3] Therefore the prevalence of Down's syndrome is likely to be higher early in pregnancy than at birth. Down's syndrome screening tests performed early in pregnancy will identify fetuses that may be lost spontaneously later in pregnancy. This affects the accuracy of cut-off rates in the determination of women who are 'high risk' or will be offered a diagnostic test and becomes relevant when the 'detection rate' of an earlier screening test is compared with that of a later screening test. A later screening test may not identify as high a proportion of Down's syndrome fetuses as an earlier test. However, it should not necessarily be interpreted that the later test is less efficient than the earlier test. Adjustment for the loss of Down's syndrome fetuses that have been terminated or spontaneously aborted needs to be made in order to provide accurate estimates of risk and screening performance.

Methods of screening for Down's syndrome

The risk of Down's syndrome increases with maternal age. The odds of having a baby affected by Down's syndrome at age 20 years are approximately 1 : 1,440 rising to 1 : 338 at 35 years and 1 : 32 at 45 years.311 [EL = 3] Therefore, before the development of biochemical and ultrasound screening methods, screening for Down's syndrome was based on maternal age only and all women over the age of 35 to 37 years were offered amniocentesis as a screening test. In 2000, in England and Wales, 16.5% of mothers were older than 35 years at the birth of their baby312 and would have been offered invasive diagnostic testing, based on a policy of screening by maternal age alone.

Invasive diagnostic testing and karyotyping is the gold standard test for confirming the diagnosis but it is associated with an excess risk for fetal loss of 1% compared with women with no invasive diagnostic testing.307 In 1998, a survey found that 8% of UK health authorities screened on the basis of maternal age alone.313 One study estimated that screening by maternal age alone detected 53% of Down's syndrome cases antenatally over a 3 year period, though this was thought to be an overestimate, as the total number of liveborn Down's syndrome babies was not obtainable.314

In the 1980s, a number of biochemical markers were found to be associated with Down's syndrome and this marked the advent of screening being offered to women younger than 35 years. This was important because, although the risk of Down's syndrome increases with age, younger women have the majority of pregnancies and therefore give birth to the majority of children with Down's syndrome. First-trimester biochemical markers now include hCG (total and free beta) and PAPP-A. hCG may also be measured in the second trimester. Other second-trimester biochemical markers include alpha-fetoprotein (AFP), unconjugated oestriol (uE_3) and dimeric inhibin A.

The associations between specific ultrasonographic markers and Down's syndrome have also been identified. One meta-analysis assessed which second-trimester ultrasound markers were effective for the detection of fetuses with Down's syndrome. The findings suggested that a thickened nuchal fold was the most accurate ultrasound marker in the second trimester. The six other markers that were assessed were reported to be of little value in screening for Down's syndrome, as they would result in more fetal losses than cases of Down's syndrome detected.315 [EL = 2a and 3] However, the review concluded that the sensitivity of a thickened nuchal fold in the second trimester was not high enough to be used as a practical screening test for Down's syndrome on its own. NT measurement for Down's syndrome screening commonly occurs between 11 and 14 weeks of gestation and detection rates for this are reported below. The presence or absence of fetal nasal bone, another possible ultrasound marker, is currently being researched.

Current screening for Down's syndrome

There is an extensive body of literature on Down's syndrome screening that investigates the numerous combinations of individual and multimarker screening in the first or second trimester, ultrasound screening and the integrated approach, which includes screening tests in the both the first and second trimester. If PAPP-A, hCG and NT are used as a first-trimester screening test (at 10 to 12 weeks), this is commonly referred to as the 'combined test'. When hCG and AFP are used between 14 to 20 weeks as a screening test, this is often called the 'double test'. If uE_3 is added to the double test combination, it becomes known as the 'triple test'. The addition of inhibin A to the triple test comprises the 'quadruple test'. The 'integrated test' uses NT and PAPP-A at 10 to 12 weeks of gestation with hCG, AFP, uE_3 and inhibin A at 14 to 20 weeks of gestation, requiring women to be managed through the first and second trimester for screening. Although the efficacy of this test is known, the acceptability of this approach to testing to pregnant women is not known. The 'serum integrated test' is the same as the integrated test without NT.

A 2001 survey of all maternity centres and primary care trusts in England indicated that the majority of units offered some form of screening for Down's syndrome. However, a variety of screening tests are used including: first-trimester NT screening with or without biochemical markers or biochemical marker screening in the second trimester (personal communication, Helen Janecek, 2003). In addition, an HTA monograph presented results for the integrated test.[316] The detection rates for each of these screening test combinations are presented in Table 9.2.

Table 9.2 Detection and false positive rates for various combinations of markers used for Down's syndrome screening

Measurements (cut-off)	False positive rate (%)	Detection rate (%)
Nuchal translucency at 9 to 14 weeks* (13 cohort studies, n = 170 343)[317]	4.7	77
Combined test : NT plus serum screening (10 studies, range reported)[318]	5	85–89
Double test (6 cohort studies, n = 110 254)[319]	Not reported**	66
Triple test (20 cohort studies, n = 194, 326, medians and ranges reported)[320]		
For a risk cut-off 1 : 190–200	4 (range 3–7)	67 (range 48–91)
For a risk cut-off 1 : 250–295	6 (range 4–7)	71 (range 48–80)
For a risk cut-off 1 : 350–380	8 (range 7–13)	73 (range 70–80)
Quadruple test (1 cohort study, n = 46 193)[321]	5	75 (95% CI 66–84)
Serum integrated test (1 nested case–control study, n = 28 434)[316]	2.7	85
Integrated test (1 nested case–control study, n = 28 434)[316]	1.3	85

* These data are from published cohort studies; data from the SURUSS report[316] have not been included as this was a nested case–control study and higher level evidence was available
** Due to variation in practice between screening programmes being compared

Considerable discrepancy between reported detection and false positive rates between studies often exist, due to differences in study design, varying cut-off rates, skill of the ultrasound operator, and the times at which the screening was conducted. All these factors should be taken into account when planning which screening method will be used for a pregnant population. In addition, other factors, such as the practicality of managing women through two trimesters for screening or the introduction of NT for Down's syndrome screening in the context of extra time required for ultrasound (assuming that a unit already offers first-trimester dating scans) should also be considered.

Diagnosis after a positive screening result

Diagnostic tests are offered to women identified as at high risk of having an affected pregnancy. Antenatal diagnosis of Down's syndrome is currently done by culture of fetal cells and fetal cells can currently only be acquired by invasive methods: amniocentesis, chorionic villus sampling (CVS) or fetal blood sampling. All of these methods carry a risk of miscarriage. The excess risk of miscarriage following amniocentesis is approximately 1%.[307] [EL = 1b] Among women who were screened in the first trimester and had a positive result, the reported rate of uptake for invasive testing for prenatal diagnosis was 77%.[322] [EL = 2a] Among women who were screened in the second trimester and had a positive result, reported uptake of invasive testing ranged from 43% to 74%, depending upon the magnitude of the risk.[321]

CVS is commonly performed between 11 and 13 weeks of gestation and amniocentesis after 15 weeks of gestation. However, first-trimester CVS is associated with a higher sampling failure rate (Peto OR 2.86, 95% CI 1.93 to 4.24) and also a higher pregnancy loss rate (Peto OR 1.33, 95% CI 1.17 to 1.52) than second-trimester amniocentesis.[323] [EL = 1a] Amniocentesis should not be carried out in the first trimester. When compared with CVS, early amniocentesis was associated with a higher failure rate (0.4% versus 2%, RR 0.23, 95% CI 0.08 to 0.65) though there was no significant difference in pregnancy loss between the two procedures (6.2% versus 5%, RR 1.24, 95% CI 0.85 to 1.81)[324] [EL = 1a] When early amniocentesis (before 14 weeks) was compared with amniocentesis at 15 weeks or later, however, a significantly higher rate of fetal loss (7.6% versus 5.9%, $P = 0.012$), fetal talipes (1.3% versus 0.1%, $P = 0.0001$) and sampling difficulty has been reported.[307] [EL = 1b] Therefore, associated risks are lowest for amniocentesis performed after fifteen weeks and highest for CVS at all times during pregnancy.

When a pregnant woman is offered a diagnostic test after a positive screening result, she should be informed of the risks associated with invasive testing and that other chromosomal anomalies, not just Down's syndrome, may be identified and that in some cases the prognosis for the fetus may not be clear. Although considerable anxiety is reported to be associated with diagnostic testing for Down's syndrome,[325,326] uptake of diagnostic testing after a high-risk screening result (1 : 250–300) in UK populations has been reported to range from 43% to 77%.[321,322]

A recent study examining the effect of prenatal diagnosis on infant mortality reported a decline in infant deaths due to congenital anomalies.[327] The authors suggested that the increased availability of reproductive choice upon diagnosis of congenital anomaly was related to the observed decrease in overall infant mortality. [EL = 3]

The future of Down's syndrome screening

The recommendations stated below accord with the current recommendations of the Antenatal Subcommittee of the UK National Screening Committee (NSC). However, as some screening tests for Down's syndrome are performed early in pregnancy, consideration should be given to ensuring that pregnant women who present late for antenatal care can also be offered screening for Down's syndrome.

Research surrounding the issue of screening for Down's syndrome is moving quickly and, while the NSC hopes that all units will achieve the standard of a 60% detection rate with a 5% false positive rate by April 2004, they also propose that a 75% detection rate with a less than 3% false positive rate should be achieved by April 2007 (www.nelh.nhs.uk/screening/dssp/home. htm). These performance meaures should be age standardised and based on a cut-off of 1/250 at term. A pilot programme in preparation for the introduction of inhibin A for Down's syndrome screening to address concerns about its reliability is currently under way. The feasibility and acceptability of the integrated and serum-integrated approach are also being explored.

Recommendations

Pregnant women should be offered screening for Down's syndrome with a test that provides the current standard of a detection rate above 60% and a false positive rate of less than 5%. The following tests meet this standard:

- From 11 to 14 weeks:
  - nuchal translucency (NT)
  - the combined test (NT, hCG and PAPP-A)
- From 14 to 20 weeks:
  - the triple test (hCG, AFP and uE3)
  - the quadruple test (hCG, AFP, uE3, inhibin A)
- From 11 to 14 weeks AND 14 to 20 weeks:
  - the integrated test (NT, PAPP-A + hCG, AFP, uE3, inhibin A)
  - the serum integrated test (PAPP-A + hCG, AFP, uE3, inhibin A). [B]

By April 2007, pregnant women should be offered screening for Down's syndrome with a test which provides a detection rate above 75% and a false positive rate of less than 3%. These performance measures should be age standardised and based on a cut-off of 1/250 at term. The following tests currently meet this standard:

- From 11 to 14 weeks:
  - the combined test (NT, hCG and PAPP-A)
- From 14 to 20 weeks:
  - the quadruple test (hCG, AFP, uE3, inhibin A)
- From 11 to 14 weeks AND 14 to 20 weeks:
  - the integrated test (NT, PAPP-A + hCG, AFP, uE3, inhibin A)
  - the serum integrated test (PAPP-A + hCG, AFP, uE3, inhibin A). [B]

Pregnant women should be given information about the detection rates and false positive rates of any Down's syndrome screening test being offered and about further diagnostic tests that may be offered. The woman's right to accept or decline the test should be made clear. [D]

10.1   Asymptomatic bacteriuria

Recommendation

Pregnant women should be offered routine screening for asymptomatic bacteriuria by midstream urine culture early in pregnancy. Identification and treatment of asymptomatic bacteriuria reduces the risk of preterm birth. [A]

10.3   *Chlamydia trachomatis*

Chlamydia trachomatis is a common sexually transmitted infection in European countries.[364] Chlamydia prevalence during pregnancy has been estimated at 6% in one English study.[365] [EL = 3] It is more frequent in women who are younger, black, single and those attending genitourinary medicine clinics.[365,366] [EL = 3]

Chlamydia infection during pregnancy is associated with higher rates of preterm birth (OR 1.6, 90%CI 1.01 to 2.5) and intrauterine growth restriction (OR 2.5, 90%CI 1.32 to 4.18). 367 [EL = 2a] Left untreated, it has also been associated with increased low birthweight and infant mortality.[368] [EL = 2b] In a review of randomised control trials, the number of women with positive cultures for chlamydia was reduced by 90% when treated with antibiotics compared with placebo (OR 0.06, 95% CI 0.03 to 0.12). [EL = 1a] However this did not alter the incidence of birth before 37 weeks.

In studies of infants born to mothers who have cultured positive to *C. trachomatis*, approximately 25% of the infants have subsequently cultured positive to *C. trachomatis*.[370,371] [EL = 3] These infants are also reported to have higher rates of neonatal conjunctivitis, lower respiratory tract infections and pneumonia.[370,371] [EL = 3]

Currently, no simple inexpensive laboratory tests for diagnosing *C. trachomatis* exist and different screening tests require samples to be taken from different anatomical sites. Tissue culture is expensive and, although it has good specificity, its sensitivity ranges from 75% to 85% because of inadequate sampling techniques (e.g., not rotating the swab firmly against the tissue for 15 to 30 seconds, removal from os must be without touching vaginal mucosa, use of lubricating jelly decreases chance of detection) and because the bacteria do not always survive transportation to the laboratory.[372] [EL = 4] Rapid tests include direct fluorescent antibody staining (50% to 90% sensitive), enzyme-linked immunoassays (sensitivity 75% to 80% and specificity 85% to 100%) and RNA-DNA hybridisation (sensitivity 70% to 85%).[364,372] [EL = 4] Direct fluorescent antibody staining, however, is labour intensive and therefore unsuitable for large numbers of samples.[364] [EL = 4] Serology is not useful in the diagnosis of acute chlamydial infection.[364,372] [EL = 4]

Nucleic acid amplification has sensitivity of 70% to 95% and specificity of 97% to 99%, with the advantage of being able to test invasive as well as noninvasive samples (e.g. urine) and it is suitable for large numbers of samples. However, it is an expensive test and inhibitors may be a problem in urine samples in pregnancy.[364,372] [EL = 4]

Due to the high rates of chlamydial infection observed among 16- to 24-year-olds in England, Wales and Northern Ireland, the UK Department of Health (DoH) has initiated a national opportunistic screening programme for all men and women under the age of 25 years. The first phase to roll out this programme has commenced in ten areas in England and the second phase is expected to commence by 2004. One of the healthcare settings for opportunistic screening is antenatal clinics. Therefore, when the roll out is complete, all pregnant women under the age of 25 years attending antenatal clinics will be offered screening for chlamydia.

Further information on screening for chlamydia in pregnant women can be found in the Scottish Intercollegiate Guidelines Network (SIGN) guideline, *Management of genital Chlamydia trachomatis infection*.[373]

Recommendation

Pregnant women should not be offered routine screening for asymptomatic chlamydia because there is insufficient evidence on its effectiveness and cost-effectiveness. However, this policy is likely to change with the implementation of the national opportunistic chlamydia screening programme. [C]

Future research

Further investigation into the benefits of screening for chlamydia in pregnancy is needed.

11.1 Gestational diabetes mellitus

There is no consensus on the definition, management or treatment of gestational diabetes mellitus (GDM).[480] According to WHO, GDM is defined as 'carbohydrate intolerance resulting in hyperglycaemia of variable severity with onset or first recognition during the pregnancy'.[481] This definition, however, encompasses women diagnosed with diabetes mellitus or impaired glucose tolerance (IGT) during pregnancy, using the same cut-off levels as for non-pregnant women.[482] In pregnancy, glucose levels are usually raised above the level considered 'normal' in non-pregnant women. Therefore, GDM, by the WHO definition, includes all IGT pregnancies and is based on non-pregnant standards that do not take into account the physiological increase in glucose levels during pregnancy. This results in a large range of women who will have gestational 'diabetes' and who may not be at increased risk for adverse pregnancy outcomes.

In a review commissioned by the NHS, it was concluded that there remains considerable debate regarding the definition of gestational diabetes. There is no evidence-based threshold for diagnosis and no standardisation for the use of the terms GDM and IGT in pregnancy.[483]

The incidence of GDM varies according to how it is defined but is reported to range from 3% to 10% in developed countries[484] and to be around 2% in the UK.[483] Women who develop GDM are more likely to develop type-2 diabetes later in life.[485] [EL = 2a] However, it is unclear whether the detection of GDM delays or prevents the subsequent development of diabetes mellitus and there are potentially increased adverse outcomes associated with screening, such as increased obstetric intervention.[486] [EL = 3] Therefore, without specific advantages for the mother, pregnancy is not an ideal time to conduct population screening for diabetes mellitus.

Observational studies indicate an association between GDM and an increase in mortality rates in babies.[487] [EL = 3] Because mortality is rare, measuring more common adverse events as a composite measure of perinatal morbidity has also been used. Morbidity measures include factors such as neonatal encephalopathy, neonatal seizures and birth trauma. GDM has been shown to be associated with fetal macrosomia;[486] [EL = 3] fetal macrosomia may be associated with birth trauma as a result of shoulder dystocia. However, while macrosomia may be associated with some poor outcomes (as a marker) there is not a direct causal relationship between macrosomia, shoulder dystocia and birth trauma. Factors such as maternal size and post-maturity are also closely associated with macrosomia.[488] The use of macrosomia as a surrogate outcome is further complicated by the variation in definitions used.[483]

To be effective, a screening programme should identify women at risk and there should be an effective intervention that improves the pregnancy outcome. The rationale for screening for gestational diabetes is to reduce poor perinatal outcome. There is global variation in screening patterns, which reflects the lack of evidence about the value of screening.[489] There are several methods used for GDM screening, which may be used independently or in combination.

Risk-factor screening

The use of risk-factor screening has led to high numbers of diagnostic tests being performed but high proportions of women with GDM being missed. In one US study, 42% of pregnant women had risk factors for GDM, but the same proportion of women with GDM was found among women with risk factors as women without risk factors (3.2% versus 2.4%, $P = 0.57$).[490] [EL = 2b] There was also no association found between the number of risk factors and risk of GDM.[490] [EL = 2b] In an older US study, similar results were reported with 44% of pregnant women without GDM having at least one risk factor.[491] [EL = 2a] Risk factor screening on its own is 50% sensitive and 58% specific.[490] [EL = 2b]

Universal screening

In Canada, a comparison was made with an area of universal screening and an area that did not implement screening for GDM. From 1990 to 1996, the incidence of GDM increased in the area of universal screening but not in the area of no screening (1.6% to 2.2% versus 1.4% to 1.0%, respectively). Rates of pre-eclampsia, fetal macrosomia, caesarean delivery, polyhydramnios and amniotic infections, however, remained the same in both regions.[492] [EL = 3]

Urinanalysis

Urine testing has low sensitivity and is a poor screening test for GDM. Reported sensitivities for urine testing for the presence of glucose range from 7% to 46%, but with high specificities ranging from 84% to 99% when compared with the 50 g glucose challenge test (GCT).[493] [EL = 2b] [494,495] [EL = 3] Glucosuria is also common in pregnant women unaffected by GDM (i.e., a high number of false positives).[493] [EL = 2b]

Blood tests

Blood tests include the measurement of glucose in the blood or plasma, with or without prior intake of oral glucose, and the measurement of fructosamine and glycosylated haemoglobin levels (HbA1c). There exists debate regarding cut-off levels for diagnosis, the amount of oral glucose that should be administered and whether glucose testing should be preceded by fasting.

Random plasma glucose (RPG), which measures non-fasting glucose levels, is measured without administration of a glucose load and at no particular fixed time after meals. Analysis can be on plasma or whole blood. Wide variations in the sensitivity of this test have been reported, depending upon the time of day the test is administered and the threshold that is used. One study reported a sensitivity of 46% and specificity of 86% (at a threshold of 6.1 mmol/litre) with the RPG in pregnant women who had eaten in the last two hours.[496] [EL = 2b] Another study reported a range of sensitivities and specificities, depending upon what time the test was taken. For a threshold of 5.6 mmol/litre, sensitivity was 29% to 80% and specificity was 74% to 80%. For a threshold of 6.1 mmol/litre, sensitivity ranged from 41% to 58% and specificity ranged from 74% to 96%. The highest sensitivity for both thresholds was found at 3 p.m.[497] [EL = 3]

Fasting plasma glucose is meant to be measured after a period of fasting, usually overnight. The following studies that reported sensitivities and specificities did not report the period of fasting used. In Brazil, examining a range of thresholds, maximum sensitivity (88%) and specificity (78%) was found at 4.9 mmol/litre.[498] [EL = 2a] In Switzerland, maximum sensitivity and specificity (81% and 76%, respectively) was found at a threshold of 4.8 mmol/litre.[499] [EL = 2a]

The 1 hour, 50 g GCT measures the blood glucose 1 hour after taking 50 g glucose (plus 150 ml fluid) orally; usually performed between 24 and 28 weeks of gestation. The sensitivity and specificity of this test is reported to be 79% and 87%, respectively.[491] [EL = 2a] Although glucose testing is usually performed with no regard to fasting status, studies have suggested that time since the last meal affects glucose levels. A test evaluation study compared glucose levels in women with and without GDM after three 50 g GCT tests: one after fasting, 1 hour after a meal and one 2 hours after a meal. In the control group, the fasting GCT was significantly higher than 1 or 2 hours after a meal ($P < 0.01$), leading to a false positive rate of 58% in the fasting state. Among the women with GDM, glucose levels 2 hours after the GCT were significantly lower than in the fasting state or 1 hour after the test ($P < 0.03$).[500] [EL = 3]

The optimal time for screening in pregnancy has been evaluated in several studies. Screening in the third trimester is reported to be the optimal time for the GCT. However, studies have also shown success with repeat testing during the three trimesters. In studies that only confirmed GDM (with 3 hour, 100 g glucose tolerance test, GTT) in women who screened positive with the 1 hour, 50 g GCT, women were screened three times during pregnancy. In one study, an estimated 11% of the GDM population would have been missed if screening had not continued past 28 weeks.[501] [EL = 3] In another study, 33% of the GDM population would have been missed had screening not continued past 31 weeks of gestation.[502] [EL = 3]

The GTT is regarded as the gold standard for the diagnosis of GDM after a positive screening result. However, the quantity of glucose load and threshold for diagnosis lack consistency. Commonly used criteria are summarised in Table 11.1.

Table 11.1 Examples of diagnostic criteria employed for gestational diabetes mellitus

	75 g glucose load (mmol/litre)		
	American Diabetic Association[503]	SIGN[480]	WHO[481]
Fasting	5.3	5.5	7.0
1 hour	10.0	–	–
2 hour	8.6	9.0	11.1
Minimum required criteria (n)	2	1	1

The first line of intervention for all pregnant women diagnosed with gestational diabetes is diet. However, a systematic review of RCTs found no difference between women treated with diet compared with women who received no dietary advice in frequencies of birthweight greater than 4000 g or 4500 g, caesarean section rates, preterm birth, birth trauma or maternal hypertensive disorders.[504] [EL = 1a] Although most pregnant women are treated with diet alone, 15% to 20% are thought to need insulin.[483]

In a trial that randomised women to diet alone or to diet plus insulin, no difference in outcomes was found. However, 14% of the diet-alone group received insulin owing to poor control and this may explain the lack of difference observed between the two groups.[505] [EL = 1b] Another study found that, while detection and treatment of GDM normalised birthweights, rates of caesarean delivery were still higher among pregnant women with GDM compared with pregnant women without GDM (34% versus 20%, RR 1.96, 95% CI 1.40 to 2.74).[506] [EL = 2a]

In an RCT of exercise as an intervention for GDM, in which only 29 out 144 subjects were successfully recruited and the method of randomisation was not clear, no differences in outcomes were seen.[507] [EL = 1b]

Intensive glucose monitoring has been reported to reduce incidence of macrosomia from 24% to 9% ($P < 0.05$) through the detection of women with high glucose levels who were then treated with insulin.[508] [EL = 3]

At present, screening for gestational diabetes appears to be hampered by the lack of a clear definition, agreed diagnostic criteria and evidence to show that intervention and treatment for this condition leads to improved outcomes for the mother and fetus. Although fasting plasma glucose and GCT have the highest reported sensitivities and specificities in the literature, there also exists considerable debate about which screening test should be used if there is to be screening. A continuum of risk for GDM should be researched and risk of adverse pregnancy outcomes clarified on such a continuum. This would help to form the basis for diagnosis. The most appropriate strategies for screening, diagnosing and managing asymptomatic GDM remain controversial.

The results of two ongoing studies are expected to resolve some of the issues surrounding the question of whether women should be routinely screened for gestational diabetes. The ACHOIS (Australian Carbohydrate Intolerance in Pregnancy Study) trial is assessing two forms of care for treating women with glucose intolerance of pregnancy detected through screening and includes 1000 women in Australia. The results of this study are expected to be available in 2004. The second trial, the Hyperglycaemia and Adverse Pregnancy Outcomes (HAPO) study, aims to define uniform standards for the detection and diagnosis of diabetes occurring in pregnancy to reduce adverse effects on mother and baby. It is an international study of 25 000 pregnant women and results are also expected to be available in 2004.

Recommendation

The evidence does not support routine screening for gestational diabetes mellitus and therefore it should not be offered. [B]

11.2 Pre-eclampsia

Pre-eclampsia is a multisystem disorder associated with increased maternal and neonatal morbidity and mortality. The incidence of pre-eclampsia ranges from 2% to 10%, depending upon the population studied and the criteria used to diagnose the disorder. Maternal symptoms of advanced pre-eclampsia may include (www.apec.org.uk/index.htm):

- bad headache
- problems with vision, such as blurring or flashing before the eyes
- bad pain just below the ribs
- vomiting
- sudden swelling of face, hands or feet.

Definitions

Pre-eclampsia	Hypertension new to pregnancy manifesting after 20 weeks of gestation that is associated with a new onset of proteinuria, which resolves after delivery.
Pregnancy-induced hypertension	Hypertension new to pregnancy that resolves after delivery but is not associated with proteinuria.
Chronic hypertension	Hypertension that predates a pregnancy or appears prior to 20 weeks of gestation.

This categorisation is helpful as it relates to the prognostic outcome of the pregnancy. Most women with hypertension in pregnancy have no clinical symptoms. Hypertension is frequently the only early sign that predates serious disease. Blood pressure measurement is routinely performed in antenatal care to allow the diagnosis and classification of hypertension in pregnancy.

Pre-eclampsia is thought to be caused by widespread endothelial cell damage secondary to an ischaemic placenta.[509] Hypertension and proteinuria are two easily measured signs associated with pre-eclampsia, although they are surrogate markers indicating end-organ damage.

Eclampsia is rare. It occurs in nearly 1/2000 pregnancies in the UK.[510] It is associated with high maternal morbidity and it accounts for over 50% of the maternal deaths associated with hypertensive disorders in pregnancy. Blood pressure may be of limited importance in identifying women who are going to develop eclampsia as about one-third of first fits occur in women with normal or a mild increase in blood pressure.[510]

Oedema was originally part of the triad of signs describing pre-eclampsia but it occurs in too many pregnant women (up to 80%) to be discriminatory and has been abandoned as a marker in classification schemes.[511a]

Physiological changes to blood pressure during pregnancy

In normal pregnancies, blood pressure usually falls during the first part of pregnancy before rising again towards term to a level similar to the value in the non-pregnant population.[512] Women with chronic hypertension may become normotensive by 10 to 13 weeks of gestation when antenatal care is usually initiated.

Defining hypertension during pregnancy

Blood pressure is a continuous variable and a cut-off point is employed to define 'normal' from 'abnormal' values. In defining an abnormal value, we should aim to identify those women who are at greater risk of an adverse outcome than those who are 'normal'. The conventional definition of hypertension in pregnancy is two readings of 140/90 mmHg taken at least 4 hours apart. Perinatal mortality is increased above this level.[513] However, about 20% of pregnant women in the UK have this reading at least once after 20 weeks of gestation. This will lead to intervention in 10% of all pregnant women but pre-eclampsia will develop only in 2% to 4% of pregnant women.[514] In a case series of 748 women who developed hypertension in pregnancy between 24 and 35 weeks (defined as greater than or equal to 140 mmHg systolic or greater than or equal to 90 mmHg diastolic), 46% later developed proteinuria greater than or equal to 1+ by dipstick on at least two occasions and 9.6% progressed to 'severe pre-eclampsia' (defined as hypertension greater than 160/110 mmHg with proteinuria, greater than 3+ of protein or thrombocytopenia).[515] The rate of progression to proteinuria was greater in those who enrolled in the study before 30 weeks. Pre-eclampsia was associated with a higher stillbirth and perinatal death rate. [EL = 3]

A large cohort study (n = 14 833) found that women with mean arterial pressure in the second trimester above 85 mmHg experienced a continuum of increased perinatal death, postnatal morbidity and small-for-gestational-age infants.[516a] In the third trimester, a similar continuum of increasing fetal deaths and morbidity was observed with mean arterial pressure above 95 mmHg.[516b] With or without proteinuria, an increased mean arterial pressure, at or above 90 mmHg, of extended duration in the second trimester, was associated with a higher stillbirth rate, pre-eclampsia and small-for-gestational-age infants. [EL = 2a]

The figure of 90 mmHg for the diastolic value corresponds approximately to 3 SD above the mean in early and mid pregnancy, 2 SD above the mean between 34 and 38 weeks of gestation and to 1.5 SD above the mean at term.[517] The finding of such a reading may therefore be more significant at 28 weeks of gestation than at term.

The diagnostic criteria of a 90 mmHg threshold with a 25 mmHg incremental rise is a definition based on evidence,[518–520] rather than the previously recommended diagnostic criteria by the American College of Obstetricians and Gynecologists (ACOG) (a rise in systolic blood pressure of 30 mmHg or of 15 mmHg in the diastolic pressure compared with booking or early pregnancy values),[511b] which included women who were not likely to suffer increased adverse outcomes. Subsequent guidelines from the US National Institutes of Health have advocated the abandonment of the ACOG diagnostic criteria.[511a]

Measuring blood pressure

The diagnosis of hypertension is dependent upon the accurate measurement of blood pressure. This accuracy depends largely on minimising measurement error. Failure to standardise technique will increase error and variability in measurement. A survey of midwives and obstetricians in one UK district general hospital reported in 1991 showed that compliance with recommendations on blood pressure measurement technique in pregnancy was poor.[521] The recommendations below relate to the American Heart Association guidelines produced in 1987,[522] which echoed previous expert opinion,[523] and concur with Shennan and Halligan's recommendations.[524]

- Use accurate equipment (mercury sphygmomanometer or validated alternative method).
- Use sitting or semi-reclining position so that the arm to be used is at the level of the heart. The practice of taking the blood pressure in the upper arm with the woman on her side will give falsely lower readings.
- Use appropriate size of cuff: at least 33 x 15 cm. There is less error introduced by using too large a cuff than by too small a cuff.
- Deflate slowly with a rate of 2 mmHg to 3 mmHg per second, taking at least 30 seconds to complete the whole deflation.
- Measure to nearest 2 mmHg to avoid digit preference.
- Obtain an estimated systolic pressure by palpation, to avoid auscultatory gap.
- Use Korotkoff V (disappearance of heart sounds) for measurement of diastolic pressure, as this is subject to less intra-observer and inter-observer variation than Korotkoff IV (muffling of heart sounds) and seems to correlate best with intra-arterial pressure in pregnancy. In the

15% of pregnant women whose diastolic pressure falls to zero before the last sound is heard, then both phase IV and phase V readings should be recorded (e.g. 148/84/0 mmHg).

- If two readings are necessary, use the average of the readings and not just the lowest reading, in order to minimise threshold avoidance.

As mercury will soon be eliminated from health settings (EU directive, EN 1060–2), a meta-analysis of validation studies of automated devices for blood pressure monitoring in pregnancy was conducted.[525] The findings indicated that, while the automated devices were accurate in pregnancy, they under-read by clinically significant amounts in women with pre-eclampsia. [EL = 3] This makes it important for automated devices to be assessed for accuracy before use, by a recognised protocol such as that recommended by the British Hypertension Society, and for readings from automated devices to be interpreted with caution.

A 15 cm cuff size may not be appropriate to use in the case of very thin arms, as blood pressure may be underestimated in those with arm circumferences less than 33 cm. For women with an arm circumference greater than 33 cm but less than 41 cm, a larger cuff should be used. In the case of very obese women, (arm circumference greater than 41 cm) thigh cuffs should be used.[526]

Regarding the use of which sound to use when recording diastolic blood pressure, an RCT of pregnancies managed by Korotkoff phase IV or phase V found that, although more episodes of severe hypertension were recorded with the use of the fourth Korotkoff sound, no differences in requirements for antihypertensive treatment, birthweight, fetal growth restriction or perinatal mortality were reported.[527] [EL = 1b] The fifth Korotkoff sound is also closer to the actual intra-arterial pressure and more reliably detected than the fourth Korotkoff sound.[528]

Assessment of risk factors for pre-eclampsia

Risk factors for pre-eclampsia are thought to include older age,[529] nulliparity,[530] long pregnancy interval,[531] a prior history of pre-eclampsia,[530] presence of a multiple pregnancy,[532] genetic susceptibility,[533] high BMI at first contact, and the presence of microvascular medical conditions such as diabetes or hypertension.[534] In the context of frequency of antenatal appointments, the assessment of a pregnant woman's overall level of risk for pre-eclampsia should be assessed at her first antenatal appointment so that a tailored plan of antenatal care can be formulated. Women with any of the following risk factors should be considered for an increased schedule of blood pressure screening [EL = 2b and 3]:[512]

- nulliparity (OR 2.71, 95% CI 1.16 to 6.34)
- age of 40 years and above (nulliparous OR 2.17, 95% CI 1.36 to 3.47; parous OR 2.05, 95% CI 1.47 to 2.87)
- family history of pre-eclampsia (e.g., pre-eclampsia in a mother or a sister, OR 5.27, 95% CI 1.57 to 17.64)
- history of previous pre-eclampsia (in first pregnancy, OR 8.23, 95% CI 6.49 to 10.45)
- BMI at or above 35 at first contact (OR 2.29, 95% CI 1.61 to 3.24)
- presence of multiple pregnancy (OR 2.76, 95% CI 1.99 to 3.82)
- pre-existing vascular disease (e.g., hypertension or diabetes).

Frequency of blood pressure monitoring

No evidence was found on when and how often blood pressure measurements should be taken. However, in a systematic review of RCTs comparing a reduced number of antenatal appointments with the standard number of antenatal appointments, no difference in the rates of pre-eclampsia were reported (pooled OR 0.37, 95% CI: 0.22 to 1.64).32 [EL = 1a]

Urinalysis

The diagnosis of pre-eclampsia depends on the presence of significant proteinuria as well as raised blood pressure. Reagent strips or 'dipsticks' are commonly used to detect proteinuria. The incidence of false positive results in random urine specimens may be up to 25% in trace reactions and 6% with 1+ reactions.[535] Therefore, dipsticks can only be a screening test and will not have much utility when not used in combination with blood pressure measurements.[536]

Due to considerable observer errors involved in dipstick urinanalysis, an RCOG Study Group recommended that automated dipstick readers be employed.[537] This can significantly improve false positive and false negative rates. An initial sample of 1+ or greater should be confirmed by a 24 hour urinary protein measurement or protein/creatinine ratio determination.[538] Although a finding of 300 mg/24 hours or more or a protein/creatinine ratio of 30 mg/mmol of creatinine is customarily regarded as significant,[539,540] a proteinuria threshold of 500 mg/24 hours has been suggested to be more predictive in relation to the likelihood of adverse outcome.[537]

Recommendation

At first contact, a woman's level of risk for pre-eclampsia should be evaluated so that a plan for her subsequent schedule of antenatal appointments can be formulated. The likelihood of developing pre-eclampsia during a pregnancy is increased in women who:

- are nulliparous
- are age 40 years or older
- have a family history of pre-eclampsia (e.g., pre-eclampsia in a mother or sister)
- have a prior history of pre-eclampsia
- have a BMI at or above 35 at first contact
- have a multiple pregnancy or pre-existing vascular disease (for example, hypertension or diabetes). [C]

Whenever blood pressure is measured in pregnancy, a urine sample should be tested at the same time for proteinuria. [C]

Standardised equipment, techniques and conditions for blood-pressure measurement should be used by all personnel whenever blood pressure is measured in the antenatal period, so that valid comparisons can be made. [C]

Pregnant women should be informed of the symptoms of advanced pre-eclampsia because these may be associated with poorer pregnancy outcomes for the mother or baby. Symptoms include headache, problems with vision, such as blurring or flashing before the eyes, bad pain just below the ribs, vomiting, and sudden swelling of face, hands or feet. [D]

Future research

Research is needed to determine the optimal frequency and timing of blood pressure measurement and on the role of screening for proteinuria.

11.3   Preterm birth

Preterm birth, or the birth of a baby before 37 weeks of gestation (less than 259 days) is one of the largest contributors to neonatal morbidity and mortality in industrialised countries. It is estimated to occur in 6% of babies in the UK, although this is difficult to assess since the UK does not collect gestational-age data at a national level.[541] Trials for the antenatal detection of preterm birth through routine cervical assessment or risk factor assessment have proved largely unsuccessful.

Vaginal examination assesses the maturation of the cervix, its dilatation at the internal os, length, consistency and position. Criteria for an abnormal 'test' result vary. A European multicentre RCT of 5440 women compared routine cervical examination at each antenatal appointment with a policy of avoiding cervical examination unless medically indicated.[542] Preterm birth occurred in 5.7% and 6.4% of the women assigned to the two groups (RR 0.88, 95% CI 0.72 to 1.09). The results of this study do not suggest a benefit from routine cervical examination. [EL = 1b]

A prospective multicentre study of vaginal ultrasonography assessed the association between cervical length and risk of preterm delivery.[543] A total of 2915 women were assessed at 24 weeks and 2531 of these women were assessed again at 28 weeks. The risk of preterm delivery was found to increase as the length of the cervix decreased. Women with shorter cervices were compared with women whose cervical lengths were above the 75th percentile. The relative risks are shown in Table 11.2. The sensitivity of this method as a screening test, however, was low at 54% and 70% for women with cervical lengths at or below 30 mm for 24 weeks and 28 weeks, respectively. [EL = 2a] Although transvaginal ultrasound screening appears to be able to predict increase risk of preterm birth, there is no evidence that this information can be used to improve outcomes.

Table 11.2   Relative risk of preterm delivery at 24 and 28 weeks of gestation by cervical length

Cervical length		24 weeks		28 weeks	
Percentile	(mm)	RR	95% CI	RR	95% CI
≤ 75th	40	1.98	1.2 to 3.27	2.8	1.41 to 5.56
≤ 50th	35	2.35	1.42 to 3.89	3.52	1.79 to 6.92
≤ 25th	30	3.79	2.32 to 6.19	5.39	2.82 to 10.28
≤ 10th	26	6.19	3.84 to 9.97	9.57	5.24 to 17.48
≤ 5th	22	9.49	5.95 to 15.15	13.88	7.68 to 25.10
≤ 1st	13	13.99	7.89 to 24.78	24.94	13.81 to 45.04

The same multicentre study also assessed the use of fetal fibronectin to predict preterm birth.[544] Measurements of fetal fibronectin in 10 456 women at 22 weeks were taken and high values after 13 weeks of gestation (with the exception of those in weeks 17 to 18) were found to be associated with a two- to three-fold increased risk of preterm birth (defined as less than 35 weeks of gestation). [EL = 2a] A slightly older multicentre cohort study reported that the presence of fetal fibronectin in the cervix and vagina from 22 to 24 weeks of gestation had a sensitivity of 63% for the prediction of preterm birth at less than 28 weeks.[545] [EL = 2a]

Using clinical risk assessment at 23 to 24 weeks of gestation, 2929 women were evaluated to assess the ability of this method to predict preterm birth.[546] Demographic factors, socioeconomic status, home and work environment, drug and alcohol use, and clinical history as well as current pregnancy factors were evaluated. Although specific risk factors were highly associated with preterm birth, this risk factor assessment failed to identify most women who subsequently had a preterm delivery. [EL = 2a]

Recommendation

Routine vaginal examination to assess the cervix is not an effective method of predicting preterm birth and should not be offered. [A]

Although cervical shortening identified by transvaginal ultrasound examination and increased levels of fetal fibronectin are associated with an increased risk for preterm birth, the evidence does not indicate that this information improves outcomes; therefore neither routine antenatal cervical assessment by transvaginal ultrasound nor the measurement of fetal fibronectin should be used to predict preterm birth in healthy pregnant women. [B]

11.4   Placenta praevia

Recommendation

Because most low-lying placentas detected at a 20 week anomaly scan will resolve by the time the baby is born, only a woman whose placenta extends over the internal cervical os should be offered another transabdominal scan at 36 weeks. If the transabdominal scan is unclear, a transvaginal scan should be offered. [C]

12.2   Measurement of symphysis–fundal distance

Use of measurement of symphysis–fundal height (in centimetres) may assist in recording an objective measure of uterine size. Interpretation of fetal growth from changes in fundal height measurement or palpation should bear in mind the errors intrinsic in the use of this technique in predicting placental insufficiency. Sequential measurements of symphysis–fundal height offer the potential to observe changes in fetal growth rate. The common causes of a size-for-dates discrepancy are:

- small-for-gestational-age
- hydramnios
- multifetal pregnancies
- molar pregnancy
- errors in estimating gestational age.

A systematic review of controlled trials compared symphysis–fundal height measurement with assessment by abdominal palpation alone.[566] Only one trial was included and no differences were detected in any of the outcomes measured, i.e. perinatal mortality, Apgar score less than 4 at 1 minute and 5 minutes, umbilical artery pH less than 7.15, admission to neonatal unit, antenatal hospitalisation for small-for-gestational-age, labour induction for small-for-gestational-age, caesarean section for small-for-gestational-age, birthweight less than tenth centile.

There is not enough evidence to evaluate the use of symphysis–fundal height measurement during antenatal care and it would seem unwise to abandon its use unless a much larger trial shows that it is unhelpful. Symphysis–fundal height measurement is among the least expensive tools in antenatal care, requiring minimal equipment, training and time.

The use of customised fundal height charts as a screening method to detect fetal growth anomalies was assessed in a non-RCT.[567] Customised fundal height charts display curves for fetal weight and fundal height while adjusting for maternal height, weight, parity and ethnic group. In this study, fundal height measurements were taken and plotted by community midwives in the intervention area at each antenatal appointment. In the control area, women received usual management, including fundal height assessment by abdominal palpation and standard recording. A significantly higher antenatal detection rate of small- and large-for-gestational-age babies was observed in the group from the study area compared with the women from the control area (OR 2.2, 95% CI 1.1 to 4.5 for small-for-gestational-age; OR 2.6, 95% CI 1.3 to 5.5 for large babies) with no increase in number of scans, but a reduction in the number of referrals for further investigation. No differences in perinatal outcome were reported. [EL = 2a] While this study showed that the use of customised growth charts might reduce false positive rates, the benefits of detecting small- or large-for-gestational-age infants without effective interventions remain unclear.

Recommendation

Pregnant women should be offered estimation of fetal size at each antenatal appointment to detect small- or large-for-gestational-age infants. [A]

Symphysis–fundal height should be measured and plotted at each antenatal appointment. [Good practice point]

Future research

Further research on more effective ways to detect and manage small- and large-for-gestational age fetuses is needed.

12.7 Umbilical and uterine artery Doppler ultrasound

One systematic review of five RCTs concluded that routine use of umbilical Doppler ultrasound had no effect on obstetric or neonatal outcomes, including perinatal mortality. The routine use of umbilical Doppler ultrasound increased the likelihood of needing further diagnostic interventions.[575] [EL = 1a]

A second systematic review of 27 primary observational studies examined the use of uterine Doppler ultrasound for the prediction of pre-eclampsia, fetal growth restriction and perinatal death in low- and high-risk populations. The predictive value was poor in women who were healthy and who had uncomplicated pregnancies (i.e. low-risk populations).[576] [EL = 2a]

Recommendations

The use of umbilical artery Doppler ultrasound for the prediction of fetal growth restriction should not be offered routinely. [A]

The use of uterine artery Doppler ultrasound for the prediction of pre-eclampsia should not be offered routinely. [B]

15 Auditable standards

Criterion	Exception	Definition of terms
A pregnant woman has the offer of an HIV test documented in her notes	A woman known to have HIV infection	
A pregnant woman has the offer of a hepatitis B virus test documented in her notes	A woman known to have hepatitis B viral infection	
A pregnant woman has the offer of a syphilis serology test documented in her notes		
A pregnant woman has the offer of a rubella susceptibility test documented in her notes		
A pregnant woman has the offer of a Down's syndrome screening test documented in her notes		An acceptable test is currently one with a minimum detection rate of 60% and an FPR no greater than 5% (see guideline recommendation in Section 9.2)

Appendix 1

Routine antenatal care for healthy pregnant women. Understanding NICE guidance: information for pregnant women, their families and the public

About this information

This information describes the guidance that the National Institute for Clinical Excellence (called NICE for short) has issued to the NHS on antenatal care. It is based on *Antenatal care: routine antenatal care for healthy pregnant women*, which is a clinical guideline produced by NICE for doctors, midwives and others working in the NHS in England and Wales. Although this information has been written chiefly for women who are pregnant or thinking of becoming pregnant, it may also be useful for family members and anyone with an interest in pregnancy or in healthcare in general.

Clinical guidelines

Clinical guidelines are recommendations for good practice. The recommendations in NICE guidelines are prepared by groups of health professionals, lay representatives with experience or knowledge of the condition being discussed, and scientists. The groups look at the evidence available on the best way of treating or managing a condition and make recommendations based on this evidence.

There is more about NICE and the way that the NICE guidelines are developed on the NICE website (www.nice.org.uk). You can download the booklet *The guideline development process – information for the public and the NHS* from the website, or you can order a copy by phoning 0870 1555 455.

What the recommendations cover

NICE clinical guidelines can look at different areas of diagnosis, treatment, care, self-help or a combination of these. The areas that a guideline covers depend on the topic. They are laid out at the start of the development of the guideline in a document called the scope.

The recommendations in *Antenatal care: routine antenatal care for healthy pregnant women*, which are also described here, cover:

- the care you can expect to receive from your midwife and doctors during your pregnancy, whether you plan to give birth at home or in hospital
- the information you can expect to receive
- what you can expect from antenatal appointments
- aspects of your lifestyle that you may want to consider (such as diet, exercise, alcohol and drug intake, sexual activity and smoking)
- routine screening tests for specific conditions
- occupational risk factors in pregnancy
- what will happen if your pregnancy goes beyond 41 weeks
- what will happen if your baby is bottom first (known as the breech position) for the birth.

They do not cover:

- information on birth or parenthood and on preparing for them
- extra care you may need if you are expecting more than one baby
- extra care you may need if you develop additional problems (such as pre-eclampsia) or if your unborn baby has any anomalies.

The information that follows tells you about the NICE guideline on antenatal care. It doesn't attempt to explain pregnancy or describe any extra care you may need for specific problems. If you want to find out more about pregnancy and antenatal care, or if you have questions about the specific treatments and options mentioned in this booklet, talk to your local midwife or doctor.

How guidelines are used in the NHS

In general, health professionals working in the NHS are expected to follow NICE's clinical guidelines. But there will be times when the recommendations won't be suitable for someone because of a specific medical condition, general health, their wishes or a combination of these. If you think that the treatment or care you receive does not match the treatment or care described in the pages that follow, you should discuss your concerns with your midwife or doctor.

If you want to read the other versions of this guideline

There are three versions of this guideline:

- this one
- the 'NICE guideline' *Antenatal care: routine antenatal care for healthy pregnant women*, which has been issued to people working in the NHS
- the full guideline, which contains all the details of the guideline recommendations, how they were developed and information about the evidence on which they are based.

All versions of the guideline are available from the NICE website (www.nice.org.uk/). This version and the NICE guideline are also available from the NHS Response Line – phone 0870 1555 455 and give the reference number(s) of the booklet(s) you want (N0310 for this version, N0311 for this version in English and Welsh, and N0309 for the NICE guideline).

Guideline recommendations

The guideline recommendations cover the routine care that all healthy pregnant women can expect to receive during their pregnancy.

You will receive extra care, in addition to what we describe here, if you are pregnant with more than one baby, if you already have certain medical conditions or if you develop a health problem during your pregnancy.

The guideline does not cover the care that women receive during or after a birth.

About antenatal care

Antenatal care is the care that you receive from health professionals during your pregnancy. It includes information on services that are available and support to help you make choices. You should be able to access antenatal care services that are readily and easily available and sensitive to your needs.

During your pregnancy you should be offered a series of antenatal appointments to check on your health and the health of your baby. During these appointments you should be given information about your care.

Your midwife or doctor should give you information in writing or in some other form that you can easily access and understand. If you have a physical, cognitive or sensory disability, for example, or if you do not speak or read English, they should provide you with information in an appropriate format.

A record should be kept of the care you receive. You should be asked to keep your maternity notes at home with you and to bring them along to all your antenatal appointments.

You have a right to take part in making decisions about your care. To be able to do this you will need to feel confident that you:

- understand what is involved
- feel comfortable about asking questions
- can discuss your choices with your antenatal care team.

Your care team should support you in this by making sure you have access to antenatal classes and information that is based on the best research evidence available.

While you are pregnant you should normally see a small number of health practitioners, led by your midwife and/or doctor (GP), on a regular basis. They should be people with whom you feel comfortable.

Antenatal appointments

The exact number of antenatal appointments and how often you have them will depend on your individual situation. If you are expecting your first child, you are likely to have up to ten appointments. If you have had children before, you should have around seven appointments. Some of them may take place at your home if this suits you. Your antenatal appointments should take place in a setting where you feel able to discuss sensitive issues that may affect you (such as domestic violence, sexual abuse, mental illness or drug use).

Early in your pregnancy your midwife or doctor should give you appropriate written or other information about the likely number, timing and purpose of your appointments, according to the options that are available to you. You should have a chance to discuss the schedule with them.

The table on page xx [20] gives a brief guide to what usually happens at each antenatal appointment.

What should happen at the appointments
The aim of antenatal appointments is to check on you and your baby's progress and to provide you with clear information and explanations, in discussions with you, about your care. At each appointment you should have the chance to ask questions and discuss any concerns you have with your midwife or doctor.

Each appointment should have a specific purpose. You will need longer appointments early in your pregnancy to allow plenty of time for your midwife or doctor to assess you and discuss your care. Wherever possible the appointments should include any routine tests you need, to cut down on any inconvenience to you.

Appointments in early pregnancy
Your first appointment should be fairly early in your pregnancy (before 12 weeks). Your midwife or doctor should use it to identify your needs (such as whether you need additional care) and should ask you about your health and any previous physical or mental illness you have had, so that you can be referred for further assessment or care, if necessary.

They should also give you an opportunity to let them know, if you wish, if you are in a vulnerable situation or if you have experienced anything which means you might need extra support, such as domestic violence, sexual abuse or female genital mutilation (such as female circumcision).

Your midwife or doctor should give you information on pregnancy care services and the options available, maternity benefits, diet, other aspects of your life which may affect your health or the health of your baby, and on routine screening tests. They should explain to you that decisions on whether to have these tests rest with you, and they should make sure that you understand what those decisions will mean for you and your baby.

During one of these early appointments your midwife or doctor should check your blood pressure and test your urine for the presence of protein. They should also weigh you and measure your height. If you are significantly overweight or underweight you may need extra care. You should not usually be weighed again.

Appointments in later pregnancy

The rest of your antenatal appointments should be tailored according to your individual health needs. They should include some routine tests (see page 120) which are used to check for certain conditions or infections. Most women are not affected by these conditions, but the tests are offered so that the small number of women who are affected can be identified and offered treatment.

Your midwife or doctor should explain to you in advance the reason for offering you a particular test. When discussing the test with you, they should make it clear that you can choose whether or not to have the test, as you wish.

During your appointments your midwife or doctor should give you the results of any tests you have had. You should be able to discuss your options with them and what you want to do.

Checking on your baby's development

At each antenatal appointment your midwife or doctor should check on your baby's growth. To do this, they should measure the distance from the top of your womb to your pubic bone. The measurement should be recorded in your notes.

The rest of this information tells you more about what you can expect from your midwife and/or doctor during your pregnancy and about the tests that you should be offered. It also tells you what you can expect if your pregnancy continues a week or more beyond your due date or if your baby is in the breech position (that is, bottom first) prior to birth.

Advice on money matters and work

Your midwife or doctor should give you information about your maternity and benefits rights. You can also get information from the Department of Trade and Industry – phone the helpline on 08457 47 47 47, call 08701 502 500 for information leaflets or visit the website at www.dti. gov.uk/er/workingparents.htm. The Government's interactive guidance website (www.tiger.gov. uk) also has information. Up-to-date information on maternity benefits can also be found on the Department for Work and Pensions website (www.dwp.gov.uk).

Your midwife or doctor should ask you about the work that you do, and should tell you about any possible risks to your pregnancy. For most women it is safe to continue working while you are pregnant, but there are hazards in some jobs that could put you at risk. More information about risks at work is available from the Health and Safety Executive; the website address is www.hse. gov.uk/mothers/index.htm or you can phone 08701 545 500 for information.

Lifestyle advice

There are a number of things you can do to help yourself stay healthy while you are pregnant. Your midwife or doctor can tell you more about them.

Exercise

You can continue or start moderate exercise before or during your pregnancy. Some vigorous activities, however, such as contact sports or vigorous racquet games, may carry extra risks, such as falling or putting too much strain on your joints. You should avoid scuba diving while you are pregnant as this can cause problems in the developing baby.

Alcohol

Excess alcohol can harm your unborn baby. If you do drink while you are pregnant, it is better to limit yourself to one standard unit of alcohol a day (roughly the equivalent of 125 ml – a small glass – of wine, half a pint of beer, cider or lager, or a single measure of spirits).

Smoking

Smoking increases the risks of your baby being underweight or being born too early – in both instances, your baby's health may be affected. You will reduce these risks if you can give up smoking, or at least smoke less, while you are pregnant. You and your baby will benefit if you can give up, no matter how late in your pregnancy.

If you need it, your midwife or doctor should offer you help to give up or cut down on smoking or to stay off it if you have recently given up. The NHS pregnancy smoking helpline can also provide advice and support – the phone number is 0800 169 9 169.

Cannabis

If you use cannabis, and especially if you smoke it, it may be harmful to your baby.

Sexual activity

There is no evidence that sexual activity is harmful while you are pregnant.

Travel

When you travel by car you should always wear a three-point seatbelt above and below your bump (not over it).

If you are planning to travel abroad you should talk to your midwife or doctor, who should tell you more about flying, vaccinations and travel insurance.

The risk of deep vein thrombosis from travelling by air may be higher when you are pregnant. Your midwife or doctor can tell you more about how you may be able to reduce the risk by wearing correctly fitted compression stockings.

Prescription and over-the-counter medicines

Only a few prescription and over-the-counter medicines have been shown to be safe for pregnant women by good-quality studies. While you are pregnant, your doctor should only prescribe medicines where the benefits are greater than the risks. You should use as few over-the counter-medicines as possible.

Complementary therapies

Few complementary therapies are known to be safe and effective during pregnancy. You should check with your midwife, doctor or pharmacist before using them.

Diet and food

Folic acid

Your midwife or doctor should give you information about taking folic acid (400 micrograms a day). If you do this when you are trying to get pregnant and for the first 12 weeks of your pregnancy it reduces the risk of having a baby with conditions which are known as neural tube defects, such as spina bifida (a condition where parts of the backbone do not form properly, leaving a gap or split which causes damage to the baby's central nervous system).

Vitamin A

Excess levels of vitamin A can cause abnormalities in unborn babies. You should avoid taking vitamin A supplements (with more than 700 micrograms of vitamin A) while you are pregnant. You should also avoid eating liver (which may contain high levels of vitamin A), or anything made from liver.

Other food supplements

You do not need to take iron supplements as a matter of routine while you are pregnant. They do not improve your health and you may experience unpleasant side effects, such as constipation.

You should not be offered vitamin D supplements as a matter of routine while you are pregnant. There is not enough evidence to tell whether they are of any benefit to pregnant women.

Food hygiene

Your midwife or doctor should give you information on bacterial infections such as listeriosis and salmonella that can be picked up from food and can harm your unborn baby. In order to avoid them while you are pregnant it is best:

- if you drink milk, to keep to pasteurised or UHT milk
- avoid eating mould-ripened soft cheese such as Camembert or Brie and blue-veined cheese (there is no risk with hard cheese such as Cheddar, or with cottage cheese or processed cheese)
- avoid eating paté (even vegetable paté)
- avoid eating uncooked or undercooked ready?prepared meals
- avoid eating raw or partially cooked eggs or food that may contain them (such as mayonnaise)
- avoid raw or partially cooked meat, especially poultry.

Toxoplasmosis is an infection that does not usually cause symptoms in healthy women. Very occasionally it can cause problems for the unborn baby of an infected mother. You can pick it up from undercooked or uncooked meat (such as salami, which is cured) and from the faeces of infected cats or contaminated soil or water. To help avoid this infection while you are pregnant it is best to:

- wash your hands before you handle food
- wash all fruit and vegetables, including ready?prepared salads, before you eat them
- make sure you thoroughly cook raw meats and ready?prepared chilled meats
- wear gloves and wash your hands thoroughly after gardening or handling soil
- avoid contact with cat faeces (in cat litter or in soil).

Screening tests

Early in your pregnancy you should be offered a number of tests. The purpose of these tests is to check whether you have any conditions or infections that could affect you or your baby's health.

Your doctor or midwife should tell you more about the purpose of any test you are offered. You do not have to have a particular test if you do not want it. However, the information they can provide may help your antenatal care team to provide the best care possible during your pregnancy and the birth. The test results may also help you to make choices during pregnancy.

Ultrasound scans

Early in your pregnancy (usually around 10 to 13 weeks) you should be offered an ultrasound scan to estimate when your baby is due and to check whether you are expecting more than one baby. If you see your midwife or doctor for the first time when you are more than 13 weeks pregnant, they should offer you a scan then.

Between 18 and 20 weeks you should be offered another scan to check for physical anomalies in your baby. You should not have any further routine scans, as they have not been shown to be useful.

Blood tests

Anaemia

You should be offered two tests for anaemia: one at your first antenatal appointment and another between your 28th and 30th week. Anaemia is often caused by a lack of iron. If you develop anaemia while you are pregnant it is usually because you do not have enough iron to meet your baby's need for it in addition to your own; you may be offered further blood tests. You should be offered an iron supplement if appropriate.

Blood group and rhesus D status

Early in your pregnancy you should be offered tests to find out your blood group and your Rhesus D (RhD) status. Your midwife or doctor should tell you more about them and what they are for. If you are RhD negative you should be offered an anti-D injection to prevent future babies developing problems. Your partner may also be offered tests to confirm whether you need an anti-D injection. You can find more information about this in Guidance on the routine use of anti-D prophylaxis for RhD negative women: information for patients, published by NICE in 2002 and available at www.nice.org.uk/pdf/Anti_d_patient_leaflet.pdf.

Early in your pregnancy, and again between your 28th and 36th week, you should be offered tests to check for red cell antibodies. If the levels of these antibodies are significant, you should be offered a referral to a specialist centre for more investigation and advice on managing the rest of your pregnancy.

Screening for infections

Your midwife or doctor should offer you a number of tests, as a matter of routine, to check for certain infections. These infections are not common, but they can cause problems if they are not detected and treated.

Asymptomatic bacteriuria

Asymptomatic bacteriuria is a bladder infection that has no symptoms. Identifying and treating it can reduce the risk of giving birth too early. It can be detected by testing a urine sample.

Hepatitis B virus

Hepatitis B virus is a potentially serious infection that can affect the liver. Many people have no symptoms, however. It can be passed from a mother to her baby (through blood or body fluids), but may be prevented if the baby is vaccinated at birth. The infection can be detected in the mother's blood.

HIV

HIV usually causes no symptoms at first but can lead to AIDS. HIV can be passed from a mother to her baby, but this risk can be greatly reduced if the mother is diagnosed before the birth. The infection can be detected through a blood test. If you are pregnant and are diagnosed with HIV you should receive specialist care.

German measles (rubella)

Screening for German measles (rubella) is offered so that if you are not immune you can choose to be vaccinated after you have given birth. This should usually protect you and future pregnancies. Testing you for rubella in pregnancy does not aim to identify it in the baby you are carrying.

Syphilis

Syphilis is rare in the UK. It is a sexually transmitted infection that can also be passed from a mother to her baby. Mothers and babies can be successfully treated if it is detected and treated early. A person with syphilis may show no symptoms for many years. A positive test result does not always mean you have syphilis, but your healthcare providers should have clear procedures for managing your care if you test positive.

Screening tests for Down's syndrome

Down's syndrome is a condition caused by the presence of an extra chromosome in a baby's cells. It occurs by chance at conception and is irreversible.

In the first part of your pregnancy you should be offered screening tests to check whether your baby is likely to have Down's syndrome. Your midwife or doctor should tell you more about Down's syndrome, the tests you are being offered and what the results may mean for you. You have the right to choose whether to have all, some or none of these tests. You can opt out of the screening process at any time if you wish.

Screening tests will only indicate that a baby may have Down's syndrome. If the test results are positive, you should be offered further tests to confirm whether your baby does, in fact, have Down's syndrome. The time at which you are tested will depend on what kinds of tests are used.

Screening tests for Down's syndrome are not always right. They can sometimes wrongly show as positive, suggesting the baby does have Down's syndrome when in fact it does not. This type of result is known as a 'false positive'. The number of occasions on which this happens with a particular test is called its 'false positive rate'.

At present you should be offered screening tests with a false positive rate of less than 5 out of 100 and which detect at least 60 out of 100 cases of Down's syndrome. The tests which meet this standard are:

- from 11 to 14 weeks:
  - nuchal translucency (an ultrasound scan)
  - combined test (an ultrasound scan and blood test)
- from 14 to 20 weeks:
  - triple test (a blood test)
  - quadruple test (a blood test)
- from 11 to 14 weeks and 14 to 20 weeks:
  - integrated test (an ultrasound scan and blood test)
  - serum integrated test (a blood test).

By April 2007 all pregnant women should be offered screening tests for Down's syndrome with a false positive rate of less than 3 out of 100 and which detect more than 75 out of 100 cases. The tests which meet this standard are:

- from 11 to 14 weeks
  - combined test
- from 14 to 20 weeks
  - quadruple test
- from 11 to 14 weeks and 14 to 20 weeks
  - integrated test
  - serum integrated test.

Pre-eclampsia

Pre-eclampsia is an illness that happens in the second half of pregnancy. Although it is usually mild, it can cause serious problems for you and your baby if it is not detected and treated.

Your midwife or doctor should tell you more about the symptoms of advanced pre-eclampsia, which include:

- headache
- problems with vision, such as blurred vision or lights flashing before the eyes
- bad pain just below the ribs
- vomiting
- sudden swelling of the face, hands or feet.

They should assess your risk of pre-eclampsia at your first antenatal appointment in order to plan for the rest of your appointments.

You are more likely to develop pre-eclampsia when you are pregnant if you:

- have had it before
- have not been pregnant before
- are 40 years old or more
- have a mother or sister who has had pre-eclampsia
- are overweight at the time of your first antenatal appointment
- are expecting more than one baby or you already have high blood pressure or diabetes.

Whenever your blood pressure is measured during your pregnancy, a urine sample should be tested at the same time for protein (as this can be another sign of pre-eclampsia).

Whenever a member of your healthcare team measures your blood pressure they should use the same type of equipment, method and conditions so that the results at different times of your pregnancy can be compared.

Placenta praevia

Placenta praevia is when the placenta is low lying in the womb and covers all or part of the entrance (the cervix). In most women, the placenta usually goes back into a normal position before the birth and does not cause a problem. If it does not, you may need a Caesarean section.

If the 20th week ultrasound scan shows that your placenta extends over the cervix you should be offered another abdominal scan at 36 weeks. If this second abdominal scan is unclear, you should be offered a vaginal scan.

Tests not offered as a matter of routine

There are a number of screening tests which have sometimes been offered to women in the past or have been suggested for routine antenatal care. The following tests should not be offered to you as a matter of routine because they have not been shown to improve outcomes for mothers or babies:

- cardiotocography (a record of the trace of a baby's heartbeat, which is monitored through electronic sensors placed on the mother's abdomen, sometimes called a trace or CTG)
- Doppler ultrasound (an ultrasound scan which measures the blood flow between the baby and the mother)
- vaginal examinations to predict whether a baby may be born too early
- routine breast and pelvic examinations

- screening for gestational diabetes mellitus (a form of diabetes triggered by pregnancy)
- daily counting and recording of the baby's movements
- routine screening for infection with:
  - group B streptococcus (GBS); this is a bacterial infection that can affect the baby (if you have previously had a baby with neonatal GBS, you should be offered treatment around the time of your labour)
  - toxoplasmosis (see page 120)
  - asymptomatic bacterial vaginosis (a vaginal infection which produces no symptoms)
  - cytomegalovirus; infection with this virus can affect the baby
  - chlamydia trachomatis (a vaginal infection) where there are no symptoms (a national screening programme for chlamydia is due to start soon, so arrangements for this will probably change).

There is not enough evidence about the effectiveness or cost-effectiveness of routine screening for hepatitis C virus to justify it.

Managing common problems

Pregnancy brings a variety of physical and emotional changes. Many of these changes are normal, and pose no danger to you or your baby, even though some of them may cause you discomfort. If you want to discuss these things, your midwife or doctor is there to give you information and support.

Nausea and sickness

You may feel sick or experience vomiting in the early part of your pregnancy. This does not indicate that anything is wrong. It usually stops around your 16th to 20th week. Your midwife or doctor should give you information about this. You may find that using wrist acupressure or taking ginger tablets or syrup helps to relieve these symptoms. If you have severe problems your doctor may give you further help or prescribe antihistamine tablets for sickness.

Heartburn

Your midwife or doctor should give you information about what to do if you suffer from heartburn during your pregnancy. If it persists they should offer you antacids to relieve the symptoms.

Constipation

If you suffer from constipation while you are pregnant your midwife or doctor should tell you ways in which you can change your diet (such as eating more bran or wheat fibre) to help relieve the problem.

Haemorrhoids

There is no research evidence on how well treatments for haemorrhoids work. If you suffer from haemorrhoids, however, your midwife or doctor should give you information on what you can do to change your diet. If your symptoms continue to be troublesome they may offer you a cream to help relieve the problem.

Backache

Backache is common in pregnant women. You may find that massage therapy, exercising in water or going to group or individual back care classes may help you to relieve the pain.

Varicose veins

Varicose veins are also common. They are not harmful during pregnancy. Compression stockings may relieve the symptoms (such as swelling of your legs), although they will not stop the veins from appearing.

Vaginal discharge

You may get more vaginal discharge than usual while you are pregnant. This is usually nothing to worry about. However, if the discharge becomes itchy or sore, or smells unpleasant, or you have pain on passing urine, tell your midwife or doctor, as you may have an infection.

Thrush

If you have thrush (a yeast infection – also known as Candida or vaginal candidiasis) your doctor may prescribe cream and/or pessaries for you to apply to the area for 1 week.

While you are pregnant it is best to avoid taking any medicine for thrush that needs to be swallowed. There is no evidence about how safe or effective these are for pregnant women.

If you are pregnant beyond 41 weeks

If your pregnancy goes beyond 41 weeks there is a greater risk of certain problems for your baby. You should be offered a 'membrane sweep', which involves having a vaginal examination; this stimulates the neck of your womb (known as the cervix) to produce hormones which may trigger spontaneous labour. If you choose not to have a membrane sweep, or it does not cause you to go into labour, you should be offered a date to have your labour induced (started off).

If you decide against having labour induced and your pregnancy continues to 42 weeks or beyond, you should be offered ultrasound scans and may have your baby's heartbeat monitored regularly, depending on your individual care plan.

You can find more information about what induction of labour means from the guideline, which you can find on the NICE website at: www.nice.org.uk/pdf/inductionoflabourinfoforwomen.pdf.

If your baby is positioned bottom first

At around 36 weeks your midwife or doctor will check your baby's position by examining your abdomen. If they think the baby is not in a 'head down' position, which is best for the birth, you should be offered an ultrasound scan to check.

If your baby is bottom first (known as the breech position) your midwife or doctor should offer you a procedure called external cephalic version (ECV). ECV means they will gently push the baby from outside, to move it round to 'head first'. It does not always work.

Your midwife or doctor should give you more information about what ECV involves.

You should not be offered ECV if you:

- are in labour
- have a scar or abnormality in your womb
- have vaginal bleeding
- have a medical condition

or if:

- your waters have broken
- your baby's health seems fragile.

If you choose to have ECV and it cannot be done at 37 weeks, it should be done at 36 weeks.

Where you can find more information

If this is your first pregnancy, your midwife or doctor should give you a copy of *The pregnancy book* (published by Health Departments in England and Wales). It tells you about many aspects of pregnancy including: how the baby develops; deciding where to have a baby; feelings and relationships during pregnancy; antenatal care and classes; information for expectant fathers; problems in pregnancy; when pregnancy goes wrong; and rights and benefits information. It also contains a list of useful organisations.

If you need further information about any aspects of antenatal care or the care that you are receiving, please ask your midwife, doctor or a relevant member of your health team. You can discuss this guideline with them if you wish, especially if you aren't sure about anything in this booklet. They will be able to explain things to you.

For further information about the National Institute for Clinical Excellence (NICE), the Clinical Guidelines Programme or other versions of this guideline (including the sources of evidence used to inform the recommendations for care), you can visit the NICE website at www.nice.org.uk.

At the NICE website you can also find information for the public about other maternity-related guidance on:

- pregnancy and childbirth: electronic fetal monitoring (guideline C)
- pregnancy and childbirth: induction of labour (guideline D)
- pregnancy – routine anti-D prophylaxis for rhesus negative women (technology appraisal no. 41).

You can get information on common problems during pregnancy from NHS Direct (telephone 0845 46 47; website www.nhsdirect.nhs.uk).

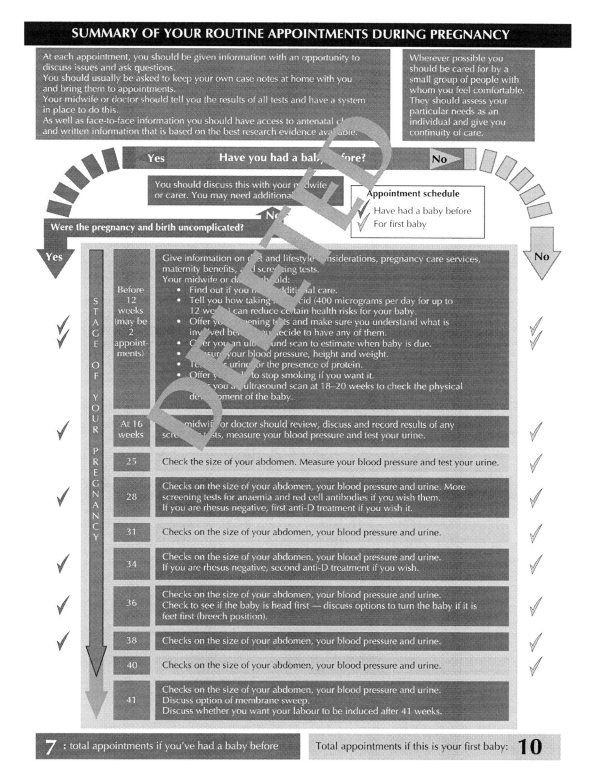

SUMMARY OF YOUR ROUTINE APPOINTMENTS DURING PREGNANCY

At each appointment, you should be given information with an opportunity to discuss issues and ask questions.
You should usually be asked to keep your own case notes at home with you and bring them to appointments.
Your midwife or doctor should tell you the results of all tests and have a system in place to do this.
As well as face-to-face information you should have access to antenatal classes and written information that is based on the best research evidence available.

Wherever possible you should be cared for by a small group of people with whom you feel comfortable. They should assess your particular needs as an individual and give you continuity of care.

Have you had a baby before? — Yes / No

You should discuss this with your midwife or carer. You may need additional...

Appointment schedule
✓ Have had a baby before
✓ For first baby

Were the pregnancy and birth uncomplicated? — Yes / No

STAGE OF YOUR PREGNANCY

Give information on diet and lifestyle considerations, pregnancy care services, maternity benefits, and screening tests.
Your midwife or doctor should:
- Find out if you need additional care.
- Tell you how taking folic acid (400 micrograms per day for up to 12 weeks) can reduce certain health risks for your baby.
- Offer you screening tests and make sure you understand what is involved before you decide to have any of them.
- Offer you an ultrasound scan to estimate when baby is due.
- Measure your blood pressure, height and weight.
- Test your urine for the presence of protein.
- Offer you help to stop smoking if you want it.
- Offer you an ultrasound scan at 18–20 weeks to check the physical development of the baby.

Before 12 weeks (may be 2 appointments)

At 16 weeks — midwife or doctor should review, discuss and record results of any screening tests, measure your blood pressure and test your urine.

25 — Check the size of your abdomen. Measure your blood pressure and test your urine.

28 — Checks on the size of your abdomen, your blood pressure and urine. More screening tests for anaemia and red cell antibodies if you wish them. If you are rhesus negative, first anti-D treatment if you wish it.

31 — Checks on the size of your abdomen, your blood pressure and urine.

34 — Checks on the size of your abdomen, your blood pressure and urine. If you are rhesus negative, second anti-D treatment if you wish.

36 — Checks on the size of your abdomen, your blood pressure and urine. Check to see if the baby is head first — discuss options to turn the baby if it is feet first (breech position).

38 — Checks on the size of your abdomen, your blood pressure and urine.

40 — Checks on the size of your abdomen, your blood pressure and urine.

41 — Checks on the size of your abdomen, your blood pressure and urine. Discuss option of membrane sweep. Discuss whether you want your labour to be induced after 41 weeks.

7 : total appointments if you've had a baby before

Total appointments if this is your first baby: **10**

References

(2003 version)

1. Expert Maternity Group. Woman centred care. In: Department of Health. *Changing Childbirth. Report of the Expert Maternity Group.* London: HMSO; 1993. p. 5–8.

2. Garcia J, Loftus-Hills A (National Perinatal Epidemiology Unit: Oxford University). An overview of research on women's views of antenatal care. Personal communication 2001.

3. Singh D, Newburn M, editors. *Access to Maternity Information and Support; the Experiences and Needs of Women Before and After Giving Support.* London: National Childbirth Trust; 2000.

4. Cochrane AL. *Effectiveness and efficiency. Random reflections on health services.* London: Nuffield Provincial Hospitals Trust; 1972.

5. Department of Health. Screening for infectious diseases in pregnancy: standards to support the UK antenatal screening programme. [In preparation]. 2003.

6. National Institute for Clinical Excellence. *Information for national collaborating centres and guideline development groups.* Guideline development process series 3. London: Oaktree Press; 2001.

7. Henderson J, McCandlish R, Kumiega L, Petrou S. Systematic review of economic aspects of alternative modes of delivery. *BJOG* 2001;108:149–57.

8. Bekker H, Thornton JG, Airey CM, Connelly JB, Hewison J, Robinson MB, *et al.* Informed decision making: An annotated bibliography and systematic review. *Health Technology Assessment* 1999;3(1):1–156.

9. Department of Health. *Changing childbirth. Report of the Expert Maternity Group.* London: HMSO; 1993.

10. Audit Commission for Local Authorities, NHS in England and Wales. *First class delivery: improving maternity services in England and Wales.* London: Audit Commission Publications; 1997. p. 1–98.

11. Murray J, Cuckle H, Sehmi I, Wilson C, Ellis A. Quality of written information used in Down syndrome screening. *Prenatal Diagnosis* 2001;21:138–42.

12. Thornton JG, Hewison J, Lilford RJ, Vail A. A randomised trial of three methods of giving information about prenatal testing. *British Medical Journal* 1995;311:1127–30.

13. O'Cathain A, Walters SJ, Nicholl JP, Thomas KJ, Kirkham M. Use of evidence based leaflets to promote informed choice in maternity care: randomised controlled trial in everyday practice. [comment]. *British Medical Journal* 2002;324:643.

14. Stapleton H. Qualitative study of evidence based leaflets in maternity care. *British Medical Journal* 2002;324:639.

15. Dodds R, Newburn M. Support during screening: an NCT report. *Modern Midwife* 1997;7:23–6.

16. Carroll JC, Brown JB, Reid AJ, Pugh P. Women's experience of maternal serum screening. *Canadian Family Physician* 2000;46:614–20.

17. Marteau TM, Slack J, Kidd J, Shaw, RW. Presenting a routine screening test in antenatal care: practice observed. *Public Health* 1992;106(2):131–41.

18. Smith D, Shaw RW, Marteau T. Lack of knowledge in health professionals: a barrier to providing information to patients. *Quality in Health Care* 1994;3:75–8.

19. Smith DK, Shaw RW, Slack J, Marteau TM. Training obstetricians and midwives to present screening tests: evaluation of two brief interventions. *Prenatal Diagnosis* 1995;15:317–24.

20. Green JM. Serum screening for Down's syndrome: experiences of obstetricians in England and Wales. *British Medical Journal* 1994;309:769–72.

21. Michie S, Marteau TM. Non-response bias in prospective studies of patients and health care professionals. *International Journal of Social Research Methodology* 1999;2:203–12.

22. Marteau TM. Towards informed decisions about prenatal testing: a review. *Prenatal Diagnosis* 1995;15(13):1215–26.

23. National Health Service. *The Pregnancy Book.* London: Health Promotion England; 2001.

24. Bro Taf Health Authority. *Tests for you and your baby during pregnancy.* Cardiff, Wales: Bro Taf Health Authority; 2000.

25. Nolan ML, Hicks C. Aims, processes and problems of antenatal education as identified by three groups of childbirth teachers. *Midwifery* 1997;13:179–88.

26. Johnson R, Slade P. Does fear of childbirth during pregnancy predict emergency caesarean section? *BJOG* 2002;109:1213–21.

27. Gagnon AJ. Individual or group antenatal education for childbirth/parenthood. *Cochrane Database of Systematic Reviews* 2001;(3).

28. Hibbard BM, Robinson JO, Pearson JF, Rosen M, Taylor A. The effectiveness of antenatal education. *Health Education Journal* 1979;38:39–46.

29. Rautauva P, Erkkola R, Sillanpaa M. The outcome and experiences of first pregnancy in relation to the mother's childbirth knowledge: The Finnish Family Competence Study. *Journal of Advanced Nursing* 1991;16:1226–32.

30. Lumley J, Brown S. Attenders and nonattenders at childbirth education classes in Australia: how do they and their births differ? *Birth* 1993;20:123–30.

31. Sullivan P. Felt learning needs of pregnant women. *Canadian Nurse* 1993;89:42.

32. Villar J, Khan-Neelofur D. Patterns of routine antenatal care for low–risk pregnancy. *Cochrane Database of Systematic Reviews* 2003;(1).

33. Hodnett ED. Continuity of caregivers for care during pregnancy and childbirth. *Cochrane Database of Systematic Reviews* 2001;(3).

34. Waldenstrom U, Turnbull D. A systematic review comparing continuity of midwifery care with standard maternity services. *British Journal of Obstetrics and Gynaecology* 1998;105:1160–70.

35. North Staffordshire Changing Childbirth Research Team. A randomised study of midwifery caseload care and traditional 'shared care'. *Midwifery* 2000;16:295–302.

36. Homer CS, Davis GK, Brodie PM, Sheehan A, Barclay LM, Wills J, *et al.* Collaboration in maternity care: a randomised controlled trial comparing community-based continuity of care with standard hospital care. *BJOG* 2001;108:16–22.

37. Homer CS, Davis GK, Brodie PM. What do women feel about community-based antenatal care? *Australian and New Zealand Journal of Public Health* 2000;24:590–5.

38. Biro MA, Waldenstrom U. Team midwifery care in a tertiary level obstetric service: a randomized controlled trial. *Birth* 2000;27:168–73.

39. Waldenstrom U. Does team midwife care increase satisfaction with antenatal, intrapartum, and postpartum care? A randomized controlled trial. [see comments.]. *Birth* 2000;27:156–67.

40. Blondel B, Breart G. Home visits for pregnancy complications and management of antenatal care: an overview of three randomized controlled trials. *British Journal of Obstetrics and Gynaecology* 1992;99:283–6.

41. Lilford RJ, Kelly M, Baines A, Cameron S, Cave M, Guthrie K, *et al*. Effect of using protocols on medical care: randomised trial of three methods of taking an antenatal history. *British Medical Journal* 1992;305:1181–4.

42. Elbourne D, Richardson M, Chalmers I, Waterhouse I, Holt E. The Newbury Maternity Care Study: a randomized controlled trial to assess a policy of women holding their own obstetric records. *British Journal of Obstetrics and Gynaecology* 1987;94:612–19.

43. Homer CS, Davis GK, Everitt LS. The introduction of a woman-held record into a hospital antenatal clinic: the bring your own records study. *Australian and New Zealand Journal of Public Health* 1999;39:54–7.

44. Lovell A, Zander LI, James CE, Foot S, Swan AV, Reynolds A. The St. Thomas's Hospital maternity case notes study: a randomised controlled trial to assess the effects of giving expectant mothers their own maternity case notes. *Paediatric and Perinatal Epidemiology* 1987;1:57–66.

45. Petrou S, Kupek E, Vause S, Maresh M. Antenatal visits and adverse perinatal outcomes: results from a British population-based study. *European Journal of Obstetrics Gynecology and Reproductive Biology* 2003;106:40–9.

46. Carroli G, Villar J, Piaggio G, Khan-Neelofur D, Gulmezoglu M, Mugford M, *et al*. WHO systematic review of randomised controlled trials of routine antenatal care. *Lancet* 2001;357:1565–70.

47. Clement S, Sikorski J, Wilson J, Das S, Smeeton N. Women's satisfaction with traditional and reduced antenatal visit schedules. *Midwifery* 1996;12:120–8.

48. Hildingsson I, Waldenstrom U, Radestad I. Women's expectations on antenatal care as assessed in early pregnancy: Number of visits, continuity of caregiver and general content. *Acta Obstetricia et Gynecologica Scandinavica* 2002;81:118–25.

49. Henderson J, Roberts T, Sikorski J, Wilson J, Clement S. An economic evaluation comparing two schedules of antenatal visits. *Journal of Health Services and Research Policy* 2000;5:69–75.

50. Kaminski M, Blondel B, Breart G. Management of pregnancy and childbirth in England and Wales and in France. *Paediatric and Perinatal Epidemiology* 1988;2:13–24.

51. Ryan, M, Ratcliffe, J, Tucker, J. Using willingness to pay to value alternative models of antenatal care. *Social Science and Medicine* 1997;44(3):371–80.

52. Crowther CA, Kornman L, O'Callaghan S, George K, Furness M, Willson K. Is an ultrasound assessment of gestational age at the first antenatal visit of value? A randomised clinical trial. [see comments]. *British Journal of Obstetrics and Gynaecology* 1999;106:1273–9.

53. Savitz DA, Terry JW Jr, Dole N, Thorp JM Jr, Siega-Riz AM, Herring AH. Comparison of pregnancy dating by last menstrual period, ultrasound scanning, and their combination. *American Journal of Obstetrics and Gynecology* 2002;187:1660–6.

54. Backe B, Nakling J. Term prediction in routine ultrasound practice. *Acta Obstetricia et Gynecologica Scandinavica* 1994;73:113–8.

55. Tunon K, Eik-Nes SH, Grottum P. A comparison between ultrasound and a reliable last menstrual period as predictors of the day of delivery in 15000 examinations. *Ultrasound in Obstetrics and Gynecology* 1996;8:178–85.

56. Blondel B, Morin I, Platt RW, Kramer MS, Usher R, Breart G. Algorithms for combining menstrual and ultrasound estimates of gestational age: consequences for rates of preterm and post-term birth. *BJOG* 2002;109:718–20.

57. Neilson JP. Ultrasound for fetal assessment in early pregnancy. *Cochrane Database of Systematic Reviews* 1999;(2).

58. Moutquin J-M, Gagnon R, Rainville C, Giroux L, Amyot G, Bilodeau R, *et al*. Maternal and neonatal outcome in pregnancies with no risk factors. *Canadian Medical Association Journal* 1987;137:728–32.

59. Mohamed H, Martin C, Haloob R. Can the New Zealand antenatal scoring system be applied in the United Kingdom? *Journal of Obstetrics and Gynaecology* 2002;22:389–91.

60. Doyle P, Roman E, Beral V, Brookes M. Spontaneous abortion in dry cleaning workers potentially exposed to perchloroethylene. *Occupational and Environmental Medicine* 1997;54:848–53.

61. Kolstad HA, Brandt LP, Rasmussen K. [Chlorinated solvents and fetal damage. Spontaneous abortions, low birth weight and malformations among women employed in the dry-cleaning industry]. [Danish]. *Ugeskrift for Laeger* 1990;152:2481–2.

62. Kyyronen P, Taskinen H, Lindbohm ML, Hemminki K, Heinonen OP. Spontaneous abortions and congenital malformations among women exposed to tetrachloroethylene in dry cleaning. *Journal of Epidemiology and Community Health* 1989;43:346–51.

63. Mozurkewich EL, Luke B, Avni M, Wolf FM. Working conditions and adverse pregnancy outcome: A meta-analysis. *Obstetrics and Gynecology* 2000;95:623–35.

64. Hanke W, Kalinka J, Makowiec-Dabrowska T, Sobala W. Heavy physical work during pregnancy: a risk factor for small-forgestational-age babies in Poland. *American Journal of Industrial Medicine* 1999;36:200–5.

65. Kramer, MS. Nutritional advice in pregnancy. *Cochrane Database of Systematic Reviews* 2003;(1):1–10.

66. Abramsky L, Botting B, Chapple J, Stone D. Has advice on periconceptional folate supplementation reduced neural-tube defects? *Lancet* 1999;354:998–9.

67. Lumley J, Watson L, Watson M, Bower C. Periconceptional supplementation with folate and/or multivitamins for preventing neural tube defects. *Cochrane Database of Systematic Reviews* 2002;(1).

68. Li Z, Gindler J, Wang H, Berry RJ, Li S, Correa A, *et al*. Folic acid supplements during early pregnancy and likelihood of multiple births: a population-based cohort study. *Lancet* 2003;361:380–4.

69. Royal College of Obstetricians and Gynaecologists. *Periconceptual folic acid and food fortification in the prevention of neural tube defects*. Scientific Advisory Committee Opinion Paper No. 4, London: RCOG; 2003.

70. Daly LE, Kirke PN, Molloy A, Weir DG, Scott JM. Folate levels and neural tube defects. Implications for prevention. *JAMA* 1995;274:1698–702.

71. Expert Advisory Group. Department of Health, Scottish office Home and Health Department, Welsh Office, and Department of Health and Social Services, Northern Ireland. *Folic acid and the prevention of neural tube defects*. London: HMSO; 1992.

72. Prevention of neural tube defects: results of the Medical Research Council Vitamin Study. MRC Vitamin Study Research Group [see comments]. *Lancet* 1991;338:131–7.

73. Wald NJ, Law MR, Morris JK, Wald DS. Quantifying the effect of folic acid. *Lancet* 2001;358:2069–73.

74. Mahomed K. Iron and folate supplementation in pregnancy. *Cochrane Database of Systematic Reviews* 2001;(2).

75. Hemminki E, Rimpela U. A randomized comparison of routine versus selective iron supplementation during pregnancy. *Journal of the American College of Nutrition* 1991;10:3–10.

76. Mahomed K. Iron supplementation in pregnancy. *Cochrane Database of Systematic Reviews* 2001;(2).

77. British Medical Association, Royal Pharmaceutical Society of Great Britain. *British National Formulary*. London: March 2003. p. 439–40.

78. van den Broek N, Kulier R, Gulmezoglu AM, Villar J. Vitamin A supplementation during pregnancy. *Cochrane Database of Systematic Reviews* 2003;(1):1–21.

79. Dolk HM, Nau H, Hummler H, Barlow SM. Dietary vitamin A and teratogenic risk: European Teratology Society discussion paper. *European Journal Obstetrics and Gynecology Reproductive Biology* 1999;83:31–6.

80. Oakley GP Jr, Erickson JD. Vitamin A and birth defects. Continuing caution is needed. *New England Journal of Medicine* 1995;333:1414–15.

81. Rothman KJ, Moore LL, Singer MR, Nguyen US, Mannino S, Milunsky A. Teratogenicity of high vitamin A intake. *New England Journal of Medicine* 1995;333:1369–73.

82. Mahomed K, Gulmezoglu, A. M. Vitamin D supplementation in pregnancy. *Cochrane Database of Systematic Reviews* 2000;(1).

83. Southwick FS, Purich DL. Intracellular pathogenesis of listeriosis. *New England Journal of Medicine* 1996;334:770–6.

84. Public Health Laboratory Service Press Release. Disease Facts: Salmonella. 2001.

85. British Nutrition Foundation. BNF Information. Diet through Life: Pregnancy. 2003. [www.nutrition.org.uk/] Accessed 20 August 2003.

86. Ledward RS. Drugs in pregnancy. In: Studd J, editor *Progress in Obstetrics and Gynaecology*. Edinburgh: Churchill Livingstone; 1998. p. 19–46.

87. Fugh-Berman A, Kronenberg F. Complementary and alternative medicine (CAM) in reproductive-age women: a review of randomized controlled trials. *Reproductive Toxicology* 2003;17:137–52.

88. Moore ML. Complementary and alternative therapies. *Journal of Perinatal Education* 2002;11:39–42.

89. Pinn G, Pallett L. Herbal medicine in pregnancy. *Complementary Therapies in Nursing and Midwifery* 2002;8:77–80.

90. Leung K-Y, Lee Y-P, Chan H-Y, Lee C-P, Tang MHY. Are herbal medicinal products less teratogenic than Western pharmaceutical products? *Acta Pharmacologica Sinica* 2002;23:1169–72.

91. Hepner DL, Harnett M, Segal S, Camann W, Bader AM, Tsen LC. Herbal medicine use in parturients. *Anesthesia and Analgesia* 2002;94:690–3.

92. Maats FH, Crowther CA. Patterns of vitamin, mineral and herbal supplement use prior to and during pregnancy. *Australian and New Zealand Journal of Obstetrics and Gynaecology* 2002;42:494–6.

93. Tsui B, Dennehy CE, Tsourounis C. A survey of dietary supplement use during pregnancy at an academic medical center. *American Journal of Obstetrics and Gynecology* 2001;185:433–7.

94. Medicines Control Agency. *Safety of Herbal Medicinal Products*. London; 2002. p. 22–23.

95. Ernst E. Herbal medicinal products during pregnancy: are they safe? *BJOG* 2002;109:227–35.

96. Dove D, Johnson P. Oral evening primrose oil: Its effect on length of pregnancy and selected intrapartum outcomes in low-risk nulliparous women. *Journal of Nurse-Midwifery* 1999;44:320–4.

97. Simpson M. Raspberry leaf in pregnancy; its safety and efficacy in labor. *Journal of Midwifery and Women's Health* 2001;46:51–9.

98. Gallo M, Sarkar M, Au W, Pietrzak K, Comas B, Smith M, *et al.* Pregnancy outcome following gestational exposure to Echinacea: a prospective controlled study. *Archives of Internal Medicine* 2000;160:3141–3.

99. Goldman RD, Koren G, Motherisk Team. Taking St John's wort during pregnancy. *Canadian Family Physician* 2003;49:29–30.

100. Clapp JF III, Simonian S, Lopez B, Appleby-Wineberg S, Harcar-Sevcik R. The one-year morphometric and neurodevelopmental outcome of the offspring of women who continued to exercise regularly throughout pregnancy. *American Journal of Obstetrics and Gynecology* 1998;178:594–9.

101. Kramer MS. Aerobic exercise for women during pregnancy. *Cochrane Database of Systematic Reviews* 2002;(4).

102. Camporesi EM. Diving and pregnancy. *Seminars in Perinatology* 1996;20:292–302.

103. Read JS, Klebanoff MA. Sexual intercourse during pregnancy and preterm delivery: effects of vaginal microorganisms. *American Journal of Obstetrics and Gynecology* 1993;168:514–19.

104. Klebanoff MA, Nugent RP, Rhoads GG. Coitus during pregnancy: is it safe? *Lancet* 1984;2:914–7.

105. Berghella V, Klebanhoff M, McPherson C. Sexual intercourse association with asymptomatic bacterial vaginosis and *Trichomonas vaginalis* treatment in relationship to preterm birth. *American Journal of Obstetrics and Gynecology* 2002;187:1277–82.

106. Walpole I, Zubrick S, Pontre J. Is there a fetal effect with low to moderate alcohol use before or during pregnancy? *Journal of Epidemiology and Community Health* 1990;44:297–301.

107. Borges G, Lopez-Cervantes M, Medina-Mora ME, Tapia-Conyer R, Garrido F. Alcohol consumption, low birth weight, and preterm delivery in the national addiction survey (Mexico). *International Journal of the Addictions* 1993;28(4):355–68.

108. Holzman C, Paneth N, Little R, Pinto-Martin J. Perinatal brain injury in premature infants born to mothers using alcohol in pregnancy. *Pediatrics* 1995;95:66–73.

109. Aronson M, Hagberg B, Gillberg C. Attention deficits and autistic spectrum problems in children exposed to alcohol during gestation: A follow-up study. *Developmental Medicine and Child Neurology* 1997;39:583–7.

110. Abel EL. Fetal alcohol syndrome: the 'American Paradox'. *Alcohol and Alcoholism* 1998;33:195–201.

111. Royal College of Obstetricians and Gynaecologists. *Alcohol consumption in pregnancy*. Guideline No. 9. London: RCOG; 1999.

112. Lumley J, Oliver S, Waters E. Interventions for promoting smoking cessation during pregnancy. *Cochrane Database of Systematic Reviews* 2001;(2). 2001.

113. Owen L, McNeill A, Callum C. Trends in smoking during pregnancy in England, 1992–7: quota sampling surveys. *British Medical Journal* 1998;317:728.

114. DiFranza JR, Lew, RA. Effect of maternal cigarette smoking on pregnancy complications and sudden infant death syndrome. *Journal of Family Practice* 1995;40:385–394.

115. Ananth CV, Smulian JC, Vintzileos AM. Incidence of placental abruption in relation to cigarette smoking and hypertensive disorders during pregnancy: A meta-analysis of observational studies. *Obstetrics and Gynecology* 1999;93:622–8.

116. Castles A, Adams EK, Melvin CL, Kelsch C, Boulton ML. Effects of smoking during pregnancy: Five meta-analyses. *American Journal of Preventive Medicine* 1999;16:208–15.

117. Shah NR, Bracken MB. A systematic review and meta-analysis of prospective studies on the association between maternal cigarette smoking and preterm delivery. *American Journal of Obstetrics and Gynecology* 2000;182:465–72.

118. Wyszynski DF, Duffy DL, Beaty TH. Maternal cigarette smoking and oral clefts: a meta-analysis. *Cleft Palate-Craniofacial Journal* 1997;34:206–10.

119. Conde-Agudelo A, Althabe F, Belizan JM, Kafury-Goeta AC. Cigarette smoking during pregnancy and risk of preeclampsia: a systematic review. *American Journal of Obstetrics and Gynecology* 1999;181:1026–35.

120. Clausson B, Cnattingius S, Axelsson O. Preterm and term births of small for gestational age infants: A population-based study of risk factors among nulliparous women. *British Journal of Obstetrics and Gynaecology* 1998;105:1011–7.

121. Raymond EG, Cnattingius S, Kiely JL. Effects of maternal age, parity and smoking on the risk of stillbirth. *British Journal of Obstetrics and Gynaecology* 1994;101:301–6.

122. Kleinman JC, Pierre MB Jr, Madans JH, Land GH, Schramm WF. The effects of maternal smoking on fetal and infant mortality. *American Journal of Epidemiology* 1988;127:274–82.

123. Lumley J. Stopping smoking. *British Journal of Obstetrics and Gynaecology* 1987;94:289–92.

124. MacArthur C, Knox EG, Lancashire RJ. Effects at age nine of maternal smoking in pregnancy: experimental and observational findings. *BJOG* 2001;108:67–73.

125. von Kries R, Toschke AM, Koletzko B, Slikker W Jr. Maternal smoking during pregnancy and childhood obesity. *American Journal of Epidemiology* 2002;156:954–61.

126. Faden VB, Graubard BI. Maternal substance use during pregnancy and developmental outcome at age three. *Journal of Substance Abuse* 2000;12:329–40.

127. Thorogood M, Hillsdon M, Summerbell C. Changing behaviour: cardiovascular disorders. *Clinical Evidence* 2002;8:37–59.

128. Law M, Tang JL. An analysis of the effectiveness of interventions intended to help people stop smoking. *Archives of Internal Medicine* 1995;155:1933–41.

129. Wisborg K, Henriksen TB, Jespersen LB, Secher NJ. Nicotine patches for pregnant smokers. *Obstetrics and Gynecology* 2000;96:967–71.

130. Hajek P, West R, Lee A, Foulds J, Owen L, Eiser JR, et al. Randomized controlled trial of a midwife-delivered brief smoking cessation intervention in pregnancy. *Addiction* 2001;96:485–94.

131. Stotts A, DiClemente CC, Dolan-Mullen P. One-to-one. A motivational intervention for resistant pregnant smokers. *Addictive Behaviors* 2002;27:275–92.

132. Moore L, Campbell R, Whelan A, Mills N, Lupton P, Misselbrook E, et al. Self help smoking cessation in pregnancy: cluster randomised controlled trial. *British Medical Journal* 2002;325:1383–6.

133. Li C, Windsor R, Perkins L, Lowe J, Goldenberg R. The impact on birthweight and gestational age of cotinine validated smoking reduction during pregnancy. *JAMA* 1993;269:1519–24.

134. Windsor R, Li C, Boyd N, Hartmann K. The use of significant reduction rates to evaluate health education methods for pregnant smokers: a new harm reduction – behavioral indicator. *Health Education and Behavior* 1999;26:648–62.

135. Fergusson DM, Horwood LJ, Northstone K, ALSPAC Study Team, Avon Longitudinal Study of Pregnancy and Childhood. Maternal use of cannabis and pregnancy outcome. *BJOG* 2002;109:21–7.

136. English DR, Hulse GK, Milne E, Holman CD, Bower CI. Maternal cannabis use and birth weight: a meta-analysis. *Addiction* 1997;92:1553–60.

137. Royal College of Obstetricians and Gynaecologists. Advice on preventing deep vein thrombosis for pregnant women travelling by air. Scientific Advisory Committee Opinion paper No. 1. London: RCOG; 2001.

138. James KV, Lohr JM, Deshmukh RM, Cranley JJ. Venous thrombotic complications of pregnancy. *Cardiovascular Surgery* 1996;4:777–82.

139. McColl MD, Ramsay JE, Tait RC, Walker ID, McCall F, Conkie JA, et al. Risk factors for pregnancy associated venous thromboembolism. *Thrombosis and Haemostasis* 1997;78:1183–8.

140. Kierkegaard A. Incidence and diagnosis of deep vein thrombosis associated with pregnancy. *Acta Obstetricia et Gynecologica Scandinavica* 1983;62:239–43.

141. Scurr JH, Machin SJ, Bailey-King S, Mackie IJ, McDonald S, Coleridge Smith PD. Frequency and prevention of symptomless deep-vein thrombosis in long-haul flights: a randomised trial. *Lancet* 2001;357:1485–9.

142. World Health Organization. Travellers with special needs. In: Martinez L, editor. *International Travel and Health*. Geneva: World Health Organization; 2002.

143. Lewis G, Drife J, editors. *Why mothers die 1997–1999: The fifth report of the Confidential Enquiries into Maternal Deaths in the United Kingdom*. London: RCOG Press; 2001.

144. Johnson HC, Pring DW. Car seatbelts in pregnancy: the practice and knowledge of pregnant women remain causes for concern. *BJOG* 2000;107:644–7.

145. Chang A, Magwene K, Frand E. Increased safety belt use following education in childbirth classes. *Birth* 1987;14:148–52.

146. Klinich KD, Schneider LW, Moore JL, Pearlman MD. Investigations of crashes involving pregnant occupants. *Annual Proceedings, Association for the Advancement of Automotive Medicine* 2000;44:37–55.

147. Crosby WM, Costiloe JP. Safety of lap-belt restraint for pregnant victims of automobile collisions. *New England Journal of Medicine* 1971;284:632–6.

148. Crosby WM, King AI, Stout LC. Fetal survival following impact: improvement with shoulder harness restraint. *American Journal of Obstetrics and Gynecology* 1972;112:1101–6.

149. Wolf ME, Alexander BH, Rivara FP, Hickok DE, Maier RV, Starzyk PM. A retrospective cohort study of seatbelt use and pregnancy outcome after a motor vehicle crash. *Journal of Trauma-Injury Infection and Critical Care* 1993;34:116–19.

150. World Health Organization. Special groups. In: Martinez L, editor. *International Travel and Health*. Geneva: World Health Organization; 2002.

151. Hurley PA. International travel and the pregnant women. In: Studd J, editor. *Progress in Obstetrics and Gynaecology*. Edinburgh: Churchill Livingstone; 2003. p. 45–55.

152. Hurley P. Vaccination in pregnancy. *Current Obstetrics and Gynaecology* 1998;8:169–75.

153. Jothivijayarani A. Travel considerations during pregnancy. *Primary Care Update for Ob/Gyns* 2002;9:36–40.

154. World Health Organization. Treatment of P. vivax, P. ovale and P. malariae infections. In: Martinez L, editor. *International Travel and Health*. Geneva: World Health Organization; 2002. [www.who.int/ith/chapter07_04.html] Accessed 4 September 2003.

155. Luxemburger C, McGready R, Kham A, Morison L, Cho T, Chongsuphajaisiddhi T, et al. Effects of malaria during pregnancy on infant mortality in an area of low malaria transition. *American Journal of Epidemiology* 2001;154:459–65.

156. World Health Organization. World malaria situation in 1993, Part 1. *Weekly Epidemiological Record* 1996;71:17–24.

157. Linday S, Ansell J, Selman C, Cox V, Hamilton K, Walraven G. Effect of pregnancy on exposure to malaria mosquitoes. *Lancet* 2000;355:1972.

158. Schaefer C, Peters PW. Intrauterine diethyltoluamide exposure and fetal outcome. *Reproductive Toxicology* 1992;6:175–6.

159. Dolan G, ter Kuile FO, Jacoutot V. Bed nets for the prevention of malaria and anaemia in pregnancy. *Transactions of the Royal Society of Tropical Medicine and Hygiene* 1993;87:620–6.

160. Pearce G. Travel insurance and the pregnant woman. *MIDIRS Midwifery Digest* 1997;7:164.

161. Brown H, Campbell H. Special considerations for pregnant travellers. *Modern Medicine of Australia* 1999;42:17–20.

162. Tucker R. Ensure pregnant travellers know the risks. *Practice Nurse* 1999;18:458–66.

163. Rose SR. Pregnancy and travel. *Emergency Medicine Clinics of North America* 1997;15:93–111.

164. Baron TH, Ramirez B, Richter JE. Gastrointestinal motility disorders during pregnancy. *Annals of Internal Medicine* 1993;118:366–75.

165. Weigel RM, Weigel MM. Nausea and vomiting of early pregnancy and pregnancy outcome. A meta-analytical review. *British Journal of Obstetrics and Gynaecology* 1989;96:1312–8.

166. Whitehead SA, Andrews PL, Chamberlain GV. Characterisation of nausea and vomiting in early pregnancy: a survey of 1000 women. *Journal of Obstetrics and Gynaecology* 1992;12:364–9.

167. Gadsby R, Barnie-Adshead AM, Jagger C. A prospective study of nausea and vomiting during pregnancy. *British Journal of General Practice* 1993;43:245–8.

168. Feldman M. Nausea and vomiting. In: Sleisenger MH, Fordtran JS, editors. *Gastrointestinal disease*. Philadelphia: WB Saunders; 1989. p. 229–31.

169. Klebanoff MA, Mills JL. Is vomiting during pregnancy teratogenic? *British Medical Journal* 1986;292:724–6.

170. Smith C, Crowther C, Beilby J, Dandeaux J. The impact of nausea and vomiting on women: a burden of early pregnancy. *Australian and New Zealand Journal of Obstetrics and Gynaecology* 2000;40:397–401.

171. Attard CL, Kohli MA, Coleman S, Bradley C, Hux M, Atanackovic G, et al. The burden of illness of severe nausea and vomiting of pregnancy in the United States. *American Journal of Obstetrics and Gynecology* 2002;186:S220–7.

172. Vutyavanich T, Kraisarin T, Ruangsri R. Ginger for nausea and vomiting in pregnancy: randomized, double-masked, placebo-controlled trial. *Obstetrics and Gynecology* 2001;97:577–82.

173. Jewell D, Young G. Interventions for nausea and vomiting in early pregnancy. *Cochrane Database of Systematic Reviews* 2001;(2).

174. Murphy PA. Alternative therapies for nausea and vomiting of pregnancy. *Obstetrics and Gynecology* 1998;91:149–55.

175. Keating A, Chez RA. Ginger syrup as an antiemetic in early pregnancy. *Alternative Therapies in Health and Medicine* 2002;8:89–91.

176. Vickers AJ. Can acupuncture have specific effects on health? A systematic review of acupuncture antiemesis trials. *Journal of the Royal Society of Medicine* 1996;89:303–11.

177. Norheim AJ, Pedersen EJ, Fonnebo V, Berge L. Acupressure treatment of morning sickness in pregnancy. A randomised, double-blind, placebo-controlled study. *Scandinavian Journal of Primary Health Care* 2001;19:43–7.

178. Knight B, Mudge C, Openshaw S, White A, Hart A. Effect of acupuncture on nausea of pregnancy: a randomized, controlled trial. *Obstetrics and Gynecology* 2001;97:184–8.

179. Werntoft E, Dykes AK. Effect of acupressure on nausea and vomiting during pregnancy: a randomized, placebo-controlled, pilot study. *Journal of Reproductive Medicine* 2001;46:835–9.

180. Smith C, Crowther C, Beilby J. Acupuncture to treat nausea and vomiting in early pregnancy: a randomized controlled trial. *Birth* 2002;29:1–9.

181. Smith C, Crowther C, Beilby J. Pregnancy outcome following womens' participation in a randomised controlled trial of acupuncture to treat nausea and vomiting in early pregnancy. *Complementary Therapies in Medicine* 2002;10:78–83.

182. Mazzotta P, Magee LA. A risk–benefit assessment of pharmacological and nonpharmacological treatments for nausea and vomiting of pregnancy. *Drugs* 2000;59:781–800.

183. Magee LA, Mazzotta P, Koren G. Evidence-based view of safety and effectiveness of pharmacologic therapy for nausea and vomiting of pregnancy (NVP). *American Journal of Obstetrics and Gynecology* 2002;186:S256–61.

184. Marrero JM, Goggin PM, Caestecker JS. Determinants of pregnancy heartburn. *British Journal of Obstetrics and Gynaecology* 1992;99:731–4.

185. Knudsen A, Lebech M, Hansen M. Upper gastrointestinal symptoms in the third trimester of the normal pregnancy. *European Journal of Obstetrics Gynecology and Reproductive Biology* 1995;60:29–33.

186. Bainbridge ET, Temple JG, Nicholas SP, Newton JR, Boriah V. Symptomatic gastro-esophageal reflux in pregnancy. A comparative study of white Europeans and Asians in Birmingham. *British Journal of Clinical Practice* 1983;37:53–7.

187. Shaw RW. Randomized controlled trial of Syn-Ergel and an active placebo in the treatment of heartburn of pregnancy. *Journal of International Medical Research* 1978;6:147–51.

188. Lang GD, Dougall A. Comparative study of Algicon suspension and magnesium trisilicate mixture in the treatment of reflux dyspepsia of pregnancy. *British Journal of Clinical Practice* 1989;66:48–51.

189. Association of the British Pharmaceutical Industry. *ABPI Compendium of Data Sheets and Summaries of Product Characteristics. Medicines Compendium*. London: Datapharm Communications; 2001.

190. Atlay RD, Parkinson DJ, Entwistle GD, Weekes AR. Treating heartburn in pregnancy: comparison of acid and alkali mixtures. *British Medical Journal* 1978;2:919–20.

191. Rayburn W, Liles E, Christensen H, Robinson M. Antacids vs. antacids plus non-prescription ranitidine for heartburn during pregnancy. *International Journal of Gynaecology and Obstetrics* 1999;66:35–7.

192. Larson JD, Patatanian E, Miner PB Jr, Rayburn WF, Robinson MG. Double-blind, placebo-controlled study of ranitidine for gastroesophageal reflux symptoms during pregnancy. *Obstetrics and Gynecology* 1997;90:83–7.

193. Magee LA, Inocencion G, Kamboj L, Rosetti F, Koren G. Safety of first trimester exposure to histamine H2 blockers. A prospective cohort study. *Digestive Diseases and Sciences* 1996;41:1145–9.

194. Nikfar S, Abdollahi M, Moretti ME, Magee LA, Koren G. Use of proton pump inhibitors during pregnancy and rates of major malformations: a meta-analysis. *Digestive Diseases and Sciences* 2002;47:1526–9.

195. Meyer LC, Peacock JL, Bland JM, Anderson HR. Symptoms and health problems in pregnancy: their association with social factors, smoking, alcohol, caffeine and attitude to pregnancy. *Paediatric and Perinatal Epidemiology* 1994;8:145–55.

196. Jewell DJ, Young G. Interventions for treating constipation in pregnancy. *Cochrane Database of Systematic Reviews* 2003;(1).

197. Abramowitz L, Sobhani I, Benifla JL, Vuagnat A, Darai E, Mignon M, *et al.* Anal fissure and thrombosed external hemorrhoids before and after delivery. *Diseases of the Colon and Rectum* 2002;45:650–5.

198. Wijayanegara H, Mose JC, Achmad L, Sobarna R, Permadi W. A clinical trial of hydroxyethylrutosides in the treatment of haemorrhoids of pregnancy. *Journal of International Medical Research* 1992;20:54–60.

199. Buckshee K, Takkar D, Aggarwal N. Micronized flavonoid therapy in internal hemorrhoids of pregnancy. *International Journal of Gynecology and Obstetrics* 1997;57:145–51.

200. Saleeby RG Jr, Rosen L, Stasik JJ, Riether RD, Sheets J, Khubchandani IT. Hemorrhoidectomy during pregnancy: risk or relief? *Diseases of the Colon and Rectum* 1991;3445:260–1.

201. Thaler E, Huch R, Huch A, Zimmermann R. Compression stockings prophylaxis of emergent varicose veins in pregnancy: A prospective randomised controlled study. *Swiss Medical Weekly* 2001;131:659–62.

202. Gulmezoglu, AM. Interventions for trichomoniasis in pregnancy. *Cochrane Database of Systematic Reviews* 2002;(3). CD000220.

203. French JI, McGregor JA, Draper D, Parker R, McFee J. Gestational bleeding, bacterial vaginosis, and common reproductive tract infections: risk for preterm birth and benefit of treatment. *Obstetrics and Gynecology* 1999;93:715–24.

204. Young GL, Jewell MD. Topical treatment for vaginal candidiasis in pregnancy. *Cochrane Database of Systematic Reviews* 2001;(2).

205. Greenwood CJ, Stainton MC. Back pain/discomfort in pregnancy: invisible and forgotten. *Journal of Perinatal Education* 2001;10:1–12.

206. Kristiansson P, Svardsudd K, von Schoultz B. Back pain during pregnancy: A prospective study. *Spine* 1996;21:702–9.

207. Ostgaard HC, Andersson GBJ, Karlsson K. Prevalence of back pain in pregnancy. *Spine* 1991;16:549–52.

208. Fast A, Shapiro D, Ducommun EJ, Friedman LW, Bouklas T, Floman Y. Low-back pain in pregnancy. *Spine* 1987;12:368–71.

209. Stapleton DB, MacLennan AH, Kristiansson P. The prevalence of recalled low back pain during and after pregnancy: A South Australian population survey. *Australian and New Zealand Journal of Obstetrics and Gynaecology* 2002;42:482–5.

210. Mantle MJ, Greenwood RM, Currey HL. Backache in pregnancy. *Rheumatology and Rehabilitation* 1977;16:95–101.

211. Young G, Jewell, D. Interventions for preventing and treating pelvic and back pain in pregnancy. *Cochrane Database of Systematic Reviews* 2003;(1).

212. Field T, Hernandez-Reif M, Hart S, Theakston H, Schanberg S, Kuhn C. Pregnant women benefit from massage therapy. *Journal of Psychosomatic Obstetrics and Gynecology* 1999;20:31–8.

213. Ostgaard HC, Zetherstrom G, Roos-Hansson E, Svanberg B. Reduction of back and posterior pelvic pain in pregnancy. *Spine* 1994;19:894–900.

214. Noren L, Ostgaard S, Nielsen TF, Ostgaard HC. Reduction of sick leave for lumbar back and posterior pelvic pain in pregnancy. *Spine* 1997;22:2157–60.

215. Tesio L, Raschi A, Meroni M. Autotraction treatment for low-back pain in pregnancy: A pilot study. *Clinical Rehabilitation* 1994;8:314–19.

216. Guadagnino MR III. Spinal manipulative therapy for 12 pregnant patients suffering from low back pain. *Chiropractic Technique* 1999;11:108–11.

217. McIntyre IN, Broadhurst NA. Effective treatment of low back pain in pregnancy. *Australian Family Physician* 1996;25:S65–7.

218. Requejo SM, Barnes R, Kulig K, Landel R, Gonzalez S. The use of a modified classification system in the treatment of low back pain during pregnancy: A case report. *Journal of Orthopaedic and Sports Physical Therapy* 2002;32:318–26.

219. Owens K, Pearson A, Mason G. Symphysis pubis dysfunction: a cause of significant obstetric morbidity. *European Journal of Obstetrics Gynecology and Reproductive Biology* 2002;105:143–6.

220. Fry D, Hay-Smith J, Hough J, McIntosh J, Polden M, Shepherd J, *et al.* National clinic guideline for the care of women with symphysis pubis dysfunction. *Midwives* 1997;110:172–3.

221. Gould JS, Wissinger HA. Carpal tunnel syndrome in pregnancy. *Southern Medical Journal* 1978;71:144–5,154.

222. Voitk AJ, Mueller JC, Farlinger DE, Johnston RU. Carpal tunnel syndrome in pregnancy. *Canadian Medical Association Journal* 1983;128:277–81.

223. Padua L, Aprile I, Caliandro P, Carboni T, Meloni A, Massi S, *et al.* Symptoms and neurophysiological picture of carpal tunnel syndrome in pregnancy. *Clinical Neurophysiology* 2001;112:1946–51.

224. Courts RB. Splinting for symptoms of carpal tunnel syndrome during pregnancy. *Journal of Hand Therapy* 1995;8:31–4.

225. Ekman-Ordeberg G, Salgeback S, Ordeberg G. Carpal tunnel syndrome in pregnancy. A prospective study. *Acta Obstetricia et Gynecologica Scandinavica* 1987;66:233–5.

226. Stahl S, Blumenfeld Z, Yarnitsky D. Carpal tunnel syndrome in pregnancy: Indications for early surgery. *Journal of the Neurological Sciences* 1996;136:182–4.

227. Dawes MG, Grudzinskas JG. Repeated measurement of maternal weight during pregnancy. Is this a useful practice? *British Journal of Obstetrics and Gynaecology* 1991;98:189–94.

228. National Academy of Sciences, Institute of Medicine, Food and Nutrition Board, Committee on Nutritional Status During Pregnancy and Lactation, Subcommittee on Dietary Intake and Nutrient Supplements During Pregnancy, Subcommittee on Nutritional Status and Weight Gain During Pregnancy. *Nutrition during pregnancy*. Washington DC: National Academy Press; 1990.

229. Siega-Riz AM, Adair LS, Hobel CJ. Maternal underweight status and inadequate rate of weight gain during the third trimester of pregnancy increases the risk of preterm delivery. *Journal of Nutrition* 1996;126:146–53.

230. Bergmann MM, Flagg EW, Miracle-McMahill HL, Boeing H. Energy intake and net weight gain in pregnant women according to body mass index (BMI) status. *International Journal of Obesity and Related Metabolic Disorders* 1997;21:1010–7.

231. Alexander JM, Grant AM, Campbell MJ. Randomised controlled trial of breast shells and Hoffman's exercises for inverted and non-protractile nipples. *British Medical Journal* 1992;304:1030–2.

232. Pattinson RE. Pelvimetry for fetal cephalic presentations at term. *Cochrane Database of Systematic Reviews* 2001;(3). 2001.

233. Lenihan JP Jr. Relationship of antepartum pelvic examinations to premature rupture of the membranes. *Obstetrics and Gynecology* 1984;83:33–7.

234. Goffinet F. [Ovarian cyst and pregnancy]. [French]. *Journal de Gynecologie, Obstetrique et Biologie de la Reproduction* 2001;30:4S100–8.

235. O'Donovan P, Gupta JK, Savage J, Thornton JG, Lilford RJ. Is routine antenatal booking vaginal examination necessary for reasons other than cervical cytology if ultrasound examination is planned? *British Journal of Obstetrics and Gynaecology* 1988;95:556–9.

236. World Health Organization. *Female genital mutilation*. WHO Information Fact Sheet No. 241. Geneva: World Health Organization; 2000.

237. British Medical Association. *Female genital mutilation: caring for patients and child protection*. London: BMA; 2001.

238. Momoh C, Ladhani S, Lochrie DP, Rymer J. Female genital mutilation: Analysis of the first twelve months of a southeast London specialist clinic. *BJOG* 2001;108:186–91.

239. World Health Organization. *A systematic review of the health complications of female genital mutilation including sequelae in childbirth.* Geneva: WHO; 2000.

240. McCaffrey M, Jankowska A, Gordon H. Management of female genital mutilation: The Northwick Park Hospital experience. *British Journal of Obstetrics and Gynaecology* 1995;102:787–90.

241. Jordan JA. Female genital mutilation (female circumcision). *British Journal of Obstetrics and Gynaecology* 1994;101:94–5.

242. British Medical Association. *Domestic violence: a health care issue?* London: BMA; 1998.

243. Tjaden P, Thoennes N. *Full report of the prevalence, incidence, and consequences of violence against women. Findings from the National Violence Against Women Survey. NCJ 183781, 1–61.* Washington DC: US Department of Justice, National Institute of Justice; 2000.

244. Canadian Centre for Justice Statistics. *Family violence in Canada: A statistical profile 2002.* 85–224-XIE. Ottawa: Statistics Canada; 2002. [www.statcan.ca/english/IPS/Data/85-224-XIE.htm] Accessed 20 August 2003.

245. Jones AS, Carlson Gielen A, Campbell JC. Annual and lifetimes prevalence of partner abuse in a sample of female HMO enrollees. *Women's Health Issues* 1999;9:295–305.

246. Ballard TJ, Saltzman LE, Gazmararian JA, Spitz AM, Lazorick S, Marks JS. Violence during pregnancy: measurement issues. *American Journal of Public Health* 1998;88:274–6.

247. Royal College of Obstetricians and Gynaecologists. *Violence against women.* London: RCOG Press; 1997.

248. Johnson JK, Haider F, Ellis K, Hay DM, Lindow SW. The prevalence of domestic violence in pregnant women. *BJOG* 2003;110:272–5.

249. Newberger EH, Barkan SE, Lieberman ES, McCormick MC, Yllo K, Gary LT, et al. Abuse of pregnant women and adverse birth outcome: current knowledge and implications for practice. *Journal of the American Medical Association* 1992;267:2370–2.

250. Murphy CC, Schei B, Myhr TL, Du MJ. Abuse: a risk factor for low birth weight? A systematic review and meta-analysis. [see comments]. *Canadian Medical Association Journal* 2001;164:1567–72.

251. Cokkinides VE, Coker AL, Sanderson M, Addy C, Bethea L. Physical violence during pregnancy: maternal complications and birth outcomes. *Obstetrics and Gynecology* 1999;93:661–6.

252. Janssen PA, Holt VL, Sugg NK, Emanuel I, Critchlow CM, Henderson AD. Intimate partner violence and adverse pregnancy outcomes: A population-based study. *American Journal of Obstetrics and Gynecology* 2003;188:1341–7.

253. Royal College of Midwives. *Domestic abuse in pregnancy.* London: RCM; 1999.

254. Royal College of Psychiatrists. *Domestic violence.* CR102. London: RCPsych; 2002.

255. Wathen CN, MacMillan HL. Interventions for violence against women. Scientific review. *JAMA* 2003;289:589–600.

256. Ramsay J, Richardson J, Carter YH, Davidson LL, Feder G. Should health professionals screen women for domestic violence? Systematic review. *British Medical Journal* 2002;325:314–18.

257. Cann K, Withnell S, Shakespeare J, Doll H, Thomas J. Domestic violence: a comparative survey of levels of detection, knowledge, and attitudes in healthcare workers. *Public Health* 2001;115:89–95.

258. Department of Health. *Domestic violence: A resource manual for health care professionals.* London: Department of Health; 2000.

259. Wilson LM, Reid AJ, Midmer DK, Biringer A, Carroll JC, Stewart DE. Antenatal psychosocial risk factors associated with adverse postpartum family outcomes. *Canadian Medical Association Journal* 1996;154:785–99.

260. Perkin MR, Bland JM. The effect of anxiety and depression during pregnancy on obstetric complications. *British Journal of Obstetrics and Gynaecology* 1993;100:629–34.

261. Dayan J, Creveuil C, Herlicoviez M. Role of anxiety and depression in the onset of spontaneous preterm labor. *American Journal of Epidemiology* 2002;155:293–301.

262. Lundy BL, Jones NA, Field T. Prenatal depression effects on neonates. *Infant Behavior and Development* 1999;22:119–29.

263. Murray D, Cox JL. Screening for depression during pregnancy with the Edinburgh Depression Scale (EPDS). *Journal of Reproductive and Infant Psychology* 1990;8:99–107.

264. Bolton HL, Hughes PM, Turton P. Incidence and demographic correlates of depressive symptoms during pregnancy in an inner London population. *Journal of Psychosomatic Obstetrics and Gynecology* 1998;19:202–9.

265. Evans J, Heron J, Francomb H, Oke S, Golding J. Cohort study of depressed mood during pregnancy and after childbirth. *British Medical Journal* 2001;323:257–60.

266. Austin M-P, Lumley J. Antenatal screening for postnatal depression: a systematic review. *Acta Psychiatrica Scandinavica* 2003;107:10–17.

267. Hayes BA, Muller R, Bradley BS. Perinatal depression: a randomized controlled trial of an antenatal education intervention for primiparas. *Birth* 2001;28:28–35.

268. Brugha TS, Wheatly S, Taub NA, Culverwell A, Friedman T, Kirwan P. Pragmatic randomized trial of an antenatal intervention to prevent postnatal depression by reducing psychosocial risk factors. *Psychological Medicine* 2000;30:1273–81.

269. Hytten F. Blood volume changes in normal pregnancy. *Clinical Haematology* 1985;14:601–12.

270. Ramsey M, James D, Steer P, Weiner C, Gornik B. *Normal values in pregnancy.* 2nd ed. London: WB Saunders; 2000.

271. Steer P, Alam MA, Wadsworth J, Welch A. Relation between maternal haemoglobin concentration and birth weight in different ethnic groups. *British Medical Journal* 1995;310:489–91.

272. Zhou LM, Yang WW, Hua JZ, Deng CQ, Tao X, Stoltzfus RJ. Relation of hemoglobin measured at different times in pregnancy to preterm birth and low birth weight in Shanghai, China. *American Journal of Epidemiology* 1998;148:998–1006.

273. Breymann C. Iron supplementation during pregnancy. *Fetal and Maternal Medicine Review* 2002;13:1–29.

274. Cuervo LG, Mahomed K. Treatments for iron deficiency anaemia during pregnancy. *Cochrane Database of Systematic Reviews* 2001;(2).

275. Davies SC, Cronin E, Gill M, Greengross P, Hickman M, Normand C. Screening for sickle cell disease and thalassaemia: a systematic review with supplementary research. *Health Technology Assessment* 2000;4:1–119.

276. Modell B, Harris R, Lane B, Khan M, Darlison M, Petrou M, et al. Informed choice in genetic screening for thalassaemia during pregnancy: audit from a national confidential inquiry. *British Medical Journal* 2000;320:337–41.

277. Modell B, Petrou M, Layton M, Varnavides L, Slater C, Ward RH, et al. Audit of prenatal diagnosis for haemoglobin disorders in the United Kingdom: the first 20 years. [see comments]. *British Medical Journal* 1997;315:779–84.

278. Department of Health. *Sickle cell, thalassaemia and other haemoglobinopathies. Report of a Working Party of the Standing Medical Advisory Committee.* London: DoH; 1999.

279. Zeuner D, Ades AE, Karnon J, Brown JE, Dezateux C, Anionwu EN. Antenatal and neonatal haemoglobinopathy screening in the UK: review and economic analysis. *Health Technology Assessment* 1999;3(11):1–186.

280. Streetly A. A national screening policy for sickle cell disease and thalassaemia major for the United Kingdom. Questions are left after two evidence based reports. *British Medical Journal* 2000;320:1353–4.

281. Aspinall PJ, Dyson SM, Anionwu EN. The feasibility of using ethnicity as a primary tool for antenatal selective screening for sickle cell disorders: pointers from the research evidence. *Social Science and Medicine* 2003;56:285–97.

282. Petrou M, Brugiatelli M, Ward RHT, Modell B. Factors affecting the uptake of prenatal diagnosis for sickle cell disease. *Journal of Medical Genetics* 1992;29:820–3.

283. Modell B, Ward RH, Fairweather DV. Effect of introducing antenatal diagnosis on reproductive behaviour of families at risk for thalassaemia major. *British Medical Journal* 1980;280:1347–50.

284. Ahmed S, Saleem M, Sultana N, Raashid Y, Waqar A, Anwar M, et al. Prenatal diagnosis of beta-thalassaemia in Pakistan: experience in a Muslim country. *Prenatal Diagnosis* 2000;20:378–83.

285. UK Blood Transfusion Services. Guidelines for the Blood Transfusion Service. 6th ed. London; TSO; 2002. [www.transfusionguidelines.org.uk/uk_guidelines/ukbts6_$01.html] Accessed 20 August 2003.

286. Whittle MJ. Antenatal serology testing in pregnancy. *British Journal of Obstetrics and Gynaecology* 1996;103:195–6.

287. Brouwers HA, Overbeeke MA, van E, I, Schaasberg W, Alsbach GP, van der HC, et al. What is the best predictor of the severity of ABO-haemolytic disease of the newborn? *Lancet* 1988;2:641–4.

288. Mollison PL, Engelfriet CP, Contreras M. *Haemolytic disease of the fetus and newborn. Blood transfusion in clinical medicine.* Oxford: Blackwell Science. 1997. p. 390–424.

289. Shanwell A, Sallander S, Bremme K, Westgren M. Clinical evaluation of a solid-phase test for red cell antibody screening of pregnant women. *Transfusion* 1999;39:26–31.

290. Filbey D, Hanson U, Wesstrom G. The prevalence of red cell antibodies in pregnancy correlated to the outcome of the newborn: a 12 year study in central Sweden. *Acta Obstetrica et Gynecologica Scandinavica* 1995;74:687–92.

291. British Committee for Standards in Haematology, Blood Transfusion Task Force. Guidelines for blood grouping and red cell antibody testing during pregnancy. *Transfusion Medicine* 1996;6:71–4.

292. National Institute for Clinical Excellence. *Guidance on the use of routine antenatal anti-D prophylaxis for RhD-negative women.* Technology Appraisal Guidance, No. 41. London: National Institute for Clinical Excellence; 2002. [www.nice.org.uk/pdf/prophylaxisFinalguidance.pdf] Accessed 20 August 2003.

293. Royal College of Obstetricians and Gynaecologists. *Ultrasound screening for fetal abnormalities: report of the RCOG working party.* London: RCOG Press; 1997.

294. Jepsen RG, Forbes CA, Sowden AJ, Lewis RA. Increasing informed uptake and non-uptake of screening: evidence from a systematic review. *Health Expectations* 2001;4:116–26.

295. Department of Health, social Services and Public Safety, Northern Ireland, National Assembly for Wales, Scottish Executive, Department of Health. *Second report of the UK National Screening Committee.* London: DoH; 2000. [www.nsc.nhs.uk/pdfs/secondreport.pdf] Accessed 21 August 2003.

296. Royal College of Obstetricians and Gynaecologists. *Report of the RCOG working party on biochemical markers and the detection of Down's syndrome.* London: Royal College of Obstetricians and Gynaecologists; 1993.

297. Bricker L, Garcia J, Henderson J, Mugford M, Neilson J, Roberts T, et al. Ultrasound screening in pregnancy: a systematic review of the clinical effectiveness, cost-effectiveness and women's views. *Health Technology Assessment* 2000;4:1–193.

298. Williamson P, Alberman E, Rodeck C, Fiddler M, Church S, Harris R. Antecedent circumstances surrounding neural tube defect births in 1990–1991. *British Journal of Obstetrics and Gynaecology* 1997;104:51–6.

299. Saari-Kemppainen A, Karjalainen O, Ylostalo P, Heinonen OP. Fetal anomalies in a controlled one-stage ultrasound screening trial. A report from the Helsinki Ultrasound Trial. *Journal of Perinatal Medicine* 1994;22(4):279–289.

300. Whitlow BJ, Chatzipapas IK, Lazanakis ML, Kadir RA, Economides DL. The value of sonography in early pregnancy for the detection of fetal abnormalities in an unselected population. *British Journal of Obstetrics and Gynaecology* 1999;106:929–36.

301. National Assembly for Wales/Velindre NHS Trust Antenatal Project Team Steering Board. *Choices: Recommendations for the provision and management of antenatal screening in Wales.* Cardiff: Velindre NHS Trust; March 2002. [www.velindretr.wales.nhs.uk/antenatal/consult_doc/choices.pdf] Accessed 21 August 2003.

302. Royal College of Obstetricians and Gynaecologists. *Routine ultrasound screening in pregnancy, protocols, standards and training. Supplement to ultrasound screening for fetal abnormalities. Report of the RCOG Working Party.* London: RCOG Press; 2000.

303. Office for National Statistics. *Child health statistics.* London: National Statistics; 2000. p. 1–26.

304. Noble J. Natural history of Down's syndrome: a brief review for those involved in antenatal screening. *Journal of Medical Screening* 1998;5:172–7.

305. Marteau TM, Dormandy E. Facilitating informed choice in prenatal testing: how well are we doing? *American Journal of Medical Genetics* 2001;106:185–90.

306. Smith DK, Shaw RW, Marteau TM. Informed consent to undergo serum screening for Down's syndrome: the gap between policy and practice. *British Medical Journal* 1994;309:776.

307. Royal College of Obstetricians and Gynaecologists. *Amniocentesis.* Guideline No. 8. London: Royal College of Obstetricians and Gynaecologists; 2000.

308. Deeks JJ. Systematic reviews of evaluations of diagnostic and screening tests. *British Medical Journal* 2001;323:157–62.

309. Lijmer JG, Mol BW, Heisterkamp S, Bonsel GJ, Prins MH, van der Meulen JH, et al. Empirical evidence of design-related bias in studies of diagnostic tests. *JAMA* 1999;282:1061–6.

310. Hook EB. Spontaneous deaths of fetuses with chromosomal abnormalities diagnosed prenatally. *New England Journal of Medicine* 1978;299:1036–8.

311. Morris JK, Mutton DE, Alberman E. Revised estimates of the maternal age specific live birth prevalence of Down's syndrome. *Journal of Medical Screening* 2002;9:2–6.

312. Paranjothy S, Thomas J. National Sentinel Caesarean Section Audit. *MIDIRS Midwifery Digest* 2001;11:S13–15.

313. Wald NJ, Huttly WJ, Hennessy CF. Down's syndrome screening in the UK in 1998. *Lancet* 1999;354:1264.

314. Youings S, Gregson N, Jacobs P. The efficacy of maternal age screening for Down's syndrome in Wessex. *Prenatal Diagnosis* 1991;11:419–25.

315. Smith-Bindman R, Hosmer W, Feldstein VA, Deeks JJ, Goldberg JD. Second-trimester ultrasound to detect fetuses with Down's syndrome. *JAMA* 2001;285:1044–55.

316. Wald NJ, Rodeck C, Hackshaw AK, Walters J, Chitty L, Mackinson AM. First and second trimester antenatal screening for Down's syndrome: the results of the serum, urine and ultrasound screening study (SURUSS). *Health Technology Assessment* 2003;7:1–88.

317. Bindra R, Heath V, Nicolaides KH. Screening for chromosomal defects by fetal nuchal translucency at 11 to 14 weeks. *Clinical Obstetrics and Gynecology* 2002;45:661–70.

318. Niemimaa M, Suonpaa M, Perheentupa A, Seppala M, Heinonen S, Laitinen P, *et al.* Evaluation of first trimester maternal serum and ultrasound screening for Down's syndrome in Eastern and Northern Finland. *European Journal of Human Genetics* 2001;9:404–8.

319. Wald NJ, Kennard A, Hackshaw A, McGuire A. Antenatal screening for Down's syndrome. *Health Technology Assessment* 1998;2:1–112.

320. Conde-Agudelo A, Kafury-Goeta AC. Triple-marker test as screening for Down syndrome: a meta-analysis. *Obstetrical and Gynecological Survey* 1998;53:369–76.

321. Wald NJ, Huttly WJ, Hackshaw AK. Antenatal screening for Down's syndrome with the quadruple test. *Lancet* 2003;361:835–6.

322. Spencer K, Spencer CE, Power M, Dawson C, Nicolaides KH. Screening for chromosomal abnormalities in the first trimester using ultrasound and maternal serum biochemistry in a one-stop clinic: a review of three years prospective experience. *BJOG* 2003;110:281–6.

323. Alfirevic Z, Gosden C, Neilson, JP. Chorion villus sampling versus amniocentesis for prenatal diagnosis. *Cochrane Database of Systematic Reviews* 1998;(4):1–8.

324. Alfirevic, Z. Early amniocentesis versus transabdominal chorion villus sampling. *Cochrane Database of Systematic Reviews* 2000;(1), 1.

325. Tercyak KP, Johnson SB, Roberts SF, Cruz AC. Psychological response to prenatal genetic counseling and amniocentesis. *Patient Education and Counseling* 2001;43:73–84.

326. Green JM. Women's experiences of prenatal screening and diagnosis. In: Abramsky L, Chapple J, editors. Prenatal diagnosis: the human side. London: Chapman and Hall; 1994. p. 37–53.

327. Liu S, Joseph KS, Kramer MS, Allen AC, Sauve R, Rusen ID, *et al.* Relationship of prenatal diagnosis and pregnancy termination to overall infant mortality in Canada. *JAMA* 2002;287:1561–7.

328. Whalley P. Bacteriuria of pregnancy. *American Journal of Obstetrics and Gynecology* 1967;97:723–38.

329. Little PJ. The incidence of urinary infection in 5000 pregnant women. *Lancet* 1966;2:925–8.

330. Campbell-Brown M, McFadyen IR, Seal DV, Stephenson ML. Is screening for bacteriuria in pregnancy worth while? *British Medical Journal* 1987;294:1579–82.

331. Foley ME, Farquharson R, Stronge JM. Is screening for bacteriuria in pregnancy worthwhile? *British Medical Journal* 1987;295:270.

332. LeBlanc AL, McGanity WJ. The impact of bacteriuria in pregnancy: a survey of 1300 pregnant patients. *Biologie Medicale* 1964;22:336–47.

333. Kincaid-Smith P, Bullen M. Bacteriuria in pregnancy. *Lancet* 1965;395–9.

334. Thomsen AC, Morup L, Hansen KB. Antibiotic elimination of group-B streptococci in urine in prevention of preterm labour. *Lancet* 1987;591–3.

335. Elder HA, Santamarina BAG, Smith S, Kass EH. The natural history of asymptomatic bacteriuria during pregnancy: the effect of tetracycline on the clinical course and the outcome of pregnancy. *American Journal of Obstetrics and Gynecology* 1971;111:441–62.

336. Gold EM, Traub FB, Daichman I, Terris M. Asymptomatic bacteriuria during pregnancy. *Obstetrics and Gynecology* 1966;27:206–9.

337. Mulla N. Bacteriuria in Pregnancy. *Obstetrics and Gynecology* 1960;16:89–92.

338. Savage WE, Hajj SN, Kass EH. Demographic and prognostic characteristics of bacteriuria in pregnancy. *Medicine* 1967;46:385–407.

339. Mittendorf R, Williams MA, Kass EH. Prevention of preterm delivery and low birth weight associated with asymptomatic bacteriuria. *Clinical Infectious Diseases* 1992;14:927–32.

340. Patterson TF, Andriole VT. Bacteriuria in pregnancy. *Infectious Disease Clinics of North America* 1987;1:807–22.

341. Screening for asymptomatic bacteriuria, hematuria and proteinuria. The US Preventive Services Task Force. *American Family Physician* 1990;42:389–95.

342. Etherington IJ, James DK. Reagent strip testing of antenatal urine specimens for infection. *British Journal of Obstetrics and Gynaecology* 1993;100:806–8.

343. Shelton SD, Boggess KA, Kirvan K, Sedor F, Herbert WN. Urinary interleukin-8 with asymptomatic bacteriuria in pregnancy. *Obstetrics and Gynecology* 2001;97:583–6.

344. Millar L, Debuque L, Leialoha C, Grandinetti A, Killeen J. Rapid enzymatic urine screening test to detect bacteriuria in pregnancy. *Obstetrics and Gynecology* 2000;95:601–4.

345. McNair RD, MacDonald SR, Dooley SL, Peterson LR. Evaluation of the centrifuged and Gram-stained smear, urinalysis, and reagent strip testing to detect asymptomatic bacteriuria in obstetric patients. *American Journal of Obstetrics and Gynecology* 2000;182:1076–9.

346. Robertson AW, Duff P. The nitrite and leukocyte esterase tests for the evaluation of asymptomatic bacteriuria in obstetric patients. *Obstetrics and Gynecology* 1988;71:878–81.

347. Bachman JW, Heise RH, Naessens JM, Timmerman MG. A study of various tests to detect asymptomatic urinary tract infections in an obstetric population. *JAMA* 1993;270:1971–4.

348. Tincello DG, Richmond DH. Evaluation of reagent strips in detecting asymptomatic bacteriuria in early pregnancy: prospective case series. *British Medical Journal* 1998;316:435–7.

349. Abyad A. Screening for asymptomatic bacteriuria in pregnancy: urinalysis vs. urine culture. *Journal of Family Practice* 1991;33:471–4.

350. Graninger W, Fleischmann D, Schneeweiss B, Aram L, Stockenhuber F. Rapid screening for bacteriuria in pregnancy. *Infection* 1992;20:9–11.

351. Smaill, F. Antibiotic treatment for symptomatic bacteriuria: antibiotic vs. no treatment for asymptomatic bacteriuria in pregnancy. *Cochrane Database of Systematic Reviews* 2002;(3):1–5.

352. Villar J, Lydon-Rochelle MT, Gulmezoglu AM. Duration of treatment for asymptomatic bacteriuria during pregnancy. *Cochrane Database of Systematic Reviews* 2001;(2).

353. Centers for Disease Control and Prevention. Sexually transmitted diseases treatment guidelines 2002. *Morbidity and Mortality Weekly Report* 2002;51:1–80.

354. Joesoef M, Schmid G. Bacterial vaginosis. *Clinical Evidence* 2002;7:1400–8.

355. Goldenberg RL, Klebanoff MA, Nugent R, Krohn MA, Hilliers S, Andrews WW. Bacterial colonization of the vagina during pregnancy in four ethnic groups. Vaginal Infections and Prematurity Study Group. *American Journal of Obstetrics and Gynecology* 1996;174:1618–21.

356. Hay PE, Morgan DJ, Ison CA, Bhide SA, Romney M, McKenzie P, *et al.* A longitudinal study of bacterial vaginosis during pregnancy. *British Journal of Obstetrics and Gynaecology* 1994;101:1048–53.

357. Flynn CA, Helwig AL, Meurer LN. Bacterial vaginosis in pregnancy and the risk of prematurity: a meta-analysis. *Journal of Family Practice* 1999;48:885–92.

358. Gratacos E, Figueras F, Barranco M, Vila J, Cararach V, Alonso PL, *et al.* Spontaneous recovery of bacterial vaginosis during pregnancy is not associated with an improved perinatal outcome. *Acta Obstetricia et Gynecologica Scandinavica* 1998;77:37–40.

359. Amsel R, Totten PA, Spiegel CA. Nonspecific vaginitis: diagnostic criteria and microbial and epidemiological associations. *American Journal of Medicine* 1983;74:14–22.

360. Nugent RP, Krohn MA, Hillier SL. Reliability of diagnosing bacterial vaginosis is improved by a standardised methods of Gram stain interpretation. *Journal of Clinical Microbiology* 1991;29:297–301.

361. Thiagarajan M. Evaluation of the use of yogurt in treating bacterial vaginosis in pregnancy. *Journal of Clinical Epidemiology* 1998;51:22S.

362. McDonald H, Brocklehurst P, Parsons J, Vigneswaran R. Interventions for treating bacterial vaginosis in pregnancy. *Cochrane Database of Systematic Reviews* 2003;(2):1–30.

363. Ugwumadu A, Manyonda I, Reid F, Hay P. Effect of early oral clindamycin on late miscarriage and preterm delivery in asymptomatic women with abnormal vaginal flora and bacterial vaginosis: a randomised controlled trial. *Lancet* 2003;361:983–8.

364. Stary A. European guideline for the management of chlamydial infection. *International Journal of STD and AIDS* 2001;12:30–3.

365. Preece PM, Ades A, Thompson RG, Brooks JH. Chlamydia trachomatis infection in late pregnancy: A prospective study. *Paediatric and Perinatal Epidemiology* 1989;3:268–77.

366. Goh BT, Morgan-Capner P, Lim KS. Chlamydial screening of pregnant women in a sexually transmitted diseases clinic. *British Journal of Venereal Diseases* 1982;58:327–9.

367. Association of chlamydia trachomatis and mycoplasma hominis with intrauterine growth restriction and preterm delivery. The John Hopkins Study of Cervicitis and Adverse Pregnancy Outcome. *American Journal of Epidemiology* 1989;129:1247–51.

368. Ryan GM, Jr, Abdella TN, McNeeley SG, Baselski VS, Drummond DE. Chlamydia trachomatis infection in pregnancy and effect of treatment on outcome. [see comments.]. *American Journal of Obstetrics and Gynecology* 1990;162:34–9.

369. Brocklehurst P, Rooney G. Interventions for treating genital chlamydia trachomatis infection in pregnancy. *Cochrane Database of Systematic Reviews* 2002;(3).

370. Preece PM, Anderson JM, Thompson RG. Chlamydia trachomatis infection in infants: A prospective study. *Archives of Disease in Childhood* 1989;64:525–9.

371. Schachter J, Grossman M, Sweet RL, Holt J, Jordan C, Bishop E. Prospective study of perinatal transmission of Chlamydia trachomatis. *JAMA* 1986;255:3374–7.

372. FitzGerald MR, Welch J, Robinson AJ, Ahmed-Jushuf IH. Clinical guidelines and standards for the management of uncomplicated genital chlamydial infection. *International Journal of STD and AIDS* 1998;9:253–62.

373. Scottish Intercollegiate Guidelines Network. *Management of genital Chlamydia trachomatis* Infection. SIGN Publication No. 42. Edinburgh: Scottish Intercollegiate Guideline Network; 2000.

374. Ryan M, Miller E, Waight P. Cytomegalovirus infection in England and Wales: 1992 and 1993. *Communicable Diseases Report* 1995;5: R74–6.

375. Preece PM, Tookey P, Ades A, Peckham CS. Congenital cytomegalovirus infection: predisposing maternal factors. *Journal of Epidemiology and Community Health* 1986;40:205–9.

376. Peckham CS, Coleman JC, Hurley R, Chin KS, Henderson K, Preece PM. Cytomegalovirus infection in pregnancy: preliminary findings from a prospective study. *Lancet* 1983;1352–5.

377. Bolyard EA, Tablan OC, Williams WW, Pearson ML, Shapiro CN, Deitchmann SD. Guideline for infection control in health care personnel. Centers for Disease Control and Prevention. *Infection Control and Hospital Epidemiology* 1998;19:407–63. Erratum 1998;19:493

378. Stagno S, Whitley RJ. Herpesvirus infections of pregnancy. Part 1: Cytomegalovirus and Epstein-Barr virus infections. *New England Journal of Medicine* 1985;313:1270–4.

379. Boxall E, Skidmore S, Evans C, Nightingale S. The prevalence of hepatitis B and C in an antenatal population of various ethnic origins. *Epidemiology and Infection* 1994;113:523–8.

380. Brook MG, Lever AM, Kelly D, Rutter D, Trompeter RS, Griffiths P, *et al*. Antenatal screening for hepatitis B is medically and economically effective in the prevention of vertical transmission: three years experience in a London hospital. *Quarterly Journal of Medicine* 1989;71:313–7.

381. Chrystie I, Sumner D, Palmer S, Kenney A, Banatvala J. Screening of pregnant women for evidence of current hepatitis B infection: selective or universal? *Health Trends* 1992;24:13–5.

382. Derso A, Boxall EH, Tarlow MJ, Flewett TH. Transmission of HBsAg from mother to infant in four ethnic groups. *British Medical Journal* 1978;15(6118):949–952.

383. Beasley RP, Trepo C, Stevens CE, Szmuness W. The e antigen and vertical transmission of hepatitis B surface antigen. *American Journal of Epidemiology* 1977;105:94–8.

384. Beasley RP, Hwang L-Y. Epidemiology of hepatocellular carcinoma. In: Vyas GN, Dienstag JL, Hoofnagle JH, editors. *Viral hepatitis and liver disease*. Orlando, FL: Grune and Stratton; 1984. p. 209–24.

385. Ramsay M, Gay N, Balogun K, Collins M. Control of hepatitis B in the United Kingdom. *Vaccine* 1998;16 Suppl:S52–5.

386. Sehgal A, Sehgal R, Gupta I, Bhakoo ON, Ganguly NK. Use of hepatitis B vaccine alone or in combination with hepatitis B immunoglobulin for immunoprophylaxis of perinatal hepatitis B infection. *Journal of Tropical Pediatrics* 1992;38:247–51.

387. Wong VC, Ip HM, Reesink HW, Lelie PN, Reerink-Brongers EE, Yeung CY, *et al*. Prevention of the HBsAg carrier state in newborn infants of mothers who are chronic carriers of HBsAg and HBeAg by administration of hepatitis-B vaccine and hepatitis-B immunoglobulin. Double-blind randomised placebo-controlled study. *Lancet* 1984;1:921–6.

388. Zhu Q. A preliminary study on interruption of HBV transmission in uterus. *Chinese Medical Journal* 1997;110:145–7.

389. Lo K, Tsai Y, Lee S, Yeh C, Wang J, Chiang BN, *et al*. Combined passive and active immunization for interruption of perinatal transmission of hepatitis B virus in Taiwan. *Hepato-gastroenterology* 1985;32:65–8.

390. Beasley RP, Hwang LY, Lee GC, Lan CC, Roan CH, Huang FY, *et al*. Prevention of perinatally transmitted hepatitis B virus infections with hepatitis B virus infections with hepatitis B immune globulin and hepatitis B vaccine. *Lancet* 1983;2:1099–102.

391. Nair PV, Weissman JY, Tong MJ, Thursby MW, Paul RH, Henneman CE. Efficacy of hepatitis B immune globulin in prevention of perinatal transmission of the hepatitis B virus. *Gastroenterology* 1984;87:293–8.

392. Xu Z-Y, Liu C-B, Francis DP. Prevention of perinatal acquisition of hepatitis B virus carriage using vaccine: preliminary report of a randomized, double-blind placebo-controlled and comparative trial. *Pediatrics* 1985;76:713–18.

393. Balmer S, Bowens A, Bruce E, Farrar H, Jenkins C, Williams R. *Quality management for screening: report to the National Screening Committee*. Leeds: Nuffield Institute for Health; 2000.

394. Summers PR, Biswas MK, Pastorek JG, Pernoll ML, Smith LG, Bean BE. The pregnant hepatitis B carrier: evidence favoring comprehensive antepartum screening. *Obstetrics and Gynecology* 1987;69:701–4.

395. Chaita TM, Graham SM, Maxwell SM, Sirivasin W, Sabcharoen A, Beeching NJ. Salivary sampling for hepatitis B surface antigen carriage: a sensitive technique suitable for epidemiological studies. *Annals of Tropical Paediatrics* 1995;15:135–9.

396. Pembrey L, Newell ML, Tovo PA. Hepatitis C virus infection in pregnant women and their children. *Italian Journal of Gynaecology and Obstetrics* 2000;12:21–8.

397. Whittle M, Peckham C, Anionwu E, et al. Antenatal screening for hepatitis C. Working party report on screening for hepatitis C in the UK. January 2002. [www.nelh.nhs.uk/screening/antenatal_pps/Hep_C_NSC.pdf] Accessed 4 September 2003.

398. Ades AE, Parker S, Walker J, Cubitt WD, Jones R. HCV prevalence in pregnant women in the UK. *Epidemiology and Infection* 2000;125:399–405.

399. Okamoto M, Nagata I, Murakami J, Kaji S, Iitsuka T, Hoshika T, et al. Prospective reevaluation of risk factors in mother-to-child transmission of hepatitis C virus: high virus load, vaginal delivery, and negative anti-NS4 antibody. *Journal of Infectious Diseases* 2000;182:1511–4.

400. Tajiri H, Miyoshi Y, Funada S, Etani Y, Abe J, Onodera T, et al. Prospective study of mother-to-infant transmission of hepatitis C virus. *Pediatric Infectious Disease Journal* 2001;20:10–4.

401. Paccagnini S, Principi N, Massironi E, Tanzi E, Romano L, Muggiasca ML, et al. Perinatal transmission and manifestation of hepatitis C virus infection in a high risk population. *Pediatric Infectious Disease Journal* 1995;14:195–9.

402. Tovo PA, Pembrey L, Newell M-L. Persistence rate and progression of vertically acquired hepatitis C infection. *Journal of Infectious Diseases* 2001;181:419–24.

403. Ketzinel-Gilad M, Colodner SL, Hadary R, Granot E, Shouval D, Galun E. Transient transmission of hepatitis C virus from mothers to newborns. *European Journal of Clinical Microbiology and Infectious Diseases* 2000;19:267–74.

404. Lin HH, Kao J-H. Effectiveness of second- and third-generation immunoassays for the detection of hepatitis C virus infection in pregnant women. *Journal of Obstetrics and Gynaecology Research* 2000;26:265–70.

405. Vrielink H, Reesink HW, van den Burg PJ. Performance of three generations of anti-hepatitis C virus enzyme-linked immunosorbent assays in donors and patients. *Vox Sanguinis* 1997;72:67–70.

406. Zaaijer HL, Vrielink H, Van Exel-Oehlers PJ, Cuypers HT, Lelie PN. Confirmation of hepatitis C infection: a comparison of five immunoblot assays. *Transfusion* 1993;33:634–8.

407. Unlinked Anonymous Surveys Steering Group. *Prevalence of HIV and hepatitis infections in the United Kingdom 2001. Annual report of the Unlinked Anonymous Prevalence Monitoring Programme.* London: Department of Health; 2002. [www.doh.gov.uk/hivhepatitis/ hivhepatitis2001.pdf] Accessed 21 August 2003.

408. Unlinked Anonymous Surveys Steering Group. *Prevalence of HIV and hepatitis infections in the United Kingdom 2000. Annual report of the Unlinked Anonymous Prevalence Monitoring Programme.* London: Department of Health; 2001. p. 5, 7, 24–30.

409. Connor EM, Sperling RS, Gelber R, Kiselev P, Scott G, O'Sullivan MJ, et al. Reduction of maternal–infant transmission of human immunodeficiency virus type 1 with zidovudine treatment. Pediatric AIDS Clinical Trials Group Protocol 076 Study Group. *New England Journal of Medicine* 1994;331:1173–80.

410. Mandelbrot L, Le Chenadec J, Berrebi A, Bongain A, Benifla J-L, Delfraissy JF, et al. Perinatal HIV-1 transmission. Interaction between zidovudine prophylaxis and mode of delivery in the French perinatal cohort. *JAMA* 1998;280:55–60.

411. Duong T, Ades AE, Gibb DM, Tookey PA, Masters J. Vertical transmission rates for HIV in the British Isles: estimates based on surveillance data. *British Medical Journal* 1999;319:1227–9.

412. AIDS and HIV infection in the United Kingdom: monthly report. *CDR Weekly* 2001;11(17):10–15. [www.phls.org.uk/publications/cdr/ PDFfiles/2001/cdr1701.pdf] Accessed 4 September 2003.

413. Samson L, King S. Evidence-based guidelines for universal counselling and offering of HIV testing in pregnancy in Canada. *Canadian Medical Association Journal* 1998;158:1449–57 [erratum appears in *CMAJ* 1999;159(1):22.

414. Van Doornum GJJ, Buimer M, Gobbers E, Bindels PJ, Coutinho RA. Evaluation of an expanded two-ELISA approach for confirmation of reactive serum samples in an HIV-screening programme for pregnant women. *Journal of Medical Virology* 1998;54:285–90.

415. Public Health Laboratory Service AIDS Diagnosis Working Group. Towards error free HIV diagnosis: notes on laboratory practice. *PHLS Microbiology Digest* 1992;9:61–4.

416. Brocklehurst P, Volmink J. Antiretrovirals for reducing the risk of mother-to-child transmission of HIV infection. *Cochrane Database of Systematic Reviews* 2002;(3).

417. European Mode of Delivery Collaboration. Elective caesarean-section versus vaginal delivery in prevention of vertical HIV-1 transmission: a randomised clinical trial. The European Mode of Delivery Collaboration. *Lancet* 1999;353:1035–9. [published erratum appears in *Lancet* 1999;353:1714].

418. Ricci E, Parazzini F. Caesarean section and antiretroviral treatment. *Lancet* 2000;355:496.

419. Cunningham CK, Chaix ML, Rekacewicz C, Britto P, Rouzioux C, Gelber RD, et al. Development of resistance mutations in women receiving standard antiretroviral therapy who received intrapartum nevirapine to prevent perinatal human immunodeficiency virus type 1 transmission: a substudy of pediatric AIDS clinical trials group protocol 316. *Journal of Infectious Diseases* 2002;186:181–8.

420. Palumbo P, Holland B, Dobbs T, Pau CP, Luo CC, Abrams EJ, et al. Antiretroviral resistance mutations among pregnant human immunodeficiency virus type 1-infected women and their newborns in the United States: vertical transmission and clades. *Journal of Infectious Diseases* 2001;184:1120–6.

421. Control and prevention of rubella: evaluation and management of suspected outbreaks, rubella in pregnant women, and surveillance for congenital rubella syndrome. *Morbidity and Mortality Weekly Report* 2001; 50:1–23.

422. Tookey P. Antenatal screening for rubella. Personal communication; 2002.

423. Miller E, Waight P, Gay N, Ramsay M, Vurdien J, Morgan-Capner P, et al. The epidemiology of rubella in England and Wales before and after the 1994 measles and rubella vaccination campaign: fourth joint report from the PHLS and the National Congenital Rubella Surveillance Programme. *Communicable Diseases Report* 1997;7:R26–32.

424. Tookey PA, Corina-Borja M, Peckham CS. Rubella susceptibility among pregnant women in North London, 1996–1999. *Journal of Public Health Medicine* 2002;24:211–6.

425. Miller E, Cradock-Watson JE, Pollock TM. Consequences of confirmed maternal rubella at successive stages of pregnancy. *Lancet* 1982;2:781–4.

426. Grangeot-Keros L, Enders G. Evaluation of a new enzyme immunoassay based on recombinant Rubella virus-like particles for detection of immunoglobulin M antibodies to Rubella virus. *Journal of Clinical Microbiology* 1997;35:398–401.

427. Morgan-Capner P, Crowcroft NS. Guidelines on the management of, and exposure to, rash illness in pregnancy (including consideration of relevant antibody screening programmes in pregnancy). On behalf of the PHLS joint working party of the advisory committees of virology and vaccines and immunisation. *Communicable Disease and Public Health/PHLS* 2002;5(1):59–71.

428. Grillner L, Forsgren M, Barr B. Outcome of rubella during pregnancy with special reference to the 17th–24th weeks of gestation. Scandinavian Journal of Infectious Diseases 1983;Vol 15:321–5.

429. Morgan-Capner P, Hodgson J, Hambling MH. Detection of rubella-specific IgM in subclinical rubella reinfection in pregnancy. *Lancet* 1985;1:244–6.

430. Revised ACIP recommendation for avoiding pregnancy after receiving a rubella-containing vaccine. *MMWR–Morbidity and Mortality Weekly Report* 2001;50:1117.

431. Health Protection Agency. Incidence of Group B streptococcal disease in infants aged less than 90 days old. *CDR Weekly* 2002;12(16):3. [193.129.245.226/publications/cdr/archive02/News/news1602.html gpB] Accessed 21 August 2003.

432. Merenstein GB, Todd WA, Brown G. Group B beta-hemolytic streptococcus: Randomized controlled treatment study at term. *Obstetrics and Gynecology* 1980;55:315–8.

433. Regan JA, Klebanoff MA, Nugent RP. The epidemiology of Group B streptococcal colonization in pregnancy. *Obstetrics and Gynecology* 1991;77:604–10.

434. Hastings MJ, Easmon CS, Neill J, Bloxham B, Rivers RP. Group B streptococcal colonisation and the outcome of pregnancy. *Journal of Infection* 1986;12:23–9.

435. Oddie S, Embleton ND. Risk factors for early onset neonatal group B streptococcal sepsis: case–control study. *British Medical Journal* 2002;325:308.

436. Centers for Disease Control and Prevention. Prevention of perinatal group B streptococcal disease. Revised Guidelines from CDC. *Morbidity and Mortality Weekly Report* 2002;51(RR11):1–25. [www.cdc.gov/mmwr/preview/mmwrhtml/rr5111a1.htm] Accessed 21 August 2003.

437. Fey R, Stuart J, George R. Neonatal group B streptococcal disease in England and Wales 1981–1997. *Archives of Disease in Childhood* 1999;80:A70.

438. Bignardi GE. Surveillance of neonatal group B streptococcal infection in Sunderland. *Communicable Disease and Public Health/PHLS* 1999;2(1):64–5.

439. Yancey MK, Schuchat A, Brown LK, Ventura VL, Markenson GR. The accuracy of late antenatal screening cultures in predicting genital group B streptococcal colonization at delivery. *Obstetrics and Gynecology* 1996;88:811–5.

440. Boyer KM, Gadzala CA, Kelly PD, Burd LI, Gotoff SP. Selective intrapartum chemoprophylaxis of neonatal group B streptococcal early-onset disease. II. Predictive value of prenatal cultures. *Journal of Infectious Diseases* 1983;148:802–9.

441. Molnar P, Biringer A, McGeer A, McIsaac W. Can pregnant women obtain their own specimens for group B streptococcus? A comparison of maternal versus physician screening. The Mount Sinai GBS Screening Group. *Family Practice* 1997;14:403–6.

442. Spieker MR, White DG, Quist BK. Self-collection of group B Streptococcus cultures in pregnant women. *Military Medicine* 1999;164:471–4.

443. Schrag SJ, Zell ER, Lynfield R, Roome A, Arnold KE, Craig AS, et al. A population-based comparison of strategies to prevent early-onset group B streptococcal disease in neonates. *New England Journal of Medicine* 2002;347:233–9.

444. Smaill, F. Intrapartum antibiotics for group B streptococcal colonisation. *Cochrane Database of Systematic Reviews* 1999;(3):1–5.

445. Benitz WE, Gould JB, Druzin ML. Antimicrobial prevention of early-onset group B streptococcal sepsis: estimates of risk reduction based on a critical literature review. *Pediatrics* 1999;103:e78.

446. Gibbs RS, McNabb F. Randomized clinical trial of intrapartum clindamycin cream for reduction of group B streptococcal maternal and neonatal colonization. *Infectious Disease in Obstetrics and Gynecology* 1996;41:25–7.

447. Schrag SJ, Zywicki S, Farley MM, Reingold AL. Group B streptococcal disease in the era of intrapartum antibiotic prophylaxis. *New England Journal of Medicine* 2000;342:15–20.

448. Jeffery HE, Moses LM. Eight-year outcome of universal screening and intrapartum antibiotics for maternal group B streptococcal carriers. *Pediatrics* 1998;101:E2.

449. Egglestone SI, Turner AJL. Serological diagnosis of syphilis. *Communicable Disease and Public Health/PHLS* 2000;3:158–62.

450. Doherty L, Fenton KA, Jones J, Paine TC, Higgins SP, Williams D, et al. Syphilis: old problem, new strategy. *British Medical Journal* 2002;325:153–6.

451. Division of STD/HIV Prevention. *Sexually Transmitted Disease Surveillance 1993*. Atlanta, GA: Centers for Disease Control and Prevention;1994.

452. Flowers J, Camilleri-Ferrante. *Antenatal screening for syphilis in East Anglia: a cost-benefit analysis*. Cambridge: Institute of Public Health; 1996.

453. STD Section, HIV and STD Division, PHLS Communicable Disease Surveillance Centre, with the PHLS Syphilis Working Group. Report to the National Screening Committee. *Antenatal Syphilis Screening in the UK: A Systematic Review and National Options Appraisal with Recommendations*. London: PHLS; 1998.

454. Public Health Laboratory Service, DHSS & PS, Scottish ISD D 5 Collaborative Group. *Sexually transmitted infections in the UK: new episodes seen at Genitourinary Medicine Clinics, 1995–2000*. London: PHLS; 2001.

455. Ingraham NR Jr. The value of penicillin alone in the prevention and treatment of congenital syphilis. *Acta Dermato-Venereologica* 1951;31:60–88.

456. Association of Genitourinary Medicine and the Medical Society for the Study of Venereal Diseases, Clinical Effectiveness Group. *UK national guidelines on the management of early syphilis*. London: Medical Society for the Study of Venereal Diseases; 2002. p. 1–18.

457. Goh BT, van Voorst Vader PC. European guideline for the management of syphilis. *International Journal of STD and AIDS* 2001;12:14–26.

458. Fiumara NJ, Fleming WL, Downing JG, Good FL. The incidence of prenatal syphilis at the Boston City Hospital. *New England Journal of Medicine* 1952;247:48–52.

459. Rotchford K, Lombard C, Zuma K, Wilkinson D. Impact on perinatal mortality of missed opportunities to treat maternal syphilis in rural South Africa: baseline results from a clinic randomized controlled trial. *Tropical Medicine and International Health* 2000;5:800–4.

460. Young H, Moyes A, McMillan A, Patterson J. Enzyme immunoassay for anti-treponemal IgG: Screening of confirmatory test? *Journal of Clinical Pathology* 1992;45:37–41.

461. Young H, Moyes A, McMillan A, Robertson DHH. Screening for treponemal infection by a new enzyme immunoassay. *Genitourinary Medicine* 1989;65:72–8.

462. Walker, GJA. Antibiotics for syphilis diagnosed during pregnancy [protocol]. *Cochrane Database of Systematic Reviews* 2001;(2).

463. Alexander JM, Sheffield JS, Sanchez PJ, Mayfield J, Wendel GD Jr. Efficacy of treatment for syphilis in pregnancy. *Obstetrics and Gynecology* 1999;93:5–8.

464. Watson-Jones D, Gumodoka B, Weiss H, Changalucha J, Todd J, Mugeye K, et al. Syphilis in pregnancy in Tanzania. II. The effectiveness of antenatal syphilis screening and single-dose benzathine penicillin treatment for the prevention of adverse pregnancy outcomes. *Journal of Infectious Diseases* 2002;186:948–57.

465. Hashisaki P, Wertzberger GG, Conrad GL, Nicholes CR. Erythromycin failure in the treatment of syphilis in a pregnant woman. *Sexually Transmitted Diseases* 1983;10:36–8.

466. Eskild A, Oxman A, Magnus P, Bjorndal A, Bakketeig LS. Screening for toxoplasmosis in pregnancy: what is the evidence of reducing a health problem? *Journal of Medical Screening* 1996;3:188–94.

467. Ades AE, Parker S, Gilbert R, Tookey PA, Berry T, Hjelm M, *et al*. Maternal prevalence of toxoplasma antibody based on anonymous neonatal serosurvey: a geographical analysis. *Epidemiology and Infection* 1993;110:127–33.

468. Allain JP, Palmer CR, Pearson G. Epidemiological study of latent and recent infection by toxoplasma gondii in pregnant women from a regional population in the UK. *Journal of Infection* 1998;36:189–96.

469. Lebech M, Andersen O, Christensen NC, Hertel J, Nielsen HE, Peitersen B, *et al*. Feasibility of neonatal screening for toxoplasma infection in the absence of prenatal treatment. *Lancet* 1999;353:1834–7.

470. Cook AJ, Gilbert RE, Buffolano W, Zufferey J, Petersen E, Jenum PA, *et al*. Sources of toxoplasma infection in pregnant women: European multicentre case–control study. European Research Network on Congenital Toxoplasmosis. *British Medical Journal* 2000;321:142–7.

471. Pratlong F, Boulot P, Villena I, Issert E, Tamby I, Cazenave J, *et al*. Antenatal diagnosis of congenital toxoplasmosis: evaluation of the biological parameters in a cohort of 286 patients. British Journal of Obstetrics and Gynaecology 1996;103:552–7.

472. Dunn D, Wallon M, Peyron F, Petersen E, Peckham C, Gilbert R. Mother-to-child transmission of toxoplasmosis: risk estimates for clinical counselling. *Lancet* 1999;353:1829–33.

473. Foulon W, Villena I, Stray-Pedersen B, Decoster A, Lappalainen M, Pinon JM, *et al*. Treatment of toxoplasmosis during pregnancy: a multicenter study of impact on fetal transmission and children's sequelae at age 1 year. *American Journal of Obstetrics and Gynecology* 1999;180:410–5.

474. Cubitt WD, Ades AE, Peckham CS. Evaluation of five commercial assays for screening antenatal sera for antibodies to Toxoplasma gondii. *Journal of Clinical Pathology* 1992;45:435–8.

475. Gilbert RE, Peckham CS. Congenital toxoplasmosis in the United Kingdom: to screen or not to screen? *Journal of Medical Screening* 2002;9:135–41.

476. Peyron, F, Wallon, M, Liou, C, and Garner, P. Treatments for toxoplasmosis in pregnancy. *Cochrane Database of Systematic Reviews* 2002;(3).

477. Wallon M, Liou C, Garner P, Peyron F. Congenital toxoplasmosis: systematic review of evidence of efficacy of treatment in pregnancy. *British Medical Journal* 1999;318:1511–14.

478. Garland SM, O'Reilly MA. The risks and benefits of antimicrobial therapy in pregnancy. *Drug Safety* 1995;13:188–205.

479. Bader TJ, Macones GA, Asch DA. Prenatal screening for toxoplasmosis. *Obstetrics and Gynecology* 1997;90:457–64.

480. Scottish Intercollegiate Guidelines Network. Management of diabetes: a national clinical guideline. SIGN Publication No. 55Edinburgh: SIGN; 2001. [www.sign.ac.uk/guidelines/fulltext/55/index.html] Accessed 21 August 2003.

481. World Health Organization, Department of Noncommunicable Disease Surveillance. *Definition, diagnosis and classification of diabetes mellitus and its complications. Report of a WHO consultation. Part 1: diagnosis and classification of diabetes mellitus.* Geneva: World Health Organization; 1999.

482. Alberti KGMM, Zimmet PZ. Definition, diagnosis and classification of diabetes mellitus and its complications. Part 1: Diagnosis and classification of diabetes mellitus. Provisional report of a WHO consultation. *Diabetic Medicine* 1998;15:539–53.

483. Scott DA, Loveman E, McIntyre L, Waugh N. Screening for gestational diabetes: a systematic review and economic evaluation. *Health Technology Assessment* 2002;6:1–172.

484. World Health Organization. *Prevention of diabetes mellitus: report of a WHO study group.* WHO Technical Report Series No. 844. Geneva: WHO; 1994.

485. Mestman JH, Anderson GV, Guadalupe V. Follow-up study of 360 subjects *with abnormal carbohydrate metabolism during pregnancy. Obstetrics* and Gynecology 1972;39:421–5.

486. Jensen DM, Sorensen B, Feilberg-Jorgensen N, Westergaard JG, Beck-Neilsen H. Maternal and perinatal outcomes in 143 Danish women with gestational diabetes mellitus and 143 controls with a similar risk profile. *Diabetic Medicine* 2000;17:281–6.

487. O'Sullivan JB, Charles D, Mahan CM, Dandrow RV. Gestational diabetes and perinatal mortality rate. *American Journal of Obstetrics and Gynecology* 1973;116:901–4.

488. Essel JK, Opai-Tetteh ET. Macrosomia: maternal and fetal risk factors. *South African Medical Journal* 1995;85(1):43–6.

489. Vogel N, Burnand B, Vial Y, Ruiz J, Paccaud F, Hohlfeld P. Screening for gestational diabetes: variation in guidelines. *European Journal Obstetrics, Gynecology and Reproductive Biology* 2000;91:29–36.

490. Marquette GP, Klein VR, Niebyl JR. Efficacy of screening for gestational diabetes. *American Journal of Perinatology* 1985;2:7–9.

491. O'Sullivan JB, Mahan CM, Charles D, Dandrow RV. Screening criteria for high-risk gestational diabetic patients. *American Journal of Obstetrics and Gynecology* 1973;116:895–900.

492. Wen SW, Liu S, Kramer MS, Joseph KS, Levitt C, Marcoux S, *et al*. Impact of prenatal glucose screening on the diagnosis of gestational diabetes and on pregnancy outcomes. *American Journal of Epidemiology* 2000;152:1009–14.

493. Watson WJ. Screening for glycosuria during pregnancy. *Southern Medical Journal* 1990;83:156–8.

494. Gribble RK, Meier PR, Berg RL. The value of urine screening for glucose at each prenatal visit. *Obstetrics and Gynecology* 1995;86:405–10.

495. Hooper DE. Detecting GD and preeclampsia. Effectiveness of routine urine screening for glucose and protein. *Journal of Reproductive Medicine* 1996;41:885–8.

496. McElduff A, Goldring J, Gordon P, Wyndham L. A direct comparison of the measurement of a random plasma glucose and a post50 g glucose load glucose, in the detection of gestational diabetes. *Australian and New Zealand Journal of Obstetrics and Gynaecology* 1994;34:28–30.

497. Jowett NI, Samanta AK, Burden AC. Screening for diabetes in pregnancy: is a random blood glucose enough? *Diabetic Medicine* 1987;4:160–3.

498. Reichelt AJ, Spichler ER, Branchtein L, Nucci LB, Franco LJ, Schmidt MI. Fasting plasma glucose is a useful test for the detection of gestational diabetes. Brazilian Study of Gestational Diabetes (EBDG) Working Group. *Diabetes Care* 1998;21:1246–9.

499. Perucchini D, Fischer U, Spinas GA, Huch R, Huch A, Lehmann R. Using fasting plasma glucose concentrations to screen for gestational diabetes mellitus: prospective population based study. *British Medical Journal* 1999;319:812–5.

500. Lewis GF, McNally C, Blackman JD, Polonsky KS, Barron WM. Prior feeding alters the response to the 50 g glucose challenge test in pregnancy. The Staub-Traugott Effect revisited. *Diabetes Care* 1993;16:1551–6.

501. Watson WJ. Serial changes in the 50-g oral glucose test in pregnancy: implications for screening. *Obstetrics and Gynecology* 1989;74:40–3.

502. Jovanovic L, Peterson CM. Screening for gestational diabetes. Optimum timing and criteria for retesting. *Diabetes* 1985;34:21–3.

503. Expert Committee on the Diagnosis and Classification of Diabetes Mellitus Report of the expert committee on the diagnosis and classification of diabetes mellitus. *Diabetes Care 2000*;26 Supplement 1:S5–S20.

504. Walkinshaw SA. Dietary regulation for 'gestational diabetes'. *Cochrane Database of Systematic Reviews* 2000;(2).

505. Persson B, Stangenberg M, Hansson U, Nordlander E. Gestational diabetes mellitus (GDM). Comparative evaluation of two treatment regimens, diet versus insulin and diet. *Diabetes* 1985;34:101–4.

506. Naylor CD, Sermer M, Chen E, Sykora K. Cesarean delivery in relation to birth weight and gestational glucose tolerance. Pathophysiology or practice style? *JAMA* 1996;275:1165–70.

507. Avery MD, Leon AS, Kopher RA. Effects of a partially home-based exercise program for women with gestational diabetes. *Obstetrics and Gynecology* 1997;89:10–5.

508. Goldberg JD, Franklin B, Lasser D, Jornsay DL, Hausknecht RU, Ginsberg-Fellner F, *et al*. Gestational diabetes: impact of home glucose monitoring on neonatal birth weight. *American Journal of Obstetrics and Gynecology* 1986;154:546–50.

509. Roberts JM, Redman CW. Pre-eclampsia: more than pregnancy-induced hypertension. *Lancet* 1993;341:1447–51.

510. Douglas KA, Redman CW. Eclampsia in the United Kingdom. *British Medical Journal* 1994;309:1395–400.

511a. National High Blood Pressure Education Programme. *Working Group Report on high blood pressure in pregnancy.* NIH Publication 00–3029. Bethesda, MD: National Institutes of Health, National Heart, Lung and Blood Institute; 2000.

511b. National High Blood Pressure Education Program Working Group. Report on high blood pressure in pregnancy. *American Journal of Obstetrics and Gynecology* 1990;163:1691–712.

512. Duckitt, K. Risk factors for pre-eclampsia that can be assessed at the antenatal booking visit: a systematic review. Presented at the International Society for the Study of Hypertension in Pregnancy Conference, 24–25 July 2003, Glasgow. 2003.

513. Friedman EA. *Blood pressure, edema and proteinuria in pregnancy.* Oxford: Elsevier Scientific; 1976.

514. Redman CW. Hypertension in pregnancy. pp 182–225. 1995.

515. Barton JR, O'Brien JM, Bergauer NK, Jacques DL, Sibai BM. Mild gestational hypertension remote from term: progression and outcome. American Journal of *Obstetrics and Gynaecology* 2001;184:979–83.

516a. Page EW, Christianson R. The impact of mean arterial pressure in the middle trimester upon the outcome of pregnancy. *American Journal of Obstetrics and Gynecology* 1976;125:740–6.

516b. Page EW, Christianson R. Influence of blood pressure changes with and without proteinuria upon outcome of pregnancy. *American Journal of Obstetrics and Gynecology* 1976;126:821–33.

517. Greer IA. Hypertension. In Dunlop W, Calder AA, editors. *High risk pregnancy.* Oxford: Butterworth Heinemann; 1992. p. 30–93.

518. Redman CW, Jefferies M. Revised definition of pre-eclampsia. *Lancet* 1988;1:809–12.

519. North RA, Taylor RS, Schellenberg JC. Evaluation of a definition of pre-eclampsia. *British Journal of Obstetrics and Gynaecology* 1999;106:767–73.

520. Levine RJ. Should the definition of preeclampsia include a rise in diastolic blood pressure > 15 mmHg to a level < 90 mmHg in association with proteinuria? *American Journal of Obstetrics and Gynecology* 2000;183:787–92.

521. Perry IJ, Wilkinson LS, Shinton RA, Beevers DG. Conflicting views on the measurement of blood pressure in pregnancy. *British Journal of Obstetrics and Gynaecology* 1991;98:241–3.

522. Frohlich ED, Grim C, Labarthe DR, Maxwell MH, Perloff D, Weidman WH. Recommendations for human blood pressure determination by sphygmomanometers: Report of a special task force appointed by the Steering Committee, American Heart Association. *Hypertension* 1988;11:210A–22A.

523. Petrie JC, O'Brien ET, Littler WA, de Swiet M. Recommendations on blood pressure measurement. *British Medical Journal* 1986;293:611–5.

524. Shennan AH, Halligan AWF. Measuring blood pressure in normal and hypertensive pregnancy. *Baillieres Clinical Obstetrics and Gynaecology* 1999;13(1):1–26.

525. Cuckson AC, Golara M, Reinders A, Shennan AH. Accuracy of automated devices in pregnancy and pre-eclampsia: a metaanalysis. *Journal of Obstetrics and Gynaecology* 2002;22:S43.

526. Mattoo TK. Arm cuff in the measurement of blood pressure. *American Journal of Hypertension* 2002;15:675–85.

527. Brown MA, Buddle ML, Farrell T, Davis G, Jones M. Randomised trial of management of hypertensive pregnancies by Korotkoff phase IV or phase V. *Lancet* 1998;352:777–81.

528. Shennan A, Gupta M, Halligan A, Taylor DJ, de Swiet M. Lack of reproducibility in pregnancy of Korotkoff phase IV as measured by mercury sphygmomanometry. *Lancet* 1996;347:139–42.

529. MacGillivray I. *Pre-eclampsia. The hypertensive disease of pregnancy.* London: WB Saunders; 1983.

530. Stamilio DM, Sehdev HM, Morgan MA, Propert K, Macones GA. Can antenatal clinical and biochemical markers predict the development of severe preeclampsia? *American Journal of Obstetrics and Gynecology* 2000;182:589–94.

531. Skjaerven R, Wilcox AJ, Lie RT. The interval between pregnancies and the risk of preeclampsia. *New England Journal of Medicine* 2002;346:33–8.

532. Taylor DJ. The epidemiology of hypertension during pregnancy. In: Rubin PC, editor. *Hypertension in pregnancy.* Amsterdam: Elsevier Science; 1988. p. 223–40.

533. Salonen-Ros H, Lichtenstein P, Lipworth W. Genetic effects on the liability of developing pre-eclampsia and gestational hypertension. *American Journal of Medical Genetics* 2000;91:256–60.

534. Sibai BM, Caritis S, Hauth J. Risks of preeclampsia and adverse neonatal outcomes among women with progestational diabetes mellitus. *American Journal of Obstetrics and Gynecology* 2000;182:364–9.

535. Davey DA, MacGillivray I. The classification and definition of the hypertensive disorders of pregnancy. *American Journal of Obstetrics and Gynecology* 1988;158(4):892–898.

536. Murray N, Homer LS, Davis GK, Curtis J, Manzos G, Brown MA. The clinical utility of routine urinalysis in pregnancy: a prospective study. *Medical Journal of Australia* 2002;177:477–80.

537. Shennan AH, Waugh JJS. The measurement of blood pressure and proteinuria. In: Critchley H, MacLean AB, Poston L, Walker JJ, editors. *Pre-eclampsia.* London: RCOG Press; 2003. p. 305–24.

538. Rodriguez-Thompson D, Lieberman ES. Use of a random urinary protein-to-creatinine ratio for the diagnosis of significant proteinuria during pregnancy. *American Journal of Obstetrics and Gynecology* 2001;185:808–11.

539. Ferrazzani S, Caruso A, De Carolis S, Martino IV, Mancuso S. Proteinuria and outcome of 444 pregnancies complicated by hypertension. *American Journal of Obstetrics and Gynecology* 1990;162:366–71.

540. Waugh JJS, Clark TJ, Divakaran TG, Khan KS, Kilby MD. A systematic review and meta-analysis comparing protein/creatinine ratio measurements and dipstick urinalysis in predicting significant proteinuria in pregnancy. Presented at the British Maternal and Fetal Medicine Society, University of York, 20–21 March 2003.

541. Chamberlain G, Morgan M. *ABC of Antenatal Care*. London: BMJ Publishing; 2002.

542. Buekens P, Alexander S, Boutsen M, Blondel B, Kaminski M, Reid M. Randomised controlled trial of routine cervical examinations in pregnancy. European Community Collaborative Study Group on Prenatal Screening. *Lancet* 1994;344:841–4.

543. Iams JD, Goldenberg RL, Meis PJ. The length of the cervix and the risk of spontaneous premature delivery. *New England Journal of Medicine* 1996;334:567–72.

544. Goldenberg RL, Klebanoff M, Carey JC. Vaginal fetal fibronectin measurements from 8 to 22 weeks' gestation and subsequent spontaneous preterm birth. *American Journal of Obstetrics and Gynecology* 2000;183:469–75.

545. Goldenberg RL, Mercer BM, Meis PJ, Copper RL, Das A, McNellis D. The preterm prediction study: fetal fibronectin testing predicts early spontaneous birth. *Obstetrics and Gynecology* 1996;87:643–8.

546. Mercer BM, Goldenberg RL, Das A. The preterm prediction study: a clinical risk assessment system. *American Journal of Obstetrics and Gynecology* 1996;174:1885–95.

547. Newton ER, Barss V, Cetrulo CL. The epidemiology and clinical history of asymptomatic midtrimester placenta previa. *American Journal of Obstetrics and Gynecology* 1984;148:743–8.

548. Lauria MR, Smith RS, Treadwell MC, Comstock CH, Kirk JS, Lee W, et al. The use of second-trimester transvaginal sonography to predict placenta previa. *Ultrasound in Obstetrics and Gynecology* 1996;8:337–40.

549. Leerentveld RA, Gilberts EC, Arnold MJ, Wladimiroff JW. Accuracy and safety of transvaginal sonographic placental localization. *Obstetrics and Gynecology* 1990;76:759–62.

550. Oppenheimer L, Holmes P, Simpson N, Dabrowski A. Diagnosis of low-lying placenta: can migration in the third trimester predict outcome? *Ultrasound in Obstetrics and Gynecology* 2001;18:100–2.

551. Sherman SJ, Carlson DE, Platt LD, Medearis AL. Transvaginal ultrasound: does it help in the diagnosis of placenta previa? *American Journal of Obstetrics and Gynecology* 1991;164:344.

552. Farine D, Peisner DB, Timor-Tritsch IE. Placenta previa: is the traditional diagnostic approach satisfactory? *Journal of Clinical Ultrasound* 1990;18:328–30.

553. Taipale P, Hiilesmaa V, Ylostalo P. Diagnosis of placenta previa by transvaginal sonographic screening at 12–16 weeks in a nonselected population. *Obstetrics and Gynecology* 1997;89:364–7.

554. Taipale P, Hiilesmaa V, Ylostalo P. Transvaginal ultrasonography at 18–23 weeks in predicting placenta previa at delivery. *Ultrasound in Obstetrics and Gynecology* 1998;12:422–5.

555. Hill LM, DiNofrio DM, Chenevey P. Transvaginal sonographic evaluation of first-trimester placenta previa. *Ultrasound in Obstetrics and Gynecology* 1995;5:301–3.

556. Dashe JS, McIntire DD, Ramus RM. Persistence of placenta previa according to gestational age at ultrasound detection. *Obstetrics and Gynecology* 2002;99:692–7.

557. Groo KM, Paterson-Brown S. Placenta praevia and placenta praevia accreta: A review of aetiology, diagnosis and management. *Fetal and Maternal Medicine Review* 2001;12:41–66.

558. Ananth CV, Smulian JC, Vintzileos AM. The association of placenta previa with history of cesarean delivery and abortion: a metaanalysis. *American Journal of Obstetrics and Gynecology* 1997;177:1071–8.

559. Ananth CV, Demissie K, Smulian JC. Placenta previa in singleton and twin births in the United States, 1989 through 1998: a comparison of risk factor profiles and associated conditions. *American Journal of Obstetrics and Gynecology* 2003;188:275–81.

560. Royal College of Obstetricians and Gynaecologists. *Placenta praevia: diagnosis and management*. Guideline No. 27. London: RCOG; 2001.

561. Neilson JP. Interventions for suspected placenta praevia. *Cochrane Database of Systematic Reviews* 2003;(1):1–19.

562. McFarlin BL, Engstrom JL, Sampson MB, Cattledge F. Concurrent validity of Leopold's maneuvers in determining fetal presentation and position. *Journal of Nurse-Midwifery* 1985;30:280–4.

563. Vause S, Hornbuckle J, Thornton JG. Palpation or ultrasound for detecting breech babies? *British Journal of Midwifery* 1997;5:318–9.

564. Thorp JM Jr, Jenkins T, Watson W. Utility of Leopold maneuvers in screening for malpresentation. *Obstetrics and Gynecology* 1991;78:394–6.

565. Olsen K. Midwife to midwife. 'Now just pop up here, dear...' revisiting the art of antenatal abdominal palpation. *Practising Midwife* 1999;2:13–5.

566. Neilson JP. Symphysis-fundal height measurement in pregnancy. *Cochrane Database of Systematic Reviews* 2001;(2).

567. Gardosi J, Francis A. Controlled trial of fundal height measurement plotted on customised antenatal growth charts. *British Journal of Obstetrics and Gynaecology* 1999;106:309–317.

568. Macones GA, Depp R. Fetal monitoring. In: Wildschut HIJ, Weiner CP, Peters TJ, editors. *When to screen in obstetrics and gynaecology*. London: WB Saunders; 1996. p. 202–18.

569. Grant A, Elbourne D, Valentin L, Alexander S. Routine formal fetal movement counting and risk of antepartum late death in normally formed singletons. *Lancet* 1989;ii:345–9.

570. Divanovic E, Buchmann EJ. Routine heart and lung auscultation in prenatal care. *International Journal of Gynecology and Obstetrics* 1999;64:247–51.

571. Sharif K, Whittle M. Routine antenatal fetal heart rate auscultation: is it necessary? *Journal of Obstetrics and Gynaecology* 1993;13:111–3.

572. Garcia J, Corry M, MacDonald D, Elbourne D, Grant A. Mothers' views of continuous electronic fetal heart monitoring and intermittent auscultation in a randomized controlled trial. *Birth* 1985;12:79–86.

573. Pattison N, McCowan L. Cardiotocography for antepartum fetal assessment. *Cochrane Database of Systematic Reviews* 2001;(2).

574. Bricker L, Neilson JP. Routine ultrasound in late pregnancy (> 24 weeks gestation). *Cochrane Database of Systematic Reviews* 2001;(2).

575. Bricker L, Neilson JP. Routine Doppler ultrasound in pregnancy. *Cochrane Database of Systematic Reviews* 2001;(2).

576. Chien PF, Arnott N, Gordon A, Owen P, Khan KS. How useful is uterine artery Doppler flow velocimetry in the prediction of preeclampsia, intrauterine growth retardation and perinatal death? An overview. *BJOG* 2000;107:196–208.

577. Hilder L, Costeloe K, Thilaganathan B. Prolonged pregnancy: evaluating gestation-specific risks of fetal and infant mortality. *British Journal of Obstetrics and Gynaecology* 1998;105:169–73.

578. Crowley, P. Interventions for preventing or improving the outcome of delivery at or beyond term. *Cochrane Database of Systematic Reviews* 2003;(1).

579. Boulvain M, Fraser WD, Marcoux S, Fontaine JY, Bazin S, Pinault JJ, Blouin D. Does sweeping of the membranes reduce the need for formal induction of labour? A randomised controlled trial. *British Journal of Obstetrics and Gynaecology* 1998;105:34–40.

580. Melzack R. The short-form McGill pain questionnaire. *Pain* 1987;30:191–7.

581. Royal College of Obstetricians and Gynaecologists, Clinical Effectiveness Support Unit. *National Sentinel Caesarean Section Audit Report.* London: RCOG Press; 2001.

582. Nelson KB, Ellenberg JH. Antecedents of cerebral palsy. Multivariate analysis of risk. *New England Journal of Medicine* 1986;315:81–6.

583. Kitchen WH, Yu VY, Orgill AA, Ford G, Rickards A, Astbury J, et al. Infants born before 29 weeks gestation: survival and morbidity at 2 years of age. *British Journal of Obstetrics and Gynaecology* 1982;89:887–91.

584. Lau TK, Lo KW, Rogers M. Pregnancy outcome after successful external cephalic version for breech presentation at term. *American Journal of Obstetrics and Gynecology* 1997;176:218–23.

585. Brocks V, Philipsen T, Secher NJ. A randomized trial of external cephalic version with tocolysis in late pregnancy. *British Journal of Obstetrics and Gynaecology* 1984;91:653–6.

586. Van Veelan AJ, Van Cappellen AW, Flu PK, Straub MJPF, Wallenburg HC. Effect of external cephalic version in late pregnancy on presentation at delivery: a randomized controlled trial. *British Journal of Obstetrics and Gynaecology* 1989;96:916–21.

587. Dugoff L, Stamm CA, Jones OW, Mohling SI, Hawkins JL. The effect of spinal anesthesia on the success rate of external cephalic version: a randomized trial. *Obstetrics and Gynecology* 1999;93:345–9.

588. Van Dorsten JP, Schifrin BS, Wallace RL. Randomized control trial of external cephalic version with tocolysis in late pregnancy. *American Journal of Obstetrics and Gynecology* 1981;141:417–24.

589. Hofmeyer GJ. External cephalic version for breech presentation before term. *Cochrane Database of Systematic Reviews* 2001;(2).

590. Hofmeyer GJ. External cephalic version facilitation for breech presentation at term. *Cochrane Database of Systematic Reviews* 2001;(2).

591. Mahomed K, Seeras R, Coulson R. External cephalic version at term. A randomized controlled trial using tocolysis. *British Journal of Obstetrics and Gynaecology* 1991;98:8–13.

592. Hofmeyr GJ. Effect of external cephalic version in late pregnancy on breech presentation and caesarean section rate: a controlled trial. *British Journal of Obstetrics and Gynaecology* 1983;90:392–9.

593. Mushambi M. External cephalic version: new interest and old concerns. *International Journal of Obstetric Anesthesia* 2001;10:263–6.

594. Hofmeyr GJ. Interventions to help external cephalic version for breech presentation at term. *Cochrane Database of Systematic Reviews* 2002;(4).

595. van Loon AJ, Mantingh A, Serlier EK, Kroon G, Mooyaart EL, Huisjes HJ. Randomised controlled trial of magnetic-resonance pelvimetry in breech presentation at term. *Lancet* 1997;350:1799–804.

596. Walkinshaw SA. Pelvimetry and breech at term. *Lancet* 2002;350:1791–2.

597. Hofmeyr GJ, Kulier, R. Cephalic version by postural management for breech presentation. *Cochrane Database of Systematic Reviews* 2003;(1).

598. Cardini F, Weixin H. Moxibustion for correction of breech presentation: a randomized controlled trial. *JAMA* 1998;280:1580–4.

599. Li Q. Clinical observation on correcting malposition of fetus by electro-acupuncture. *Journal of Traditional Chinese Medicine* 1996;16:260–2.

600. Rouse DJ, Andrews WW, Goldenberg RL, Owen J. Screening and treatment of asymptomatic bacteriuria of pregnancy to prevent pyelonephritis: a cost-effectiveness and cost-benefit analysis. *Obstetrics and Gynecology* 1995;86:119–23.

601. Petrou S, Sach T, Davidson L. The long-term costs of preterm birth and low birth weight: results of a systematic review. *Child: Care, Health and Development* 2001;27:97–115.

602. Connor N, Roberts J, Nicoll A. Strategic options for antenatal screening for syphilis in the United Kingdom: a cost effectiveness analysis. *Journal of Medical Screening* 2000;7:7–13.

603. Read JS, Klebanoff MA. Sexual intercourse during pregnancy and preterm delivery: effects of vaginal microorganisms. *American Journal of Obstetrics and Gynecology* 1993;168:514–19.

604. Raymond EG, Cnattingius S, Kiely JL. Effects of maternal age, parity, and smoking on the risk of stillbirth. *British Journal of Obstetrics and Gynaecology* 1994;101:301–6.

605. Ho KY, Kang JY, Viegas OA. Symptomatic gastro-oesophageal reflux in pregnancy: a prospective study among Singaporean women. *Journal of Gastroenterology and Hepatology* 1998;13:1020–6.

606. Kovacs GT, Campbell J, Francis D, Hill D, Adena A. Is Mucaine an appropriate medication for the relief of heartburn during pregnancy? *Asia-Oceania Journal of Obstetrics and Gynaecology* 1990;16:357–62.

607. Briggs DW, Hart DM. Heartburn of pregnancy. A continuation study. *British Journal of Clinical Practice* 1972;26:167–9.

608. Dick PT, with the Canadian Task Force on the Periodic Health Examination. Prenatal screening and diagnosis of Down Syndrome. 84–98. 1994. [www.ctfphc.org/Full_Text/Ch08full.htm] Accessed 4 September 2003.

609. Bindra R, Heath V, Liao A, Spencer K, Nicolaides KH. One-stop clinic for assessment of risk for trisomy 21 at 11–14 weeks: a prospective study of 15030 pregnancies. *Ultrasound in Obstetrics and Gynecology* 2002;20:219–25.

610. Mastrobattista JM, Bishop KD, Newton ER. Wet smear compared with gram stain diagnosis of bacterial vaginosis in asymptomatic pregnant women. *Obstetrics and Gynecology* 2000;96:504–6.

611. Krohn MA, Hillier SL, Eschenbach DA. Comparison of methods of diagnosing bacterial vaginosis among pregnant women. *Journal of Clinical Microbiology* 1990;27:1266–71.

612. Royal College of Obstetricians and Gynaecologists. *Induction of labour.* Evidence-based Clinical Guideline No. 9. London: RCOG Press; 2001.

613. Department of Health. Unlinked Anonymous Prevalence Monitoring Programme in the United Kingdom. *Summary Report from the Unlinked Anonymous Surveys Steering Group. Data to the end of 1998.* London: DoH; 1999.

614. Balano K, Beckerman K, Ng V. Rapid HIV screening during labor. *JAMA* 1998;280:1664.

615. Postma MJ, Beck EJ, Mandalia S, Sherr L, Walters MDS, Houweling H, et al. Universal HIV screening of pregnant women in England: cost effectiveness analysis. *British Medical Journal* 1999;318:1656–60.

616. Shey Wiysonge CU, Brocklehurst P, Sterne JAC. Vaginal disinfection during labor for reducing the risk of mother-to-child transmission of HIV infection. *Cochrane Database of Systematic Reviews* 2002;(3).

617. Kind C, Rudin C, Siegrist C, Wyler C, Biedermann K, Lauper U, et al. Prevention of vertical HIV transmission: additive protective effect of elective cesarean section and zidovudine prophylaxis. *AIDS* 1998;12:205–10.

618. Shey Wiysonge CU, Brocklehurst P, Sterne, JAC. Vitamin A supplementation for reducing the risk of mother-to-child transmission of HIV infection. *Cochrane Database of Systematic Reviews* 2002;(3).

619. Stray-Pedersen B. Economic evaluation of different vaccination programmes to prevent congenital rubella. *NIPH Annals* 1982;5:69–83.

620. Hurtig AK, Nicoll A, Carne C, Lissauer T, Connor N, Webster JP, *et al.* Syphilis in pregnant women and their children in the United Kingdom: results from national clinician reporting surveys 1994–97. *British Medical Journal* 1998;317:1617–19.

621. Ryan M, Hall SM, Barrett NJ, Balfour AH, Holliman RE, Joynson DH. Toxoplasmosis in England and Wales 1981 to 1992. *CDR Review* 1995;5: R13–21.

622. Lappalainen M, Koskiniemi M, Hiilesmaa V, Ammala P, Teramo K, Koskela P, *et al.* Outcome of children after maternal primary Toxoplasma infection during pregnancy with emphasis on avidity of specific IgG. *Pediatric Infectious Disease Journal* 1995;14:354–61.

623. Danielian PJ, Wang J, Hall MH. Long-term outcome by method of delivery of fetuses in breech presentation at term: population based follow up. *British Medical Journal* 1996;312:1451–3.

624. Krebs L, Topp M, Langhoff-Roos, J. The relation of breech presentation at term to cerebral palsy. *British Journal of Obstetrics and Gynaecology* 1999;106:943–7.

625. Milsom I, Ladfors L, Thiringer K, Niklasson A, Odeback A, Thornberg E. Influence of maternal, obstetric and fetal risk factors on the prevalence of birth asphyxia at term in a Swedish urban population. *Acta Obstetricia et Gynecologica Scandinavica* 2002;81:907–17.

626. van Loon AJ, Mantingh A, Thijn CJP, Mooyaart EL. Pelvimetry by magnetic resonance imaging in breech presentation. *American Journal of Obstetrics and Gynecology* 1990;163:1256–60.

627. Hofmeyr GJ, Hannah ME. Planned caesarean section for term breech delivery. *Cochrane Database of Systematic Reviews* 2000;(2).

628. Hannah ME, Hannah WJ, Hewson SA, Hodnett ED, Saigal S, Willan AR. Planned caesarean section versus planned vaginal birth for breech presentation at term: a randomised multicentre trial. *Lancet* 2000;356:1375–83.

629. Gimovsky ML, Wallace RL, Schifrin BS, Paul RH. Randomized management of the nonfrank breech presentation at term: a preliminary report. *American Journal of Obstetrics and Gynecology* 1983;146:34–40.

630. Collea JV, Chein C, Quilligan EJ. The randomized management of term frank breech presentation: a study of 208 cases. *American Journal of Obstetrics and Gynecology* 1980;137:235–44.

631. Royal College of Obstetricians and Gynaecologists. *The Management of Breech Presentation*. Guideline No. 20. London: RCOG; April 2001. [www.rcog.org.uk/guidelines.asp?PageID=106&GuidelineID=19] Accessed 8 September 2003.

References

(2008 update)

632. National Institute for Health and Clinical Excellence. *The Guidelines Manual 2006*. London: NICE; 2006.

633. National Institute for Health and Clinical Excellence. *The Guidelines Manual 2007*. London: NICE; 2007.

634. National Collaborating Centre for Women's and Children's Health. *Intrapartum Care*. London: RCOG Press; 2007.

635. Department of Health. *Maternity Matters: Choice, Access and Continuity of Care in a Safe Service*. London: Department of Health; 2007.

636. National Collaborating Centre for Women's and Children's Health. *Diabetes in Pregnancy: Management of Diabetes and its Complications from Preconception to the Postnatal Period*. London: RCOG Press; 2008.

637. Dyson L, McCormick F, Renfrew MJ. Interventions for promoting the initiation of breastfeeding. (Cochrane Review). In: *Cochrane Database of Systematic Reviews*, Issue 2, 2007. Chichester: Wiley Interscience.

638. Fairbank L, O'Meara S, Renfrew MJ, et al. A systematic review to evaluate the effectiveness of interventions to promote the initiation of breastfeeding. *Health Technology Assessment* 2000; 4:(25)i-171.

639. Lavender T. Breastfeeding expectations versus reality: a cluster randomised controlled trial. *BJOG: an International Journal of Obstetrics and Gynaecology* 2005;112(8):1047–53.

640. Mattar CN, Chong YS, Chan YS, et al. Simple antenatal preparation to improve breastfeeding practice: a randomized controlled trial. *Obstetrics and Gynecology* 2007;109(1):73–80.

641. Noel-Weiss J. Randomized controlled trial to determine effects of prenatal breastfeeding workshop on maternal breastfeeding self-efficacy and breastfeeding duration. *JOGNN: Journal of Obstetric, Gynecologic, and Neonatal Nursing* 2006;35(5):616–24.

642. Reifsnider E and Eckhart. Prenatal breastfeeding education: its effect on breastfeeding among WIC participants. *Journal of Human Lactation* 1997;13(2):121–5.

643. Wiles LS. The effect of prenatal breastfeeding education on breastfeeding success and maternal perception of the infant. *JOGNN: Journal of Obstetric, Gynecologic, and Neonatal Nursing* 1984;13(4):253–7.

644. Pugin E, Valdes V, et al. Does prenatal breastfeeding skills group education increase the effectiveness of a comprehensive breastfeeding promotion program? *Journal of Human Lactation* 1996;12(1):15–19.

645. Sheehan A. Australian women's stories of their baby-feeding decisions in pregnancy. *Midwifery* 2003;19(4):259–66.

646. Gulick EE. Informational correlates of successful breast-feeding. *MCN: The American Journal of Maternal/Child Nursing* 1982;7(6):370–5.

647. Campbell MK, Carbone E, Honess-Morreale L, et al. Randomized trial of a tailored nutrition education CD-ROM program for women receiving food assistance. *Journal of Nutrition Education and Behavior* 2004;36(2):58–66.

648. Olson CM, Strawderman MS, Reed RG. Efficacy of an intervention to prevent excessive gestational weight gain. *American Journal of Obstetrics and Gynecology* 2004;191(2):530–6.

649. Szwajcer EM, Hiddink GJ, Koelen MA, et al. Nutrition-related information-seeking behaviours before and throughout the course of pregnancy: consequences for nutrition communication. *European Journal of Clinical Nutrition* 2005;59 Suppl 1:S57-S65.

650. Orstead C. Efficacy of prenatal nutrition counseling: weight gain, infant birth weight, and cost-effectiveness. *Journal of the American Dietetic Association* 1985;85(1):40–5.

651. Lumley J, Oliver SS, Chamberlain C, Oakley K. Interventions for promoting smoking cessation during pregnancy. (Cochrane Review). In: *Cochrane Database of Systematic Reviews*, Issue 2, 2004. Chichester: Wiley Interscience.

652. Acharya G, Jauniaux E, Sathia L, et al. Evaluation of the impact of current antismoking advice in the UK on women with planned pregnancies. *Journal of Obstetrics and Gynaecology* 2002;22(5):498–500.

653. Rigotti NA, Park ER, Regan S, et al. Efficacy of telephone counseling for pregnant smokers: a randomized controlled trial. *Obstetrics and Gynecology* 2006;108(1):83–92.

654. Byrd JC. Smoking cessation among pregnant women in an urban setting. *Wisconsin Medical Journal* 1993;92(11):609–12.

655. McLeod D. Can support and education for smoking cessation and reduction be provided effectively by midwives within primary maternity care? *Midwifery* 2004;20(1):37–50.

656. Goodson JG. Prenatal child safety education. *Obstetrics and Gynecology* 1985;65(3):312–15.

657. Greenberg LW. A prenatal and postpartum safety education program: influence on parental use of infant car restraints. *Journal of Developmental and Behavioral Pediatrics* 1982;3(1):32–4.

658. Waterson E, Murray-Lyon IM. Preventing fetal alcohol effects: A trial of three methods of giving information in the antenatal clinic. *Health Education Research* 1990;5(1):53–61.

659. Smits MW, Paulk TH, Kee CC. Assessing the impact of an outpatient education program for patients with gestational diabetes. *Diabetes Educator* 1995;21(2):129–34.

660. Graham W, Smith P, Kamal A, et al. Randomised controlled trial comparing effectiveness of touch screen system with leaflet for providing women with information on prenatal tests. *British Medical Journal* 2000;320(7228):155–60.

661. Glazier R, Goel V, Holzapfel S, et al. Written patient information about triple-marker screening: a randomized, controlled trial. *Obstetrics and Gynecology* 1997;90(5):769–74.

662. Bekker HL. Applying decision analysis to facilitate informed decision making about prenatal diagnosis for Down syndrome: a randomised controlled trial. *Prenatal Diagnosis* 2004;24(4):265–75.

663. Leung KY, Lee CP, Chan HY, et al. Randomised trial comparing an interactive multimedia decision aid with a leaflet and a video to give information about prenatal screening for Down syndrome. *Prenatal Diagnosis* 2004;24(8):613–18.

664. Hewison J, Cuckle H, Baillie C, et al. Use of videotapes for viewing at home to inform choice in Down syndrome screening: a randomised controlled trial. *Prenatal Diagnosis* 2001;21(2):146–9.

665. Andersen HF, Freda MC, Damus K, et al. Effectiveness of patient education to reduce preterm delivery among ordinary risk patients. *American Journal of Perinatology* 1989;6(2):214–17.

666. Simpson WM, Johnstone FD, Boyd FM, *et al*. Uptake and acceptability of antenatal HIV testing: randomised controlled trial of different methods of offering the test. *British Medical Journal* 1998;316(7127):262–7.

667. Hunt LM, de Voogd KB, Castaneda H. The routine and the traumatic in prenatal genetic diagnosis: does clinical information inform patient decision-making? *Patient Education and Counseling* 2005;56(3):302–12.

668. Williams C, Alderson P, Farsides B. What constitutes 'balanced' information in the practitioners' portrayals of Down's syndrome?[erratum appears in Midwifery. 2003 Mar;19(1):75]. *Midwifery* 2002;18(3):230–7.

669. Jaques AM, Bell RJ, Watson L, Halliday JL. People who influence women's decisions and preferred sources of information about prenatal testing for birth defects. *Australian and New Zealand Journal of Obstetrics and Gynaecology* 2004;44(3):233–8.

670. Soltani H. Exploring women's views on information provided during pregnancy. *British Journal of Midwifery* 2005;13(10):633–6.

671. Lavender T. Research. Do we provide information to women in the best way? *British Journal of Midwifery* 2000;8(12):769–75.

672. Nolan ML. Antenatal education: failing to educate for parenthood. *British Journal of Midwifery* 1997;5(1):21–6.

673. Jacoby A. Mothers' views about information and advice in pregnancy and childbirth: Findings from a national study. *Midwifery* 1988;4(103):110.

674. Bennett I. 'Breaking it down': Patient-clinician communication and prenatal care among African American women of low and higher literacy. *Annals of Family Medicine* 2006;4(4):334–40.

675. Vonderheid SC, Montgomery KS, Norr KF. Ethnicity and prenatal health promotion content. *Western Journal of Nursing Research* 2003;25(4):388–404.

676. Benn C. Women planning and experiencing pregnancy and childbirth: information needs and sources. *Nursing Praxis in New Zealand* 1999;14(3):4–15.

677. Ussher M. Perceived barriers to and benefits of attending a stop smoking course during pregnancy. *Patient Education and Counseling* 2006;61(3):467–72.

678. Cates SC, Carter-Young HL, Conley S, *et al*. Pregnant women and listeriosis: preferred educational messages and delivery mechanisms. *Journal of Nutrition Education and Behavior* 2004;36(3):121–7.

679. Orr RD. Nutritional care in pregnancy: the patient's view. II. Perceptions, satisfaction, and response to dietary advice and treatment. *Journal of the American Dietetic Association* 1979;75(2):131–6.

680. Spiby H, Slade P, Escott D, *et al*. Selected coping strategies in labor: an investigation of women's experiences. *Birth* 2003;30(3):189–94.

681. Maestas LM. The effect of prenatal education on the beliefs and perceptions of childbearing women: 2000 Virginia Larsen Research Grant winner. *International Journal of Childbirth Education* 2003;18(1):17–21.

682. Hart MA. Self-care agency before and after childbirth education classes. *International Orem Society Newsletter* 1998;6(2):10–11.

683. Rolls C. Pregnancy-to-parenting education: creating a new approach. *Birth Issues* 2001;10(2):53–8.

684. Redman S, Oak S, Booth P, *et al*. Evaluation of an antenatal education programme: characteristics of attenders, changes in knowledge and satisfaction of participants. *Australian and New Zealand Journal of Obstetrics and Gynaecology* 1991;31(4):310–16.

685. Schmied V, Myors K, Wills J, *et al*. Preparing expectant couples for new-parent experiences: a comparison of two models of antenatal education. *Journal of Perinatal Education* 2002;11(3):20–7.

686. Schneider Z. Antenatal education classes in Victoria: what the women said. *Australian Journal of Midwifery* 2001;14(3):14–21.

687. Lee H. Childbirth education: do classes meet consumer expectations? *Birth Issues* 1998;7(4):137–42.

688. Stewart P. Promoting first trimester prenatal classes: a survey. *Canadian Journal of Public Health* 1993;84(5):331–3.

689. Schneider Z. An Australian study of women's experiences of their first pregnancy. *Midwifery* 2002;18(3):238–49.

690. Alexander GR, Tompkins ME, Petersen DJ, *et al*. Discordance between LMP-based and clinically estimated gestational age: implications for research, programs, and policy. *Public Health Reports* 1995;110(4):395–402.

691. Olesen AW. Prediction of delivery date by sonography in the first and second trimesters. *Ultrasound in Obstetrics and Gynecology* 2006;28(3):292–7.

692. Taipale P. Predicting delivery date by ultrasound and last menstrual period in early gestation. *Obstetrics and Gynecology* 2001;97(2):189–94.

693. Neufeld LM, Haas JD, Grajeda R, Martorell R. Last menstrual period provides the best estimate of gestation length for women in rural Guatemala. *Paediatric and Perinatal Epidemiology* 2006;20(4):290–8.

694. Mustafa G, David RJ. Comparative accuracy of clinical estimate versus menstrual gestational age in computerized birth certificates. *Public Health Reports* 2001;116(1):15–21.

695. Johnsen SL, Rasmussen S, Sollien R, Kiserud T. Accuracy of second trimester fetal head circumference and biparietal diameter for predicting the time of spontaneous birth. *Journal of Perinatal Medicine* 2006;34(5):367–70.

696. Nguyen TH. Evaluation of ultrasound-estimated date of delivery in 17,450 spontaneous singleton births: do we need to modify Naegele's rule? *Ultrasound in Obstetrics and Gynecology* 1999;14(1):23–8.

697. Rowlands S, Royston P. Estimated date of delivery from last menstrual period and ultrasound scan: which is more accurate? *British Journal of General Practice* 1993;43(373):322–5.

698. Okonofua FE. Accuracy of prediction of gestational age by ultrasound measurement of biparietal diameter in Nigerian women. *International Journal of Gynecology and Obstetrics* 1989;28(3):217–19.

699. Campbell S, Warsof SL, Little D, Cooper DJ. Routine ultrasound screening for the prediction of gestational age. *Obstetrics and Gynecology* 1985;65(5):613–20.

700. Kopta MM, May RR, Crane JP. A comparison of the reliability of the estimated date of confinement predicted by crown-rump length and biparietal diameter. *American Journal of Obstetrics and Gynecology* 1983;145(5):562–5.

701. Selbing A. The pregnant population and a fetal crown-rump length screening program. *Acta Obstetricia et Gynecologica Scandinavica* 1983;62(2):161–4.

702. Bennett KA, Crane JM, O'shea P, *et al*. First trimester ultrasound screening is effective in reducing postterm labor induction rates: a randomized controlled trial. *American Journal of Obstetrics and Gynecology* 2004;190(4):1077–81.

703. Waldenstrom U, Axelsson O, Nilsson S, *et al*. Effects of routine one-stage ultrasound screening in pregnancy: a randomised controlled trial. *Lancet* 1988;2:585–8.

704. Eik-Nes SH, Salvesen KA, Okland O, *et al*. Routine ultrasound fetal examination in pregnancy: The 'alesund' randomized controlled trial. *Ultrasound in Obstetrics and Gynecology* 2000;15(6):473–8.

705. Morin I. Determinants and consequences of discrepancies in menstrual and ultrasonographic gestational age estimates. *BJOG: an International Journal of Obstetrics and Gynaecology* 2005;112(2):145–52.

706. Scientific Advisory Committee on Nutrition. *Update on Vitamin D*. Position statement by the Scientific Advisory Committee on Nutrition. 2007.

707. Gray R, Henderson J. Review of the fetal effects of prenatal alcohol exposure. Oxford: National Perinatal Epidemiology Unit; 2006.

708. Mariscal M. Pattern of alcohol consumption during pregnancy and risk for low birth weight. *Annals of Epidemiology* 2006;16(6):432–8.

709. Weatherhead SC, Wahie S, Reynolds NJ, *et al.* An open-label, dose-ranging study of methotrexate for moderate-to-severe adult atopic eczema. *British Journal of Dermatology* 2007;156(2):346–51.

710. Ostrowsky JT, Lippman A, Scriver CR. Cost-benefit analysis of a thalassemia disease prevention program. *American Journal of Public Health* 1985;75(7):732–6.

711. Chasen ST, Loeb-Zeitlin S, Landsberger EJ. Hemoglobinopathy screening in pregnancy: comparison of two protocols. *American Journal of Perinatology* 1999;16(4):175–80.

712. Phelan L, Bain BJ, Roper D, *et al.* An analysis of relative costs and potential benefits of different policies for antenatal screening for beta thalassaemia trait and variant haemoglobins. *Journal of Clinical Pathology* 1999;52(9):697–700.

713. Cronin EK, Normand C, Henthorn JS, *et al.* Organisation and cost-effectiveness of antenatal haemoglobinopathy screening and follow up in a community-based programme. *BJOG: an International Journal of Obstetrics and Gynaecology* 2000;107(4):486–91.

714. Rogers M, Phelan L, Bain B. Screening criteria for beta thalassaemia trait in pregnant women. *Journal of Clinical Pathology* 1995;48(11):1054–6.

715. Bain BJ. Screening of antenatal patients in a multiethnic community for beta thalassaemia trait. *Journal of Clinical Pathology* 1988;41(5):481–5.

716. Sirichotiyakul S, Maneerat J, Sa-nguansermsri T, *et al.* Sensitivity and specificity of mean corpuscular volume testing for screening for alpha-thalassemia-1 and beta-thalassemia traits. *Journal of Obstetrics and Gynaecology Research* 2005;31(3):198–201.

717. Ghosh A, Woo JS, Wan CW, *et al.* Evaluation of a prenatal screening procedure for beta-thalassaemia carriers in a Chinese population based on the mean corpuscular volume (MCV). *Prenatal Diagnosis* 1985;5(1):59–65.

718. Sin SY, Ghosh A, Tang LC, *et al.* Ten years' experience of antenatal mean corpuscular volume screening and prenatal diagnosis for thalassaemias in Hong Kong. *Journal of Obstetrics and Gynaecology Research* 2000;26(3):203–8.

719. Yeo GS, Tan KH, Liu TC. Screening for beta thalassaemia and HbE traits with the mean red cell volume in pregnant women. *Annals of the Academy of Medicine, Singapore* 1994;23(3):363–6.

720. Modell B, Darlison M, Khan M, *et al.* Role of genetic diagnosis registers in ongoing consultation with the community. *Community Genetics* 2000;3(3):144–7.

721. Ahmed S, Green JM, Hewison J. Attitudes towards prenatal diagnosis and termination of pregnancy for thalassaemia in pregnant Pakistani women in the North of England. *Prenatal Diagnosis* 2006;26(3):248–57.

722. Ahmed S, Green J, Hewison J. Antenatal thalassaemia carrier testing: women's perceptions of "information" and "consent". *Journal of Medical Screening* 2005;12(2):69–77.

723. Durosinmi MA, Odebiyi AI, Akinola NO, *et al.* Acceptability of prenatal diagnosis of sickle cell anaemia by a sample of the Nigerian population. *African Journal of Medicine and Medical Sciences* 1997;26(1–2):55–8.

724. Dyson SM, Culley L, Gill C, *et al.* Ethnicity questions and antenatal screening for sickle cell/thalassaemia [EQUANS] in England: a randomised controlled trial of two questionnaires. *Ethnicity and Health* 2006;11(2):169–89.

725. Greengross P, Hickman M, Gill M, *et al.* Outcomes of universal antenatal screening for haemoglobinopathies. *Journal of Medical Screening* 1999;6(1):3–10.

726. Thomas P, Oni L, Alli M, *et al.* Antenatal screening for haemoglobinopathies in primary care: a whole system participatory action research project. *British Journal of General Practice* 2005;55(515):424–8.

727. Eurenius K, Axelsson O, Cnattingius S, *et al.* Second trimester ultrasound screening performed by midwives; sensitivity for detection of fetal anomalies. *Acta Obstetricia et Gynecologica Scandinavica* 1999;78(2):98–104.

728. Stefos T, Plachouras N, Sotiriadis A, *et al.* Routine obstetrical ultrasound at 18–22 weeks: our experience on 7,236 fetuses. *Journal of Maternal-Fetal Medicine* 1999;8(2):64–9.

729. Taipale P, Ammala M, Salonen R, *et al.* Two-stage ultrasonography in screening for fetal anomalies at 13–14 and 18–22 weeks of gestation. *Acta Obstetricia et Gynecologica Scandinavica* 2004;83(12):1141–6.

730. Nakling J, Backe B. Routine ultrasound screening and detection of congenital anomalies outside a university setting. *Acta Obstetricia et Gynecologica Scandinavica* 2005;84(11):1042–8.

731. Souka AP, Pilalis A, Kavalakis I, *et al.* Screening for major structural abnormalities at the 11- to 14-week ultrasound scan. *American Journal of Obstetrics and Gynecology* 2006;194(2):393–6.

732. Nikkila A, Rydhstroem H, Kallen B, *et al.* Ultrasound screening for fetal anomalies in southern Sweden: a population-based study. *Acta Obstetricia et Gynecologica Scandinavica* 2006;85(6):688–93.

733. Stoll C, Clementi M, and EUROSCAN Study Group. Prenatal diagnosis of dysmorphic syndromes by routine fetal ultrasound examination across Europe. *Ultrasound in Obstetrics and Gynecology* 2003;21(6):543–51.

734. Grandjean H, Larroque D, Levi S. The performance of routine ultrasonographic screening of pregnancies in the Eurofetus Study. *American Journal of Obstetrics and Gynecology* 1999;181(2):446–54.

735. Levi S, Zhang WH, Alexander S, *et al.* Short-term outcome of isolated and associated congenital heart defects in relation to antenatal ultrasound screening. *Ultrasound in Obstetrics and Gynecology* 2003;21(6):532–8.

736. Hughes PF, Agarwal M, Newman P, *et al.* An evaluation of fructosamine estimation in screening for gestational diabetes mellitus. *Diabetic Medicine* 1995;12(8):708–12.

737. Zhang WH, Levi S, Alexander S, *et al.* Sensitivity of ultrasound screening for congenital anomalies in unselected pregnancies. *Revue d Epidemiologie et de Sante Publique* 2002;50(6):571–80.

738. Smith NC, Hau C. A six year study of the antenatal detection of fetal abnormality in six Scottish health boards. *British Journal of Obstetrics and Gynaecology* 1999;106(3):206–12.

739. Taipale P, Ammala M, Salonen R, *et al.* Learning curve in ultrasonographic screening for selected fetal structural anomalies in early pregnancy. *Obstetrics and Gynecology* 2003;101(2):273–8.

740. Carvalho MH, Brizot ML, Lopes LM, *et al.* Detection of fetal structural abnormalities at the 11–14 week ultrasound scan. *Prenatal Diagnosis* 2002;22(1):1–4.

741. Tabor A, Zdravkovic M, Perslev A, *et al.* Screening for congenital malformations by ultrasonography in the general population of pregnant women: factors affecting the efficacy. *Acta Obstetricia et Gynecologica Scandinavica* 2003;82(12):1092–8.

2008 update

742. Royal College of Obstetricians and Gynaecologists. Recommendations arising from the 26th Annual RCOG Study Group: Intrapartum Fetal Surveillence. London: RCOG Press; 1998.

743. Whitlow BJ, Economides DL. First trimester detection of fetal abnormalities in an unselected population. *Contemporary Reviews in Obstetrics and Gynaecology* 1998;10(4):245–53.

744. Srisupundit K, Tongsong T, Sirichotiyakul S, *et al.* Fetal structural anomaly screening at 11–14 weeks of gestation at Maharaj Nakorn Chiang Mai Hospital. *Journal of the Medical Association of Thailand* 2006;89(5):588–93.

745. Cedergren M, Selbing A. Detection of fetal structural abnormalities by an 11–14-week ultrasound dating scan in an unselected Swedish population. *Acta Obstetricia et Gynecologica Scandinavica* 2006;85(8):912–15.

746. Guariglia L, Rosati P. Transvaginal sonographic detection of embryonic-fetal abnormalities in early pregnancy. *Obstetrics and Gynecology* 2000;96(3):328–32.

747. Westin M, Saltvedt S, Bergman G, *et al.* Routine ultrasound examination at 12 or 18 gestational weeks for prenatal detection of major congenital heart malformations? A randomised controlled trial comprising 36,299 fetuses. *BJOG: an International Journal of Obstetrics and Gynaecology* 2006;113(6):675–82.

748. Saltvedt S, Almstrom H, Kublickas M, *et al.* Detection of malformations in chromosomally normal fetuses by routine ultrasound at 12 or 18 weeks of gestation-a randomised controlled trial in 39,572 pregnancies. *BJOG: an International Journal of Obstetrics and Gynaecology* 2006;113(6):664–74.

749. Randall P, Brealey S, Hahn S, *et al.* Accuracy of fetal echocardiography in the routine detection of congenital heart disease among unselected and low risk populations: a systematic review. *BJOG: an International Journal of Obstetrics and Gynaecology* 2005;112(1):24–30.

750. Buskens E, Grobbee DE, Frohn-Mulder IM, *et al.* Efficacy of routine fetal ultrasound screening for congenital heart disease in normal pregnancy. *Circulation* 1996;94(1):67–72.

751. Tegnander E, Williams. Prenatal detection of heart defects in a non-selected population of 30,149 fetuses – detection rates and outcome. *Ultrasound in Obstetrics and Gynecology* 2006;27(3):252–65.

752. Wessel H, Reitmaier P, Dupret A, *et al.* Deaths among women of reproductive age in Cape Verde: causes and avoidability. *Acta Obstetricia et Gynecologica Scandinavica* 1999;78(3):225–32.

753. Khoshnood B, De VC, Vodovar V, *et al.* Trends in prenatal diagnosis, pregnancy termination, and perinatal mortality of newborns with congenital heart disease in France, 1983–2000: A population-based evaluation. *Pediatrics* 2005;115(1):95–101.

754. Makrydimas G, Sotiriadis A, Ioannidis JP. Screening performance of first-trimester nuchal translucency for major cardiac defects: a meta-analysis. *American Journal of Obstetrics and Gynecology* 2003;189(5):1330–5.

755. Bahado-Singh RO, Wapner R, Thom E, *et al.* Elevated first-trimester nuchal translucency increases the risk of congenital heart defects. *American Journal of Obstetrics and Gynecology* 2005;192(5):1357–61.

756. Atzei A, Gajewska K, Huggon IC, *et al.* Relationship between nuchal translucency thickness and prevalence of major cardiac defects in fetuses with normal karyotype. *Ultrasound in Obstetrics and Gynecology* 2005;26(2):154–7.

757. Westin M. Is measurement of nuchal translucency thickness a useful screening tool for heart defects? A study of 16,383 fetuses. *Ultrasound in Obstetrics and Gynecology* 2006;27(6):632–9.

758. Simpson LL, Malone FD, Bianchi DW, *et al.* Nuchal translucency and the risk of congenital heart disease. *Obstetrics and Gynecology* 2007;109(2 Pt 1):376–83.

759. Benn PA, Horne D, Craffey A, *et al.* Maternal serum screening for birth defects: results of a Connecticut regional program. *Connecticut Medicine* 1996;60(6):323–7.

760. Norem CT, Schoen EJ, Walton DL, *et al.* Routine ultrasonography compared with maternal serum alpha-fetoprotein for neural tube defect screening. *Obstetrics and Gynecology* 2005;106(4):747–52.

761. Cristofalo EA, DiPietro JA, Costigan KA, *et al.* Women's response to fetal choroid plexus cysts detected by prenatal ultrasound. *Journal of Perinatology* 2006;26(4):215–23.

762. Kemp J, Davenport M, Pernet A. Antenatally diagnosed surgical anomalies: the psychological effect of parental antenatal counseling. *Journal of Pediatric Surgery* 1998;33(9):1376–9.

763. Hyett J, Perdu M, Sharland G, *et al.* Using fetal nuchal translucency to screen for major congenital cardiac defects at 10–14 weeks of gestation: population based cohort study. *British Medical Journal* 1999;318(7176):81–5.

764. Schwarzler P, Carvalho JS, Senat MV, *et al.* Screening for fetal aneuploidies and fetal cardiac abnormalities by nuchal translucency thickness measurement at 10–14 weeks of gestation as part of routine antenatal care in an unselected population. *BJOG: an International Journal of Obstetrics and Gynaecology* 1999;106(10):1029–34.

765. Michailidis GD, Economides DL. Nuchal translucency measurement and pregnancy outcome in karyotypically normal fetuses. *Ultrasound in Obstetrics and Gynecology* 2001;17(2):102–5.

766. Mavrides E, Cobian-Sanchez F, Tekay A, *et al.* Limitations of using first-trimester nuchal translucency measurement in routine screening for major congenital heart defects. *Ultrasound in Obstetrics and Gynecology* 2001;17(2):106–10.

767. Crossley JA, Aitken DA, Cameron AD, *et al.* Combined ultrasound and biochemical screening for Down's syndrome in the first trimester: a Scottish multicentre study. *BJOG: an International Journal of Obstetrics and Gynaecology* 2002;109(6):667–76.

768. Nicolaides KH, Spencer K, Avgidou K, *et al.* Multicenter study of first-trimester screening for trisomy 21 in 75 821 pregnancies: results and estimation of the potential impact of individual risk-orientated two-stage first-trimester screening. *Ultrasound in Obstetrics and Gynecology* 2005;25(3):221–6.

769. Wapner R, Thom E, Simpson JL, *et al.* First-trimester screening for trisomies 21 and 18. *New England Journal of Medicine* 2003;349(15):1405–13.

770. Stenhouse EJ, Crossley JA, Aitken DA, *et al.* First-trimester combined ultrasound and biochemical screening for Down syndrome in routine clinical practice. *Prenatal Diagnosis* 2004;24(10):774–80.

771. Malone FD, Ball RH, Nyberg DA, *et al.* First-trimester nasal bone evaluation for aneuploidy in the general population. *Obstetrics and Gynecology* 2004;104(6):1222–8.

772. Cicero S, Avgidou K, Rembouskos G, *et al.* Nasal bone in first-trimester screening for trisomy 21. *American Journal of Obstetrics and Gynecology* 2006;195(1):109–14.

773. Prefumo F, Sairam S, Bhide A, *et al.* First-trimester nuchal translucency, nasal bones, and trisomy 21 in selected and unselected populations. *American Journal of Obstetrics and Gynecology* 2006;194(3):828–33.

774. Ramos-Corp, Santiago JC, Montoya F. Ultrasonographic evaluation of fetal nasal bone in a low-risk population at 11–13 + 6 gestational weeks. *Prenatal Diagnosis* 2006;26(2):112–17.

775. Kozlowski P, Knippel AJ, Froehlich S, *et al.* Additional performance of nasal bone in first trimester screening: Nasal bone in first trimester screening. *Ultraschall in der Medizin* 2006;27(4):336–9.

776. Zoppi MA, Ibba RM, Axiana C, *et al.* Absence of fetal nasal bone and aneuploidies at first-trimester nuchal translucency screening in unselected pregnancies. *Prenatal Diagnosis* 2003;23(6):496–500.

777. Viora E, Masturzo B, Errante G, *et al.* Ultrasound evaluation of fetal nasal bone at 11 to 14 weeks in a consecutive series of 1906 fetuses. *Prenatal Diagnosis* 2003;23(10):784–7.

778. Rozenberg P. Screening for Down syndrome using first-trimester combined screening followed by second-trimester ultrasound examination in an unselected population. *American Journal of Obstetrics and Gynecology* 2006;195(5):1379–87.

779. Weingertner AS, Kohler M, Firtion C, *et al.* Interest of foetal nasal bone measurement at first trimester trisomy 21 screening. *Fetal Diagnosis and Therapy* 2006;21(5):433–8.

780. Orlandi F, Rossi C, Orlandi E, *et al.* First-trimester screening for trisomy-21 using a simplified method to assess the presence or absence of the fetal nasal bone. *American Journal of Obstetrics and Gynecology* 2005;192(4):1107–11.

781. Avgidou K, Papageorghiou A, Bindra R, *et al.* Prospective first-trimester screening for trisomy 21 in 30,564 pregnancies. *American Journal of Obstetrics and Gynecology* 2005;192(6):1761–7.

782. Jaques AM, Collins VR, Haynes K, *et al.* Using record linkage and manual follow-up to evaluate the Victorian maternal serum screening quadruple test for Down's syndrome, trisomy 18 and neural tube defects. *Journal of Medical Screening* 2006;13(1):8–13.

783. Sotiriadis A, Makrydimas G, Ioannidis JP. Diagnostic performance of intracardiac echogenic foci for Down syndrome: a meta-analysis. *Obstetrics and Gynecology* 2003;101(5 Pt 1):1009–16.

784. Coco C, Jeanty P. Isolated fetal pyelectasis and chromosomal abnormalities. *American Journal of Obstetrics and Gynecology* 2005;193(3 Pt 1):732–8.

785. Malone FD, Canick JA, Ball RH, *et al.* First-trimester or second-trimester screening, or both, for Down's syndrome. *New England Journal of Medicine* 2005;353(19):2001–11.

786. Knight GJ, Palomaki GE, Neveux LM, *et al.* Integrated serum screening for Down syndrome in primary obstetric practice. *Prenatal Diagnosis* 2005;25(12):1162–7.

787. Platt LD, Greene N, Johnson A, *et al.* Sequential pathways of testing after first-trimester screening for trisomy 21. *Obstetrics and Gynecology* 2004;104(4):661–6.

788. Gafvels C, Lithner F. Lifestyle as regards physical exercise, smoking and drinking, of adult insulin-treated diabetic people compared with non-diabetic controls. *Scandinavian Journal of Social Medicine* 1997;25(3):168–75.

789. Wright D, Bradbury I, Cuckle H, *et al.* Three-stage contingent screening for Down syndrome. *Prenatal Diagnosis* 2006;26(6):528–34.

790. Wald NJ, Rudnicka AR, Bestwick JP. Sequential and contingent prenatal screening for Down syndrome. *Prenatal Diagnosis* 2006;26(9):769–77.

791. Saltvedt S, Almstrom H, Kublickas M, *et al.* Screening for Down syndrome based on maternal age or fetal nuchal translucency: a randomized controlled trial in 39,572 pregnancies. *Ultrasound in Obstetrics and Gynecology* 2005;25(6):537–45.

792. Biggio JR, Jr., Morris TC, Owen J, *et al.* An outcomes analysis of five prenatal screening strategies for trisomy 21 in women younger than 35 years. *American Journal of Obstetrics and Gynecology* 2004;190(3):721–9.

793. Comstock CH, Malone FD, Ball RH, *et al.* Is there a nuchal translucency millimeter measurement above which there is no added benefit from first trimester serum screening? *American Journal of Obstetrics and Gynecology* 2006;195(3):843–7.

794. Green JM, Hewison J, Bekker HL, *et al.* Psychosocial aspects of genetic screening of pregnant women and newborns: A systematic review. *Health Technology Assessment (Winchester, England)* 2004;8(33):iii-87.

795. Rowe HJ, Fisher JRW, Quinlivan JA. Are pregnant Australian women well informed about prenatal genetic screening? A systematic investigation using the Multidimensional Measure of Informed Choice. *Australian and New Zealand Journal of Obstetrics and Gynaecology* 2006;46(5):433–9.

796. Georgsson OS, Saltvedt S, Grunewald C, *et al.* Does fetal screening affect women's worries about the health of their baby? A randomized controlled trial of ultrasound screening for Down's syndrome versus routine ultrasound screening. *Acta Obstetricia et Gynecologica Scandinavica* 2004;83(7):634–40.

797. Lawson KL, Turriff-Jonasson SI. Maternal serum screening and psychosocial attachment to pregnancy. *Journal of Psychosomatic Research* 2006;60(4):371–8.

798. Rowe RE, Garcia J, Davidson LL. Social and ethnic inequalities in the offer and uptake of prenatal screening and diagnosis in the UK: a systematic review. *Public Health* 2004;118(3):177–89.

799. Dormandy E, Michie S, Hooper R, *et al.* Low uptake of prenatal screening for Down syndrome in minority ethnic groups and socially deprived groups: a reflection of women's attitudes or a failure to facilitate informed choices? *International Journal of Epidemiology* 2005;34(2):346–52.

800. Spencer K, Aitken D. Factors affecting women's preference for type of prenatal screening test for chromosomal anomalies. *Ultrasound in Obstetrics and Gynecology* 2004;24(7):735–9.

801. Wald NJ, Bestwick JP, Morris JK. Cross-trimester marker ratios in prenatal screening for Down syndrome. *Prenatal Diagnosis* 2006;26(6):514–23.

802. Gilbert RE, Augood C, Gupta R, *et al.* Screening for Down's syndrome: effects, safety, and cost effectiveness of first and second trimester strategies. *British Medical Journal* 2001; 323:1–6.

803. Roberts T, Mugford M, Piercy J. Choosing options for ultrasound screening in pregnancy and comparing cost effectiveness: a decision analysis approach. *British Journal of Obstetrics and Gynaecology* 1998;105(9):960–70.

804. Ritchie K, Bradbury I, Slattery J, *et al.* Economic modelling of antenatal screening and ultrasound scanning programmes for identification of fetal abnormalities. *BJOG: an International Journal of Obstetrics and Gynaecology* 2005;112(7):866–74.

805. Smith JW, Rogers RE, Katz BP, *et al.* Diagnosis of chlamydial infection in women attending antenatal and gynecologic clinics. *Journal of Clinical Microbiology* 1987;25(5):868–72.

806. Baselski VS, McNeeley SG, Ryan. A comparison of nonculture-dependent methods for detection of Chlamydia trachomatis infections in pregnant women. *Obstetrics and Gynecology* 1987;70(1):47–52.

807. Stamm WE, Harrison HR, Alexander ER, *et al.* Diagnosis of Chlamydia trachomatis infections by direct immunofluorescence staining of genital secretions. A multicenter trial. *Annals of Internal Medicine* 1984;101(5):638–41.

808. Garland SM, Tabrizi S, Hallo J, Chen S. Assessment of Chlamydia trachomatis prevalence by PCR and LCR in women presenting for termination of pregnancy. *Sexually Transmitted Infections* 2000;76(3):173–6.

809. Andrews WW, Lee HH, Roden WJ, *et al.* Detection of genitourinary tract Chlamydia trachomatis infection in pregnant women by ligase chain reaction assay. *Obstetrics and Gynecology* 1997;89(4):556–60.

810. Thejls H, Gnarpe J, Gnarpe H, *et al.* Expanded gold standard in the diagnosis of Chlamydia trachomatis in a low prevalence population: diagnostic efficacy of tissue culture, direct immunofluorescence, enzyme immunoassay, PCR and serology. *Genitourinary Medicine* 1994;70(5):300–3.

811. Macmillan S, McKenzie H, Templeton A. Parallel observation of four methods for screening women under 25 years of age for genital infection with Chlamydia trachomatis. *European Journal of Obstetrics, Gynecology, and Reproductive Biology* 2003;107(1):68–73.

812. Renton A. Chlamydia trachomatis in cervical and vaginal swabs and urine specimens from women undergoing termination of pregnancy. *International Journal of STD and AIDS* 2006;17(7):443–7.

813. Hosein IK, Kaunitz AM, Craft SJ. Detection of cervical Chlamydia trachomatis and Neisseria gonorrhoeae with deoxyribonucleic acid probe assays in obstetric patients. *American Journal of Obstetrics and Gynecology* 1992;167(3):588–91.

814. Yang LI, Panke ES, Leist PA, *et al.* Detection of Chlamydia trachomatis endocervical infection in asymptomatic and symptomatic women: comparison of deoxyribonucleic acid probe test with tissue culture. *American Journal of Obstetrics and Gynecology* 1991;165(5 Pt 1):1444–53.

815. Asbill KK, Higgins RV, Bahrani-Mostafavi Z, *et al.* Detection of Neisseria gonorrhoeae and Chlamydia trachomatis colonization of the gravid cervix including commentary by Mammel JB with author response. *American Journal of Obstetrics and Gynecology* 2000;183(2):340–6.

816. Spence MR. A correlative study of Papanicolaou smear, fluorescent antibody, and culture for the diagnosis of Chlamydia trachomatis. *Obstetrics and Gynecology* 1986;68(5):691–5.

817. Martin DH, Eschenbach DA, Cotch MF, *et al.* Double-blind placebo-controlled treatment trial of chlamydia trachomatis endocervical infections in pregnant women. *Infectious Diseases in Obstetrics and Gynecology* 1997;5(1):10–17.

818. Ryan Jr GM, Abdella TN, McNeeley SG, *et al.* Chlamydia trachomatis infection in pregnancy and effect of treatment on outcome. *American Journal of Obstetrics and Gynecology* 1990;162(1):34–9.

819. Cohen I, Veille J-C, Calkins BM. Improved pregnancy outcome following successful treatment of chlamydial infection. *JAMA: the journal of the American Medical Association* 1990; 263:3160–3.

820. Black-Payne C, Ahrabi MM, Bocchini JA, Jr. *et al.* Treatment of Chlamydia trachomatis identified with Chlamydiazyme during pregnancy. Impact on perinatal complications and infants. *Journal of Reproductive Medicine* 1990;35(4):362–7.

821. Rivlin ME, Morrison JC, Grossman JH. Comparison of pregnancy outcome between treated and untreated women with chlamydial cervicitis. *Journal of the Mississippi State Medical Association* 1997;38(11):404–7.

822. McMillan JA, Weiner LB, Lamberson HV, *et al.* Efficacy of maternal screening and therapy in the prevention of chlamydia infection of the newborn. *Infection* 1985;13(6):263–6.

823. American Diabetes Association. Gestational Diabetes Mellitus. *Diabetes Care* 2004;27(Suppl 1):S88–90.

824. Crowther CA, Hiller JE, Moss JR, *et al.*; Australian Carbohydrate Intolerance Study in Pregnant Women (ACHOIS) Trial Group. Effect of treatment of gestational diabetes mellitus on pregnancy outcomes. *New England Journal of Medicine* 2005;352(24):2477–86.

825. Mires GJ, Williams FL, Harper V. Screening practices for gestational diabetes mellitus in UK obstetric units. *Diabetic Medicine* 1999;16(2):138–41.

826. Nelson-Piercy C, Gale EAM. Do we know how to screen for gestational diabetes? Current practice in one regional health authority. *Diabetic Medicine* 1994;11(5):493–8.

827. Chiaffarino F, Parazzini F, Bortolotti A, *et al.* Debate over screening for gestational diabetes. Scientific uncertainty is mirrored in clinical practice in Italy. *British Medical Journal* 1998;316(7134):861.

828. Rouse DJ, Owen J, Goldenberg RL, *et al.* The effectiveness and costs of elective cesarean delivery for fetal macrosomia diagnosed by ultrasound. *JAMA: the journal of the American Medical Association* 1996;276(18):1480–6.

829. Dornhorst A, Paterson CM, Nicholls JSD, *et al.* High prevalence of gestational diabetes in women from ethnic minority groups. *Diabetic Medicine* 1992; 9:820–5.

830. Moses R, Griffiths R, Davis W. Gestational diabetes: do all women need to be tested? *Australian and New Zealand Journal of Obstetrics and Gynaecology* 1995;35(4):387–9.

831. Davey RX, Hamblin PS. Selective versus universal screening for gestational diabetes mellitus: an evaluation of predictive risk factors. *Medical Journal of Australia* 2001;174(3):118–21.

832. Griffin ME, Coffey M, Johnson H, *et al.* Universal vs. risk factor-based screening for gestational diabetes mellitus: detection rates, gestation at diagnosis and outcome. *Diabetic Medicine* 2000;17(1):26–32.

833. Schytte T, Jorgensen LG, Brandslund I, *et al.* The clinical impact of screening for gestational diabetes. *Clinical Chemistry and Laboratory Medicine* 2004;42(9):1036–42.

834. Weijers RN, Bekedam DJ, Goldschmidt HM, *et al.* The clinical usefulness of glucose tolerance testing in gestational diabetes to predict early postpartum diabetes mellitus. *Clinical Chemistry and Laboratory Medicine* 2006;44(1):99–104.

835. Ostlund I, Hanson U. Occurrence of gestational diabetes mellitus and the value of different screening indicators for the oral glucose tolerance test. *Acta Obstetricia et Gynecologica Scandinavica* 2003;82(2):103–8.

836. Kim C, Berger DK, Chamany S. Recurrence of gestational diabetes mellitus: a systematic review. *Diabetes Care* 2007;30(5):1314–19.

837. Ostlund I, Hanson U. Repeated random blood glucose measurements as universal screening test for gestational diabetes mellitus. *Acta Obstetricia et Gynecologica Scandinavica* 2004;83(1):46–51.

838. Nasrat AA, Johnstone FD, Hasan SAM. Is random plasma glucose an efficient screening test for abnormal glucose tolerance in pregnancy? *BJOG: an International Journal of Obstetrics and Gynaecology* 1988; 95:855–60.

839. Lind T. Antenatal screening using random blood glucose values. *Diabetes* 1985; 34 Suppl 2:17–20.

840. Seshiah V, Balaji V, Balaji MS, *et al.* Gestational diabetes mellitus in India. *Journal of the Association of Physicians of India* 2004; 52:707–11.

841. Cetin M, Cetin A. Time-dependent gestational diabetes screening values. *International Journal of Gynaecology and Obstetrics* 1997;56(3):257–61.

842. O'Sullivan JB, Mahan CM, Charles D, *et al.* Screening criteria for high-risk gestational diabetic patients. *American Journal of Obstetrics and Gynecology* 1973;116(7):895–900.

843. Buhling KJ, Henrich W, Kjos SL, *et al.* Comparison of point-of-care-testing glucose meters with standard laboratory measurement of the 50g-glucose-challenge test (GCT) during pregnancy. *Clinical Biochemistry* 2003;36(5):333–7.

844. Murphy NJ, Meyer BA, O'Kell RT, *et al.* Carbohydrate sources for gestational diabetes mellitus screening. A comparison. *Journal of Reproductive Medicine* 1994;39(12):977–81.

845. Court DJ, Mann SL, Stone PR, *et al.* Comparison of glucose polymer and glucose for screening and tolerance tests in pregnancy. *Obstetrics and Gynecology* 1985;66(4):491–9.

846. Fadl H, Ostlund I, Nilsson K, *et al.* Fasting capillary glucose as a screening test for gestational diabetes mellitus. *BJOG: an International Journal of Obstetrics and Gynaecology* 2006;113(9):1067–71.

847. Lamar ME, Kuehl TJ, Cooney AT, *et al.* Jelly beans as an alternative to a fifty-gram glucose beverage for gestational diabetes screening. *American Journal of Obstetrics and Gynecology* 1999;181(5 Pt 1):1154–7.

848. Boyd KL, Ross EK, Sherman SJ. Jelly beans as an alternative to a cola beverage containing fifty grams of glucose. *American Journal of Obstetrics and Gynecology* 1995;173(6):1889–92.

849. Rajab KE, Mehdi S. Pregnancy outcome among gestational diabetics with blood glucose levels between 7.7 and 8.3 mmol/l. *International Journal of Gynaecology and Obstetrics* 1998;63(1):59–61.

850. Yogev Y, Langer O, Xenakis EM, *et al.* The association between glucose challenge test, obesity and pregnancy outcome in 6390 non-diabetic women. *Journal of Maternal-Fetal and Neonatal Medicine* 2005;17(1):29–34.

851. Dietrich ML, Dolnicek TF, Rayburn WF. Gestational diabetes screening in a private, midwestern American population. *American Journal of Obstetrics and Gynecology* 1987;156(6):1403–8.

852. Sun B, Wang X, Song Q, *et al.* Prospective studies on the relationship between the 50 g glucose challenge test and pregnant outcome. *Chinese Medical Journal* 1995;108(12):910–13.

853. Rumbold AR. Women's experiences of being screened for gestational diabetes mellitus. *Australian and New Zealand Journal of Obstetrics and Gynaecology* 2002;42(2):131–7.

854. Kerbel D, Glazier R, Holzapfel S, *et al.* Adverse effects of screening for gestational diabetes: a prospective cohort study in Toronto, Canada. *Journal of Medical Screening* 1997;4(3):128–32.

855. Naylor CD, Sermer M, Chen E, *et al.* Selective screening for gestational diabetes mellitus. *New England Journal of Medicine* 1997;337(22):1591–6.

856. Rayner M, Petersen S, Buckley C, Press V. Coronary heart disease statistics: diabetes supplement. London: British Heart Foundation; 2001.

857. Yaron Y, Cherry M, Kramer RL, *et al.* Second-trimester maternal serum marker screening: Maternal serum alpha- fetoprotein, beta-human chorionic gonadotropin, estriol, and their various combinations as predictors of pregnancy outcome. *American Journal of Obstetrics and Gynecology* 1999;181(4):968–74.

858. Pouta AM, Hartikainen AL, Vuolteenaho OJ, *et al.* Midtrimester N-terminal proatrial natriuretic peptide, free beta hCG, and alpha-fetoprotein in predicting preeclampsia. *Obstetrics and Gynecology* 1998;91(6):940–4.

859. Cotter AM, Martin CM, O'leary JJ, *et al.* Increased fetal DNA in the maternal circulation in early pregnancy is associated with an increased risk of preeclampsia. *American Journal of Obstetrics and Gynecology* 2004;191(2):515–20.

860. Leung TN, Zhang J, Lau TK, *et al.* Increased maternal plasma fetal DNA concentrations in women who eventually develop preeclampsia. *Clinical Chemistry* 2001;47(1):137–9.

861. Lambert-Messerlian GM, Silver HM, Petraglia F, *et al.* Second-trimester levels of maternal serum human chorionic gonadotropin and inhibin a as predictors of preeclampsia in the third trimester of pregnancy. *Journal of the Society for Gynecologic Investigation* 2000;7(3):170–4.

862. Ashour AM, Lieberman ES, Haug LE, *et al.* The value of elevated second-trimester beta-human chorionic gonadotropin in predicting development of preeclampsia. *American Journal of Obstetrics and Gynecology* 1997;176(2):438–42.

863. Sanchez-Ramos L, Jones DC, Cullen MT. Urinary calcium as an early marker for preeclampsia. *Obstetrics and Gynecology* 1991;77(5):685–8.

864. Baker PN, Hackett GA. The use of urinary albumin-creatinine ratios and calcium-creatinine ratios as screening tests for pregnancy-induced hypertension. *Obstetrics and Gynecology* 1994;83(5 Pt 1):745–9.

865. Rogers MS, Chung T, Baldwin S, *et al.* A comparison of second trimester urinary electrolytes, microalbumin, and N-acetyl-beta-glucosaminidase for prediction of gestational hypertension and preeclampsia. *Hypertension in Pregnancy* 1994;13(2):179–92.

866. Conde-Agudelo A, Belizan JM, Lede R, *et al.* Prediction of hypertensive disorders of pregnancy by calcium/creatinine ratio and other laboratory tests. *International Journal of Gynaecology and Obstetrics* 1994;47(3):285–6.

867. Kazerooni T, Hamze-Nejadi S. Calcium to creatinine ratio in a spot sample of urine for early prediction of pre-eclampsia. *International Journal of Gynaecology and Obstetrics* 2003;80(3):279–83.

868. Papageorghiou AT, Yu CK, Bindra R, *et al.* Multicenter screening for pre-eclampsia and fetal growth restriction by transvaginal uterine artery Doppler at 23 weeks of gestation. *Ultrasound in Obstetrics and Gynecology* 2001;18(5):441–9.

869. Harrington K, Carpenter RG, Goldfrad C, *et al.* Transvaginal Doppler ultrasound of the uteroplacental circulation in the early prediction of pre-eclampsia and intrauterine growth retardation. *British Journal of Obstetrics and Gynaecology* 1997;104(6):674–81.

870. Marchesoni D, Pezzani I, Springolo F, *et al.* The use of uterine artery Doppler as a screening test for pre-eclampsia. *Italian Journal of Gynaecology and Obstetrics* 2003;15(1):15–20.

871. Schwarze A, Nelles I, Krapp M, *et al.* Doppler ultrasound of the uterine artery in the prediction of severe complications during low-risk pregnancies. *Archives of Gynecology and Obstetrics* 2005;271(1):46–52.

872. Ay E, Kavak ZN, Elter K, *et al.* Screening for pre-eclampsia by using maternal serum inhibin A, activin A, human chorionic gonadotropin, unconjugated estriol, and alpha-fetoprotein levels and uterine artery Doppler in the second trimester of pregnancy. *Australian and New Zealand Journal of Obstetrics and Gynaecology* 2005;45(4):283–8.

873. Audibert F, Benchimol Y, Benattar C, *et al.* Prediction of preeclampsia or intrauterine growth restriction by second trimester serum screening and uterine Doppler velocimetry. *Fetal Diagnosis and Therapy* 2005;20(1):48–53.

874. Conde-Agudelo A, Belizan JM. Maternal morbidity and mortality associated with interpregnancy interval: cross sectional study. *British Medical Journal* 2000;321(7271):1255–9.

875. Basso O, Christensen K, Olsen J. Higher risk of pre-eclampsia after change of partner. An effect of longer interpregnancy intervals? *Epidemiology* 2001;12(6):624–9.

876. Reiss RE, O'Shaughnessy RW, Quilligan TJ, *et al.* Retrospective comparison of blood pressure course during preeclamptic and matched control pregnancies. *American Journal of Obstetrics and Gynecology* 1987;156(4):894–8.

877. Sibai BM, Gordon T, Thom E, *et al.* Risk factors for preeclampsia in healthy nulliparous women: a prospective multicenter study. The National Institute of Child Health and Human Development Network of Maternal-Fetal Medicine Units. *American Journal of Obstetrics and Gynecology* 1995;172(2 Pt 1):642–8.

878. Odegard RA, Vatten LJ, Nilsen ST, *et al.* Risk factors and clinical manifestations of pre-eclampsia. *BJOG: An International Journal of Obstetrics & Gynaecology* 2000;107(11):1410–16.

879. Stettler RW, Cunningham FG. Natural history of chronic proteinuria complicating pregnancy. *American Journal of Obstetrics and Gynecology* 1992;167(5):1219–24.

880. Goldenberg RL. The preterm prediction study: the value of new vs standard risk factors in predicting early and all spontaneous preterm births. NICHD MFMU Network. *American Journal of Public Health* 1998;88(2):233–8.

2008 update

881. Iams JD, Goldenberg RL, Mercer BM, *et al.* The Preterm Prediction Study: recurrence risk of spontaneous preterm birth. National Institute of Child Health and Human Development Maternal-Fetal Medicine Units Network. *American Journal of Obstetrics and Gynecology* 1998;178(5):1035–40.

882. Kristensen J, Langhoff-Roos J, Kristensen FB. Implications of idiopathic preterm delivery for previous and subsequent pregnancies. *Obstetrics and Gynecology* 1995;86(5):800–4.

883. Iams JD, Goldenberg RL, Mercer BM. The preterm prediction study: can low-risk women destined for spontaneous preterm birth be identified? *American Journal of Obstetrics and Gynecology* 2001;184:652–5.

884. Blondel B, Le Coutour X, Kaminski M, *et al.* Prediction of preterm delivery:is it substantially improved by routine vaginal examinations? *American Journal of Obstetrics and Gynecology* 1990;162:1042–8.

885. Chambers S, Pons JC, Richard A, *et al.* Vaginal infections, cervical ripening and preterm delivery. *European Journal of Obstetrics, Gynecology and Reproductive Biology* 1991;38(2):103–8.

886. Parikh MN, Mehta AC. Internal cervical os during the second half of pregnancy. *Journal of Obstetrics and Gynaecology of the British Empire* 1961; 68:818–21.

887. Leveno KJ, Cox K, Roark ML. Cervical dilatation and prematurity revisited. *Obstetrics and Gynecology* 1986;68(3):434–5.

888. Heath VC, Daskalakis G, Zagaliki A, *et al.* Cervicovaginal fibronectin and cervical length at 23 weeks of gestation: relative risk of early preterm delivery. *BJOG: an International Journal of Obstetrics and Gynaecology* 2000;107(10):1276–81.

889. Chang TC, Chew TS, Pang M, *et al.* Cervicovaginal foetal fibronectin in the prediction of preterm labour in a low-risk population. *Annals of the Academy of Medicine, Singapore* 1997;26(6):776–80.

890. Faron G, Boulvain M, Lescrainier JP, *et al.* A single cervical fetal fibronectin screening test in a population at low risk for preterm delivery: an improvement on clinical indicators? *British Journal of Obstetrics and Gynaecology* 1997;104(6):697–701.

891. Daskalakis G, Papapanagiotou A, Mesogitis S, *et al.* Bacterial vaginosis and group B streptococcal colonization and preterm delivery in a low-risk population. *Fetal Diagnosis and Therapy* 2006;21(2):172–6.

892. Crane JM, Armson BA, Dodds L, *et al.* Risk scoring, fetal fibronectin, and bacterial vaginosis to predict preterm delivery. *Obstetrics and Gynecology* 1999;93(4):517–22.

893. Lockwood CJ, Ghidini A, Wein R, *et al.* Increased interleukin-6 concentrations in cervical secretions are associated with preterm delivery. *American Journal of Obstetrics and Gynecology* 1994;171(4):1097–102.

894. Inglis SR, Jeremias J, Kuno K, *et al.* Detection of tumor necrosis factor-alpha, interleukin-6, and fetal fibronectin in the lower genital tract during pregnancy: relation to outcome. *American Journal of Obstetrics and Gynecology* 1994;171(1):5–10.

895. Goepfert AR, Goldenberg RL, Andrews WW, *et al.* The Preterm Prediction Study: association between cervical interleukin 6 concentration and spontaneous preterm birth. National Institute of Child Health and Human Development Maternal-Fetal Medicine Units Network. *American Journal of Obstetrics and Gynecology* 2001;184(3):483–8.

896. Sakai M, Sasaki Y, Yoneda S, *et al.* Elevated interleukin-8 in cervical mucus as an indicator for treatment to prevent premature birth and preterm, pre-labor rupture of membranes: a prospective study. *American Journal of Reproductive Immunology* 2004;51(3):220–5.

897. Sakai M, Ishiyama A, Tabata M, *et al.* Relationship between cervical mucus interleukin-8 concentrations and vaginal bacteria in pregnancy. *American Journal of Reproductive Immunology* 2004;52(2):106–12.

898. Simpson JL, Palomaki GE, Mercer B, *et al.* Associations between adverse perinatal outcome and serially obtained second- and third-trimester maternal serum alpha-fetoprotein measurements. *American Journal of Obstetrics and Gynecology* 1995;173(6):1742–8.

899. Dugoff L, Hobbins JC, Malone FD, *et al.* Quad screen as a predictor of adverse pregnancy outcome. *Obstetrics and Gynecology* 2005;106(2):260–7.

900. Morssink LP, Kornman LH, Beekhuis JR, *et al.* Abnormal levels of maternal serum human chorionic gonadotropin and alpha-fetoprotein in the second trimester: relation to fetal weight and preterm delivery. [see comment]. *Prenatal Diagnosis* 1995;15(11):1041–6.

901. Ong CYT, Liao AW, Spencer K, *et al.* First trimester maternal serum free beta human chorionic gonadotrophin and pregnancy associated plasma protein a as predictors of pregnancy complications. *BJOG: an International Journal of Obstetrics and Gynaecology* 2000;107(10):1265–70.

902. Yaron Y, Ochshorn Y, Heifetz S, *et al.* First trimester maternal serum free human chorionic gonadotropin as a predictor of adverse pregnancy outcome. *Fetal Diagnosis and Therapy* 2002;17(6):352–6.

903. Hvilsom GB, Thorsen P, Jeune B, *et al.* C-reactive protein: a serological marker for preterm delivery? *Acta Obstetricia et Gynecologica Scandinavica* 2002;81(5):424–9.

904. Karinen L, Pouta A, Bloigu A, *et al.* Serum C-reactive protein and Chlamydia trachomatis antibodies in preterm delivery. *Obstetrics and Gynecology* 2005;106(1):73–80.

905. Wren BG. Subclinical renal infection and prematurity. *Medical Journal of Australia* 1969;1:596–600.

906. Robertson JG, Livingstone JR, Isdale MH. The managment and complications of asymptomatic bacteriuria in pregnancy. Report of a study on 8,275 patients. *Journal of Obstetrics and Gynaecology of the British Commonwealth* 1968;75(1):59–65.

907. Uncu Y, Uncu G, Esmer A, *et al.* Should asymptomatic bacteriuria be screened in pregnancy? *Clinical and Experimental Obstetrics and Gynecology* 2002;29(4):281–5.

908. Layton R. Infection of the urinary tract in pregancy: an investigation of a new routine in antenatal care. *Journal of Obstetrics and Gynaecology of the British Commonwealth* 1964;71:927–33.

909. Klebanoff MA, Hillier SL, Nugent RP, *et al.* Is bacterial vaginosis a stronger risk factor for preterm birth when it is diagnosed earlier in gestation? *American Journal of Obstetrics and Gynecology* 2005;192(2):470–7.

910. Hillier SL, Nugent RP, Eschenbach DA, *et al.* Association between bacterial vaginosis and preterm delivery of a low-birth-weight infant. The Vaginal Infections and Prematurity Study Group. [see comment]. *New England Journal of Medicine* 1995;333(26):1737–42.

911. Purwar M, Ughade S, Bhagat B, *et al.* Bacterial vaginosis in early pregnancy and adverse pregnancy outcome. *Journal of Obstetrics and Gynaecology Research* 2001;27(4):175–81.

912. Taipale P, Hiilesmaa V. Sonographic measurement of uterine cervix at 18–22 weeks' gestation and the risk of preterm delivery. *Obstetrics and Gynecology* 1998;92(6):902–7.

913. Leung TN, Pang MW, Leung TY, *et al.* Cervical length at 18–22 weeks of gestation for prediction of spontaneous preterm delivery in Hong Kong Chinese women. *Ultrasound in Obstetrics and Gynecology* 2005;26(7):713–17.

914. Fukami T, Ishihara K, Sekiya T, *et al.* Is transvaginal ultrasonography at mid-trimester useful for predicting early spontaneous preterm birth? *Journal of Nippon Medical School = Nihon Ika Daigahu Zasshi* 2003;70(2):135–40.

915. To MS, Skentou C, Liao AW, *et al.* Cervical length and funneling at 23 weeks of gestation in the prediction of spontaneous early preterm delivery. *Ultrasound in Obstetrics and Gynecology* 2001;18(3):200–3.

2008 update

916. Bais JM, Eskes M, Pel M, *et al.* Effectiveness of detection of intrauterine growth retardation by abdominal palpation as screening test in a low risk population: an observational study. *European Journal of Obstetrics, Gynecology, and Reproductive Biology* 2004;116(2):164–9.

917. Secher NJ, Lundbye-Christensen S, Qvist I, Bagger P. An evaluation of clinical estimation of fetal weight and symphysis fundal distance for detection of SGA infants. *European Journal of Obstetrics Gynecology and Reproductive Biology* 1991;38(2):91–6.

918. Rosenberg K. Measurement of fundal height as a screening test for fetal growth retardation. *British Journal of Obstetrics and Gynaecology* 1982;89(6):447–50.

919. Persson B, Stangenberg M, Lunell NO, Brodin U, Holmberg NG, Vaclavinkova V. Prediction of size of infants at birth by measurement of symphysis fundus height. *British Journal of Obstetrics and Gynaecology* 1986;93(3):206–11.

920. Harding K. Screening for the small fetus: A study of the relative efficacies of ultrasound biometry and symphysiofundal height. *Australian and New Zealand Journal of Obstetrics and Gynaecology* 1995;35(2):160–4.

921. Grover V. Altered fetal growth: Antenatal diagnosis by symphysis-fundal height in India and comparison with western charts. *International Journal of Gynecology and Obstetrics* 1991;35(3):231–4.

922. Rogers MS. Evaluation of fundal height measurement in antenatal care. *Australian and New Zealand Journal of Obstetrics and Gynaecology* 1985;25(2):87–90.

923. Warsof SL, Cooper DJ, Little D, Campbell S. Routine ultrasound screening for antenatal detection of intrauterine growth retardation. *Obstetrics and Gynecology* 1986;67(1):33–9.

924. Skovron ML, Berkowitz GS, Lapinski RH, *et al.* Evaluation of early third-trimester ultrasound screening for intrauterine growth retardation. *Journal of Ultrasound in Medicine* 1991;10(3):153–9.

925. Newnham JP, Patterson LL, James IR, *et al.* An evaluation of the efficacy of Doppler flow velocity waveform analysis as a screening test in pregnancy. *American Journal of Obstetrics and Gynecology* 1990;162(2):403–10.

926. Hedriana HL. A comparison of single versus multiple growth ultrasonographic examinations in predicting birth weight. *American Journal of Obstetrics and Gynecology* 1994;170(6):1600–4.

927. Lin CC. The association between oligohydramnios and intrauterine growth retardation. *Obstetrics and Gynecology* 1990;76(6):1100–4.

928. Chauhan SP, Scardo JA, Hendrix NW, *et al.* Accuracy of sonographically estimated fetal weight with and without oligohydramnios. A case-control study. *Journal of Reproductive Medicine* 1999;44(11):969–73.

929. Beattie RB. Antenatal screening for intrauterine growth retardation with umbilical artery Doppler ultrasonography. *British Medical Journal* 1989;298(6674):631–5.

930. Todros T. Performance of Doppler ultrasonography as a screening test in low risk pregnancies: results of a multicentric study. *Journal of Ultrasound in Medicine* 1995;14(5):343–8.

931. Sijmons EA, Reuwer PJ, van Beek E, Bruinse HW. The validity of screening for small-for-gestational-age and low-weight-for-length infants by Doppler ultrasound. *British Journal of Obstetrics and Gynaecology* 1989;96(5):557–61.

932. Atkinson MW, Maher JE, Owen J, *et al.* The predictive value of umbilical artery Doppler studies for preeclampsia or fetal growth retardation in a preeclampsia prevention trial. *Obstetrics and Gynecology* 1994;83(4):609–12.

933. Owen P. Prediction of intrauterine growth restriction with customised estimated fetal weight centiles. *BJOG: an International Journal of Obstetrics and Gynaecology* 2003;110(4):411–15.

934. Okonofua FE, Ayangade SO, Chan RCW, *et al.* A prospective comparison of clinical and ultrasonic methods of predicting normal and abnormal fetal growth. *International Journal of Gynecology and Obstetrics* 1986;24(6):447–51.

935. Ott WJ. Ultrasonic diagnosis of altered fetal growth by use of a normal ultrasonic fetal weight curve. *Obstetrics and Gynecology* 1984;63(2):201–4.

936. Smith-Bindman R. US evaluation of fetal growth: prediction of neonatal outcomes. *Radiology* 2002;223(1):153–61.

937. Stratton JF, Scanaill SN, Stuart B, *et al.* Are babies of normal birth weight who fail to reach their growth potential as diagnosed by ultrasound at increased risk? *Ultrasound in Obstetrics and Gynecology* 1995;5(2):114–18.

938. Zhang J. Isolated oligohydramnios is not associated with adverse perinatal outcomes. *BJOG : an international journal of obstetrics and gynaecology* 2004;111(3):220–5.

939. Biggio JR, Wenstrom KD, Dubard MB, *et al.* Hydramnios prediction of adverse perinatal outcome. *Obstetrics and Gynecology* 1999;94(5 Pt 1):773–7.

940. Clausson B, Gardosi J, Francis A, *et al.* Perinatal outcome in SGA births defined by customised versus population-based birthweight standards. *BJOG: an International Journal of Obstetrics and Gynaecology* 2001;108(8):830–4.

941. Zhang X, Platt RW, Cnattingius S, *et al.* The use of customised versus population-based birthweight standards in predicting perinatal mortality. *BJOG: an International Journal of Obstetrics and Gynaecology* 2007;114(4):474–7.

942. Confidential Enquiry into Maternal and Child Health. *Why Mothers Die 2000–2002.*Sixth Report of the Confidential Enquiries into Maternal Deaths in the United Kingdom. London: RCOG Press; 2004.

943. Department of Health. *National Service Framework for Children, Young People and Maternity Services – Core Standards.* London: Department of Health; 2004.

944. Sullivan ID. Prenatal diagnosis of structural heart disease: does it make a difference to survival? *Heart* 2002;87(5):–6, 2002.

945. Wren C, Birrell G, Hawthorne G. Cardiovascular malformations in infants of diabetic mothers. *Heart* 2003;89(10):1217–20.

946. Smith RS, Comstock CH, Lorenz RP, *et al.* Maternal diabetes mellitus: which views are essential for fetal echocardiography? *Obstetrics and Gynecology* 1997;90(4 Pt 1):575–9.

947. Ogge G, Gaglioti P, Maccanti S, *et al.* Prenatal screening for congenital heart disease with four-chamber and outflow-tract views: A multicenter study. *Ultrasound in Obstetrics and Gynecology* 2006;28(6):779–84.

948. Poncet B, Touzet S, Rocher L, *et al.* Cost-effectiveness analysis of gestational diabetes mellitus screening in France. *European Journal of Obstetrics, Gynecology and Reproductive Biology* 2002;103(2):122–9.

949. Di CG, Volpe L, Casadidio I, *et al.* Universal screening and intensive metabolic management of gestational diabetes: cost-effectiveness in Italy. *Acta Diabetologica* 2002;39(2):69–73.

950. Nicholson WK, Fleisher LA, Fox HE, *et al.* Screening for gestational diabetes mellitus: a decision and cost-effectiveness analysis of four screening strategies. *Diabetes Care* 2005;28(6):1482–4.

951. Scott DA, Loveman E, McIntyre L, *et al.* Screening for gestational diabetes: a systematic review and economic evaluation. *Health Technology Assessment* 2002;6(11):1–172.

952. Reed BD. Screening for gestational diabetes – analysis by screening criteria. *Journal of Family Practice* 1984;19(6):751–5.

953. Massion C, O'Connor PJ, Gorab R, *et al.* Screening for gestational diabetes in a high-risk population. *Journal of Family Practice* 1987;25(6):569–75.

2008 update

954. Lavin JP, Barden TP, Miodovnik M. Clinical experience with a screening program for gestational diabetes. *American Journal of Obstetrics and Gynecology* 1981;141(5):491–4.

955. Larijani B, Hossein-Nezhad A, Vassigh A-R. Effect of varying threshold and selective versus universal strategies on the cost in gestational diabetes mellitus. *Archives of Iranian Medicine* 2004;7(4):267–71.

956. National Collaborating Centre for Women's and Children's Health. *Fertility: Assessment and Management for People with Fertility Problems.* London: RCOG Press; 2004.

957. Coustan DR. Methods of screening for and diagnosing of gestational diabetes. *Clinics in Perinatology* 1993;20(3):593–602.

958. Weeks JW, Major CA, de Veciana M, *et al.* Gestational diabetes: Does the presence of risk factors influence perinatal outcome? *American Journal of Obstetrics and Gynecology* 1994;171:1003–7.

959. Curtis L, Netten A. *Unit Costs of Health and Social Care.* Canterbury: Personal and Social Services Research Unit University of Kent at Canterbury; 2006.

960. Davies LM, Drummond MF. Management of labour: consumer choice and cost implications. *Journal of Obstetrics and Gynaecology* 1991;11(Suppl 1):s28–s33.

961. Langer O, Conway DL, Berkus MD, *et al.* A comparison of glyburide and insulin in women with gestational diabetes mellitus. *New England Journal of Medicine* 2000;343(16):1134–8.

962. Briggs A, Claxton K, Sculpher M. *Decision Modelling for Health Economic Evaluation.* Oxford: Oxford University Press; 2006.

963. Goetzl L, Wilkins I. Glyburide compared to insulin for the treatment of gestational diabetes mellitus: A cost analysis. *Journal of Perinatology* 2002;22(5):403–6.

964. UK National Screening Committee. *Antenatal Screening: Working Standards Incorporating Those for the National Down Syndrome Screening Programme for England.* London: NSC; 2004.

965. Rosen DJD, Kedar I, Amiel A, *et al.* A negative second trimester triple test and absence of specific ultrasonographic markers may decrease the need for genetic amniocentesis in advanced maternal age by 60%. *Prenatal Diagnosis* 2002;22(1):59–63.

966. Binns B. Screening for Chlamydia trachomatis infection in a pregnancy counseling clinic. *American Journal of Obstetrics and Gynecology* 1988;159(5):1144–9.

967. National Institute for Health and Clinical Excellence. *Improving the Nutrition of Pregnant and Breastfeeding Mothers in Low-Income Households.* Public Health Guidance 11. London: NICE; 2008.

968. Matsuoka LY, Wortsman J, Dannenberg MJ, Hollis BW, Lu Z, Holick MF. Clothing prevents ultraviolet-B radiation-dependent photosynthesis of vitamin D3. *Journal of Clinical Endocrinology and Metabolism* 1992;75(4):1099–103.

969. Dunnigan MG, Henderson JB, Hole DJ, Berry JL. Meat consumption reduces the risk of nutritional rickets and osteomalacia. *British Journal of Nutrition* 2005;94:983–91.

970. Finch PJ, Ang L, Colston KW, Nisbet J, Maxwell JD. Blunted seasonal variation in serum 25-hydroxy vitamin D and increased risk of osteomalacia in vegetarian London Asians. *European Journal of Clinical Nutrition* 1992;46(7):509–15.

971. Brooke OG, Brown IR, Bone CD, Carter ND, Cleeve HJ, Maxwell JD, *et al.* Vitamin D supplements in pregnant Asian women: effects on calcium status and fetal growth. *British Medical Journal* 1980;280(6216):751–4.

972. Brooke OG, Butters F, Wood C. Intrauterine vitamin D nutrition and postnatal growth in Asian infants. *British Medical Journal* 1981;283:1024.

973. Maxwell JD, Ang L, Brooke OG, Brown IRF. Vitamin D supplements enhance weight gain and nutritional status in pregnant Asians. *British Journal of Obstetrics and Gynaecology* 1981;88:987–91.

974. Cockburn F, Belton NR, Purvis RJ. Maternal vitamin D intake and mineral metabolism in mothers and their newborn infants. *British Medical Journal.* 1980;281(6232):11–14.

975. Datta S, Alfaham M, Davies DP, Dunstan F, Woodhead S, Evans J, Richards B. Vitamin D deficiency in pregnant women from a non-European ethnic minority population – an interventional study. *BJOG* 2002;109(8):905–8.

976. Mallet E, Gugi B, Brunelle P, Henocq A, Basuyau JP, Lemeur H. Vitamin D supplementation in pregnancy: a controlled trial of two methods. *Obstetrics and Gynecology* 1986;68(3):300–4.

977. Delvin EE, Salle BL, Glorieux FH, Adeleine P, David LS. Vitamin D supplementation during pregnancy: effect on neonatal calcium homeostasis. *The Journal of Pediatrics* 1986;109(2):328–34.

978. Greer FR, Marshall S. Bone mineral content, serum vitamin D metabolite concentrations, and ultraviolet B light exposure in infants fed human milk with and without vitamin D2 supplements. *The Journal of Pediatrics* 1989;114(2):204–12.

979. Greer FR, Searcy JE, Levin RS. Bone mineral content and serum 25-hydroxyvitamin D concentration in breast-fed infants with and without supplemental vitamin D. *Journal of Pediatrics* 1981;98(5):696–701.

980. Greer FR, Searcy JE, Levin RS, Steichen JJ, Steichen-Asche PS, Tsang RC. Bone mineral content and serum 25-hydroxyvitamin D concentrations in breast-fed infants with and without supplemental vitamin D: one-year follow-up. *Journal of Pediatrics* 1982;100(6):919–22.

981. Congdon P, Horsman A, Kirby PA. Mineral content of the forearms of babies born to Asian and white mothers. *British Medical Journal* 1983;286(6373):1233–5.

982. Pietrek J, Preece MA, Windo J, O'Riordan JL, Dunnigan MG, McIntosh WB, Ford JA. Prevention of vitamin-D deficiency in Asians. *Lancet* 1976;1(7970):1145–8.

983. Stephens WP, Klimiuk PS, Berry JL, Mawer EB. Annual high-dose vitamin D prophylaxis in Asian immigrants. *Lancet* 1981;2(8257):1199–202.

984. Ala-Houhala M. 25-Hydroxyvitamin D levels during breast-feeding with or without maternal or infantile supplementation of vitamin D. *Journal of Pediatric Gastroenterology and Nutrition* 1985;4(2):220–6.

985. Greer FR, Marshall S. Bone mineral content, serum vitamin D metabolite concentrations, and ultraviolet B light exposure in infants fed human milk with and without vitamin D2 supplements. *The Journal of Pediatrics* 1989;114(2):204–12.

986. Hollis BW, Wagner CL. Vitamin D requirements during lactation: high-dose maternal supplementation as therapy to prevent hypovitaminosis D for both the mother and the nursing infant. *American Journal of Clinical Nutrition* 2004;80(6 Suppl):1752S–8S.

987. Smail F, Vazquez JC. Antibiotics for asymptomatic bacteriuria in pregnancy. *Cochrane Database of Systematic Reviews* 2007;CD000490(2).

988. Crowther CA, Hiller JE, Moss JR, *et al.* Effect of treatment of gestational diabetes mellitus on pregnancy outcomes. *New England Journal of Medicine* 2005;352(24):2477–86.

989. Joint Formulary Committee. *British National Formulary.* 52nd ed. London: British Medical Association and Royal Pharmaceutical Society of Great Britain; 2006.

990. NHS Sickle Cell and Thalassaemia Screening Programme. Personal communication, March 2008.

991. Danilenko-Dixon D, Van Winter J, Nelson R, Ogburn P. Universal versus selective gestational diabetes screening: application of 1997 American Diabetes Association recommendations. *American Journal of Obstetrics and Gynecology* 1999;181:798–802.

992. Williams CB, Iqbal S, Zawacki CM, Yu D, Brown MB, Herman WH. Effect of selective screening for gestational diabetes. *Diabetes Care* 1999;22:418–21.

993. Davies L, Drummond M. *The Costs of Induction of Labour by Prostaglandin E₂ or Oxytocin: Refining the Estimates.* York: University of York; 1993.

994. Redshaw M, Rowe R, Hockley C, Brocklehurst P. *Recorded Delivery: a National Survey of Women's Experience of Maternity Care.* Oxford: National Perinatal Epidemiology Unit, University of Oxford; 2007.

995 . Javaid, MK, Crozier R, Harvey NC, Gale CR, Dennison EM, Boucher BJ, *et al.*; Princess Anne Hospital Study Group. Maternal vitamin D status during pregnancy and childhood bone mass at age 9 years: a longitudinal study, *Lancet* 2006;367(9504):36–43.

996. Devereux G, Litonjua AA, Turner SW, *et al.* Maternal vitamin D intake during pregnancy and early childhood wheezing. *American Journal of Clinical Nutrition* 2007;85:853–9.

997. Gale CR, Robinson SM, Harvey MC, *et al.* Maternal vitamin D status during pregnancy and child outcomes. *European Journal of Clinical Nutrition* 2008;62(1):68–77.

998. Department of Health. *Dietary Reference Values for Food Energy and Nutrients for the United Kingdom.* Report of the panel on dietary reference values of the Committee on Medical Aspects of Food Policy. London: HMSO; 1991.

999. NCSSG. *New Frontiers: Annual Report of the National Chlamydia Screening Programme in England 2005/06.* London: HPA; 2006.

1000. Streetly A, Dick M. Screening for haemoglobinopathies. *Current Paediatrics* 2005;15(1):32–9.

1001. Lu MC, Tache V, Alexander GR, Kotelchuck M, Halfon N. Preventing low birth weight: is prenatal care the answer? *Journal of Matern–Fetal and Neonatal Medicine* 2003;13(6):362–80.

1002. Gueorguieva RV, Sarkar NP, Carter RL, Ariet M, Roth J, Resnick MB. A risk assessment screening test for very low birth weight. *Maternal and Child Health Journal* 2003;7(2):127–36.

1003. Gomez JL, Young BK. A weighted risk index for antenatal prediction of perinatal outcome. *Journal of Perinatal Medicine* 2002;30(2):137–42.

1004. Nelson HD, Nygren MA, MnInerney Y, Klein J. *Screening Women and Elderly Adults for Family and Intimate Partner Violence.* US Preventive Services Task Force. 2007 [www.ahrq.gov/clinic/3rduspstf/famviolence/famviolrev.htm].

1005. McDonnell E, Geary M, O'Reilly M, Collins C, Holohan M, Ward L. Acceptability of routine enquiry regarding domestic violence in the antenatal clinic. *Irish Medical Journal* 2006;99(4):123–4.

1006. Anderson BA, Marshak HH, Hebbeler DL. Identifying intimate partner violence at entry to prenatal care: clustering routine clinical information. *Journal of Midwifery and Women's Health* 2002;47(5):353–9.

1007. Webster J, Holt V. Screening for partner violence: direct questioning or self-report? *Obstetrics and Gynecology* 2004;103(2):299–303.

1008. Carroll JC, Reid AJ, Biringer A, Midmer D, Glazier RH, Wilson L et al. Effectiveness of the antenatal psychosocial health assessment (ALPHA) form in detecting psychosocial concerns: A randomized controlled trial. *CMAJ: Canadian Medical Association Journal* 2005;173(3):253–9.

1009. Carroli G, Rooney C, Villar J. How effective is antenatal care in preventing maternal mortality and serious morbidity? An overview of the evidence. *Paediatric and Perinatal Epidemiology* 2001;15 Suppl 1:1–42.

1010. Stahl K, Hundley V. Risk and risk assessment in pregnancy - do we scare because we care? *Midwifery* 2003;19(4):298–309.

1011. Cancer Research UK. *SunSmart: Stay Safe.* 2006 [http://info.cancerresearchuk.org/healthyliving/sunsmart/].

1012. NHS Direct. *Cancer of the Skin: Prevention.* 2006. [http://www.nhsdirect.nhs.uk/articles/article.aspx?articleId=83&sectionId=9].

1013. Zlotkin S. Vitamin D concentrations in Asian children living in England. Limited vitamin D intake and use of sunscreens may lead to rickets. *British Medical Journal* 1999;318(7195):1417.

1014. Hypponnen E, Power C. Hypovitaminosis D in British adults at age 45y: nationwide cohort study of diet and lifestyle predictors. *American Journal of Clinical Nutrition* 2007;85:860–8.

1015. Pan W, Wu GP, Li YF, *et al.* The experience of diagnosis the abnormal fetal heart by fetal echocardiography to 900 fetuses. Guangzhou, China: Guangdong Cardiovascular Institute; undated [available from www.unepsa.org/china/ab/1327.HTM; accessed 30 August 2006].

1016. Bonnet D, Coltri A, Butera G, *et al.* Detection of transposition of the great arteries in fetuses reduces neonatal morbidity and mortality. *Circulation* 1999;99(7):916–18.

1017. Bonnet D, Jouannic JM, Fermont L. Impact of prenatal diagnosis on perinatal care of transposition of the great arteries. *Ultrasound in Obstetrics and Gynecology* 2003;22(S1):66–7.

1018. Kumar RK, Newburger JW, Gauvreau K, *et al.* Comparison of outcome when hypoplastic left heart syndrome and transposition of the great arteries are diagnosed prenatally versus when diagnosis of these two conditions is made only postnatally. *American Journal of Cardiology* 1999;83(12):1649–53.

1019. Streetly A, Maxwell K, Mejia A. *Sickle Cell Disorders in Greater London: a needs assessment of screening and care services.* Fair Shares for London Report. London: United Medical and Dental Schools Department of Public Health Medicine; 1997.

1020. Wilson JM, Jungner G. Principles and practice of screening for disease. *WHO Chronicle* 1968;22(11):473.

1021. Weisz B, Pandya P, Chitty L, *et al.* Practical issues drawn from the implementation of the integrated test for Down Syndrome screening into routine clinical practice. *BJOG: an International Journal of Obsterics and Gynaecology* 2007;114(4):493–7.

1022. Ego A, Subtil D, Grange G, Thiebaugeorges O, Senat MV, Vayssiere C, Zeitlin J. Customized versus population-based birth weight standards for identifying growth restricted infants: a French multicenter study. *American Journal of Obstetrics and Gynecology* 2006;194(4):1042–9.

1023. Figueras F, Figueras J, Meler E, Eixarch E, Coll O, Gratacos E, Gardosi J, Carbonell X. Customised birthweight standards accurately predict perinatal morbidity. *Archives of Disease in Childhood Fetal and Neonatal edition* 2007; 92(4): F277-80.

1024. Wren C, Richmond S, Donaldson L. Temporal variability in birth prevalence of cardiovascular malformations. *Heart* 2000;83(4):414–9.

2008 update

Index

2008 update

2008 update

2008 update

2008 update

2008 update

2008 update

2008 update

2008 update